PLATE 1. General view of the western end of the Altınova, looking north from the top of site 054/7 (Könk), site 054/2 (Tepecik) in the right background.

MEMOIRS OF THE MUSEUM OF ANTHROPOLOGY
UNIVERSITY OF MICHIGAN
NUMBER 11

AN ARCHAEOLOGICAL SURVEY OF THE KEBAN RESERVOIR AREA OF EAST-CENTRAL TURKEY

by

ROBERT WHALLON

ANN ARBOR
1979

© 1979 Regents of the University of Michigan
The Museum of Anthropology
All rights reserved
Printed in the
United States of America

ISBN 0-932206-84-0

For Robert J. and Linda Braidwood

Contents

FIGURES iii
TABLES vii
PLATES vii
ACKNOWLEDGMENTS viii

CHAPTER 1: THE SURVEY
INTRODUCTION 1
THE SURVEY AREA
- Location and topography 2
- Climate 5
- Vegetation 8
- Fauna 9
- Mineral resources 9

ARCHAEOLOGICAL SURVEY
- Previous investigations 10
- Initial survey 11
- Intensive survey 11
- Survey coverage 12
- Site numbering system 12
- Site recording 13
- Controlled surface collection ... 14
- Summary of sites found, recorded and collected 16

CHAPTER 2: THE POTTERY
INTRODUCTION 17
CERAMIC WARES
- Chalcolithic Ware 18
- Graphite Slipped Ware 19
- Cream Chaff Ware 20
- Late Chalcolithic Grit Tempered Ware 22
- Reserved Slip Ware 23
- Plain Simple Ware 23
- Fine Grooved Ware 24
- Early Bronze Age Burnished Ware 25
- Early Bronze Age Relief Decorated Ware 28
- Early Bronze Age Lids 28
- Early Bronze Age Polished Ware . 28
- Early Bronze Age Red Slipped Ware 29
- Early Bronze Age Plain Ware .. 30
- Early Bronze Age Thick Ware . 30
- Early Bronze Age Red Painted Ware 31
- Early Bronze Age Black Painted Ware 32
- Middle Bronze Age Gritty Ware 33
- Old Hittite Gray Ware 34
- Old Hittite Light Faced Gray Ware 35
- Old Hittite Black Faced Gray Ware 35
- Middle Bronze Age Gray Ware . 36
- Hittite Red Ware 36
- Hittite Plain Ware 37
- Hittite Fine Ware 38
- Hittite Thick Ware 39
- Hittite Exterior Wheel-Marked Ware 39
- Hittite Buff-Orange Burnished Ware 39
- Hittite Chaff Faced Ware 41
- Hittite Orange Smoothed Ware 42
- Hittite Red-Brown Burnished Ware 42
- Hittite Brown Burnished Ware . 43
- Hittite White Slipped Ware 44
- Hittite Painted Ware 45
- Hittite Brown Gritty Cooking Ware 45
- Iron Age Ware 46
- Iron Age Painted Ware 49
- Iron Age Thick Ware 49
- Medieval Brick Ware 50
- Medieval Thick Ware 52
- Medieval Coarse Ware 52
- Medieval Glazed Ware 53
- Medieval Sgraffiato Ware 53
- Medieval Red Slipped Ware ... 54
- Medieval White Slipped Ware .. 55
- Medieval Painted Ware 55
- Medieval Cooking Ware 55
- Medieval Modeled Ware 56

Archaeological Survey of the Keban Reservoir

    Roman Red Ware 57
    DEFINITION OF CHRONOLOGICAL
    PERIODS 57

CHAPTER 3: THE SITES
    INTRODUCTION
Site	Page
N52/1 (Taşkun Mevkii)	161
N52/2 (Taşkun Kalesi)	164
N52/3 (Fatmalı-Kalecik)	166
N52/4 (Aşvan Kalesi)	168
N52/5 (Pulur)	171
N52/6 (Kalaycık)	171
N52/7	172
N52/8	173
N52/9 (Çay Boyu)	173
N52/10	175
N52/11	176
N53/1	177
N53/3 (Hanibrahimşah)	178
N55/1	179
O54/1 (Tülin Tepe)	180
O54/2 (Tepecik)	182
O54/3 (Değirmen Tepe)	187
O54/4	194
O54/5	194
O54/6	195
O54/7 (Könk)	198
O54/8 (Norşun Tepe)	199
O54/9	211
O54/10	213
O54/11	216
O54/12	218
O54/13	221
O54/14	222
O54/15	225
O54/16	226
O54/17	227
O54/18	228
O54/19	228
O54/20	229
O54/21	230
O54/22	231
O54/23	232
O54/24	233
O54/25	235
O54/26	237
O54/27	238
O54/28	240
O55/1 (Korucu Tepe)	241
O55/2	244
O55/3 (Boy Tepe)	246
O55/4	249
O55/5	251
O55/6	252
O55/7	252
O55/8-9 (Habusu Körtepe)	253
O55/10	257

CHAPTER 4: SETTLEMENT PATTERNS
    ESTIMATION OF OCCUPATION AREA 259
    GEOGRAPHICAL BASES OF
    SETTLEMENT PATTERN 263
    DEFINING SETTLEMENT PATTERNS 264
        Early Chalcolithic 265
        Halaf 266
        Late Chalcolithic 266
        Chalcolithic-Early Bronze Age
        Transitional 268
        Early Bronze Age I-II 268
        Early Bronze Age IIIA 270
        Early Bronze Age IIIB 270
        Middle Bronze Age 270
        Late Bronze Age (Hittite) 273
        Iron Age 274
        Hellenistic-Roman 274
        Medieval (Byzantine-Selcuk) ... 274
        Medieval (Ottoman-Recent and
        Unspecified) 276
    POPULATION TRENDS 276

CHAPTER 5: EVALUATION OF CONTROLLED SURFACE COLLECTION
    COMPARISON AMONG METHODS 288
    COMPARISON OF SURVEY AND
    EXCAVATION RESULTS 292
        O54/2 (Tepecik) 293
        O54/8 (Norşun Tepe) 294
        N52/2 (Taşkun Kalesi) 296
        N52/3 (Fatmalı-Kalecik) ... 296
        O54/3 (Değirmen Tepe) 296
        N52/1 (Taşkun Mevkii) 297
        N52/4 (Aşvan Kalesi) 297
        N52/9 (Çay Boyu) 298
        O55/8-9 (Habusu Körtepe) .. 298
        N52/5 (Pulur) 299
        N52/6 (Kalaycık) 299
        N53/3 (Hanibrahimşah) 299
    SUMMARY 299

BIBLIOGRAPHY 301

APPENDIX
    Sherd Counts of the
    Wares Recovered by the
    Controlled Collections in the
    Keban Reservoir Survey 306

Figures

1. Location of the Keban Reservoir in east-central Turkey ... 2
2. Map of the Keban Reservoir ... 3
3. Map of the Aşvan area ... 4
4. Map of the Altınova ... 6
5. Reference grid for the site numbering system in the region around the Keban Reservoir ... 13
6. Chalcolithic Ware ... 60
7. Chalcolithic Ware ... 63
8. Chalcolithic Ware ... 64
9. Graphite Slipped Ware, Late Chalcolithic Grit Tempered Ware, Reserved Slip Ware, Plain Simple Ware, Fine Grooved Ware ... 67
10. Cream Chaff Ware ... 68
11. Cream Chaff Ware ... 71
12. Early Bronze Age Burnished Ware ... 72
13. Early Bronze Age Burnished Ware ... 75
14. Early Bronze Age Burnished Ware ... 76
15. Early Bronze Age Relief Decorated Ware, Early Bronze Age Lids ... 79
16. Early Bronze Age Polished Ware, Early Bronze Age Red Slipped Ware, Early Bronze Age Plain Ware, Early Bronze Age Thick Ware ... 80
17. Early Bronze Age Thick Ware, Early Bronze Age Red Painted Ware ... 83
18. Early Bronze Age Black Painted Ware ... 84
19. Early Bronze Age Red Painted Ware, Early Bronze Age Black Painted Ware ... 87
20. Middle Bronze Age Gritty Ware ... 88
21. Old Hittite Gray Ware ... 91
22. Middle Bronze Age Gray Ware, Old Hittite Light Faced Gray Ware ... 92
23. Hittite Plain Ware ... 95
24. Hittite Plain Ware ... 96
25. Hittite Plain Ware ... 99
26. Hittite Plain Ware, Hittite Fine Ware ... 100
27. Hittite Thick Ware ... 103
28. Hittite Thick Ware, Hittite Exterior Wheel-Marked Ware, Hittite Buff-Orange Burnished Ware ... 104
29. Hittite Buff-Orange Burnished Ware ... 107
30. Hittite Buff-Orange Burnished Ware, Hittite Chaff Faced Ware ... 108
31. Hittite Orange Smoothed Ware, Hittite Red-Brown Burnished Ware ... 111
32. Hittite Brown Burnished Ware ... 112
33. Hittite White Slipped Ware ... 115
34. Hittite Painted Ware ... 116
35. Hittite Painted Ware, Hittite Brown Gritty Cooking Ware ... 119
36. Iron Age Ware ... 120
37. Iron Age Ware ... 123
38. Iron Age Ware, Iron Age Painted Ware ... 124
39. Iron Age Thick Ware ... 127
40. Medieval Brick Ware ... 128
41. Medieval Brick Ware ... 131
42. Medieval Brick Ware ... 132
43. Medieval Brick Ware ... 135
44. Medieval Brick Ware ... 136
45. Medieval Thick Ware ... 139
46. Medieval Thick Ware ... 140
47. Medieval Coarse Ware, Medieval Glazed Ware, Medieval Sgraffiato Ware ... 143
48. Medieval Red Slipped Ware ... 144
49. Medieval Red Slipped Ware, Medieval White Slipped Ware ... 147
50. Medieval White Slipped Ware, Medieval Painted Ware ... 148
51. Medieval Painted Ware ... 151
52. Medieval Cooking Ware ... 152
53. Medieval Cooking Ware, Medieval Modeled Ware ... 155
54. Medieval Modeled Ware ... 156
55. Medieval Modeled Ware, Halafian Ware, Hittite Red Ware, Phrygian(?) Ceramics, Roman Red Ware ... 159
56. N52/1 - Site plan and profile ... 162
57. N52/1 - Density contours of Early Chalcolithic ceramics ... 163
58. N52/1 - Density contours of Early Bronze Age I-II ceramics ... 163

59. N52/1 - Density contours of Hittite ceramics .. 163
60. N52/1 - Counts of Medieval sherds 164
61. N52/2 - Site plan and profile 164
62. N52/2 - Density contours of Medieval ceramics . 166
63. N52/3 - Site plan and profile 167
64. N52/3 - Density contours of Early Chalcolithic ceramics 168
65. N52/3 - Density contours of Late Chalcolithic ceramics 168
66. N52/4 - Site plan and profiles 168
67. N52/5 - Site plan and profile 171
68. N52/6 - Site plan and profile 172
69. N52/8 - Site plan and profile 173
70. N52/9 - Site plan and profile 174
71. N52/9 - Density contours of Late Chalcolithic ceramics 174
72. N52/9 - Density contours of Early Bronze Age I-II ceramics 175
73. N52/9 - Density contours of Hittite ceramics .. 175
74. N52/9 - Density contours of Medieval ceramics . 175
75. N52/10 - Site plan and profile 176
76. N52/11 - Site plan and profile 177
77. N53/1 - Site plan and profile 177
78. N53/3 - Site plan and profile 178
79. N55/1 - Site plan and profile 179
80. O54/1 - Site plan 181
81. O54/2 - Site plan and profiles 183
82. O54/2 - Density contours of Early Bronze Age I-II ceramics 188
83. O54/2 - Density contours of Early Bronze Age IIIA ceramics 188
84. O54/2 - Density contours of Early Bronze Age IIIB ceramics 189
85. O54/2 - Density contours of Middle Bronze Age ceramics 189
86. O54/2 - Density contours of Hittite ceramics .. 190
87. O54/2 - Density contours of Iron Age ceramics . 190
88. O54/2 - Density contours of Medieval ceramics . 191
89. O54/2 - Counts of Medieval Glazed Ware sherds . 191
90. O54/3 - Site plan and profile 192
91. O54/3 - Density contours of Early Bronze Age I-II ceramics 193
92. O54/3 - Density contours of Hittite ceramics .. 193
93. O54/3 - Density contours of Iron Age ceramics . 193
94. O54/3 - Density contours of Medieval ceramics . 194
95. O54/5 - Site plan and profile 195
96. O54/6 - Site plan and profile 195
97. O54/6 - Density contours of Early Chalcolithic ceramics 197
98. O54/6 - Density contours of Late Chalcolithic ceramics 197
99. O54/6 - Density contours of Hittite ceramics .. 197
100. O54/6 - Density contours of Medieval ceramics . 198
101. O54/7 - Site plan and profiles 198
102. O54/8 - Site plan and profiles 200
103. O54/8 - Counts of Early Chalcolithic sherds .. 204
104. O54/8 - Counts of Late Chalcolithic sherds ... 204
105. O54/8 - Density contours of Early Bronze Age I-II ceramics 206
106. O54/8 - Density contours of Early Bronze Age III ceramics 206
107. O54/8 - Density contours of Middle Bronze Age ceramics 207
108. O54/8 - Density contours of Hittite ceramics .. 207
109. O54/8 - Density contours of Iron Age ceramics . 208
110. O54/8 - Counts of Early Iron Age rim sherds . 209
111. O54/8 - Counts of Middle Iron Age rim sherds . 209
112. O54/8 - Density contours of Medieval ceramics . 210
113. O54/9 - Site plan and profile 211
114. O54/9 - Density contours of Hittite ceramics .. 212
115. O54/9 - Density contours of Medieval ceramics . 213
116. O54/10 - Site plan and profiles 213
117. O54/10 - Density contours of Early Bronze Age I-II ceramics 215
118. O54/10 - Density contours of Middle Bronze Age ceramics 215
119. O54/10 - Density contours of Hittite ceramics . 216
120. O54/10 - Density contours of Medieval ceramics . 216
121. O54/11 - Site plan and profile 216
122. O54/11 - Density contours of Middle Bronze Age ceramics 217
123. O54/11 - Density contours of Hittite ceramics . 218
124. O54/11 - Density contours of Medieval ceramics . 218
125. O54/12 - Site plan and profile 219
126. O54/12 - Density contours of Early Bronze Age I-II ceramics 220
127. O54/12 - Density contours of Hittite ceramics . 220
128. O54/12 - Density contours of Medieval ceramics . 221
129. O54/13 - Site plan and profile 221
130. O54/14 - Site plan and profile 222
131. O54/14 - Density contours of Early Chalcolithic ceramics 223
132. O54/14 - Density contours of Early Bronze Age I-II ceramics 223

Figures

133. O54/14 - Density contours of Middle Bronze Age ceramics 224
134. O54/14 - Density contours of Hittite ceramics . 224
135. O54/14 - Density contours of Medieval ceramics . 224
136. O54/15 - Site plan and profiles 225
137. O54/15 - Counts of Hittite sherds 226
138. O54/15 - Density contours of Medieval ceramics . 226
139. O54/16 - Site plan and profile 227
140. O54/16 - Density contours of Medieval ceramics . 227
141. O54/19 - Site plan and profiles 229
142. O54/20 - Site plan and profile 229
143. O54/21 - Site plan and profiles 230
144. O54/21 - Density contours of Hittite ceramics . 231
145. O54/21 - Density contours of Medieval ceramics . 231
146. O54/22 - Site plan and profile 232
147. O54/23 - Site plan and profile 232
148. O54/24 - Site plan and profile 233
149. O54/24 - Counts of Early Chalcolithic sherds . 234
150. O54/24 - Density contours of Early Bronze Age I-II ceramics 235
151. O54/24 - Density contours of Hittite ceramics . 235
152. O54/24 - Density contours of Medieval ceramics . 235
153. O54/25 - Site plan and profile 236
154. O54/25 - Density contours of Hittite ceramics . 237
155. O54/25 - Density contours of Medieval ceramics . 237
156. O54/26 - Site plan and profile 237
157. O54/27 - Site plan and profile 238
158. O54/27 - Density contours of Hittite ceramics . 239
159. O54/27 - Density contours of Medieval ceramics . 240
160. O54/28 - Site plan and profile 240
161. O55/1 - Site plan and profiles 241
162. O55/1 - Profile of large cut on northwest side of mound 243
163. O55/2 - Site plan and profile 245
164. O55/2 - Density contours of Early Bronze Age I-II ceramics 245
165. O55/2 - Density contours of Hittite ceramics .. 246
166. O55/3 - Site plan and profile 246
167. O55/3 - Counts of all obsidian 248
168. O55/3 - Counts of all ceramics 248
169. O55/3 - Counts of Chalcolithic-Early Bronze Age Transitional sherds 248
170. O55/3 - Counts of Early Bronze Age I-II sherds . 248
171. O55/3 - Counts of Middle Bronze Age sherds . 249
172. O55/3 - Counts of Hittite sherds 249
173. O55/3 - Counts of Medieval sherds 249
174. O55/4 - Site plan and profile 250
175. O55/4 - Density contours of Hittite ceramics .. 250
176. O55/4 - Density contours of Iron Age ceramics . 251
177. O55/4 - Density contours of Medieval ceramics . 251
178. O55/5 - Site plan and profile 251
179. O55/6 - Site plan and profile 252
180. O55/7 - Site plan and profile 253
181. O55/8-9 - Site plan and profile 253
182. O55/8-9 - Density contours of Early Chalcolithic ceramics 255
183. O55/8-9 - Density contours of Late Chalcolithic ceramics 256
184. O55/8-9 - Density contours of Chalcolithic-Early Bronze Age Transitional ceramics 256
185. O55/8-9 - Density contours of Early Bronze Age I-II ceramics 257
186. O55/8-9 - Density contours of Hittite ceramics . 257
187. O55/8-9 - Density contours of Medieval ceramics . 258
188. O55/10 - Site plan and profile 258
189. Plot of total site size against measured and average sizes of occupation areas in the Keban survey data 262
190. Log-log plot of total site size against average size of occupation at sites in the Keban Reservoir survey 262
191. Relative proportions of total measured to total estimated occupation area by period within the Altınova and the survey area in general 263
192. Distribution map of Early Chalcolithic occupations by size class in the Aşvan area 265
193. Distribution map of Early Chalcolithic occupations by size class in the Altınova 266
194. Distribution map of Late Chalcolithic occupations by size class in the Aşvan area 267
195. Distribution map of Late Chalcolithic occupations by size class in the Altınova 267
196. Distribution map of Chalcolithic-Early Bronze Age Transitional occupations by size class in the Altınova 268
197. Distribution map of Early Bronze Age I-II occupations by size class in the Aşvan area 269
198. Distribution map of Early Bronze Age I-II occupations by size class in the Altınova 269
199. Distribution map of Early Bronze Age IIIA occupations by size class in the Aşvan area 270
200. Distribution map of Early Bronze Age IIIA occupations by size class in the Altınova 271
201. Distribution map of Early Bronze Age IIIB occupations by size class in the Aşvan area 271
202. Distribution map of Early Bronze Age IIIB occupations by size class in the Altınova 272

203. Distribution map of Middle Bronze Age occupations by size class in the Altınova 272
204. Distribution map of Late Bronze Age (Hittite) occupations by size class in the Aşvan area ... 273
205. Distribution map of Late Bronze Age (Hittite) occupations by size class in the Altınova 274
206. Distribution map of Iron Age (Early and Unspecified) occupations by size class in the Altınova 275
207. Distribution map of Medieval (Byzantine-Selcuk) occupations by size class in the Aşvan area . 275
208. Distribution map of Medieval (Byzantine-Selcuk) occupations by size class in the Altınova . 276
209. Distribution map of Medieval (Ottoman-Recent and Unspecified) occupations by size class in the Aşvan area 277
210. Distribution map of Medieval (Ottoman-Recent and Unspecified) occupations by size class in the Altınova 277
211. Total measured and estimated area of occupation by period within the Altınova and other parts of the survey area 278

Tables

1. Temperature and frost data from Elâzığ 7
2. Monthly precipitation at Elâzığ and Çemişkezek . 7
3. Survey coverage of the Keban Reservoir 12
4. Methods of controlled collection applied in the Keban survey 15
5. Identified ceramics from the controlled surface collection of site N52/4 (Aşvan Kalesi) 170
6. Stratified random grid sampling scheme for site O54/2, Makaraz Tepe (Tepecik) 185
7. Sherd counts from stratigraphic units in the large profile collected at O55/1 (Korucu Tepe) 242
8. Summary of site sizes and known and measured occupations on surveyed sites in the Keban Reservoir area 260
9. Fractional multipliers for estimating average occupation size from total site size 263
10. Early Chalcolithic occupation areas 279
11. Late Chalcolithic occupation areas 280
12. Chalcolithic-Early Bronze Age Transitional occupation areas 280
13. Early Bronze Age I-II occupation areas 281
14. Early Bronze Age IIIA occupation areas 282
15. Early Bronze Age IIIB occupation areas 282
16. Middle Bronze Age occupation areas 283
17. Late Bronze Age (Hittite) occupation areas ... 284
18. Iron Age (Early and Unspecified) occupation areas 285
19. Medieval (Byzantine-Selcuk) occupation areas . 286
20. Medieval (Ottoman-Recent and Unspecified) occupation areas 287

Plates

Plate 1: General view of the western end of the Altınova .... Frontispiece

Plate 2: Characteristic examples of Cream Chaff Ware 160

Acknowledgments

A great number of people helped in a multitude of ways to carry out the research reported in this monograph. By no means can all of these individuals be thanked properly here. However, it has been largely through their efforts that much of this work came to be done well or at all and that it can now, finally, be presented as a contribution to public knowledge. If a few are selected here for special mention, this does not lessen in any way my gratitude or debt to the many others whose help, advice, and encouragment were essential to the final success of my work.

Special thanks must go first to Robert J. and Linda Braidwood, who, although never quite directly involved in the Keban survey, were always behind me and this project in many ways—from my first experiences in eastern Anatolia through years of advice, encouragment, and support—to the point that this work is dedicated to them.

In Turkey I met with invaluable help from all sides. First and foremost, my thanks go to Professor Halet Çambel, under whose auspices my work was done. I am also greatly indebted to her for an introduction to Turkey and its people, in depth and in ways that few are fortunate enough to experience. Through her, my contact with this part of the world went far beyond the archaeology I was doing, and my involvement was thus more than a simple commitment to my work.

I am also particularly appreciative of my relationship with Sönmez Kantman, who jointly directed the field survey in the Keban Reservoir area. The cooperation we enjoyed was outstanding, and fieldwork has seldom gone so well or effectively.

Thanks must also be extended to all the local officials who actively aided our project. I note particularly the Vali of Elâzığ, Zekeriya Çelikbilekli, the Director of the Elâzığ-Harput Museum, Ferhan Memişoğlu, and the officials of the Elâzığ State Engineering and Architecture Academy. A number of other officials in several state and local agencies were also most cooperative, and much of the success of the survey was due to their generous help.

I also received a great deal of support and advice during the analysis of the survey materials. This was particularly important in the effort to classify properly the enormous variety of ceramics we encountered. Special thanks for extensive help in this regard go to Maurits van Loon and to Shan Winn. Without their expertise and suggestions it would have been infinitely more difficult to develop a satisfactory classification of the pottery collected during the survey. My debt to them is substantial; a large part of the value of this report is due to their generous help, and I am grateful in due measure.

In addition, it gives me pleasure to thank here the many students who have been involved in this project—the Turkish students who so ably and willingly carried out the demanding and often exhausting work in the field, the American students who endured both exceptional heat and tedium in the laboratory in Elâzığ, and the students at the University of Michigan who coded, drew, programmed, tabulated, etc., until the seemingly endless tasks of organization and preparation of both data and manuscript were brought under control. Their work was invaluable. To mention only one of many, particular thanks go to

Archaeological Survey of the Keban Reservoir

Susan Loving, whose fine maps, plans, and graphs grace these pages, allowing at last the publication of this work.

A year at the Netherlands Institute for Advanced Study in the Humanities and Social Science (N.I.A.S.) provided valuable time for the organization and writing of substantial portions of this monograph.

The enormous task of editing the final manuscript and seeing it through the printing process was undertaken by Mary Shimizu and David Victor, to whom I obviously am very grateful.

Finally, I would like to thank my wife, Barbara, for her patience, critical reading and comments.

This survey of the Keban Reservoir area was made over ten years ago. The laboratory analyses of the collected materials were completed within a few years after the field survey. In retrospect, I see problems with this work and report. There is much I now would do differently. There comes a point, however, at which such considerations at last are outweighed by the responsibility to put on record the data and conclusions as they stand, making them available to all archaeologists to use and criticize. The omissions and errors of fact and judgment in this work are mine. I hope, however, that at least a significant portion of it will prove useful and valuable.

This material is based upon work supported by the National Science Foundation under grants GS-1618 and GS-3025. Any opinions, findings, and conclusions or recommendations expressed in this publication are those of the author and do not necessarily reflect the views of the National Science Foundation.

1

The Survey

INTRODUCTION

The archaeological survey reported in this monograph was carried out in 1967 as a cooperative project between the Prehistory Section, Faculty of Letters, Istanbul University, and the University of Michigan Museum of Anthropology. Field work was done under the auspices of Istanbul University. It was directed jointly by the author and Sönmez Kantman, then an assistant at Istanbul University acting for Prof. Dr. Halet Çambel who was officially responsible for the field project (Whallon and Kantman 1969, 1970). The later analysis of the survey materials was carried out under the author's supervision.

Our attention was first drawn to eastern Anatolia as an area in which early stages of plant and animal domestication might have occurred. Although Flannery (1969: 80–81) has proposed an alternative view, it has been thought generally that the transition from food-gathering to food-producing began within the limits of the natural geographical ranges of the wild ancestors of the early domesticates (e.g. Braidwood and Howe 1960, 1962; Braidwood 1972). Also, the present evidence seems to point to the piedmont and intermontane valleys along the mountain chains from Palestine through the Taurus and Zagros ranges as the main geographic context of this transition. These areas are described as being of "open mixed-oak woodland and grassland country, perhaps most characteristically manifested at ca. 1000 meters in elevation" (Braidwood and Howe 1962: 132).

Turkey occupies a more or less central position with respect to this geographical zone and to the ranges of several of the major domesticated plants and animals. Recent work has indicated that village communities in Turkey, on the southern edge of the great northward arch of the Taurus Mountains above the Mesopotamian plain, participated in the transition to food-production at an early date and in a preceramic stage (Çambel and Braidwood 1970; Braidwood, Çambel, Redman and Watson 1971). After Braidwood and Çambel's first season of survey and excavation in southeastern Turkey, our survey was conceived as an extension of the archaeological search for evidence of the early stages of domestication into the high intermontane valleys of Anatolia.

Conversations with members of the Braidwood-Çambel expedition staff had suggested that these high valleys, with their broad, well-watered floors, might be rich in natural stands of the wild ancestors of the common domesticated grains. Also, the original range of wild sheep and goats

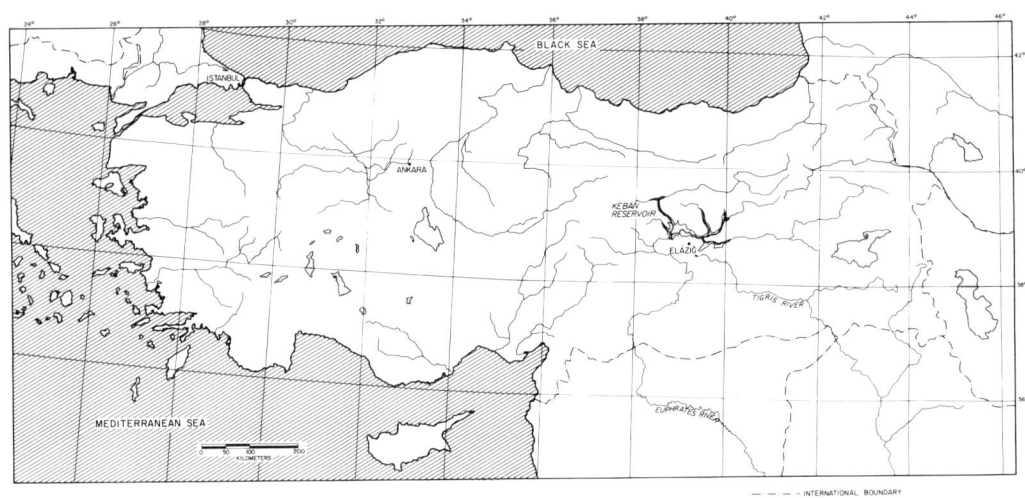

FIGURE 1. Location of the Keban Reservoir in east-central Turkey.

certainly had included these valleys. We therefore hoped that investigation here would find substantial archaeological remains of communities from the period of incipient food production. In addition to their environmental characteristics, these intermontane valleys offered several geographical advantages for archaeological research. They are relatively restricted in size, and their boundaries are relatively clear-cut. These features clearly limit local populations and constrain external contacts, facilitating the archaeological definition of former population density, distribution, and external relations. The intermontane valleys of eastern Anatolia thus appeared appropriate for the investigation of local sequences of development from the appearance of early farming villages to later, complex, urban societies.

Several high, intermontane valleys of eastern Anatolia were considered in selecting our survey area. The plain of Elbistan was at first thought to be a desirable area. However, the ongoing construction of the Keban Dam across the upper Euphrates brought our attention to the area of the future Keban Reservoir, in particular to the plain of Elâzığ. The imminent threat of losing this area to future archaeological investigation was decisive in our selection. The Elâzığ plain and much of the rest of the reservoir area were, in our thinking at the time, geographically and environmentally appropriate for our project. The area was, in addition, the nearest of all areas considered to the site of Çayönü, where the earliest evidence for domestication in Turkey had recently been unearthed (Çambel and Braidwood 1970; Braidwood, Çambel, Redman and Watson 1971).

The results of our survey showed that we had been wrong in our supposition that archaeological remains from the period of early plant and animal domestication would be abundant in this area. However, the geographical characteristics of the survey area did set off neatly a separate and well-delimited center of population which could be studied conveniently as a unit and whose growth, cultural development, and external relations could be defined rather clearly.

The Survey Area

LOCATION AND TOPOGRAPHY

The Keban Reservoir is located in east-central Turkey, roughly between 38°45' and 39°30' E. longitude and 38°30' and 39° N. latitude (Fig. 1). It was created by a dam on the Euphrates River (Fırat Nehri) just upstream from the old lead-silver mining village of Keban, and is fed by the waters of two major rivers—the Euphrates (also known as the Karasu above its junction with the Murat) and the Murat River (Murat Suyu). These two rivers joined slightly above the site of the dam and continued as the Euphrates past Keban and on to the plain of Malatya before cutting through the Taurus mountains to the Mesopotamian flatlands. From the dam the reservoir forms an irregular, generally narrow and very long, extended lake (Fig. 2), covering a total area of

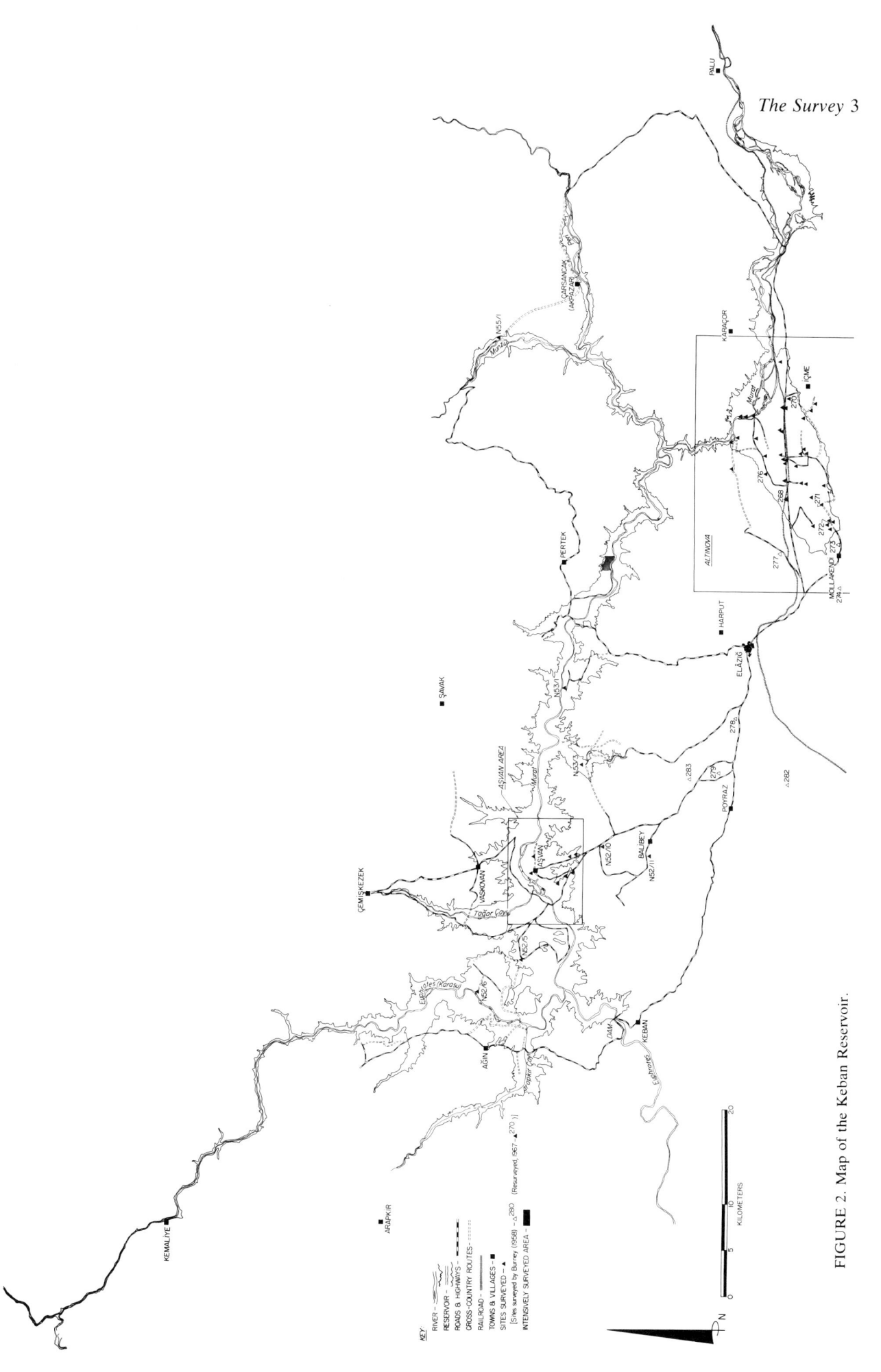

FIGURE 2. Map of the Keban Reservoir.

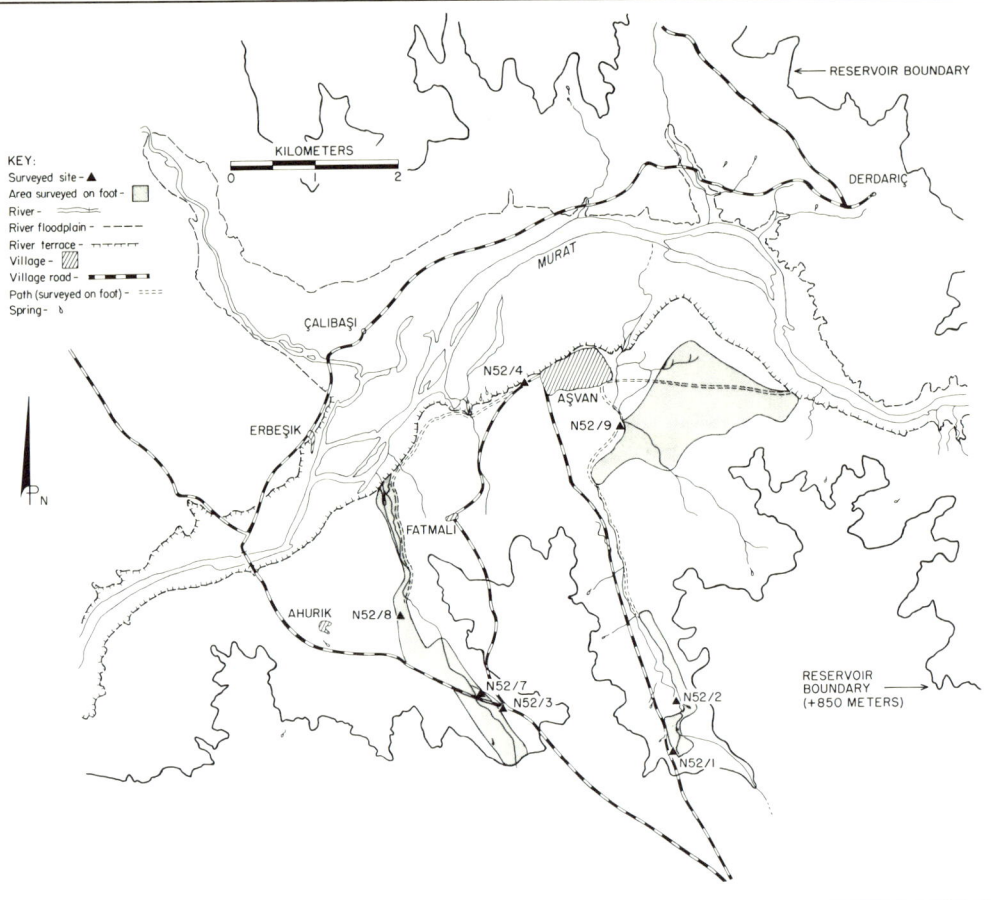

FIGURE 3. Map of the Aşvan area.

roughly 680 km (EBASCO Services, Inc. 1964; *Doomed by the Dam* 1967: 4), making the Keban Reservoir about the sixteenth largest in the world (*World Almanac* 1978: 452).

The reservoir is confined largely within deep, narrow, rocky valleys cut into igneous and metamorphic rocks (Baykal and Erentöz 1966; Altınlı, Pamir, and Erentöz 1963). This gives the reservoir area its narrow, elongated character. Two major arms run up to the northeast of the dam, the shorter one up the valley of the Arapkir Çayı and a very long one up the narrow valley of the Euphrates. The major length of the reservoir extends to the east and southeast of the dam, however, along the valley of the Murat River and to a lesser extent up the Munzur and Peri rivers. Most of these stretches of the reservoir are again elongated and narrow, in relatively deep valleys, with only small, scattered patches of more level, recent alluvial land here and there between the river and the steep valley walls (Altınlı, Pamir and Erentöz 1963; Baykal and Erentöz 1966). Such patches of fertile land tend to occur at points where tributary valleys enter the main valley. They are small, however, and although there were recently villages in almost all such places, they were often poor in comparison with villages on larger areas of deep alluvial soil. While the lower reaches of the valleys included in the reservoir are narrow and steep-sided, the long, extended upper reaches are even more so. These are extremely narrow, deep valleys, often virtually gorges through which the rivers and streams trace their narrow beds. Although the population is not sparse in these upper valley regions, it is definitely concentrated on the high plateaus and hills above the valley floor. The river valley is too narrow and deep to be inhabited effectively, and alluvial soil apparently too rare and inaccessible to be of more than minor importance in the agricultural lands of the people in these areas.

The reservoir opens up into broader, more

expansive areas in two places. Directly to the north and east of the dam lies an area partially in the valley of the Euphrates but mainly spreading along the lower reaches of the Murat River in the vicinity of the village of Aşvan (Figs. 2 and 3). This is an area of continental neogene and other sedimentary rocks. The other important widening of the reservoir is in the area to the east of Elâzığ, where the narrow line of the reservoir pool, running east along the valley of the Murat River, sweeps back to the west up a broad, flat plain to form a major embayment (Figs. 2 and 4). This area is the lowest and easternmost part of the valley plain called the Altınova (formerly also Uluova or "Great Plain," Saraçoğlu 1956:378; Sarıbeyoğlu 1951:16, or occasionally Mollakendi Ovası, Saraçoğlu 1956:378), which continues to the west beyond the bounds of the reservoir, running south of, and reaching a point somewhat to the southwest of, Elâzığ.

The Altınova or Uluova consists of a broad sheet of alluvium. This is Pleistocene alluvium in the eastern end of the valley which is to be flooded, but the upper, western end is covered by recent alluvium (Altınlı, Pamir and Erentöz 1963). This alluvium is covered with a thick and very fertile soil, and the plain, particularly the lower part to the east, is well watered by many small, spring-fed streams running into the Haringet stream (Saraçoğlu 1956:379). Villages were numerous here, and crops were varied and abundant. Indeed, the local name, Altınova, translates as "golden plain," possibly a reflection of its fertility and productivity (Pl. 1). Certainly the center of prehistoric and early historic occupation of the region covered this plain.

In and near the Keban Reservoir these broad valleys form, together with the Malatya plain to the west, the major intermontane basins between the southwestern Taurus mountains and the eastern Anti-Taurus or Munzur mountain range, between what Sarıbeyoğlu (1951:13) calls the Inner and Outer Taurus Mountains. The valley floors are not especially high in this region, although the uplands surrounding the Keban reservoir run 1500-2000 m in elevation, the first Taurus ranges flanking the Altınova to the south rise to 2000-2500 m and the Munzur range has several peaks above 3000 m (Tanoğlu, Erinç and Tümertekin 1961). The Keban Dam is based at approximately 700 m elevation, and the outlines of the reservoir trace the contour of approximately 845 m (EBASCO Services, Inc. 1964). Elâzığ, outside and above the reservoir, has an elevation of about 1020 m.

These elevations are quite comparable to those of the northern fringe of the Mesopotamian plain just over the Taurus Mountains to the south. There the plain is about 700 m in elevation, rising to roughly 1000 m in the first foothills of the Taurus Mountains, as at Ergani. Thus the preceramic village site of Çayönü Tepesi (Braidwood, Çambel and Watson 1969; Çambel and Braidwood 1970; Braidwood, Çambel, Redman and Watson 1971) near Ergani is found at approximately the same altitude as the base of the Keban Dam.

CLIMATE

Climatically, the most striking feature of the survey area is the fact that it comes alternately under the influence of cold, east Anatolian winter conditions and the hot, Mesopotamian summer regime (Tanoğlu, Erinç and Tümertekin 1961; Maps 8–13—other map references are all from this source). In terms of overall, mean annual temperature, the Altınova lies in the belt of temperatures from 17.5°–20° C, while the Aşvan area just falls into the next colder zone of 15°–17.5° C (Map 7). For the reservoir area as a whole, then, the average annual temperature must be close to 17.5° C. This is a reflection of the fact that the area is under the cold climatic regime of east Anatolia in the winter (Map 8), but that the zone of hot, Mesopotamian climatic conditions rapidly expands northward to encompass the Keban area in the summer (Maps 10–12). The cold is relatively short-lived, and along the river valleys of the reservoir area the average annual number of frost days is only 75–100 (Map 18). The averages for Elâzığ are given (Table 1) from data presented in Sarıbeyoğlu (1951:19). They may be taken as generally characteristic of the reservoir area, although as Sarıbeyoğlu notes (1951:20) there is much variation about this picture which is primarily related to variation in altitude. The area is thus characterized by a strong contrast between short, cold winters, roughly from December through February, and relatively long, hot summers, approximately from May through September.

Most of the reservoir area falls into the zone of 40–60 cm mean annual precipitation, while the Altınova, next to the Taurus Mountains, lies on

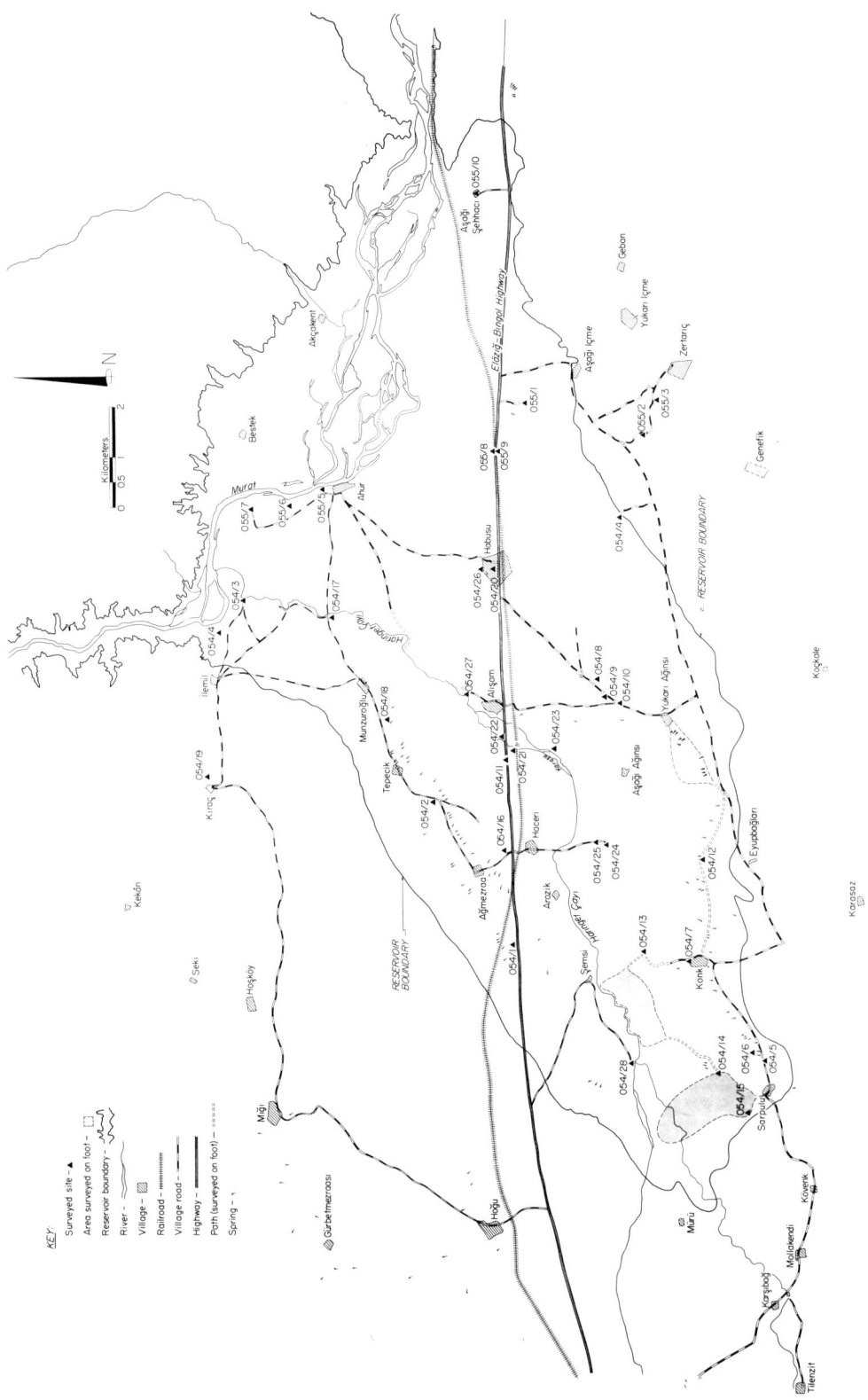

FIGURE 4. Map of the Altınova.

TABLE 1 Temperature and Frost Data from Elâzığ*

Month	Average Temperature (°C)	No. of Frost Days
12	−0.5	25
1	−2.4	27
2	0.3	18
3	4.1	12
4	12.5	2
5	18.7	0
6	24.2	0
7	27.8	0
8	27.6	0
9	22.1	0
10	13.7	0
11	7.8	7

*Sarıbeyoğlu 1951:19

TABLE 2 Monthly Precipitation at Elâzığ and Çemişkezek*

Month	Elâzığ§ Precipitation (mm)	Percent	Çemişkezek‡ Precipitation (mm)	Percent
12	48.6	11	119.7	17
1	33.3	7	119.7	17
2	57.7	13	73.7	11
Total Winter Precipitation (%)		31		45
3	40.3	9	60.6	9
4	72.4	16	103.6	15
5	55.3	12	45.1	6
Total Spring Precipitation (%)		37		30
6	24.2	5	9.3	1
7	4.2	1	3.6	1
8	2.1	0	1.9	0
Total Summer Precipitation (%)		6		2
9	10.4	2	9.0	1
10	42.5	9	65.9	10
11	66.5	15	82.5	12
Total Fall Precipitation (%)		26		23

*From Sarıbeyoğlu 1951:23
§Measurements taken over 10 years
‡Measurements taken over 3 years

the edge of the zone of 60–80 cm average yearly precipitation. Precipitation is very unevenly distributed over the year, however. The Elâzığ-Keban area lies on the border between regions characterized by greatest proportion of precipitation in the winter and greatest proportion in the spring (Map 49). Over the Keban Reservoir as a whole, then, the winter and spring precipitation should be closely equal, the Altınova perhaps falling more under the mountain regime with higher proportions of winter precipitation, and spring rains being somewhat more predominant in other parts of the reservoir.

Data from Sarıbeyoğlu (Table 2) illustrate this general picture and give some feeling for the degree of variability to be expected within the area covered by the reservoir. Elâzığ exhibits the typical pattern for the area with 26 percent of the yearly precipitation falling in the autumn, 30 percent in the winter, 37 percent in the spring and only 7 percent in the summer. The figures for Çemişkezek show a fairly strong trend towards a pattern of dominant winter precipitation as well as a much higher overall annual amount of precipitation, but it is likely that this is at least in part due to the short period of observation and that these strong deviations from the picture presented by Elâzığ would be moderated over the course of a longer period of recording.

Most of the precipitation is rain. There are, on the average, only 30–40 days with snow cover in the area (Map 40), while the mean annual number of rainy days is 75–100 for most of the reservoir, with the Altınova falling just inside the zone of 60–75 days (Map 47). There are thus about twice as many rainy days in the area as days with snow cover. Looking at these patterns of precipitation throughout the year (Maps 26–31), it is clear that the Elâzığ-Keban area comes alternately under the influence of the rain and snow belt associated with the highlands of the Taurus mountains and the dry climate of the Mesopotamian plain. The high precipitation along the mountains and adjacent upland areas prevails in the winter and spring, from November to April. After that, the dry Mesopotamian climatic zone rapidly encompasses the area, to dominate it over the summer, from May to October.

In short, the survey area is characterized by strong climatic contrasts due to its falling alternately under the influence of different climatic regimes. In has cold, wet winters, cool wet springs, a long, dry, hot summer and a short, cool, and moderately wet fall. Very much the same can be said for the area near the site of Çayönü.

VEGETATION

The Keban Reservoir lies within the region of natural oak-juniper forest (Sarıbeyoğlu 1951:28; Saraçoğlu 1956:432; Walter 1956:312; Gökmen 1962). The most common trees characteristic of this woodland include oaks (*Quercus* sp.), maples (*Acer* sp.), juniper (*Juniperus oxycedrus*), hackberry (*Celtis tournefortii*), ash (*Fraxinus rotundifolia*), almond (*Amygdalus* sp.) and East Indian mastic (*Pistacia khinjuk*) (van Zeist 1972:16). This natural vegetation must have originally covered the whole survey area, although today most of it no longer exists due to land clearance for fields and general deforestation by man. Even in the area of and around the Keban Reservoir, where much of the land consists of steep, rocky slopes and mountains, there was only roughly 23 percent forest cover in about 1950 (Sarıbeyoğlu 1951:26). Nevertheless, there are enough forest remnants to give a good picture of the composition of the natural vegetation in the area. The best description of the natural vegetation specific to the region within which the survey area lies is given by Sarıbeyoğlu (1951:28–29) from his personal observations.

In terms of forest trees, oak was the dominant genus. Juniper was also found throughout the region. Hackberry was found near Tunceli, and northeast of Tunceli, in the Harçik valley, there was ash (*Fraxinus oxycarpa* Willd.). Ascending in elevation, mountain poplar (*Populus tremuloides*) increased in frequency. Along the upper Munzur valley alder mixed with birch occurred, and just to the north, on one of the eastern peaks of the Munzur range, a unique stand of pine was noted. Willow and poplar were found in large numbers along watercourses.

Fruiting plants included wild Neopolitan medlar (Turk. *alıç*) and pear (*Pyrus elaeagnifolia*), which were both found everywhere except at extremely high elevations. Gum mastic trees (*Pistacia terebinthus*) grew in the areas of Çemişkezek and Harput. Sumac was encountered in large quantities in lower areas, and from place to place in the Harçik, Munzur, and Murat valleys wild grapes were found. Walnut trees were also found along many valleys, especially near Tunceli. Several types of short, alpine grass grew in the high mountain areas.

The various species noted by Sarıbeyoğlu in his geographical survey are typical of the southeast Anatolian oak-juniper woodland. The restricted distributions of several of these species undoubtedly are due to the influence of man. Originally this vegetation must have covered the whole region, with the major variation being between those areas along watercourses or by springs, the drier valley and upland, and the high, alpine meadows. From the recent work of van Zeist, it appears that this vegetation type was established in southeastern Turkey sometime after ca. 7000 B.C. (van Zeist 1972:16–17). At about 7000 B.C. the region from southeastern Turkey to the Zagros Mountains of western Iran appears to have been covered by an oak-pistachio steppe forest, and we can probably safely assume that this steppe forest was also characteristic of our area. It is likely, then, that the oak-juniper forest became established in these areas sometime between 6000–4000 B.C.

The early historical evidence concerning the vegetation of this area is extremely spotty and difficult to interpret. Still, it seems that the mountainous country above Mesopotamia was viewed as a forest domain throughout the Bronze Age and even after it, i.e. roughly from 3000 B.C. on, for a considerable period (Rowton 1967). Rowton (1967:268) even suggests that the whole of the eastern Taurus Mountains and part of the northern Zagros were referred to very early as the "wild cypress mountains." The term is largely confined to religious, mythical or epic contexts in Sumerian and is replaced elsewhere by an Akkadian loan word, which suggests to Rowton that the tree-epithet for this geographical area might go back to a very early phase in the Sumerian literary tradition, far back into the Bronze Age or perhaps even earlier. It therefore seems fairly certain that the steppe had been replaced by full forest cover well before 3000 B.C. The wild cypress (*Cupressus sempervirens horizontalis*) after which this region was supposedly named is no longer found there, however, but only in the southern Caucasus and northern Persia. Rowton suggests that it disappeared from the region because of heavy logging. The wood was exceptionally fragrant and therefore in great demand in Mesopotamia as timber for temples and palaces. It grew only at relatively low altitudes, making it readily accessible for cutting.

Not only the wild cypress, but also other trees may have been extensively cut and transported as timber to southern Mesopotamia from the eastern Taurus. Specifically, in later texts Rowton notes,

> From the Diyala to the Lebanon there is only one major gap in the sylvan horizon of Mesopotamia. That is the vast catchment area of the Euphrates in the region above Malatya. At no time is there any reference to timber in that region and today it is almost completely bare and severely eroded. Caution is of course necessary when faced with this sort of negative evidence. But there are widespread reasons, though by no means free from uncertainty, which suggest, in conjunction with the negative evidence, that this region is likely to have been deforested at an early date, most probably in the third millennium B.C. (Rowton 1967:274).

This area is, of course, where the Keban Reservoir is located. The logistics of transporting timber from here to lower Mesopotamia were easy, as the Murat River and the Euphrates formed a waterway directly connecting the two regions. There are numerous examples of the use of these rivers for just such transportation. In addition to undoubtedly extensive forest cutting for local use in building and for fuel for the smelting of local ores, then, there is a further possibility that the logging of timber was of substantial economic importance to the Keban Reservoir area for trade with the developing states of Mesopotamia. It may be useful to consider this possibility in interpreting and explaining the temporal trends of population growth and settlement pattern change revealed by the survey.

FAUNA

There are very little data on the natural fauna of this area. In the British Admiralty's geographical handbook of Turkey (Great Britain, Admiralty 1942:251) a general list is given. Of larger mammals, bear, hyena, lynx, fox, wild pig, big-horned ibex, and wild goat near the Euphrates are reported. Wild goat is still extensively hunted and bear also, to a limited extent. Small game and wildfowl are numerous, including a number of species potentially important for food or pelts. Trout are abundant in cold streams at high elevations. In the larger rivers are other fish, mostly of medium size, 2–6 lb., but including one species which may be 6 ft. long and over 100 lb. in weight.

MINERAL RESOURCES

The hard crystalline rocks forming the hills and mountains of the region around the Keban Reservoir are rich in many mineral ores. Some of these, such as the extremely rich chromium deposits at Guleman, are only of modern industrial importance, but there are significant occurrences of minerals which were of widespread use and importance in prehistoric and early historic times, also.

The largest and best known of these occurrences is the great copper deposit at Maden or Ergani Maden (Ryan 1957:60). This deposit is today one of the largest in Turkey, with reserves of several million tons of ore (Ryan 1957:25, 60). Other, minor copper deposits occur elsewhere in the region, at Hozat (Altınlı, Pamir and Erentöz 1963:112; Ryan 1957:59), and near Ovacik, Harput, Palu, and Sivrice (Ryan 1957:59–61). Some of these sources, but most probably the huge deposit at Maden, were exploited very early in prehistory. Artifacts hammered from native copper have been found at Çayönü Tepesi, where they date somewhere between 7500–6500 B.C. (Çambel and Braidwood 1970; Braidwood, Çambel and Watson 1969; van Zeist 1972). Later, with the advent of true metallurgy in the Chalcolithic and Early Bronze Age, the rich copper lodes of this region may have been important sources of ore.

Tin is rare in all of Turkey; in east Anatolia the only source mentioned is near Hozat, not far to the north of the survey area (Ryan 1957:63). It is, however, not at all sure that this source would have been of much use in pre-industrial times. Ryan's description makes it clear that this is not a rich nor an easily worked source: "... near Hozat there are several granite areas one or more of which contain small amounts of tin" (Ryan 1957:63).

Iron ore is found in several locations around the survey area. At least one of them is quite rich in ore. This is just up the Murat River from the Altınova, near the village of Genç where there are at least four occurrences of ore. The ore is easily visible. It "is seen over a large area covered by soil and forest" (Ryan 1957:108), and it is rich, containing almost 58 percent iron. There are also minor occurrences of iron oxide in the mountains to the south of the Altınova (Ryan 1957:111). Some other sources exist well to the north of the reservoir, north of Hozat (Ryan 1957:108).

Precious metals also come from the region. The best known and formerly most important source is the lead-silver mine at Keban. This mine has been worked off and on for a considerable period of time. The earliest workings are unknown but it presumably was worked in pre-Ottoman times (Saraçoğlu 1956:382). It was an important mine in late Ottoman times, with Keban being an administrative center from 1784–1834 for a large surrounding region including Harput, Diyarbakır, Sivas, Malatya and Erzincan (Sarıbeyoğlu 1951:76). Ryan reports a record of peak production in 1833 with 4–5 tons of silver being produced (Ryan 1957:24). Gold is not extensively discussed in the literature, but the mineral resources map of Turkey indicates a source on the south side of the Altınova (*Türkiye Maden Zuhurları* 1960).

Clearly, the region of the Keban Reservoir is rich in mineral resources. This does not mean that all of these resources were actually exploited in prehistoric or early historic times. There is, unfortunately, no direct information on prehistoric or early historic mining in this region. Most mining probably was open pit mining, the traces of which disappeared rapidly, and in the cases of some of the richest sources such as the Maden copper mines and the Keban lead-silver mines, modern mining operations have destroyed any traces of earlier operations. These deposits were potentially exploitable, however, and it is useful to bear this in mind when considering the nature and course of early cultural developments in the Elâzığ-Keban region, given the importance of metallurgy in several of the prehistoric and early historic cultures whose remains were found in the course of our survey in this area.

Archaeological Survey

Previous Investigations

An excellent review of early travels and observations in the region of Elâzığ has been given by Hauptmann (1969/1970:21–30) and will not be repeated here. To our knowledge, the first serious attempt at a general archaeological survey of this area was made by Kökten (1947). Kökten noted the presence of numerous mounds and remarked on the desirability of extensive excavations here, in what was obviously a center of early cultural development. Specific mention was made of several mounds within the area of the later Keban Reservoir, including at least Pulur (N52/5, called Kültepe by Kökten), Aşvan (N52/4, called Avşan), Könk (054/7), a mound called Şemsi (054/1, Tülin Tepe?), the four small mounds around Sarpulu (054/5,6,14,15), and Norşun Tepe (054/8), clearly recognized by Kökten as the biggest mound in the region and probably the center of early cultural developments here (Kökten 1947:461–462). However, the only ceramics illustrated, dated and discussed by Kökten are from Mollakendi and Kövenk (Kökten 1947:470–471, Pl. CIII, CIV). The sites are outside of the reservoir area and therefore not included in our survey, but these are Early Bronze Age sherds and, along with Burney's later data from this area, help somewhat to fill out the picture of Early Bronze Age settlement pattern developed by our survey within the Keban Reservoir area alone.

The most important precursor to our work was an extensive survey of eastern Anatolia made by C.A. Burney in 1956 (Burney 1958). In his survey of the Elâzığ plain, Burney's attention was concentrated on the higher portions of the plain from northwest to southeast of Elâzığ. The lower valley areas near the Murat and Euphrates were investigated only in the Altınova, southeast of Elâzığ (Burney 1958:204). Burney reported five mounds from the area later to be incorporated within the Keban Reservoir, and illustrated ceramic materials from them, largely of Early Bronze Age date. Interestingly, Burney omits mention of Norşun Tepe (054/8), the largest mound in the valley, although it had been noted specifically by Kökten, and Hauptmann (1970:115) seemed to be under the impression that Burney had presented material from it. Most of the smaller mounds were not noted or collected, and Burney naturally did not see any of the mounds in other areas of the reservoir.

A later survey in 1966 by the Middle East Technical University Department of Restoration was made in the reservoir area explicitly for the purpose of locating and recording antiquities which were threatened with flooding (*Doomed by the Dam* 1967). The orientation of this survey was toward historical periods, particularly as evidenced by standing architectural monuments. A certain amount of attention was given to mounds, however, and five of the large mounds in the reservoir were photographed and reported (*Doomed by the Dam* 1967:63). These mounds included three from the Altınova and also two from other areas of the reservoir.

Only two of the mounds reported by Burney and by the group from the Middle East Technical University are the same, however. There thus had been eight mounds from the Keban Reservoir recorded and reported by archaeological groups prior to our survey in 1967. Our group revisited these eight sites to the extent that was possible, one site having been destroyed in 1966, and investigated them more thoroughly and systematically. In addition, 44 new mound sites were discovered and similarly thoroughly investigated. We did not extend our survey to standing architectural features. Our interests in prehistoric material led us to concentrate only on mounds and other surface scatters of artifacts. This report, then, is a description of the 52 archaeological sites investigated by our group, of the methods by which these sites were investigated, the analyses of the materials from them, and of the patterns of prehistoric settlement in the Keban Reservoir area revealed by this work.

INITIAL SURVEY

The survey began with general reconnaissance of the area and rapidly developed into a more intensive search for sites to examine. It was our ultimate goal to make a systematic surface collection of materials from as many sites as possible. We were largely successful in doing this in the areas of intensive survey, but materials were obtained from every site located in these areas whether or not systematic collections were made.

At first a series of wide-ranging trips were made by jeep in and around the future reservoir area. These were intended to give us a rough impression of the region, of the reservoir, and of the general distribution of mounds in the various areas within the reservoir (Fig. 2). Most major areas of the reservoir were at least traversed. Every arm of the reservoir was at least partially covered.

Immediately striking were the sharp differences between the broad areas of deep alluvial soil and those areas where steep, rocky walls closely confined a narrow valley floor with only small patches of alluvium. The latter areas were the narrow valleys of the Arapkir Çayı, the upper Euphrates valley, the valleys of the Munzur and Peri rivers, and a good stretch of the lower valley of the Murat River between Aşvan and the Altınova. The Altınova and the area around Aşvan were the main expanses of alluvial terrain in the reservoir.

Not all wide valley areas were characterized by a dense contemporary population, rich fields or prehistoric mounds, however. Those wider areas which roll gently up out of the reservoir to the surrounding uplands are generally relatively poor in springs and small streams and consequently were less densely inhabited and less intensively cultivated than the better watered areas. Rows of springs and small streams are found in those places where a wide valley floor rises gently to meet steeply rising valley walls rather abruptly. Here, water from the surrounding uplands or mountains reappears at or near where the rocky valley walls meet the alluvial bottomlands.

Within the reservoir, the Altınova and the area around Aşvan were the best representatives of this latter situation, and it was in these areas, primarily that of the Altınova, that the largest concentrations of present-day population and fields were to be found. It was also soon apparent that the majority of the mounds in the reservoir were to be found in these two areas, and in the most dense concentration. The largest mounds and the greatest density of large mounds were clearly in the Altınova. A few sites were located elsewhere, and an intensive walking survey was made in one area along the Murat River south of Pertek to reconfirm the results obtained from general inspection. However, the obvious choices for further intensive survey were the Aşvan area and the Altınova (Figs. 3 and 4).

INTENSIVE SURVEY

In both of these areas, as well as the small area on the Murat south of Petek, almost every possible location for prehistoric sites was visited. A more extensive coverage by jeep, which quickly located the major, higher mounds was supplemented by a close coverage on foot of large portions of these areas. The five or six members of the survey party would space themselves 100–200 m apart and would walk over large swaths from one landmark to another. Many of the lower mounds or non-mound sites, not visible from the jeep, were found in these walking surveys. Inquiries of the local villagers, often accompanied by showing of obsidian, flint, and ceramics, frequently confirmed the results of our searches and occasionally revealed the existence of small

12 Archaeological Survey of the Keban Reservoir

TABLE 3 Survey coverage of the Keban Reservoir

Location	Area covered in sq. km:			
	General Survey	Intensive Survey	Reservoir Area (%)	Surveyed Area (%)
Altınova	—	180	26.5	56
Aşvan	—	28	4	8.5
Other	114	1	17	35.5
Total	114	209	47.5	100
Reservoir area (%)	17	31		
Surveyed area (%)	35	65		

sites not yet located by us. In these ways we convinced ourselves that we had located virtually all of the significant sites and the majority of all occupations which were represented by surface remains in the Aşvan area and the Altınova.

SURVEY COVERAGE

Of the 680 km^2 covered by the Keban Reservoir, approximately 323 km^2 were covered by the survey. This is about 47.5 percent of the reservoir area. Most of the area covered was in the Altınova and the Aşvan area. About 180 km^2 were surveyed in the Altınova and about 28 km^2 in the Aşvan area. All of this was intensive survey. In addition a little over one km^2 was covered intensively in the Murat River valley south of Pertek, giving a total of almost 210 km^2 covered by intensive survey. The other areas covered by us consisted of a series of smaller strips and areas in the different branches of the reservoir which were examined during our general reconnaissance of the region (Fig. 2). These smaller areas ranged from roughly 75 km^2 in the broad and open but dry area northeast of the Murat-Euphrates junction down to small areas 5–6 km^2 in size in the narrow valley arms of the reservoir. The areas covered may be roughly summarized in Table 3.

The portions of the reservoir not covered by our surveys consist in large part of narrower, steep-sided valleys. There are sites in these areas. A few were visited or seen by us in our general survey (e.g. N55/1 and an unvisited site east of Çarsancak, cf. Fig. 2), and a few were subsequently discovered by others. Sites in these areas are sparsely scattered relative to those in the intensive survey areas, however, and we feel fairly sure that the intensive coverage of these more limited but richer areas has provided us with the most useful data on the area which we could have gathered in the time available.

SITE NUMBERING SYSTEM

The sites located or visited and collected by the survey were numbered according to a regular system. This system was devised by Drs. Halet Çambel and Robert J. Braidwood in 1963 for the recording of sites located by their survey for prehistoric materials in the provinces of Siirt, Diyarbakır and Urfa. Our survey group, having similar aims, decided to adhere to the same system in the hopes of promoting its more widespread application.

The system is of universal applicability within Turkey. It is based upon a grid formed by dividing each degree of latitude and longtitude into units of 15' (Fig. 5). The horizontal rows of this grid, each 15' of latitude in width, are identified by sequential letters of the alphabet running from north to south. The vertical or north-south columns of the grid are numbered from west to east and are each 15' of longitude in width. A grid square is thus designated by the letter of the row and the number of the column within which it lies. The designation O54, for example, indicates the rectangle or area from 38° 30' to 38°45' N. latitude and from 39°15' to 39°30'E. longitude (Fig. 5). Within each of these grid units sites are numbered sequentially, usually in the order of discovery or of incorporation into the system, O54/1, O54/2, etc. Such a system is useful in several ways. It provides an accurate way of recording and referring to sites which are not named or whose name is unknown, and it easily and immediately differentiates sites with the same name (certain names for mounds are very common and are found repeatedly). Most important, the grid designation immediately locates a site to within a relatively

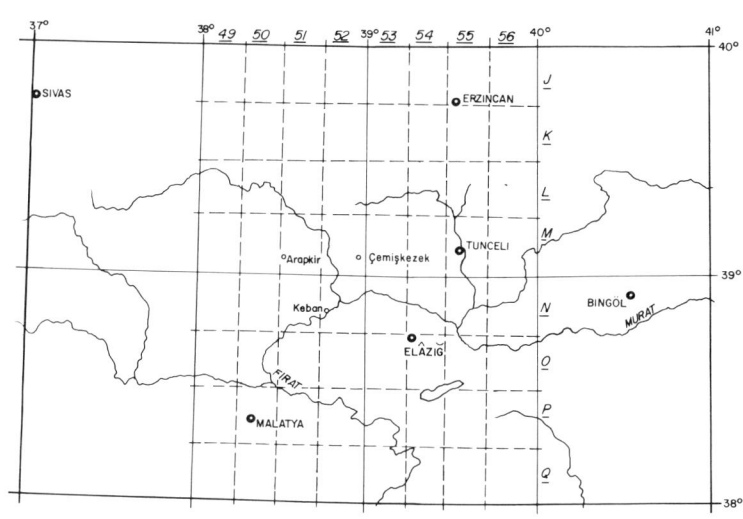

FIGURE 5. Reference grid for the site numbering system in the region around the Keban Reservoir.

small area within Turkey. In our area the average size of a grid unit is approximately 22x28 km. This system for recording archaeological sites should be useful for the rapid identification and retrieval of sites within specified areas, for studying distributional patterns of archaeological materials, etc., given its eventual widespread and uniform adoption.

SITE RECORDING

When a site was found or visited, a series of basic observations were made. The site was first approximately located on our maps of the reservoir area. If its position on the map was unmistakably clear or obvious from its direct relation to other features on the map, it was accepted as adequate. If, however, the site was found far from obvious landmarks, its position on the map was checked by a series of compass readings from the site to the most obvious landmarks or nearby villages. Insofar as possible the local name of the site and the administrative boundaries (village, *nahiye, kaza, vilayet*) within which it fell were recorded. These were usually elicited from local residents.

A brief description accompanied by a sketch plan and side view was then made. The nature of the site (mound, surface scatter, etc.), its general shape, its condition, and its present use (fields, village, pasture, etc.) were described. Its position with respect to significant features of the landscape such as springs, streams, valleys, etc. was mentioned. A sketch was then made to illustrate this description, often supplemented by photographs. The dimensions of the site were then estimated or roughly paced off, and the survey team ranged over the site, collecting what appeared to them to be a good sample of both typical and striking surface materials. The site location, this description, and the general surface collection constituted our basic data which was assembled for every site found.

Later, certain sites were revisited for controlled surface collection. In these cases much more detailed measurements and drawings of the sites were usually made. It was our aim to make such thorough and systematic examination of as many sites as possible. With the exception of a tiny, late (probably Ottoman) site in the Altınova, we were successful in doing this for every site where such work was possible within the areas of intensive survey. (Sites which were largely destroyed, covered by tough meadow grass, or underneath contemporary villages obviously could not be investigated in this way). In addition, two sites just outside of the reservoir area were treated similarly, in one case because of the particularly interesting materials found on the site and in the other because of the proximity of the site to a series of other mounds of the same period in the reservoir area, which made it appear that they, together, might form a group.

CONTROLLED SURFACE COLLECTION

The use of systematic collections of surface materials to infer something of the subsurface structure of archaeological sites was proposed and used quite some time before our survey in the case of shallow, non-mound sites (Binford, Binford, Whallon and Hardin 1970). From this earlier work we developed the idea that controlled surface collections on mounds might also be informative as to the subsurface structure of the mounds. This idea was first tested on a small mound in the province of Siirt, in the course of the Istanbul University—University of Chicago Joint Prehistoric Project survey in 1963 (Whallon n.d.). This work utilized regularly spaced collection squares arranged over the site in areas of different density. The results could be interpreted readily and allowed a reconstruction of the stratigraphy of the mound and of the differences in size and location of the three major levels inferred to exist.

These results led also to our consideration of a number of other possible ways in which such surface collections might be carried out so as to similarly disclose something of the internal structure of a mound before excavation. All of these ideas were tested in our survey of the Keban Reservoir area. All of the various methods of surface collection considered were applied here, some on several sites. It was hoped that these collections would serve as test cases which would allow us to evaluate the relative effectiveness and efficiency of the different methods. It was further hoped that eventual excavations in the area might provide some test of the relative accuracy of the reconstructions of mound structure made from surface materials collected according to these different methods. Another isolated test case is the work done to the south of the Keban area at Çayönü Tepesi (Redman and Watson 1970). This work is also an offshoot from our original work near Siirt, carried out after consultation and advice from us, to test one of the several possible alternative methods suggested by our original project.

In our original application of systematic surface collection on a mound, the distributions of materials of different periods exhibited a pattern of generally concentric oval bands in which older materials appeared generally peripheral to younger materials. This pattern was interpreted as a manifestation of the concentration of materials of different periods at the point on the mound where they were eroding out of the edge of the occupation layer to which they belonged. Since older materials would naturally lie under younger materials, they would lie outside of or peripheral to materials eroding from a higher, younger stratum where the edge of the older stratum was exposed and eroding rather than completely capped by later deposits.

It was known that such a pattern could be detected by the collection of surface materials from regularly spaced squares. Obviously it would also be detected by the collection of all surface materials from a complete grid of squares covering a site. It seemed clear that the tremendous increase in effort and time required to totally collect a site would far outweigh the value of any added detail or precision that might result. Total collection was applied at one site (055/3) found by our survey, because of our interest in the apparently very early obsidian assemblage found there in abundance.

Random selection of a certain proportion of the squares from a grid seemed a possibly good alternative to the regular selection or spacing of grid squares over a site. In considering this alternative we were guided by many of the arguments in favor of random sampling which have appeared recently in the archaeological literature. The central point of most of these arguments is that a random sample should give an unbiased and truly representative sample of the population being investigated, in this case the surface materials on a site. At five sites (N52/9, 054/2, 054/14, 054/21, 055/8–9) therefore, a grid was established over the site, and squares for collection were chosen randomly from this grid. In almost all cases we attempted to cover ca. 10 percent of the surface area of the mound with our sample, but on the largest site collected in this matter (054/2, Tepecik) this proved to be simply too great an effort for the time available. Only an average of ca. 6 percent of the surface of this site was collected, but this varied over the mound, being ca. 10 percent in the center, on the high peak of the mound, and dropping to ca. 4 percent–5 percent on the lower, surrounding terrace and peripheral slopes.

A variant of this method was applied to a single, almost circular site (N52/3). Here a randomized circular distribution of collection squares was designed. The number of 4x4 m squares necessary to cover ca. 10 percent of the mound surface was determined. The mound was divided into a series of concentric, 4 m wide bands radiating from its center, and the squares to be collected were divided among these bands proportionately to the areas covered by each band. The positions of the squares falling in each band were then determined by randomly selecting from the center of the mound compass headings whose intersections with the band gave the points on the band at which squares were to be placed.

The fact that the basic stratigraphic structure of the mound on which we originally applied a method of systematic surface collection was revealed by concentric bands of distribution of the materials of different periods led to two non-grid-based methods for collection. One was simply to collect materials from the surface in concentric bands, round or oval following the general shape of the mound, radiating outward from the center of the mound. This method was used only once, on a site (N52/4) which was largely covered with grass, leaving relatively little material visible on the surface. On most sites where surface collection was feasible, surface material was too abundant to collect entire bands in this manner.

Thinking again of the pattern of results obtained in our first experience near Siirt, it seemed plausible that collection from one or more strips of grid squares running straight across a mound or up from the edge to the center would reveal the location and superposition of major occupation layers whose edges were exposed and eroding along the slopes of the mound. If a clear pattern of concentric bands of materials did exist in the surface materials on a site, it seemed reasonable that a strip of collection units running at or close to a right angle across such bands would allow us to identify and define them as peaks in the frequency of materials of a given age at a given point or points along the strip. The peak frequencies of materials of different ages should be arrayed sequentially along the strip according to the stratigraphic relations among them. If, as was thought highly likely, erosion was moving materials a considerable distance down the slopes of high, steep-sided mounds, this also ought to be detectable in a strip collection. Although materi-

TABLE 4 Methods of controlled surface collection applied in the Keban survey

Method	No. of sites at which applied
Gridded strip	16
Randomized grid	5
Randomized circular grid	1
Complete grid	1
Complete concentric annular bands	1
Total	24

als of all ages would accumulate near the bottom of the slope, the materials pertaining to any one period or occupation level should be found running up the slope to the level from which they were being eroded, beyond which they should decline abruptly in frequency. Materials from different periods or occupation levels consequently should be traceable to different heights along the slopes of such mounds, reflecting the stratigraphic relations among them. Based on the preceeding considerations, the gridded strip method of surface collection was also applied on sites investigated by our survey, and because it proved to be an extremely fast and efficient method, was applied at 16 sites, far more than any other form of collection (N52/1, N52/2, 054/3, 054/6, 054/8, 054/9, 054/10, 054/11, 054/12, 054/15, 054/16, 054/24, 054/25, 054/27, 055/2, 055/4).

Finally, in one instance we were fortunate enough at one site (055/1, Korucu Tepe) to find a deep cut made far into the site, revealing a number of major strata. In this instance we simply made a rough sketch of the profile exposed and collected materials from a number of natural and artificial strata. This procedure is not, of course, a method for systematic surface survey, although it does give us much more information about a site than a normal, general surface pick-up usually can.

The different methods of controlled surface collection and the number of times which they were applied are summarized in Table 4.

We applied this wide variety of methods experimentally to compare and to test, at least partially, different ways of using surface materials to infer something of the subsurface structure of mounds in the Near East. The results obtained are discussed individually below, and their relative effectiveness in indicating periods of occupation, the size and location of each occupation layer, and the nature or condition of occupation layers in a site is evaluated in Chapter 5.

SUMMARY OF SITES FOUND, RECORDED AND COLLECTED

A total of 52 archaeological sites were recorded by our survey. A single additional mound was seen but not visited in the valley of the Peri River east of Çarsancak (Akpazar) (Fig. 2). Of the 52 sites investigated, five had previously been listed by Burney (1958:204). Bronze Age materials from these five sites were illustrated and discussed by Burney, but no general description of the mounds themselves nor any mention of materials from other periods was made. It thus seemed worthwhile and reasonable to revisit the sites mentioned by Burney. Sporadic references to these and other sites in this area, in particular those in the Altınova, are found scattered throughout the literature of travellers and archaeologists from an early date up to the Middle East Technical University's recent survey for historic sites. In all cases these are brief and quite incomplete. Again, it seemed necessary, for thorough coverage and adequate documentation, to record uniformly all sites located by our survey. We thus reduplicate only a very small amount of data already in the literature and are able to contribute 45 or more new sites to our knowledge of the archaeological remains in this area. Most of the sites were mounds, but eight of the 52 were not. Six were simply concentrations of surface materials, and two were small ruins, partially standing.

Of the 52 sites recorded, 47 are actually within the area flooded by the Keban Reservoir. Five recorded sites are outside the reservoir area. Such sites outside the reservoir area were visited, recorded, and collected because they were immediately adjacent to a group of sites which did fall in the reservoir, because they had particularly interesting materials on the surface, or because they seemed isolated and not likely to be found again except by intensive surveys. All of the sites recorded outside of the reservoir were mounds.

In the Aşvan area of intensive survey eight sites were found, seven in the reservoir and one outside. Six of these sites were mounds. In the Altınova, intensive survey disclosed 38 sites, 35 within the reservoir. Of these latter, six were not mounds.

General surface collections were made from all of the sites recorded by the survey. Of these, 33 were judged suitable for controlled surface collection. In total, 24 of these sites were actually collected in this manner. In the reservoir area there were 28 sites where controlled collection was possible, 22 of which were done. In the Aşvan survey area five sites within and one outside the reservoir were collectable. All five sites in the reservoir were collected. The one outside the reservoir was not collected. Twenty-one sites in the Altınova, 18 within and three outside of the area to be flooded, were potential candidates for controlled collection procedures. Seventeen of those within and two of those outside the future reservoir were collected in a controlled manner. No sites from other areas were collected in this way.

A great deal of site area was covered, and a tremendous amount of archaeological material was obtained from the controlled surface collections. A total of 1,623 grid squares were collected, covering 21,722 m^2 of site area (1,059 grid squares of 3x4 m, 563 squares of 4x4 m, and one 2x3 m square). Of these totals, 18,796 m^2 were collected in the Altınova and 2,926 m^2 in the Aşvan area. Gridded strips accounted for 12,714 m^2, randomized grids for 5,424 m^2, the randomized circular grid for 768 m^2, and the complete gridded collection for 2,816 m^2 of area covered by the controlled collections. The collection of complete, concentric, annular circles adds a substantial but not precisely measured amount to the above figures. We have not totaled the artifact counts from the various sites, but our collections were enormous, weighing an estimated three tons and containing perhaps over 200,000 sherds. But these are only impressive figures. The interesting results are the distributional patterns of materials found on and among the sites visited.

2

The Pottery

Introduction

Pottery was by far the most abundant material collected during surface survey and was really the only effective material for characterizing and dating the occupations present at most of the sites. However, a serious problem was the lack of information on the ceramic sequence in the area. All archaeological investigations previous to our survey had been limited also to surface survey (e.g. Kökten 1947; Burney 1958), and no excavations had been made anywhere within the region. Therefore, the first classification of the ceramics collected in our survey was rough and based primarily on characteristics of paste and temper, although a number of similarities with pottery from excavations outside the Keban region were seen. This was not a particularly satisfactory classification, and many of our first efforts to define periods of occupation at the sites surveyed were not very convincing or successful.

However, the first excavations in the Keban Reservoir provided an outline of the ceramic sequence in the area, and we were much better able to define chronologically relevant classes of pottery among our survey materials, using the initial information from several of the major excavations, along with more numerous and detailed comparisons with pottery from sequences known in other regions. The ceramics from our survey were thus classified into a series of wares, which are described in roughly chronological order.

A standard format has been adopted for these descriptions, giving the identifying features of paste, temper, colors, surface treatment, decoration, manufacture, firing, etc. In addition, each of these wares is illustrated in a series of figures presenting virtually every variety of rim profile found in the survey materials. Not all of these profiles occurred with the same frequency, and note is usually made in the ware descriptions of which forms are common, typical, rare, or unusual.

This amount of detail is provided to allow other workers to assess for themselves the accuracy of our ware definitions and chronological assignments. We are quite aware that the classification presented here is a general one. There is often reason to suspect that a fairly broad range of time may be spanned by a ware, and there is undoubtedly a certain amount of mixture in some wares of pottery from different periods. We hope that the presentation of our primary data in this detailed manner will allow other archaeologists to judge the extent to which our wares, as here defined, are chronologically or culturally meaningful. Our present belief is that mixture and lack of chronological precision are not significant enough to prohibit a generally accurate division of the survey ceramics into major temporal phases at the end of this chapter. If this is true, then the picture of settlement patterns derived from this data is also generally sound.

In the descriptions of the wares, firing is characterized impressionistically as "low," "medium," "high," etc., referring thus to sherds that give out a dull, hollow click, a sharp, crisp tap, and a clear, ringing sound respectively when struck with or on a hard object. The percentages of tempering were measured in a manner similar to that of Braidwood and Braidwood (1960:33–34), consisting of a quick, visual comparison of the number of particles seen in the cross-section of the paste to a series of squares drawn with differing densities of points in them. These are not percentages by weight or volume, therefore, but rather a measure of the relatively sparse to dense appearance of the tempering material in the paste. Descriptions of paste and surface colors were made directly from observation of the mass of survey materials. However, the illustrated sherds were chosen to be representative of the range of form in each ware, not the typical pastes, surfaces, colors, etc., and although the correspondence is generally good, some illustrated rims of typical form will be found to represent the unusual rather than the characteristic in these other features.

CHALCOLITHIC WARE

PASTE: Rough and moderately porous. Usually has a moderate amount of chaff temper and a moderate amount of grit or coarse sand temper. The grit or sand temper is very irregular in size with many small particles, commonly 1–1.5 mm but with some ranging up to 3 mm in size. Some sherds have small to large flakes of iron pyrites mixed in the paste.

  Color: Usually gray to dark gray in the core, but occasionally black and occasionally buff-brown to light buff. The core is most commonly dark and the surfaces lighter.
  Firing: Low to medium.
  Manufacture: Hand.

SURFACES: Both interior and exterior are almost always burnished, sometimes highly polished, and at least well smoothed. An occasional sherd is simply smoothed over. Interior and exterior surfaces are usually at least somewhat different in color, but in no fixed pattern. There is a wide variety of color—light buff, buff-brown, brown, red-brown, dirty brown, gray-brown, light gray, dark gray-brown, and dark gray. Almost all are mottled in lighter and darker shades, sometimes with stripe or occasionally cross-hatch or crisscross burnishing. Mottled brown to gray, irregularly burnished, predominates.

DECORATION: Lugs or knobs are common, usually simple, rounded knobs or simple, vertically flattened lugs (Fig. 6:i–k, y, z, ee). Horizontal appliqué ridges are not uncommon, usually with vertical cuts at slightly irregular intervals along the ridge (Fig. 6:h; Fig. 7:f). A variant may be short, appliqué ridges, sometimes in pairs (Fig. 8:f).

FORM: The most common form is a bowl with straight to very slightly outflaring sides and a simple, rounded to slightly pointed lip (Fig. 6:a–k). Some bowls may be deeper, with thin, straight sides (Fig. 6:l,m). Small examples of the most common form seem more like small cups than true bowls (Fig. 6:n,o). An apparent variant on this theme occurs at site N52/1 in the form of simple bowls with broadly rounded, slightly outflaring lips (Fig. 6:p–s). Occasional bowls exhibit a lip which is slightly beveled to the interior and slightly protruding to the outside (Fig. 6:t,u), while a few from site N52/1 have flattened lips (Fig. 6:v,w). More distinctive are simple bowls with slightly inturned sides and slightly pointed lips (Fig. 6:x–aa).

Hole-mouth bowls are not uncommon, usually with simple, round to pointed lip profiles (Fig. 6:bb–ee), but also sometimes with flattened lips (Fig. 6:ff,gg). Some sherds seem to represent very large, deep bowls with a simple profile of straight sides which angle outwards (Fig. 7:a–c), though these might possibly be from very large jars. Occasional rare sherds which may belong in this ware come from bowls with various forms of beaded rims (Fig. 8:i,j).

Jars are less common than bowls in this ware, but are found regularly. Some have broad, high, outflaring rims (Fig. 7:d,e). Rare examples have a very short, barely outflaring neck with a pointed lip (Fig. 7:g,h). Some jars have more broadly and gently outcurving rims. Larger varieties (Fig. 7:i,j) and smaller varieties (Fig. 7:k,l) exist. (The profiles of some of the larger varieties approach Early Bronze Age forms very closely (e.g. Fig. 7:l).

Bases are virtually always flat (Fig. 7:m–s), with varying degrees of rounding of the edges. Some bases may be round, or half-round, (e.g. Figs. 6:g and 7:s).

There are two different sorts of handles, as distinct from lugs. One is a horizontal strap or barrel handle (Fig. 8:a), which is often too small to be a true handle and must represent some means for suspension. The other is a simple, loop handle with a triangular cross-section (Fig. 8:g), but it is not known what orientation this sort of handle may have had on the vessel.

Sieves, or vessels pierced with many small holes, are not uncommon, and are typical of this type (Fig. 8:c). One example of a strainer spout is known (Fig. 8:h). Perforated or partially perforated sherds of this type may be spindle whorls (Fig. 8:d,e). Occasionally, miniature vessels of various sorts are found, sometimes looking like tiny ceramic boxes (Fig. 8:b).

THICKNESS: There is a continuous variation from thin (4 mm) through medium (5–7 mm) to thick (10–12 mm).

COMPARISONS AND DATING: This ware closely resembles the Dark Faced Burnished Ware of the Amuq' sequence (Braidwood and Braidwood 1960; 49–52, 73–77, Pls. 12, 80), although the Keban material has a more limited range of form. The comparisons are best with the Dark Faced Burnished Ware of Amuq' A and B (compare Figs. 6 and 7 with the Braidwoods' Figs. 105, 107, 121, 123, 137). The comparison with the earlier phases in the Amuq' sequence is strengthened by the resemblances of the Keban pottery with appliqué ridges, and ridges with incisions, to some of the Coarse Simple Ware in Amuq' A and B (cf. Braidwoods' Figs. 21 and 40:9–13). These comparisons suggest a very early date for this ware of ca. 6000–5000 B.C.

However, the few available radiocarbon dates from the Keban area indicate a much later temporal placement of at least some occupations characterized by this pottery. One date, from N52/3 (Fatmalı-Kalecik), is 4225 ± 50 B.C. (GrN-5284), and a date of 4259 ± 71 B.C. (P-1929) for levels with these ceramics at Korucu Tepe has been reported by Brandt (1973:444).

In the latter case, Halaf and 'Ubaid-like sherds were occasionally found alongside the plain Chalcolithic Ware, a situation similar to Amuq' D, which corresponds entirely with the carbon-14 date. In fact, the Dark Faced Burnished Ware in the Amuq' sequence lasts until phase E (Braidwood and Braidwood 1960:106), thus being found first with no painted ceramics, then with Halaf ware, with Halaf and 'Ubaid, and finally with 'Ubaid pottery.

Therefore, until the early range of the sequence in the Keban area is more thoroughly investigated, this pottery must be dated simply as earlier than 4000 B.C., possibly extending as far back as 6000 B.C. In most cases Halafian and 'Ubaid-like ceramics are so rare that we cannot rely on their occurrence in even a large surface collection to date more closely an occupation otherwise characterized by this Chalcolithic Ware.

Some may object to calling this ware "Chalcolithic." If, indeed, it extends to a very early time here, well prior to the occupations in which it is found associated with Halaf and/or 'Ubaid materials, it may well represent a "Neolithic" period in the Keban area. It has been called Neolithic by Esin (1971:157) at Tepecik (054/2) on the basis of the same comparisons with the Amuq' phases A and B that were made above, as well as comparison with the Tarsus Neolithic. However, both Brandt (1973:440–444) and Hauptmann (1976c:34) call it Chalcolithic, and wider comparisons are possible with materials called Chalcolithic in central Anatolia (cf. Horoztepe—Özgüç and Akok 1958:34–35, Figs. 61–119, and the comparisons made therein with Büyük Güllücek, Alişar, Dundartepe, and Alacahüyük; cf. also Gölhüyük—Kökten 1947: Pl. XCI).

Given the above comparisons, we will retain the name "Chalcolithic" for this ware. Future revision of this terminology may be necessary when the earlier ranges of the sequence in the Elâzığ area become better known.

GRAPHITE SLIPPED WARE

PASTE: Relatively compact but rough, moderately well levigated. Relatively little to no chaff temper. Small quantity of sand or fine grit temper, ca. 5 percent–10 percent. Usually only very small particles, but occasionally one as large as 1 mm.

Color: Core is black to dark gray, turning to light brown, red-brown, or occasionally light gray toward the surface on both sides. Browns are the normal colors.
Firing: Low to medium high.
Manufacture: Hand, often with "lumpy" or "bumpy" surfaces.

SURFACES: Both surfaces are slipped with black, graphite slip and then almost always burnished or polished. The graphite sparkles and shines in the light and generally rubs off easily on the fingers. The burnishing is usually striped and irregular, and the brown undersurface often shows through in stripes where the graphite slip is worn away.

DECORATION: Usually undecorated. One sherd has slight ribbing or grooving on the exterior (Fig. 9:b). Knobs or lugs, vertically flattened, are not uncommon.

FORM: Usually a simple bowl with straight, vertical to slightly outsloping sides and rounded to somewhat pointed lip forms (Fig. 9:a–e). One sherd comes from a jar with gently outcurving rim (Fig. 9:f).

THICKNESS: Medium, 6–10 mm.

COMPARISONS AND DATING: The rim forms and lugs or knobs of this pottery are all virtually identical to those of our Chalcolithic Ware. An exception is the slight ribbing or grooving (Fig. 9:b) which does not occur on the Chalcolithic Ware. On the basis of the extremely close parallels between this pottery and our Chalcolithic Ware, we assign them both the same dating. In the excavated levels characterized by Chalcolithic Ware at N52/3 (Fatmalı-Kalecik) two sherds with light, fugitive graphite slip were found. However, within our survey area, the Graphite Slipped Ware appears to be very largely restricted to the Altınova.

Cream Chaff Ware (Pl. 2)

PASTE: Light and porous, moderately well to poorly levigated. Abundant chaff temper, from 10 percent–25 percent. Other tempering material is essentially absent, but very rarely a sherd will have white grit inclusions.

Color: Generally light gray to gray in the center, ranging to buff, light buff or cream towards the surfaces. Sometimes light buff or cream all the way through.
Firing: Medium to high. Mostly rather high.
Manufacture: Both handmade and wheelmade. Handmade examples largely predominate, but some pieces clearly look wheelmade.

SURFACES: The inner and outer surfaces are generally the same, but there are occasional slight differences in color. Usually the surfaces are simply smoothed over, leaving moderately abundant chaff markings. Surfaces are often soft. Occasionally, better smoothed to lightly burnished examples are found. A number of sherds from the survey collections are slipped in a whitish to cream or cream-buff slip, with one example of a red-orange slip (Fig. 10:nn).

In the excavated sample from site N52/3, Fatmalı-Kalecik (Whallon and Wright 1970), none of the sherds of this ware were obviously slipped. This sample was our standard of comparison, and we therefore may have underestimated the importance and frequency of slipping on this ware at other sites. Sherds with slipped surfaces from the survey collections were included in this ware on the basis of their overall similarity to normal, unslipped examples in ware and form. The patterns of distribution seem roughly the same for both slipped and unslipped sherds, and at least two examples (Fig. 10:b,p) of slipped Cream Chaff sherds were collected from exposed levels in the cut at site O55/1 (Korucu Tepe), in which houses with typical Cream Chaff Ware are exposed. It is sometimes difficult to separate the slipped examples of this ware from the much later Hittite White Slipped Ware, without the aid of vessel form, as discussed below. The available evidence however, seems to argue in favor of the inclusion of the otherwise typical slipped ceramics within the category of Cream Chaff Ware, although the characteristic surface of the ware is simply smoothed.

Surfaces are generally light in color, the most common colors being light cream to light buff, with some gray-buff, orange and occasional red and light gray to brown-gray examples.

DECORATION: Other than occasional slipping, decoration is not known for this ware from the surface collected material. In the excavated sample from N52/3, however, there are a few rare sherds which are painted in black-brown or red to crimson in simple bands or cross-hatched lines (Whallon and Wright 1970).

FORM: There is a series of distinctive and characteristic forms of Cream Chaff Ware, alongside a number of relatively simple, undiagnostic vessel forms. A number of simple bowls of open form with rounded lips (Fig. 10:a–d) are common but not diagnostic. Occasionally the lip is slightly flattened horizontally (Fig. 10:e). More typical are simple bowls with an inwardly bevelled lip, leaving a ridge running around the inside of the bowl just below the lip (Fig. 10:f–o). Also typical are simple, open bowls with flat, grooved lips (Fig. 10: p–s). A few rims are vertical, with flat, grooved lips and a slight bulge at the beginning of the vessel body, like slightly collared bowls (Fig. 10:t) or incipient jars (Fig. 10:u). An open bowl with an inward-beveled, grooved lip (Fig. 10:v) is rare but clearly related to the bowls with flat, grooved lips.

Very characteristic of Cream Chaff Ware is a series of bowls with "beaded" rims or rounded protrusions of the lip running around the exterior of the vessel. These are usually deep bowls with vertical or, more typically, slightly incurving rims (Fig. 10:w–ee), but there are also more open, shallow varieties (Fig. 10:ff–ii). Similar rims are found on deeper, larger bowls (Fig. 10:jj–ll). An extreme example of such bowls has a heavy bead with a broadly grooved lip (Fig. 10:mm). Somewhat similar beaded rim bowls are found in our Hittite White Slipped Ware (Fig. 33:o), and it is occasionally quite difficult to distinguish some Cream Chaff bowls of this form from their Hittite parallels.

Simple, incurved bowls with round lips (Fig. 11:a–d) and bowls with simple, round lips and in-sloping sides, bordering on hole-mouth jars (Fig. 11:e, f) also occur. A few uncommon, open bowl forms (Fig. 11:g, h) complete the series of Cream Chaff bowls.

Simple jars with sharply out-angled rims, which exhibit a clearly defined inner angle, with plain, rounded lips (Fig. 11:i–l) or a square lip (Fig. 11:m) have been found in the excavated sample and the surface collections. These jars are not frequently paralleled in other, technologically similar wares. There are several variants on this form of simple jar: with a more excurvate neck (Fig. 11:o), and with a short, out-angled rim (Fig. 11:p). Quite characteristic for this ware are relatively large jars with out-angled rims and "beaded" lips (i.e., with a rounded external protrusion), which are not common in the excavated sample from N52/3 but are rather well represented in the surface collections from other sites (Fig. 11:q–v). Jars with out-angled or excurvate rims and flat or slightly beveled, grooved lips (Fig. 11:w–cc) are also most characteristic of this ware. Jars with outflaring rims terminating in triangular or trianguloid lip profiles, which result in an external protrusion of the rim (Fig. 11:dd–gg) are distinctive but relatively uncommon. A simple jar with broad, rounded lip, slightly out-turned (Fig. 11:hh), and two unusual forms with interior ledges, probably both bowls, one shallow (Fig. 11:ii) and one deeper (Fig. 11:jj) complete the range of shapes of this ware.

No bases were found in this ware. We therefore suppose them to have been gently rounded and now indistinguishable in sherd material.

THICKNESS: There are generally two rather easily distinguishable classes of thickness, or size, in the vessels of this ware. Medium-thick sherds, which range from 6–10 mm in thickness, and thick sherds which are roughly 18–20 mm thick.

COMPARISONS AND DATING: It was at first very difficult to distinguish this ware in the surface collections, and many of the sherds which were eventually assigned to this category were originally placed either in Hittite White Slipped or, more commonly, in Hittite Chaff Faced Wares. From the description of the ware, it is easy to see the high degree of technological resemblance among these three wares. It was really the finding of an assemblage consisting purely of Cream Chaff Ware in the upper levels of the excavation of the site N52/3 (Fatmalı-Kalecik—Whallon and Wright 1970) which definitively established for us the existence of this ware and its characteristic forms, quite distinct from the Hittite wares and undoubtedly of quite a different date. The finding of sherds of this ware in lower levels at 055/1 (Korucu Tepe), below Early Bronze Age levels, confirmed our impression of the early dating of this ware, which had been based largely on general parallels in form with dated ceramics from areas outside the Elâzığ plain. In retrospect, then, although a number of sherds, especially body sherds, were quite likely misclassified in the sorting of the survey materials, the reality of this ware as a chronologically significant class of ceramics seems sound to us, and its presence at a number of sites has been firmly recorded and confirmed by the tabulation of vessel forms. Where misclassification has occurred, it has tended strongly to be in the direction of classifying sherds of Cream Chaff Ware as Hittite sherds, primarily because of our doubts about Cream Chaff Ware and our difficulty in defining it from the survey materials. In all cases where this sort of misclassification was extensive, it has been detected by the discordance between the frequency of occurrence of the Hittite White Slipped and Chaff Faced Wares and other Hittite wares, or by the study of the rim forms of the ceramics involved, and largely has been corrected. Errors in tabulating body sherds undoubtedly still exist here and there, but are, in general, of little consequence when compared to the patterns of occurrence and distribution of the much larger number of correctly classified sherds.

The Cream Chaff Ware assemblage from the Keban area has numerous far-flung parallels from the Amuq' to southwestern Iran. In the Amuq' the materials from phase F are very similar to our group of Cream Chaff ceramics, particularly the Chaff-faced Simple ware (Braidwood and Braidwood 1960: Figs. 174, 176, Pls. 24:8–14; 84:6), and some Smooth-faced Simple ware from the same phase (Fig. 171-esp. 1, 4, 7, 21, 27). This would put the date of this ware between 3500–3000 B.C. Recent dates from excavated levels at Korucu Tepe (055/1) characterized by Cream Chaff Ware are 3380 ± 40 B.C. (GrN-5287) and 3420 ± 40 B.C. (GrN-5286), in perfect accord with the comparisons with Amuq' F materials (Brandt 1973:444).

Similar comparisons extend across northern Mesopotamia. Good parallels for Cream Chaff forms are found at Tepe Gawra in strata IX–XI (Tobler 1950:153–159), where wheel-made pottery also makes its first appearance as a part of the ceramic assemblage. The Braidwoods (1960:513–514) also relate their Amuq' F material to the "Gawra period" of northern Mesopotamia, pointing to similar ceramics from Tell Halaf and Carchemish as well as from Cilicia (Gözlu Kule–Tarsus) and Malatya (Arslan Tepe). More recently, this same ceramic assemblage has been reported from southwestern Iran (Wright, Neely, Johnson and Speth 1975) where it has been called Terminal 'Ubaid or 'Ubaid-Uruk Transitional and compared directly to the materials from the Keban site N52/3 (Fatmalı-Kalecik). In southwestern Iran this material has been dated to ca. 4000–3700 B.C. in corrected radiocarbon dates—again in perfect concordance with the standard radiocarbon dating, just after the middle of the fourth millennium, for the Keban materials and Amuq' F.

LATE CHALCOLITHIC GRIT TEMPERED WARE

DESCRIPTION: The description of this ware is the same as for ordinary Chalcolithic Ware with the one exception of form.

FORM: Jars with outflaring rims (Fig. 9:g,h). The rims are relatively low with respect to the vessel size, and the angle of flare is moderate, giving an impression of angling out rather than of outcurving. Open bowls with bead rims, one larger, and with a heavier, rounder bead on the exterior (Fig. 9:i), and the other smaller and finer, with a smaller bead (Fig. 9:j). Flat plates with low, vertical rims and a round lip (Fig. 9:k).

COMPARISONS AND DATING: This ware would be confused completely with ordinary Chalcolithic Ware except for its distinctive forms. Only rim sherds can be assigned to this category, therefore.

Distinction from other Chalcolithic ceramics was recognized only after the excavations at N52/3 (Fatmalı-Kalecik—Whallon and Wright 1970) and at 055/1 (Korucu Tepe—Brandt 1973:441).

Chronologically, these vessels belong with the ceramics of Cream Chaff Ware. They are found stratigraphically with this latter pottery, and parallels in Cream Chaff Ware are found for both the jar forms (Fig. 11:o) and the two bowl forms (Fig. 10:z,bb) of this ware. At N52/3 there is no obvious break between the earlier Chalcolithic occupation and the later occupation characterized by Cream Chaff Ware. Chalcolithic Ware continues in some of its distinctive shapes and in the forms of Late Chalcolithic Grit Tempered Ware alongside the new forms and new fabric of Cream Chaff Ware. There is thus good evidence for the chronological succession of a period characterized by Chalcolithic Ware exclusively, followed immediately by the period of Cream Chaff pottery, with some degree of continuity between these periods.

RESERVED SLIP WARE

PASTE: The paste of this ware is fine, compact and tough. It is well levigated. Temper is sand and is very variable in quantity. The most common paste contains ca. 10 percent light colored sand. The sand is mainly white, rarely with some iron pyrites included. The particle size is very fine, seldom reaching .5–1.0 mm in size. Other pastes vary, from having 5 percent or less, very fine, dark sand, to up to 25 percent light sand. Some very fine sand is included in all of them giving a typical impression of a fine sandy paste.
- Color: The most common color is a light brown to light buff. There are some instances of light gray, dark gray, dark reddish (maroon) brown. Occasionally the core is light gray grading into light olive-green surfaces.
- Firing: High to very high.
- Manufacture: Mixed wheel and hand? Perhaps slow wheel or well wiped hand manufacture.

SURFACES: The surfaces were first simply roughly smoothed. The exterior surface was then covered with a reserve or wiped slip. The basic surface colors run from light buff or brown to light or dark gray, with a number of sherds being greenish buff to olive-green. The slip is cream.

DECORATION: The slip applied to the vessel exterior is reserved or wiped in simple patterns. The most common is a series of obliquely radiating lines (Fig. 9:m). These usually radiate from a horizontal line at the vessel neck. They are irregular in width and often in angle. The other design found in this ware is a horizontal, ladder-like motif, or a series of reserve horizontal lines with short, reserve vertical lines, which do not reach the horizontal lines, running along between the horizontals (Fig. 9:n,o).

FORM: Almost no rims of this ware were recovered or recognized by the survey. The one clear rim of this ware belongs to a simple jar form with a slightly outcurving rim, which is quite thick in relation to the thickness of the body wall on the shoulder of the vessel (Fig. 9:l). One bowl of this ware was found with a flat ledge-like lip protruding to the exterior from a slightly incurving vessel wall.

THICKNESS: Medium-thick, ranging from 4–10 mm with a rough average of 6 mm.

COMPARISONS AND DATING: In the Amuq', this is "quite characteristic Phase G pottery" (Braidwood and Braidwood 1960:275). However, it is also found in Phase H, alongside the typical Early Bronze Age Red-Black Burnished ware. Reserved Slip Ware in the Keban area compares closely to that from the Amuq' (Braidwood and Braidwood 1960: Fig. 218). Therefore, a range of ca. 3000–2500 B.C. is suggested for this ware, with the period of its most characteristic occurrence falling in the earlier half of this range.

PLAIN SIMPLE WARE

PASTE: Plain Simple Ware is characterized by an extremely fine and compact, well-levigated paste. It is generally so dense, homogeneous, and compact that it forms a solid, with only occasional, pinprick-size holes in it. In spite of its fineness and homogeneity, it is soft, and lighter cream-white pieces are often chalky, leaving white powder on the fingers. The paste is usually just slightly too hard for this, however. There seems to be no tempering material added to the clay, perhaps an occasional rare speck of fine sand is to be seen in some sherds.
- Color: The color of the paste is light, ranging from a light whitish cream or light greenish cream through cream-buff to a light buff. An occasional rare piece is fired harder, to a light olive color with a cream tinge. The color is generally uniform throughout the thickness of the sherd, only sometimes exhibiting a very thin layer near the surfaces which is slightly lighter than the core.
- Firing: Generally highly fired, perhaps ranging down to medium-high firing for the softer pieces.
- Manufacture: Wheel. The wheel-marks are clearly visible on the vessel interiors, sometimes also with some slight grooving. The exteriors also usually show fine wheel-marks, although they are sometimes completely smoothed over.

SURFACES: The surfaces are smooth and unburnished. On occasional fine pieces the smoothing almost reaches the point of a burnish, but not quite.

DECORATION: Virtually none. Only an occasional piece is simply incised.

FORM: Very few rims of this ware were recovered, and the range of forms represented is certainly limited to an unrepresentative sample. One simple bowl form, with a very slight, rounded or beaded lip is known (Fig. 9:p), and a simple outflaring profile from a broad, open bowl or from a simple jar (Fig. 9:q) was also found.

Bases were much more frequent. They are both flat and ring bases. Flat bases are either sharply angled at the edge (Fig. 9:r,s) or are gently rounded from the base up to the vessel wall (Fig. 9:t,u). Bases sometimes show some irregular, interior grooving, perhaps resulting from the manufacturing process as the vessel was turned (Fig. 9:r,s). This feature is more common on simple, sharp-angled bases than on others, and on bases in general in comparison with the rest of the vessel. Simple, low, ring bases are also common (Fig. 9:v–x).

In addition to the usual rims and bases, stems of vessels in this ware are also found, representing a class of hollow-footed goblets or chalices (Fig. 9:y,z), for which we unfortunately do not know either the rim forms or the full bases.

THICKNESS: This fine ware is moderately thin, generally ranging around 4–5 mm in thickness.

COMPARISONS AND DATING: Similar Plain Simple Ware occurs in a number of Amuq' phases. Parallels for this ware from the Keban are difficult to demonstrate precisely because of the paucity of rim sherds and the very fragmentary condition of our surface-collected material. This enormously restricts our ability to compare forms between the two regions. However, the simple beaded rim bowl seems to find its best parallels in Amuq' G (Braidwood and Braidwood 1960: Fig. 206:4) and H (Figs. 269:1; 270:3). Also, the high, pedestal bases typical for this ware (Fig. 9:y,z) are most common in Amuq' G (Braidwood and Braidwood 1960: Fig. 214:18–24, Pl. 26:5–6), and the small ring bases of the Keban material are most like those illustrated from Phase H (Braidwood and Braidwood 1960: Fig. 269:9–12). In addition, the rare incised pieces in the survey collections show close parallels with similar pottery from Amuq' G (Braidwood and Braidwood 1960: Fig. 221:5–8). However, the simple jar rim (Fig. 9:q), insofar as so small a piece can be compared, shows most resemblance to forms in Amuq' I (Braidwood and Braidwood 1960: Fig. 312:21 or 25). Low ring bases are also typical of Phase I (Braidwood and Braidwood 1960: Fig. 313:17–18), and chalice bases are found in Phases I–J (Braidwood and Braidwood 1960: Pl. 40:5). Flat bases are common throughout the sequence, from Phase G to J. It is said that the best comparisons for the excavated Plain Simple Ware from Korucu Tepe (055/1) are with Amuq' I–J (Kelly-Buccellati 1974:44).

In terms of dating, this gives a possible range of 1000 years for this ware—from 3000–2000 B.C. Our feeling is that the survey materials show a slightly better resemblance to the Amuq' G–H materials than to the later forms, and we have here treated them as early third millennium ceramics. However, the Korucu Tepe finds indicate that this may be wrong—that this ware may have a later date in the Keban area, or that it may even span the entire third millennium here.

FINE GROOVED WARE

PASTE: The paste of this ware is extremely fine, extremely compact, tough, non-porous, and extremely well levigated. There is no true visible temper, although there are very rare, tiny, white particles in the paste of some sherds.

    Color: The core is often banded in layers of different colors. The colors of these bands vary from orange through light buff to light gray. Some sherds are homogeneous light gray or light buff throughout, but there is usually a mixture and alternation of colors. The most typical colors in this alternation are light gray with orange.
    Firing: Very high.
    Manufacture: Wheel.

SURFACES: The surfaces of this ware are always very well smoothed, but not burnished. On both inside and outside surfaces there are usually very evident, fine to moderately pronounced grooves, presumably made as the vessels were being turned, but these are grooves made by the fingers, rather than wheel-markings in the normal sense.

The colors of the surfaces range from orange through deep red, light buff, dark brown, to dark gray. A mixture is occasionally seen, particularly of orange and gray. In these instances, the sherds typically have grooved stripes of lighter gray with occasional intermediate streaks of orange.

DECORATION: None known.

FORM: Relatively few rims of this ware were recovered from the surface survey, and the range of forms represented is undoubtedly very restricted and probably not really representative of the ware. At least one small, hole-mouth bowl is present, with a simple rounded lip profile and, in this case, a shallow exterior groove just below the lip (Fig. 9:aa). Another bowl form is rather unusual, with a broad, flat lip, protruding to both the interior and the exterior and a body wall which thins rapidly as it descends from this thick, T-shaped rim (Fig. 9:bb).

The known bases are flat, and the typical grooves of this ware are particularly pronounced on vessel interiors near the base (Fig. 9:cc).

THICKNESS: Very thin with a range of 3–7 mm, but with 3–4 mm typical.

COMPARISONS AND DATING: This rare ware is apparently an import to the Keban area from northern Mesopotamia. There it is known from Early Dynastic III and Akkadian levels and can be dated to ca. 2600–2300 B.C. (Mallowan 1947: 29–31; van Loon 1973:362, Kelly-Buccellati 1974:44).

Early Bronze Age Burnished Ware

PASTE: The fabric of this ware is generally moderately coarse and poorly levigated. The tempering material is variable, but there is virtually always some quantity of chaff. There may or may not be grit tempering also. The most common fabrics have either abundant chaff inclusions (20 percent–30 percent) and little (less than 5 percent) grit of irregular size, or have less than 10 percent chaff temper but are then rough with irregular-sized grits in moderate abundance (15 percent–20 percent). The grit temper ranges from very tiny sand-sized particles up to larger, angular fragments 2–3 mm in size. The grit is generally light in color, ranging to pure white.

Color: The paste color is variable. The core is quite often distinct from the surfaces, being usually dark gray to black while the surfaces are lighter. Sometimes the cross section of the sherd shows two zones, corresponding to the usual variation in surface color, running from lighter on one side to darker on the other, with a rather sharp boundary between the two zones. Only rare examples show a uniform color throughout the core. These pieces are generally either the high-fired gray or black sherds, or the lighter chaff-tempered, low-fired, buff-colored sherds.

Firing: Low to medium. Occasionally medium-high.

Manufacture: Hand, generally smoothly shaped.

SURFACES: The interior and exterior surfaces are almost always different. This is usually simply a matter of color, in which case the interior surface is quite often lighter than the exterior. Not uncommonly, however, the interior surface is left unburnished, being only smoothed, while the exterior is burnished. The exterior surfaces are always burnished, usually to a moderate polish, though sometimes just lightly. The degree of burnishing does not run continuously from lightly burnished to highly polished, but there is an apparent break between moderate burnishing and very high polishing to a glossy finish. A separate ware has been recognized, therefore—Early Bronze Age Polished, to accomodate these extremely well finished sherds, and Early Bronze Age Burnished contains only ceramics which are lightly to moderately well burnished.

Exterior surfaces range in color from pure black through dark gray to an occasional gray-brown and on to a series of lighter browns, ranging through red-brown to a light buff. There is sometimes some variation in color on the same piece, but generally the colors seem to be rather uniform on a single vessel. In terms of exterior surface color, blacks and grays make up an estimated 40 percent–50 percent of the total number of sherds, as compared to the buffs and browns.

Interiors range through roughly the same colors, but with greater emphasis on the lighter shades of gray, buff, and brown. The interiors of many vessels are significantly lighter in color than the exterior surface.

DECORATION: Pottery of this type is occasionally decorated with grooves or with appliqué ridges in patterns, but this decoration is so distinctive, with definite foreign affiliations, that sherds exhibiting such decoration were assigned to another "ware"—Early Bronze Age Relief Decorated.

FORM: This ware occurs in a wide variety of forms, a number of which are very distinctive and diagnostic. Some of this variability may reflect chronological differences in form which were unrecognized at the time of the survey and of the analysis of the survey materials. We present all the forms together, however, just as they were tabulated in analyzing the survey materials, and will comment below under "Comparisons and dating" on some of the recent information available concerning forms in this series.

The most common, and the most diagnostic and characteristic form in which this ceramic occurs is a vessel with a broad, flat "groove," impression or indentation running around the neck. This depression creates above it a relatively short rim which usually has a flat or partially flattened exterior face, forming what has formerly been called a "rail-rim" by Burney (1958:165ff.). The lower edge of this depression usually also is marked by a sharp or clear break. This sometimes takes the form of a shoulder on the vessel but more often simply marks the edge of the neck indentation, while the body continues smoothly from this point down. We therefore describe this typical profile of this ware as an impressed or indented neck, rather than follow Burney in calling the shape a "rail-rim." There are occasional sherds which have the characteristic rim form but which have either so broad a neck indentation that the lower border is not preserved on even quite large sherds, or which actually have no sharply defined lower border. Such sherds really do have the appearance of vessels with "rail-rims," but, relying on the evidence from numerous sherds, in which an impression with consistently clear upper and lower edges is the prominent feature of vessel form, we are treating all these sherds as members of a single large class of "impressed neck" vessels.

The specific forms or profiles of these impressed neck vessels are quite variable. There are some bowl-like forms with vertical to very slightly in-sloping necks (Fig. 12:a–e). These forms grade rapidly into jar forms with more and more steeply in-turned necks (Fig. 12:f–i). The typical or most common form seems to be a relatively squat jar with a slightly in-sloping neck surmounted by a slightly out-turned rim above the neck depression. (From this it can easily be seen why the form early acquired the name of "rail-rim" jar.)

The rim form shows many varieties, running from flattened and squared-off (Fig. 12:j–n), through shapes which are rounded from the inside to a point or peak above the flat outer face (Fig. 12:o–t), to various forms and degrees of rounding (Fig. 12:u–z). A few profiles show such faint or subtle neck indentations that the characteristic profile is almost lost, just detectable, often more with the fingers than by eye (Fig. 12:aa–cc).

Larger vessels occur, sometimes with high necks hinting at more elongated jar forms (Fig. 12:dd), but more often being simply larger variants of forms found in the more typical smaller vessels (Fig. 12:ee–hh). Some peculiarities in form do occur among these larger vessels, however (e.g. Fig. 12:ee,hh). Very large, storage vessels of "impressed neck" (or "rail-rim") type also regularly occur, but we have generally placed them in our category of Early Bronze Age Thick ceramics.

A series of small bowl forms in this ware, with more or less sharply out-turned lips which are often thickened or somewhat squared-off (Fig. 12:ii–ll), are quite reminiscent of the common "impressed neck" vessels even though lacking the true characteristics of that form. These small bowls seem to represent some sort of degenerate or secondary, related form of the true impressed rim vessel type.

Plain bowls also occur, most simply with a square, horizontally flattened lip profile (Fig. 12:mm–qq). The rims of such bowls are occasionally ornamented with a modeled spur or projection which seems more decorative than possibly functional (Fig. 12:nn). The flat lip is rarely tilted outward (Fig. 12:rr). A few miscellaneous shallow bowl profiles have various rounded lip forms (Fig. 12:ss,tt).

There are two other rather unusual bowl forms.

One is a shallow bowl with a thickened, bead-like lip (Fig. 13:a,b). The other comprises a series of bowls with simple, rounded, outward-protruding ledge rims (Fig. 13:c–f).

There are some deeper bowls with slightly pointed lips and a profile which swings up to become almost vertical near the lip (Fig. 13:g–i). These bowl forms seem to grade into forms in which the body becomes thickened just below the lip on the outside, leaving a narrow lip with an exterior bulge in the body below the lip (Fig. 13:j–l). These forms in turn seem to continue on into true hole-mouth jars (Fig. 13:m–y). Some of these hole-mouth jars are sharply in-turned, with a large sweep to the body profile (Fig. 13:o–q), and sometimes have slight exterior grooves on the in-turned part (Fig. 13:r), but the majority of the various forms of hole-mouth jars have only slightly in-turned profiles. Some small vessels have a tiny upward or outward-flaring lip around their hole-mouth (Fig. 13:w,x). Other hole-mouth vessels have occasional lugs (Fig. 13:y), but the examples at hand are too fragmentary to allow any detailed description of such lugs.

There are some other unusual and peculiar bowl forms (Fig. 13:z–bb) and some simple vertical lip profiles from vessels which may be either deep bowls or simple jars (Fig. 13:cc–ee).

The last important bowl form is what we may call the V-profile hole-mouth jar (Fig. 13:ff–ii). These are vessels whose body walls angle smoothly outward until, at a point close to the top of the vessel, they sharply angle inwards for a short distance to a simple rounded or squared-off lip. The whole profile thus looks somewhat like an asymmetrical V on its side. The form is characteristic, and, as we will discuss below, seems to be chronologically restricted to a very late phase of this ware.

In addition to the typical impressed neck jars, there are also a number of simple jar forms in this ware. Many are jars with short rims out-turned above an inwardly sloping body wall (Fig. 13:jj–tt). A special rim form has a band of exterior grooves or corrugations (Fig. 13:uu,vv). There is a flat panel above this band of grooves, just below the lip. The lip is rounded from the inside to a round point. For this form, also, there now appears to be a specific chronological position which will be discussed below.

A wide range of other jar profiles is also present in our sample (Fig. 14:a–z). There are many variations in vessel shape and lip profile in this mixed group, but it is not easy to subdivide it into definite classes, and none are particularly distinctive.

One specific and diagnostic feature, however, is the triangular ledge handle on jars with slightly excurvate necks (Fig. 14:aa,bb). This feature is very characteristic of this ware.

Some odd forms occur. Vessels with some sort of interior ledge (Fig. 14:cc,dd), a flat, plate-like form with a broad, flat rim (Fig. 14:ee), a graceful bowl form which in some ways looks Iron Age, but which is definitely of this ware (Fig. 14:ff), and two rims from either broad bowls or unusual jar forms (Fig. 14:gg,hh).

Bases are more varied in this ware than in most others. There are simple flat bases (Fig. 14:ii), flat bases with an external bead running around the foot (Fig. 14:jj), at least two types of ring bases (Fig. 14:kk,ll), and at least one vessel foot pierced by a hole (Fig. 14:mm). Unfortunately, because of the lack of complete vessels in our collection, it is impossible to begin to associate specific forms of bases with forms of rims.

THICKNESS: Obviously, thickness varies a great deal in this ware, but the majority of pieces are of medium (6–10 mm) thickness.

COMPARISONS AND DATING: This is the typical burnished pottery of the East Anatolian Early Bronze Age (Burney 1958), otherwise known as the Early Trans-Caucasian Culture (Burney and Lang 1972:44). Its origins have been traced to Armenia and Georgia (Kelly-Buccellati 1974:49–51). Closely related pottery is found in the Amuq' Phases H and I, as Red-Black Burnished ware (Braidwood and Braidwood 1960), and as far south as Palestine, as Khirbet Kerak ware (Amiran 1952; Whallon and Kantman 1969). In general, then, this ware dates to roughly 3000–2000 B.C. (cf. van Loon 1973:361–368; Kelly-Buccellati 1974:52–54).

More specifically, the impressed neck or "rail-rim" vessels occur throughout the Early Bronze Age sequence (Kelly-Buccellati (1974:48), although they appear most characteristic of the early and middle ranges of this span of time. The sharply angled-in or V-profiled hole-mouth jars (Fig. 13:ff–ii) are typical for the Early Bronze III period and directly develop into similar Middle Bronze Age forms (Kelly-Buccellati 1974:66).

Jars with exterior grooving or fluting on the neck (Fig. 13:uu,vv) may also be referred to the Early Bronze III period (Kelly-Buccellati 1974:48).

EARLY BRONZE AGE RELIEF DECORATED WARE

DESCRIPTION: The description of this ware is the same as for the Early Bronze Age Burnished, except for the following:

DECORATION: The exterior surface is decorated with geometrical reliefs formed by small, raised ribs (Fig. 15:a–c). In the cases examined, these ribs seem to be built up from the body material and are not appliqué strips.

FORM: The only example of this ware on which the rim profile was also preserved exhibits a typical Early Bronze Age Burnished profile of the "impressed neck" sort (Fig. 15:a).

THICKNESS: Moderately thick in the examples seen (15–18 mm).

COMPARISONS AND DATING: Obviously closely related to Early Bronze Age Burnished Ware in general, and characteristic for the East Anatolian Early Bronze Age or the Early Trans-Caucasian Culture (Burney 1958; Burney and Lang 1972), this particular variety of ceramics is typical of the earlier periods of the Early Bronze Age. At Korucu Tepe (O55/1) it is found only in the Early Bronze II levels, but elsewhere it occurs earlier, in Early Bronze I contexts (Kelly-Buccellati 1974; 48, 51–54). This particular ware thus dates ca. 3000–2300 B.C.

EARLY BRONZE AGE LIDS

DESCRIPTION: This category is not really a proper ceramic ware at all, but is a convenient pigeon-hole in which to put this rather characteristic class of artifacts, distinct from ordinary sherds. These lids have technological characteristics in common with the typical Early Bronze Age Burnished Ware. They are sometimes less highly burnished than the vessels themselves, however. They have a characteristic lenticular shape with one flat side. The upper side arches up to a high point from which it drops abruptly into a groove encircling the center of the lid. The handle is not preserved on most examples. In some cases it seems likely to have been a knob of some sort, while in one case the beginning of a strap handle is present on the lid (Fig. 15:g).

The lids are often decorated with grooved lines radiating out in various manners from the center (Fig. 15:d–f). An occasional lid appears to have been plain (Fig. 15:g).

COMPARISONS AND DATING: The same as for Early Bronze Age Burnished Ware generally.

EARLY BRONZE AGE POLISHED WARE

PASTE: The paste ranges all the way from very fine and smooth to relatively rough. It is generally moderately fine-textured with a small amount (ca. 15 percent) of fine chaff temper and a little (usually only 5 percent or less) grit temper composed mainly of gray-white grits of medium size (.5–1 mm).

- Color: Black to dark gray. There are occasional light-colored sherds with a lighter-colored paste, light gray in the core grading to brown or light buff at the surfaces.
- Firing: Ranges again all the way from medium low to high. The average is a good medium.
- Manufacture: Vessels of this ware are finely made by hand. On sherds with unburnished interiors many smoothing marks are visible on the interior.

SURFACES: Both surfaces are generally treated in the same manner. Interior and exterior surface colors also are usually the same, although the interior surface is occasionally lighter than the exterior surface, as is typical for much of the Early Bronze Age pottery in this area. The great majority of the sherds of this ware are black. However, there are occasional light gray or light brown surfaces.

The surfaces seem to be slipped, or else they are wet-smoothed carefully before burnishing. Typically, they are both then extremely highly burnished to a lustrous polish. There seems to be a definite break here between the degree to which these vessels are polished to a luster and the ordinary burnishing of Early Bronze Age Burnished ceramics. Occasional sherds show the typical high polish only on the exterior surface, having a less well burnished or even unburnished interior.

DECORATION: None.

FORM: The majority of vessel forms in this ware parallel the typical Early Bronze Age Burnished "impressed neck" forms. They also run the same range, from impressed neck bowls (Fig. 16:a,b) to impressed neck jars (Fig. 16:c–e). Some very small jars have the typical shoulder of such forms, but lack the "rail–rim" (Fig. 16:f), other small jars seem to have simply a strongly out-curving neck (Fig. 16:g), while some jars of normal size have the "rail–rim," but lack the shoulder characteristic of the "impressed neck" (Fig. 16:h).

Several other bowl forms occur, mostly very simple profiles with out-sloping sides (Fig. 16:i), slight in-turned rims (Fig. 16:j), or, apparently, simply straight sides (Fig. 16:k).

A relatively unusual form is a round pot stand (Fig. 16:l), obviously for relatively small vessels, and, interestingly, exhibiting the same sort of "impressed" or "rail–rim" profile as many of the ordinary vessels in this ware.

THICKNESS: Sherds of this ware run from thin to medium thick (4–8 mm), congruent with the range from medium to tiny vessels represented.

COMPARISONS AND DATING: The same as for Early Bronze Age Burnished. The Polished ceramics are just a finer variety of this ware. Profiles are closely comparable with those of ordinary Early Bronze Age Burnished pottery, including the unusual pot-stand (cf. Kelly-Bucellati 1974: Fig. 24:E42).

EARLY BRONZE AGE RED SLIPPED WARE

DESCRIPTION: The same as Early Bronze Age Burnished except for the following:

SURFACES: The surfaces are thinly to moderately thickly slipped with a red to orange-red to dark red-brown slip and then burnished, often irregularly in stripes. The slipped surface is therefore often worn or eroded in stripes (or patches), revealing the underlying light buff to dark gray surface of the paste.

Usually both surfaces are treated the same way, but occasionally only the exterior surface is slipped and the interior is left smooth but otherwise unfinished.

FORM: A number of simple forms, and some rather unusual ones characterize this ware. Some are similar to forms which are found also in Early Bronze Age Burnished and Early Bronze Age Polished, such as the large "rail–rim" or impressed neck jar (Fig. 16:m). Others are simpler and are not so diagnostic. There is a jar with a gently outcurving neck (Fig. 16:n). Bowls seem to be represented by a deep, straight-sided form with either a pointed lip (Fig. 16:o) or a broad, flat lip (Fig. 16:p), although these could be the rims of large jars with vertical necks. Unmistakable bowls include a simple hemispherical form (Fig. 16:q), and simple hole-mouth forms (Fig. 16:r,s).

More unusual and distinctive for this ware are a hole-mouth jar with sharply pointed lip and outer collar (Fig. 16:t), and two bowls with grooves on the outer surfaces, one with simple, out-angling sides (Fig. 16:u), the other with a faintly S-shaped profile (Fig. 16:v).

THICKNESS: Medium thick to thick (10–30 mm).

COMPARISONS AND DATING: Finding comparable materials and dating this ware are difficult. The bulk of it seemed to us to relate to the Early Bronze Age, such judgment being based on technological similarities between this ware and Early Bronze Age Burnished Ware, and on parallels in form between these two wares, specifically impressed neck or "rail–rim" profiles, excurvate jars, some simple bowl forms (Fig. 16:p,q), and the simple hole-mouth jars described above. It has been suggested that other forms may be related to Late Chalcolithic (Fig. 16:o), Middle to Late Bronze Age (Fig. 16:t), or Iron Age (Fig. 16:u,v) ceramics (van Loon, personal communication). On the other hand, a very similar ware is found in Amuq' B—the Braidwoods' Coarse Red-Slipped Ware. The sherds illustrated on their Pl. 11:8–9 look to us virtually identical to our Early Bronze Age Red Slipped Ware, and at least some forms seem similar between the two wares (compare Braidwood and Braidwood 1960: Fig. 41:3 with Fig. 16:u; Fig. 41:5–6 with Fig. 16:r).

It seems clear that this is not a single "ware," but that our classification has grouped together a somewhat heterogeneous collection of material. Fortunately, this material is not common and a large proportion of it does seem to belong to the

Early Bronze Age. Therefore, our inclusion of it in the general assemblage of Early Bronze Age ceramics is not likely to significantly distort the results of the analysis of the survey data, either by the incorporation of extraneous materials in the Early Bronze Age counts or by the deletion of sherds from the counts for other periods. Nevertheless, an eventual reclassification of these ceramics would be highly desirable.

Early Bronze Age Plain Ware

PASTE: The paste is very coarse, porous, and light. It contains a large amount of chaff temper which shows up clearly and frequently on the surface of the vessels, while the paste is usually riddled with holes as a result of the burning out of the vegetal temper. The paste is poorly levigated, which also often results in actual holes in the paste. There is a moderate amount (ca. 10 percent) of medium to large, coarse grit temper. This grit is angular and often white, though sometimes it may be ordinary stream gravel rather than prepared, crushed tempering material.
> Color: The core is usually distinct from the two surfaces. It is often black to gray while the surfaces are lighter. Occasional sherds are black all the way through and then contain much carbonized vegetal material, which remains in the paste. Some sherds are uniformly light brown all the way through the cross-section.
> Firing: Generally low.
> Manufacture: Hand, but well smoothed.

SURFACES: Both surfaces are plain, smoothed, but there are no traces of any attempt to burnish them. Colors range from black to light brown or reddish brown.

DECORATION: None.

FORM: Few forms were found in this ware. There is a hole-mouth jar of a simple form (Fig. 16:w), and two bowl forms with slightly incurved sides (Fig. 16:x,y). Other bowl forms include a beaded-rim bowl (Fig. 16:z), and a bowl with a very slight groove under the rim, somewhat giving the impression of a beaded rim (Fig. 16:aa). A jar with excurvate rim (Fig. 16:bb) and a jar with a vertical, squared-off rim (Fig. 16:cc) complete the range of forms found in our sample.

THICKNESS: Medium, 5–12 mm.

COMPARISONS AND DATING: Most of the rim forms seen in this ware are similar to simple forms of Early Bronze Age Burnished Ware. We therefore assigned this plain ware to the same period, although later information indicates that the plain ware is more common at the end of the Early Bronze Age sequence, in Early Bronze III times (van Loon, personal communication).

Early Bronze Age Thick Ware

PASTE: The paste of this ware is light, porous, relatively rough, and poorly levigated. There is relatively abundant chaff temper (ca. 15 percent–20 percent), and a small quantity (5 percent or less) of medium sized (up to 1 mm) grit inclusions.
> Color: The cross-section of the sherd either shows a dark gray core with lighter, buff, or orange surfaces, or is orange to bright orange all the way through.
> Firing: Low.
> Manufacture: Hand.

SURFACES: The inner and outer surfaces are often different, typical for ceramics of this period. The exterior is often darker, and the interior lighter. The surfaces are either simply smoothed or lightly to moderately well burnished.
Surface colors range from dark to light gray to buff-brown, orange-brown, or brown.

DECORATION: None.

FORM: This ware seems to represent only large storage jars. Profiles are primarily variants, on a large scale, of the familiar "impressed neck" or "rail–rim" profile of Early Bronze Age Burnished Ware (Fig. 16:dd–ff, Fig. 17:a–d). Unusual forms are a jar with a short, angled-out rim (Fig. 17:e—perhaps also a sort of variant on the "rail–rim" theme), a jar with a gently outcurved rim (Fig. 17:f), and a jar with a heavy, rounded, and undercut bead rim (Fig. 17:g).

THICKNESS: Thick by definition, 14–34 mm, tending more to the larger end of this range.

COMPARISONS AND DATING: The same as for Early Bronze Age Burnished Ware.

EARLY BRONZE AGE RED PAINTED WARE

PASTE: Very fine, compact, well levigated, and homogeneous, with a moderate amount of very fine sand temper (ca. 10 percent). The sand particles are white. Very occasionally, larger white particles, up to 3 mm in size, occur.

    Color: Buff to buff-brown, but also occasionally darker buff-orange.

    Firing: Medium to high, with high being somewhat more common.

    Manufacture: Hand, but finely made and well shaped and smoothed.

SURFACES: Both surfaces are slipped a cream to light buff color. Rarely, there appears a deep orange slip, probably the same slip as on other vessels but fired differently.

The exterior surface is painted with geometric designs in red to deep red to red-brown, matt paint. The lines are of medium thickness to thin (particularly in contrast to Early Bronze Age Black Painted). There may be, rarely, a bichrome effect given by the application of thicker paint on the borders of designs and thinner, lighter application of paint on the filler lines of the design.

DECORATION: Painted, geometric designs in red as mentioned above. The designs are built up out of a series of simple elements, of which the most prominent are simple horizontal lines, wavy horizontal lines, cross-hatching, and triangles, either as rows of pendant triangles, or running rows of standing triangles, often filled with opposing diagonal lines.

Simple designs run from a stripe of paint on the rim (Fig. 17:l), or a row of tiny dabs of paint pendant from the rim (Fig. 19:d), to the extension of a series of plain bands of paint over a strap handle (Fig. 17:k). Other small and fragmentary examples of such simple bands are too incomplete to tell if this represents the totality of the design or not (e.g. Fig. 17:i,q). In one case (Fig. 17:q), a bichrome band occurs on a sherd with thin lines in black on the lip. This sherd may not actually belong in this ware, but the prominence of the broad red band made us inclined to place it here. In general, bichrome designs occur on otherwise typical Early Bronze Age Black Painted sherds, and then the red paint occurs only as a plain band, a minor element within the total design.

More complicated designs include a wavy, horizontal line above a row of triangles composed of opposing diagonal lines (Fig. 17:h; Fig. 19:a). The same sort of horizontal line also occurs enclosed between two straight, horizontal lines above a filled-triangle motif (Fig. 19:b), and again alone above a panel of cross-hatching (Fig. 17:m). Cross-hatched panels recur on several sherds, between single or multiple horizontal lines, and below either a row of short diagonal lines on the lip (Fig. 17:n) or a row of solid triangles pendant from the lip (Fig. 17:j). Similar triangles overhang diagonal lines from a motif which, unfortunately, is largely missing in another example (Fig. 17:o). They also are found, in one case, above two horizontal lines and a row of large, open triangles (Fig. 17:r).

The most complicated designs consist of complex combinations of diagonal rows of pendant triangles and triangular or rhomboidal panels filled with oblique filler lines (Fig. 17:p; Fig. 19:c,e).

FORM: Vessel forms in this ware are quite varied. Jars similar to, or variants of, the typical Early Bronze Age "impressed neck" or "rail–rim" form occur (Fig. 17:h–k), although most of these vessels are only generally related to this form and do not directly reproduce it. In some cases (Fig. 17:i,j), the small panel formed at the rim by this lip thickening or neck impressing is used as a design panel for the painted design. Other jars have excurvate rims with an asymmetrical thickening of the lip from the outside, often called cambering (Fig. 17:l). There are also simple jars with an outcurving profile and a slightly pointed lip (Fig. 17:m).

Bowls almost always show some sort of incurvate or hole-mouth form. One form, with a flat exterior facet on the lip, is identical to a typical Early Bronze Age Black Painted bowl (Fig. 18:a–e). An interesting form has a thickening of the body wall, forming the outward curvature, or belly, of the bowl under a small bead rim (Fig. 17:n). The bead rim itself serves as the panel for the upper border of the painted design. Simple hole-mouth forms (Fig. 17:o,p) and hole-mouth forms with various sorts of thickened lips also occur (Fig. 17:q,r).

The only sure base of this ware is flat, with a

sort of small "step," elevating the body wall above the actual vessel base (Fig. 17:s).

THICKNESS: The usual vessel thickness is moderate, with a wall approximately 5–9 mm thick. Rare sherds are very thin, running about 2.5 mm in thickness.

COMPARISONS AND DATING: This ware is subsumed under the Black-on-White Painted ware at Korucu Tepe (055/1), although the detailed description of this ware (Griffin 1974:56) makes it clear that "reddish brown" painting and the characteristic designs of our Red Painted ware are typical of an earlier period than the Black Painted ware described below. The more open designs, hatched chevrons and triangles, and the solid triangles painted on vessel lips are diagnostic (Griffin 1974:56, and compare her Fig. 25, particularly C and D, to our Fig. 17, particularly m and h; cf. van Loon 1973: Pl.11). This particular style of painted ware is characteristic of the Early Bronze Age IIIA, dated to ca. 2300–2150 B.C. (van Loon 1973:364).

Early Bronze Age Black Painted Ware

PASTE: Very fine, compact, well levigated, and homogeneous. Tempered with a moderate amount of very fine, white sand particles (ca. 10 percent). Very occasionally there are larger white particles, up to 3 mm in size.
  Color: Light beige or buff to light brown, occasionally darker olive green or reddish buff.
  Firing: Medium to high, with high being more common.
  Manufacture: Hand, but well made, carefully shaped and smoothed.

SURFACES: Interior and exterior: light cream (occasionally light buff) slipped. Smoothed but never burnished. Exterior then painted in matt black paint. Occasional pieces are bichrome, with some bands of deep, matt red paint sandwiched within broader bands of black.

DECORATION: Painted geometric motifs. These motifs are painted with bold, broad lines, with some more finely drawn hatching or motifs between the broader lines. The hallmark of this ware is, therefore, the closely spaced, broad, black bands running horizontally (Fig. 18: a–i,p; Fig. 19:k–r).

Thinner lines occur, usually, as filler lines in a total design, but they sometimes occupy a more prominent place. The most common thin-line motif is a series of zig-zag lines running parallel to each other, horizontally between thicker, horizontal bands (Fig. 18:b,p; Fig. 19:i,j). Another thin-line design consists of opposing diagonal lines (Fig. 19:f,g), most typically occurring between thicker lines in triangular and rhomboidal panels (Fig. 18:n).

Most sherds, however, exhibit designs composed only of broad bands or of broad bands between which are designs in medium-broad lines. These sherds may show only horizontal lines (Fig. 19:m), sometimes only a thin one on a tiny vessel (Fig. 18:m). More commonly, there are more complicated patterns. Usually these consist of a panel squeezed in between multiple, broad bands. Such panels contain cross-hatching (Fig. 18:a,c; Fig. 19:k), a wavy, horizontal line or lines (Fig. 18:g–i), panels of vertical lines (Fig. 18:d), occasionally alternate vertical and diagonal lines (Fig. 19:h), and finally, sometimes, opposed diagonals, whose overall patterns are not clear from the examples recovered in the survey (Fig. 18:e).

The bichrome sherds are incomplete, but seem to exhibit an interesting type of design. Here, deep red bands are enclosed between the usual broad and closely-spaced black bands, but not symmetrically. The red bands usually run obliquely through the width of the black band within which they occur (Fig. 19:p–r).

All of the above designs may be enclosed between an upper and a lower border. The upper border is frequent, and is, in our sample, very uniformly a row of relatively short, diagonal lines. This row of lines is usually applied as a panel on a flat facet on the vessel rim. Otherwise it is usually applied quite simply on the lip of the vessel (Fig. 18:a–e,g,h,j–l,n–p). One unusual exception is a jar with a row of pendant triangles along the rim, reminiscent of the pendant triangles of Early Bronze Age Red Painted, but here occurring in black on a different vessel form (Fig. 18:q).

Lower boundaries are, perhaps, somewhat less common than the upper row of diagonal lines, although our sample of sherds hardly allows a reliable quantitative estimate. Lower design boundaries consist of a sort of "fringe" formed by short oblique lines or trianguloid "teeth" flaring obliquely away along the lower edge of the bottom band of the design (Fig. 19:j,l,o,p). A variation on this theme is a row of scallops running along this edge in the same way (Fig. 19:n).

A single strap handle also shows the typical parallel black bands characteristic of the body design of this ware (Fig. 18:r).

FORM: A common form for this ware is a hole-mouth jar with a flat facet built up or projecting out from the rim, on which the upper panel or border of the design, a row of short oblique lines, is painted (Fig. 18:a–e). In some ways this form is quite reminiscent of the "rail-rim" or "impressed neck" characteristic of many Early Bronze Age Burnished vessels, but in detail it is noticeably different.

Simple hole-mouth vessels also occur (Fig. 18:f,g), as well as bowls with in-turned sides (Fig. 18:h).

Bowls are also represented by a simple, hemispherical form (Fig. 18:i), and by a series of open forms with short, rolled out lips (Fig. 18:j,k). A similar sort of lip also occurs on what may be a jar with excurvate neck (Fig. 18:l). A miniature version of this same bowl form is represented by one example (Fig. 18:m).

There is a rather graceful carinated bowl shape (Fig. 18:n).

Jars with short, out-angled or sharply out-turned rims are found (Fig. 18:o–q).

A strap handle is known (Fig. 18:r).

Bases are flat, either simple (Fig. 18:s), or elevated on a short pedestal, creating a short "foot" at the base of the vessel (Fig. 18:t).

THICKNESS: Vessels run from small, with thin body sherds (4–6 mm), to large, with thicker walls (13–14 mm).

COMPARISONS AND DATING: Stylistically, this ware is rather different from the preceding Red Painted ware, although the two are considered together in the excavated materials from Korucu Tepe, 055/1 (Griffin 1974). The designs are more "closed" or dense, with thicker horizontal bands, typical diagonal strokes on the lip, and small fringing strokes or triangles below the design panel (Griffin 1974:56, and compare her Figs. 26A with our Fig. 18:f; 26D with Fig. 18:a–d; and 26E with Fig. 18:o,p). At Korucu Tepe, these ceramics occur in Middle Bronze Age I levels, ca. 2000–1800 B.C. but they are also typical of Early Bronze Age IIIB levels, which were found at other excavated sites in the Keban area but not at Korucu Tepe (van Loon 1973:368, and personal communication). This would give a total range of time for the occurrence of this style of painted pottery of ca. 2150–1800 B.C.

The wide distribution of this ware in the Malatya-Elâzığ regions was discussed by Burney (1958:170–171, 205–208), who also pointed out its general resemblance to central Anatolian Cappadocian ware. These resemblances are considered in more detail by Griffin (1974:81–82), building the case for contemporaneity of the Black Painted ware of the Keban area and the Cappadocian ware of Kültepe Early Bronze IIIB to Karum II times (roughly 2300–1500 B.C.— Mellink 1965:126).

A radiocarbon date obtained from material collected from an exposed profile with levels producing this Black Painted ware at 054/2 (Tepecik) was 2030 ± 70 B.C. (GrN-5285). This corresponds well with a general Early Bronze Age IIIB date for this pottery.

MIDDLE BRONZE AGE GRITTY WARE

PASTE: The paste is relatively rough, only moderately well levigated. It contains an abundant amount (30 percent–50 percent or more) of coarse grit temper. The grit temper is a light-colored, crushed, crystalline rock, perhaps a light-colored granite. There is a wide range of particle sizes, but with most ranging from medium (1–1.5 mm) to large (up to 5 mm) in size.

> Color: Paste is usually black to dark gray to dark gray-brown in color. It is occasionally brown to orange-brown. Sometimes the core is distinguishable in color from the surfaces of a sherd. In these cases, the core is frequently lighter in color than the surfaces.
>
> On the whole, the impression is of a coarse, dark paste which has been made very gritty by the addition of a large amount of light-colored temper.
>
> Firing: Low.
> Manufacture: Hand.

SURFACES: Both the interior and exterior are usually identical, with the interior surface very occasionally being lighter than the exterior. Surfaces are usually burnished, rarely only lightly smoothed. The burnish is usually moderately good, but it is always striped (stroke-burnished). The gritty character of the paste is not frequently seen on the surfaces, but there are sherds with surfaces almost as rough as the paste itself. Colors are usually black, dark gray, dark brown or dark gray-brown. Lighter colors such as brown to slightly orange-brown are also sometimes seen.

DECORATION: Generally undecorated, but simple geometric designs are sometimes found in broad-line incising on the vessel exteriors (Fig. 20:ee). The designs are smaller but reminiscent of the relief and incised designs on Early Bronze Age wares.

FORM: Forms are rather varied. There are a few open bowl forms—one with a simple inward-beveled rim (Fig. 20:a), another with an interior ridge or facet (Fig.20:b), and finally a strange form with a broad, flat, flange rim (Fig. 20:c).

More common are hole-mouth jars of various kinds. There are simple forms with square lips (Fig. 20:d) and round lips (Fig. 20:e–h). Sometimes there is a sort of interior bead lip (Fig. 20:i). Other forms have various thickened or "club-shaped" profiles (Fig. 20:j,k). There is also a form with a tiny, flared-out rim which could grade easily into a normal jar profile (Fig. 20:l).

Normal jars with various forms of outcurved rims are quite common (Fig. 20:m–r). Variants with shorter (Fig. 20:s), more angled-out (Fig. 20:t) and squatter (Fig. 20:u) rims occur. A distinctive form is a jar with a relatively heavy rolled-out rim (Fig. 20:v,w). Also distinctive are jars with a broad, more or less folded-out, ledge-like rim (Fig. 20:x,y). One jar rim with an exterior "rail" is reminiscent of Early Bronze Age profiles (Fig. 20:z). Several other miscellaneous forms are also found in this ware (Fig. 20:aa–dd).

THICKNESS: Medium thick, 8–12 mm.

COMPARISONS AND DATING: This is the Brown Gritty Burnished ware of Griffin (1974:55; cf. van Loon and Buccellati 1970:93). As Griffin notes (1974:66–67), this ware developed from local Early Bronze Age pottery, and a number of similarities in form can be found between this ware and the various Early Bronze Age ceramics. It is found as early as Early Bronze Age III at Norşun Tepe (054/8) and lasts as late as the Late Bronze Age I at Korucu Tepe (055/1), but its period of greatest abundance and characteristic occurrence is the Middle Bronze Age, ca. 2000–1600 B.C. (Griffin 1974:82; van Loon 1973:368–369).

OLD HITTITE GRAY WARE

PASTE: The paste of this ware is distinctive. It is fine, compact, hard, sometimes "rocky," slightly rough and sandy, with occasionally somewhat laminar structure. It is tempered with fine sand, with mostly light, white or gray, particles, rarely light brown. The proportion is generally 10 percent–15 percent, rarely up to 20 percent. The particles are usually .25 mm in size or less. They range up to 1 or 1.5 mm on occasion, but they are typically tiny, "pinprick" size.

- Colors: Colors are gray—light gray, dark gray, medium gray, dark brown-gray, light blue-green gray. The simple range of light to dark gray is most common and most aptly characterizes this ware.
- Firing: High. The sherds characteristically "clink."
- Manufacture: Wheeled. The wheelmarks are sometimes completely smoothed over, but it is typical that they are lightly visible on both the exterior and interior surfaces.

SURFACES: Both surfaces are usually slipped and burnished, although they are sometimes only smoothed. The interior surface is occasionally left unslipped and merely smoothed. Wheelmarks are typically visible on both surfaces, although this varies with the degree to which the surface is smoothed and burnished.

- Color: Surface colors range from gray-browns to gray to deep brown. Light gray sometimes also occurs, especially on unslipped surfaces. The interior surface is frequently lighter than the exterior.

DECORATION: Usually none, but there are some sherds with bands of grooves on the exterior surface.

FORM: Most characteristic of this ware are the various forms of hole-mouth jars. Typically, these show some sort of thickened facet or collar running around the rim on the exterior (Fig. 21:a–c). Frequently, the facet or collar is ribbed (Fig. 21:d,e). Simple hole-mouth jars are common, however (Fig. 21:f,g). Some hole-mouth jars have a single groove on the outside, either well below the lip (Fig. 21:h) or just under it (Fig. 21:i). One form seems intermediate between a true hole-mouth jar and a simple, straight-sided bowl (Fig. 21:j).

Open bowls occur, but almost always with a complex rim having some sort of external protrusion, collar or bead (Fig. 21:k–n).

Jars are typically straight-sided, or with slightly inward-sloping walls, and have heavy rims. The rims are either greatly thickened and slightly rolled out, with a gentle, down and outward-sloping, beveled lip (Fig. 21:o,p), or they are bent or angled out in various ways, sometimes with some grooving on the underside of the lip on the outside (Fig. 21:q–u). Simple, excurvate jar rims are not entirely unknown (Fig. 21:v), although they most often occur on thin vessels (Fig. 21:z,aa). More common are small jars with short, out-angled lips (Fig. 21:w–y). One unusual form is a straight-sided jar with a bead rim (Fig. 21:bb).

Bases are largely ring bases. These are found both on more or less straight-sided vessels and on normal, curved vessel forms (Fig. 21:cc–ff). Flat bases with a small step at the vessel foot also occur (Fig. 21:gg).

Small strap handles are found in this ware (Fig. 21:hh).

THICKNESS: Medium thin, 5–6 mm, to typically medium, 5–9 mm. There are some thick sherds up to 16–17 mm.

COMPARISONS AND DATING: Gray, wheeled ceramics are the hallmark of the Middle Bronze Age in the Keban area, dated to ca. 2000–1600 B.C., roughly contemporary to, though ending slightly earlier than, the Old Hittite period at Boğazköy (van Loon and Buccellati 1970: 94–96; van Loon 1973:368–369; Griffin 1974:55; Fischer 1963:101; Bittel 1970:ix). Griffin (1974:66,83) sees these gray wares as a local development from Early Bronze Age III wares, but there are ties to other regions. The gray "Minyan" ware in the Amuq' phases K–M is said possibly to be a cognate ware (Griffin 1974:83; Bier 1973:431), and there may be parallels to the Keban area gray wares in Azerbaijan and Elbistan (Griffin 1974:83). Our Old Hittite Gray Ware is apparently most typically what Griffin and van Loon refer to as Middle Bronze Age Gray Wheelmarked ware, but their category also includes our Middle Bronze Age Gray and Old Hittite Light Faced Gray wares as variants.

OLD HITTITE LIGHT FACED GRAY WARE

DESCRIPTION: The same as for Old Hittite Gray Ware except:

SURFACES: The inner surface is usually simply smoothed and is light gray, i.e. relatively unfinished. It is very occasionally finished in the same way as the exterior surface. The exterior surface is slipped and always moderately well burnished. Colors are many and varied, but always lighter than the color of the paste in the core. Orange-brown, buff-orange, brown, deep coffee brown, gray, buff, etc. all occur. Impressionistically, brown to buff-brown colors predominate in this variety.

FORM: Very few vessel forms are known in this ware. One is a plate with an inner thickening of the rim (Fig. 22:z). Bases are flat with a facet at the foot (Fig. 22:aa) or ring bases (Fig. 22:bb,cc).

THICKNESS: Medium, 5–8 mm.

COMPARISONS AND DATING: This is simply a variant of Old Hittite Gray Ware with particularly light and well-finished surfaces.

OLD HITTITE BLACK FACED GRAY WARE

DESCRIPTION: The same as for Old Hittite Gray Ware except:

SURFACES: The inner surface is usually simply light gray and smoothed, i.e. relatively unfinished. It is occasionally finished in the same way as the outer surface. The exterior surface is slipped with a black slip and moderately well burnished. The burnishing is usually striped or is a criss-cross pattern burnish.

FORM: The vessel forms are not known.

THICKNESS: Medium, 5–7 mm.

COMPARISONS AND DATING: This seems to be simply a variety of Old Hittite Gray Ware and should in all likelihood be of the same date. It may be the same as the Black Smoothed Ware found in Middle Bronze Age levels at Korucu Tepe (055/1—Griffin 1974:55,66) although her description of the "blue black" surface which "crackles" does not correspond very well with our observations.

MIDDLE BRONZE AGE GRAY WARE

PASTE: The paste is generally relatively fine in texture, but only moderately well levigated, leaving the paste moderately porous with many small holes in it (occurring at a density of roughly 10 percent–15 percent of the surface area in cross-section). There is a moderate amount of sandy temper, including a high proportion of white particles, and occasionally a fleck of iron pyrites in some sherds. The proportion of temper is variable, being usually 10 percent–15 percent, but running occasionally up to 20 percent–25 percent. The size of the particles is very small. They are rarely as large as .5 mm, mostly much smaller. An exceptional particle as large as 1 mm is possible, however.

> Color: The color of cores is variable, and a cross-section of a sherd frequently shows a layering of colors in the core. The colors range from a typical gray, dark gray, or black to brown or dark brown.
> Firing: Low. Occasionally medium.
> Manufacture: Wheel.

SURFACES: The interior and exterior surfaces are often identical in color. It also not infrequently happens that the interior surface is lighter than the exterior of the sherd. Both surfaces may vary from a smoothed or well-smoothed, uniform surface finish to well burnished. Colors are very restricted and typically range from medium to dark gray. Black also occurs, and gray-brown to dark brown or reddish brown are also seen. Burnishing is sometimes incomplete and striped. On simply smoothed, unburnished interior surfaces wheelmarks are sometimes fairly evident.

DECORATION: None specifically known, unless perhaps the occasional stripe burnishing can be counted as decorative.

FORM: Not a very wide range of form is known for this ware and there are few really characteristic shapes. The ware is more readily identified by its qualities of paste and color.

Simple, shallow bowls are known, both with squared-off lips (Fig. 22:a,b) and with rounded lips (Fig. 22:c–f). Three unusual rim forms are also found on simple open bowls—a flat, grooved rim with an interior bead (Fig. 22:g), a rounded-outward lip with a short outward projection (Fig. 22:h), and a complex, shouldered form (Fig. 22:i).

More characteristic perhaps are hole-mouth jars (Fig. 22:j–m). Mostly these are simple (Fig. 22:j,k), but a sort of shoulder or inset lip occurs on one form (Fig. 22:l), and another form has an exaggerated exterior carination, accentuating a gently incurved, interior profile (Fig. 22:m).

Jars with excurvate rims are known, sometimes with beveled lips (Fig. 22:n), sometimes with flat, outward-protruding lips (Fig. 22:o), and also with simple rounded lips (Fig. 22:p). Jars also occur with simple, very short, bent-out lips (Fig. 22:q), and with a slightly thickened exterior facet or collar (Fig. 22:r,s). Probably the most distinctive jar form in this ware, however, is one with a relatively thin body wall leading up to a much thicker, angled to somewhat rolled-out, broad rim or lip (Fig. 22:t,u).

Bases are both simple, flat bases (Fig. 22:v,w) and ring bases (Fig. 22:x,y).

THICKNESS: Usually medium, 4–8 mm, but sometimes medium-thick, up to 12 mm.

COMPARISONS AND DATING: The appearance of wheel-made gray wares is taken to be characteristic of the Middle Bronze Age (cf. Old Hittite Gray Ware). Our Middle Bronze Age Gray Ware is apparently Griffin's "coarser gray variant" among these ceramics (1974:55). The comparisons and dating are otherwise the same as for Old Hittite Gray Ware.

HITTITE RED WARE

PASTE: Very fine and well levigated. Tough and hard, but with a slightly laminar structure. Sand-tempered with numerous light, white to brown, particles and some glittering particles, probably mica.

> Color: Dark gray to black or light gray,

sometimes with a brown layer near the surface.

Firing: Medium.

Manufacture: Wheel.

SURFACES: Both surfaces are usually the same. They are slipped with a thick, dark red slip and highly burnished, often to a fine polish. The interior surface is occasionally plain, unfinished brown or dark reddish brown, smoothed but with clear wheel marks and sometimes distinct ridges.

DECORATION: None.

FORM: This ware is very rare, and only one rim form was found, an open bowl form with subtriangular, in-tilted lip (Fig. 55:e).

THICKNESS: Medium, 4–8 mm, generally 6–8 mm.

COMPARISONS AND DATING: This distinctive but very uncommon ware strongly resembles certain central Anatolian Hittite wares. Griffin (1974:67) even suggests that it may have been imported into the Keban region. Certainly, it occurs only rarely. Only nine sherds of this ware were recovered from all of our controlled surface collections. The parallels in ware are with central Anatolian wares of the Kültepe Karum period (Griffin 1974:84; Hauptmann 1969/70:39). Griffin also points out similarities in form between the excavated vessels in the Keban area and other, later wares at Tarsus and Boğazköy. Comparisons for the one rim form recovered by the surface survey are difficult to find. Among the closest are certain shallow bowls from Boğazköy with narrow, inturned lips (Fischer 1963: Pls. 85–89, especially Nos. 750, 760). Such bowls occur throughout the sequence at Boğazköy. The closest parallels in shape to our Fig. 55:e are from the later phases of this sequence but are found there in a different ware. Red polished bowls of this general type are found in the earlier, Karum-period levels of the Boğazköy sequence, however, and we assume that our example is a variant of this general form of bowl. Hittite Red, then, is probably a ware of the Middle Bronze Age, and in spite of the later parallels in form, it probably belongs to the early part of the second millennium B.C., Middle Bronze Age I, ca. 2000–1800 B.C.

HITTITE PLAIN WARE

PASTE: Moderately fine to fine and generally well levigated, compact and tough. Temper is usually medium-fine sand, occasionally fine sand, in moderate to abundant quantities (15 percent–30 percent averaging ca. 20 percent–25 percent). In pieces with finer paste the temper is almost absent or is very fine sand in very small amounts (usually less than 5 percent). Pieces with coarser, less well levigated paste are tempered with coarser sand, including some larger, rough particles up to 8 mm in size. In such sherds, coarse temper seems to occur in proportions of about 10 percent–15 percent.

Color: Color of the paste is generally on the lighter side, typically comprising buffs, red-buffs, and orange to light brown. Occasionally, darker brown to gray-brown or light gray pastes are found.

Firing: Typically high or very high, sometimes medium-high.

Manufacture: Wheel, but most wheel-marks are usually smoothed away.

SURFACES: The exterior and interior vessel surfaces are most commonly treated in the same way. Both are simply smoothed without burnishing. The smoothing is typically very well done, eliminating all wheel-marks and leaving few or no traces. Some sherds do show traces of smoothing and some still show wheel-markings, however.

Surface colors are typically light buffs, orange-buffs, or light browns. The most common colors are light cream-buff to light orange-buff. Red-buff is not uncommon. Medium browns occur but are rare. Deep red browns are somewhat more common, and there are rare instances of a dirty, deep maroon. The general and typical impression is of a variety of light-colored surfaces, however. The exterior and interior surfaces normally are the same color.

DECORATION: None.

FORM: There is an incredible variety of forms in this ware. Quite characteristic are plates (Fig. 23:a–l), in addition to bowls and jars. Open-mouthed bowls appear in a wide range of lip forms and rim profiles (Fig. 23:m–eee; Fig. 24:a–bb). Among these are smooth profiled simple bowls (Fig. 23:m–v), as well as simple bowls with an angular profile (Fig. 23:w,x), and those with a "broken profile" (Fig. 23:y). Typical in the class of bowls are the thickened rim or "club-rim" forms (Fig. 23:bb,dd–ff). Many bowls have an exterior bead or protrusion at the rim (Fig. 23:hh–eee; Fig. 24:a–f), which becomes a ledge rim in the case of some forms (Fig. 24:g–l). Other profiles are S-shaped (Fig. 24:p), becoming almost carinated bowls (Fig. 24:q–t). The profiles of open bowls grade gradually into those of hole-mouth jars (Fig. 24:cc–nn; Fig. 25:z,jj,mm,ss). Again, there is a wide variety of specific profiles, but in general it appears that the hole-mouth jars have not as sharply in-turned rim profiles as in some other wares.

Jars exhibit as wide a range of form as bowls. There are a number of jars with short, sharply out-turned or out-angled rims (Fig. 25:a–l). Many jars have out-curving necks, with lips formed by exterior beads of various forms (Fig. 25:m–u). A simple excurvate neck and plain lip is also a common jar form (Fig. 25:v–y,bb–ii,kk,ll). Among the jars are a number of thickened lip or "club rim" profiles (Fig. 25:aa,oo–rr), similar to those among the bowls. A few unusual shapes complete the series of jars (Fig. 24:ss–uu). In most cases it is hard to discern anything other than a simple circular vessel mouth, but at least one clear example of a shaped or "trefoil" mouth was found (Fig. 25:nn).

As might be expected in a ware which encompasses such wide variation in form, there are a number of different kinds of bases. Simple flat bases, with either a rounded (Fig. 26:a,b) or angular (Fig. 26:c–e) bottom profile are followed by occasional round bases (Fig. 26:f) and a relatively high frequency and variety of ring bases (Fig. 26:g–m).

Handles are usually round (Fig. 26:o–q) to sub-rectangular (Fig. 26:n) loop handles (Fig. 25:i,p; Fig. 26:u), although there are also some pierced lugs (Fig. 26:s,t). Some vessels were equipped with large pouring spouts (Fig. 26:r).

THICKNESS: Vessel walls are generally of medium thickness, ca. 5–9 mm.

COMPARISONS AND DATING: This ware probably corresponds at least roughly to Griffin's (1974:60) "Orange Self-Slipped or Smoothed Ware." In any case, it forms part of the series of orange wares that are diagnostic of the Late Bronze Age (ca. 1500–1200 B.C.) at Korucu Tepe (055/1—van Loon 1973:369–372; Griffin 1974:56–60) and in the Keban area generally. This series is discussed as a whole under Hittite Buff-Orange Burnished Ware.

HITTITE FINE WARE

PASTE: Very fine, compact, hard, very well levigated and very smooth. There is usually no visible temper. Sometimes there is a very sparse (less than 5 percent), extremely fine sand temper of both light and dark colors. This may be just a natural constituent of the clay.

> Color: Color is usually constant from surface to surface, through the core. There is quite a wide range of paste color. It is usually light buff to light orange-buff. Some pieces are orange, deep red, light or medium gray, brown, and even olive green, however.
>
> Firing: Very high, sherds "clink" with a high tone.
>
> Manufacture: Wheel, very finely made.

SURFACES: Exterior and interior surfaces are normally the same in treatment and color (which is thus normally identical with that of the paste itself). The interior surface is occasionally lighter in color. Colors run the same gamut as for the paste. Both surfaces are usually simply well smoothed, eliminating all wheel and smoothing marks, although wheel marks do sometimes remain evident. Vessels then may be burnished or simply left smooth. If burnished, the burnishing is very finely done, either on both surfaces or on the exterior alone.

DECORATION: None.

FORM: There is a full range of forms in this fine ware. There are simple open bowls (Fig. 26:v–x,z,pp). There are hole-mouth jars of simple profile (Fig. 26:y), and also hole-mouth jars with beaded lip (Fig. 26:aa,bb), or with other, less usual lip profiles (Fig. 26:cc). Some bowls have quite unusual lip forms—rolled in (Fig. 26:dd) or with a tiny interior ledge (Fig. 26:ee). A series of vessels represent small bowls or cups with slightly constricted necks (Fig. 26:ff–hh), or tiny jars with a very short out-turned rim (Fig. 26:ii,jj). One form is close to a ledge-rim bowl (Fig. 26:kk).

There are other occasional and unusual bowl forms (e.g. Fig. 26:ll). True jars are infrequent and only occur as simple forms with a short out-folded rim (Fig. 26:mm) or with a gently out-angled rim (Fig. 26:oo). There is one "double profile," or somewhat S-shaped, bowl or jar profile (Fig. 26:nn).

THICKNESS: Thin, 3–5 mm, to very thin, 2–3 mm.

COMPARISONS AND DATING: No ware like this is considered explicitly or separately in the discussions of the excavated materials from Korucu Tepe (055/1). It nonetheless seems evident that this pottery falls within the general class of Late Bronze Age orange wares from that site and is to be dated along with them to ca. 1500–1200 B.C. (van Loon 1973:369–372; Griffin 1974:56–60).

HITTITE THICK WARE

DESCRIPTION: The same as for Hittite Plain Ware with the following exceptions:

SURFACES: In addition to the range of treatment and color typical of Hittite Plain Ware, buff-orange to red-brown burnished exterior and interior surfaces are also found.

FORM: This ware consists primarily of heavy storage jars. Some are thick-walled with straight, vertical rims (Fig. 27:a–c). Some hole-mouth vessel forms occur, with square, block-like rims (Fig. 27:d) or more commonly with angled-out rims (Fig. 27:e–g). These hole-mouth forms grade into bowls with slightly incurving walls and sharply angled-out rims (Fig. 27:h,i).

The remainder of the vessel forms are all of jars with various simple excurvate, out-turned, or exterior protruding rim profiles (Fig. 27:j–y). Some more uncommon forms include those with a kind of interior ledge (Fig. 27:p,q), and an excurvate, thickening, or "club" rim (Fig. 27:v), which is similar to forms occurring in Hittite Plain Ware.

Bases are generally flat, with sharp (Fig. 28:a,b) or rounded (Fig. 28:c) base angles. One high ring-foot was placed in this ware because of its size (Fig. 28:d), but it is possible that this is just a large vessel of Hittite Plain Ware. Handles are massive and oval in cross-section (Fig. 28:e).

COMPARISONS AND DATING: The same as for the other orange wares of the Hittite or Late Bronze Age Period, cf. Hittite Buff-Orange Burnished Ware.

HITTITE EXTERIOR WHEEL-MARKED WARE

DESCRIPTION: The same as for Hittite Plain or Hittite Fine (unburnished) wares, except that the surfaces show clear, fine wheel-markings near the rim. Wheel-marks are always present on the exterior and are usually equally clearly visible on the interior surface.

FORM: Known are a straight-sided bowl or jar rim with short, horizontal lip (Fig. 28:f), a bowl with a vertical rim and distinct shoulder, or "broken profile," above a curved, basin-shaped body (Fig. 28:g), and a simple, open bowl (Fig. 28:h).

COMPARISONS AND DATING: This ware seems to correspond to Griffin's (1974:60) "Orange to Buff Wheelmarked Ware," forming part of the large series of orange wares characteristic of the Late Bronze Age in the Keban area (van Loon 1973:369–372; Griffin 1974:56–60), cf. Hittite Buff-Orange Burnished Ware.

HITTITE BUFF-ORANGE BURNISHED WARE

DESCRIPTION: The same as for Hittite Plain Ware except:

SURFACES: The interior and exterior are virtually always the same. Both are slipped and burnished. The interior is occasionally simply smoothed, or not as carefully slipped and not as highly burnished as the exterior. On a number of pieces with more abundant, dark sand temper, the surface is speckled with the tiny black or gray sand grains showing through the slip.
 Color: The most common colors are buff, light buff-orange, buff-brown, or light cream orange. There are occasional deeper oranges and lighter cream-buffs.

DECORATION: Very, very rarely are fragments found with incised decoration. These have been too small to determine the total design, but there seem to be panels or areas outlined by incisions which are then filled in with a whole series of short, incised strokes. An occasional sherd has multiple, shallow, parallel grooves (Fig. 30:i).

FORM: The variety of forms is great in this ware, just as for Hittite Plain Ware, and many specific forms are shared or are similar between the two wares.

Plates are present (Fig. 28:i–l). Simple, smooth-profiled, open bowls (Fig. 28:m–p), bowls with ledge-like exterior protrusions (Fig. 28:q–t), bowls with angular (Fig. 28:w–bb) and S-shaped (Fig. 28:cc–ee) profiles, the "broken profile" bowl form (Fig. 28:ff), a large series of bowls with different forms of exterior bead or protrusion at the rim (Fig. 28:u,v,gg–rr,uu), some with an interior bead or protrusion at the rim (Fig. 28:vv,ww), and occasional strange forms with interior ledges or grooving (Fig. 28:ss,tt) illustrate the wide variety of bowls in this ware.

Hole-mouth jars occur in a number of forms (Fig. 29:a–t). In contrast to the bowls, there appears to be relatively little similarity between hole-mouth forms specific to this ware and those typical of Hittite Plain Ware.

Jars show many variations on simple themes. Most common is some sort of bending or angling out of the rim, often with an exterior thickening or bead (Fig. 29:u–jj). A few forms are excurvate or out-angled with the general thickening of the lip typical of "club rims" in other Hittite wares (Fig. 29:kk,mm). There are also several varieties of simple outward-bent or curved jar rims (Fig. 29:nn–uu). Somewhat more unusual forms do occur, however (Fig. 29:vv–yy).

Handles are common. All are loop handles with cross-sections which are oval to typically sub-rectangular with a groove down one side (Fig. 30:a–h). Simple loop handles are normal, but there are occasional more elaborate ways of joining a handle to the vessel rim (Fig. 30:c).

Bases are commonly flat, angling or sometimes curving up into the vessel body profile (Fig. 30:j–l). There is a class of flat bases which show an incipent to distinct thickening at the foot of the vessel, separating base from body (Fig. 30:m–o). In one instance this approaches a true ring base (Fig. 30:p), a form which also occasionally occurs in this ware (Fig. 30:q).

THICKNESS: Medium, 5–9 mm.

COMPARISONS AND DATING: Hittite Buff-Orange Burnished, Red-Brown Burnished, and Brown Burnished wares all fall either under the category of "Orange Burnished Ware" or of "Orange Slipped Ware" at Korucu Tepe (055/1—Griffin 1974:60). They, along with Hittite Plain and some less common wares—Hittite Thick, Orange Smoothed, Fine, Exterior Wheel-Marked, and Chaff Faced, comprise the orange wares which were early recognized as the diagnostic and typical ceramics for the Hittite Empire Levels in the Korucu Tepe excavations (van Loon and Buccellati 1970:96–99). These levels belong to the Late Bronze Age of the Keban area, ca. 1500–1200 B.C. (van Loon 1973:369–371).

A tremendous variety of form is found in these wares. Many of these forms are distinctive to these wares and to the Late Bronze Age. However, a number of forms are carried over from quite different, Middle Bronze Age wares, to be made in the new wares, either directly or with slight modification (compare Fig. 21:a–c with Fig. 29:b; Fig. 22:k with Fig. 29:f; Fig. 22:i with Fig. 24:q,r; Fig. 21:i with Fig. 32:z).

Griffin (1974:84–87) summarizes her comparisons of the excavated material from Korucu Tepe with other Anatolian sites by linking the Late Bronze Age I in the Keban area with the Tarsus Late Bronze Age I and Boğazköy Büyükkale IV c–d, and the Late Bronze Age II at Korucu Tepe with Tarsus Late Bronze Age II and Boğazköy Büyükkale III and Unterstadt level 1, among others. However, van Loon states that it is hard to draw good parallels between the Keban area ceramics and those of Boğazköy except for the typical and numerous platters (cf. Fig 23:a–l; Fig. 28:i–l). He sees stronger connections to Tarsus and further suggests that the abundant orange wares characteristic of this ceramic assemblage appear in the Keban area as a result of the spread of mass production of pottery in this period from the area of Tarsus over east Anatolia and, eventually, to central Anatolia (van Loon 1973:370–371).

In fact, a number of other, close comparisons of rim forms can be made with the pottery from Boğazköy. Some of these are with Old Hittite examples from Boğazköy, e.g. Fig. 29:kk, a "club lip," which is quite typical for our assemblage in the Keban area, can be compared with a vessel from the Unterstadt level 3 (Fischer

1963: Pl. 60:545). A similar comparison can be made between Fig. 29:ll and Fischer's Pl. 60:551, an example also from the same level. Fig. 32:g, a bowl with inward beveled, triangular lip in Brown Burnished Ware, is similar in form to bowls from Boğazköy Büyükkale IVc (Fischer 1963:Pl.93:842,838), considered by Fischer (1963:101) to be contemporary with the Unterstadt level 3 and to be pre-Empire in date.

Other parallels with pre-Empire materials from Boğazköy involve either forms which continue into later periods or a series of related forms which develop, one from another, within the sequence of Hittite ceramics. For example, Fig. 23:cc, a shallow, flat-lipped bowl with a small protrusion or ledge on the inside of the rim, is similar to examples from Boğazköy Büyükkale IVc (Fischer 1963:Pl. 93:840) and Büyükkale III (Pl. 94:852). Also, a series of open bowls with S-shaped rim profiles, typical for the Late Bronze Age ceramics in the Keban area, is paralleled in the materials from virtually all periods at Boğazköy. The best comparisons are Fig. 28:dd with Fischer's Pl. 97:877–878 (Büyükkale IVd, Old Hittite), Fig. 24:q with Fischer's Pl. 98:890 (Büyükkale IVb), and Fig. 28:ee with Fischer's Pl. 103:935 (Unterstadt level 1b). These selected comparisons thus span almost the entire range of the Hittite occupation of Boğazköy.

Most additional parallels between the Keban area ceramics and those from Boğazköy pertain to the period of the Hittite Empire, however. Compare, for example, Fig. 29:n, a "knob-lipped," hole-mouth jar, with Fischer's Pl. 51:500 (Büyükkale III); Fig. 25:l, a square-lipped jar rim, with Fischer's Pl. 56:531 (Unterstadt level 2); Fig. 24:g–l, thick shallow bowls with heavy horizontal lip, with Fischer's Pl. 119:1062 (Unterstadt level 2).

A number of other specific parallels or comparisons can be drawn with the material from Boğazköy. The above is a selection of some of the more distinctive forms which can be compared. The general picture is clear, however. For the survey materials as a whole, just as for the excavated materials from Korucu Tepe, the best parallels seem to be with ceramics from the latter part of the Old Hittite period through the whole period of the Hittite Empire. This comprises the Late Bronze Age as a whole in the Keban area and dates to ca. 1500–1200 B.C. (Fischer 1963:101, van Loon 1973:369–371).

HITTITE CHAFF FACED WARE

PASTE: Moderately compact, fine to medium-fine with a small to medium amount of chaff temper, ca. 5 percent–15 percent. The paste is fairly well levigated so that the chaff temper is often more visible on the face of a sherd than in its cross-section. It is nevertheless relatively porous, with fine holes visible in the cross-section in all but the hardest, high-fired pieces. There is usually also a sparse amount, 5 percent or less, of medium to fine, white or sometimes gray grit temper.

    Color: The color of the paste is quite variable. Most commonly there is a tough, hard, dark gray core which breaks roughly, in a "rocky" manner, with orange to orange-buff layers on both sides of this core. These lighter colored layers near the surfaces of the sherds are of varying thickness, often thin but not uncommonly representing a significant proportion of the vessel thickness. Some cores are of lighter gray with buff edges. Less common pieces have orange-buff, light brown, or buff, softer, sandy cores.

    Firing: Medium high to high.

    Manufacture: Wheel, but marks are only occasionally visible.

SURFACES: The vessel surfaces are slipped with a light buff to light cream-buff slip. Both surfaces are usually the same in treatment and color, although the interior surfaces are sometimes less well slipped and finished than the exteriors, and they are also occasionally darker in color. The lighter colored slips run on into the cream-white of Hittite White Slipped Ware. Most slips tend to be brown to orange-buff in Hittite Chaff Faced Ware, rather than truly cream-white, but there seems to be an overlap in color between the two wares. The slip is usually well smoothed to occasionally lightly burnished. Sometimes it is matt. On both surfaces chaff marks are clearly visible, and are sparse (ca. 5 percent) to moderately abundant (10 percent–15 percent).

DECORATION: None.

FORM: Bowls sometimes have the familiar "club-rim" profile (Fig. 30:r). Others are slightly constricted at the rim, which is thickened with a slight outward protrusion (Fig. 30:u), as is an apparently carinated form (Fig. 30:v), and one with a rim with an exterior ledge (Fig. 30:w).

Jars can have a short, thick, slightly out-angled rim (Fig. 30:x,y). Smoothly excurvate jar forms are found with exterior grooving at or slightly below the point of constriction of the neck (Fig. 30:z,aa). Other jars have slightly in-sloping necks with short lips which are bent out rather abruptly (Fig. 30:bb,cc). One unusual hole-mouth jar profile is also known (Fig. 30:dd).

THICKNESS: Medium to medium-thick, 6–12 mm.

COMPARISONS AND DATING: This ware corresponds to Griffin's (1974:60) "Chaff-faced Ware." It is included by her in the series of Late Bronze Age orange wares from Korucu Tepe (055/1), but appears in her Table 4 as occurring infrequently throughout the Middle and Late Bronze Age. Therefore, it may span a period from ca. 2000–1200 B.C. In our analysis of the survey materials, we considered this ware to be related to other "Hittite" or Late Bronze Age wares, particularly on the basis of similarities in rim profiles (e.g., Fig. 30:r–y,bb,cc). In retrospect we can also see some resemblances to typical Middle Bronze Age profiles (e.g. Fig. 30:z,aa). We have tabulated this ware with the other Late Bronze Age ceramics and feel that confusion between Middle and Late Bronze Age materials due to this practice has probably been slight. The ware is relatively rare, and the majority of the rim forms seem typical for other Late Bronze Age materials rather than for the Middle Bronze Age.

HITTITE ORANGE SMOOTHED WARE

DESCRIPTION: The same as for Hittite Plain Ware except:

PASTE:
> Color: The core is most commonly orange to buff-orange. Sometimes it is light brown-buff to light to dark gray.

SURFACES: The exterior and interior surfaces are usually identical. The interior is sometimes slightly lighter in color than the exterior. Both are typically covered with an orange to buff-orange slip. Red-orange or dark orange is not uncommon, and occasional pieces are light orange-buff to light buff. The surfaces are then partially smoothed, with the smoothing being done in bands or stripes around the vessel. The entire surface is sometimes smoothed, but facets produced by the smoothing are usually evident.

FORM: Not a large number of vessel forms is known from this ware, but there is some variety among those that are known. Many of the profiles are similar to those in other Hittite wares.

Plates (Fig. 31:a) and bowls (Fig. 31:b) with flat, ledge rims are known. There are bowls with outward-protruding beads (Fig. 31:c), and with heavy rims having both inside and outside beads (Fig. 31:h). Simple bowls may be straight-sided (Fig. 31:d), basin-shaped (Fig. 31:f), or have a "broken profile" (Fig. 31:e). A simple, hole-mouth jar occurs (Fig. 31:g), as well as a series of jars with excurvate or out-angled rims (Fig. 31:i–m).

THICKNESS: Medium, 7–12 mm.

COMPARISONS AND DATING: This ware is probably included within Griffin's (1974:60) "Orange Slipped Ware," although a precise comparison is difficult. The agreement seems better with the description of the ware itself than with the forms mentioned by Griffin. There are close resemblances between other forms illustrated for the Hittite series as a whole from Korucu Tepe and our Orange Smoothed Ware (Griffin 1974:Fig. 27; cf. van Loon and Buccellati 1970: Fig. 8). It is clear that this ware forms part of the Hittite or Late Bronze Age assemblage and is therefore to be dated in the same way as Hittite Plain, Buff-Orange Burnished Ware, etc.—ca. 1500–1200 B.C.

HITTITE RED-BROWN BURNISHED WARE

DESCRIPTION: The same as for Hittite Plain Ware except:

PASTE:
> Color: Cores are more often light gray to gray, and outer layers of the cross-section are more often orange to orange-buff than in Hittite Plain Ware.

SURFACES: Both surfaces are usually the same, but the interior surface may occasionally be lighter in color than the exterior surface. They are slipped and moderately to highly burnished. Burnishing is very occasionally striped. Rare sherds have simply smoothed, unburnished surfaces.

> Colors: By far the most common color is dark red-brown. There are some dark red-oranges, and examples of bright orange-brown or lighter red-brown are found but are very unusual.

FORM: A moderate variety of vessel shapes and profiles is known, most of which parallel the forms of other Hittite wares.

Again, there are plates (Fig. 31:n–p). Bowls occur in many varieties, some with interior bead (Fig. 31:q), most with some sort of exterior bead or protrusion (Fig. 31:r–y). These protrusions rarely approach a ledge form (Fig. 31:s,t). There is a possible example of a "broken profile" bowl (Fig. 31:z), and one S-shaped bowl profile (Fig. 31:aa). A rim with exterior grooves and a flat exterior lip facet appears in both hole-mouth (Fig. 31:bb) and straight-sided (Fig. 31:cc) varieties. A simple bowl with in-turned rim (Fig. 31:dd), and a hole-mouth jar (Fig.31:ee) are also present.

Jars range from straight-sided specimens with short, out-turned lips (Fig. 31:ff), through forms with simple, excurvate necks and round or flat lips (Fig. 31:gg–kk), to a series of forms with excurvate rims with exterior protrusions at the lip (Fig. 31:ll–pp).

Handles have sub-rectangular (Fig. 31:qq) to flattened oval (Fig. 31:rr) cross-sections. One example of a perforated strainer, probably from a spout, was found (Fig. 31:ss).

THICKNESS: Medium 5–10 mm.

COMPARISONS AND DATING: The same as for Hittite Buff-Orange Burnished Ware.

Hittite Brown Burnished Ware

DESCRIPTION: The same as for Hittite Plain Ware except:

PASTE: Occasional sherds contain large quantities (15 percent–25 percent) of crushed white grit. Large (1 mm) particles are common and sizes range up to 2 mm. The paste of these sherds has some resemblance to that of Hittite Brown Gritty Cooking Ware.

SURFACES: The exterior surfaces are slipped and burnished. They are most commonly brown, usually a dark brown to a slightly reddish or maroon-brown, rarely a dark gray-brown. Occasional sherds are lighter brown to buff-brown. The interiors are often the same as the exteriors but they are also frequently less well burnished.

FORM: This ware occurs in many forms. Some of these are known also in other Hittite wares.

Plates seem to be absent. Bowls are not uncommon. There are simple, basin-shaped bowls with rounded lips, usually with some elaboration of the lip profile such as slight flaring and thickening with (Fig. 32:a) or without (Fig. 32:b) interior groove. Other varieties have well formed "collars" (Fig. 32:c), pointed lips with flat, exterior facet (Fig. 32:d), or flat, squared-off lips (Fig. 32:e). Some open bowls have an interior protuberance at the rim (Fig. 32:f), grading into an interior-beveled lip with inner protrusion (Fig. 32:g). Others have a slight exterior protuberance (Fig. 32:h), but more common is an exterior flange, usually angled downward (Fig. 32:i,j), but sometimes forming a horizontal ledge (Fig. 32:k). Also common is a triangular lip form with an exterior ridge or spur (Fig. 32:l–o), which is sometimes above a broad groove and angle in the vessel wall (Fig. 32:l).

These last bowl forms grade directly into similar shapes in hole-mouth jars (Fig. 32:p,q). These and other hole-mouth jars are found in a wide variety of specific rim profiles and constitute the most varied class of vessels in this ware. Some have triangular collars (Fig. 32:r) or exterior flattening at the lip (Fig. 32:s). Some have heavy thickened, triangular lips which may be oriented in various ways (Fig. 32: t–v). Other lips have both interior and exterior beads (Fig. 32:w,x). Simple rim profiles also are found (Fig. 32:y,z), although even these often have a groove on the exterior. Some profiles have a strange, inset lip which is slightly separated from the body wall profile (Fig. 32:aa,bb). Most common, however, is a hole-mouth form with a short, round, exterior bead at the lip (Fig. 32:cc–gg). This grades through a simple, excurvate lip (Fig. 32:hh) to a series of forms with out-folded, flat, ledge rims (Fig. 32:ii–ll).

True jars are often closely related to this last type of hole-mouth jar. Most forms have straight-sided necks and an exterior ledge (Fig. 32:mm), or angled-out rim (Fig. 32:nn–pp), ranging to an exterior bead (Fig. 32:qq–ss). Simple, excurvate or out-angled necks and rims are also found (Fig. 32:tt–ww). Unusual shapes include those with an incipient (Fig. 32:xx) or true (Fig. 32:yy,zz) inner ledge, and those with a triangular collar (Fig. 32:aaa).

Bases are flat with a sharp angle at the foot of the vessel which may be accentuated (Fig. 32:bbb) or not (Fig. 32:ccc). Handles are round in cross-section (Fig. 32:ddd,eee).

COMPARISONS AND DATING: The same as for Hittite Buff-Orange Burnished Ware.

HITTITE WHITE SLIPPED WARE

PASTE: The texture is medium fine to fine, usually compact and moderately well levigated. Rare pieces are poorly levigated and show a laminar structure. Such pieces are an unusual light cream in color. Temper is grit in moderate amounts (10 percent–15 percent, usually ca. 10 percent). The grit is multi-colored, both light and dark, and is of medium size, ca. 0.5 mm and smaller, with occasional particles up to 2–3 mm in size. There is occasionally a moderate amount of chaff temper in the paste. The center of the core is usually dark to light grey in these sherds.

    Color: With the exceptions mentioned above, colors are mostly orange to buff. There are occasional light grays and light browns. In some sherds (not only those with chaff temper), the centers of the core are light gray, and rare pieces are dark gray all the way through, except for a thin, light buff layer at the exterior surface.

    Firing: Medium–high to high.

    Manufacture: Wheel.

SURFACES: Vessel exteriors are slipped in a generally dirty, cream–white or whitish gray, sometimes a light whitish buff, and occasionally a pure white. Slip of this last color is thickly applied. Otherwise, slips are usually thin, allowing the underlying surface to show through. This surface is typically orange or buff, and only infrequently other colors. Slips are typically matt, rarely slightly burnished.

The interior surfaces are often identical, but they are perhaps somewhat more commonly simply orange, buff or red-orange, well smoothed, and slightly to moderately well burnished.

Chaff-tempered pieces have a very slight to moderate chaff-faced appearance.

DECORATION: None.

FORM: Simple, open bowls with slightly thickened rims are common (Fig. 33: a–e), as are other simple bowls (Fig. 33:f–h), sometimes with interior bead (Fig. 33:i) or exterior grooving (Fig. 33:j,k). A form with an angled profile occurs (Fig. 33:l), as well as some thick-walled, relatively straight-sided bowls with flat lips (Fig. 33:m,n). A number of bowls have a round to slightly pointed exterior bead at the rim (Fig. 33: o–t). One has a sort of downward-angled flange (Fig. 33:u).

A simple, semi-hole-mouth jar (Fig. 33:v) and a hole-mouth jar with a thickened and horizontally flattened rim (Fig. 33:w) are found.

Simple jars with excurvate necks and plain rims are relatively common (Fig. 33:x–bb). The lip is sometimes thickened (Fig. 33:cc). Other jars with out-curved necks have round, exterior beads at the rim (Fig. 33:dd,ee), grading into horizontal (Fig. 33:ff–hh) to down-turned (Fig. 33:ii) ledge rims. One unusual shape has an interior bead rim (Fig. 33:jj).

Bases are flat (Fig. 33:kk) or ring (Fig. 33:ll,mm). There are some round, loop handles (fig. 33:nn).

THICKNESS: Medium, 5–10 mm, but also thick, ca. 18 mm.

COMPARISONS AND DATING: This ware was found in the "Hittite Empire" levels at Korucu Tepe (055/1—van Loon and Buccellati 1970:95–97), forming part of the ceramic assemblage characterized by various orange wares. In fact, this simply seems to be a white-slipped variety of orange ware, usually containing a noticeable amount of chaff temper. It is not discussed by Griffin (1974) but is clearly to be dated, along with the rest of this distinctive assemblage, to ca. 1500–1200 B.C. (cf. Hittite Buff-Orange Burnished Ware).

HITTITE PAINTED WARE

This category covers a wide range of pastes, shapes, and paints. It perhaps represents a composite of wares from different periods or of different functions. In general:

PASTE: The most common and typical sherds are the same as Hittite Plain. Pastes vary from fine and well levigated with little or no temper to coarse, with abundant (up to 25 percent–30 percent) grit, usually whole. Some sherds have a moderate amount (10 percent–15 percent) of chaff temper.

>Color: Again, the range is mostly the same as for Hittite Plain—buffs and buff-oranges. There are a few grays and a few light buffs or creams.
>Firing: Medium to high.
>Manufacture: Wheel.

SURFACES: The vessel surfaces are mainly buff, brown-buff, orange-buff, or cream-buff. Sometimes they are cream slipped, and there are a few darker grays or browns. Surfaces are occasionally burnished.

DECORATION: Vessels are painted in soft matt red to light red, scarlet or red-orange. Paint color sometimes varies to brown, dark brown or black. It is almost always the exterior which is painted. Very rarely is the only paint found inside the rim (e.g. Fig. 34:m). Paint was applied in broad bands around the vessel (Fig. 34:a–d,f,h–j,n), in irregular diagonal or vertical stripes (Fig. 34:e,g,o; Fig. 35:a–c), or roughly wavy lines (Fig. 34:l; Fig. 35:e). A few designs are more even and regular geometric patterns such as cross-hatching (Fig. 35:d,f). More unusual designs include pendant "blades" (Fig. 35:g) and occasional festoons and "sprigs" protruding from other design elements. Sometimes only the flat surface of the lip is painted as a band of color, on both outward (Fig. 34:k) and inward-facing (Fig. 34:m) lips.

FORM: Both bowls and jars were painted. Bowls are usually of simple profile (Fig. 34:a,b), or have an exterior bead or molding along the lip (Fig. 34:c–e). Semi-ledges are found (Fig. 34:f), as well as a sort of "splayed" lip (Fig. 34:g). The S-shaped bowl profile is also found in this ware (Fig. 34:j).

Jars exhibit mostly simple excurvate forms (Fig. 34:h,i,k,n). Hole-mouth jars, both with exterior bead rim (Fig. 34:l) and interior beveled lip (Fig. 34:m) are known.

Bases are flat (Fig. 34:p), sometimes with a short basal elevation (Fig. 34:q).

THICKNESS: Medium, 6–11 mm.

COMPARISONS AND DATING: This ware is described by Griffin (1974:60) as her "Red-on-Buff Painted Ware." She describes two varieties of this ware, one with large X's on the shoulder of the vessel, and one with one or two painted bands around the rim or shoulder. These correspond to the examples on Fig. 34 (with the exception of Fig. 34:m, which may well be a rim of cream Chaff Ware that has been misclassified by us as a Hittite sherd—compare this sherd to one illustrated by Esin 1970: Pl. 114:2, T 70–80$_{22}$). This particular style of Hittite Painted Ware appears to be characteristic for the Keban area (cf. Esin 1971:Pl.93:2). Griffin (1974:85) points to comparable painting on a jar from early second millennium B.C. levels at Boğazköy, but finds the vessel shapes of the Keban area painted ware to be most similar to those from Hittite Empire levels at Boğazköy. Such forms apparently begin already in Karum times at Kültepe and elsewhere (Griffin 1974:85). On the other hand, a number of other designs found on sherds of this ware in the survey collections are closely paralleled at Boğazköy by materials from the most part from Büyükkale III–IVB, Hittite Empire levels (Fischer 1963:Pls. 15–20; compare particularly his Pl. 20:200 to our Fig. 35:a, his Pl. 19:186 to our Fig. 35:d, his Pl. 20:193–194 to our Fig. 35:g, and examples from his Pl. 16 to our Fig. 35:f).

In general, therefore, we consider this ware to belong primarily to Hittite Empire, or Late Bronze Age, times and to date to ca. 1500–1200 B.C.

HITTITE BROWN GRITTY COOKING WARE

PASTE: Medium texture, sandy, with rough breaks. Feels relatively light and porous, although holes are seldom actually visible in the paste. Fine to medium sand of all colors, dark to light, was used as tempering material, usually moderately abundantly (15 percent–25 percent), and sometimes exceedingly abundantly (30 percent–50 percent). The paste is thus quite soft and crumbly with a gritty, sandpaper-like feel.

> Color: Generally brown to deep reddish brown or dark red-gray. Gray also occurs. The cross-section is usually homogeneous in color. Very occasionally is the center of the core darker.
>
> Firing: Low.
>
> Manufacture: Wheeled. The marks are usually smoothed over but are still clearly visible on many pieces.

SURFACES: Vessel interiors and exteriors are generally identical. The interior is sometimes slightly darker, rarely somewhat lighter, than the exterior. Surfaces are simply smoothed in most cases, but are occasionally lightly burnished, especially on the rim. The sandy temper usually shows through clearly on the surfaces, which typically feel rough, gritty, and sandy, like medium to fine sandpaper. Colors are generally dirty browns or dark browns ranging to deep red brown. Some browns are lighter, with a slight buff-orange tinge. A few examples of reddish-grays to grays have been found.

DECORATION: None.

FORM: The range of form is quite restricted in this ware relative to other Hittite pottery. Simple, straight-sided bowls with lugs (Fig. 35:h), straight-sided bowls with exterior beads at the rim (Fig. 35:i), open bowls with similar beads (Fig. 35:j,l), and forms with gently incurved sides (Fig. 35:k) exhaust the variety of bowls.

Most common are hole-mouth jars, typically with an exterior flange, or undercut groove (Fig. 35:m–p). One form of hole-mouth jar has a short, out-angled lip (Fig. 35:q). Only one type of simple jar rim with excurvate neck and exterior lip protrusion is known (Fig. 35:r).

THICKNESS: Typically medium-thin, 5–8 mm, some medium, up to 10 mm.

COMPARISONS AND DATING: This ware is little discussed by Griffin. It seems to be part of her "Buff Cooking Ware" (1974:55), although it is clear that she includes much more in that category than our Hittite Brown Gritty Cooking Ware. However, she describes some cooking ware from Late Bronze Age levels at Korucu Tepe (055/1) in terms very close to the specific description for our ware, referring to the frequent dark brown color, burnishing, and similarity to her brown gritty burnished ware (Griffin 1974:55,69,72). The cooking pot forms to which she apparently largely restricts this last ware (Griffin 1974: 69, Fig. 27:314,318–21) are those which we have described above as most common for Hittite Brown Gritty Cooking Ware (cf. Fig. 35:m–p). Earlier, van Loon and Buccellati (1970:94–95) described a dark brown cooking ware from the Hittite Empire levels at Korucu Tepe, which sounds very much like our ware. It is clear the Hittite Brown Gritty Cooking Ware is another member of the Late Bronze Age or Hittite Empire period ceramic assemblage in the Keban area, dating ca. 1500–1200 B.C.

IRON AGE WARE

PASTE: Paste is fairly well levigated and compact. It shows a moderately rough and irregular break. Temper is grit, which is apparently crushed and is usually very fine. Particles range up to 1 mm in size in some sherds, however, and rare examples have relatively large quantities of large particles. Quantity of temper is quite variable, ranging from 5 percent–15 percent, with an average of ca. 10 percent. The grit occurs in all colors from white to black. The general impression is of a hard, tough, moderately coarse paste.

In some pieces, usually those of lighter color, the paste may be somewhat more porous and slightly laminated in texture. In these pieces there is usually a small to moderate amount (5 percent–10 percent, occasionally 15 percent) of chaff temper. Grit temper is then sparse (5 percent–10 percent). A generally tough and hard impression is still given by this paste. Very rarely is fine homogeneous paste with 5 percent–10 percent fine chaff temper and no grit found.

> Color: Paste colors range from light brown through buff, buff-orange, and brown to dark brown, dark red-brown, or deep buff-orange. With any of these colors, the center of the core may be light or dark gray, particularly in sherds with somewhat coarser paste and temper. In rare instances a sherd may be gray through its whole cross-section.
>
> Firing: Medium to high. Medium is more common with sherds in the brown to

buff range of surface colors. Higher firing is more characteristic of red and cream-surfaced sherds.

Manufacture: This ware appears to be handmade. Some vessels may be wheeled, but none show unmistakable wheel marks. This is perhaps surprising in view of some of the rather complex profiles which are common and typical of this ware.

SURFACES: Vessel surfaces show a wide range of variation, primarily in color. Iron age ceramics were initially subdivided into Red, Brown, and Cream wares, but were eventually combined into a single ware since the intergradation among these color categories was so great that it proved impossible to separate them consistently. Surface treatment is more uniform, however.

Both interior and exterior vessel surfaces are slipped, typically thickly, so that the color of the underlying paste does not show through. The surfaces are then moderately to well burnished, the separate burnishing strokes typically being clearly visible. There is a slight tendency for the lighter colored sherds to be less well burnished, or even matt surfaced, in contrast to darker pieces. However, most light colored sherds are well burnished.

Color varies from dark, almost black, to light cream. What was originally called Iron Age Red is characterized by buff-reds, reds, deep reds, deep browns, maroon-red, maroon with black or dark gray blotches, and occasional almost black sherds. The lighter end of this scale grades imperceptibly into the reddish buffs of our former Iron Age Brown. This latter was typified by light colors, however—light reddish buffs, light buff-brown, light brown, to light buff. Light buff was also common in the original Iron Age Cream category, along with very light buffs, light cream-buff, and light cream-gray. This continuous gradation from the darkest to the lightest colors, the general similarity of pastes, and the identical range of vessel forms present in each of the original categories led to their being combined into the single Iron Age Ware described here.

DECORATION: There is one class of decoration, quite uniform in kind. On certain bowls and jars there are one or two bands of short, elongated, oval grooves. These grooves are diagonal and usually run parallel to each other on any one band (Fig. 38:f–i,k), but they are generally at opposite angles to each other on paired bands (Fig. 38:l,m). Occasionally the grooves occur in pairs which alternate in orientation on a single band (Fig. 38:j). On jars, the bands are formed of a ridge or raised strip and are located either in the neck constriction (Fig. 38:f), or more commonly on the vessel body (Fig. 38:j–m). On bowls, the bands are created as panels defined by two or more parallel grooves running horizontally around the rim of the bowl (Fig. 38:g–i). These are all simple, open bowls. An occasional body sherd is also found with a groove and/or some fragment of such a band (e.g. Fig. 38:n).

Certain bowl forms are decorated with a panel of horizontal, parallel grooves as described below.

FORM: A very characteristic bowl shape has a slightly in-turned rim with a complex series of exterior protrusions or ridges at and just below the lip, on the vessel exterior (Fig. 36:a–f). These bowls are generally light in color, varying from brown through buff-brown to cream. Somewhat similar but quite simple, bent or S-shaped bowl profiles (Fig. 36:g–i) are found in all colors. There is also a large series of simple, open bowls with a slight nick or groove in the neck just under the lip and occasionally one or more shallow grooves on the lower body (Fig. 36:j–r). These bowls are found in all colors. They grade through a few examples with very shallow but more regularly spaced grooves (Fig. 36:s,t) into a group of bowls of simple profile with a series of relatively narrow, but clearly defined, regularly spaced, parallel grooves forming a horizontal band on the vessel exterior, just below the lip (Fig. 36:u–z). Very closely related to this group is a series of slightly hole-mouth jars, rarely with subtle, shallow grooves (Fig. 36:aa,bb), typically with a number of clear, narrow, and relatively regularly spaced grooves, usually on the in-turned portion of the rim (Fig. 36:cc–hh). These grooved bowls and hole-mouth jars are quite characteristic among Iron Age ceramics and occur in all shades of color, although there is a definite tendency for them to be on the dark side, with brown, buff-orange and red common.

There are also several simply in-curved (Fig. 36:ii–kk) to angled-in (Fig. 36:ll), hole-mouth vessels, and a series of very simple, shallow, open bowl profiles (Fig. 36:mm–qq). Such forms grade gradually into shallow, open bowls with an exterior bead at the lip (Fig. 36:rr), which in turn run on into a wide variety of bowls with exterior beads or protrusions at the lip, and open basin-shaped to deep, straight-sided profiles (Fig. 36:ss–uu; Fig. 37:a–o). These bowls may be of any color. A few examples occur of bowls with interior bead (Fig. 37:p,q). A strange form, having a splayed lip with parallel grooves running along the surface of the lip, is also found (Fig. 37:r,s). One bowl form has a sharply angled-out ledge rim (Fig. 37:t).

There are a few profiles which are difficult to place exactly in bowl or jar categories, being sometimes almost intermediate. These are slightly offset, or S-shaped profiles on almost vertical-sided vessels, sometimes looking like a slightly hole-mouth jar (Fig. 37:u,v), sometimes clearly like a bowl (Fig. 37:w).

Jars include relatively tall-necked examples with short, slightly out-angled, thickened lips (Fig. 37:x), often with grooves on the neck at the point of bending and below (Fig. 37:y,z). The majority of jars have gently excurvate to moderately angled necks (Fig. 37:aa–qq). A number of minor varieties of form are found in this category. Particularly characteristic is a broadly excurvate neck with a short band of parallel grooves approximately on the middle of the shoulder of the vessel (Fig. 37:aa). Some jar rims have heavier, thicker lips, often with exterior protrusions or beads. (Fig. 37:rr–tt). A few show thickened, practically flat lips on a short, vertical rim (Fig. 37:aa; Fig. 38:a).

Bases are flat, with slightly rounded edge (Fig. 37:vv,ww) or ring bases (Fig. 37:xx,yy). Spouts occur on some jars (Fig. 38:a–c). Handles are either sub-rectangular in cross-section, with slightly grooved, broad sides (Fig. 38:d) or round (Fig. 38:e).

THICKNESS: Medium to medium-thick, 6–12 mm.

COMPARISONS AND DATING: We have described and generally treated this ware as a unit. However, there is good evidence for a subdivision of at least some of this material into Early and Middle periods on the basis of several specific rim forms. Our knowledge of the Early Iron Age forms comes primarily from comparisons with excavated material from Korucu Tepe (055/1). Middle Iron Age forms can be identified and dated from comparisons with excavated material from Norşun Tepe (054/8) and with materials from Urartian sites in the Lake Van region.

We have given a single description of Iron Age Ware for both periods. In fact, there does appear to be considerable continuity in ware between them. We began our analysis of the Iron Age ceramics with a more detailed classification of several wares but found that there was so much intergradation among these categories that it was necessary to group them into the single ware described here. However, there is some indication of variation from Early to Middle Iron Age in terms of manufacture. The typically complex rim forms of the Middle Iron Age were apparently produced on a wheel (Hauptmann 1971:88). We had wondered at the complex profiles found in this supposedly handmade ware but had failed to find definitive evidence for the use of a wheel on the sherds in our surface collections. Thus, although at least some Middle Iron Age vessels must have been wheelmade, the bulk of what we have classified as Iron Age pottery was made by hand.

The Early Iron Age ceramics were definitely handmade (Hauptmann 1969/70:58; van Loon 1973:373) and comprise at least two very distinctive types. The most common of these is made up of the bowls with vertical to in-turned rims and several grooves running around the outside of the vessel above the shoulder (cf. Fig. 36:u–hh). These have been discussed as quite characteristic of our Iron Age Ware, and numerous examples can be found in the excavated materials from a number of sites in the Keban area (e.g., Korucu Tepe, 055/1—van Loon 1973: Pl. 19c; Norşun Tepe, 054/8—Hauptmann 1969/70: Pls. 16–19; Tepecik, 054/2—Esin 1970: Pl. 6:5–6, Pl. 7:1–2,9). The second type of distinctive pottery from this period is the decorated ware discussed earlier (cf. Fig. 38:f–m). This decorated ware is found regularly in association with the grooved-rim ceramics in the Keban area (e.g., van Loon 1973:373, Pl. 19A; Hauptmann 1969/70: Pl. 16:6, Pl. 17:7; Esin 1970: Pl. 7:3, 6–8). In addition to these two distinctive kinds of pottery, jars with excurvate rims and grooves on the shoulder of the vessel, just below the neck may also belong in the Early Iron Age ceramic assemblage (compare Fig. 37:aa with van Loon 1973: Pl. 19B, and with Hauptmann 1969/70:Pl. 17:4).

This Early Iron Age assemblage has been dated to ca. 1200–800 B.C. (van Loon 1973:372–373), and van Loon suggests possible cultural ties with the Lake Van region in this period. Hauptmann points only to similarities with materials from Arslan Tepe in Malatya (Hauptmann 1969/70:63).

Middle Iron Age rim forms are no less distinctive. They are the complex profiles about which we were concerned when considering whether or not some Iron Age pottery might be wheelmade (Fig. 36:a–f). Such ceramics were not found at Korucu Tepe but were present at Norşun Tepe (054/8). They are discussed by Hauptmann (1969/70:67–72), who points out their general relationship with Urartian pottery from the Lake Van region. Middle Iron Age occupation is dated by him to roughly the second quarter of the first milennium B.C.—Norşun Tepe, after this occupation, being abandoned in the sixth century B.C. The material illustrated by Hauptmann is very similar to ours, much of which was actually collected from the surface of Norşun (054/8). Good parallels are also found at Altıntepe. (cf. Emre 1969: Figs. 8,10, with Fig. 36:a–e). In addition to these rather striking forms, several other rim profiles can be compared to those at Altıntepe. Compare Emre 1969: Fig. 2 to Fig. 37:oo; his Fig. 21 to Fig. 37:u,v; and his Fig. 22 to Fig. 37:aa—although in the last two cases the Altıntepe pottery is painted while the same forms in the Keban are not. The Urartian materials from Altıntepe comparable to the Middle Iron Age ceramics in the Keban area are dated ca. 750–600 B.C. (Emre 1969).

Iron Age Painted Ware

PASTE: Extremely fine and well levigated, tough, homogeneous and compact. Temper appears to be absent or sparse (5 percent or less), tiny, pinprick-size white grits.
    Color: Light buff to orange-buff, uniform throughout the thickness of the sherd.
    Firing: High.
    Manufacture: Appears handmade, perhaps wheeled.

SURFACES: Interior surfaces are simply smoothed, light buff to orange buff. The exterior surfaces are well smoothed to lightly burnished orange-buff to dark orange-buff.

DECORATION: The vessel exteriors are painted in red-orange to dark red-brown paint. Designs appear to be roughly rectilinear, geometrical patterns executed in irregular, "blobby" lines and irregular round dots and ovals (Fig. 38:o–q).

FORM: Only body sherds were found to be painted. No rim profiles can be associated with this painting from our sample, but it is probable that these body sherds belong to vessels whose profiles can be found in our category of Iron Age Ware.

THICKNESS: Medium, 6–8 mm.

COMPARISONS AND DATING: This ware was found in excavated levels of the Early Iron Age at Norşun Tepe (054/8) and is apparently restricted to this period (cf. Hauptmann 1969/70:63–64, Pl. 16:1–5).

Iron Age Thick Ware

DESCRIPTION: The same as for Iron Age Ware except:

PASTE: Paste is somewhat more porous than the thinner ware but is still compact and tough. Chaff temper is more common and is found as larger pieces, but still in moderately low density, ca. 10 percent.
    Color: Occurs in lighter shades, ranging from browns to cream.
    Firing: Medium-high.

DECORATION: On some vessels with exterior ridges at the rim, a row of shallow, irregular, slightly diagonal, oval grooves or depressions is present (Fig. 39:a).

FORM: A common form of large bowl or slightly hole-mouth jar has a rim profile characterized by pronounced external beads or ridges and grooves very similar to profiles typical of ordinary Iron Age Ware (Fig. 39:a–c). Other large, open bowls have a lip with a thick, exterior bead or protrusion (Fig. 39:d,e). Another open bowl form is shallow, with a simple, rounded lip undercut by a narrow groove (Fig. 39:j), very similar again to forms common for thinner vessels. Massive bowls with splayed walls and plain lips are also found (Fig. 39:k).

Jars have very short rims with exterior protrusions or ledges on a vertical or slightly in-sloping neck (Fig. 39:f,h). In addition to the other hole-mouth forms described above, a jar with gently incurving walls and a thickened, well-rounded lip is also known (Fig. 39:i).

THICKNESS: Thick, 18–28 mm.

COMPARISONS AND DATING: The same as for Iron Age Ware generally.

Medieval Brick Ware

PASTE: Typically slightly rough, moderately well levigated, tempered with ca. 15 percent crushed grit. The grit is largely light in color with many white particles, but also ranging through gray to occasional black particles. It is of moderate size, probably about .5 mm on the average, with pieces of 1 mm not uncommon, and some particles of 2 mm or more, depending on the thickness of the vessel.

> Color: Sherds often have gray or light gray cores, sometimes light brown or even light buff. Near the surfaces, colors are typically deep red-brown to bright orange, roughly the color of building bricks, from which this ware gets its name. Other colors may occur from time to time, including light buff, light gray-buff, gray, and dark, coffee-chocolate brown.

Some pastes are much finer, well levigated, and harder, with no temper, or sparse (5 percent or less) grit temper, as above, but generally in smaller particles. These pastes are typically bright orange to red-orange in color.

Rare pieces have chaff temper up to an abundant 15 percent–20 percent or more, making a light coarse, very porous paste with some (ca. 5 percent) relatively large grits (up to 3 mm). These pieces generally have gray cores and brick red to orange paste near the surfaces.

> Firing: Usually medium, some low. Thinner sherds with fine paste are sometimes highly fired.
>
> Manufacture: Wheel. Wheelmarks are generally light and hard to see on the rough surfaces of most sherds, but are clear on thinner sherds.

SURFACES: Both surfaces are usually the same, although a slight color difference is not uncommon, in which case the interior may be either lighter or darker. Surfaces are usually simply smoothed. The gritty paste typically gives a "bumpy" character to the surface, and the grit particles occasionally show clearly on the surface, giving the sherd a gritty feel. It is, however, not uncommon to find better smoothed, self-slipped pieces and even a few irregularly to moderately well burnished ones.

Surface colors vary around the typical brick orange-red, from dark maroon to dark gray and from bright orange to light buff-orange, light buff and gray-buff. However, all colors give a generally drab impression.

DECORATION: This is typically a plain ware category, but a variety of combing, incision, grooving, and light smearing is sporadically found. Sometimes simple finger tip impressions are used (Fig. 44:g). This decoration is never very extensive on the vessels and there are no consistently repeated patterns except for rows of shallow, parallel grooves on the rims of certain bowls, described below.

FORM: The range of form in this category is great. This is fairly recent material. It was not our greatest interest, and it is therefore probable that this great diversity of form is at least partly the result of our lumping together a variety of ceramics which represent a significant span of time. All these forms share great similarities in ware, however, and no consistent associations between particular vessel forms and specific varieties of ceramic ware were readily apparent, on which a sub-division might have been made.

Plates, both simple and with more complex rims, were occasionally found (Fig. 40:a–d). There were some shallow bowls with simple, squared-off lips (Fig. 40:e,f). Deep bowls with similar simple, flat, or slightly rounded lips were relatively more common (Fig. 40:g–o). These bowls are sometimes handled, either with an arch modeled on the body under the lip (Fig. 40:g) or with a heavy strap handle, having a sub-rectangular cross section, and coming directly off the lip (Fig. 40:m). Another series of deep bowls have flat lips with a sharp, inward protrusion (Fig. 40:p–r). One of these bowls has an oval strap handle beginning from the vessel wall below the lip (Fig. 40:p). These bowls grade into a series with outward beveled lips or rounded lips, all with inner protrusions (Fig. 40:s–w). These in turn seem to grade through an intermediate form (Fig. 40:x) into several bowls with exterior protrusions or beaded rims (Fig. 41:a–c).

One variety of bowls with beaded rims has a sharply angled body profile (Fig. 41:e–g). Somewhat similar are simple bowl rims with an inset or "broken" profile (Fig. 41:h,i), which are not far from bowls with S-shaped profiles (Fig. 41:j). A related form is a broad, shallow bowl with a short, vertical rim, grooved to create a slightly S-shaped profile (Fig. 41:k,l). A distinctive class of bowls has a broader, vertical rim which is decorated with narrow, shallow, parallel exterior grooves (Fig. 41:m–o).

Other simple bowls have a single, deeper indentation or groove under the lip, giving a "beaded" effect (Fig. 41:p–s). Sometimes these are heavy, thick-walled vessels (Fig. 41:t), grading into forms with outward beveled rims with an exterior bead, both in thick (Fig. 41:u,v) and normal (Fig. 41:w–z) varieties. Bowls with exterior ledge rims in a number of shapes (Fig. 41:aa–ii) are relatively common. One deep bowl with a stubby, squared-off ledge rim also has a large oval lug handle (Fig. 41:ii). The range of open bowls extends finally to a simple form with a tapered rim and rounded lip (Fig. 41:jj).

Hole-mouth jars are quite common. A number have simple forms with gently in-curved walls and rounded lips (Fig. 41:kk–nn). Some of these have exterior grooves (Fig. 41:ll,nn). Simple hole-mouth jars with slightly up-turned, pointed lips occur (Fig. 41:oo,pp), again sometimes with exterior grooves (Fig. 41:oo).

An angled form is known also (Fig. 42:a), but the most frequently found hole-mouth jars have a clear exterior protrusion or bead. These occur in a large number of specific shapes (Fig. 42:b–q,s,v,w,y–bb). Occasional forms have a squared-off lip, thickened on both sides (Fig. 42:r), a modeled internal flange with slight external protrusion (Fig. 42:t), a thickened, beveled lip (Fig. 42:u), or a simple, flatly beveled lip (Fig. 42:x).

True jars most typically have an excurvate neck and a bead, ledge, thickening, or similar exterior protrusion at the lip (Fig. 42:cc–uu; Fig. 43:a,n–r,t–z). Almost all these jar necks are gently excurvate. Occasionally, they are almost straight (Fig. 42:ff,hh,ii; Fig. 43:w,y,z), and they are rarely angled outward (Fig. 42:oo). Some of these jars have flat or turned-down, triangular, ledge handles (Figs. 42:kk; Fig. 43:ee). Other jar forms are also generally gently excurvate, with plain, square or rounded lips (Figs. 42:vv–aaa; Fig. 43:b–m,s,dd). Again, occasional examples have straight necks (Fig. 43:i,k,dd) or angled necks (Fig. 42:yy). The triangular ledge rim also sometimes appears on these jars (Fig. 43:h). A rare example of a trefoil-mouthed pitcher (Fig. 43:k) can also be noted. A few jars have more complex rims, with an internal ledge (Fig. 43:aa–cc).

Triangular ledge handles have been mentioned above. There are also ovoid, projecting handles with one grooved side (fig. 44:a). The most common handles, however, are semi-oval to sub-rectangular, loop handles (Fig. 44:b,f) and broad, flat, oval strap handles (Fig. 44:c–e). Both classes have single or multiple grooves on the outside, and the strap handles often have finger-tip impressions at the base. Simple lugs have been mentioned, but they also occasionally have slightly more complex forms (e.g. Fig. 44:h).

Bases are usually flat, with or without a slight foot (Fig. 44:i–m). A few ring bases do occur (Fig. 44:n,o).

THICKNESS: Medium to medium thick, 6–14 mm.

COMPARISONS AND DATING: This ware was identified primarily from its occurrence on sites in the survey area. It, and its varieties—Medieval Thick, White Slipped, and Red Slipped wares—are occasionally found on sites from which no other kinds of pottery were recovered. These wares therefore seemed to form a group or assemblage. They were often found in great abundance on sites in this area. A number of these sites still had partially standing stone foundation walls either on the surface or only lightly covered by earth and vegetation, giving a strong impression that the pottery found on them was recent or modern. Some similar or identical pottery could be seen in the market in Elâzığ, and such observations extend back to the turn of the century when Huntington noted the manufacture and use of a "coarse red pottery" in this area (Huntington 1902:390). Similarly, Medieval Cooking Ware and green Glazed Ware, which are often found with Brick, White Slipped, and Red Slipped ceramics, can also be closely approximated or matched in the Elâzığ market.

However, the above group of wares is not entirely recent. It is also found associated with typical Byzantine-Selcuk Sgraffiato Ware. This is true at a number of sites. At Korucu Tepe (055/1), this complex has been specifically dated to Late Selcuk-Early Mongol times, ca. 1200–1400 A.D. (van Loon 1973:373). However, it may possibly also be slightly earlier than this at other sites in the area.

We therefore take all these "Medieval" wares—Brick, Thick, White Slipped, Red Slipped, Cooking, Glazed, and the uncommon or rare Painted and Coarse wares— as representative of a broad range of time from the Byzantine period virtually to the present day. The occupation of a surveyed site producing these wares is more specifically identified as Byzantine-Selcuk if it contains Sgraffiato Ware or Medieval Modeled Ware with Islamic designs (cf. description of this ware). Otherwise, unless there is evidence for recent or modern occupation, it is simply called "other Medieval," which may mean any date from these earlier periods up to some time in this century.

The great range of variation in vessel form, rim profile, etc., which can be seen in our "Medieval" wares is undoubtedly due in large part to the great range of time spanned by this grouping of pottery, and the several cultural groups which are probably represented by these "Medieval" assemblages. Clearly, much better and more accurate divisions and dating of these ceramics can be made. They fall far from our range of interest and competence, however, and the rough classification presented and used here was the best possible in the limited time available to process the enormous quantity of data from our survey.

Medieval Thick Ware

PASTE: Dense, compact and moderately coarse. Abundant (10 percent–20 percent) temper, consisting of moderately coarse, crushed grit of all colors, .5–1 mm particles are common, with larger particles running up to 4–5 mm.
    Color: Center of the core is usually dark gray, varying to brown or buff. Toward the vessel surface it becomes brown, buff, or brick orange.
    Firing: Variable.
    Manufacture: Wheel.

SURFACES: All the different surface colors and treatments of Medieval Brick, Medieval White Slipped and Medieval Red Slipped wares are found. The most common surfaces are simply smoothed and are brick orange, brown, or light buff in color.

DECORATION: On occasional pieces rows of broad, shallow indentations, usually fingertip impressions, are found, sometimes accompanied by a groove or a ridge (Fig. 46:a,l,m).

FORM: A number of jars, hole-mouth vessels, and occasional bowls, all with heavy exterior ledges or beads, are found (Fig. 45:a–p; Fig. 46:a–j). Some examples of hole-mouth jars and bowls have simpler, plain or flat lips (Fig. 46:k–m).

THICKNESS: Thick, 15–40 mm.

COMPARISONS AND DATING: The same as for Medieval Brick Ware.

Medieval Coarse Ware

PASTE: Typically very coarse, rough, and poorly levigated with many holes and fissures in the paste. Breaks often appear very rough and "rocky." Temper is usually mixed chaff and grit, with variable proportions of both, but temper is usually abundant. There is generally ca. 5 percent–15 percent chaff temper and 10 percent–15 percent grit. The grits are normally large and coarse, with particles over 1 mm being common and sizes up to 3–4 mm often found. The grit is dark, brown to gray and black.
    Color: The cores are usually dark gray to dark gray-brown, changing near the surface to dirty, dark brown or light buff. Some pieces are buff-brown to buff.
    Firing: Low to moderately low.
    Manufacture: Characteristically hand, with very bumpy, irregular surfaces.

SURFACES: Surfaces are very irregular or "bumpy," simply smoothed or self-slipped with very occasional, slight burnished smoothing on the self-slipped pieces. Colors range from "dirty" brown, red-brown and dark red to maroon and buff.

DECORATION: None.

FORM: Simple hole-mouth forms (Fig. 47:a), bowls with a stubby ledge rim (Fig. 47:b), and simple excurvate jar forms (Fig. 47:c) are known. Horizontally pierced lugs (Fig. 47:c) and round, loop handles (Fig. 47:d) are known. Spouts occur (Fig. 47:e). Bases are flat, with or without a slight foot (Fig. 47:f,g).

THICKNESS: Medium-thick, 10–15 mm.

COMPARISONS AND DATING: This ware is rare. When found, it is always in association with large quantities of Medieval Brick and other Medieval wares. We assume it forms part of this same general assemblage, discussed under Medieval Brick Ware.

Medieval Glazed Ware

PASTE: Paste is fine and compact. It is tempered with abundant but extremely fine sand, probably over 20 percent, but quantities cannot be seen clearly. The paste thus has the feel of very fine sandpaper. There is also often 5 percent–10 percent fine, visible particles, usually of a pinprick size, but occasionally up to 1 mm. These are usually light in color—white, light gray or brown.
> Color: Typically orange, dark brick-red, or brick-brown. Dark brown, buff brown, or buff are not uncommon, however.
> Firing: Varies from moderately low to medium high.
> Manufacture: Wheel.

SURFACE: One or both surfaces are glazed. The unglazed surfaces are simply smoothed and not further finished. The glazes are usually monochrome greens of all shades, to an occasional blue-green.

DECORATION: Vessel exteriors are occasionally decorated with low ribbing, consisting of shallow, parallel grooves (Fig. 47:o).

FORM: Bowls range from simple basins (Fig. 47:h–j) to forms with an angled-out rim (Fig. 47:p) and broad, shallow kinds, almost like dishes (Fig. 47:q). Jars are present in tiny (Fig. 47:k) to medium sized varieties. Some are slightly hole-mouth (Fig. 47:m), but most have an out-angled neck (Fig. 47:l), usually with an exterior beaded rim (Fig. 47:n,r).

Handles are broad, flattened oval strap handles (Fig. 47:s). Bases are high and low pedestals (Fig. 47:t,u), rings (Fig. 47:v), and occasionally flat (Fig. 47:w).

THICKNESS: Medium, 6–8 mm. Occasionally thick, up to 13–14 mm.

COMPARISON AND DATING: This is very clearly a "late" ceramic type. Nevertheless, it seems to cover a relatively long period of time. At Korucu Tepe (055/1) it is found in Late Selcuk-Early Mongol levels dated to 1200–1400 A.D. (van Loon 1973:373). The comparisons are the same as for Sgraffiato Ware for this period. However, the range of variation in the Glazed Ware is greater than for Sgraffiato Ware, and green glazed pottery is common even today in the Elâzığ market. Undoubtedly, differences exist between the early green glazed ceramics and those sold today in Elâzığ, but we were not able to identify such differences visually in the sherds from the survey. We therefore treat plain green glazed pottery as part of the varied group of medieval to virtually modern materials discussed under Medieval Brick Ware.

Medieval Sgraffiato Ware

PASTE: Very fine textured but only moderately to poorly levigated. Some pieces are well levigated, but there are virtually always many small holes in the paste. Temper appears to be very sparse (less than 5 percent) and consists of very fine, usually pinprick-size, white grits.
> Color: Buff-brown to orange-buff. Occasionally light to dark gray.
> Firing: Very variable from low to high. Most medium.
> Manufacture: Wheel.

SURFACES: The inner surface is glazed in light green, green, or bluish green. The exterior is sometimes also glazed, particularly near the rim, but, over most of the vessel body and near the base, it is usually plain, smoothed, and the color of the paste.

DECORATION: The inner surface is covered with curvilinear, often floral, designs incised into the paste and thus filled with a thicker layer of glaze, forming black or sometimes dark blue-green lines on the lighter glazed surface (Fig. 47:x,ff). The exterior surface, when glazed, may also have some similar designs near the rim.

FORM: This ware occurs primarily as bowls, usually open, but some deeper, basin or cup-shaped forms also occur (Fig. 47:x–dd). Bases appear to be pedestals or very high ring bases (Fig. 47:ee,ff).

THICKNESS: Medium, 5–9 mm.

COMPARISONS AND DATING: This distinctive ware has a more clearly restricted time span than the other "Medieval" wares discussed. At Korucu Tepe (055/1) it is typical of Late Selcuk-Early Mongol levels dated to ca. 1200–1400 A.D. (van Loon 1973:373). The comparisons are close between the survey material and that from the excavations at Korucu Tepe. The common shape is a small, ring-based bowl (cf. van Loon 1973:373). Compare the bases in Bakırer (1974:Figs. 34–35) with Fig. 47, especially Fig. 47:ee, and the simple bowl rim profiles on Fig. 47:x–dd with Bakırer's Fig. 32.

At least some of the material from N52/2 (Taşkun Kale) has been dated to this same range of time (McNicoll 1974:50–51). However, at Taşkun Kale there is possibly earlier, Christian (Byzantine?) occupation, and the Sgraffiato Ware may easily also be associated with such occupations here and at other sites (cf. Mitchell 1973:134). We therefore date this ware generally as representative of Byzantine-Selcuk occupation.

MEDIEVAL RED SLIPPED WARE

DESCRIPTION: The same as for Medieval Brick except:

SURFACES: One or both surfaces are slipped with a dark or deep red to maroon slip. The slip is medium thick, i.e. not usually thin enough to let the underlying surface be exposed, but not as thick as Iron Age Slips. The slipped surface is usually simply smoothed but it is occasionally slightly to moderately well burnished.

DECORATION: Edges of rims are sometimes nicked (Fig. 48:a,nn; Fig. 49:a), some forms are grooved on the outside as described below, and rare pieces have stamped decoration on the rim or elsewhere (e.g. Fig. 48:nn).

FORM: A wide variety of profiles is represented in this ware. The most common vessels are bowls and hole-mouth jars. Good examples of other jars are rare. A flat plate or lid is also present (Fig. 48:a).

Simple, shallow, open bowls with a number of lip profiles are common (Fig. 48:b–j). These are rarely grooved on the outside, and a flat, vertically pierced, triangular ledge handle is known on this form (Fig. 48:b). Another form has a broad groove under the lip, giving the lip the appearance of a semi-separate bead (Fig. 48:k–m). This profile occurs on deep and on open bowls, grading into hole-mouth forms with exterior beads or flanges (Fig. 48:n–q). Other hole-mouth jars have plainer lips, squared or beveled (Fig. 48:r–x). One variety has a grooved lip (Fig. 48:s,t). Some of these vessels have exterior grooves under the lip (Fig. 48:w,x). On one of these a small, vertically pinched lug is present (Fig. 48:x). Such vessels are similar to bowls with vertical rims and exterior grooves (Fig. 48:y), running on into open bowls with angled profiles and a single groove under the lip (Fig. 48:z,aa).

Jars are represented by a series of generally larger and heavier vessels with generally straight necks and thick, usually flat, ledge or bead rims (Fig. 48:bb–ff,hh–jj,ll,nn; Fig. 49:a). Frequently, these are hard to distinguish from large, deep, straight-sided bowls, and there are some clear bowl forms with similar exterior ledge or bead rims (Fig. 48:gg,kk).

An occasional simple, deep, cup-shaped bowl occurs (Fig. 48:mm). There is also a distinctive class of open to slightly incurvate bowls with an exterior flange or ledge at the rim, and a sharp, triangular ridge on the body below the rim, usually at a point of inflection in the body profile (Fig. 49:b–f).

Handles are most commonly oval to broad, flattened loop handles (Fig. 49:g–k). Bases are flat, often with a small "foot" (Fig. 49:l,m).

COMPARISONS AND DATING: See Medieval Brick Ware.

Medieval White Slipped Ware

DESCRIPTION: The same as for Medieval Brick except:

SURFACES: One or both surfaces are slipped with a medium thick, cream-white to light grayish white slip, usually simply smoothed over, very rarely slightly burnished. On many pieces the slip is worn through in spots, revealing a typical brick red-orange surface.

FORM: Simple, open bowls (Fig. 49:n–t; Fig. 50:k) and open bowls with exterior beads or thickened rims (Fig. 49:u–aa) are common.

Hole-mouth vessels are not uncommon. There is one sharply angled form (Fig. 49:bb) and a number of in-sloping rims with beaded or slightly out-turned lip (Fig. 49:cc–ee; Fig. 50:c,d,g,j).

True jars are found in several simple excurvate or out-angled forms (Fig. 49:ff–jj; Fig. 50:a). There are also several thick-walled jars with excurvate or vertical necks, and heavy lips of various forms (Fig. 50:b,e,f,h,i).

Round loop handles (Fig. 50:l) and flattened, strap handles (Fig. 50:m) are found. One base is known. It is flat with a small "foot" (Fig. 50:n).

THICKNESS: Both medium, as in Medieval Brick Ware, and thick, as in Medieval Thick Ware.

COMPARISONS AND DATING: See Medieval Brick Ware.

Medieval Painted Ware

PASTE: Medium fine, slightly rough, well compacted and levigated. Contains relatively abundant (10 percent–15 percent) sand temper of all colors, which gives the paste a sandpaper-like feel.
    Color: Light buff. Rarely light brown-buff or light reddish buff.
    Firing: Medium.
    Manufacture: Wheelmade. Wheelmarks are often visible on both surfaces. Perhaps a few pieces are handmade.

SURFACE: Both surfaces are simply smoothed to a rather sandy, plain finish. They are very rarely self-slipped and better smoothed. Surfaces are usually light brown, buff-brown, gray or gray-brown in color. Occasionally they are light buff.

DECORATION: One or the other surface, and frequently the lip, is painted in matt red, scarlet, or maroon to dull red paint. The paint is usually relatively thin and faint. There are some examples of thicker, more bold painting.

The designs are generally bold but very irregular. Quite typical are simple, broad stripes or bands of paint, horizontal at the rim or on the lip (Fig. 50:o,p,r,s), or vertical on handles (Fig. 51:k,l). It is hard to decipher other designs from the fragments at hand. They appear bold and simple, formed of broad, straight, or wavy lines (Fig. 51:a,d,f–j). Incising sometimes accompanies the painted decoration (Fig. 51:f,i).

FORM: The most common are open bowls, some with heavy, bead rims (Fig. 50:o–r). Others have vertical sides (Fig. 50:s), with simple internally beveled lip (Fig. 51:a), or with a turned-out rim (Fig. 51:b). Hole-mouth vessels are also found, with simple (Fig. 50:t), beaded (Fig. 51:c), or out-angled (Fig. 51:d) rims.

A few jars seem to occur, but are rare and sometimes of rather unusual shape (Fig. 51:e,h).

Handles are broad, flattened, oval straps (Fig. 51:m,n).

THICKNESS: Medium, 6–10 mm.

COMPARISONS AND DATING: This is a fairly uncommon ware. Usually it was found with Medieval Brick Ware and the other Medieval wares. We therefore have dated it in the same way as Brick Ware. In retrospect, however, we find some confusion of this ware with the Late Chalcolithic Cream Chaff Ware. Compare Fig. 51:a (and perhaps Fig. 51:d?) with Esin (1972:Pl. 114, 2:T70–759). This ambiguity is unfortunate, but will not noticeably affect the results of the survey and analysis. The misidentification affects only a few sherds of a relatively infrequent type of pottery.

Medieval Cooking Ware

PASTE: Paste is rough, coarse, and only moderately well levigated. There is ca. 10 percent–20 percent fairly large, coarse, grit temper. Particles are often 1 mm and not infrequently 2–3 mm in size. The grit is a mixture of all colors. A moderate amount of mica is typically included, though many pieces have simply mixed grit.

> Color: Black through dark brown, buff, light gray with orange borders, orange, and red-brown. A wide variety with no particularly dominant color. All are relatively dull, dark, and "dirty" except the oranges. The general impression is of a rough, coarse, gritty, dark ware of many varied colors.
> Firing: Low to occasionally medium low.
> Manufacture: Handmade and often still bumpy and irregular.

SURFACES: Both surfaces are characteristically rough, irregular and "bumpy." They are simply smoothed or self-slipped, sometimes perhaps truly slipped, but this over only roughly evened surfaces. Better smoothed examples are rarely found. Surface colors are typically very dark maroon or black to dark brown or dark red-brown. There are some brighter orange-reds mottled with gray and black. All surfaces are variable in color "blotchy," and look "dirty."

DECORATION: There is usually no decoration, but occasionally a bowl with grooved rim (Fig. 52:f) is found, sometimes with little oval incisions or impressions between the grooves (Fig. 52:d). Also, occasional sherds with shallow incision are found in this ware (Fig. 53:g).

FORM: A full range of bowls, hole-mouth vessels and jars occurs in this ware. There are both deep and shallow open bowls with several simple lip profiles (Fig. 52:a–f). These sometimes are decorated with exterior grooves and incision as noted above. A characteristic form has a relatively straight side, curving, or occasionally angling in, towards the base and loop or strap handles at or near the lip (Fig. 52:j–l). Other open bowls have beaded rims (Fig. 52:g–i), and one shape is more complex, with a grooved, ledge rim (Fig. 52:ll).

Open bowls grade directly into hole-mouth jar forms. The hole-mouth vessels have many lip profiles—simple rounded (Fig. 52:m–o,bb), squared- or beveled-off (Fig. 52:p–s), or with an exterior bead or flange (Fig. 52:t–w,z,aa). Common is a hole-mouth jar with squared-off lip and a small strap handle below the lip (Fig. 52:r).

Certain hole-mouth vessels have a distinct neck, angled up or vertical (Fig. 52:dd,ee). Jars are often difficult to separate clearly from hole-mouth vessels. In general, they seem to have constricted mouths and relatively short, slightly flaring rims (Fig. 52:x,y,cc,ff–kk). Handles are again common as relatively flat straps attached at the vessel lip (Fig. 52:cc,gg). There are also some short lugs on jar necks (Fig. 52:hh,ii).

Handles show a complete range from round loops to flat straps (Fig. 53:a,b,d–f), including elaborate modeled shapes (Fig. 53:c). Large, flat, handled lids are known (Fig. 53:h). Bases are flat, with and without a "foot" (Fig. 53:i,j).

THICKNESS: Medium, 6–10 mm.

COMPARISONS AND DATING: The same as for Medieval Brick Ware. Examples similar, if not identical, to this pottery can be found today in the market in Elâzığ. But compare also van Loon (1973:Pl. 26B) with Fig. 52:cc for a dating in the Late Selcuk-Early Mongol period (ca. 1200–1400 A.D.).

Medieval Modeled Ware

PASTE: Fine textured, moderately well levigated, with few small pinprick holes remaining in the paste. The temper is sparse (less than 5 percent–10 percent) and consists of fine sand, usually pinprick size, and usually white, with some fine gray or brown grains. In some pieces the paste is fine, compact and sandy, with 15 percent–20 percent fine sand temper.

> Color: Light brown to light orange with a light gray center. In the case of the particularly sandy pieces, colors tend to be cream to greenish cream with a light brown center.
> Firing: Medium to medium-high.
> Manufacture: Apparently a mixture of wheel and hand.

SURFACES: Interiors are plain, roughly smoothed and usually irregular. They are usually brown to dark brown, rarely cream. Exteriors are plain, smoothed brown to light brown, again rarely cream. They are always decorated.

DECORATION: Decoration is on vessel exteriors. It consists of many varieties of incised, impressed, molded or appliqué designs.

One of the most common motifs is a series of parallel, horizontal grooves on the necks of bowls, hole-mouth jars, and jars, between which are short, parallel, diagonal incisions or impressions, either straight or slightly S-shaped (Fig. 53:k–n; Fig. 54:a,b). A variation on this has opposed diagonals (Fig. 53:o,p). Another common motif is single or multiple, adjacent, shallow incisions in S-shaped, wavy, or sometimes horizontal, straight lines, either simply on the vessel wall, or on a raised panel (Fig. 53:q; Fig. 54:c,e–g).

Other decoration consists of appliqué, molded, or modeled relief figures, often simple concentric circles (Fig. 54:d,h), but also frequently delicate and approaching Arabic script in character (Fig. 54:i,j).

Lids are decorated with bold, broad, but shallow incisions in a large number of complex patterns (Fig. 54:k,l; Fig. 55:a–c). The edges are sometimes notched with finger indentations (Fig. 55:a).

FORM: Open bowls or cups are common (Fig. 53:k–n, r). Hole-mouth jars are also not infrequent (Fig. 53:o,p). Some jar rims are found, usually simple (Fig. 53:q; Fig. 54:a), but also occasionally in unusual forms (Fig. 54:b). Large lids are typical (Fig. 54:k,l; Fig. 55:a–c). Most of the decorated sherds found were body sherds, however, and although in a number of instances it seems fairly clear that they come from large (Fig. 54:c,e), or small (Fig. 54:h) jars, it is usually impossible to tell from what sort of vessel they come.

THICKNESS: Usually moderately thin, 6–7 mm.

COMPARISONS AND DATING: This pottery tends to be found with Brick Ware and other Medieval ceramics, and we have dated it generally in the same way as Brick Ware. More specific dating has been given to certain very fine modeled pieces which appear to us to be Selcuk in date (cf. Fig. 54:h,i), some clearly being decorated with Arabic script or designs derived therefrom (Fig. 54:j). These few pieces have been taken, along with Sgraffiato Ware, as indicative of Selcuk occupation. At Korucu Tepe (055/1) Selcuk occupation has been dated to ca. 1200–1400 A.D. (van Loon 1973:373), but it may also be earlier at other sites.

ROMAN RED WARE

PASTE: Very fine to extremely fine textured, homogeneous and well levigated. Ranging from a very fine paste having ca. 10 percent–15 percent fine sand tempering, mostly of pinpoint size, largely consisting of dark particles with some iron pyrites, to an extremely fine paste with no visible temper. The latter paste is very tough, with only rare pinpoint-sized holes in it.
  Color: Light buff to orange. The extremely fine pieces tend to be orange, sometimes with a light buff center.
  Firing: Ranges widely from low or medium low to high for some of the extremely fine pieces.
  Manufacture: Wheelmade with clear regular, smooth markings.

SURFACES: Both surfaces are covered with a thick, homogeneous slip. This is always well smoothed to burnished and very uniform. It is sometimes highly polished. The slip is bright orange, orange-red, deep red, or brown.

DECORATION: None known.

FORM: Very few forms are known of this relatively rare pottery. A very simple bowl (Fig. 55:i), a plate (Fig. 55:j), and a flat, ring base (Fig. 55:k) are the only definite shapes found.

THICKNESS: Moderately thin, 5–6 mm, to thin, 4 mm.

COMPARISONS AND DATING: If this is not imported *Terra Sigillata*, it must be a provincial copy of this distinctive ware and should, therefore, date somewhere between 300 B.C. and 330–400 A.D.

DEFINITION OF CHRONOLOGICAL PERIODS

It is clear from the comparisons and dating of each of these wares that they fall rather naturally into several chronological groups. The wares in each of these groups tend to be found together, and although it is an approximation, we have relied on the occurrence of these groups of ceramic wares to indicate occupation of sites in this region within broad chronological periods. In our survey and analysis, we recognized about a dozen such periods from groups of characteristic wares. These are outlined briefly below.

EARLY CHALCOLITHIC—defined by the presence of Chalcolithic Ware and, locally, Graphite Slipped Ware. In fact, the period so defined, although beginning earlier, undoubtedly lasts through our Middle Chalcolithic or Halaf period and terminates only with the succeeding Late Chalcolithic. This can be seen from the considerations brought forth in the discussion of the "comparisons and dating" of Chalcolithic Ware. The sequence of early periods as recognized in our survey is thus:

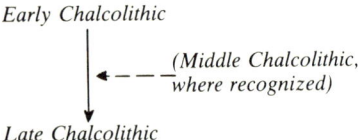

MIDDLE CHALCOLITHIC OR HALAFIAN—recognized only from the distinctive Halafian pottery or its local imitation. Since this ware is quite rare on sites in the Keban Reservoir area, occupation of this period was seldom identified. It would be reasonable to say, therefore, that we can effectively identify only a broad Early Chalcolithic and a more sharply defined Late Chalcolithic period from our survey data.

LATE CHALCOLITHIC—defined from Cream Chaff and Late Chalcolithic Grit Tempered wares. Only the Cream Chaff Ware is common. The chronological placement and external correspondences of this period are relatively sharp and clear, as discussed under the "comparisons and dating" of Cream Chaff Ware.

CHALCOLITHIC-EARLY BRONZE AGE TRANSITIONAL—defined only from the presence of Reserved-Slip and Plain Simple wares. It is clear that other wares were current in this period, but they are not distinctive to it. Unfortunately, both of the diagnostic wares for this period are uncommon, making it difficult to feel assured that all, or even most, of the occupations of this period have been identified from our survey data. Where such occupations were indicated by the presence of these two distinctive wares, it was still usually difficult or impossible to measure or estimate their importance, location, or extent on the sites. Nonetheless, we were able to identify such occupations often enough to justify the separate recognition of this period in our analysis.

EARLY BRONZE AGE I–II—an important and rather long period, reflected in the survey collections by large quantities of Early Bronze Age Burnished, Plain, and Thick wares, with less frequent but quite diagnostic and distinctive Early Bronze Age Polished and Relief Decorated wares and Early Bronze Age Lids, as well as rare examples of Fine Grooved Ware and small quantities of the uncertain category of Early Bronze Age Red Slipped Ware. As discussed in detail in the various sections on "comparisons and dating," certain of these wares were made over a longer range of time, and certain forms of some wares have specific chronological significance, both within and after this period. However, as a group, the combination of most or all of the wares listed above seems a relatively reliable indicator of occupation during this broad period.

EARLY BRONZE AGE IIIA—identified by the presence of Early Bronze Age Red Painted pottery. Identification of this period sometimes may be reinforced by the presence of large proportions of Early Bronze Age Plain Ware relative to Early Bronze Age Burnished pottery, as well as the occasional occurrence of grooved or corrugated neck jar forms in the latter ware.

EARLY BRONZE AGE IIIB—defined by the distinctive Early Bronze Age Black Painted Ware. In addition, Early Bronze Age Plain Ware may be present in large proportions relative to the Early Bronze Age Burnished Ware, and V-profiled hole-mouth jar forms of the latter ware may sometimes be found also. The painted ware by itself is diagnostic, however.

MIDDLE BRONZE AGE—characterized by gray wares, most commonly and diagnostically by Middle Bronze Age Gray and Old Hittite Gray wares, rarely with Old Hittite Light Faced and Black Faced Gray wares, very rarely with Hittite Red Ware, and occasionally accompanied by Middle Bronze Age Gritty Ware.

LATE BRONZE AGE OR HITTITE—a period of major importance in this area, and probably a time of actual incorporation of the region within the Hittite Empire. It is identified from a large series of characteristic wares, including most commonly Hittite Plain, Thick, Buff-Orange Burnished, and

Brown Burnished wares. These wares are usually abundant on sites occupied during Hittite or Late Bronze Age times. Also belonging to this period, but less common are Hittite Fine, Orange Smoothed, White Slipped, Painted, Exterior Wheel-marked, Chaff Faced, and Brown Gritty Cooking Wares.

IRON AGE—identified from Iron Age Ware as defined from our survey materials. At some sites it is possible to be more specific and to speak of Early and Middle Iron Age occupations, recognized from a few distinctive rim profiles, as discussed under the "comparisons and dating" of our Iron Age Ware. Such distinctive rims were not found at all sites, however, and in cases where they were absent, we were able to specify occupation only within the Iron Age as a single, broad period.

HELLENISTIC-ROMAN—only rarely identified as a period of occupation. This was done on the basis of finding Roman Red Ware on a site. However, this is a most infrequent ware, and the other ceramics in use during this period were not recognized by us in our survey materials. For a picture of occupation of the Keban Reservoir area in this period, one must refer, therefore, to the later excavations here (e.g. Harper 1970, 1971, 1972; Öğün 1971, 1972; Serdaroğlu 1970, 1971, 1972, 1974, 1976; French 1970, 1971; French and Mitchell 1976).

MEDIEVAL (BYZANTINE-SELCUK)—defined by the occurrence of Sgraffiato Ware and Medieval Modeled Ware with Islamic designs. These two wares are accompanied by a wide range of other Medieval ceramics, but these latter, alone, were not generally diagnostic to us of any specific period within this late range of time.

MEDIEVAL (OTTOMAN-MODERN AND UNSPECIFIED)—a very broad, recent period identified by us from the generally abundant Medieval Brick Ware, usually accompanied by some or all of the other recognized Medieval ceramics—Medieval Coarse, Glazed, Red Slipped, White Slipped, Painted, and Cooking wares. Together, these wares were not identifiable by us as belonging to any specific period. It was clear that such pottery regularly was found with Byzantine-Seluck Sgraffiato and Modeled Wares, but in many cases similar or identical vessels could be purchased in the modern bazaar in Elâzığ. Therefore, the presence of these wares alone was taken as indicative only of occupation within the broad range of medieval to modern times. More specific identification of an Ottoman-Modern period of occupation was based on other indications such as finding Ottoman pipe fragments or the ruins of a church, the name of the site, etc.

The above periods are defined only roughly, of course, by our criteria, and they vary widely in their length and the likelihood of finding sure evidence of their presence from surface collections from archaeological sites, particularly from large and deeply stratified mounds. However, given these limitations, and within the broad periods outlined above, we were able to be consistent in identifying the periods of occupation at the sites surveyed, and to sketch an outline of the sequence of settlement patterns and of the culture-history of the Keban Reservoir area.

FIGURE 6 CHALCOLITHIC WARE

a. 055/8, Sq. 23. Exterior: dark gray-brown. Core: black. Interior: brown to gray-brown. Rim diameter: 10 cm.

b. N52/3, Sq. 17. Both surfaces burnished but irregular and "lumpy." Exterior: light buff-brown with darker burnished streaks. Core: black. Interior: light buff-brown. Rim diameter: ± 16 cm.

c. N52/3, Sq. 33. Exterior and interior: mottled red-brown burnished. Core: dark to dark grayish red-brown. Rim diameter: ?

d. N52/3, Sq. 11. Exterior: light cream-brown. Core: light buff-brown. Interior: medium light brown. Rim diameter: 16 cm.

e. N52/3, Sq. 12. Exterior and interior: light cream-brown. Core: dark gray. Rim diameter: ?

f. N52/3, Sq. 11. Exterior: light mottled cream-gray. Core: dark gray. Interior: light mottled cream-brown. Rim diameter: ?

g. 055/1, Sq. 8. Exterior and interior: plain, unburnished light brown. Core: light brown. Rim diameter: 16 cm.

h. 055/8, Sq. 26. Exterior and interior: dull red-brown. Core: black. Rim diameter: ?

i. N52/3, Sq. 1. Exterior: light buff-brown burnished. Core: dark gray. Interior: light buff to dark gray burnished. Rim diameter: 20 cm.

j. 054/8, Sq. B24. Exterior: black. Core: light brown. Interior: brown to red-brown burnished. Rim diameter: 16 cm.

k. N52/3, Sq. 6. Exterior: plain dirty gray-brown. Core: dark gray. Interior: dark reddish brown. Rim diameter: 22 cm.

l. N52/3, Sq. 25. Exterior and interior: light, mottled buff-brown burnished. Core: light cream-brown. Rim diameter: 26-28 cm. ?

m. N52/3, Sq. 27. Exterior: dirty dark gray burnished. Core: dark gray. Interior: light gray-brown burnished. Rim diameter: ?

n. N52/3, Sq. 38. Exterior and interior: slightly mottled light brown-gray burnished. Core: dark brownish gray. Rim diameter: 8 cm.

o. N52/3, Sq. 3. Exterior: medium gray to red-brown smooth. Core: dark brown-gray. Interior: dark red-brown. Rim diameter: 6 (8?) cm.

p. N52/1, Sq. B6. Exterior: dark gray. Core: red-brown. Interior: medium brown. Rim diameter: ?

q. N52/1, Sq. A33. Exterior: cream-gray. Core: gray-brown. Interior: light brown. Rim diameter: ?

r. N52/1, Sq. A24. Exterior: mottled cream-gray. Core: gray-brown. Interior: light cream-gray. Rim diameter: ?

s. N52/1, Sq. A31. Exterior: mottled cream-gray. Core: dark gray to brown. Interior: red-brown. Rim diameter: ?

t. 054/8, Sq. D53. Exterior: mottled reddish gray. Core: gray-green. Interior: gray-black. Rim diameter: ?

u. N52/3, Sq. 34. Exterior and interior: light gray to pearly gray, mottled and slightly burnished. Core: light cream-gray. Rim diameter: 22 cm ?

v. N52/1, Sq. A23. Exterior: medium gray. Core: buff. Interior: light brown. Rim diameter: ?

w. N52/1, Sq. A46. Exterior: dark gray. Core: dark gray-brown. Interior: light brown. Rim diameter: ?

x. 055/8, Sq. 19. Exterior: dark brown burnished. Core: brown with thin gray streak in center. Interior: light brown burnished. Rim diameter: 12 cm.

y. N52/3, Gen'l. Exterior: mottled brown-gray burnished. Core: light buff-brown. Interior: dark mottled gray-black burnished. Rim diameter: 12 cm.

z. N52/3, Sq. 8. Exterior: light buff-brown burnished. Core: dark gray. Interior: dark gray-brown. Rim diameter: 16 cm.

aa. N52/3, Sq. 5. Exterior: plain light buff. Core: gray-brown. Interior: dark buff-gray. Rim diameter: ± 20 cm.

bb. 054/24, Sq. A6. Exterior: dark gray. Core light gray. Interior: light mottled gray. Rim diameter: ?

cc. N52/3, Gen'l. Exterior and interior: medium red-brown burnished, slightly mottled. Core: light brown to light gray. Rim diameter: ?

dd. N52/3, Gen'l. Exterior: medium gray mottled, burnished in stripes. Core: light greenish brown. Interior: dark gray-black. Rim diameter: 32 cm?

ee. 054/22, Gen'l. Exterior and interior: light brown-buff. Core: dark gray. Rim diameter: ?

ff. N52/3, Sq. 20. Exterior: light gray mottled. Core: dark gray. Interior: gray-brown. Rim diameter: ?

gg. N52/3, Sq. 36. Exterior and interior: light gray to pearly gray, slightly burnished. Core: light cream-gray. Rim diameter: ?

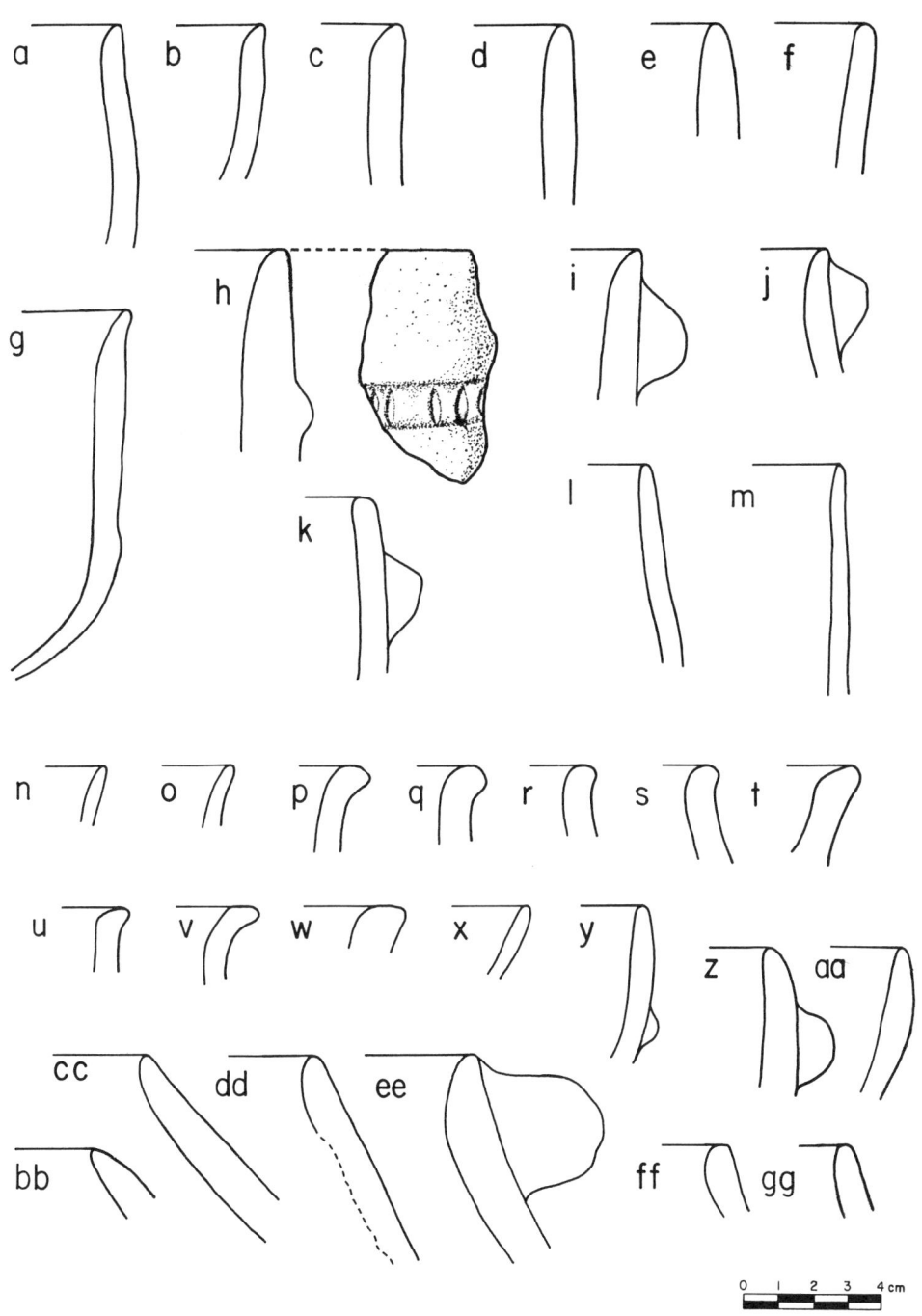

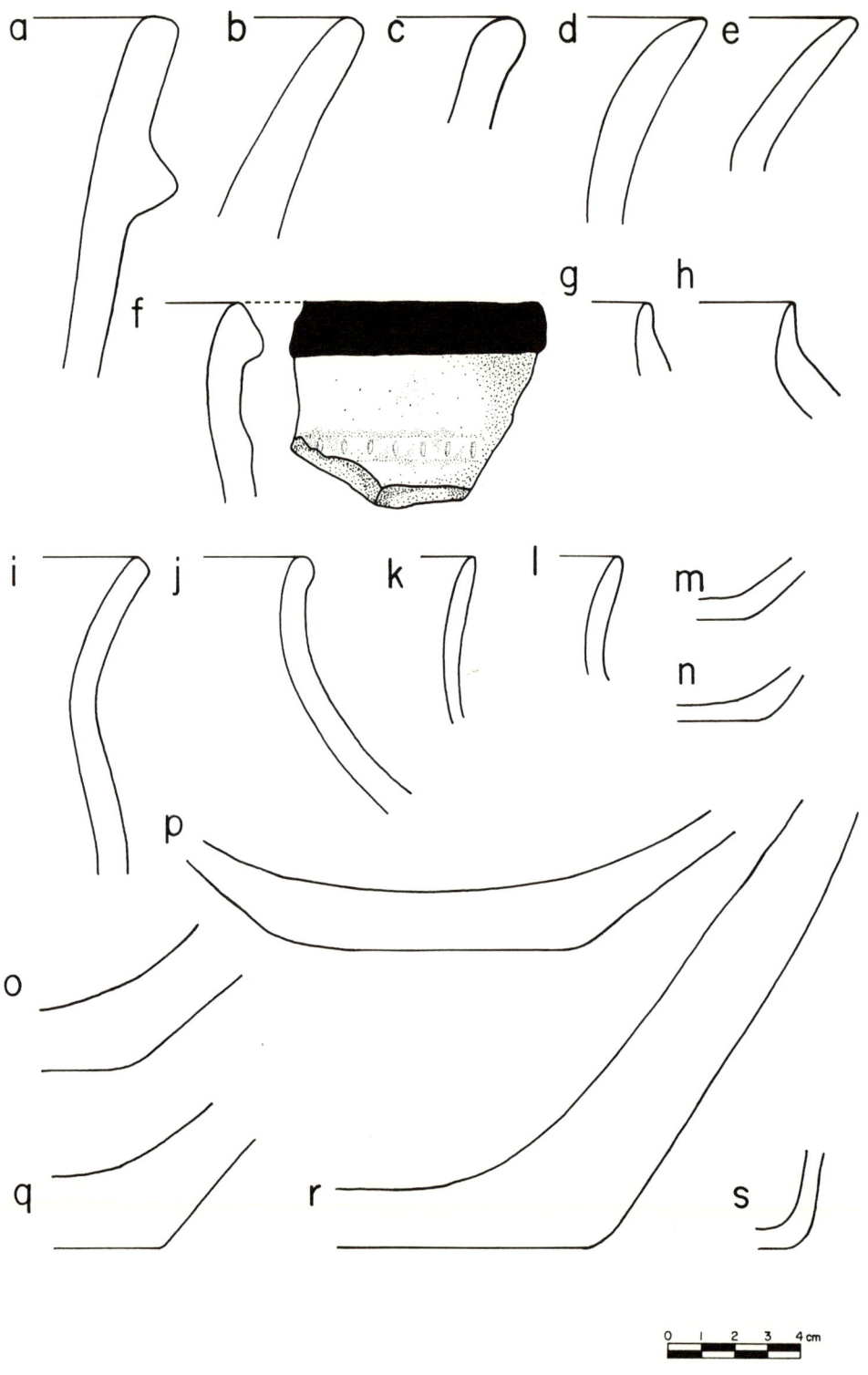

FIGURE 7 CHALCOLITHIC WARE

a. N52/3, Sq. 5. Exterior and interior: light cream–buff unburnished. Core: light–medium gray. Rim diameter: ?

b. O55/8, Sq. 19. Exterior: light buff. Core: dark gray. Interior: gray–buff. Rim diameter: 40 cm?

c. O54/6, Sq. A9. Exterior and interior: dark red–orange with dark gray mottling (graphite slip?). Core: black. Rim diameter: ?

d. N52/3, Sq. 20. Exterior: light buff, very slightly burnished. Core: gray–brown. Interior: dirty brown, very slightly burnished. Rim diameter: ?

e. O55/8, Sq. 32. Exterior: light mottled brown. Core: black. Interior: mottled gray–brown. Rim diameter: ?

f. N55/1, Gen'l. Exterior and interior: heavy white slip with red–brown paint on inside and outside of lip. Core: dark orange. Rim diameter: 20 cm.

g. O55/8, Sq. 6. Exterior and interior: light brown. Core: gray. Rim diameter: 8 cm.

h. O55/1, Sq. 24. Exterior: dark gray with light cream mottling (slip?). Core and interior: dirty brown. Rim diameter: 16 cm.

i. O55/8, Sq. 28. Exterior: light red to buff–brown. Core: dark gray. Interior: red–brown buff. Rim diameter: ± 24 cm.

j. N52/1, Sq. A26. Exterior: medium gray mottled. Core: light brown. Interior: gray–brown. Rim diameter: ± 22 cm.

k. O54/22, Gen'l. Exterior and interior: highly polished dark brown to black, slightly mottled. Core: dark brown to black. Rim diameter: 12 cm.

l. O55/8, Sq. 22. Exterior: dark mottled brown. Core: black. Interior: dark mottled brown to gray–black. Rim diameter: 16 cm.

m. N52/3, Sq. 8. Exterior: light gray to pearly gray mottled, burnished. Core: light to medium gray. Interior: light gray.

n. N52/3, Sq. 28. Exterior, core, and interior: dark gray, with occasional shades of brown–gray. Exterior burnished.

o. N52/3, Sq. 27. Exterior: light buff to buff–brown, burnished. Core and interior: dark gray–black.

p. N52/3, Sq. 27. Exterior: light gray–buff burnished. Core: dark gray–black. Interior: dark gray to gray–buff.

q. N52/3, Sq. 27. Exterior: light buff to buff–brown burnished. Core and interior: dark gray–brown.

r. N52/3, Sq. 5. Exterior: gray–buff unburnished. Core: dark gray. Interior: light gray to dark gray–buff.

s. N52/3, Sq. 5. Exterior: light gray to gray–brown, burnished. Core: dark gray. Interior: light gray.

FIGURE 8 CHALCOLITHIC WARE

a. O55/9, Gen'l. Exterior: mottled buff/brown/gray. Core: medium gray. Interior: dark gray, rough.

b. N52/3, Sq. 5. Exterior and interior: light mottled gray. Core: dark gray.

c. O55/8, Sq. 30. Sieve. No information on color.

d. N52/3, Sq. 34. Partially pierced sherd disc. No information on color.

e. N52/3, Sq. 37. Partially pierced sherd disc. No information on color.

f. O55/9, Gen'l. Exterior: dark mottled gray–brown. Core: light gray–brown. Interior: dirty gray–buff.

g. N52/3, Sq. 28. Exterior: mottled gray burnished. Core: dark gray.

h. N52/3, Sq. 25. Exterior, core, and interior: brown to light buff–brown. On exterior, spout plain, body burnished.

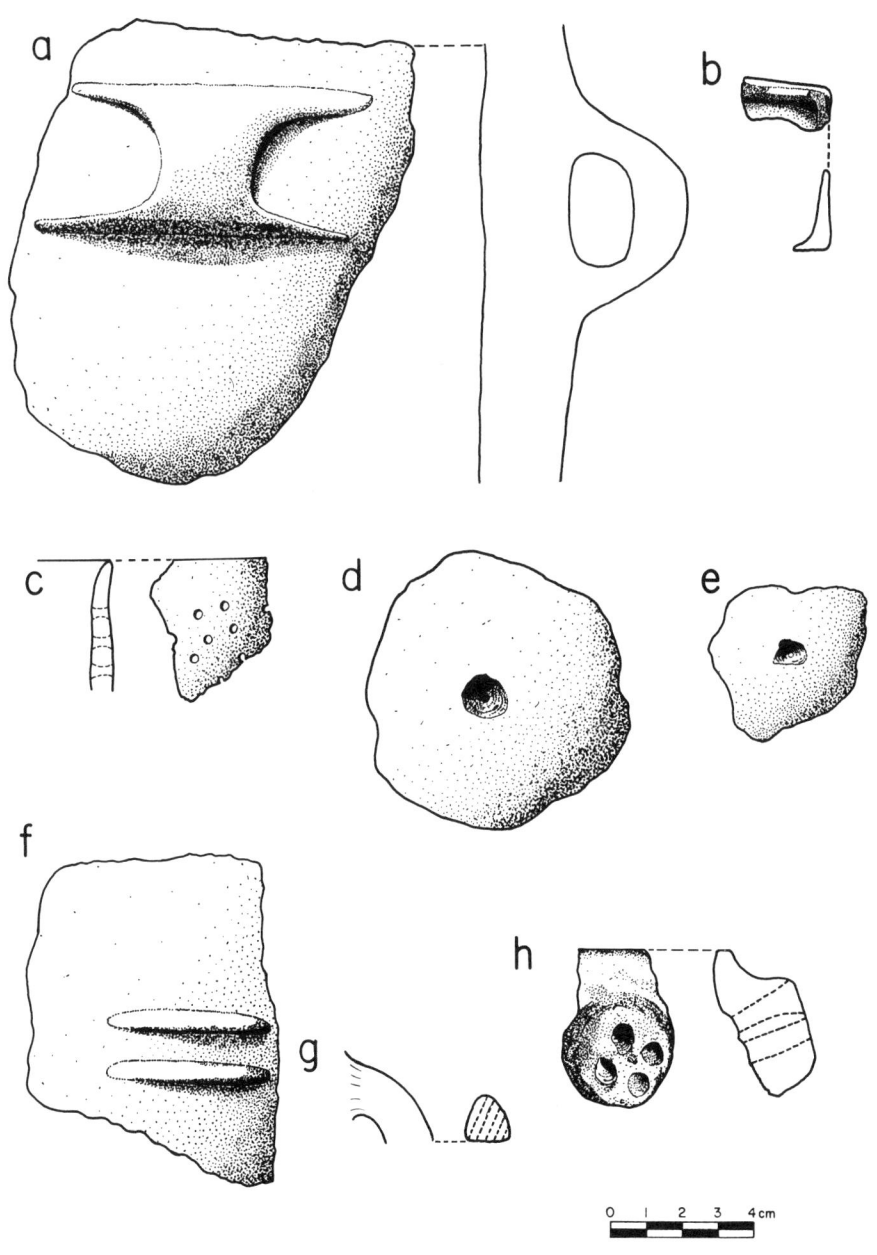

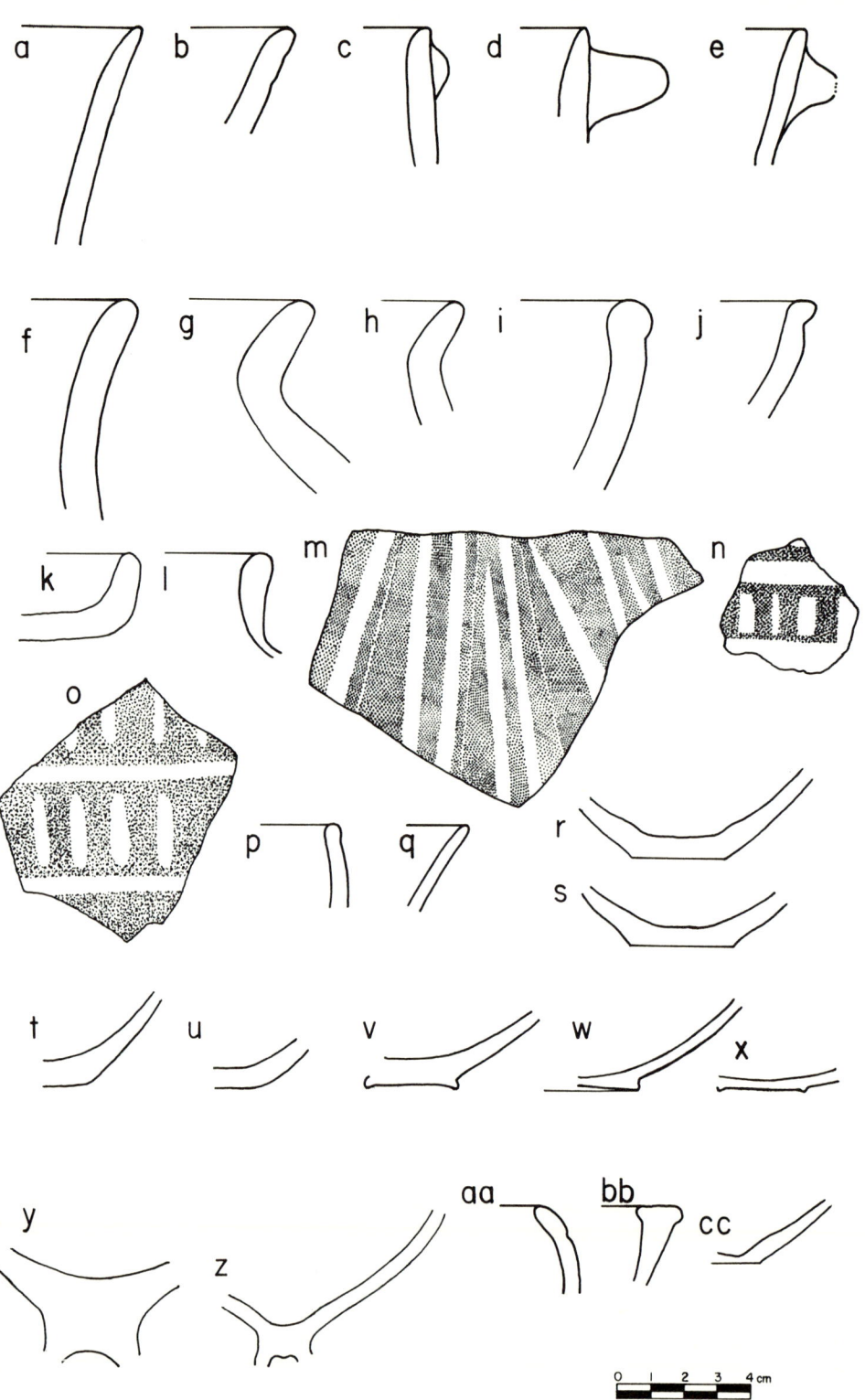

FIGURE 9

GRAPHITE SLIPPED WARE

a. 054/7, Gen'l. Exterior: graphite slipped, burnished. Core: black center with orange on both sides. Interior: black burnished. Rim diameter: 34 cm.

b. 055/8, Sq. 22. Exterior and interior: graphite slipped, burnished. Core: gray-brown, gritty. Rim diameter: 22 cm.

c. 055/8, Sq. 23. Exterior and interior: graphite slipped, burnished. Core: black. Rim diameter: 18 cm.

d. 055/8, Sq. 22. Exterior and interior: graphite slipped, burnished. Core: black-brown. Rim diameter: ?

e. 054/6, Sq. B30. Exterior and interior: graphite slipped, burnished. Core: black with orange sides, chaff-filled. Rim diameter: ?

f. 054/7, Gen'l. Exterior: graphite slipped, burnished. Core: black. Interior: dark gray burnished. Rim diameter: 38 cm.

LATE CHALCOLITHIC GRIT TEMPERED WARE

g. N52/3, Sq. 9. Exterior and interior: dirty rust-brown. Core: medium gray. Rim diameter: 28 cm.

h. N52/3, Gen'l. Exterior: dirty brown. Core: light buff-brown. Interior: light brown. Rim diameter: 18 cm.

i. 055/8, Sq. 14. Exterior and interior: light gray burnished. Core: dark gray. Rim diameter: ?

j. 055/8, Sq. 14. Exterior and interior: light gray burnished. Core: dark gray. Rim diameter: ?

k. 055/8, Sq. 16. Exterior and interior: light reddish buff, burnished. Core: light brown. Rim diameter: ?

RESERVED SLIP WARE

l. 054/2, Sq. 34. Exterior: buff-brown with cream slip on rim. Core: red center to brown. Interior: damaged and indeterminate. Rim diameter: 26 cm.

m. N52/1, Gen'l. Exterior: gray-brown with cream slip. Core: brown. Interior: brown.

n. 054/2, Sq. 80. Exterior, core, and interior: orange-brown. Cream slip on exterior.

o. 055/8, Sq. 16. Exterior, core, and interior: light brown. Cream slip on exterior.

PLAIN SIMPLE WARE

p. 055/8, Sq. 13. Exterior, core, and interior: cream-orange. Rim diameter: 10 cm.

q. 055/9, Sq. 40. Exterior, core, and interior: orange. Rim diameter: 12 cm.

r. 055/8, Sq. 14. Exterior: cream-orange. Interior and core: cream.

s. 054/8, Gen'l. Exterior, core, and interior: orange.

t. 055/9, Sq. 39. Exterior, core, and interior: cream.

u. 055/8, Sq. 13. Exterior, core, and interior: orange.

v. 055/9, Sq. 39. Exterior, core, and interior: cream.

w. 055/8, Sq. 13. Exterior, core, and interior: cream-orange.

x. 055/8, Gen'l. Exterior, core, and interior: light greenish cream.

y. 054/2, Sq. 43. Exterior and interior: cream. Core: orange.

z. N52/1, Gen'l. Exterior, core, and interior: cream.

FINE GROOVED WARE

aa. 054/8, Sq. D69. Exterior: dark brown. Core: gray center to dark brown. Interior: light brown to light gray, variegated. Rim diameter: 22 cm?

bb. 055/9, Sq. 9. Exterior: buff to orange, variegated. Core: gray center to orange. Interior: orange. Rim diameter: 24 cm.

cc. N52/1, Sq. B12. Exterior and interior: buff to orange, variegated. Core: gray center to orange.

FIGURE 10 CREAM CHAFF WARE

a. N52/9, Sq. 17. Exterior, core, and interior: cream. Rim diameter: 30 cm.
b. N52/3, Sq. 17. Exterior, core, and interior: cream. Rim diameter: 26 cm.
c. 055/8, Sq. 18. Exterior and interior: cream–orange. Core: gray center to orange. Rim diameter: 22 cm.
d. 055/1, Sq. 12. Exterior and interior: lightly slipped, white. Core: light orange. Rim diameter: 20 cm.
e. 054/6, Sq. B27. Exterior: buff–orange. Core: black center to buff. Interior: cream–orange. Rim diameter: ?
f. 055/1, Sq. 27. Exterior: buff. Core: buff–brown. Interior: buff–orange. Rim diameter: 26 cm.
g. 054/24, Sq. A21. Exterior and interior: cream. Core: gray center to brown. Rim diameter: 26 cm.
h. 055/8, Gen'l. Exterior and interior: Red–brown burnished. Core: gray center to dark orange. Rim diameter: 29 cm?
i. 055/8, Gen'l. Exterior and interior: buff smoothed. Core: charcoal gray center to buff. Rim diameter: ?
j. 055/1, Sq. 17. Exterior: orange to gray. Core: orange–brown. Interior: orange. Rim diameter: ?
k. 055/8, Sq. 14. Exterior, core, and interior: cream–orange. Rim diameter: 32 cm. (Inside of lip: often painted in a band of matt red.)
l. N52/3, Gen'l. Exterior and interior: red to red–buff. Core: dark gray to black. Rim diameter: ?
m. N52/3, Sq. 6. Exterior and interior: cream. Core: cream–orange. Rim diameter: 22 cm.
n. 055/8, Sq. 19. Exterior, core, and interior: light buff. Rim diameter: 40 cm?
o. 055/8, Sq. 19. Exterior and interior: cream slip. Core: buff–orange. Rim diameter: 40 cm.
p. N52/3, Sq. 26. Exterior and interior: cream. Core: gray center to cream. Rim diameter: 22 cm.
q. 054/6, Sq. A13. Exterior and interior: white slipped. Core: brown. Rim diameter: 18 cm.
r. 054/2, Sq. 132. Exterior: cream. Core: black center to cream. Interior: cream–orange. Rim diameter: 26 cm.
s. 055/8, Sq. 7. Exterior, core, and interior: light orange. Rim diameter: ?
t. 054/8, Sq. B53. Exterior and interior: red slipped over buff. Core: black to gray center to buff–orange. Rim diameter: 24 cm.
u. 054/3, Sq. 8. Exterior and interior: buff–orange. Core: orange. Rim diameter: 10 cm.
v. 055/8, Sq. 19. Exterior, core, and interior: bright orange. Rim diameter: 30 cm?
w. 055/8, Sq. 19. Exterior and interior: buff. Core: gray center to buff. Rim diameter: 30 cm.
x. 055/8, Sq. 21. Exterior: white slipped. Core: orange. Interior: buff–orange. Rim diameter: 18 cm.
y. 055/8, Sq. 21. Exterior: cream–orange. Core: black center to buff–orange. Interior: buff. Rim diameter: 18 cm.
z. 055/1, Sq. 12. Exterior and interior: white slipped. Core: light orange. Rim diameter: 12 cm.
aa. 055/1, Sq. 22. Exterior and interior: cream slipped. Core: light buff. Rim diameter: 38 cm.
bb. 055/8, Sq. 14. Exterior: white. Core: gray. Interior: orange. Rim diameter: 24 cm.
cc. 055/8, Sq. 19. Exterior and interior: cream slipped. Core: light buff. Rim diameter: 23 cm.
dd. 055/8, Sq. 19. Exterior and interior: orange. Core: gray center to buff–orange. Rim diameter: 20 cm.
ee. 054/10, Sq. C20. Exterior: buff. Core: gray. Interior: whitish buff. Rim diameter: 34 cm.
ff. 055/8, Sq. 14. Exterior: cream. Core: gray. Interior: cream–orange. Rim diameter: 30 cm.
gg. N52/3, Sq. 30. Exterior and interior: cream. Core: black. Rim diameter: 28 cm.
hh. 055/8, Sq. 14. Exterior and interior: buff–orange slipped. Core: gray center to buff–orange. Rim diameter: ?
ii. 054/2, Sq. 14. Exterior, core, and interior: light buff. Surfaces burnished. Rim diameter: ?
jj. 055/8, Sq. 14. Exterior and interior: orange smoothed. Core: buff–orange. Rim diameter: 40 cm?
kk. 054/24, Sq. A28. Exterior, core, and interior: gray. Rim diameter: 36 cm.
ll. 054/12, Sq. A3. Exterior: cream. Core: black center to buff. Interior: cream–orange. Rim diameter: 28 cm.
mm. N52/9, Sq. 9. Exterior, core, and interior: cream. Rim diameter: 28 cm.

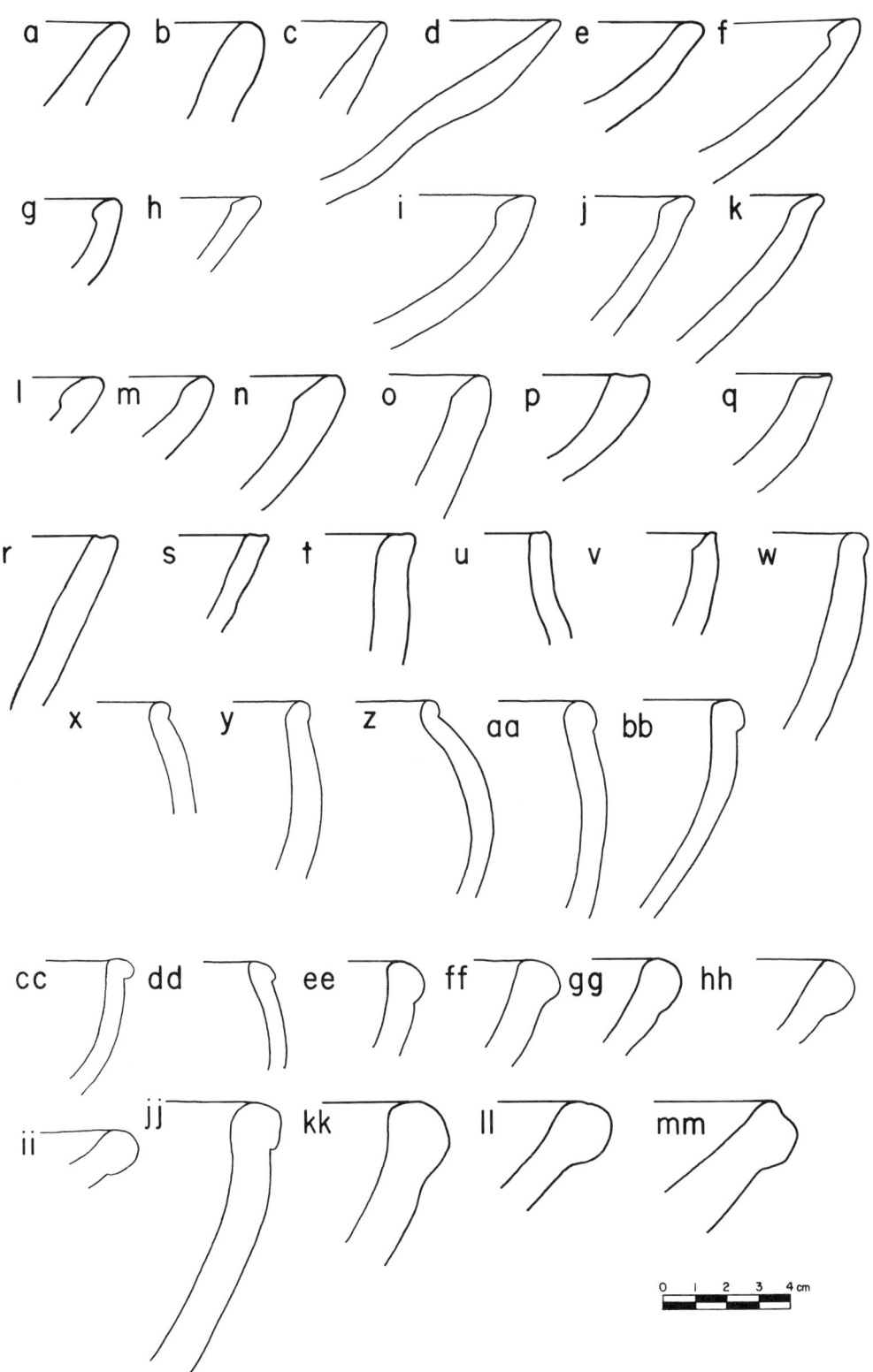

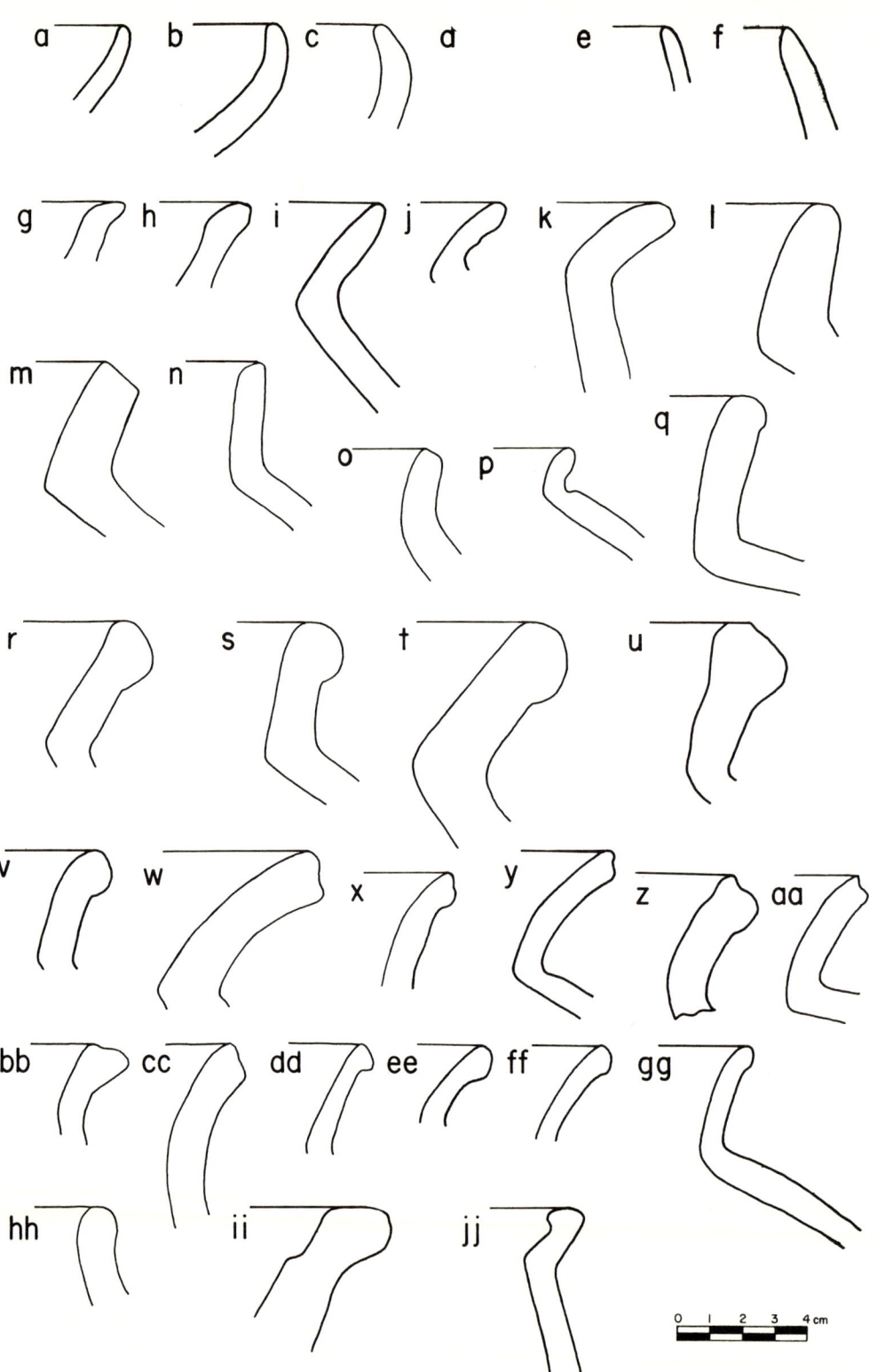

FIGURE 11 CREAM CHAFF WARE

a. 054/12, Sq. A16. Exterior: cream. Core: gray. Interior: cream–orange. Rim diameter: 20 cm.

b. N52/3, Sq. 20. Exterior: cream. Core: orange. Interior: cream–orange. Rim diameter: 26 cm.

c. 055/8, Sq.14. Exterior, core, and interior: buff. Rim diameter: 22 cm.

d. 054/24, Sq. A34. Exterior, core, and interior: cream. Rim diameter: 20 cm.

e. 054/24, Sq. A20. Exterior: cream–orange. Core: orange. Interior: cream. Rim diameter: 16 cm.

f. 055/8, Sq. 18. Exterior: cream. Core: buff–orange. Interior: cream–orange. Rim diameter: 10 cm.

g. 055/8, Sq. 3. Exterior and interior: cream smoothed. Core: dark gray center to cream–buff. Rim diameter: 20 cm?

h. 054/24, Sq. A24. Exterior, core, and interior: cream. Rim diameter: 24 cm.

i. N52/3, Sq. 17. Exterior and interior: cream. Core: gray center to buff. Rim diameter: 24 cm.

j. N52/3, Sq. 30. Exterior and interior: cream. Core: gray. Rim diameter: 20 cm.

k. 054/6, Sq. B23. Exterior: white slipped. Core: gray. Interior: buff. Rim diameter: 28 cm.

l. 055/8, Sq. 26. Exterior and interior: white slipped. Core: cream–buff. Rim diameter: 28 cm.

m. 055/8, Sq. 14. Exterior: red–buff burnished. Core: black center to orange. Interior: buff. Rim diameter: 40+ cm.

n. 055/2, Sq. A10. Exterior: buff. Core: black. Interior: cream–orange. Rim diameter: 8 cm.

o. 055/8, Sq. 18. Exterior and interior: buff. Core: black center to buff. Rim diameter: 30 cm.

p. 055/8, Gen'l. Exterior and interior: cream–orange slipped. Core: dark gray. Rim diameter: 19 cm?

q. 055/8, Sq. 19. Exterior and interior: cream. Core: dark gray center to buff. Rim diameter: 36 cm.

r. 055/8, Sq. 14. Exterior and interior: orange smoothed. Core: orange–brown. Rim diameter: 37 cm.

s. 054/8, Sq. B26. Exterior and interior: cream. Core: dark gray center to cream. Rim diameter: 30 cm.

t. 055/8, Gen'l. Exterior and interior: cream slipped. Core: orange–buff. Rim diameter: 40+ cm.

u. 055/8, Sq. 4. Exterior and interior: cream slip. Core: orange–buff. Rim diameter: 38 cm.

v. 055/8, Sq. 20. Exterior and interior: cream. Core: dark gray center to buff. Rim diameter: 18 cm.

w. 055/8, Sq. 21. Exterior and interior: white slipped. Core: brown. Rim diameter: 40+ cm.

x. 054/8, Sq. D71. Exterior and interior: white slipped. Core: gray. Rim diameter: 12 cm.

y. 055/8, Gen'l. Exterior: cream. Core: gray center to buff–orange. Interior: buff. Rim diameter: 22 cm.

z. 055/8, Sq. 4. Exterior and interior: cream–buff slipped. Core: dark red center to orange. Rim diameter: 40+ cm.

aa. 055/8, Gen'l. Exterior and interior: cream. Core: dark gray center to buff. Rim diameter: 22 cm.

bb. 054/2, Sq. 29. Exterior and interior: cream. Core: dark gray center to buff. Rim diameter: 18 cm.

cc. 054/8, Sq. C35. Exterior and interior: brown. Core: black center to buff. Rim diameter: 36 cm.

dd. 054/8, Sq. D22. Exterior and interior: red slipped. Core: black–gray center to buff–orange. Rim diameter: 20 cm.

ee. N52/3, Sq. 14. Exterior and interior: cream. Core: cream–orange. Rim diameter: 12 cm.

ff. N52/9, Sq. 20. Exterior, core, and interior: cream–orange. Rim diameter: 12 cm.

gg. 055/8, Sq. 19. Exterior and interior: cream slipped. Core: black–gray center to brown. Rim diameter: 12 cm.

hh. 054/2, Sq. 108. Exterior and interior: buff. Core: dark gray center to buff. Rim diameter: 38 cm?

ii. 055/8, Sq. 18. Exterior: cream. Core: orange–brown. Interior: buff. Rim diameter: 34 cm.

jj. 054/24, Sq. A30. Exterior and interior: cream–orange. Core: orange. Rim diameter: 22 cm.

FIGURE 12 EARLY BRONZE AGE BURNISHED WARE

a. 054/8, Sq. B14. Exterior, core, and interior: black. Rim diameter: 10 cm.
b. 054/8, Sq. C35. Exterior: buff. Core: gray. Interior: dark gray. Rim diameter: 12 cm.
c. 054/8, Sq. B29. Exterior and interior: gray. Core: black. Rim diameter: 16 cm.
d. N52/1, Sq. A11. Exterior and core: black. Interior: gray. Rim diameter: 8 cm.
e. 054/8, Sq. A11. Exterior: buff-brown. Core: black to brown. Interior: black. Rim diameter: 22 cm.
f. 054/8, Gen'l. Exterior: gray. Core: black. Interior: light gray. Rim diameter: 14 cm.
g. 054/8, Sq. B27. Exterior and core: black. Interior: brown-gray. Rim diameter: 32 cm.
h. 054/8, Sq. B15. Exterior: gray-black. Core: black. Interior: light gray. Rim diameter: 32 cm.
i. 054/8, Sq. B36. Exterior and interior: orange-brown. Core: dark gray. Rim diameter: 18 cm.
j. 054/8, Sq. A25. Exterior and interior: red. Core: black center to red. Rim diameter: 20 cm.
k. 054/2, Sq. 101. Exterior and interior: red-brown. Core: gray center to brown. Rim diameter: 24 cm.
l. 054/8, Sq. A26. Exterior: black. Core: black to buff. Interior: orange-buff. Rim diameter: 20 cm.
m. 054/8, Gen'l. Exterior: black. Core: black to buff. Interior: buff. Rim diameter: 14 cm.
n. 054/8, Sq. B37. Exterior: buff-cream. Core: buff. Interior: buff-orange. Rim diameter: 32 cm.
o. 054/8, Sq. C46. Exterior and core: black. Interior: black to buff. Rim diameter: 16 cm.
p. 054/8, Sq. C14. Exterior: orange-brown. Core: black to gray. Interior: gray-orange. Rim diameter: 20 cm.
q. 054/8, Sq. B36. Exterior: black. Core: black to buff. Interior: buff. Rim diameter: 24 cm.
r. 054/8, Sq. B31. Exterior: black. Core: black to gray. Interior: buff. Rim diameter: 26 cm.
s. 054/8, Sq. B56. Exterior and interior: buff-orange. Core: black center to orange. Rim diameter: 28 cm.
t. 054/8, Sq. B48. Exterior: buff to black. Core: black. Interior: buff-brown. Rim diameter: 20 cm.
u. 054/8, Sq. B29. Exterior: black. Core: black to brown. Interior: buff-brown. Rim diameter: 22 cm.
v. 054/2, Sq. 42. Exterior and interior: red-brown. Core: buff. Rim diameter: 16 cm.
w. 054/8, Sq. C35. Exterior and interior: gray. Core: black center to gray. Rim diameter: 22 cm.
x. 054/8, Sq. A52. Exterior and interior: buff-gray. Core: black. Rim diameter: 40+ cm.
y. 054/8, Sq. D77. Exterior: red-brown. Core: gray center to buff. Interior: buff-brown. Rim diameter: 16 cm.
z. 054/8, Sq. C27. Exterior: red-orange. Core: orange to buff. Interior: buff-cream. Rim diameter: 28 cm.
aa. 054/2, Sq. 34. Exterior and interior: orange-buff. Core: buff. Rim diameter: 10 cm.
bb. 054/3, Sq. 8. Exterior and interior: brown. Core: black center to brown. Rim diameter: 30 cm.
cc. 054/8, Sq. B35. Exterior: black. Core: black to brown. Interior: brown. Rim diameter: 22 cm.
dd. 054/8, Sq. B31. Exterior: gray. Core: gray to orange. Interior: brown. Rim diameter: 26 cm.
ee. 054/8, Gen'l. Exterior and interior: red. Core: black center to orange. Rim diameter: 36 cm.
ff. 054/8, Sq. B17. Exterior: buff-brown. Core: black. Interior: red-orange. Rim diameter: 32 cm.
gg. 054/8, Sq. B33. Exterior and core: black. Interior: buff-orange. Rim diameter: 38 cm.
hh. 054/8, Sq. B34. Exterior and core: black. Interior: buff-brown. Rim diameter: 34 cm.
ii. 054/8, Sq. B36. Exterior: gray-black. Core: black. Interior: buff. Rim diameter: 14 cm.
jj. 054/8, Gen'l. Exterior, core, and interior: black. Rim diameter: 14 cm.
kk. 054/8, Sq. C38. Exterior: red-brown. Core: brown to orange. Interior: orange. Rim diameter: 18 cm.
ll. 054/8, Gen'l. Exterior and core: black. Interior: gray. Rim diameter: 16 cm.
mm. 054/2, Sq. 96. Exterior and core: black. Interior: brown. Rim diameter: 28 cm.
nn. 054/8, Gen'l. Exterior and interior: brown. Core: black. Rim diameter: 18 cm.
oo. 054/2, Sq. 126. Exterior and interior: buff. Core: gray center to buff. Rim diameter: 16 cm.
pp. 054/8, Sq. A59. Exterior and interior: buff. Core: black center to buff. Rim diameter: 24 cm.
qq. 055/4, Sq. 39. Exterior and interior: brown. Core: gray. Rim diameter: 26 cm.
rr. 054/2, Sq. 156. Exterior, core, and interior: gray. Rim diameter: 26 cm.
ss. 054/8, Sq. C33. Exterior: buff-brown. Core: gray. Interior: brown. Rim diameter: ?
tt. N52/1, Sq. A17. Exterior: brown. Interior and core: orange. Rim diameter: 12 cm.

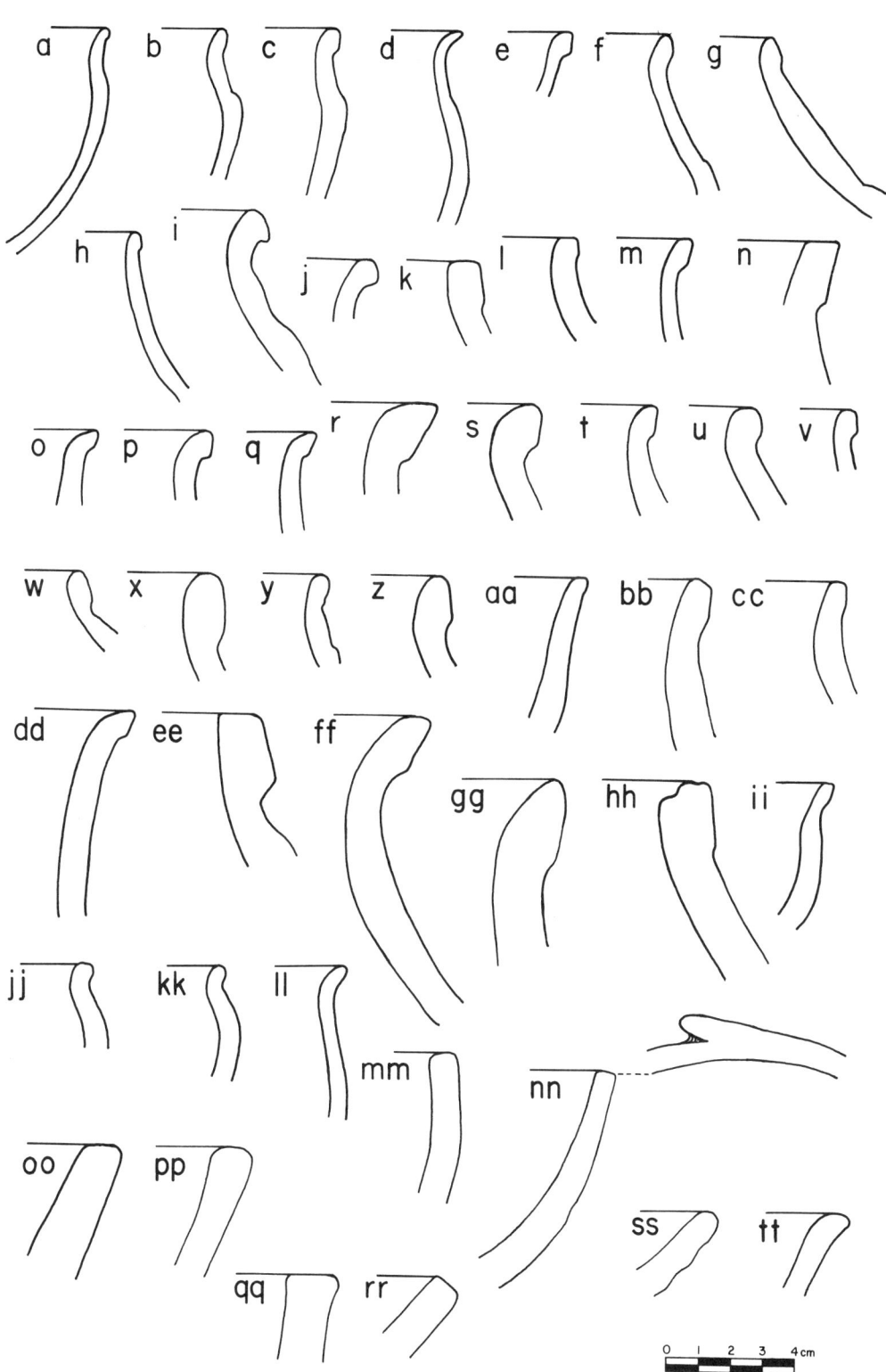

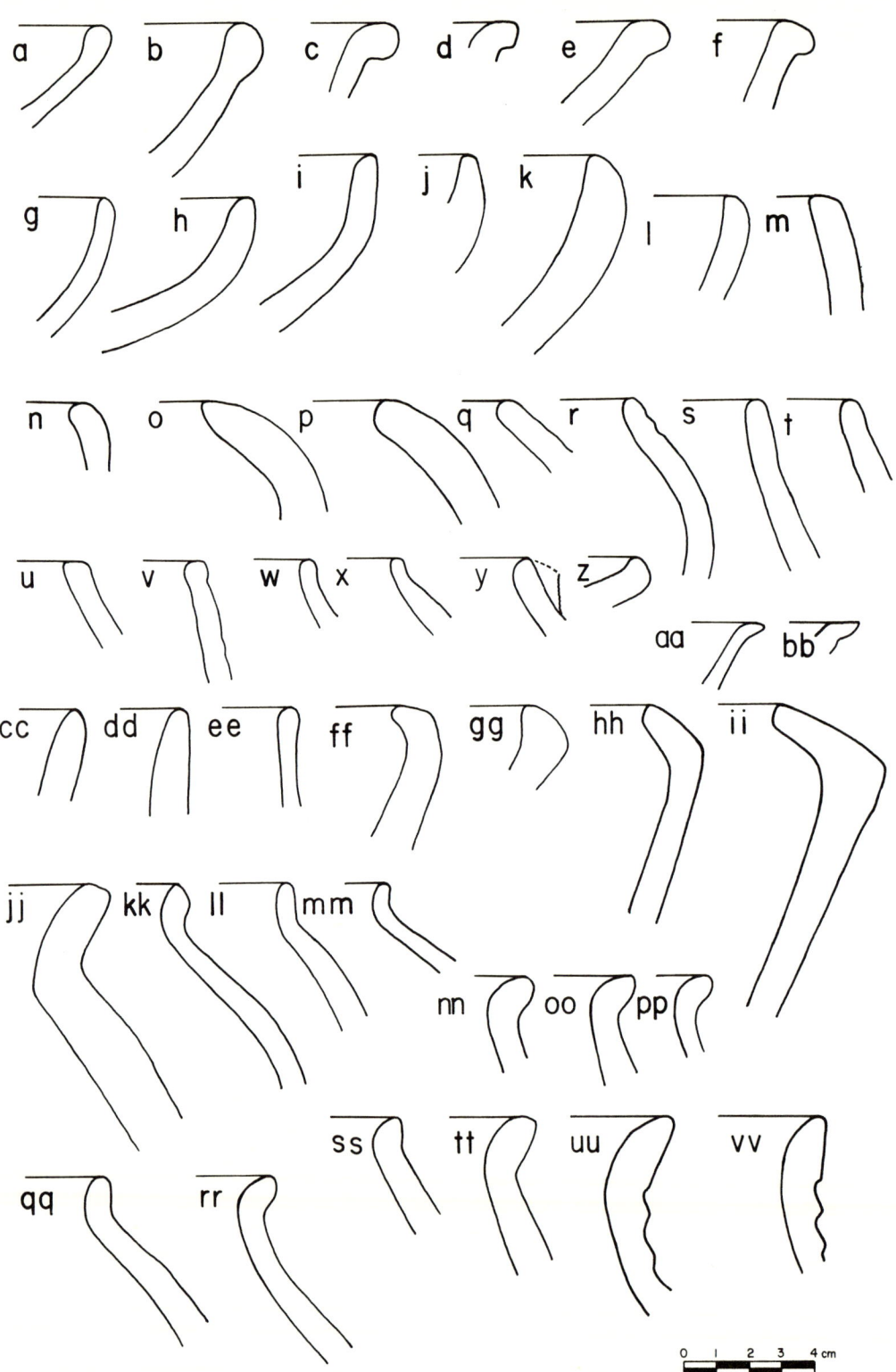

FIGURE 13 EARLY BRONZE AGE BURNISHED WARE

a. 055/8, Sq. 14. Exterior, core, and interior: buff. Rim diameter: 22 cm.
b. 054/27, Sq. A32. Exterior and interior: brown. Core: orange-buff. Rim diameter: 32 cm.
c. 055/4, Sq. 48. Exterior and interior: buff. Core: black. Rim diameter: 24 cm.
d. 054/2, Sq. 101. Exterior, core, and interior: brown. Rim diameter: 12 cm.
e. 054/8, Sq. B24. Exterior, core, and interior: brown. Rim diameter: 20 cm.
f. 054/2, Sq. 154. Exterior, core, and interior: brown. Rim diameter: 14 cm.
g. 054/8, Sq. B33. Exterior, core, and interior: black. Rim diameter: 12 cm.
h. 054/2, Sq. 131. Exterior and interior: brown. Core: black. Rim diameter: 28 cm.
i. 054/8, Sq. A15. Exterior and interior: buff-red. Core: gray center to orange. Rim diameter: 32 cm.
j. 054/8, Sq. B48. Exterior and interior: brown. Core: black. Rim diameter: 34 cm.
k. 054/8, Sq. B29. Exterior and interior: red-brown. Core: brown. Rim diameter: 28 cm.
l. 054/8, Sq. B24. Exterior and core: black. Interior: red-brown. Rim diameter: 18 cm.
m. N53/1, Gen'l. Exterior and interior: red-orange. Core: buff. Rim diameter: 18 cm.
n. 054/8, Sq. D68. Exterior and interior: buff. Core: gray. Rim diameter: 14 cm.
o. 054/8, Sq. C57. Exterior: black. Core: buff to black. Interior: brown. Rim diameter: 38 cm.
p. 054/8, Sq. A48. Exterior and interior: brown. Core: black. Rim diameter: 34 cm.
q. 054/8, Sq. A32. Exterior and interior: brown. Core: gray. Rim diameter: ?
r. 054/8, Sq. A11. Exterior and interior: buff-orange. Core: brown. Rim diameter: 14 cm.
s. 055/8, Sq. 21. Exterior: black. Core: black to brown. Interior: brown. Rim diameter: 16 cm.
t. 054/8, Sq. D36. Exterior and core: black. Interior: brown. Rim diameter: 22 cm.
u. 054/2, Sq. 98. Exterior: black. Core: brown. Interior: red-brown. Rim diameter: 14 cm.
v. 054/8, Sq. D71. Exterior and interior: red-brown. Core: brown. Rim diameter: 34 cm.
w. 054/8, Sq. C36. Exterior, core, and interior: brown. Rim diameter: 14 cm.
x. 054/8, Sq. D45. Exterior, core, and interior: gray. Rim diameter: 12 cm.
y. 054/8, Sq. A42. Exterior: black. Core: black to brown. Interior: brown. Rim diameter: 10 cm.
z. 054/12, Sq. A6. Exterior: cream. Core: black center to brown. Interior: brown. Rim diameter: 22 cm.
aa. 054/8, Sq. D35. Exterior and core: black. Interior: orange. Rim diameter: 8 cm.
bb. 054/2, Sq. 80. Exterior and interior: brown. Core: gray. Rim diameter: 10 cm.
cc. 054/8, Sq. D25. Exterior and interior: buff-brown. Core: buff. Rim diameter: 20 cm.
dd. 054/8, Sq. B33. Exterior, core, and interior: gray. Rim diameter: 22 cm.
ee. 054/8, Sq. A13. Exterior, core, and interior: buff-orange. Rim diameter: 18 cm.
ff. 054/24, Sq. A1. Exterior: buff. Core: black. Interior: brown. Rim diameter: 28 cm.
gg. 054/8, Sq. D71. Exterior: gray-black. Core: black. Interior: brown. Rim diameter: 18 cm.
hh. 054/8, Sq. D33. Exterior: black to buff. Core: black. Interior: gray-buff. Rim diameter: 36 cm.
ii. 054/8, Gen'l. Exterior: black. Core: brown to orange. Interior: gray. Rim diameter: 34 cm.
jj. 055/8, Sq. 7. Exterior: buff. Core: brown. Interior: gray. Rim diameter: ?
kk. 054/8, Sq. A28. Exterior: orange-brown. Core: dark gray. Interior: buff-brown. Rim diameter: 22 cm.
ll. 055/8, Sq. 21. Exterior and interior: buff. Core: black. Rim diameter: 8 cm.
mm. 054/8, Sq. A15. Exterior and interior: gray. Core: black. Rim diameter: 14 cm.
nn. 054/8, Sq. D39. Exterior: buff-orange. Core: black center to buff. Interior: orange. Rim diameter: 28 cm.
oo. 054/2, Sq. 180. Exterior and interior: buff-orange. Core: gray. Rim diameter: 20 cm.
pp. 054/8, Sq. A15. Exterior and interior: buff-orange. Core: black center to orange. Rim diameter: 20 cm.
qq. 054/8, Sq. A15. Exterior: orange-brown. Core: dark gray. Interior: buff-brown. Rim diameter: 24 cm.
rr. 054/2, Sq. 90. Exterior: gray to brown. Core: black to brown. Interior: red. Rim diameter: 14 cm.
ss. 054/8, Sq. A23. Exterior: black. Core: black to buff. Interior: buff. Rim diameter: 22 cm.
tt. 054/2, Sq. 37. Exterior and core: black. Interior: buff. Rim diameter: 28 cm.
uu. 054/8, Sq. D33. Exterior: black. Core: gray-black to orange-buff. Interior: red-orange. Rim diameter: ?
vv. 054/8, Sq. B15. Exterior: buff-brown. Core: black center to buff. Interior: buff-orange. Rim diameter: 24 cm.

FIGURE 14 EARLY BRONZE AGE BURNISHED WARE

a. 054/8, Sq. C18.   Exterior: buff to gray. Core: gray to orange. Interior: red-brown. Rim diameter: 20 cm.
b. 054/8, Sq. C64.   Exterior and interior: red-brown. Core: black center to orange. Rim diameter: 22 cm.
c. 054/2, Sq. 124.   Exterior: black. Core: black to buff. Interior: buff. Rim diameter: 14 cm.
d. 054/8, Sq. B68.   Exterior and interior: cream-buff. Core: buff-orange. Rim diameter: 22 cm.
e. N52/9, Sq. 13.   Exterior, core, and interior: buff. Rim diameter: 30 cm.
f. 054/8, Sq. D42.   Exterior and interior: brown. Core: gray. Rim diameter: 22 cm.
g. 054/2, Sq. 132.   Exterior and core: buff. Interior: buff-orange. Rim diameter: 10 cm.
h. 054/1, Sq. 95.   Exterior: buff. Core: brown. Interior: red-brown. Rim diameter: 10 cm.
i. 054/2, Sq. 27.   Exterior and core: black to brown. Interior: gray. Rim diameter: 12 cm.
j. 054/2, Sq. 151.   Exterior and interior: buff-orange. Core: orange. Rim diameter: 6 cm.
k. 054/8, Sq. A52.   Exterior and interior: red-brown. Core: black center to buff. Rim diameter: 12 cm.
l. 054/2, Sq. 64.   Exterior and core: brown. Interior: red-brown. Rim diameter: 24 cm.
m. N52/2, Sq. B36.   Exterior: black. Core: black to brown. Interior: brown. Rim diameter: 12 cm.
n. 054/2, Sq. 30.   Exterior and interior: buff. Core: gray. Rim diameter: 16 cm.
o. 054/8, Sq. A54.   Exterior, core, and interior: gray. Rim diameter: 20 cm.
p. 054/8, Sq. D27.   Exterior and interior: buff-gray. Core: black center to buff. Rim diameter: 26 cm.
q. 054/8, Sq. A11.   Exterior, core, and interior: brown. Rim diameter: 20 cm.
r. 054/8, Sq. D16.   Exterior and interior: red-brown. Core: black. Rim diameter: 18 cm.
s. 054/8, Sq. A19.   Exterior and interior: red-brown. Core: gray center to red-brown. Rim diameter: 26 cm.
t. 054/8, Sq. D33.   Exterior: brown. Core: black. Interior: gray. Rim diameter: 14 cm.
u. 054/8, Sq. A12.   Exterior: buff-brown. Core: gray. Interior: gray-brown. Rim diameter: 22 cm.
v. 054/10, Sq. A11.   Exterior, core, and interior: brown. Rim diameter: 40+ cm.
w. 054/8, Sq. D38.   Exterior and interior: gray. Core: black. Rim diameter: 26 cm.
x. 055/8, Sq. 19.   Exterior and interior: brown. Core: black center to buff. Rim diameter: 20 cm.
y. 054/8, Sq. D21.   Exterior: orange. Core: black center to buff. Interior: buff-orange. Rim diameter: 36 cm.
z. 055/8, Sq. 18.   Exterior and core: brown. Interior: orange-brown. Rim diameter: 20 cm.
aa. 054/8, Gen'l.   Exterior, core, and interior: brown. Rim diameter: 22 cm.
bb. 054/8, Sq. D38.   Exterior: black. Core: black to brown. Interior: buff-orange. Rim diameter: 18 cm.
cc. 055/8, Sq. 14.   Exterior and interior: buff-brown. Core: black. Rim diameter: 26 cm.
dd. 054/8, Sq. D42.   Exterior and core: brown. Interior: red-brown. Rim diameter: 28 cm.
ee. 054/8, Sq. A25.   Exterior: gray. Core: black. Interior: black-brown. Rim diameter: 22 cm.
ff. 055/8, Sq. 28.   Exterior: red-brown. Core and interior: brown. Rim diameter: 18 cm.
gg. 054/8, Sq. D64.   Exterior and core: black. Interior: red-brown. Rim diameter: 20 cm.
hh. 055/8, Sq. 27.   Exterior: brown. Core and interior: black. Rim diameter: 24 cm.
ii. 055/8, Sq. 23.   Exterior: gray. Core: brown. Interior: black. Diameter: 6 cm.
jj. 054/2, Sq. 102.   Exterior, core, and interior: brown. Diameter: 22 cm.
kk. 054/8, Sq. A36.   Exterior: brown. Core: black. Interior: gray. Diameter: 4 cm.
ll. N52/1, Sq. B6.   Exterior, core, and interior: black. Diameter: 3 cm.
mm. N53/1, Gen'l.   Exterior, core, and interior: brown.

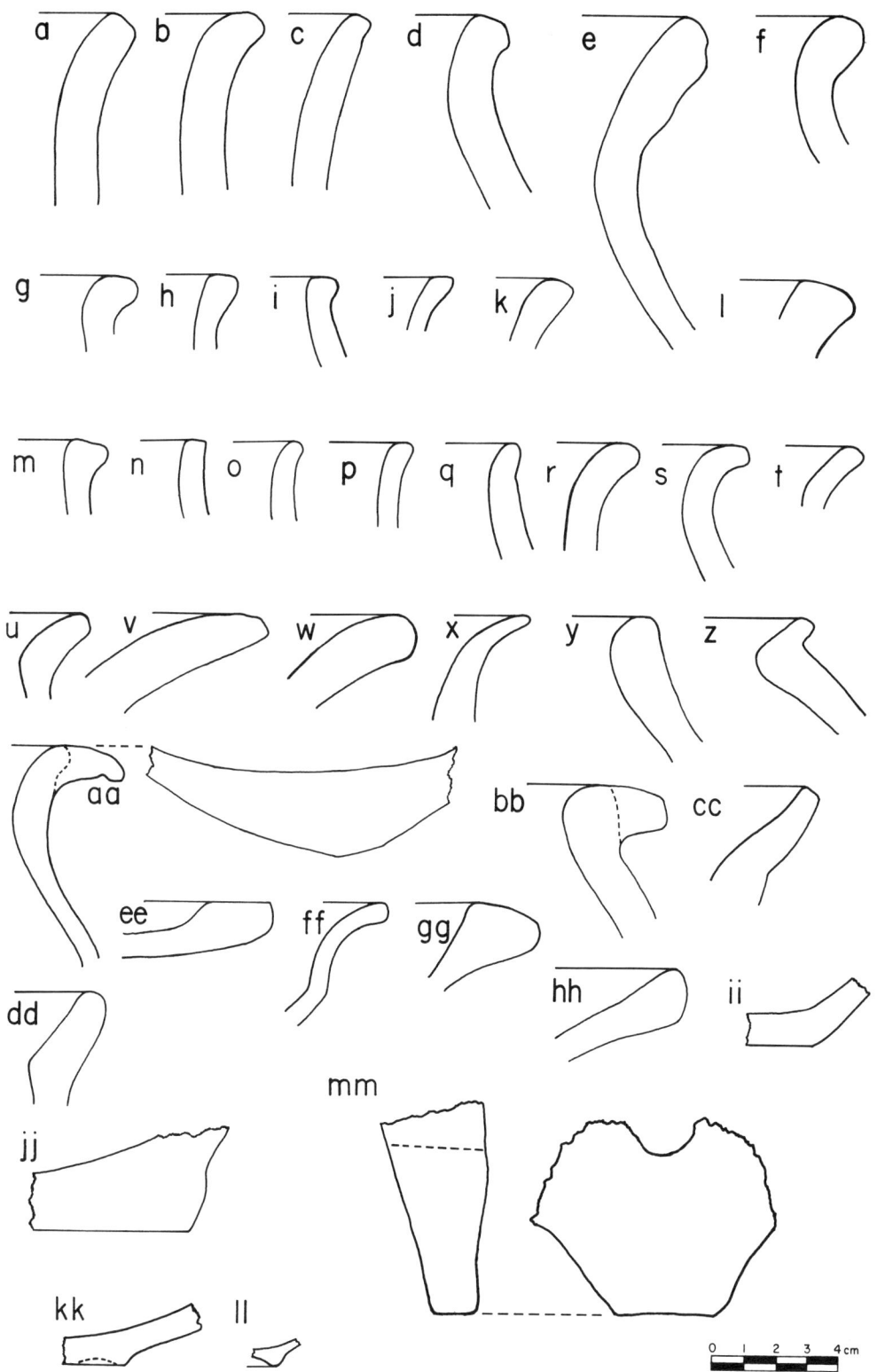

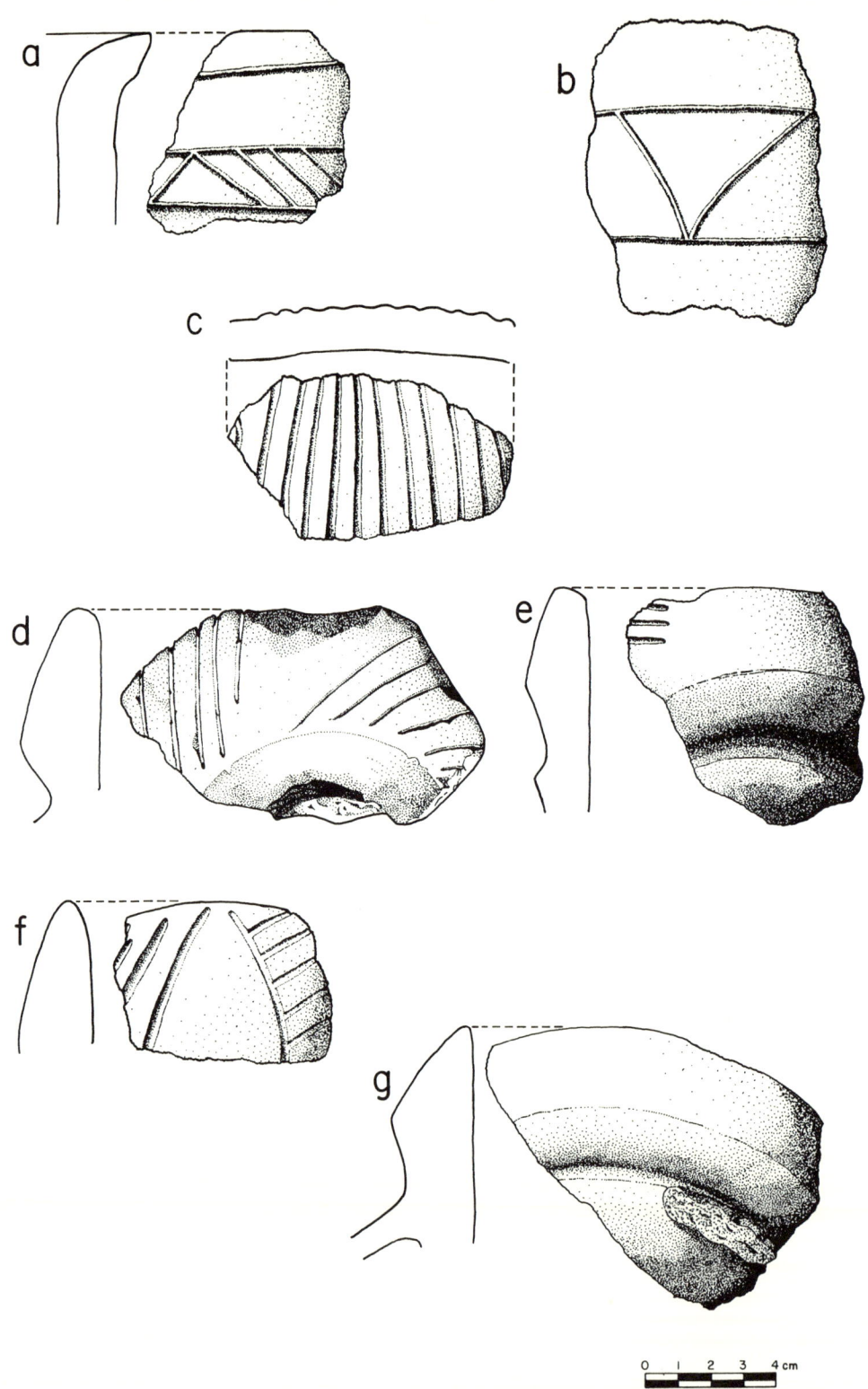

FIGURE 15

EARLY BRONZE AGE RELIEF DECORATED WARE
    a. 054/2, Gen'l.   Exterior: black. Core: gray to black. Interior: red, buff, and black.
    b. 054/8, Sq. B31.   Exterior and interior: red-brown. Core: black center to brown.
    c. 054/8, Sq. B32.   Exterior: gray-black. Core: black to gray to buff-brown. Interior: buff to gray.

EARLY BRONZE AGE LIDS
    d. 054/8, Gen'l.   Exterior and core: black. Interior: buff.
    e. 054/8, Sq. B21.   Exterior and interior: buff to brown. Core: black.
    f. 054/8, Sq. D35.   Exterior: buff mottled to gray-black. Core: black. Interior: buff.
    g. 054/8, Sq. B24.   Exterior and interior: buff to brown. Core: black with brown layer near surfaces.

FIGURE 16

EARLY BRONZE AGE POLISHED WARE
a. 054/2, Sq. 34. Exterior and interior: black polished. Core: black. Rim diameter: 16 cm.
b. 054/8, Sq. B24. Exterior: gray polished. Core: black. Interior: black polished. Rim diameter: 12 cm.
c. 054/8, Sq. B22. Exterior: buff-brown polished. Core: black center to brown. Interior: buff. Rim diameter: 16 cm.
d. 054/2, Sq. 34. Exterior: black polished. Core: black. Interior: black smoothed. Rim diameter: 16 cm.
e. 054/8, Sq. B29. Exterior: gray polished. Core: black. Interior: brown burnished. Rim diameter: 16 cm.
f. 054/8, Sq. B19. Exterior: black polished. Core: gray-black. Interior: buff polished. Rim diameter: 8 cm.
g. N53/3, Gen'l. Exterior: black polished. Core: black on exterior half, buff on interior half. Interior: brown polished. Rim diameter: 10 cm.
h. 054/8, Sq. B29. Exterior and interior: black polished. Core: black. Rim diameter: 14 cm.
i. N55/1, Gen'l. Exterior and interior: black polished. Core: black. Rim diameter: 10 cm.
j. 054/8, Sq. B29. Exterior and interior: gray polished. Core: black. Rim diameter: 16 cm.
k. N52/9, Sq. 2. Exterior and interior: black polished. Core: black. Rim diameter: ?
l. 054/2, Gen'l. Exterior and interior: black polished. Core: black. Rim diameter: 8 cm.

EARLY BRONZE AGE RED SLIPPED WARE
m. 054/8, Sq. B33. Exterior: red slip. Core: black center to orange. Interior: brown slip. Rim diameter: 34 cm.
n. 055/2, Gen'l. Exterior and interior: red slip. Core: black. Rim diameter: 30 cm.
o. 055/8, Sq. 28. Exterior and interior: red slipped. Core: black-brown. Rim diameter: 24 cm.
p. 054/2, Sq. 38. Exterior: red slip. Core: black. Interior: buff burnished. Rim diameter: 40 cm.
q. N55/1, Gen'l. Exterior and interior: red slip over cream. Core: cream (chaffy). Rim diameter: 18 cm.
r. 054/2, Sq. 6. Exterior and interior: red-brown slip. Core: black center to orange. Rim diameter: 20 cm.
s. 054/2, Sq. 170. Exterior and interior: red-brown slip. Core: black center to brown. Rim diameter: 14 cm.
t. N52/2, Sq. A12. Exterior and interior: red slip. Core: black. Rim diameter: 20 cm.
u. 055/1, Gen'l. Exterior and interior: red-brown slip. Core: orange. Rim diameter: 14 cm.
v. 054/2, Sq. 104. Exterior and interior: red slip. Core: gray center to orange. Rim diameter: 26 cm.

EARLY BRONZE AGE PLAIN WARE
w. 054/8, Sq. A48. Exterior and interior: brown. Core: gray. Rim diameter: 40+ cm.
x. 054/8, Sq. B29. Exterior: gray to black. Core: black to dark brown. Interior: gray. Rim diameter: 40+ cm.
y. 054/8, Sq. A15. Exterior, core, and interior: black. Rim diameter: 40 cm.
z. 054/2, Sq. 151. Exterior and interior: buff-brown. Core: black. Rim diameter: ?
aa. 054/2, Sq. 46. Exterior and interior: buff. Core: black. Rim diameter: ?
bb. 054/8, Sq. D37. Exterior and interior: buff to red. Core: black. Rim diameter: 30 cm?
cc. N52/1, Sq. A45. Exterior: black. Core: black to red. Interior: red. Rim diameter: 18 cm.

EARLY BRONZE AGE THICK WARE
dd. 054/8, Sq. A26. Exterior: black burnished. Core: black. Interior: red-brown burnished. Rim diameter: 40 cm.
ee. 054/8, Sq. A37. Exterior: red mottled to black burnished. Core: black to orange. Interior: brown burnished. Rim diameter: 40 cm.
ff. 054/2, Sq. 99. Exterior and interior: buff-orange burnished. Core: black. Rim diameter: ?

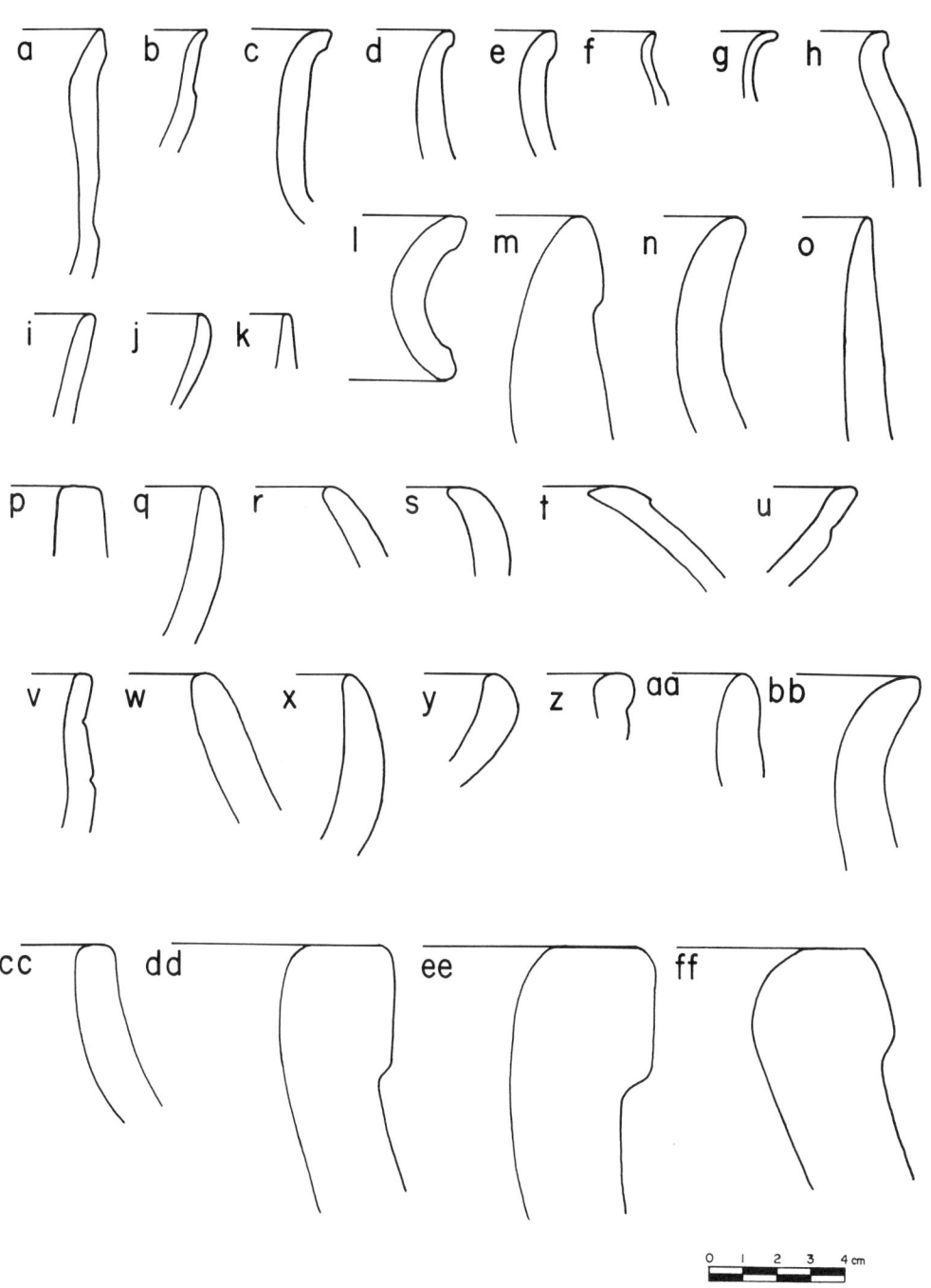

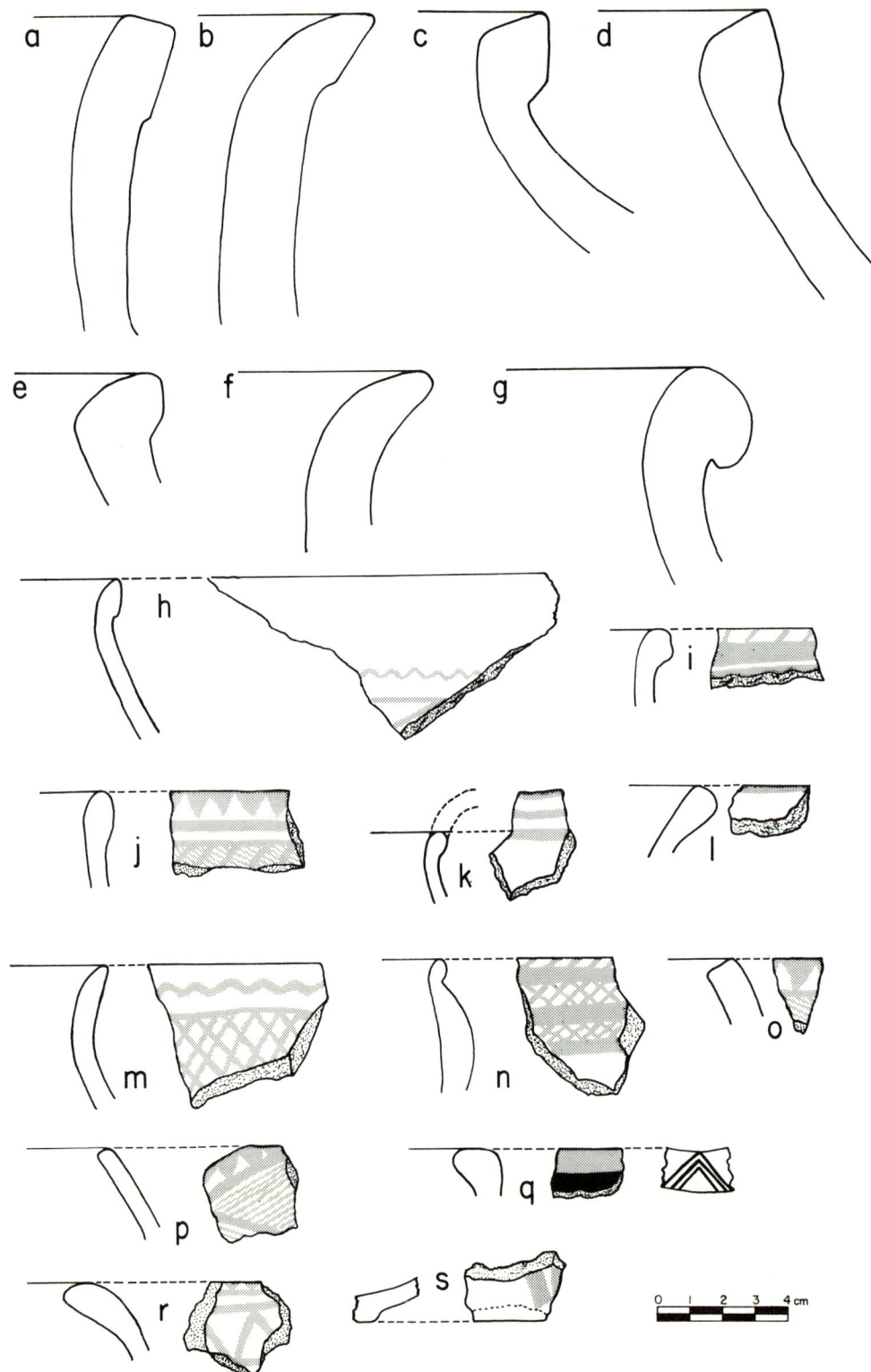

FIGURE 17

EARLY BRONZE AGE THICK WARE

a. 054/2, Gen'l. Exterior and interior: orange to black burnished. Core: orange. Rim diameter: 40+ cm.

b. 054/8, Gen'l. Exterior and interior: orange to buff to black burnished (plain examples of this form occur). Core: black to buff. Rim diameter: 39 cm.

c. N53/1, Gen'l. Exterior and interior: buff slip. Core: dark gray. Rim diameter: 20 cm.

d. N53/1, Gen'l. Exterior and interior: Orange-buff burnished. Core: dark gray to buff. Rim diameter: 30–33 cm.

e. N53/1, Gen'l. Exterior and interior: buff-gray burnished. Core: gray-buff. Rim diameter: ?

f. 054/8, Sq. D24. Exterior and interior: orange-black burnished. Core: black to orange. Rim diameter: 38 cm.

g. 055/4, Sq. 9. Color unrecorded. Rim diameter: 40+ cm.

EARLY BRONZE AGE RED PAINTED WARE

for h–s   Exterior: red painted on cream-buff slip. Core: cream-buff to orange. Interior: cream-buff slip or plain, with painting often extending slightly over the lip into the interior.

h. N52/6, Gen'l. Rim diameter: 22 cm.
i. 054/2, Sq. 98. Rim diameter: 12 cm.
j. 054/1, Gen'l. Rim diameter: 18 cm.
k. 054/2, Sq. 21. Rim diameter: ?
l. 054/8, Sq. D24. Rim diameter: 11 cm.
m. N52/9, Sq. 3. (Slip almost white). Rim diameter: 20 cm.
n. 055/1, Sq. 27. Rim diameter: 10 cm.
o. 054/2, Sq. 37. Rim diameter: ?
p. 054/2, Sq. 33. Rim diameter: ?
q. 054/8, Sq. C11. (Bichrome, red and black painted). Rim diameter: 18 cm.
r. 054/2, Gen'l. Rim diameter: 19 cm.
s. 054/8, Sq. C14. Diameter: 9 cm.

FIGURE 18 EARLY BRONZE AGE BLACK PAINTED WARE

for a–r Exterior: black painted on cream (probably slipped). Core: cream–buff. Interior: cream–buff, plain or lightly burnished.

    a. 054/8, Sq. D45.   Rim diameter: 30 cm.
    b. 054/8, Sq. B27.   Rim diameter: 18 cm.
    c. 054/8, Sq. A41.   Rim diameter: 22 cm.
    d. 054/8, Gen'l.   Rim diameter: 16 cm.
    e. 054/2, Sq. 65.   Rim diameter: 28 cm.
    f. 054/8, Sq. B55.   Three thin bands of paint on the rim, rest eroded beyond recognition. Rim diameter: 24 cm.
    g. 054/8, Sq. A12.   Rim diameter: 40+ cm?
    h. 054/8, Sq. D34.   Rim diameter: 12 cm.
    i. 054/8, Sq. D37.   Rim diameter: 26 cm.
    j. 054/8, Sq. C35.   Rim diameter: 16 cm.
    k. 054/8, Sq. C92.   Rim diameter: 15 cm.
    l. 054/2, Sq. 97.   Rim diameter: 11 cm.
    m. 054/2, Sq. 17.   Rim diameter: ?
    n. 054/2, Sq. 101.   Rim diameter: 8 cm.
    o. 054/8, Sq. B53.   Rim diameter: ?
    p. 054/8, Sq. A50.   Rim diameter: 18 cm.
    q. 054/6, Sq. B13.   Rim diameter: 26 cm.
    r. 054/8, Sq. A24.

for s–t Same, except lacking paint on the exterior.

    s. 054/2, Sq. 91.   Diameter: ?
    t. 054/2, Gen'l.   Diameter: 12 cm.

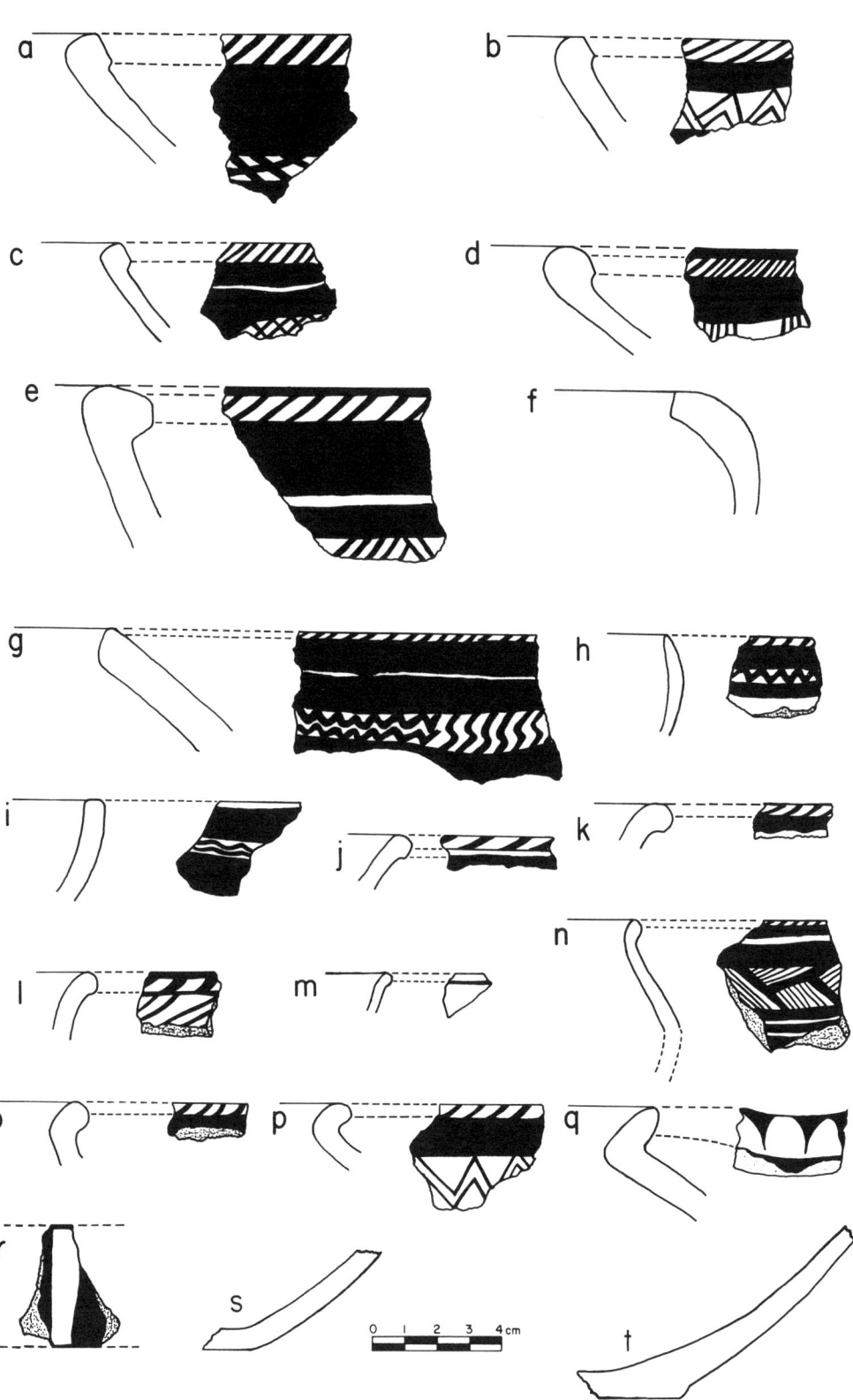

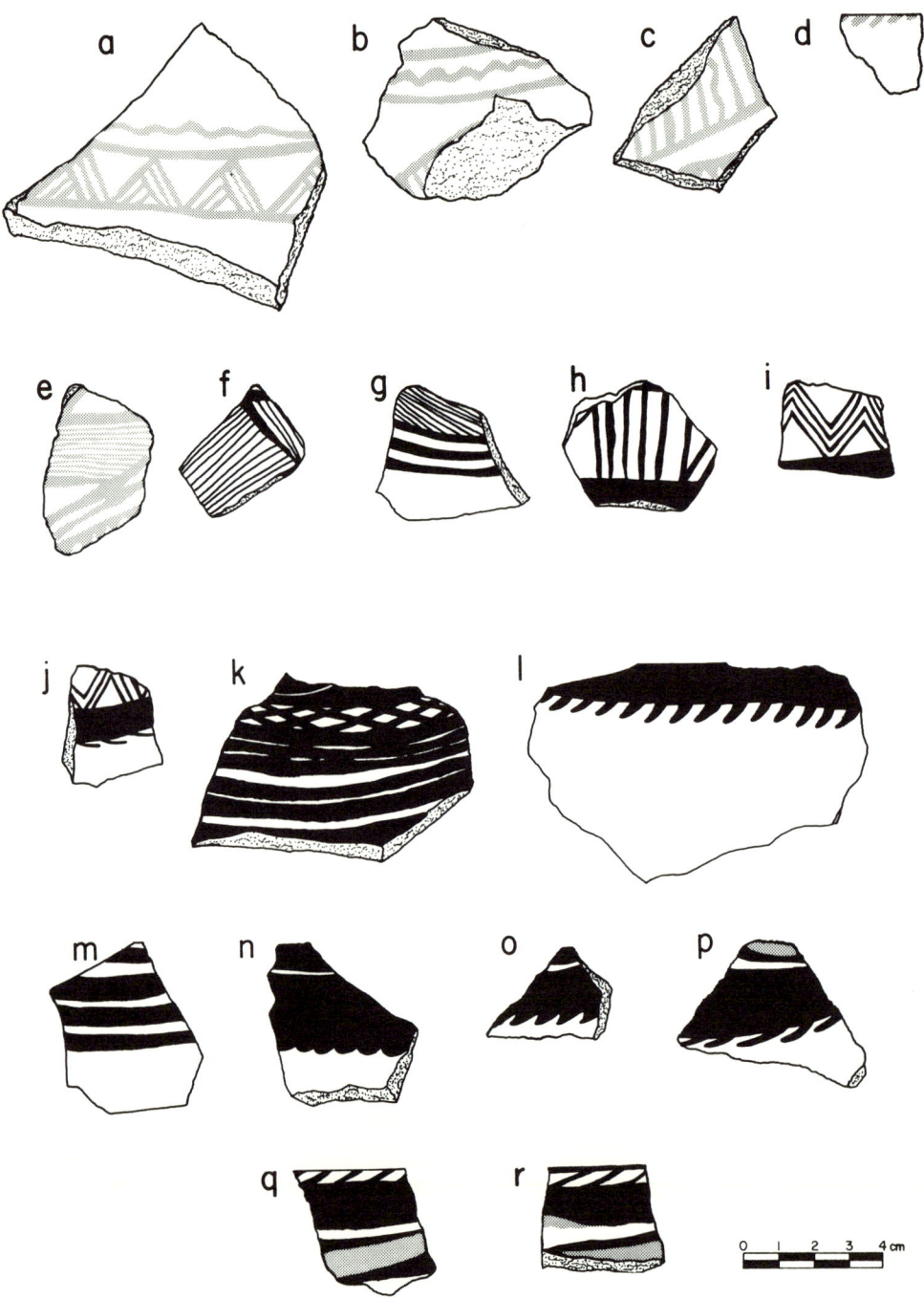

FIGURE 19

EARLY BRONZE AGE RED PAINTED WARE
for a–e   Exterior: red painted on cream–buff slip. Core: cream–buff to orange. Interior: cream–buff, plain or slipped.
    a. 054/8, Sq. B19.
    b. 054/8, Sq. B37.
    c. 054/8, Sq. B19.
    d. 054/8, Sq. D15.
    e. 054/2, Sq. 82.

EARLY BRONZE AGE BLACK PAINTED WARE
for f–o   Exterior: black painted on cream (probably slipped). Core: cream–buff. Interior: cream–buff, plain or lightly burnished.
    f. 054/8, Sq. B46.
    g. 054/8, Gen'l.
    h. 054/8, Sq. C30.
    i. 054/8, Sq. B11.
    j. 054/2, Gen'l.
    k. 054/8, Sq. A12.
    l. 054/8, Sq. D55.
    m. 054/8, Sq. A13.
    n. N52/2, Sq. B9.
    o. 054/8, Sq. D25.
for p–r   Exterior: black and red bichrome painted. Description otherwise the same as for f–o.
    p. 054/8, Gen'l.
    q. 054/8, Sq. C47.
    r. 054/8, Sq. C66.

FIGURE 20 MIDDLE BRONZE AGE GRITTY WARE

a. 054/2, Sq. 5. Exterior and interior: black, smooth. Core: black. Rim diameter: ?

b. 054/2, Sq. 5. Exterior and interior: brown, smooth. Core: brown. Rim diameter: 34 cm.

c. 054/14, Sq. I. Exterior and interior: gray-brown. Core: brown. Rim diameter: ?

d. 052/4, Gen'l. Exterior and interior: gray, smooth. Core: gray-brown. Rim diameter: 20 cm.

e. 054/8, Sq. A11. Exterior and interior: black, smooth. Core: dark gray. Rim diameter: 26 cm.

f. 054/2, Gen'l. Exterior and interior: brown burnished. Core: brown. Rim diameter: 40 cm.

g. 054/2, Sq. 91. Exterior and interior: brown burnished. Core: black center, red-brown edges. Rim diameter: 20 cm.

h. 054/2, Sq. 88. Exterior and interior: gray burnished. Core: brown. Rim diameter: 22 cm.

i. 054/8, Sq. C19. Exterior and interior: black burnished. Core: black. Rim diameter: 18 cm.

j. N52/7, Gen'l. Exterior, core, and interior: gray-black. Rim diameter: 20 cm.

k. 054/2, Sq. 136. Exterior and interior: brown burnished. Core: brown. Rim diameter: 18 cm.

l. 054/2, Sq. 96. Exterior: brown burnished. Core: brown. Interior: brown smoothed. Rim diameter: 14 cm.

m. 054/8, Sq. A42. Exterior and interior: gray-brown burnished. Core: dark gray. Rim diameter: ?

n. 054/10, Sq. C3. Exterior: black burnished. Core: black. Interior: gray burnished. Rim diameter: ?

o. 054/8, Sq. C43. Exterior and interior: gray, smooth. Core: center brown, edges black. Rim diameter: ?

p. 054/2, Sq. 88. Exterior and interior: gray, burnished. Core: gray-green. Rim diameter: 32 cm.

q. N53/1, Gen'l. Exterior and interior: brown burnished. Core: brown. Rim diameter: 10 cm.

r. N53/1, Gen'l. Exterior and core: gray. Interior: buff burnished. Rim diameter: ?

s. 054/14, Sq. J. Exterior and interior: gray burnished. Core: brown. Rim diameter: ?

t. 054/8, Sq. A45. Exterior and interior: gray burnished. Core: dark gray. Rim diameter: 36 cm.

u. 054/14, Sq. 13. Exterior and interior: gray burnished. Core: brown. Rim diameter: ?

v. 054/10, Sq. A2. Exterior and interior: gray burnished. Core: dark gray. Rim diameter: ?

w. 054/8, Sq. D55. Exterior and interior: gray burnished. Core: gray. Rim diameter: ?

x. 054/27, Sq. A11. Exterior and interior: gray burnished. Core: brown. Rim diameter: 22 cm.

y. 054/14, Sq. I. Exterior and interior: gray burnished. Core: black-brown. Rim diameter: ?

z. N53/1, Gen'l. Exterior and interior: gray burnished. Core: gray. Rim diameter: 28 cm.

aa. 054/8, Sq. A21. Exterior and interior: black, smooth. Core: black. Rim diameter: 34 cm.

bb. 054/2, Sq. 131. Exterior and interior: red-brown burnished. Core: dark brown center, red-brown edges. Rim diameter: 20 cm.

cc. 054/10, Sq. C5. Exterior: black. Core: brown center, black edges. Interior: black burnished. Rim diameter: 14 cm.

dd. 054/2, Sq. 48. Exterior: brown burnished. Core: gray-brown. Interior: brown, smooth. Rim diameter: 30 cm.

ee. 054/2, Sq. 64. Exterior: gray, smooth, incised. Core: black. Interior: gray, smooth.

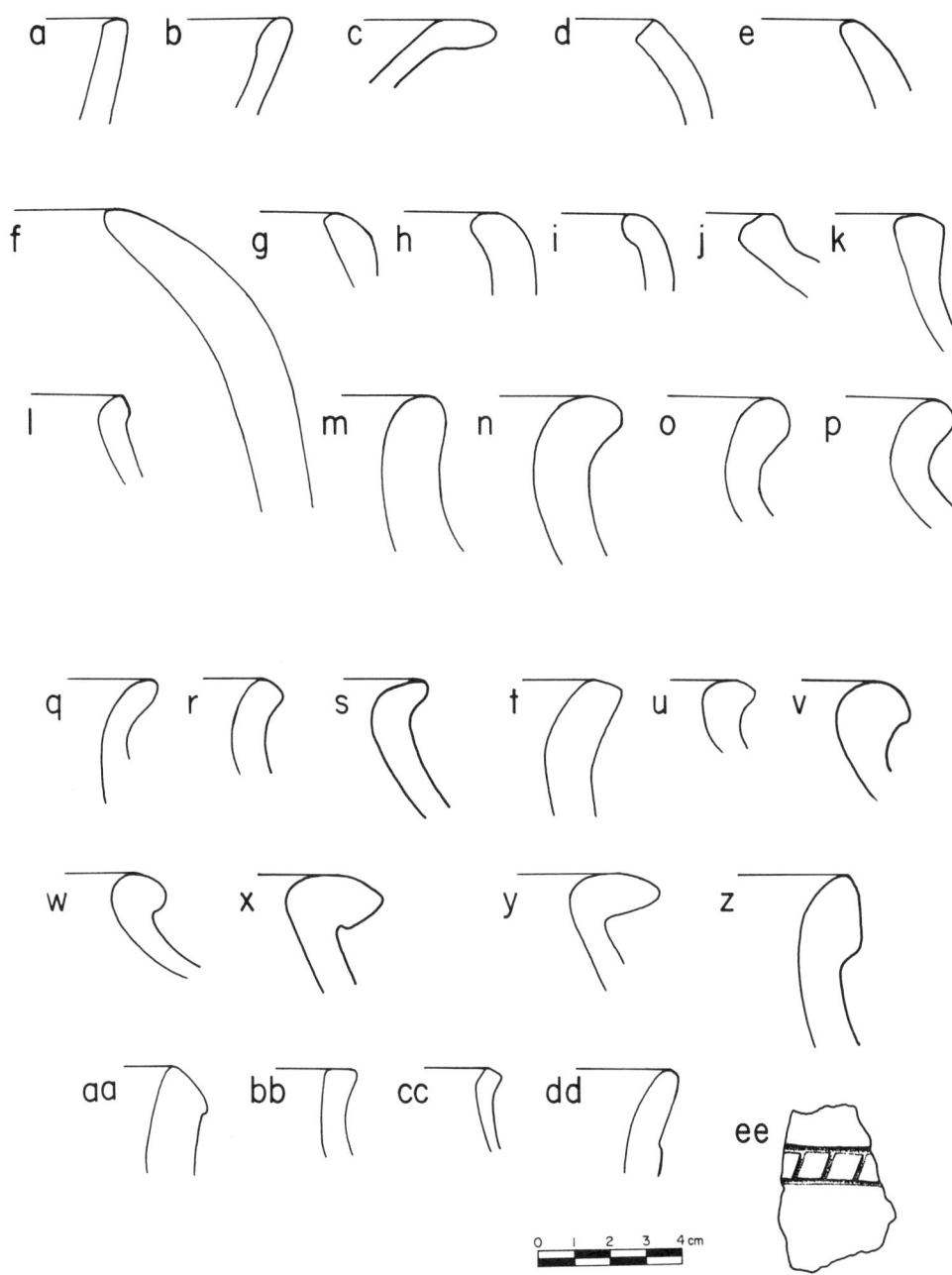

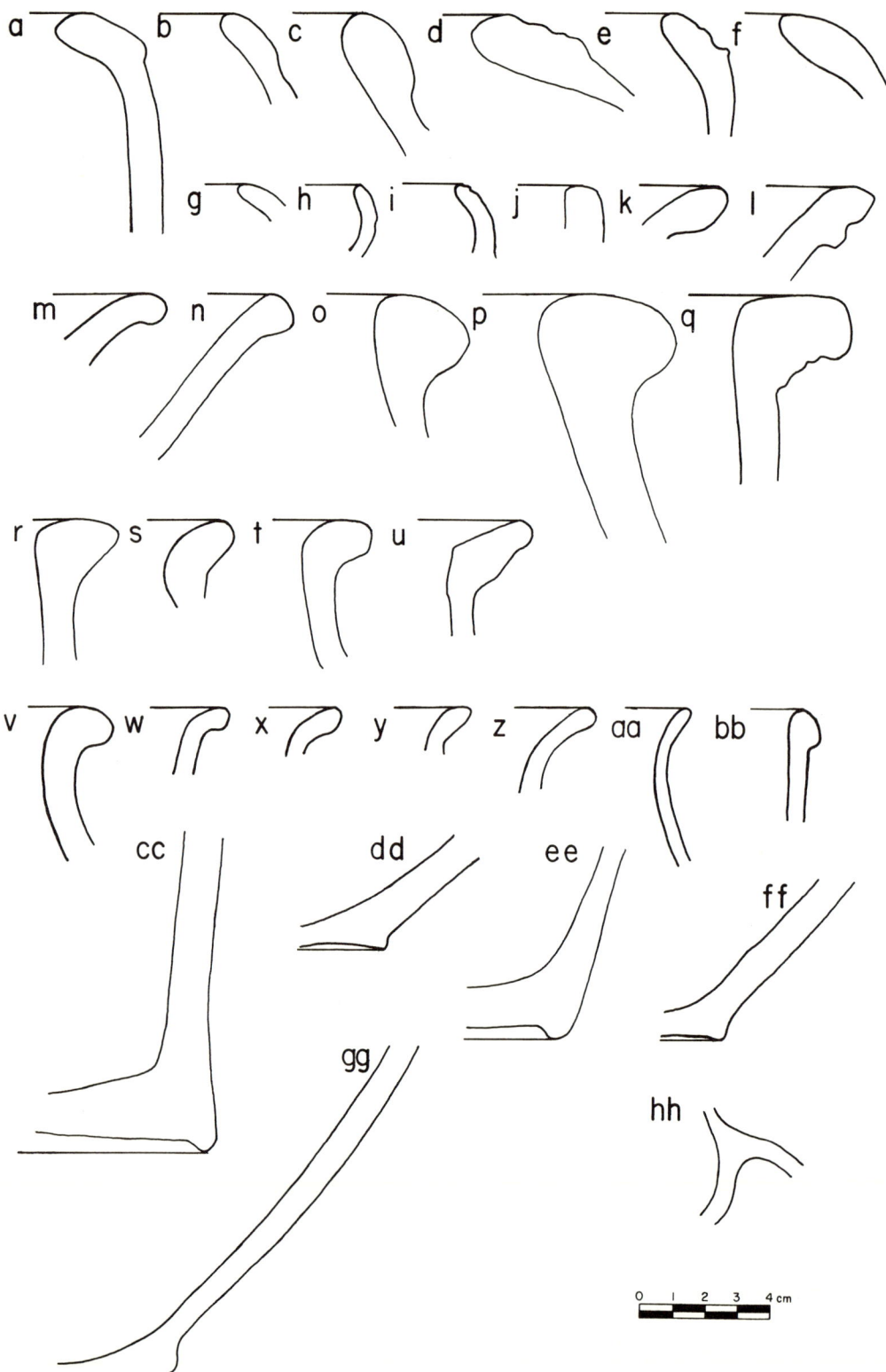

FIGURE 21 OLD HITTITE GRAY WARE

a. 054/8, Gen'l. Exterior and interior: brown burnished. Core: gray center to brown. Rim diameter: 40+ cm?

b. 054/8, Sq. C8. Exterior and interior: dark brown. Core: gray center to brown. Rim diameter: 38 cm.

c. 054/2, Sq. 39. Exterior and interior: dark gray burnished. Core: light gray, black center. Rim diameter: 40 cm.

d. 054/8, Sq. D15. Exterior: light gray with dark gray burnished stripes. Interior: light gray, lightly burnished. Core: gray. Rim diameter: 26 cm.

e. 054/10, Sq. C4. Exterior: dark gray. Core: very dark gray. Interior: light gray. Rim diameter: 30 cm.

f. 054/8, Sq. A11. Exterior and interior: gray burnished. Core: gray. Rim diameter: 34 cm.

g. 054/8, Gen'l. Exterior and interior: brown burnished. Core: black center to gray. Rim diameter: ?

h. 054/24, Sq. A30. Exterior and interior: brown–gray. Core: light gray. Rim diameter: ?

i. 054/8, Sq. C22. Exterior and interior: dark gray. Core: gray. Rim diameter: ?

j. 054/8, Sq. D89. Exterior: dark gray burnished. Core: gray. Interior: ? (damaged). Rim diameter: ?

k. 054/8, Sq. B36. Exterior and interior: brown burnished. Core: dark gray. Rim diameter: ?

l. 054/8, Sq. C32. Exterior: gray burnished. Core: gray. Interior: grayish brown. Rim diameter: 38 cm.

m. 054/2, Gen'l. Exterior: dark gray. Core: very light gray. Interior: light gray. Rim diameter: 34 cm.

n. 054/2, Gen'l. Exterior: black. Core: gray–brown. Interior: dark gray. Rim diameter: 40+ cm?

o. 054/8, Sq. A46. Exterior: gray burnished. Core: gray. Interior: light gray, lightly burnished. Rim diameter: 32 cm.

p. 054/2, Gen'l. Exterior and interior: gray–brown burnished. Core: gray. Rim diameter: 30 cm.

q. 054/8, Sq. C23. Exterior and interior: dark gray burnished. Core: gray. Rim diameter: 40 cm.

r. 054/2, Sq. 99. Exterior: dark brown burnished. Core: gray center to brown. Interior: light brown. Rim diameter: 26 cm.

s. 054/8, Sq. D40. Exterior: dark brown. Core: gray. Interior: light brown. Rim diameter: ?

t. 054/8, Sq. C18. Exterior: light gray. Core: gray. Interior: gray burnished. Rim diameter: 20 cm.

u. 054/8, Sq. D23. Exterior: brown. Core: gray. Interior: light brown. Rim diameter: 32 cm.

v. 054/8, Sq. C30. Exterior and core: dark brown. Interior: light brown. Rim diameter: 22 cm.

w. 054/14, Sq. 17. Exterior, core, and interior: gray. Rim diameter: ?

x. 054/8, Sq. C15. Exterior and interior: dark gray burnished. Core: gray. Rim diameter: 20 cm.

y. 055/1, Sq. 29. Exterior and interior: brown. Core: black. Rim diameter: 20 cm.

z. 054/19, Gen'l. Exterior and interior: dark brown burnished. Core: gray center to brown. Rim diameter: 18 cm.

aa. N52/10, Gen'l. Exterior, core, and interior: light gray. Rim diameter: ?

bb. 055/4, Sq. 14. Exterior and interior: dark gray. Core: gray–brown. Rim diameter: 26 cm.

cc. 054/19, Gen'l. Exterior: black. Core: gray–brown. Interior: light gray.

dd. 054/2, Gen'l. Exterior: dark brown burnished. Core: ? Interior: gray–brown.

ee. 054/2, Gen'l. Exterior: light to dark gray. Interior and core: Light gray.

ff. 054/8, Sq. B28. Exterior: light gray. Core: dark gray–brown. Interior: gray.

gg. 054/8, Sq. D60. Exterior: black. Core: gray. Interior: light gray.

hh. 054/8, Sq. D59. Exterior: gray burnished. Core and interior: gray.

FIGURE 22

MIDDLE BRONZE AGE GRAY WARE

a. 054/2, Sq. 122. Exterior and interior: gray burnished. Core: dark brown. Rim diameter: 20 cm.

b. 054/8, Sq. B33. Exterior and interior: gray burnished. Core: black outer half, gray inner half. Rim diameter: 22 cm.

c. 054/2, Sq. 21. Exterior and interior: gray burnished. Core: dark gray. Rim diameter: ?

d. 054/2, Sq. 122. Exterior: gray smoothed. Core: gray–brown. Interior: gray burnished. Rim diameter: 16 cm.

e. 054/2, Sq. 68. Exterior: light gray burnished. Core: gray–brown. Interior: dark gray burnished. Rim diameter: 20 cm.

f. 054/2, Sq. 64. Exterior and interior: gray–brown burnished. Core: black. Rim diameter: ?

g. 054/2, Sq. 62. Exterior: brown burnished. Core: gray. Interior: gray smoothed. Rim diameter: 22 cm.

h. 055/4, Sq. 45. Exterior and interior: gray burnished. Core: gray. Rim diameter: 10 cm.

i. 054/8, Sq. C40. Exterior and interior: gray burnished. Core: light gray. Rim diameter: 20 cm.

j. 054/10, Gen'l. Exterior: gray burnished (small incisions on rim). Core: dark gray center, brown edges. Interior: brown (slipped?) burnished. Rim diameter: 18 cm.

k. 054/8, Sq. C92. Exterior: brown–gray burnished. Core: light gray. Interior: gray burnished. Rim diameter: 24 cm.

l. 054/8, Sq. C40. Exterior and interior: gray burnished. Core: light gray. Rim diameter: 22 cm.

m. 054/2, Sq. 114. Exterior: brown–gray burnished. Core: brown. Interior: brown burnished. Rim diameter: ?

n. 054/2, Gen'l. Exterior and interior: gray burnished. Core: ? Rim diameter: 28 cm.

o. 054/25, Sq. A24. Exterior and interior: gray burnished. Core: gray–brown. Rim diameter: 10 cm.

p. 054/2, Gen'l. Exterior and interior: gray smoothed. Core: gray center to dark brown edges. Rim diameter: 20 cm.

q. 054/8, Sq. B10. Exterior and interior: Light gray burnished. Core: dark gray. Rim diameter: 20 cm.

r. 054/8, Sq. A15. Exterior and interior: brown burnished. Core: gray. Rim diameter: 18 cm.

s. 054/8, Sq. D58. Exterior: gray burnished. Core: gray. Interior: dark gray burnished. Rim diameter: 28 cm.

t. 054/8, Sq. C18. Exterior: gray–black burnished. Core: black. Interior: black smoothed. Rim diameter: 40 cm.

u. 054/8, Sq. D25. Exterior and interior: gray burnished. Core: brown center, black edges. Rim diameter: 20 cm.

v. 054/2, Sq. 110. Exterior: gray burnished. Core: dark gray. Interior: ? (damaged).

w. 054/2, Sq. 21. Exterior: gray smoothed. Core: gray. Interior: light gray smoothed.

x. 054/2, Sq. 48. Exterior: gray burnished. Core: brown–gray. Interior: gray.

y. 054/2, Sq. 68. Exterior: gray burnished. Core: dark gray. Interior: gray smoothed.

OLD HITTITE LIGHT FACED GRAY WARE

z. 054/8, Sq. A66. Exterior and interior: brown. Core: gray. Rim diameter: 26 cm.

aa. 054/2, Sq. 40. Exterior and interior: brown. Core: gray. Diameter: 12 cm.

bb. 054/2, Sq. 15. Exterior: red–brown. Core: gray interior to orange exterior. Interior: gray. Diameter: 12 cm.

cc. 054/2, Sq. 87. Exterior and interior: brown. Core: gray. Diameter: 12 cm.

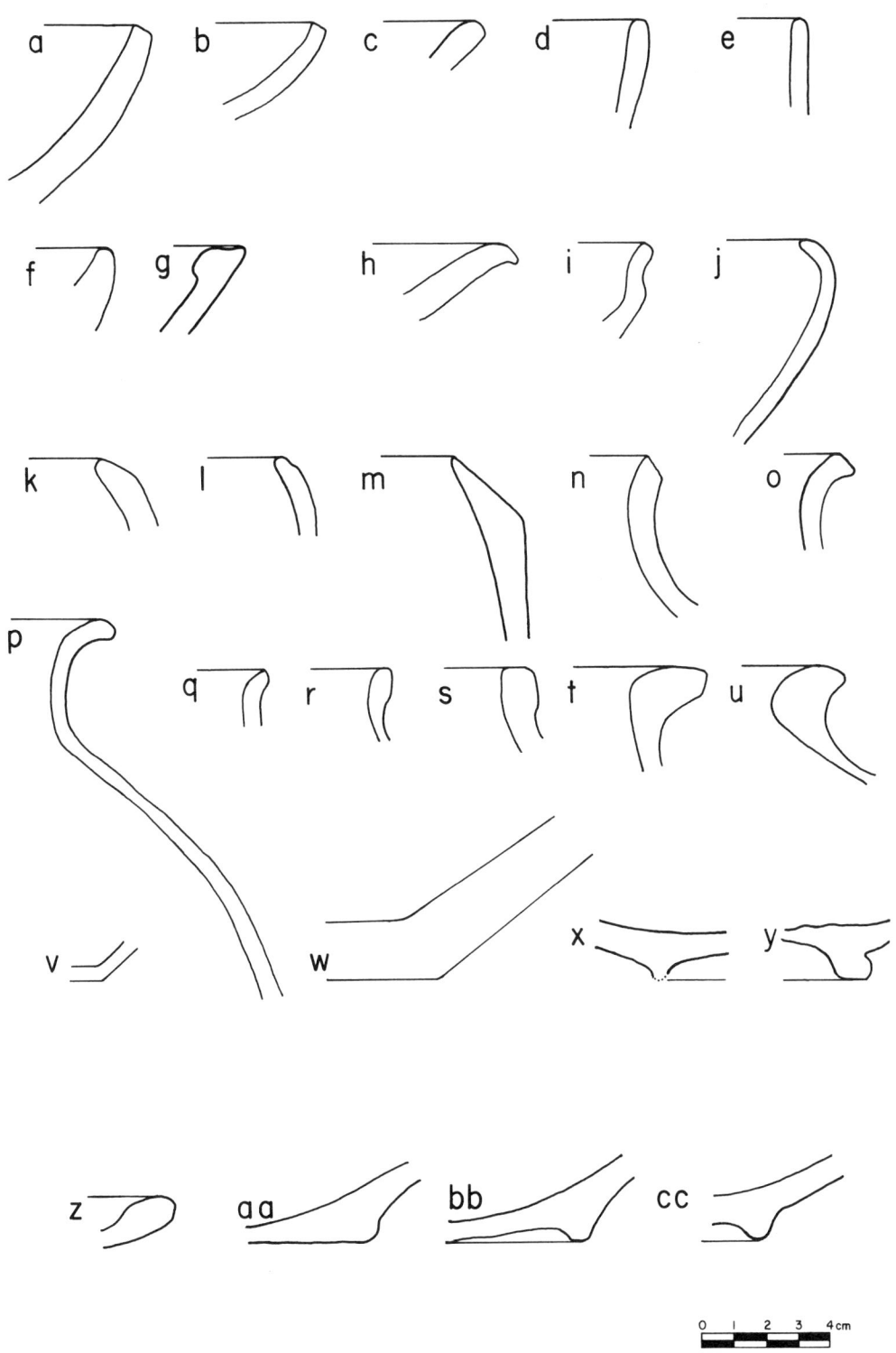

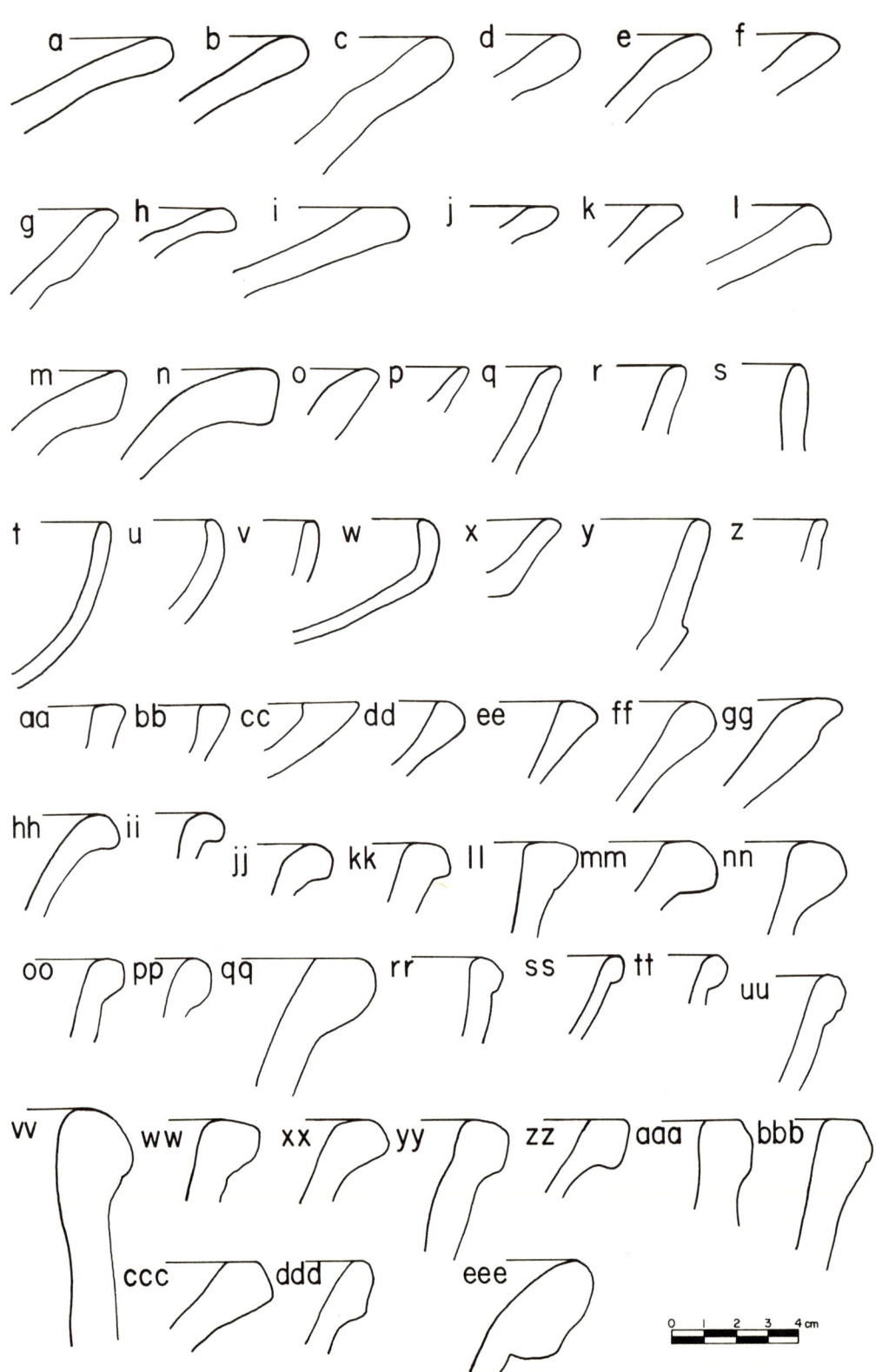

FIGURE 23 HITTITE PLAIN WARE

a. 054/8, Sq. C21. Exterior, core, and interior: brown. Rim diameter: 26 cm.
b. 054/2, Sq. 177. Exterior: red-orange. Core: brown. Interior: buff-brown. Rim diameter: 24 cm.
c. 054/8, Sq. C27. Exterior, core, and interior: buff. Rim diameter: 38 cm.
d. 054/8, Sq. C18. Exterior and interior: cream. Core: buff-brown. Rim diameter: 20 cm.
e. 054/8, Sq. B42. Exterior and interior: cream. Core: brown-gray. Rim diameter: 24 cm.
f. 054/2, Sq. 129. Exterior: red-brown. Core: brown. Interior: orange. Rim diameter: 26 cm.
g. 054/8, Sq. D64. Exterior and interior: red-brown. Core: gray center to orange. Rim diameter: 30 cm.
h. 054/2, Sq. 68. Exterior, core, and interior: cream. Rim diameter: 10 cm.
i. 054/8, Sq. D51. Exterior and interior: red-brown. Core: gray center to brown. Rim diameter: 36 cm.
j. 054/9, Sq. C15. Exterior, core, and interior: brown. Rim diameter: 14 cm.
k. 054/8, Sq. A45. Exterior, core, and interior: brown. Rim diameter: 22 cm.
l. 054/8, Sq. C15. Exterior, core, and interior: white-orange. Rim diameter: 24 cm.
m. 054/8, Sq. A43. Exterior and interior: buff-orange. Core: gray center to orange. Rim diameter: 12 cm.
n. 054/8, Sq. C43. Exterior and core: buff. Interior: buff-orange. Rim diameter: 22 cm.
o. 054/2, Sq. 41. Exterior and interior: buff-orange. Core: orange. Rim diameter: 12 cm.
p. 054/8, Sq. C46. Exterior, core, and interior: red-brown. Rim diameter: 8 cm.
q. 054/8, Sq. C51. Exterior and interior: buff-orange. Core: gray center to orange. Rim diameter: 14 cm.
r. 054/8, Sq. C20. Exterior and interior: orange-cream. Core: orange. Rim diameter: 8 cm.
s. 054/8, Sq. D32. Exterior, core, and interior: brown. Rim diameter: 10 cm.
t. 054/2, Sq. 12. Exterior: buff. Core: gray center to brown. Interior: buff-orange. Rim diameter: 16 cm.
u. 054/6, Sq. B35. Exterior: buff-orange. Core: buff. Interior: buff burnished. Rim diameter: ?
v. 054/8, Sq. A56. Exterior, core, and interior: buff. Rim diameter: 12 cm.
w. 054/9, Gen'l. Exterior, core, and interior: buff. Rim diameter: 22 cm.
x. 054/2, Sq. 113. Exterior: buff-orange. Core: brown. Interior: red-brown. Rim diameter: 24 cm.
y. 054/2, Sq. 64. Exterior and interior: cream-buff. Core: buff. Rim diameter: ?
z. 055/3, Sq. 37. Exterior and interior: buff-orange. Core: orange. Rim diameter: 8 cm.
aa. 054/8, Sq. C32. Exterior, core, and interior: brown. Rim diameter: 18 cm.
bb. 054/8, Sq. D45. Exterior: buff. Core: orange. Interior: brown. Rim diameter: 20 cm.
cc. 054/6, Sq. B16. Exterior and interior: buff-orange. Core: gray center to orange. Rim diameter: 18 cm.
dd. 054/8, Sq. D47. Exterior and interior: gray-brown. Core: gray. Rim diameter: 24 cm.
ee. 054/8, Sq. D15. Exterior, core, and interior: buff. Rim diameter: 26 cm.
ff. 054/8, Sq. A27. Exterior: orange-buff. Core and interior: orange. Rim diameter: 22 cm.
gg. 054/2, Sq. 56. Exterior and interior: buff-brown. Core: orange. Rim diameter: 12 cm.
hh. 054/8, Sq. C65. Exterior and interior: orange-buff. Core: buff. Rim diameter: 20 cm.
ii. 054/2, Sq. 115. Exterior, core, and interior: buff. Rim diameter: ?
jj. 054/8, Sq. D59. Exterior: brown. Core and interior: orange. Rim diameter: 20 cm.
kk. 054/8, Sq. D47. Exterior and interior: brown. Core: gray center to brown. Rim diameter: 16 cm.
ll. 054/8, Sq. A56. Exterior and core: brown. Interior: red-brown. Rim diameter: 22 cm.
mm. 054/2, Sq. 47. Exterior: cream. Core: gray center to buff. Interior: buff. Rim diameter: ?
nn. 054/2, Sq. 41. Exterior, core, and interior: brown. Rim diameter: ?
oo. 054/8, Sq. C21. Exterior and interior: white. Core: orange. Rim diameter: 18 cm.
pp. 054/8, Sq. A43. Exterior and interior: brown. Core: buff. Rim diameter: 12 cm.
qq. 054/8, Sq. D24. Exterior: buff. Core: orange. Interior: brown. Rim diameter: 32 cm.
rr. 054/8, Sq. D67. Exterior: brown. Core: buff. Interior: brown-buff. Rim diameter: 20 cm.
ss. N52/1, Sq. B4. Exterior and interior: cream. Core: cream-buff. Rim diameter: 14 cm.
tt. N52/1, Sq. A28. Exterior, core, and interior: cream. Rim diameter: 14 cm.
uu. 054/8, Gen'l. Exterior, core, and interior: white. Rim diameter: 28 cm.
vv. 054/2, Sq. 63. Exterior and core: buff-brown. Interior: red-brown. Rim diameter: ?
ww. 054/8, Sq. C76. Exterior and interior: brown. Core: orange. Rim diameter: 22 cm.
xx. 054/8, Sq. C44. Exterior and interior: brown. Core: orange. Rim diameter: 24 cm.
yy. 054/8, Sq. C35. Exterior and interior: brown. Core: orange. Rim diameter: 32 cm.
zz. 054/8, Sq. A27. Exterior, core, and interior: buff. Rim diameter: 22 cm.
aaa. 054/8, Sq. A9. Exterior and interior: buff-orange. Core: buff. Rim diameter: 20 cm.
bbb. 054/8, Sq. D24. Exterior: red-brown. Core and interior: orange. Rim diameter: 28 cm.
ccc. 054/8, Sq. A67. Exterior and interior: orange. Core: buff. Rim diameter: 30 cm.
ddd. 054/8, Sq. A36. Exterior and interior: cream-buff. Core: orange. Rim diameter: 18 cm.
eee. 054/8, Sq. A39. Exterior and interior: brown. Core: orange. Rim diameter: 18 cm.

FIGURE 24 HITTITE PLAIN WARE

a. 054/8, Sq. C31. Exterior and interior: red-brown. Core: orange. Rim diameter: 12 cm.
b. 054/2, Sq. 74. Exterior: brown. Core: orange-buff. Interior: buff. Rim diameter: 10 cm.
c. 054/8, Sq. C40. Exterior: brown. Core: gray. Interior: brown-gray. Rim diameter: 10 cm.
d. 054/8, Sq. C33. Exterior and interior: brown. Core: buff. Rim diameter: 30 cm.
e. 054/8, Sq. C39. Exterior, core and interior: orange. Rim diameter: 30 cm.
f. 054/8, Sq. D39. Exterior: red-brown. Core: gray center to red. Interior: brown. Rim diameter: 22 cm.
g. 055/1, Sq. 17. Exterior and interior: buff-orange. Core: orange. Rim diameter: 34 cm.
h. 054/8, Sq. A42. Exterior: brown. Core and interior: orange. Rim diameter: 36 cm.
i. 055/1, Gen'l. Exterior and interior: buff-orange. Core: gray center to orange. Rim diameter: 38 cm.
j. 054/8, Sq. A50. Exterior and interior: buff. Core: orange. Rim diameter: ±34 cm.
k. 054/8, Sq. C15. Exterior and interior: white. Core buff. Rim diameter: 36 cm.
l. 054/8, Sq. A45. Exterior and interior: brown. Core: gray center to orange. Rim diameter: 30 cm.
m. 054/8, Sq. D54. Exterior and interior: red-brown. Core: orange. Rim diameter: 10 cm.
n. 054/8, Sq. C59. Exterior and interior: cream-buff. Core: orange. Rim diameter: 14 cm.
o. 055/3, Gen'l. Exterior, core and interior: buff-orange. Rim diameter: 12 cm.
p. 054/8, Sq. C41. Exterior and interior: brown. Core: gray center to buff. Rim diameter: 26 cm.
q. 054/8, Sq. C62. Exterior: red-brown. Core: orange. Interior: brown. Rim diameter: 18 cm.
r. 054/8, Sq. C49. Exterior and core: orange. Interior: cream. Rim diameter: 20 cm.
s. 054/8, Sq. D47. Exterior and interior: buff. Core: black center to orange. Rim diameter: 30 cm.
t. 054/8, Sq. D74. Exterior, core, and interior: buff. Rim diameter: 18 cm.
u. 055/8, Gen'l. Exterior, core, and interior: cream. Rim diameter: 24 cm.
v. 054/22, Gen'l. Exterior and interior: buff-brown. Core: gray-brown. Rim diameter: 24 cm.
w. 054/8, Sq. C59. Exterior, core, and interior: cream-buff. Rim diameter: 26 cm.
x. 054/8, Sq. D57. Exterior and core: buff. Interior: orange. Rim diameter: 12 cm.
y. 054/2, Sq. 115. Exterior and interior: buff-brown. Core: gray center to brown. Rim diameter: ?
z. 055/8, Gen'l. Exterior: buff-orange. Core and interior: cream-orange. Rim diameter: 38 cm.
aa. 054/8, Sq. A13. Exterior: orange-buff. Core: buff. Interior: brown. Rim diameter: ?
bb. 054/22, Gen'l. Exterior and interior: buff-orange. Core: orange. Rim diameter: ?
cc. 054/8, Sq. C83. Exterior, core, and interior: buff. Rim diameter: 22 cm.
dd. 054/8, Sq. C85. Exterior, core, and interior: buff. Rim diameter: 20 cm.
ee. 054/8, Sq. A73. Exterior: cream. Core and interior: cream-orange. Rim diameter: 38 cm.
ff. 055/4, Sq. 42. Exterior, core, and interior: gray-buff. Rim diameter: 20 cm.
gg. 054/8, Sq. A12. Exterior and interior: brown. Core: orange. Rim diameter: 14 cm.
hh. 054/8, Sq. C11. Exterior: buff-orange. Core: brown. Interior: weathered away. Rim diameter: 18 cm.
ii. 054/2, Sq. 158. Exterior: brown. Core: brown center to buff. Interior: red-brown. Rim diameter: 20 cm.
jj. 055/9, Sq. 40. Exterior, core, and interior: cream-orange. Rim diameter: 24 cm.
kk. 054/9, Sq. A1. Exterior and interior: red-brown. Core: buff-brown. Rim diameter: 22 cm.
ll. 054/8, Sq. B33. Exterior, core, and interior: buff. Rim diameter: 18 cm.
mm. N55/1, Gen'l. Exterior and core: buff-brown. Interior: buff-orange. Rim diameter: 18 cm.
nn. 054/8, Sq. C30. Exterior, core, and interior: brown. Rim diameter: 20 cm.
oo. 054/2, Sq. 84. Exterior, core, and interior: brown. Rim diameter: 26 cm.
pp. 054/8, Sq. A63. Exterior and core: orange. Interior: buff. Rim diameter: 34 cm.

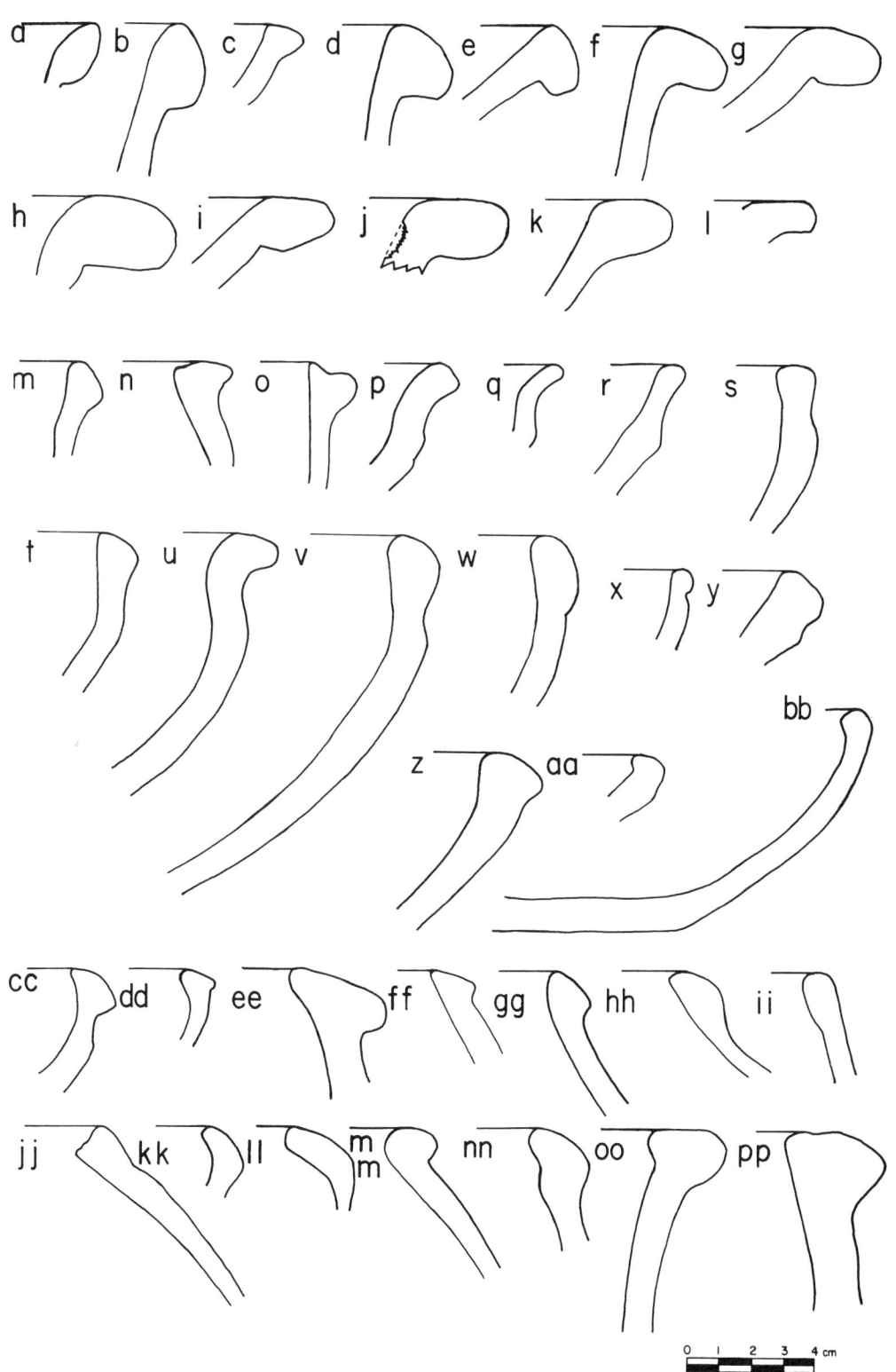

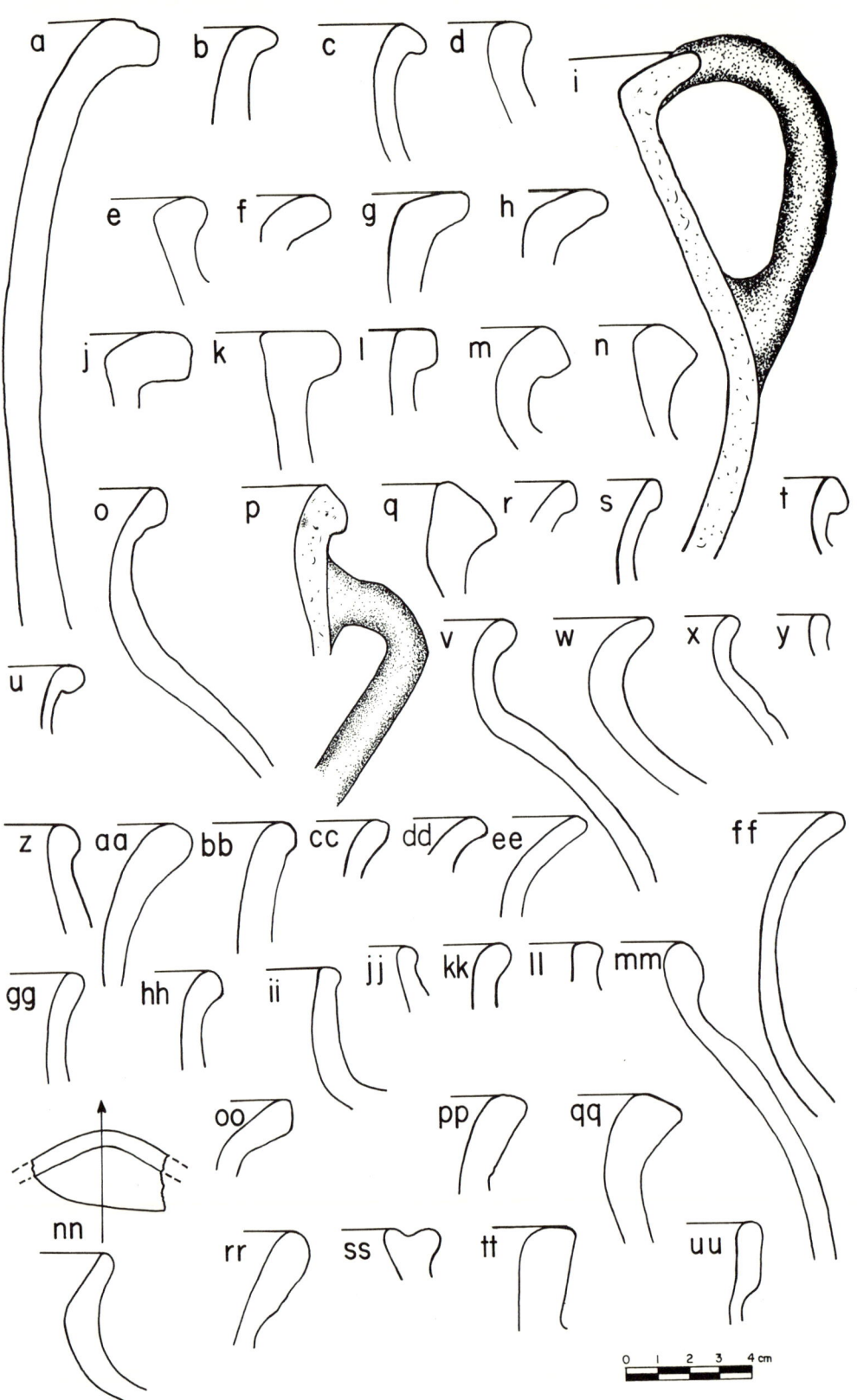

FIGURE 25 HITTITE PLAIN WARE

a. 054/8, Sq. A29. Exterior: brown. Core: black. Interior: buff. Rim diameter: 30 cm.
b. 054/8, Sq. B42. Exterior and interior: brown. Core: orange-buff. Rim diameter: 20 cm.
c. 055/4, Gen'l. Exterior and interior: buff-orange. Core: buff. Rim diameter: 8 cm.
d. 054/8, Sq. D22. Exterior and interior: brown. Core: orange. Rim diameter: 22 cm.
e. N52/7, Gen'l. Exterior and interior: buff. Core: gray center to buff. Rim diameter: 22 cm.
f. 054/8, Sq. C28. Exterior, core, and interior: orange-buff. Rim diameter: 22 cm.
g. 055/1, Sq. 29. Exterior and interior: red-brown. Core: brown. Rim diameter: 14 cm.
h. 054/8, Sq. D45. Exterior, core, and interior: orange. Rim diameter: 30 cm.
i. 055/1, Sq. 21. Exterior, core, and interior: orange. Rim diameter: 36 cm.
j. 054/8, Sq. D44. Exterior and interior: red-brown. Core: brown. Rim diameter: 32 cm.
k. 054/8, Sq. D30. Exterior and interior: brown. Core: buff. Rim diameter: 26 cm.
l. 054/8, Sq. C42. Exterior and interior: brown. Core: gray center to brown. Rim diameter: 20 cm.
m. 055/3, Sq. 51. Exterior and interior: buff. Core: gray-buff. Rim diameter: 22 cm.
n. 054/12, Sq. B14. Exterior: buff. Core: gray center to buff. Interior: buff-orange. Rim diameter: 10 cm.
o. 055/9, Gen'l. Exterior and core: buff-orange. Interior: orange. Rim diameter: 16 cm.
p. N55/1, Gen'l. Exterior and interior: buff. Core: buff-orange. Rim diameter: ?
q. 054/8, Sq. D44. Exterior: cream. Core: brown. Interior: buff. Rim diameter: 28 cm.
r. 054/8, Sq. A54. Exterior: brown. Core: orange. Interior: orange-red. Rim diameter: 22 cm.
s. N52/1, Sq. A18. Exterior, core, and interior: cream. Rim diameter: 20 cm.
t. 054/8, Sq. D11. Exterior: orange. Core: gray center to orange. Interior: buff. Rim diameter: 14 cm.
u. N53/1, Gen'l. Exterior and interior: buff. Core: orange center to buff. Rim diameter: 14 cm.
v. N52/1, Sq. B23. Exterior and interior: cream. Core: gray center to buff. Rim diameter: 16 cm.
w. 054/3, Sq. 9. Exterior and interior: buff-orange. Core: orange. Rim diameter: 10 cm.
x. 054/8, Sq. C29. Exterior: buff. Core: gray. Interior: red-brown. Rim diameter: 18 cm.
y. 054/8, Sq. A46. Exterior: orange-buff. Core and interior: orange. Rim diameter: 16 cm.
z. 054/2, Sq. 157. Exterior, core, and interior: cream. Rim diameter: 14 cm.
aa. 054/8, Sq. C84. Exterior, core, and interior: buff. Rim diameter: 16 cm.
bb. 054/8, Sq. D57. Exterior and interior: buff. Core: black center to buff. Rim diameter: 30 cm.
cc. 054/8, Sq. C9. Exterior and interior: buff. Core: gray. Rim diameter: 14 cm.
dd. 054/8, Sq. D21. Exterior and interior: orange-cream. Core: orange. Rim diameter: 12 cm.
ee. 054/8, Sq. A12. Exterior, core, and interior: white. Rim diameter: 16 cm.
ff. 054/1, Gen'l. Exterior and interior: buff-orange. Core: orange. Rim diameter: 20 cm.
gg. 054/8, Sq. A36. Exterior and interior: brown. Core: red-orange. Rim diameter: 26 cm.
hh. 054/2, Sq. 94. Exterior: cream-orange. Core and interior: cream. Rim diameter: 14 cm.
ii. 055/3, Sq. 69. Exterior, core, and interior: buff-orange. Rim diameter: 14 cm.
jj. 054/8, Sq. D67. Exterior, core, and interior: orange. Rim diameter: 10 cm.
kk. N52/1, Sq. A45. Exterior: buff-orange. Core and interior: buff-orange. Rim diameter: 16 cm.
ll. 054/2, Sq. 64. Exterior: buff. Core: gray center to brown. Interior: brown. Rim diameter: ?
mm. 055/9, Gen'l. Exterior, core, and interior: buff-orange. Rim diameter: 28 cm.
nn. 054/2, Sq. 156. Exterior: buff. Core: gray center to brown-orange. Interior: buff-brown. Rim diameter: ?
oo. 054/8, Sq. D55. Exterior and interior: buff. Core: orange. Rim diameter: 14 cm.
pp. 054/8, Sq. C17. Exterior: buff. Core and interior: orange. Rim diameter: 24 cm.
qq. 054/27, Sq. A23. Exterior and interior: red-brown. Core: orange. Rim diameter: 40+ cm?
rr. 054/8, Sq. A45. Exterior and interior: white. Core: cream. Rim diameter: 14 cm.
ss. 054/2, Sq. 54. Exterior and interior: buff. Core: orange-buff. Rim diameter: 22 cm.
tt. 055/8, Sq. 18. Exterior: buff-orange. Core and interior: gray. Rim diameter: 24 cm.
uu. 054/8, Sq. C92. Exterior: red-brown. Core and interior: brown. Rim diameter: 14 cm.

FIGURE 26

HITTITE PLAIN WARE

a. N52/1, Sq. B2. Exterior, core, and interior: buff-orange. Base diameter: 3 cm.
b. 054/2, Sq. 34. Exterior, core, and interior: cream-orange. Base diameter: 7 cm.
c. 054/2, Sq. 108. Exterior, core, and interior: red-brown. Base diameter: 12 cm.
d. N52/1, Sq. A19. Exterior, core, and interior: gray-cream. Base diameter: 10 cm.
e. N52/1, Sq. A38. Exterior and interior: buff-cream. Core: buff. Base diameter: 4 cm.
f. 054/1, Gen'l. Exterior, core, and interior: brown. Base diameter: 3.5 cm.
g. 054/8, Sq. C18. Exterior, core, and interior: cream-orange. Base diameter: 10 cm.
h. 055/1, Gen'l. Exterior: brown. Core: orange. Interior: buff. Base diameter: 12 cm.
i. 054/2, Sq. 92. Exterior and interior: buff. Core: orange. Base diameter: 14 cm.
j. 054/8, Sq. C91. Exterior and interior: brown. Core: orange. Base diameter: 10 cm.
k. 054/8, Sq. A41. Exterior and core: buff. Interior: buff-orange. Base diameter: 8 cm.
l. 054/8, Sq. D64. Exterior: buff-orange. Core: buff. Interior: red-brown. Base diameter: 12 cm.
m. 054/8, Sq. D66. Exterior: brown. Core: orange. Interior: red-brown. Base diameter: 12 cm.
n. 054/8, Gen'l. Exterior: cream-buff. Core: gray center to buff.
o. 055/1, Gen'l. Exterior and core: cream.
p. 054/8, Sq. D35. Exterior: cream-orange. Core: black.
q. 054/2, Sq. 97. Exterior: buff-orange. Core: buff.
r. 054/6, Sq. B35.
s. 054/8, Sq. D51. Exterior: red-brown. Core: buff. Interior: gray.
t. 054/2, Sq. 6. Exterior: buff-cream. Core and interior: buff-orange.
u. 055/1, Gen'l. Exterior, core, and interior: brown.

HITTITE FINE WARE

v. 055/1, Gen'l. Exterior and interior: buff burnished. Core: buff. Rim diameter: 22 cm.
w. 054/8, Sq. C22. Exterior and interior: buff burnished. Core: buff. Rim diameter: ?
x. 055/8, Sq. 14. Exterior and interior: buff-orange. Core: buff-orange. Rim diameter: ?
y. 055/1, Sq. 24. Exterior and interior: dirty buff-gray. Core: brown-gray. Rim diameter: 16 cm.
z. 054/21, Sq. 3. Exterior, core, and interior: buff. Rim diameter: 8 cm.
aa. 055/3, Sq. 13. Exterior, core, and interior: buff. Rim diameter: 6 cm.
bb. N52/2, Sq. A25. Exterior and interior: buff burnished. Core: gray center to buff. Rim diameter: 8 cm.
cc. 054/2, Sq. 6. Exterior and interior: buff-orange burnished. Core: buff. Rim diameter: 8 cm.
dd. 055/1, Gen'l. Exterior and interior: buff-orange burnished. Core: buff-orange. Rim diameter: 12 cm.
ee. 054/8, Sq. B20. Exterior and interior: buff-orange smoothed. Core: orange. Rim diameter: 8 cm.
ff. N51/1, Sq. A40. Exterior and interior: buff-orange smoothed. Core: buff-orange. Rim diameter: 14 cm.
gg. 054/8, Sq. D24. Exterior: buff smoothed. Core: buff-orange. Interior: orange smoothed. Rim diameter: ?
hh. 054/8, Sq. B29. Exterior and interior: buff burnished. Core: buff. Rim diameter: 10 cm.
ii. 054/1, Gen'l. Exterior and interior: buff-orange smoothed. Core: buff-orange. Rim diameter: 8 cm.
jj. 055/8, Sq. 16. Exterior: cream. Core: buff. Interior: cream-orange. Rim diameter: 8 cm.
kk. 054/8, Sq. C86. Exterior and interior: buff-orange burnished. Core: buff-orange. Rim diameter: 18 cm.
ll. 054/2, Sq. 162. Exterior and interior: orange burnished. Core: light brown. Rim diameter: ?
mm. 054/8, Sq. D65. Exterior and interior: buff-gray smoothed. Core: buff-gray. Rim diameter: 4 cm.
nn. 054/8, Sq. C85. Exterior and interior: buff-brown burnished. Core: orange. Rim diameter: 18 cm.
oo. 054/8, Sq. D81. Exterior and interior: buff-orange smoothed. Core: buff-orange. Rim diameter: 14 cm.
pp. 054/22, Gen'l. Exterior: light buff burnished. Core: buff-orange. Interior: buff-orange smoothed. Rim diameter: 28 cm.

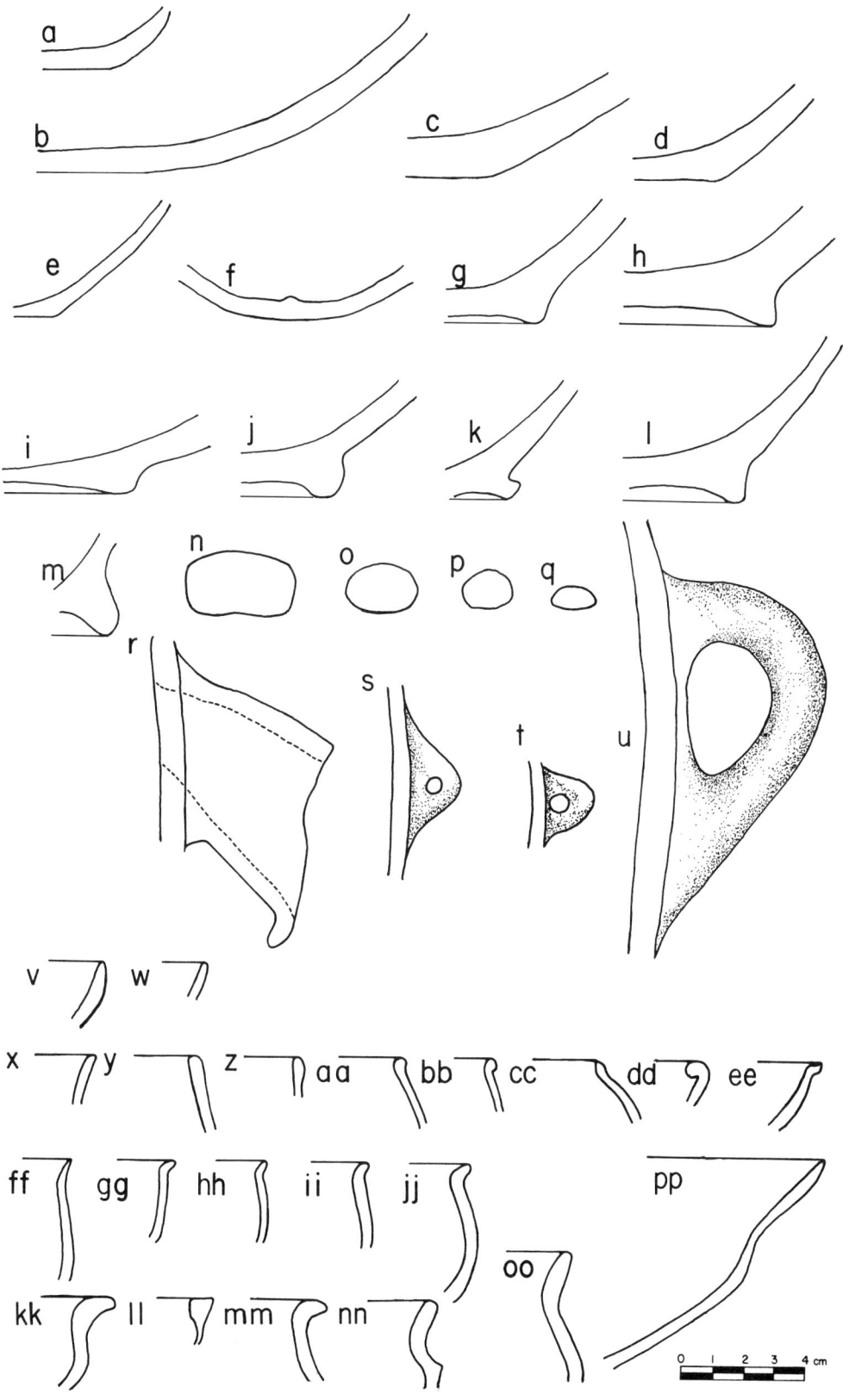

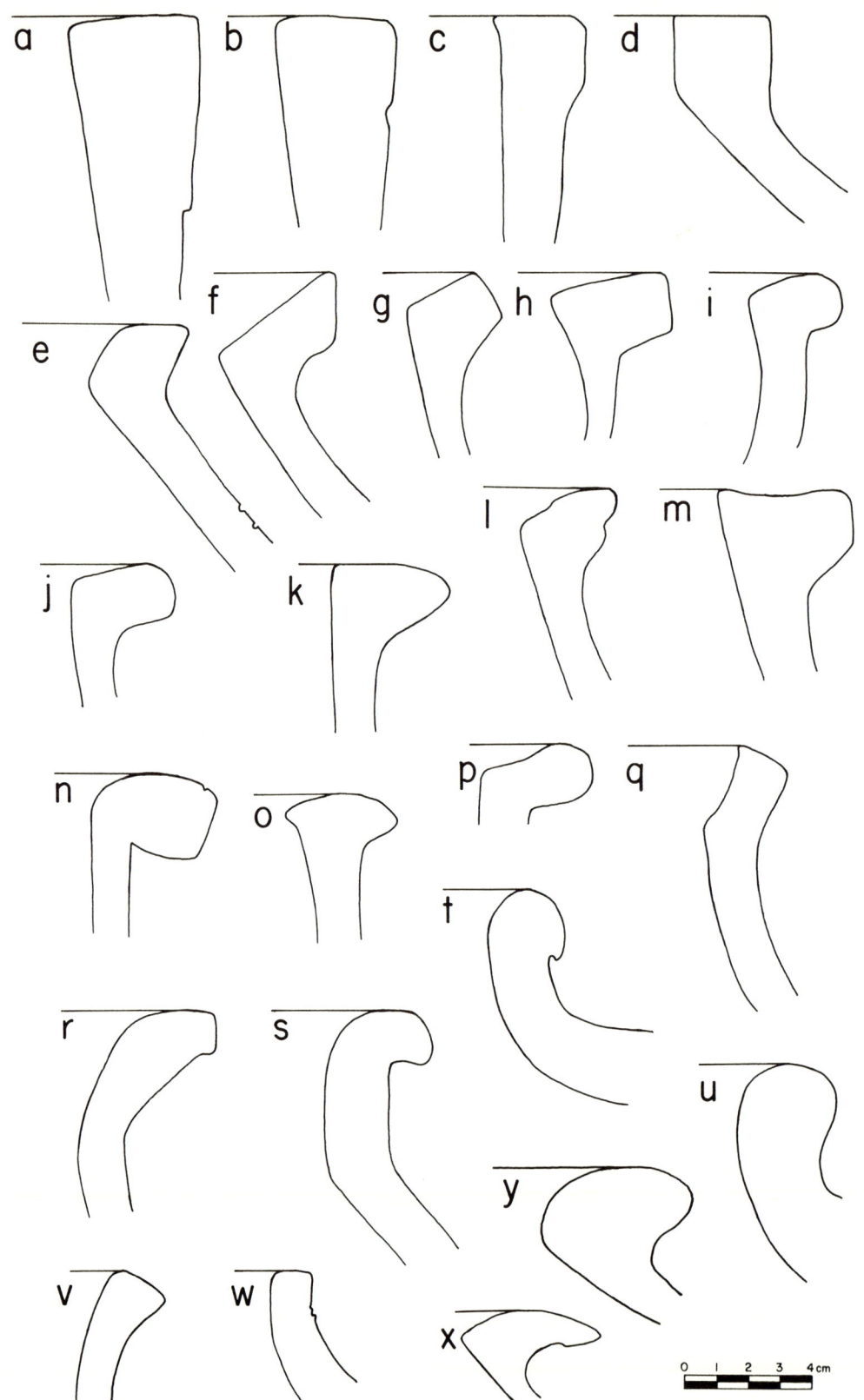

FIGURE 27 HITTITE THICK WARE

a. 054/2, Sq. 60. Exterior: buff–orange smoothed. Core: black. Interior: buff–orange. Rim diameter: ?

b. 054/2, Sq. 49. Exterior and interior: buff–orange burnished. Core: buff–orange. Rim diameter: ?

c. 054/9, Sq. B20. Exterior and interior: buff–orange burnished. Core: gray center to orange. Rim diameter: 30 cm.

d. 054/8, Sq. C40. Exterior and interior: buff–orange. Core: brown. Rim diameter: 40+ cm?

e. 054/8, Sq. C17. Exterior: red–brown smoothed. Core and interior: red–brown. Rim diameter: 32 cm.

f. 054/6, Sq. A13. Exterior and interior: brown burnished. Core: orange–brown. Rim diameter: 26 cm.

g. 055/4, Gen'l. Exterior and interior: buff–orange burnished. Core: brown. Rim diameter: 40+ cm?

h. 054/12, Sq. B8 Exterior and interior: buff–orange. Core: gray. Rim diameter: 28 cm.

i. 055/4, Gen'l. Exterior and interior: brown burnished. Core: buff. Rim diameter: 34 cm.

j. 055/4, Gen'l. Exterior: buff. Core: orange. Interior: buff–orange. Rim diameter: 32 cm.

k. 054/8, Sq. A60. Exterior and interior: buff–orange. Core: black center to orange. Rim diameter: 38 cm.

l. 055/4, Gen'l. Exterior: red–brown. Core: brown–buff. Interior: brown. Rim diameter: 34 cm.

m. 054/6, Sq. A7. Exterior: buff–brown. Core: gray–brown. Interior: buff. Rim diameter: 36 cm.

n. 054/8, Sq. C21. Exterior and interior: buff–orange smoothed. Core: buff–orange. Rim diameter: 40+ cm?

o. 055/4, Gen'l. Exterior: buff–brown. Core and interior: buff. Rim diameter: 34 cm. burnished. Rim diameter: 40+ cm.

r. 054/2, Sq. 90 Exterior, core, and interior: buff. Rim diameter: 34 cm.

s. 054/2, Sq. 135. Exterior and interior: buff–orange smoothed. Core: gray center to orange. Rim diameter: 28 cm.

t. 055/3, Sq. 46. Exterior, core, and interior: buff–orange. Rim diameter: ?

u. 055/3, Sq. 35. Exterior, core, and interior: buff. Rim diameter: 34 cm.

v. 055/4, Sq. 21. Exterior: brown burnished. Core: buff–orange. Interior: brown. Rim diameter: 30 cm.

w. 054/8, Sq. A47. Exterior and interior: orange. Core: buff center to orange. Rim diameter: ?

x. 054/2, Sq. 142. Exterior: brown burnished. Core: gray center to red–brown. Interior: brown smoothed. Rim diameter: 40+ cm?

y. 054/8, Sq. A36. Exterior and interior: brown burnished. Core: gray center to brown–buff. Rim diameter: ?

FIGURE 28

HITTITE THICK WARE
a. 054/2, Sq. 122. Exterior: red-brown. Core and interior: buff. Basal diameter: 12 cm.
b. 054/9, Sq. A7. Exterior: buff-orange burnished. Core and interior: buff. Basal diameter: ?
c. 054/2, Sq. 36. Exterior: brown burnished. Core: buff-orange. Interior: orange. Basal diameter: ?
d. 054/8, Sq. A33. Exterior and interior: buff-orange. Core: gray. Basal diameter: 16 cm.
e. 054/2, Gen'l. Exterior: buff-orange burnished. Core: orange.

HITTITE EXTERIOR WHEEL-MARKED WARE
f. 055/1, Gen'l. Exterior and interior: brown burnished. Core: red-brown. Rim diameter: ?
g. 054/4, Gen'l. Exterior and interior: buff smoothed. Core: black center to brown. Rim diameter: 10 cm.
h. 054/8, Sq. B26. Exterior and interior: buff smoothed. Core: buff. Rim diameter: 12 cm.

HITTITE BUFF-ORANGE BURNISHED WARE
i. 054/8, Sq. A39. Exterior: buff-orange. Core: gray center to buff. Interior: brown. Rim diameter: ?
j. 054/8, Sq. C28. Exterior, core, and interior: buff-orange. Rim diameter: ?
k. 054/8, Sq. C32. Exterior and interior: red-orange. Core: buff-orange. Rim diameter: ?
l. 055/1, Gen'l. Exterior and interior: buff-orange. Core: bright orange. Rim diameter: ?
m. 054/2, Sq. 56. Exterior and interior: brown-buff. Core: brown-orange. Rim diameter: ?
n. 054/8, Sq. C18. Exterior, core, and interior: buff-brown. Rim diameter: 20 cm.
o. 054/8, Sq. D47. Exterior and interior: buff-orange. Core: orange-brown. Rim diameter: ?
p. 054/8, Sq. C11. Exterior: buff-orange. Core and interior: orange-red. Rim diameter: ?
q. 054/8, Sq. D65. Exterior and interior: rust-orange. Core: orange-brown. Rim diameter: 16 cm.
r. 054/8, Sq. D17. Exterior and interior: buff-orange. Core: brown-orange. Rim diameter: ?
s. 054/2, Sq. 48. Exterior and interior: buff-brown. Core: light brown. Rim diameter: ?
t. 054/8, Sq. C27. Exterior, core, and interior: light buff. Rim diameter: 40+ cm?
u. 054/25, Sq. A6. Exterior and interior: red-brown. Core: buff-brown. Rim diameter: 20 cm.
v. 055/8, Sq. 25. Exterior: orange. Core and interior: buff-orange. Rim diameter: 18 cm?
w. 054/2, Sq. 176. Exterior, core, and interior: buff-brown. Rim diameter: 34 cm.
x. 054/7, Gen'l. Exterior and interior: light buff. Core: dark gray. Rim diameter: 24 cm.
y. 054/2, Sq. 124. Exterior and interior: light buff. Core: gray center to buff. Rim diameter: 22 cm.
z. 054/28, Gen'l. Exterior and interior: buff-orange. Core: orange. Rim diameter: 24 cm.
aa. 054/9, Sq. A11. Exterior and interior: white-buff. Core: buff. Rim diameter: 20 cm.
bb. 054/8, Sq. A52. Exterior and interior: light orange. Core: orange. Rim diameter: 24 cm.
cc. 054/9, Sq. C3. Exterior: light buff. Core: buff-brown. Interior: buff-orange. Rim diameter: 26 cm.
dd. 054/8, Sq. C47. Exterior and core: bright orange. Interior: buff. Rim diameter: ?
ee. 055/4, Sq. 13. Exterior and interior: light buff-orange. Rim diameter: ?
ff. 054/2, Sq. 64. Exterior and interior: light buff. Core: gray center to buff. Rim diameter: 26 cm.
gg. 054/8, Sq. A27. Exterior, core, and interior: bright orange. Rim diameter: ?
hh. 054/2, Sq. 74. Exterior: dark buff-brown. Core and interior: buff-brown. Rim diameter: 12 cm.
ii. 054/8, Sq. A71. Exterior, core, and interior: buff. Rim diameter: ?
jj. 054/9, Sq. B16. Exterior and interior: light buff-brown. Core: gray center to brown. Rim diameter: 16 cm.
kk. N52/1, Sq. A51. Exterior and interior: buff-brown. Core: gray center to orange. Rim diameter: 22 cm.
ll. 054/8, Sq. C30. Exterior, core, and interior: light buff. Rim diameter: 22 cm.
mm. 054/2, Sq. 65. Exterior and interior: light buff. Core: gray center to orange. Rim diameter: 16 cm.
nn. 055/8, Sq. 3. Exterior and interior: buff-brown. Core: gray center to brown. Rim diameter: ?
oo. 054/8, Sq. C92. Exterior: dark orange. Core: orange. Interior: buff-orange. Rim diameter: 24 cm.
pp. 054/8, Sq. D67. Exterior: orange-buff. Core: bright orange. Interior: orange. Rim diameter: ?
qq. 054/8, Sq. C43. Exterior and interior: orange. Core: bright orange. Rim diameter: 34 cm.
rr. 054/9, Sq. A9. Exterior and interior: light buff. Core: dark gray center to orange. Rim diameter: ?
ss. 054/8, Sq. B37. Exterior: light orange. Core: bright orange. Rim diameter: 26 cm.
tt. 054/8, Sq. C31. Exterior, core, and interior: orange. Rim diameter: 38 cm.
uu. 055/8, Sq. 14. Exterior and interior: light buff. Core: brown. Rim diameter: 24 cm.
vv. 054/4, Sq. 44. Exterior and interior: light buff over orange. Core: buff-orange. Rim diameter: 34 cm.
ww. 054/2, Sq. 142. Exterior and interior: light buff. Core: red-brown. Rim diameter: 20 cm.

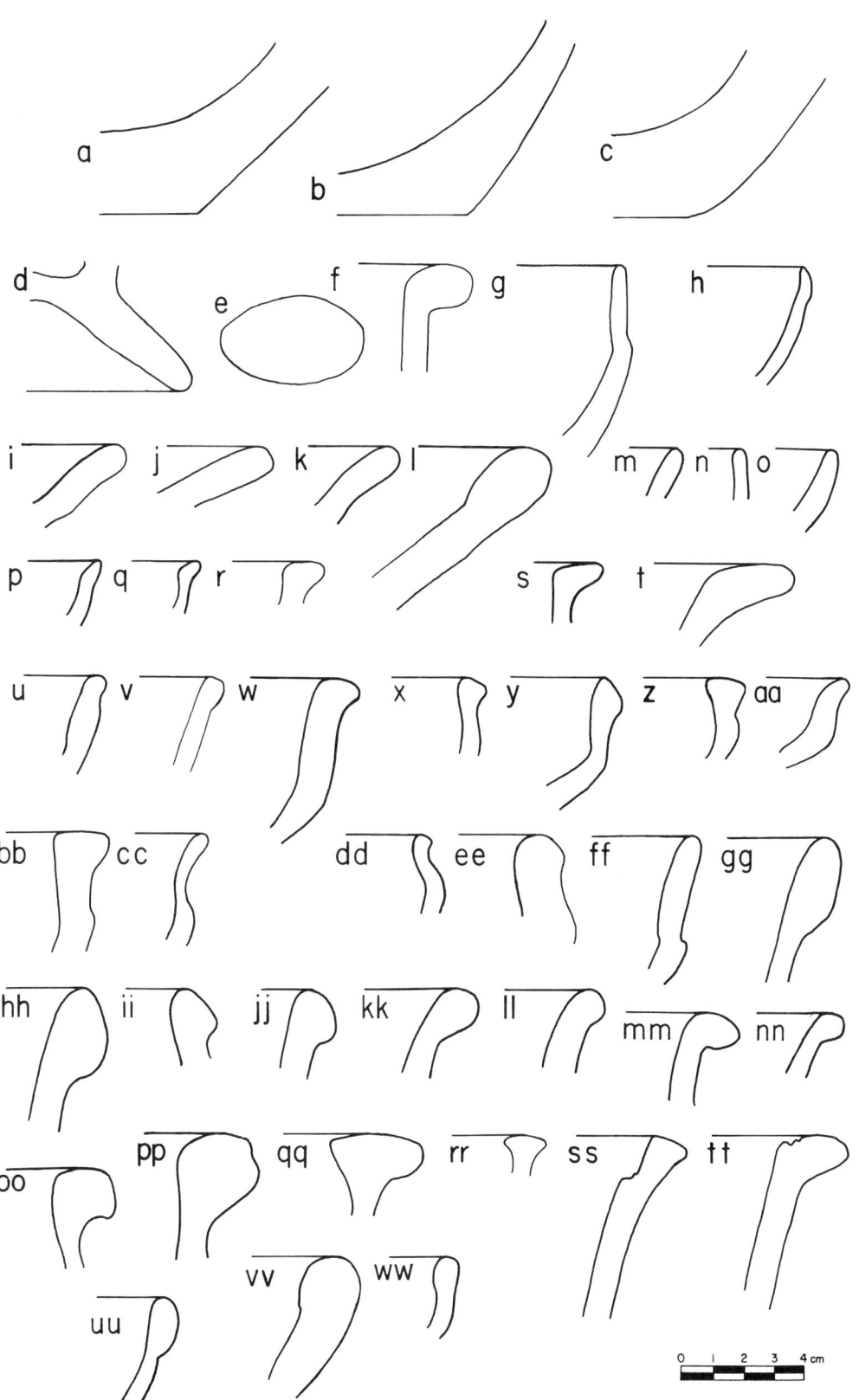

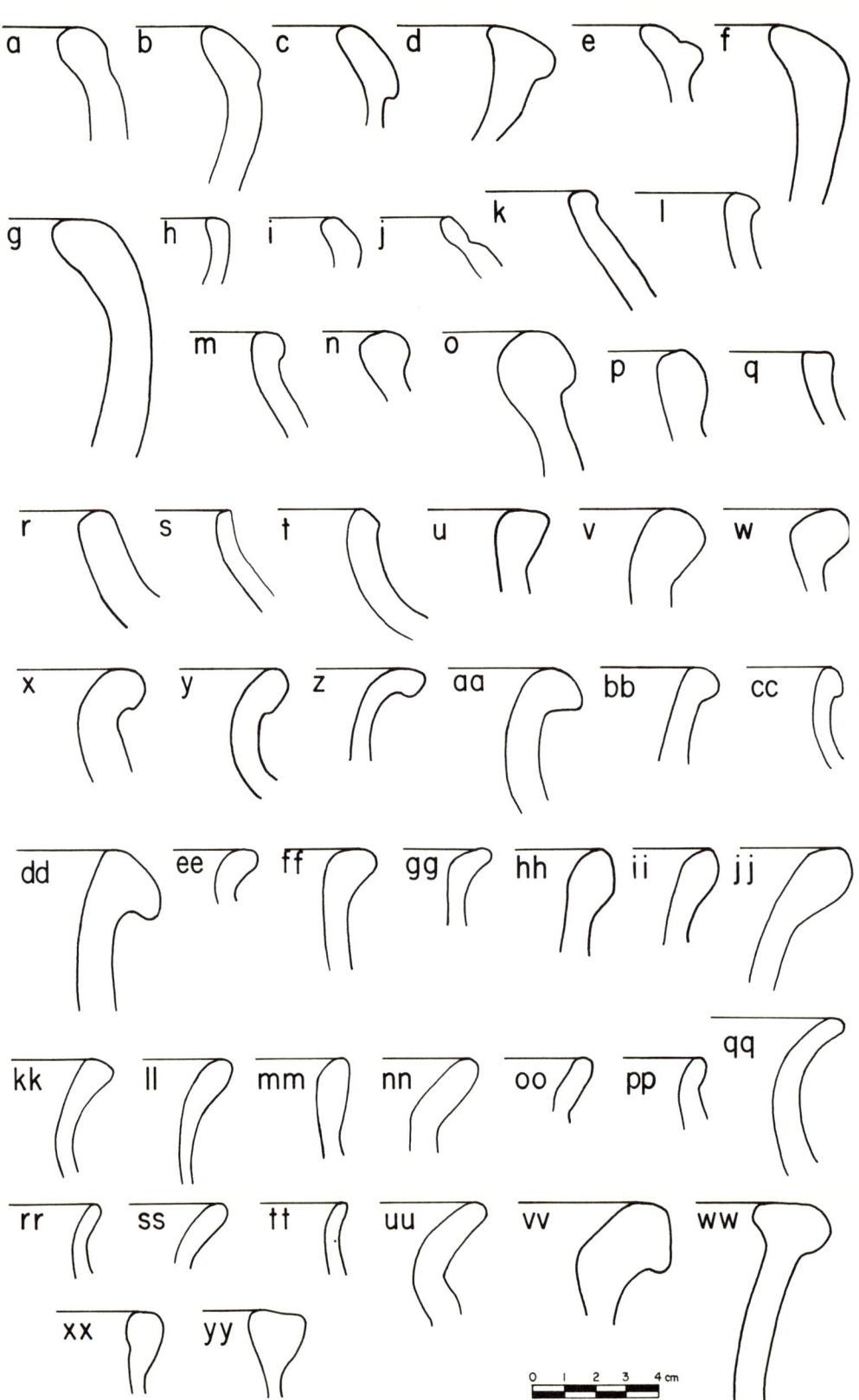

FIGURE 29 HITTITE BUFF–ORANGE BURNISHED WARE

a. 054/6, Sq. A1. Exterior: buff–white. Core buff–brown. Interior: buff–orange. Rim diameter: 28 cm.

b. 055/4, Sq. 27. Exterior: gray–buff. Core: gray center to buff. Interior: buff. Rim diameter: 22 cm.

c. 054/8, Sq. D76. Exterior and interior: buff. Core: brown–orange. Rim diameter; 34 cm.

d. 054/8, Sq. C85. Exterior and interior: buff–orange. Core: orange. Rim diameter: 28 cm.

e. 054/8, Sq. C49. Exterior and interior: buff. Core: red–brown. Rim diameter: 22 cm.

f. 054/2, Sq. 141. Exterior, core, and interior: light buff. Rim diameter: 30 cm.

g. 054/8, Sq. C24. Exterior and interior: light buff to cream. Core: orange–buff. Rim diameter: ?

h. 054/8, Sq. A56. Exterior, core, and interior: buff–brown. Rim diameter: 16 cm.

i. 054/8, Sq. C82. Exterior and interior: brown–orange. Core: gray center to orange. Rim diameter: 24 cm.

j. 054/8, Sq. A50. Exterior and interior: buff–brown. Core: dark gray center to brown. Rim diameter: ?

k. 054/27, Sq. A30. Exterior and interior: buff–brown. Core: orange–brown. Rim diameter: ?

l. 054/8, Sq. B8. Exterior: buff–cream. Core: bright orange. Interior: orange. Rim diameter: ?

m. 054/2, Sq. 157. Exterior, core, and interior: light buff. Rim diameter: 20 cm.

n. 054/2, Sq. 15. Exterior, core, and interior: brown. Rim diameter: 28 cm.

o. 054/2, Sq. 132. Exterior, core, and interior: buff–brown. Core: red–brown. Rim diameter: 32 cm.

p. 054/8, Sq. D68. Exterior, core, and interior: red–orange. Rim diameter: 24 cm.

q. 054/8, Sq. C49. Exterior and interior: buff–orange. Core: gray center to buff. Rim diameter: 26 cm.

r. 054/27, Sq. A11 Exterior and interior: light buff–brown. Core: brown–orange. Rim diameter: ?

s. 055/9, Sq. 40. Exterior, core, and interior: orange. Rim diameter: 34 cm.

t. 055/9, Sq. 38. Exterior, core, and interior: light buff. Rim diameter: 10 cm.

u. 054/8, Sq. A46. Exterior and interior: buff–brown. Core: gray. Rim diameter: 34 cm.

v. 054/2, Sq. 34. Exterior and interior: light buff. Core: light gray. Rim diameter: 26 cm.

w. 054/8, Sq. A51. Exterior and interior: brown. Core: light red–brown. Rim diameter: 30 cm?

x. 054/8, Sq. C56. Exterior and interior: red–orange. Core: gray center to orange. Rim diameter: 40+ cm.

y. N52/9, Sq. 3. Exterior and interior: orange–buff over orange. Core: bright orange. Rim diameter: ?

z. 054/14, Sq. H. Exterior: buff to light brown. Core: light orange–buff. Interior: light buff. Rim diameter: ?

aa. 054/2, Gen'l. Exterior, core, and interior: buff–brown. Rim diameter: 20 cm.

bb. 054/8, Sq. C48. Exterior: buff–orange. Core: bright orange. Interior: orange. Rim diameter: 30 cm.

cc. 054/8, Sq. C32. Exterior and interior: buff to brown. Core: gray center to orange. Rim diameter: 8 cm.

dd. 054/8, Sq. B33. Exterior, core, and interior: yellow–orange. Rim diameter: 32 cm.

ee. 054/8, Sq. A11. Exterior and interior: bright orange. Core: buff–orange. Rim diameter: 16 cm.

ff. 054/8, Sq. C22. Exterior, core, and interior: buff–orange. Rim diameter: ?

gg. 054/8, Sq. C89. Exterior and interior: buff–brown. Core: light orange. Rim diameter: 20 cm?

hh. 054/2, Sq. 177. Exterior, core, and interior: buff–brown. Rim diameter: ?

ii. 054/2, Sq. 122. Exterior, core, and interior: brown–orange. Rim diameter: 24 cm.

jj. 054/8, Sq. D40. Exterior: light buff. Core: orange–buff. Interior: yellow–orange. Rim diameter: 32 cm.

kk. 055/4, Gen'l. Exterior: buff–brown. Core: orange–buff. Interior: light buff. Rim diameter: 28 cm.

ll. 054/8, Gen'l. Exterior: buff. Core and interior: buff. Rim diameter: 10 cm.

mm. 054/8, Sq. C35. Exterior and interior: buff–brown. Core: pale orange–red. Rim diameter: 14 cm.

nn. 054/8, Sq. A22. Exterior and interior: orange–yellow. Rim diameter: 40 cm?

oo. 054/2, Sq. 182. Exterior: whitish buff. Core: pale orange–brown. Interior: brown–buff. Rim diameter: 24 cm.

pp. 054/8, Sq. C73. Exterior, core, and interior: buff. Rim diameter: 14 cm.

qq. 054/8, Sq. C64. Exterior and interior: buff–brown. Core: gray center to orange. Rim diameter: 16 cm?

rr. 054/8, Sq. C37. Exterior and interior: buff–orange. Core: red–orange. Rim diameter: 10 cm.

ss. 054/8, Sq. C84. Exterior and interior: orange. Core: gray center to orange. Rim diameter: ?

tt. 054/8, Sq. D22. Exterior and core: orange–brown. Interior: orange. Rim diameter: 18 cm.

uu. 054/8, Sq. A42. Exterior and interior: red–brown. Core: brown. Rim diameter: 26 cm.

vv. 054/8, Sq. C5. Exterior and interior: buff. Core: gray. Rim diameter: 18 cm?

ww. 054/2, Sq. 84. Exterior and interior: buff–brown. Core: brown. Rim diameter: 26 cm.

xx. 054/8, Sq. A47. Exterior, core, and interior: red–orange. Rim diameter: 16 cm.

yy. 054/3, Sq. 20. Exterior and interior: buff–orange. Core: bright orange. Rim diameter: 28 cm.

FIGURE 30

HITTITE BUFF–ORANGE BURNISHED WARE

a. 054/8, Sq. D72. Exterior and interior: light buff. Core: gray center to orange.

b. 054/8, Sq. D60. Exterior, core, and interior: white–buff.

c. 054/8, Sq. D51. Exterior and interior: light buff. Core: gray center to buff.

d. 054/8, Sq. A31. Exterior: white–buff. Core: gray center to buff. Interior: light gray.

e. 054/8, Sq. D86. Exterior, core, and interior: orange–red.

f. 054/8, Sq. D68. Exterior: buff. Core: gray center to orange.

g. 054/2, Sq. 125. Exterior and core: buff–orange.

h. 054/8, Sq. C89. Exterior: light buff. Core: orange–buff.

i. 054/2, Gen'l. Exterior, core, and interior: light buff.

j. 054/8, Sq. C18. Exterior: light buff. Core: buff to light gray. Interior: gray.

k. 054/8, Sq. B58. Exterior and interior: buff–brown. Core: light buff.

l. 054/9, Sq. A18. Exterior: white–buff. Core: gray center to buff. Interior: orange–buff.

m. 054/2, Sq. 115. Exterior: white–buff. Core: gray center to buff. Interior: buff.

n. 054/8, Sq. D68. Exterior: light buff. Core: buff to orange. Interior: light orange.

o. 054/8, Sq. C33. Exterior and interior: brown. Core: light gray.

p. 054/8, Sq. A47. Exterior: brown–orange. Core: gray center to orange. Interior: red–brown.

q. 054/9, Sq. C15. Exterior: white–buff. Core: gray center to orange. Interior: ?

HITTITE CHAFF FACED WARE

r. 054/8, Sq. D41. Exterior and interior: orange burnished. Core: orange–brown. Rim diameter: 28 cm.

s. 054/8, Sq. C18. Exterior and interior: cream, slightly burnished. Core: orange–buff. Rim diameter: 26 cm?

t. 054/8, Sq. C29. Exterior and interior: cream. Core: orange–buff. Rim diameter: 23 cm?

u. 054/9, Sq. A5. Exterior and interior: orange smoothed. Core: buff. Rim diameter: 24 cm?

v. 054/8, Sq. C18. Exterior and interior: brown smoothed. Core: buff–brown. Rim diameter: 28 cm?

w. 054/8, Sq. C20. Exterior and Interior: cream. Core: dark gray center to buff. Rim diameter: 40 cm.

x. 054/8, Sq. C49. Exterior and interior: red–brown. Core: black center to brown–buff. Rim diameter: 38 cm?

y. 054/8, Sq. C19. Exterior, core, and interior: gray. Rim diameter: ?

z. 055/1, Gen'l. Exterior: cream. Core: buff to orange. Interior: orange. Rim diameter: 26 cm.

aa. 055/8, Gen'l. Exterior and interior: orange, lightly burnished. Core: orange. Rim diameter: 14 cm.

bb. 054/8, Sq. D37. Exterior and interior: red–brown. Core: black center to brown–buff. Rim diameter: 26 cm.

cc. 054/8, Sq. C26. Exterior and interior: red–brown. Core: black center to brown–buff. Rim diameter: 38 cm?

dd. 054/9, Sq. C8. Exterior and interior: brown burnished. Core: gray center to buff. Rim diameter: 25 cm.

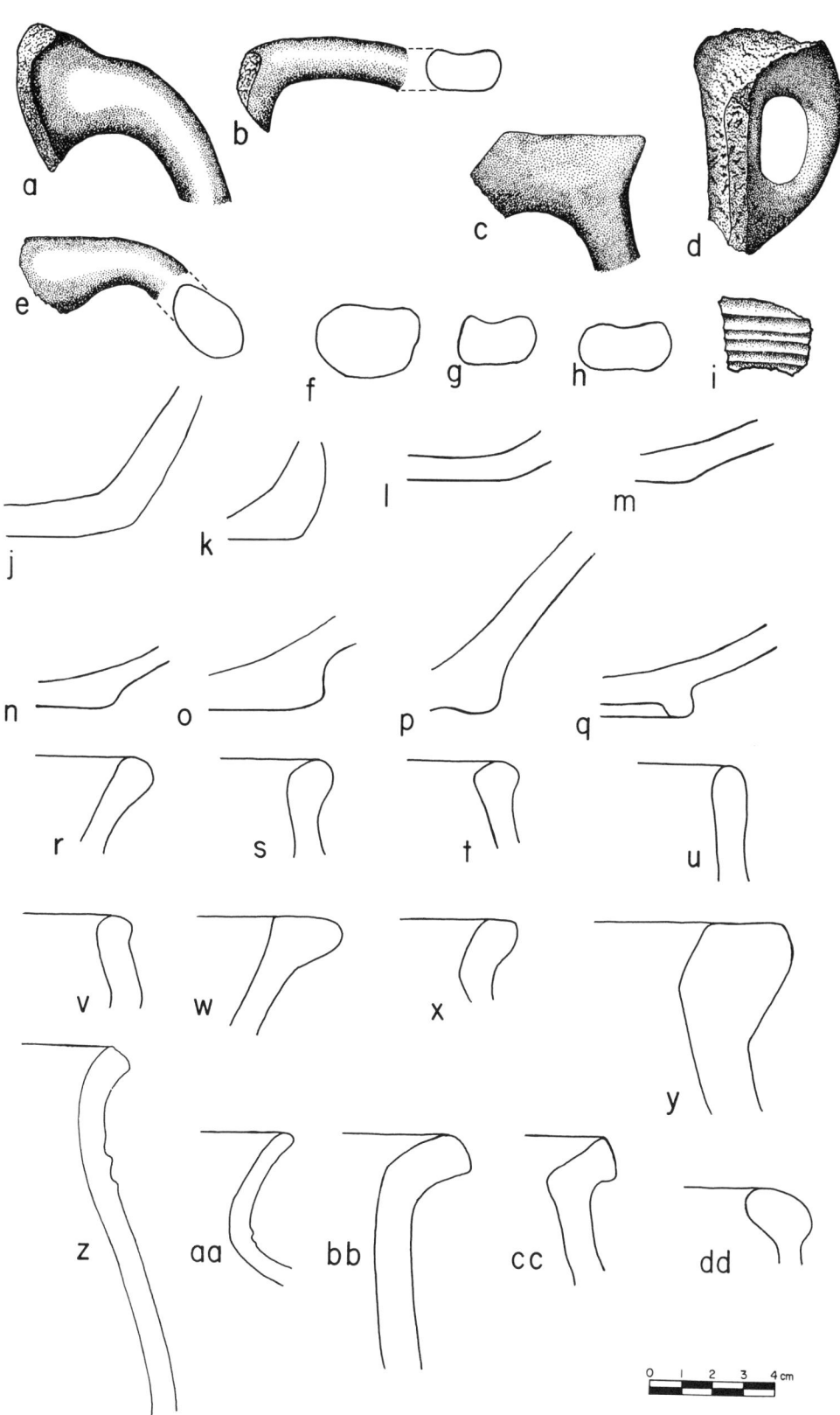

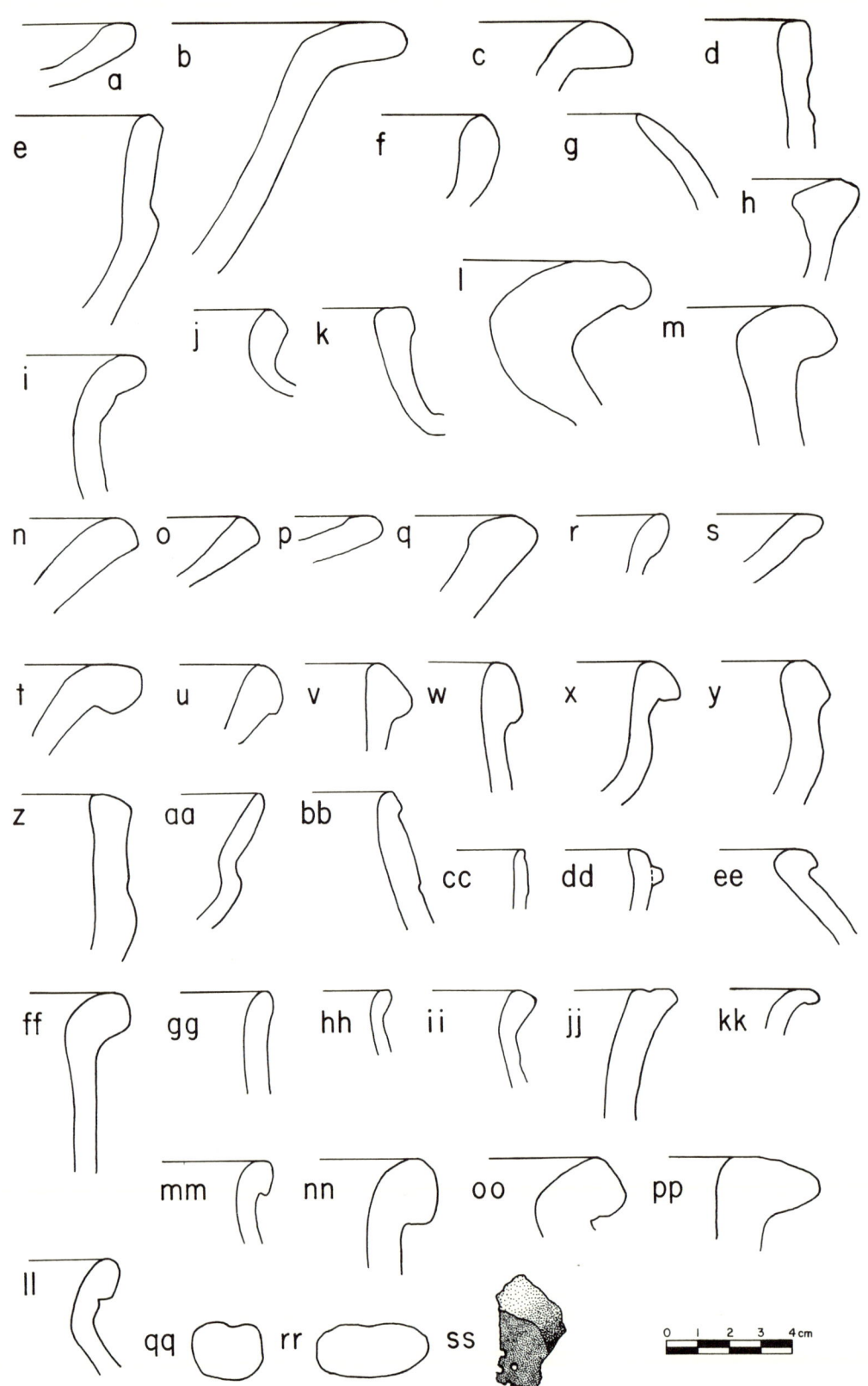

FIGURE 31

HITTITE ORANGE SMOOTHED WARE

a. 055/1, Gen'l. Exterior and interior: buff–orange. Core: buff. Rim diameter: 32 cm.
b. 055/1, Gen'l. Exterior and interior: orange wheelmarked. Core: buff–orange. Rim diameter: 32 cm.
c. 054/2, Sq. 42. Exterior and interior: dark orange. Core: orange. Rim diameter: 32 cm.
d. 054/8, Sq. C85. Exterior and interior: buff–orange. Core: buff. Rim diameter: 5 cm.
e. 054/8, Sq. C29. Exterior, core, and interior: orange. Rim diameter: 19 cm.
f. 054/8, Sq. A27. Exterior and core: orange. Interior: orange wheelmarked. Rim diameter: 10 cm.
g. 055/1, Gen'l Exterior, core, and interior: orange. Rim diameter: 18 cm.
h. 054/2, Gen'l. Exterior and interior: buff–orange. Core: buff. Rim diameter: 38 cm.
i. 055/1, Gen'l. Exterior and interior: buff–orange. Core: buff. Rim diameter: 18 cm.
j. 055/1, Gen'l. Exterior and interior: orange. Core: buff–orange. Rim diameter: 16 cm.
k. 054/8, Sq. D64. Exterior and interior: dark orange. Core: orange. Rim diameter: 16 cm.
l. 054/8, Sq. D44. Exterior and interior: dark orange. Core: black center to orange–brown. Rim diameter: 34 cm?
m. 054/8, Sq. C78. Exterior, core, and interior: orange. Rim diameter: 25 cm.

HITTITE RED–BROWN BURNISHED WARE

for n–ss Exterior: red–brown burnished. Core: gray center to orange–buff or orange–brown. Interior: red–brown.

n. 054/2, Sq. 138. Rim diameter: 26 cm?
o. 054/8, Sq. B63. Rim diameter: 22 cm.
p. 054/8, Sq. A43. Rim diameter: 32 cm?
q. 054/8, Sq. A36. Rim diameter: 38 cm.
r. 054/9, Sq. C19. Rim diameter: 5 cm.
s. 054/8, Sq. C35. Rim diameter: 23 cm.
t. 054/8, Sq. D15. Rim diameter: 26 cm.
u. 054/8, Sq. C83. Rim diameter: ?
v. 054/8, Sq. C54. Rim diameter: 8 cm.
w. 054/8, Sq. C62. Rim diameter: 20 cm.
x. 055/8, Sq. 20. Rim diameter: 22 cm?
y. 054/8, Sq. C84. Rim diameter: 26 cm.
z. 054/8, Sq. A33. Rim diameter: 24 cm.
aa. 054/9, Sq. C8. Rim diameter: 24 cm.
bb. 054/8, Sq. A48. Rim diameter: ?
cc. 054/2, Sq. 110. Rim diameter: 14 cm?
dd. 054/8, Sq. A67. Rim diameter: 20 cm.
ee. 054/8, Sq. B31. Rim diameter: 10 cm.
ff. 054/9, Sq. C6. Rim diameter: 22 cm.
gg. 054/8, Sq. A51. Rim diameter: 18 cm?
hh. 054/8, Sq. C36. Rim diameter: 12 cm.
ii. 054/8, Sq. C46. Rim diameter: 18 cm.
jj. 054/8, Sq. D5. Rim diameter: 34 cm.
kk. 054/8, Sq. C38. Rim diameter: 24 cm?
ll. 054/8, Sq. D22. Rim diameter: 18 cm.
mm. 054/8, Sq. D69. Rim diameter: 21 cm.
nn. 054/8, Sq. C24. Rim diameter: 27 cm.
oo. 054/8, Sq. D34. Rim diameter: 40+ cm?
pp. 054/8, Sq. D44. Rim diameter: 38 cm.
qq. 054/8, Sq. D54.
rr. 054/9, Sq. B19.
ss. 054/2, Sq. 166.

FIGURE 32

HITTITE BROWN BURNISHED WARE

Exterior and interior surfaces of all sherds on this figure are brown unless otherwise noted.

a. 054/3, Sq. 11. Exterior: gray-brown. Core: brown. Rim diameter: ?
b. 054/8, Sq. D17. Exterior and interior: buff-brown. Core: light brown. Rim diameter: ?
c. 054/8, Sq. C28. Core: light brown. Rim diameter: ?
d. 055/1, Sq. 21. Interior: brown smoothed. Core brown. Rim diameter: 16 cm.
e. 054/6, Sq. B8. Core: light brown. Rim diameter: 16 cm.
f. 054/8, Sq. D14. Core and interior: red-brown. Rim diameter: 30 cm.
g. 054/2, Gen'l. Core: gray center to light brown. Rim diameter: 16 cm.
h. 054/8, Sq. C84. Core: red-brown. Rim diameter: 38 cm.
i. 054/2, Sq. 74. Core: light brown. Rim diameter: 30 cm.
j. 054/8, Sq. C33. Core: black center to brown. Rim diameter: 40 cm.
k. 054/2, Gen'l. Core: gray center to red-brown. Rim diameter: 32 cm.
l. 054/3, Sq. 20. Core: gray center to brown. Rim diameter: 20 cm.
m. 054/6, Sq. B29. Core: gray. Rim diameter: ?
n. 055/4, Sq. 14. Core: brown. Rim diameter: 14 cm.
o. 054/8, Sq. C58. Core: orange. Rim diameter: 24 cm.
p. 054/9, Sq. B16. Interior: weathered. Core: gray center to light brown. Rim diameter: 34 cm.
q. 054/8, Sq. C35. Exterior, core, and interior: red-brown. Rim diameter: 20 cm.
r. 054/8, Sq. D58. Exterior: red-brown. Core: dark brown. Rim diameter: 22 cm.
s. 054/8, Sq. D70. Core: brown. Rim diameter: ?
t. 054/9, Sq. A6. Core: light brown. Rim diameter: 24 cm.
u. 055/4, Sq. 25. Core: buff-orange. Rim diameter: 26 cm.
v. 054/2, Sq. 177. Core: gray. Rim diameter: 26 cm.
w. 054/2, Sq. 147. Core: light brown. Rim diameter: ?
x. 054/6, Sq. B15. Core: light brown. Rim diameter: 20 cm.
y. 054/9, Sq. A6. Core: gray center to brown. Rim diameter: ?
z. 054/8, Sq. D52. Core: red-brown. Rim diameter: ?
aa. 054/8, Sq. C31. Core: light brown. Rim diameter: 12 cm.
bb. 054/6, Sq. A1. Core: gray center to brown. Rim diameter: ?
cc. 054/8, Sq. C58. Exterior and interior: light brown. Core: gray center to red-brown. Rim diameter: 24 cm.
dd. 054/2, Sq. 128. Core: gray center to red-brown. Rim diameter: 30 cm.
ee. 054/11, Sq. A4. Core: black. Rim diameter: ?
ff. 054/8, Sq. A15. Interior: light brown. Core: red-brown. Rim diameter: 18 cm.
gg. 054/8, Sq. A43. Core: light brown. Rim diameter: ?
hh. 054/2, Sq. 113. Exterior and interior: red-brown. Core: gray center to red-brown. Rim diameter: 22 cm.
ii. 054/2, Sq. 132. Core: gray center to brown. Rim diameter: 14 cm.
jj. 054/2, Sq. 75. Core: brown. Rim diameter: ?
kk. 054/8, Sq. A69. Core: red-brown. Rim diameter: 26 cm.
ll. 054/2, Sq. 147. Exterior and interior: buff-brown. Core: gray center to brown. Rim diameter: 38 cm?
mm. 054/8, Sq. A40. Core: gray. Rim diameter: ?
nn. 054/8, Sq. A45. Core: red-orange. Rim diameter: 22 cm.
oo. 054/2, Sq. 8. Core: brown. Rim diameter: ?
pp. 054/8, Sq. D54. Exterior: Damaged. Core: brown. Rim diameter: 26 cm.
qq. 054/8, Sq. A59. Core: light brown. Rim diameter: 28 cm.
rr. 054/8, Sq. C52. Core: orange. Rim diameter: 18 cm.
ss. 054/2, Sq. 46. Core: brown. Rim diameter: 20 cm.
tt. 054/8, Sq. C82. Core: brown. Rim diameter: ?
uu. 054/9, Sq. B15. Core: orange. Rim diameter: 26 cm.
vv. 054/8, Sq. D51. Core: light brown. Rim diameter: 14 cm.
ww. 054/8, Gen'l. Core: brown. Rim diameter: 22 cm.
xx. 054/8, Sq. A45. Core: red-orange. Rim diameter: 18 cm.
yy. 054/8, Sq. A23. Core: brown. Rim diameter: 16 cm.
zz. 054/8, Sq. D62. Core: light brown. Rim diameter: 38 cm.
aaa. 054/2, Sq. 64. Core: light brown. Rim diameter: ?
bbb. 054/2, Sq. 5. Exterior: brown-red. Core: light brown. Interior: brown smoothed.
ccc. 054/9, Sq. A18. Exterior: buff-brown. Core: red-brown. Interior: weathered.
ddd. 054/8, Gen'l. Core: orange center to light brown.
eee. 054/2, Sq. 79. Core: light brown.

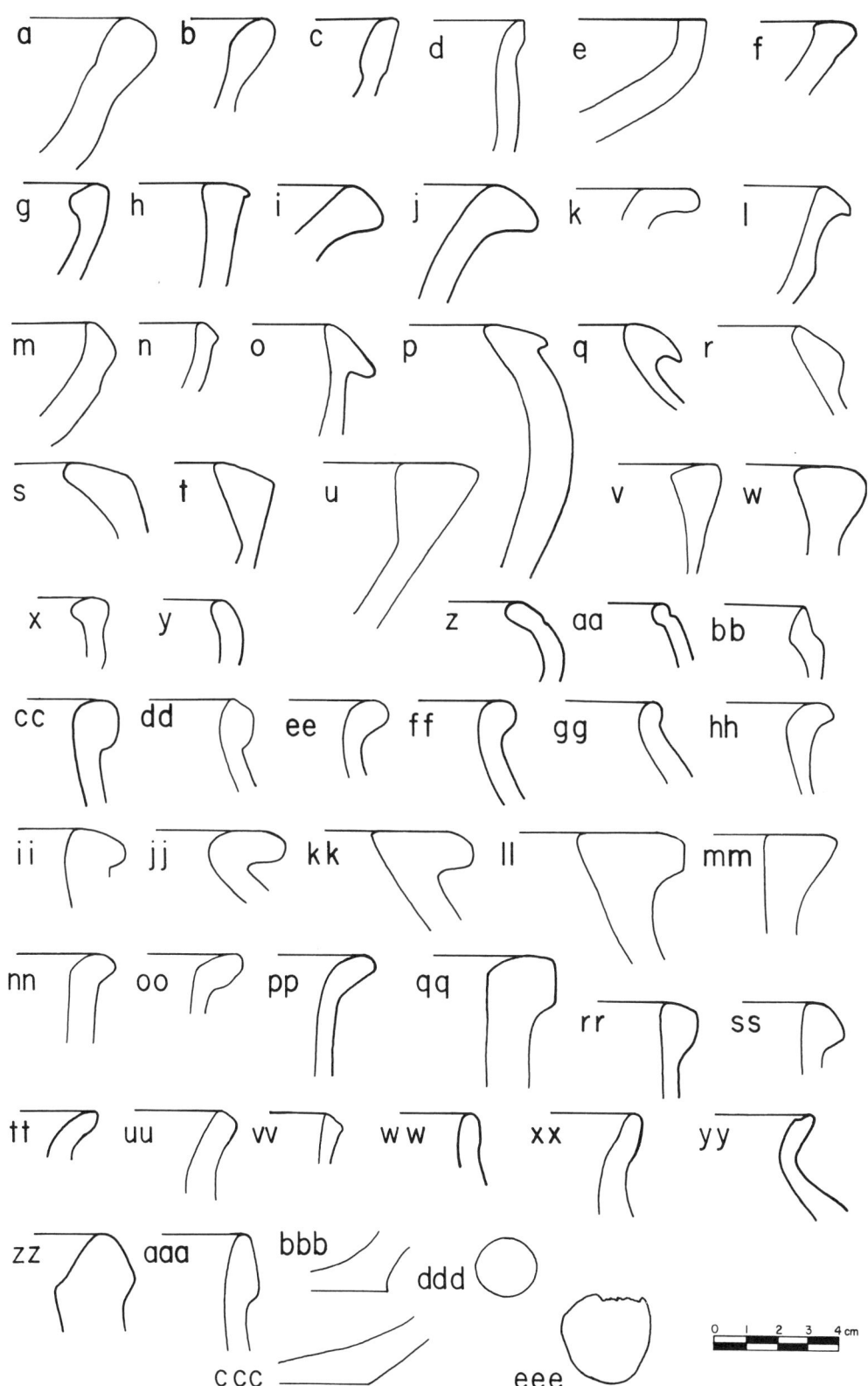

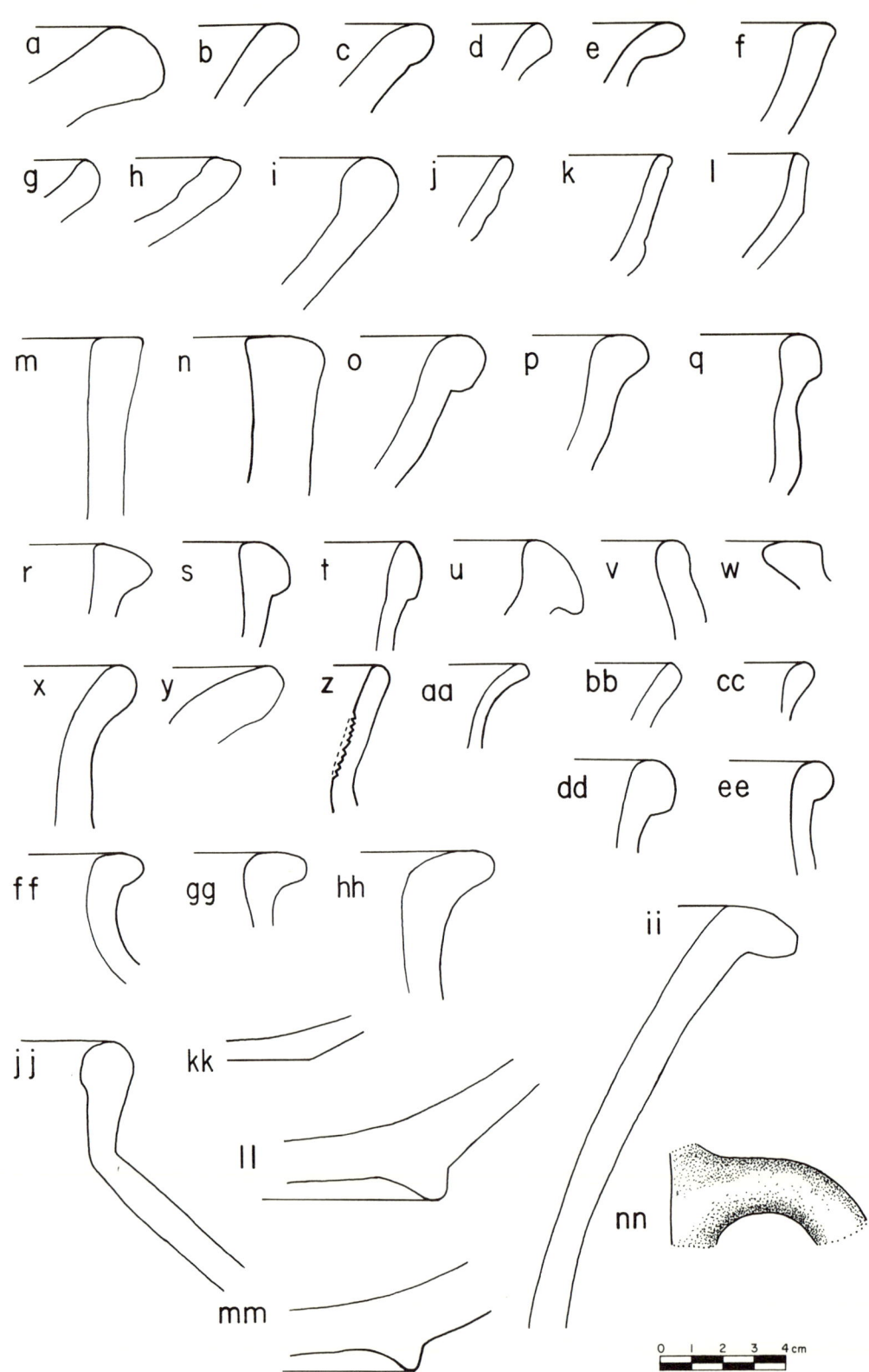

FIGURE 33 HITTITE WHITE SLIPPED WARE

Exterior and interior surfaces of all sherds on this figure are white slipped unless otherwise noted.

a. 054/2, Sq. 98. Core: orange. Rim diameter: 16 cm.
b. 054/8, Sq. D49. Interior: orange. Core: buff. Rim diameter: 34 cm.
c. 054/2, Sq. 96. Interior: gray. Core: black. Rim diameter: 16 cm.
d. 054/8, Sq. A54. Core: cream. Rim diameter: 14 cm.
e. N52/1, Sq. A16. Core: orange. Rim diameter: 14 cm.
f. 054/2, Sq. 127. Core: gray. Rim diameter: 18 cm.
g. 054/2, Sq. 22. Core: cream. Rim diameter: 22 cm.
h. 054/2, Sq. 98. Core: orange. Rim diameter: 10 cm.
i. 054/8, Sq. C34. Core: gray. Rim diameter: 20 cm.
j. 054/8, Sq. C34. Core and interior: buff. Rim diameter: 8 cm.
k. 054/27, Sq. A3. Exterior and interior: white-cream. Core: cream. Rim diameter: 26 cm.
l. 054/8, Sq. D47. Core and interior: buff. Rim diameter: 8 cm.
m. 054/12, Sq. A28. Exterior and interior: cream-buff. Core: black. Rim diameter: 12 cm.
n. 054/8, Sq. D54. Interior: buff. Core: orange. Rim diameter: 38 cm.
o. 054/8, Sq. A28. Interior: orange. Core: gray center to orange. Rim diameter: 28 cm.
p. 054/8, Sq. C91. Core: orange. Interior: buff. Rim diameter: 24 cm.
q. 054/1, Gen'l. Core: white. Rim diameter: 24 cm.
r. 054/2, Sq. 136. Core: buff. Rim diameter: 24 cm.
s. 054/9, Sq. 6. Core and interior: buff. Rim diameter: 24 cm.
t. 054/8, Sq. D13. Core: orange. Rim diameter: 8 cm.
u. 054/24, Sq. A20. Core: black. Rim diameter: 38 cm.
v. 054/2, Sq. A5. Core: black center to buff. Rim diameter: ?
w. 054/9, Sq. A6. Core and interior: buff. Rim diameter: 38 cm.
x. 054/2, Sq. 131. Core: orange. Rim diameter: 12 cm.
y. 055/8, Sq. 14. Core: gray. Rim diameter: 36 cm.
z. 054/8, Sq. C34. Core and interior: red-brown. Rim diameter: 14 cm.
aa. 054/2, Sq. 114. Core and interior: buff-orange. Rim diameter: 14 cm.
bb. 054/2, Sq. 123. Core: buff. Rim diameter: 12 cm.
cc. 054/8, Sq. C37. Core: buff. Rim diameter: 6 cm.
dd. 054/8, Sq. D22. Core: orange. Rim diameter: 24 cm.
ee. 055/9, Sq. 25. Core: orange-buff. Interior: cream. Rim diameter: 18 cm.
ff. 054/2, Gen'l. Core and interior: buff. Rim diameter: 26 cm.
gg. 054/8, Sq. D75. Core: buff. Interior: cream-orange. Rim diameter: 14 cm.
hh. 054/4, Gen'l. Core and interior: orange. Rim diameter: 24 cm.
ii. 055/1, Sq. 17. Core: gray center to brown. Interior: red-brown. Rim diameter: 40 cm.
jj. 055/8, Sq. 19. Core: black center to gray-brown. Rim diameter: 32 cm.
kk. 054/2, Sq. 6. Core and interior: orange. Basal diameter: 6 cm.
ll. 054/8, Sq. A45. Core and interior: orange. Basal diameter: 12 cm.
mm. 054/2, Sq. 65. Core: black. Interior: gray. Rim diameter: 14 cm.
nn. 054/8, Sq. D53. Core: orange. Interior: red-brown.

FIGURE 34

HITTITE PAINTED WARE

a. 054/12, Gen'l. Exterior and interior: buff plain, red paint. Core: buff-brown. Rim diameter: 18 cm.

b. 054/8, Sq. A12. Exterior: orange smoothed, brown paint. Core: buff-orange. Interior: orange smoothed. Rim diameter: 14 cm.

c. 054/2, Sq. 8. Exterior and interior: buff smoothed, light red paint. Core: buff. Rim diameter: 10 cm.

d. 054/8, Sq. A26. Exterior: buff smoothed, red paint. Core: buff. Interior: buff smoothed. Rim diameter: 8 cm.

e. 054/8, Sq. C24. Exterior: brown burnished, dark red paint. Dot of paint on lip. Core: buff. Interior: buff burnished. Rim diameter: ?

f. 054/2, Sq. 93 Exterior and interior: cream slip, red paint. Core: buff-orange. Rim diameter: 14 cm?

g. 054/2, Sq. 157. Exterior: cream slip on gray, red paint. Core: black center to gray. Interior: cream slip on gray. Rim diameter: 18 cm.

h. N52/2, Sq. B28. Exterior: cream burnished, red paint. Core: buff. Interior: cream, paint on inside of lip. Rim diameter: 24 cm.

i. 054/8, Sq. D60. Exterior: cream slip, light red paint. Core: gray center to buff. Interior: cream slip. Rim diameter: 16 cm.

j. 055/9, Sq. 22. Exterior and interior: light orange smoothed, light red paint. Core: buff. Rim diameter: 13 cm.

k. 054/8, Sq. C29. Exterior and interior: buff-orange smoothed. Core: buff-orange. Lip: red paint. Rim diameter: 10 cm.

l. 054/2, Sq. 74. Exterior: buff burnished, red paint. Core: buff. Interior: buff burnished. Rim diameter: 14 cm.

m. 055/8, Gen'l. Exterior and interior: buff slipped. Core: gray center to buff. Lip: red paint. Rim diameter: 32 cm.

n. 054/2, Gen'l. Exterior and interior: cream slip, red paint. Core: orange-brown. Rim diameter: 40 cm.

o. 054/4, Gen'l. Exterior: buff, red paint. Core and interior: buff. Neck diameter: 6 cm.

p. 054/2, Sq. 8. Exterior: red paint. Core and interior: gray. Base diameter: 12 cm.

q. 054/2, Sq. 118. Exterior: red paint. Core and interior: buff.

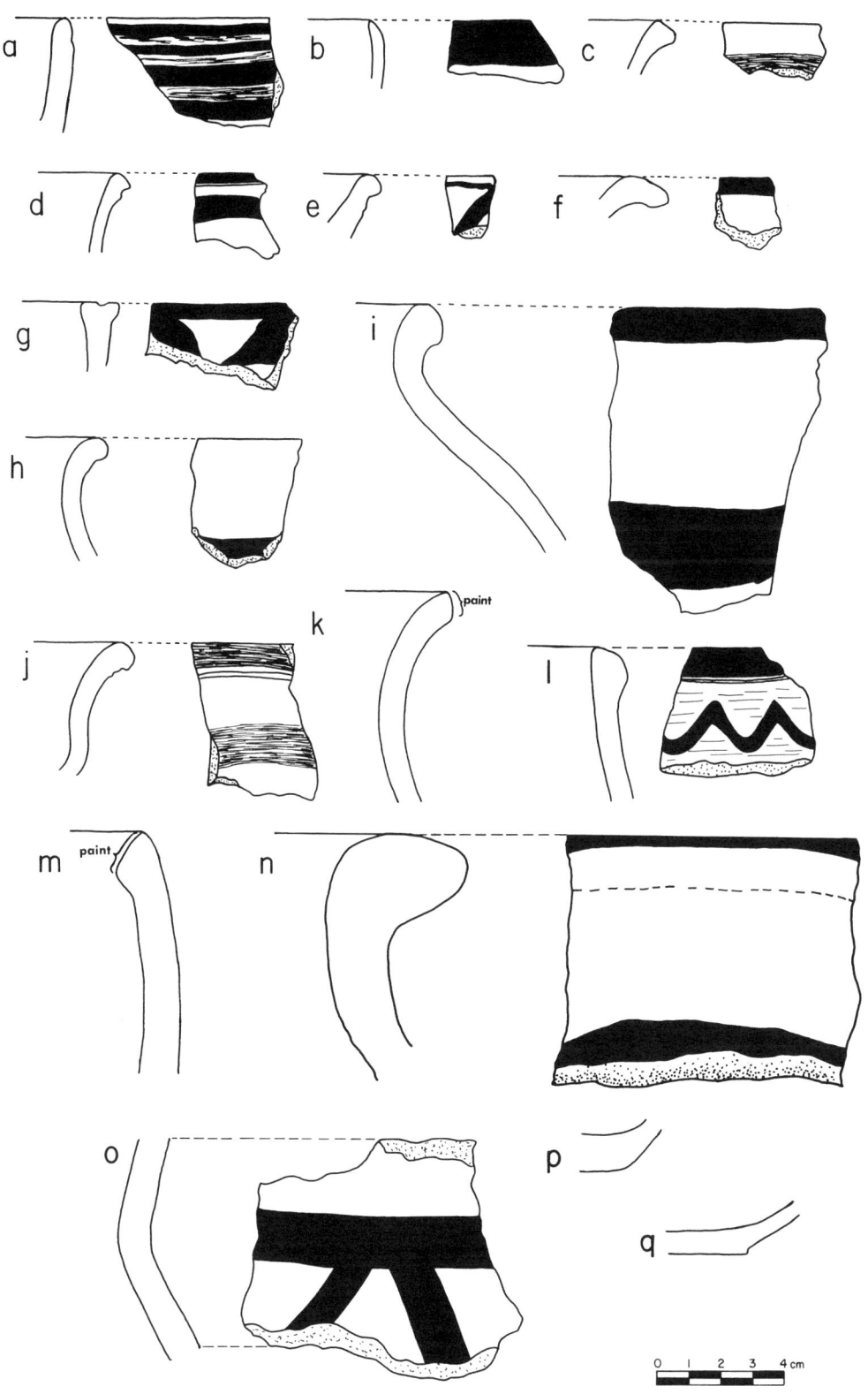

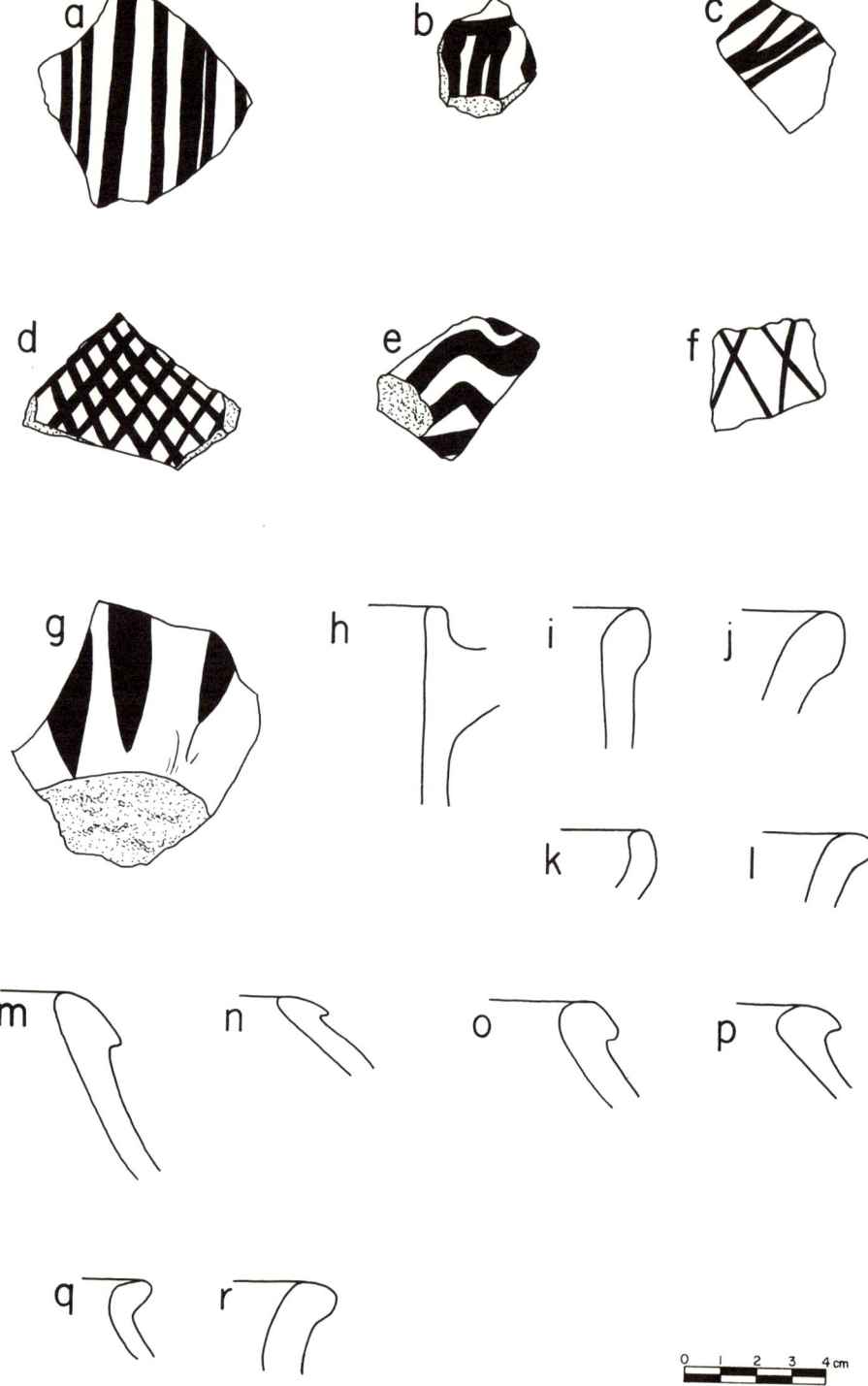

FIGURE 35

HITTITE PAINTED WARE

a. 054/2, Sq. 39. Exterior: cream-buff, black paint.
b. 055/9, Sq. 42. Exterior: gray, black paint.
c. 054/6, Sq. B12. Exterior: orange-buff, dark brown paint.
d. 054/8, Sq. B47. Exterior: cream, black paint.
e. 054/8, Sq. C42. Exterior: orange buff, dark brown paint.
f. 055/8, Sq. 19. Exterior: buff, brown paint.
g. 054/3, Gen'l. Exterior: orange-buff, red-brown paint.

HITTITE BROWN GRITTY COOKING WARE

h. N52/1, Sq. A7. Exterior, core, and interior: brown. Rim diameter: ?
i. 054/8, Sq. C17. Exterior and interior: red-brown. Core: brown. Rim diameter: 22 cm.
j. 054/2, Sq. 179. Exterior and interior: buff-brown burnished. Core: black. Rim diameter: ?
k. 054/8, Sq. A27. Exterior and interior: dark brown burnished. Core: red-brown. Rim diameter: ?
l. 054/8, Sq. A21. Exterior and interior: dark brown burnished. Core: dark brown. Rim diameter: ?
m. 054/8, Sq. C17. Exterior: brown smoothed. Core and interior: gray. Rim diameter: 22 cm.
n. 054/8, Sq. C20. Exterior and interior: gray brown. Core: brown. Rim diameter: 28 cm.
o. 055/1, Gen'l. Exterior, core, and interior: red-brown. Rim diameter: 20 cm.
p. 055/1, Gen'l. Exterior, core, and interior: buff-orange.
q. 054/12, Sq. A12. Exterior and interior: gray-brown. Core: brown. Rim diameter: 18 cm.
r. 055/9, Gen'l. Exterior and interior: brown burnished. Core: brown-black. Rim diameter: 34 cm.

FIGURE 36 IRON AGE WARE

a. 054/8, Sq. D64. Exterior and interior: light brown. Core: light gray. Rim diameter: 32 cm.
b. 054/8, Sq. D71. Exterior, core, and interior: buff-brown. Rim diameter: 28 cm.
c. 054/8, Sq. A48. Exterior, core, and interior: brown. Rim diameter: 26 cm.
d. 054/9, Sq. C13. Exterior and interior: red-brown. Core: gray center to buff-orange. Rim diameter: 30 cm.
e. 054/8, Sq. D52. Exterior and interior: brown. Core: gray center to brown. Rim diameter: 22 cm.
f. 054/8, Sq. A15. Exterior: cream. Core: black. Interior: buff-orange. Rim diameter: 16 cm.
g. 054/8, Sq. C21. Exterior and interior: cream. Core: orange. Rim diameter: 30 cm.
h. 054/8, Sq. C47. Exterior, core, and interior: brown. Rim diameter: 28 cm.
i. 054/8, Sq. D72. Exterior and interior: red. Core: orange. Rim diameter: 12 cm.
j. 054/2, Sq. 151. Exterior and interior: buff. Core: gray. Rim diameter: 22 cm.
k. 054/8, Sq. A31. Exterior, core, and interior: buff-brown. Rim diameter: 18 cm.
l. 054/8, Sq. C34. Exterior and interior: buff. Core: orange. Rim diameter: 22 cm.
m. 054/8, Sq. B32. Exterior and interior: red-brown. Core: brown. Rim diameter: 26 cm.
n. 055/3, Sq. 84. Exterior: brown. Core and interior: red-orange. Rim diameter: 26 cm.
o. 054/8, Sq. C75. Exterior: red-cream. Core: orange. Interior: red. Rim diameter: 20 cm.
p. 054/8, Sq. D65. Exterior and interior: red. Core: red-brown. Rim diameter: 20 cm.
q. 054/8, Sq. D12. Exterior and interior: cream. Core: orange. Rim diameter: 14 cm.
r. 054/8, Sq. D72. Exterior and interior: buff-brown. Core: brown. Rim diameter: 14 cm.
s. 054/2, Sq. 16. Exterior, core, and interior: cream-buff. Rim diameter: 18 cm.
t. 054/8, Sq. C38. Exterior and interior: cream. Core: buff. Rim diameter: 28 cm.
u. 054/8, Sq. B49. Exterior and interior: brown. Core: black center to buff. Rim diameter: 10 cm.
v. 054/8, Sq. D79. Exterior and interior: brown. Core: orange. Rim diameter: 10 cm.
w. 054/8, Sq. C32. Exterior and interior: red. Core: gray center to orange. Rim diameter: 34 cm.
x. 054/8, Sq. B33. Exterior and interior: brown. Core: orange-brown. Rim diameter: 32 cm.
y. 054/8, Sq. C67. Exterior and interior: buff-orange. Core: gray center to orange. Rim diameter: 20 cm.
z. 054/8, Sq. C15. Exterior and interior: buff-orange. Core: buff. Rim diameter: 12 cm.
aa. 054/8, Sq. C61. Exterior and interior: brown. Core: gray center to orange. Rim diameter: ?
bb. 054/2, Sq. 157. Exterior: red-brown. Core and interior: orange. Rim diameter: 20 cm.
cc. 054/8, Sq. A37. Exterior and interior: red. Core: red-brown. Rim diameter: 26 cm.
dd. 054/8, Sq. C35. Exterior, core, and interior: brown. Rim diameter: 16 cm.
ee. 054/8, Sq. C31. Exterior and interior: brown. Core: gray center to orange. Rim diameter: 26 cm.
ff. 054/8, Sq. C58. Exterior: cream. Core: orange. Interior: buff-cream. Rim diameter: 22 cm.
gg. 054/8, Sq. B34. Exterior, core, and interior: buff. Rim diameter: 22 cm.
hh. 054/8, Sq. C31. Exterior: cream. Core: buff. Interior: cream-buff. Rim diameter: 22 cm.
ii. 054/8, Sq. D44. Exterior and interior: buff. Core: orange. Rim diameter: 22 cm.
jj. 054/8, Sq. A45. Exterior and interior: brown. Core: black center to brown. Rim diameter: 16 cm.
kk. 054/8, Sq. D60 Exterior and interior: brown. Core: gray center to buff. Rim diameter: 22 cm.
ll. 054/8, Sq. D68. Exterior and interior: buff. Core: black. Rim diameter: 26 cm.
mm. 055/2, Gen'l. Exterior and interior: brown. Core: black center to brown. Rim diameter: 20 cm.
nn. 054/8, Sq. C42. Exterior and interior: brown. Core: gray. Rim diameter: 14 cm.
oo. 054/8, Sq. B37. Exterior: cream. Core: brown. Interior: buff-cream. Rim diameter: 36 cm.
pp. 054/8, Sq. D20. Exterior and interior: buff. Core: orange. Rim diameter: 30 cm.
qq. 054/8, Sq. A47. Exterior and interior: brown. Core: gray center to brown. Rim diameter: 22 cm.
rr. 054/8, Sq. D42. Exterior, core, and interior: brown. Rim diameter: 24 cm.
ss. 054/9, Sq. C10. Exterior: buff. Core: gray center to orange. Interior: brown. Rim diameter: 28 cm.
tt. 054/2, Sq. 53. Exterior: buff. Core and interior: brown. Rim diameter: 26 cm.
uu. 054/8, Sq. D56. Exterior, core, and interior: brown. Rim diameter: 14 cm.

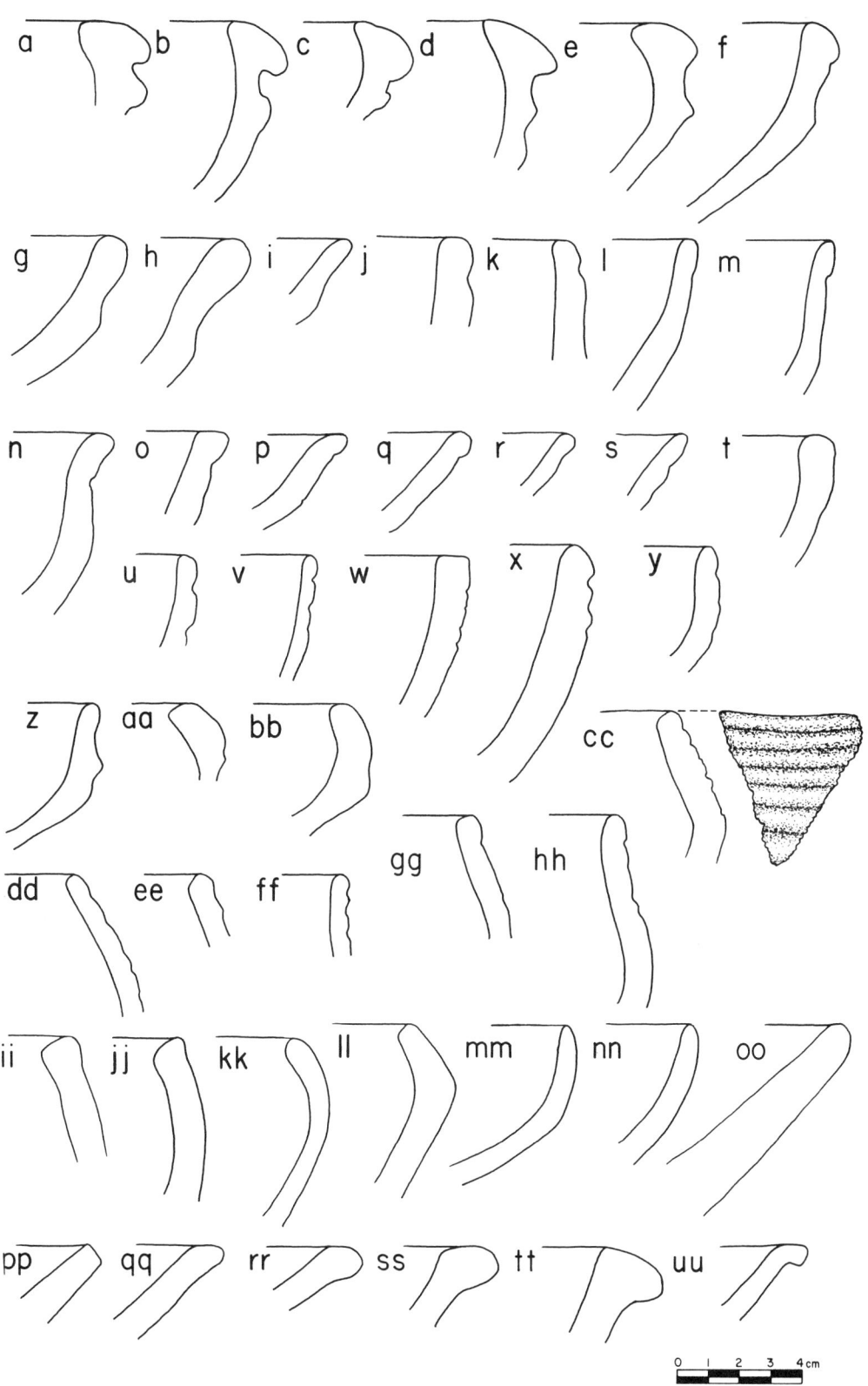

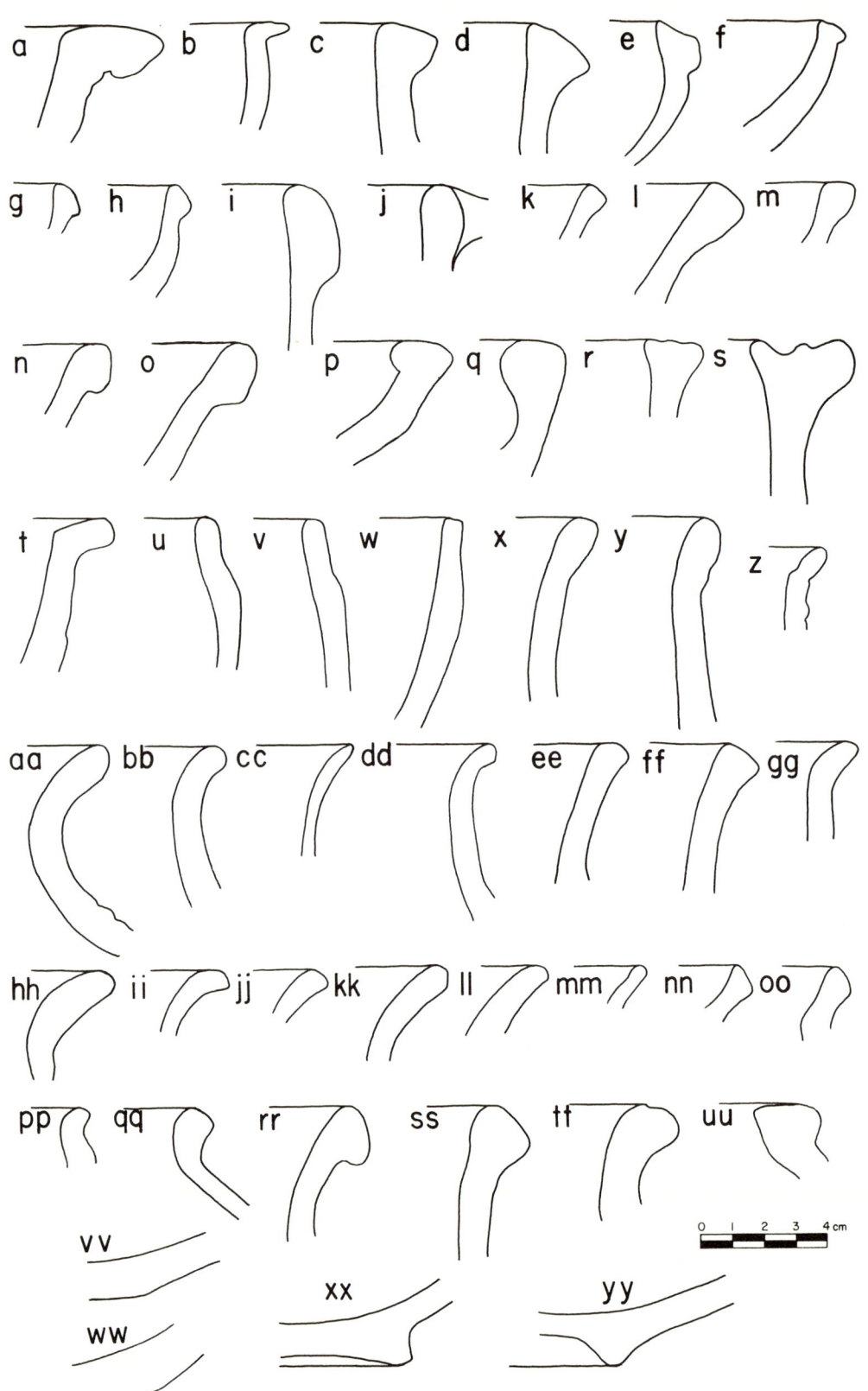

FIGURE 37 IRON AGE WARE

a. 054/2, Sq. 181. Exterior and interior: brown. Core: gray center to brown. Rim diameter: 36 cm.
b. 055/8, Sq. 18. Exterior: brown-buff. Core: black. Interior: buff. Rim diameter: 14 cm.
c. 054/8, Sq. A63. Exterior, core, and interior: brown. Rim diameter: 18 cm.
d. 054/8, Sq. C19. Exterior: buff-brown. Core: brown. Interior: buff-orange. Rim diameter: 26 cm.
e. 054/8, Sq. C87. Exterior and interior: buff-brown. Core: orange. Rim diameter: 24 cm.
f. 055/3, Sq. 41. Exterior and interior: brown. Core: orange center to brown. Rim diameter: 26 cm.
g. 054/8, Sq. A62. Exterior and interior: buff. Core: gray center to buff. Rim diameter: 16 cm.
h. 054/8, Sq. C21. Exterior and interior: brown. Core: gray. Rim diameter: 18 cm.
i. 054/8, Sq. C92. Exterior, core, and interior: brown. Rim diameter: 26 cm.
j. 054/8, Sq. C93. Exterior and interior: brown. Core: gray center to gray. Rim diameter: 10 cm.
k. 054/8, Sq. D19. Exterior, core, and interior: cream. Rim diameter: 14 cm.
l. 054/8, Sq. A41. Exterior and interior: cream. Core: gray. Rim diameter: 28 cm.
m. 054/8, Sq. D76. Exterior and interior: buff. Core: orange. Rim diameter: 12 cm.
n. 054/8, Sq. C12. Exterior, core, and interior: brown. Rim diameter: 18 cm.
o. 054/8, Sq. C15. Exterior: brown. Core: gray center to orange. Interior: black. Rim diameter: 22 cm.
p. 054/8, Sq. D43. Exterior and interior: brown. Core: orange. Rim diameter: 24 cm.
q. 054/8, Sq. C19. Exterior and interior: brown. Core: gray center to buff. Rim diameter: 20 cm.
r. 054/2, Sq. 130. Exterior, core, and interior: buff. Rim diameter: 32 cm.
s. 054/8, Sq. C78. Exterior, core, and interior: brown. Rim diameter: 38 cm.
t. 054/8, Sq. B34. Exterior and interior: brown. Core: orange. Rim diameter: 34 cm.
u. 054/8, Sq. B48. Exterior and interior: brown. Core: orange-buff. Rim diameter: 12 cm.
v. 054/8, Sq. C17. Exterior, core, and interior: light buff. Rim diameter: 23 cm.
w. 054/8, Sq. D54. Exterior and interior: brown. Core: orange. Rim diameter: ± 32 cm.
x. 054/8, Sq. A24. Exterior and interior: cream-buff. Core: orange. Rim diameter: 20 cm.
y. 055/1, Gen'l. Exterior and interior: cream. Core: black center to brown. Rim diameter: 24 cm.
z. 054/8, Sq. C43. Exterior and interior: red. Core: orange. Rim diameter: 18 cm.
aa. 054/19, Gen'l. Exterior: cream. Core: orange. Interior: cream-orange. Rim diameter: 14 cm.
bb. 054/8, Sq. A71. Exterior and interior: brown. Core: orange. Rim diameter: ?
cc. 055/4, Sq. 18. Exterior, core, and interior: red-orange. Rim diameter: 14 cm.
dd. 054/3, Sq. 20. Exterior: brown. Core: black. Interior: buff. Rim diameter: 24 cm.
ee. 054/8, Sq. C86. Exterior, core, and interior: brown. Rim diameter: 22 cm.
ff. 054/8, Sq. C61. Exterior and interior: brown. Core: gray center to buff. Rim diameter: 18 cm.
gg. 054/8, Sq. D57. Exterior, core, and interior: brown. Rim diameter: 16 cm.
hh. 054/8, Sq. D34. Exterior and interior: buff. Core: gray center to buff. Rim diameter: 20 cm.
ii. 054/8, Sq. C52. Exterior and interior: brown. Core: gray center to buff. Rim diameter: 12 cm.
jj. 054/8, Sq. D26. Exterior and interior: brown. Core: black center to brown. Rim diameter: ?
kk. 054/8, Sq. D14. Exterior and interior: brown. Core: black center to brown. Rim diameter: 14 cm.
ll. 054/2, Sq. 103. Exterior and interior: brown. Core: orange. Rim diameter: 16 cm.
mm. 054/2, Sq. 22. Exterior and interior: buff. Core: orange. Rim diameter: 14 cm.
nn. 054/8, Sq. D75. Exterior and interior: red. Core: brown. Rim diameter: 14 cm.
oo. 054/2, Sq. 175. Exterior: red. Core: orange. Interior: red-brown. Rim diameter: 24 cm.
pp. 054/2, Sq. 118. Exterior and interior: buff-brown. Core: gray. Rim diameter: 26 cm.
qq. 054/8, Sq. C62. Exterior and interior: brown. Core: gray center to brown. Rim diameter: 16 cm.
rr. 054/8, Sq. A60. Exterior and interior: brown. Core: gray center to brown. Rim diameter: 10 cm.
ss. 054/8, Sq. A68. Exterior and interior: brown. Core: orange. Rim diameter: 12 cm.
tt. 054/8, Sq. A29. Exterior and interior: brown. Core: black. Rim diameter: 26 cm.
uu. 054/8, Sq. A77. Exterior and interior: brown. Core: buff. Rim diameter: ?
vv. 054/2, Sq. 159. Exterior and interior: brown. Core: brown-gray. Base diameter: 6 cm.
ww. 054/2, Sq. 142. Exterior and interior: brown. Core: black. Base diameter: 10 cm.
xx. 054/8, Sq. C45. Exterior and interior: brown. Core: orange. Base diameter: 10 cm.
yy. 054/8, Sq. D62. Exterior: brown. Core and interior: buff. Base diameter: 12 cm.

FIGURE 38

IRON AGE WARE

a. 054/2, Sq. 88.　　Exterior, core, and interior: brown. Rim diameter: 16 cm.

b. 054/8, Sq. B33.　　Exterior and interior: brown. Core: orange-brown. Rim diameter: 12 cm.

c. 054/2, Sq. 126.　　Exterior and interior: brown. Core: buff. Rim diameter: 16 cm.

d. 054/8, Sq. A71.　　Exterior: brown. Core: gray center to buff.

e. 054/2, Gen'l.　　Exterior: red-brown. Core: brown-black.

f. 054/2, Sq. 121.　　Exterior: white slip. Core: black center to orange. Interior: brown. Rim diameter: ?

g. 054/8, Sq. C41.　　Exterior: buff. Core: orange. Interior: buff-orange burnished. Rim diameter: ?

h. 054/8, Sq. A59.　　Exterior and interior: buff-brown burnished. Core: red-brown. Rim diameter: 24 cm.

i. 054/4, Gen'l.　　Exterior and interior: buff burnished. Core: buff-brown. Rim diameter: ?

j. 054/8, Sq. C30.　　Exterior: cream. Core: brown-orange. Interior: red-brown.

k. 055/1, Gen'l.　　Exterior: white slip. Core: black. Interior: red-orange burnished.

l. 054/4, Gen'l.　　Exterior: buff. Core: gray. Interior: buff-brown.

m. 054/8, Sq. B48.　　Exterior and interior: buff-brown burnished. Core: brown.

n. 054/8, Sq. B48.　　Exterior: cream slip burnished. Core: red-brown. Interior: red-brown burnished.

IRON AGE PAINTED WARE

o. 054/8, Gen'l.　　Exterior: dark red paint on buff paste.

p. 054/8, Sq. A27.　　Exterior: dark red paint on buff paste.

q. 054/8, Sq. C46.　　Exterior: dark red paint on buff paste.

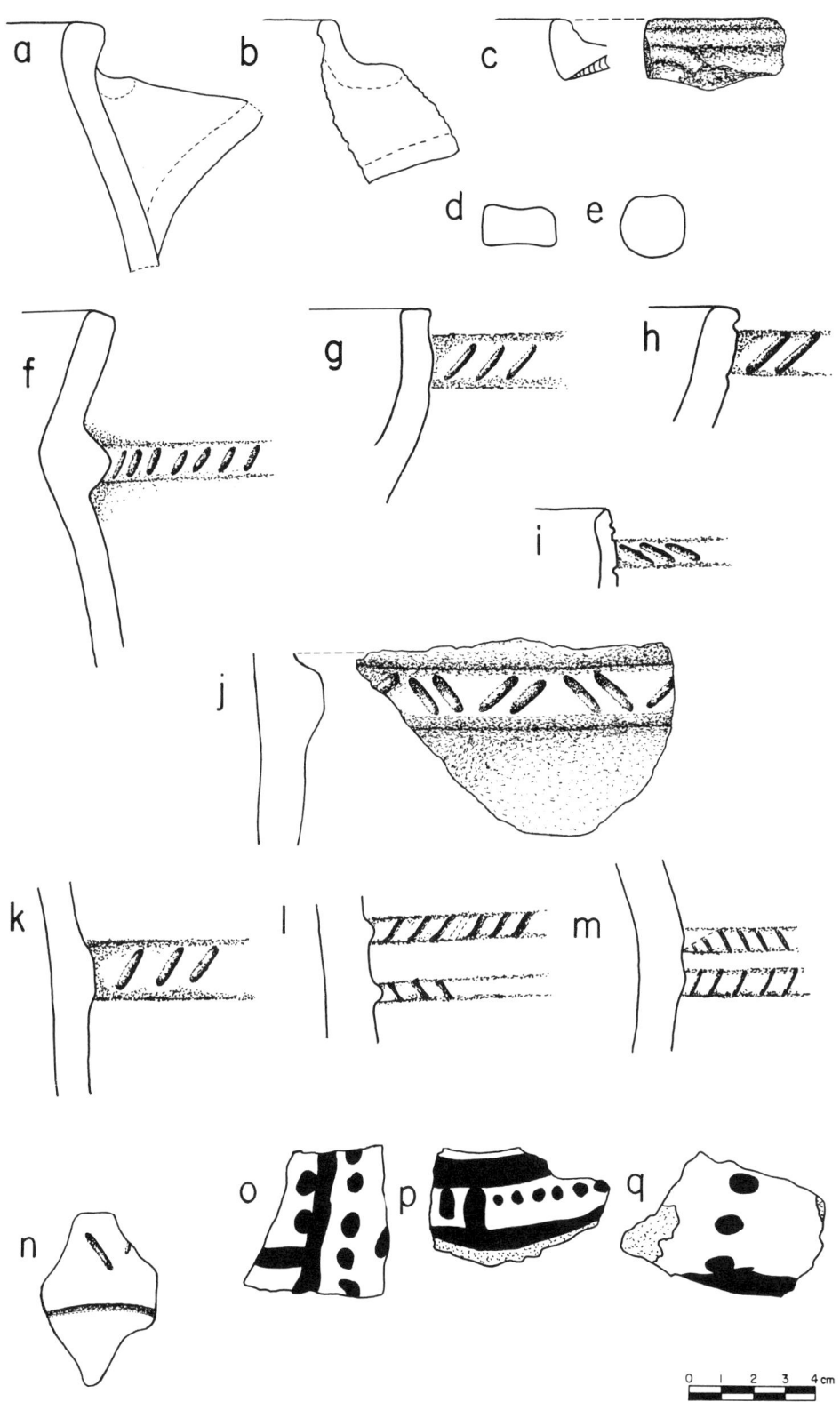

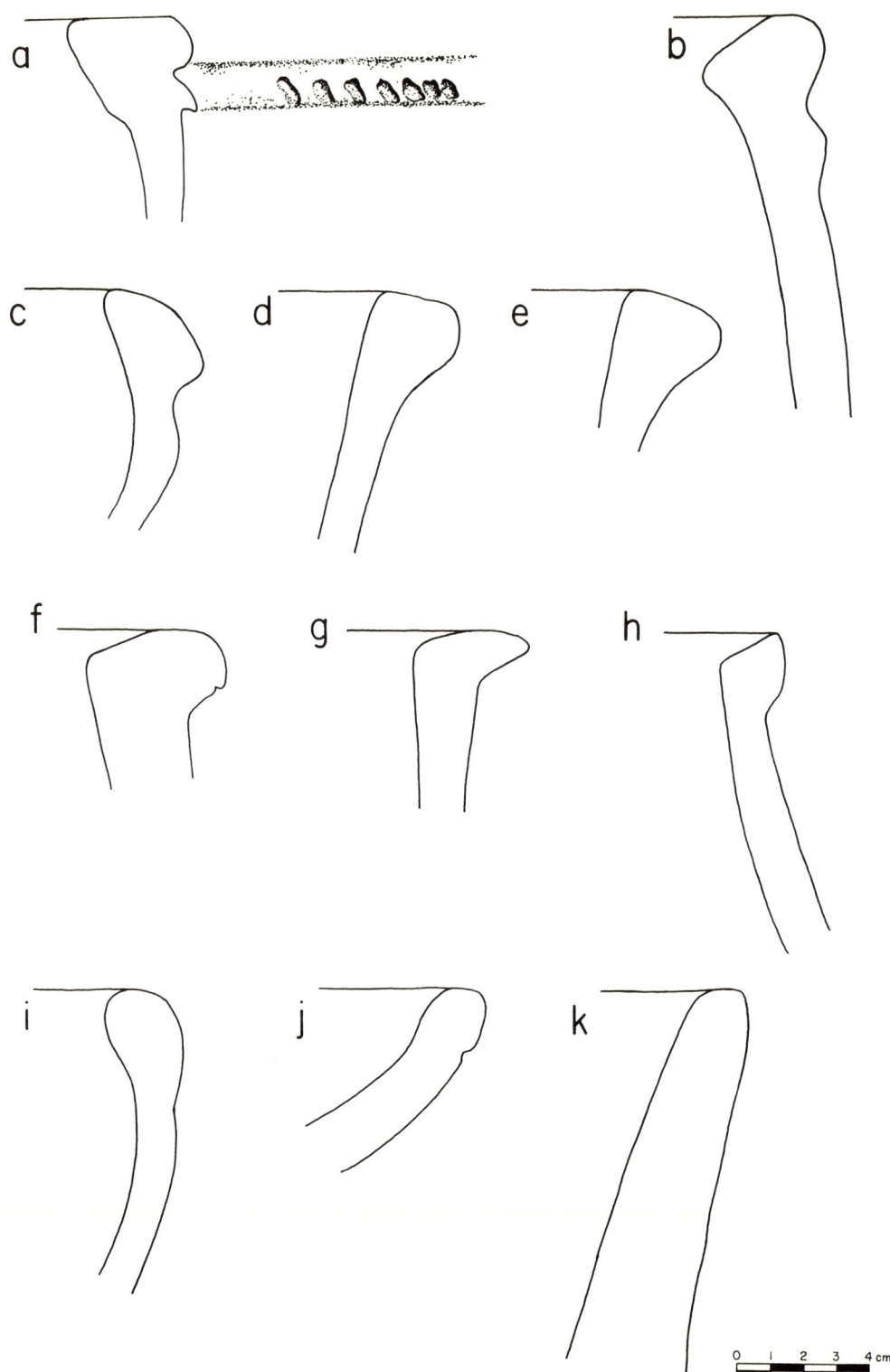

FIGURE 39 IRON AGE THICK WARE

a. 054/2, Sq. 157. Exterior and interior: buff. Core: buff–orange. Rim diameter: 40+ cm?

b. 054/9, Sq. A9. Exterior: cream slip on orange. Core: buff–orange. Interior: buff–brown. Rim diameter: 40+ cm?

c. 054/9, Sq. B19. Exterior: brown. Core: gray. Interior: buff. Rim diameter: 32 cm.

d. 054/8, Sq. D70. Exterior and interior: buff–brown burnished. Core: gray center to buff–brown. Rim diameter: 40+ cm?

e. 054/8, Sq. C31. Exterior and interior: brown burnished. Core: gray. Rim diameter: 40+ cm?

f. 054/8, Sq. D84. Exterior and interior: cream–buff slip. Core: gray. Rim diameter: 40+ cm?

g. 054/8, Sq. B26. Exterior and interior: cream slip burnished. Core: gray center to red–brown. Rim diameter: 36 cm?

h. 054/8, Sq. D21. Exterior and interior: buff–brown burnished. Core: gray center to buff–brown. Rim diameter: 40+ cm?

i. 054/9, Sq. A1. Exterior and interior: cream–buff slip. Core: gray center to buff. Rim diameter: 40+ cm?

j. 054/8, Sq. A36. Exterior and interior: red–brown burnished. Core: gray center to red. Rim diameter: ?

k. 054/8, Sq. A22. Exterior and interior: brown burnished. Core: gray center to light orange. Rim diameter: 40 cm.

FIGURE 40 MEDIEVAL BRICK WARE

a. 054/8, Sq. A50. Exterior and interior: buff. Core: orange. Rim diameter: 26 cm.

b. 054/8, Sq. C19. Exterior, core, and interior: buff. Rim diameter: 30 cm.

c. 054/10, Sq. A4. Exterior: brown. Core: black center to brown. Interior: brown-red. Rim diameter: 22 cm.

d. 054/8, Sq. D45. Exterior, core, and interior: brown. Rim diameter: 40 cm.

e. 054/8, Sq. A40. Exterior and interior: brown. Core: black. Rim diameter: 28 cm.

f. 054/8, Sq. C10. Exterior and interior: brick-brown. Core: brown. Rim diameter: 18 cm.

g. 054/2, Sq. 131. Exterior, core, and interior: gray-buff. Rim diameter: 40 cm?

h. N52/2, Sq. A35. Exterior and interior: brick-brown. Core: black center to brick-brown. Rim diameter: ?

i. 054/12, Sq. D14. Exterior and interior: brown-buff. Core: orange-red. Rim diameter: 28 cm.

j. 054/8, Sq. D24. Exterior and interior: buff. Core: black. Rim diameter: 24 cm.

k. 054/12, Sq. B11. Exterior: brown. Core: black. Interior: red-brown. Rim diameter: 14 cm.

l. 054/8, Sq. C34. Exterior: orange-red. Core: orange. Interior: red. Rim diameter: 22 cm.

m. 054/8, Sq. C51. Exterior and interior: buff. Core: red-buff. Rim diameter: 9 cm.

n. 054/8, Sq. D49. Exterior and interior: red-brown. Core: orange. Rim diameter: 24 cm.

o. 054/6, Sq. B13. Exterior, core, and interior: brown. Rim diameter: 20 cm.

p. 054/19, Gen'l. Exterior: buff with spotty red slip. Core and interior: buff. Rim diameter: 11 cm.

q. 054/10, Gen'l. Exterior and interior: buff-orange. Core: cream-orange. Rim diameter: 12 cm.

r. 054/2, Gen'l. Exterior and interior: brown. Core: gray center to buff. Rim diameter: 32 cm.

s. 054/8, Sq. B24. Exterior: brown-buff. Core: brown. Interior: brown-red. Rim diameter: 30 cm.

t. 054/8, Sq. C19. Exterior and core: brown. Interior: buff. Rim diameter: 26 cm.

u. 054/2, Gen'l. Exterior, core, and interior: brown. Rim diameter: 34 cm.

v. 054/8, Sq. A42. Exterior and interior: brown. Core: gray. Rim diameter: 28 cm.

w. 054/8, Sq. C35. Exterior and interior: black. Core: orange center to black. Rim diameter: 24 cm.

x. 054/8, Sq. A52. Exterior and interior: orange. Core: gray center to orange. Rim diameter: ?

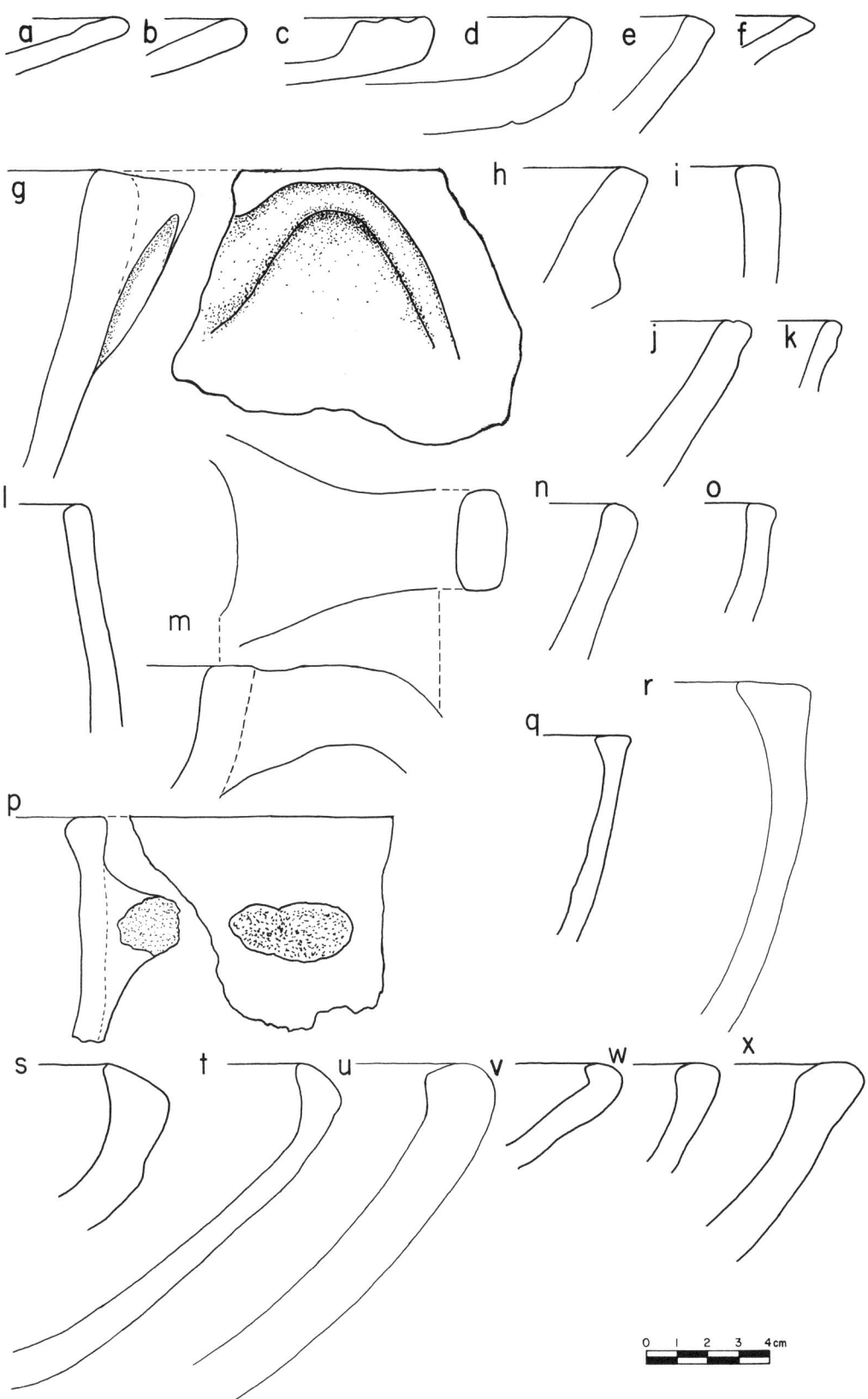

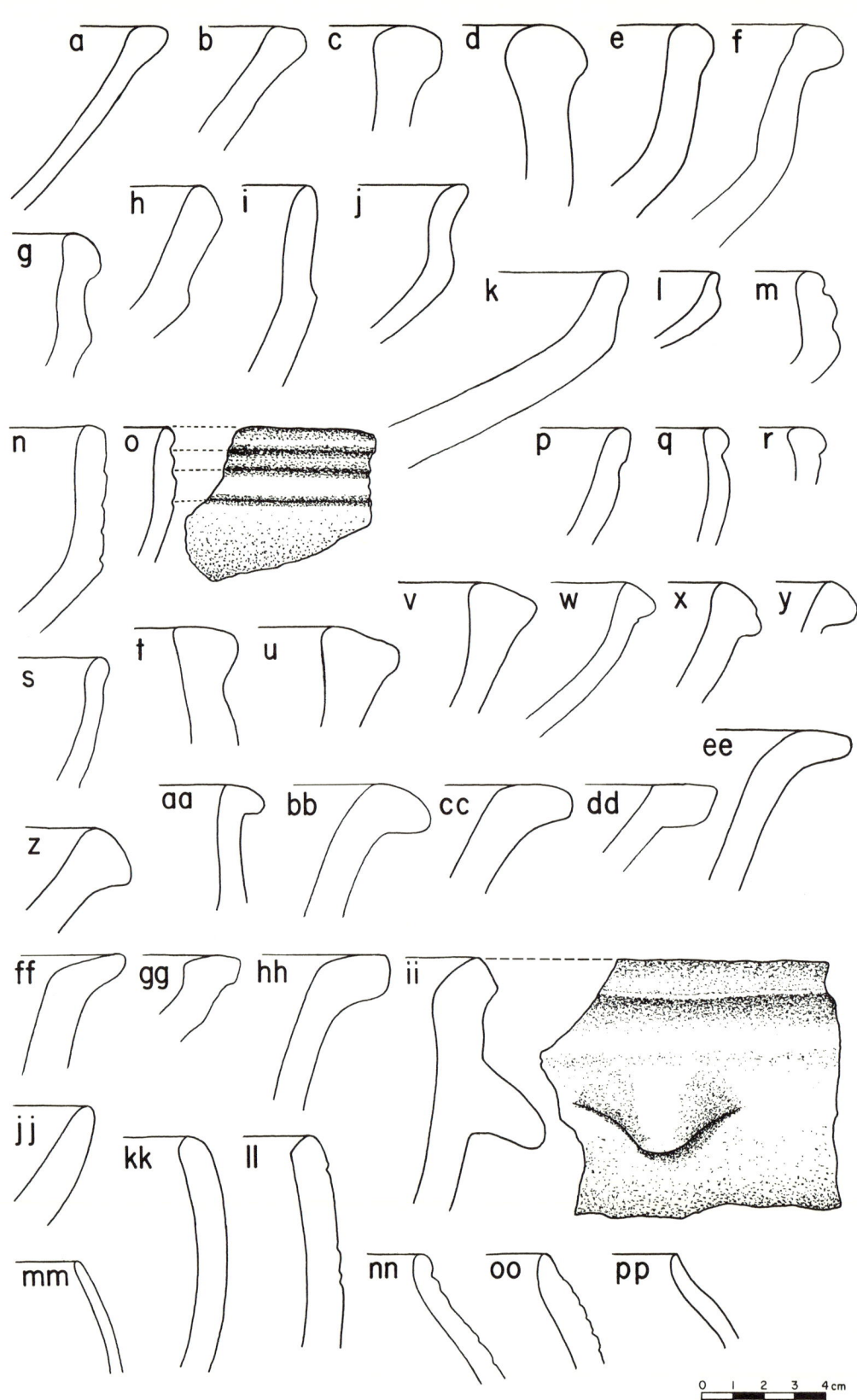

FIGURE 41 MEDIEVAL BRICK WARE

a. 055/8, Sq. 20. Exterior, core, and interior: orange–buff. Rim diameter: 24 cm.
b. 054/8, Gen'l. Exterior: red–brown. Core: orange. Interior: buff–brown. Rim diameter: 26 cm.
c. 054/8, Sq. C56. Exterior and interior: brick–brown. Core: black center to buff. Rim diameter: ?
d. 054/8, Sq. C86. Exterior and interior: buff–orange. Core: gray center to orange. Rim diameter: 40+ cm?
e. 054/8, Sq. D23. Exterior, core, and interior: brown. Rim diameter: 26 cm.
f. 055/1, Gen'l. Exterior and interior: brown. Core: brown–red. Rim diameter: 32 cm.
g. N52/2, Sq. A30. Exterior, core, and interior: red–orange. Rim diameter: 12 cm.
h. 054/8, Sq. A34. Exterior: buff. Core: orange. Interior: red. Rim diameter: 30 cm.
i. 054/8, Sq. C36. Exterior and interior: red–brown. Core: orange center to brown. Rim diameter: 40 cm?
j. 054/24, Sq. A20. .Exterior, core, and interior: brown. Rim diameter: 24 cm.
k. 054/6, Sq. A33. Exterior and interior: orange–brown. Core: black center to brown. Rim diameter: 34 cm?
l. 054/8, Sq. A12. Exterior and interior: black. Core: gray. Rim diameter: 16 cm.
m. 054/21, Gen'l. Exterior: orange–buff. Core: orange. Interior: orange–cream. Rim diameter: 26 cm.
n. 054/2, Sq. 16. Exterior and interior: red. Core: gray center to brown. Rim diameter: ?
o. 054/8, Sq. A12. Exterior, core, and interior: brown. Rim diameter: ?
p. 055/4, Sq. 29. Exterior: brown–red. Core: black. Interior: red. Rim diameter: 24 cm.
q. 055/4, Gen'l. Exterior and interior: gray–brown. Core: orange. Rim diameter: 26 cm.
r. 054/6, Sq. B2. Exterior and interior: red–brown. Core: brown to brick–brown. Rim diameter: ?
s. 054/8, Sq. C32. Exterior and interior: buff. Core: black. Rim diameter: 16 cm.
t. N52/2, Sq. A33. Exterior and interior: red–cream. Core: black center to orange. Rim diameter: 40 cm.
u. 054/25, Sq. A14. Exterior and interior: red–brown. Core: brown. Rim diameter: 34 cm.
v. 054/25, Sq. A15. Exterior and interior: brown. Core: brown–red. Rim diameter: 36 cm.
w. 054/2, Sq. 87. Exterior, core, and interior: brown. Rim diameter: 24 cm.
x. 054/8, Sq. D66. Exterior and interior: red–brown. Core: light orange buff. Rim diameter: 26 cm.
y. 054/8, Sq. A49. Exterior, core, and interior: brown. Rim diameter: 28 cm.
z. 054/8, Sq. C67. Exterior and interior: cream. Core: brown–orange. Rim diameter: 32 cm.
aa. 054/8 Sq. D23. Exterior and interior: brown. Core: black. Rim diameter: 26 cm.
bb. 055/1, Gen'l. Exterior and interior: brick red. Core: brick–red to orange. Rim diameter: 26 cm.
cc. 054/2, Sq. 107. Exterior, core, and interior: gray. Rim diameter: 24 cm.
dd. N52/2, Sq. A80. Exterior and interior: brick red–brown. Core: orange–brown. Rim diameter: 28 cm.
ee. 054/9, Sq. C9. Exterior, core, and interior: brown. Rim diameter: 40+ cm?
hh. 054/8, Sq. C53. Exterior and interior: orange. Core: gray center to orange. Rim diameter: 36 cm.
ii. N52/2, Sq. B23. Exterior, core, and interior: buff. Rim diameter: 40+ cm?
jj. 054/6, Sq. A7. Exterior and interior: red–buff. Core: black center to buff. Rim diameter: 30 cm.
kk. N52/2, Gen'l. Exterior and interior: red. Core: brown. Rim diameter: 34 cm.
ll. 054/8, Sq. C65. Exterior and interior: brown. Core: gray. Rim diameter: 34 cm.
mm. 054/2, Sq. 107. Exterior: brown. Core and interior: buff. Rim diameter: 6 cm.
nn. 054/8, Sq. C14. Exterior, core, and interior: brown. Rim diameter: ?
oo. 054/8, Sq. A3. Exterior and core: black. Interior: brown. Rim diameter: 22 cm.
pp. 054/8, Sq. D25. Exterior and interior: buff. Core: black. Rim diameter: 16 cm.

FIGURE 42 MEDIEVAL BRICK WARE

a. 054/18, Gen'l. Exterior and interior: pale orange. Core: brown center to orange. Rim diameter: 28 cm.
b. N52/2, Gen'l. Exterior and interior: brown. Core: black. Rim diameter: 24 cm.
c. 054/1, Gen'l. Exterior: brown. Core: black center to brown. Interior: brown-gray. Rim diameter: 18 cm.
d. 054/8, Sq. A23. Exterior and interior: brown. Core: gray center to brown. Rim diameter: 22 cm.
e. 054/8, Sq. C17. Exterior and interior: red-brown. Core: brown. Rim diameter: 24 cm.
f. 054/8, Sq. C38. Exterior, core, and interior: brown. Rim diameter: 18 cm.
g. 055/4, Sq. 44. Exterior and interior: brown. Core: brick-red. Rim diameter: 22 cm.
h. 055/4, Sq. 45. Exterior, core, and interior: black. Rim diameter: 20 cm.
i. 054/8, Sq. C31. Exterior and interior: red-brown. Core: orange to orange-brown. Rim diameter: ?
j. 054/8, Sq. C29. Exterior and interior: brick-red. Core: orange-brown. Rim diameter: 28 cm.
k. 054/8, Sq. D17. Exterior, core, and interior: brown. Rim diameter: 20 cm.
l. 054/8, Sq. A25. Exterior, core, and interior: brown. Rim diameter: 26 cm.
m. 054/2, Sq. 175. Exterior and interior: brown. Core: black center to gray. Rim diameter: 40+ cm?
n. 054/8, Sq. C30. Exterior, core, and interior: buff-brown. Rim diameter: 38 cm.
o. N52/10, Gen'l. Exterior and core: brown. Interior: red-brown. Rim diameter: 22 cm.
p. 054/8, Sq. A45. Exterior and interior: brick red-brown. Core: gray center to orange. Rim diameter: 26 cm.
q. N52/2, Sq. A65. Exterior and interior: light orange. Core: orange-brown. Rim diameter: ?
r. 054/24, Sq. A13. Exterior, core, and interior: brown. Rim diameter: 24 cm.
s. 054/8, Sq. D71. Exterior and interior: red-brown. Core: orange-buff. Rim diameter: 24 cm.
t. 054/18, Gen'l. Exterior: buff. Core: brown-orange. Interior: buff-red. Rim diameter: 28 cm.
u. 054/8, Sq. C29. Exterior and interior: red-brown. Core: black center to buff. Rim diameter: 36 cm.
v. 054/8, Sq. D70. Exterior, core, and interior: brown. Rim diameter: 32 cm.
w. 054/8, Sq. C54. Exterior, core, and interior: brown. Rim diameter: 20 cm.
x. 054/8, Sq. D20. Exterior and interior: dark red-brown. Core: orange-brown. Rim diameter: 32 cm.
y. 054/8, Sq. A13. Exterior, core, and interior: brown. Rim diameter: 14 cm.
z. 054/8, Sq. C22. Exterior and interior: orange-brown. Core: gray. Rim diameter: 28 cm.
aa. 054/8, Sq. D41. Exterior: brown. Core: gray center to orange. Interior: red-brown. Rim diameter: 40+ cm?
bb. 055/4, Gen'l. Exterior and interior: red-brown. Core red-orange. Rim diameter: ?
cc. 054/2, Sq. 162. Exterior and interior: deep red-brown. Core: orange-brown. Rim diameter: ?
dd. 054/8, Sq. C41. Exterior and interior: red-brown. Core: gray center to orange. Rim diameter: 38 cm.
ee. 054/8, Gen'l. Exterior: red to cream. Core: orange-brown. Interior: orange. Rim diameter: 16 cm.
ff. 054/8, Sq. C29. Exterior and interior: brown. Core: gray center to orange. Rim diameter: 16 cm.
gg. 054/8, Sq. A27. Exterior and interior: red-cream. Core: light brown. Rim diameter: 34 cm?
hh. 054/8, Sq. A58. Exterior and interior: red-brown. Core: gray center to orange. Rim diameter: 24 cm.
ii. 054/8, Sq. C18. Exterior, core, and interior: red-brown. Rim diameter: 10 cm?
jj. 054/8, Sq. A53. Exterior, core, and interior: brown. Rim diameter: 24 cm.
kk. 054/8, Sq. A15. Exterior, core, and interior: dark red. Rim diameter: 32 cm.
ll. 054/6, Sq. B11. Exterior and interior: buff-brown. Core: gray center to brown. Rim diameter: 26 cm.
mm. 054/8, Sq. D41. Exterior and interior: dark red-brown. Core: dark gray center to orange. Rim diameter: ?
nn. 054/12, Sq. B6. Exterior, core, and interior: brown. Rim diameter: 24 cm.
oo. 054/10, Sq. C1. Exterior and interior: red-brown. Core: orange center to brown. Rim diameter: 18 cm.
pp. 054/8, Sq. C34. Exterior and interior: brown. Core: brown-orange. Rim diameter: 28 cm.
qq. 054/8, Sq. C42. Exterior and interior: red-brown. Core: gray center to light orange. Rim diameter: ?
rr. 054/8, Sq. D70. Exterior: buff. Core: gray center to buff. Interior: brown. Rim diameter: 18 cm.
ss. 055/4, Sq. 48. Exterior, core, and interior: red. Rim diameter: 20 cm.
tt. 054/2, Sq. 168. Exterior: brown. Core: black. Interior: buff. Rim diameter: 16 cm.
uu. 054/8, Sq. D38. Exterior, core, and interior: brown. Rim diameter: 32 cm.
vv. 054/6, Sq. B20. Exterior and interior: brick-red. Core: red-orange. Rim diameter: 18 cm.
ww. 054/8, Sq. D71. Exterior: red-brown. Core: black. Interior: brown. Rim diameter: 22 cm.
xx. 054/8, Sq. C16. Exterior, core, and interior: brown. Rim diameter: 24 cm.
yy. 054/6, Sq. B16. Exterior and interior: brown-buff. Core: orange-brown. Rim diameter: 22 cm.
zz. 054/25, Sq. A19. Exterior: brown. Core: gray center to cream. Interior: cream. Rim diameter: 18 cm.
aaa. 054/12, Sq. B9. Exterior: cream-buff. Core: black. Interior: brown. Rim diameter: 10 cm.

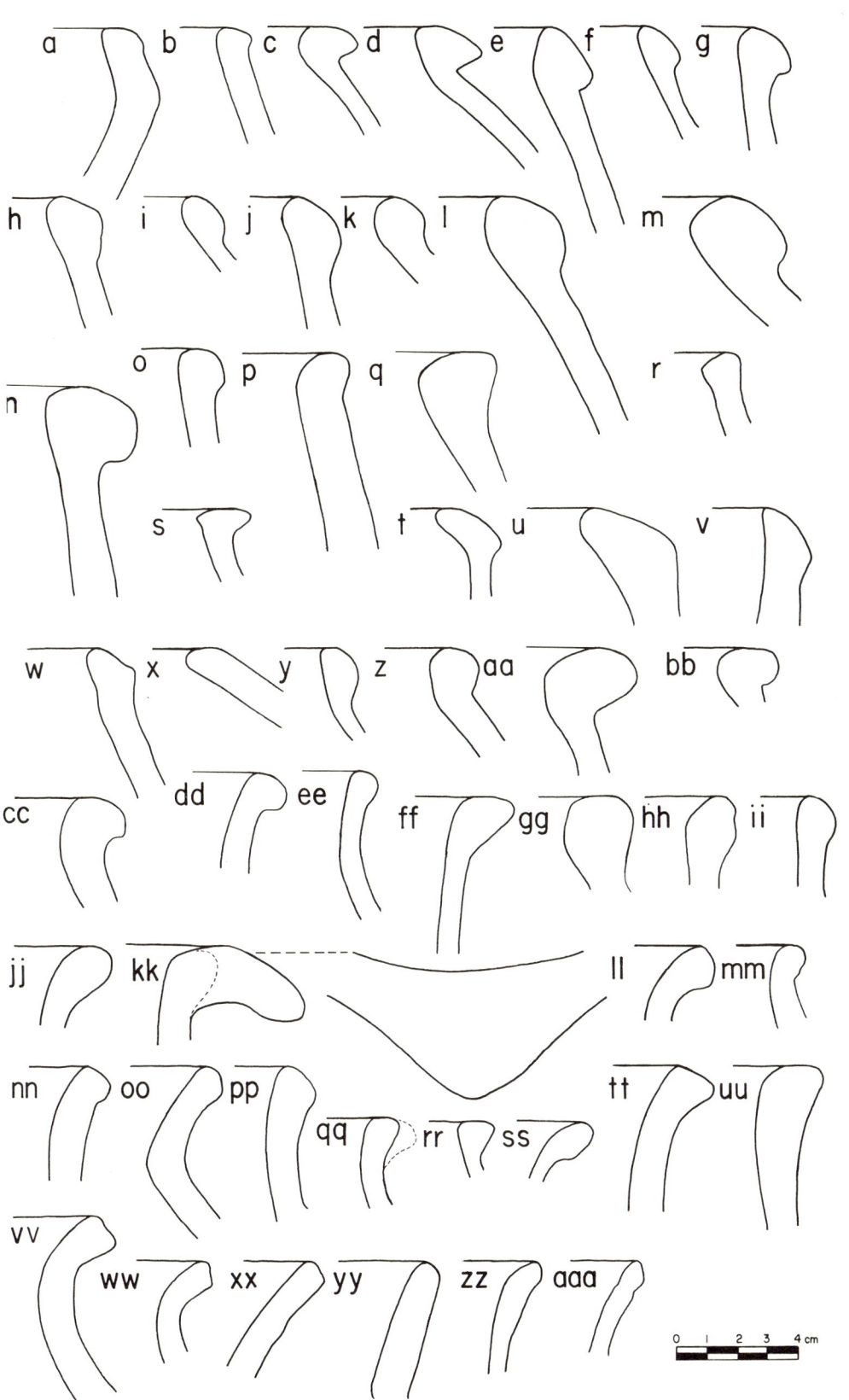

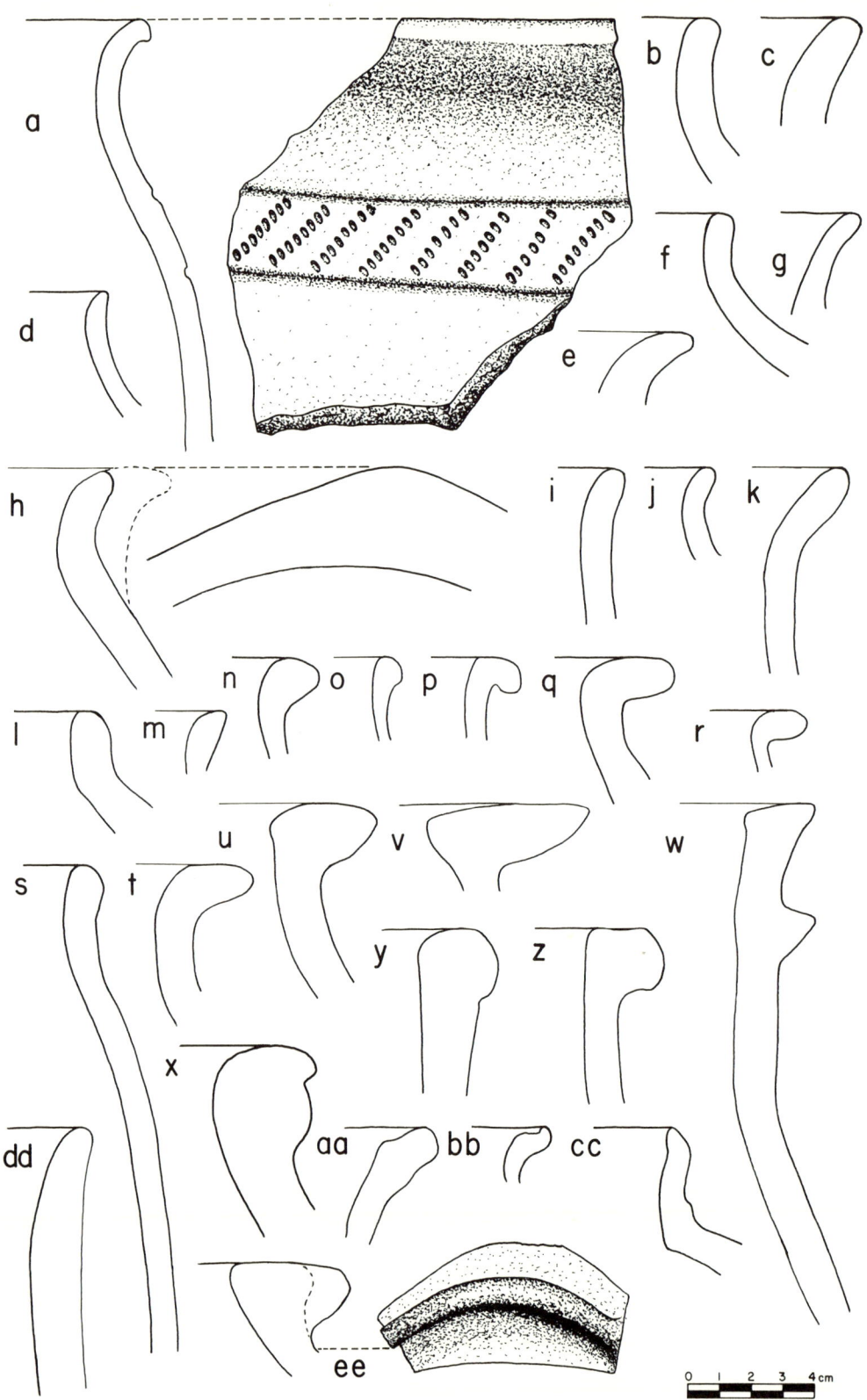

134

FIGURE 43 MEDIEVAL BRICK WARE

a. 054/8, Sq. A23. Exterior, core and interior: reddish buff. Rim diameter: 14–17 cm.

b. 054/8, Sq. D44. Exterior, core, and interior: brown. Rim diameter: 20 cm.

c. 054/27, Sq. A30. Exterior and interior: red-brown. Core: gray center to orange. Rim diameter: 34 cm.

d. 054/15, Sq. A27. Exterior and interior: dark red-brown. Core: dark orange-brown. Rim diameter: ?

e. 054/8, Sq. B31. Exterior, core, and interior: dark red-brown. Rim diameter: 32 cm.

f. 054/8, Sq. B24. Exterior, core, and interior: brown. Rim diameter: 18 cm.

g. N52/2, Sq. A43. Exterior, core, and interior: cream-orange. Rim diameter: 10 cm.

h. 054/8, Sq. A13. Exterior and interior: red-brown burnished. Core: black center to red-brown. Rim diameter: ?

i. 054/8, Sq. C29. Exterior and interior: buff-brown. Core: gray center to orange. Rim diameter: 30 cm.

j. 054/8, Sq. B36. Exterior, core, and interior: buff-brown. Rim diameter: 16 cm.

k. 054/8, Gen'l. Exterior and interior: brown. Core: orange center to brown. Rim diameter: ? (Trefoil mouth).

l. 055/3, Sq. 164. Exterior, core, and interior: orange-brown. Rim diameter: 26 cm.

m. 055/9, Sq. 27. Exterior and core: brown-black. Interior: brown. Rim diameter: ?

n. 054/2, Sq. 49. Exterior, core, and interior: buff. Rim diameter: 22 cm.

o. 054/8, Sq. A51. Exterior and interior: red-brown. Core: gray center to orange. Rim diameter: 12 cm.

p. 055/4, Gen'l. Exterior and interior: brick-red. Core: red-orange. Rim diameter: 26 cm.

q. 054/8, Sq. B51. Exterior and interior: brown. Core: gray center to orange. Rim diameter: 24 cm.

r. 054/8, Sq. C23. Exterior: buff-orange. Core: orange. Interior: dark buff-orange. Rim diameter: 18 cm.

s. 054/8, Sq. D57. Exterior: black. Core: black to brown. Interior: brown. Rim diameter: 18 cm.

t. 054/8, Sq. D41. Exterior and interior: orange-red. Core: gray center to orange. Rim diameter: 20 cm?

u. 054/8, Sq. C49. Exterior, core, and interior: brick red-brown. Rim diameter: 30 cm.

v. 054/8, Sq. D55. Exterior: red-brown. Core: gray center to red-brown. Interior: ? Rim diameter: 18 cm (inside).

w. N52/2, Sq. A40. No information.

x. 054/21, Sq. 13. Exterior and interior: brown-red. Core: orange-brown. Rim diameter: ?

y. 054/8, Sq. C32. Exterior, core, and interior: brown. Rim diameter: 34 cm.

z. 054/8, Sq. C43. Exterior and interior: brown. Core: gray-black. Rim diameter: 38 cm.

aa. 055/4, Sq. 49. Exterior: gray. Core: gray to buff. Interior: buff. Rim diameter: 22 cm.

bb. 054/6, Gen'l. Exterior: purple-black. Core: brown. Interior: deep red. Rim diameter: 8 cm.

cc. 054/6, Sq. B7. Exterior, core, and interior: orange-brown. Rim diameter: 24 cm.

dd. 055/8, Sq. 30. Exterior and interior: buff. Core: black center to buff. Rim diameter: 40 cm.

ee. 054/10, Sq. B6. Exterior and interior: brown. Core: brown-red. Rim diameter: 28 cm.

FIGURE 44 MEDIEVAL BRICK WARE

    a. 054/8, Sq. D40.   Exterior: buff. Core: dark gray center to buff.

    b. 054/8, Gen'l.   Exterior, core, and interior: dirty dull red.

    c. N52/2, Sq. A53.   Exterior: buff-brown. Core: gray center to buff.

    d. N52/2, Sq. A57.   Exterior and core: light red-brown.

    e. 054/2, Gen'l.   Exterior and interior: dark orange-brown. Core: dark buff-orange.

    f. 054/8, Sq. B12.   Exterior and core: buff.

    g. 054/21, Sq. 13.   Exterior and interior: brick red-brown. Core: orange-brown. Rim diameter: ?

    h. 054/8, Sq. D32.   Exterior and interior: dark red. Core: dark gray center to dark red.

    i. 055/9, Sq. 31.   Exterior: buff-cream. Core: orange-buff. Interior: buff. Base diameter: 8 cm.

    j. 054/2, Sq. 158.   Exterior and interior: brown. Core: black. Basal diameter: 12 cm.

    k. N52/2, Sq. B21.   Exterior and interior: buff. Core: orange. Basal diameter: 16 cm.

    l. 054/8, Sq. C75.   Exterior: buff. Core: black center to buff. Interior: gray-buff. Basal diameter: 9 cm.

    m. 054/2, Sq. 157.   Exterior: brown. Core and interior: black. Basal diameter: 14 cm.

    n. 054/8, Sq. C64.   Exterior, core, and interior: brown. Basal diameter: 8 cm.

    o. 055/1, Gen'l.   Exterior: red-brown. Core and interior: buff-brown. Basal diameter: 16 cm.

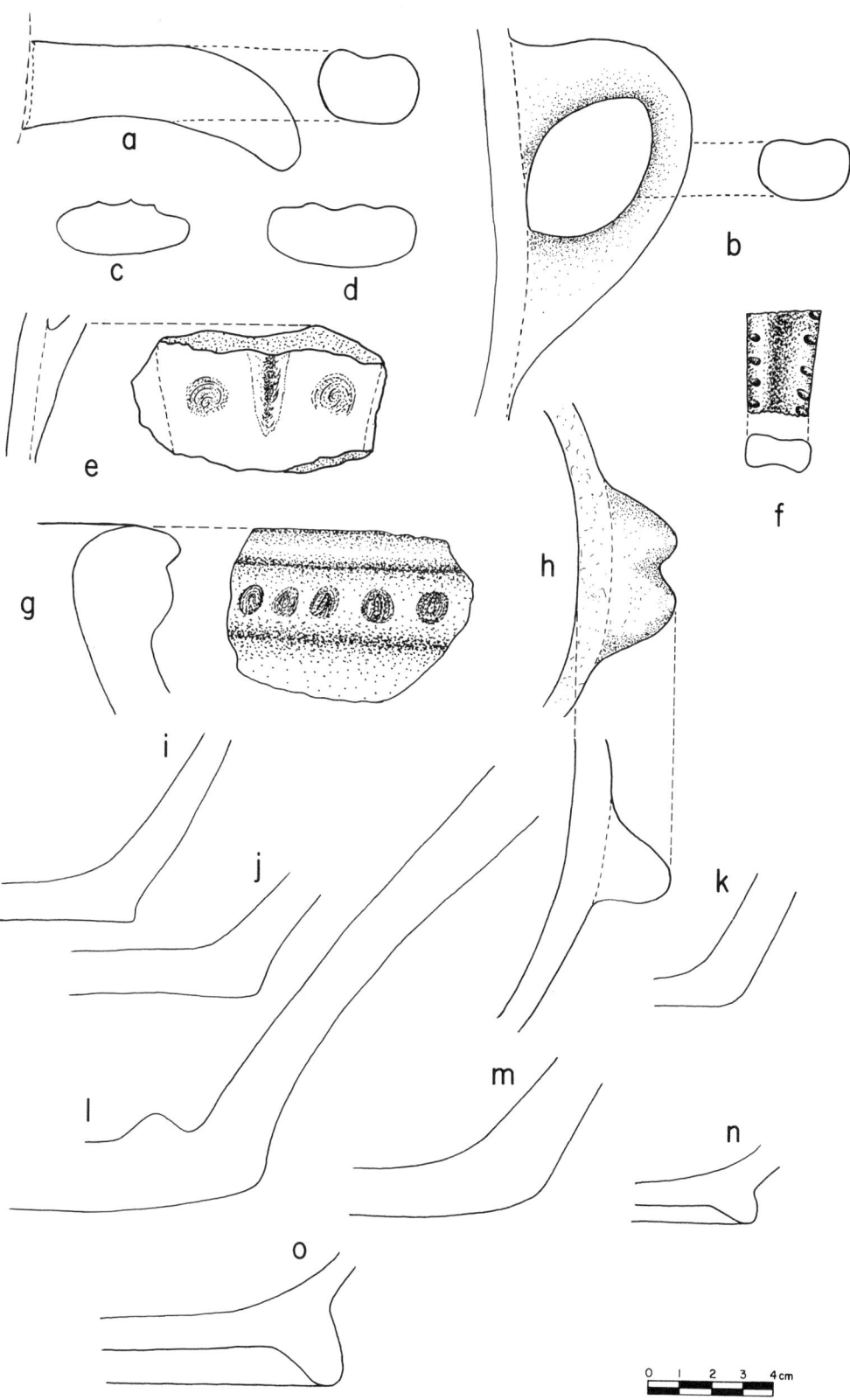

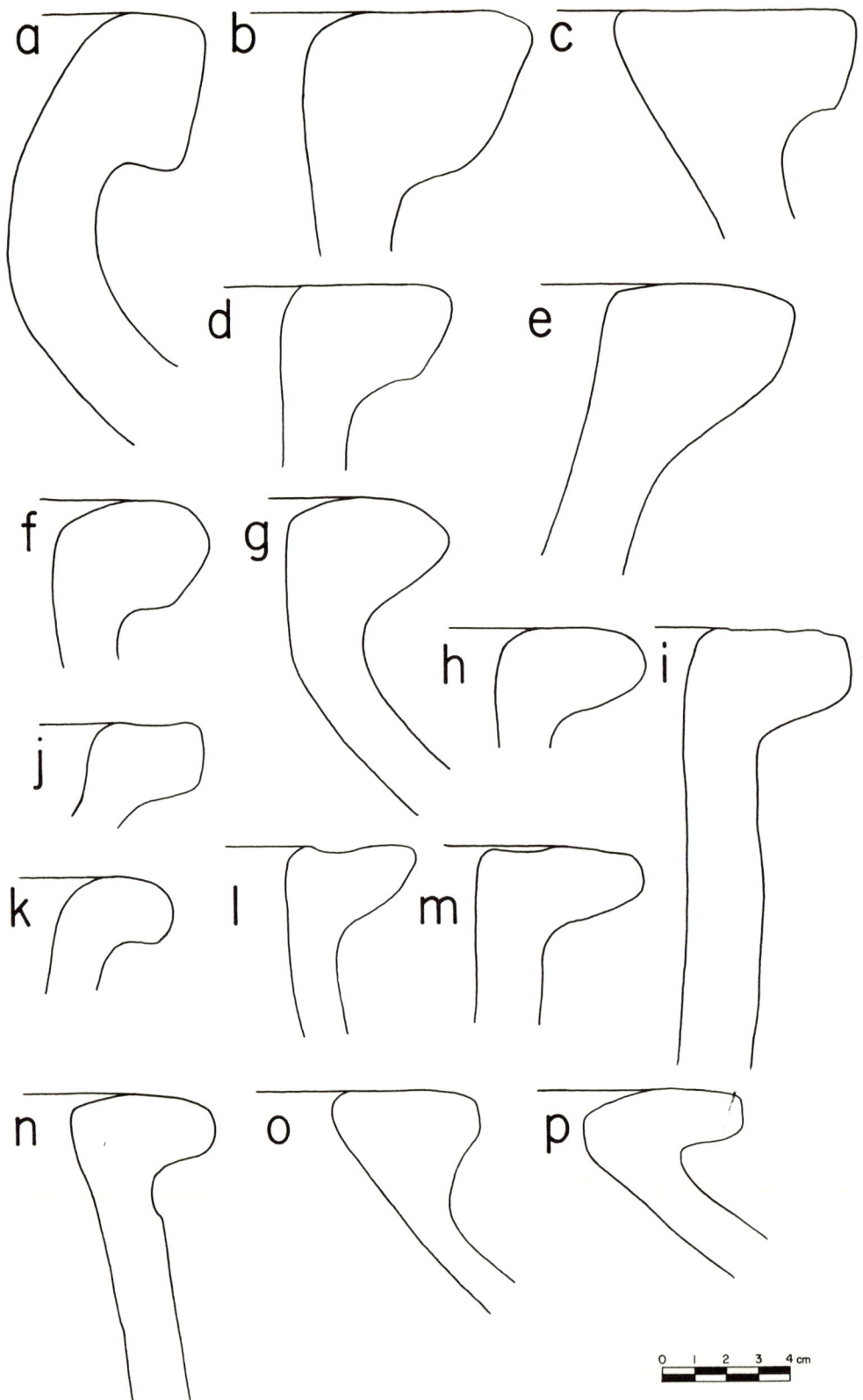

FIGURE 45 MEDIEVAL THICK WARE

a. 055/1, Gen'l. Exterior: orange–buff. Core: black. Interior: buff. Rim diameter: 40+ cm?

b. 054/13, Gen'l. Exterior, core, and interior: light buff. Rim diameter: 40 cm.

c. 054/6, Sq. A15. Exterior, core, and interior: buff–orange. Rim diameter: 40+ cm?

d. N52/2, Sq. A82. Exterior: light red slip. Core: dark gray center to light gray. Interior: gray. Rim diameter: 36–38 cm.

e. 054/8, Sq. A36. Exterior and interior: red. Core: black. Rim diameter: 26 cm.

f. N52/2, Sq. A55. Exterior and core: buff. Interior: buff–gray. Rim diameter: 40+ cm?

g. N52/2, Gen'l. Exterior, core, and interior: brown. Rim diameter: 34 cm.

h. 054/8, Sq. C36. Exterior and interior: cream–buff. Core: buff. Rim diameter: 40 cm.

i. N52/2, Sq. A45. Exterior: buff. Core red center to brown. Interior: buff–brown. Rim diameter: 40+ cm?

j. 054/2, Sq. 143. Exterior, core, and interior: cream–buff. Rim diameter: ?

k. 054/8, Sq. C30. Exterior and interior: brown–red. Core: brown. Rim diameter: 40 cm.

l. 054/8, Sq. C32. Exterior and interior: buff slip burnished over cream. Core: gray center to brownish cream. Rim diameter: 40+ cm?

m. N52/2, Sq. A87. Exterior, core, and interior: white. Rim diameter: 40+ cm?

n. N52/2, Sq. A86. Exterior, core, and interior: white. Rim diameter: ?

o. 054/9, Sq. B14. Exterior, core, and interior: brown. Rim diameter: 32 cm.

p. 054/4, Gen'l. Exterior and interior: red–brown burnished. Core: dark red. Rim diameter: 40+ cm?

FIGURE 46 MEDIEVAL THICK WARE

a. 054/13, Gen'l. Exterior, core, and interior: brown. Rim diameter: 34 cm.

b. 054/8, Sq. B26. Exterior and interior: red–buff. Core: gray center to buff. Rim diameter: 40+ cm?

c. 054/2, Sq. 43. Exterior and interior: brown. Core: buff–cream. Rim diameter: 38 cm.

d. 054/9, Sq. A20. Exterior, core, and interior: buff. Rim diameter: 26 cm.

e. 054/8, Sq. A36. Exterior and interior: red–brown. Core: orange. Rim diameter: 36 cm.

f. 054/8, Sq. A31. Exterior and interior: brown. Core: black. Rim diameter: 36 cm.

g. 054/6, Sq. A30. Exterior, core, and interior: cream–buff. Rim diameter: ?

h. N55/4, Sq. 21. Exterior and interior: red burnished. Core: brown center to light red. Rim diameter: 39 cm.

i. 055/8, Sq. 9. Exterior and interior: buff–orange. Core: cream–orange. Rim diameter: 40+ cm?

j. 055/4, Sq. 11. Exterior and interior: buff–brown burnished. Core: light orange–buff. Rim diameter: 40+ cm?

k. N52/8, Gen'l. Exterior and interior: buff. Core: gray center to buff. Rim diameter: 40+ cm?

l. 054/25, Sq. A14. Exterior and interior: buff. Core: dark gray center to buff. Rim diameter: ?

m. N52/2, Sq. C6. Exterior, core, and interior: brown. Rim diameter: 40+ cm?

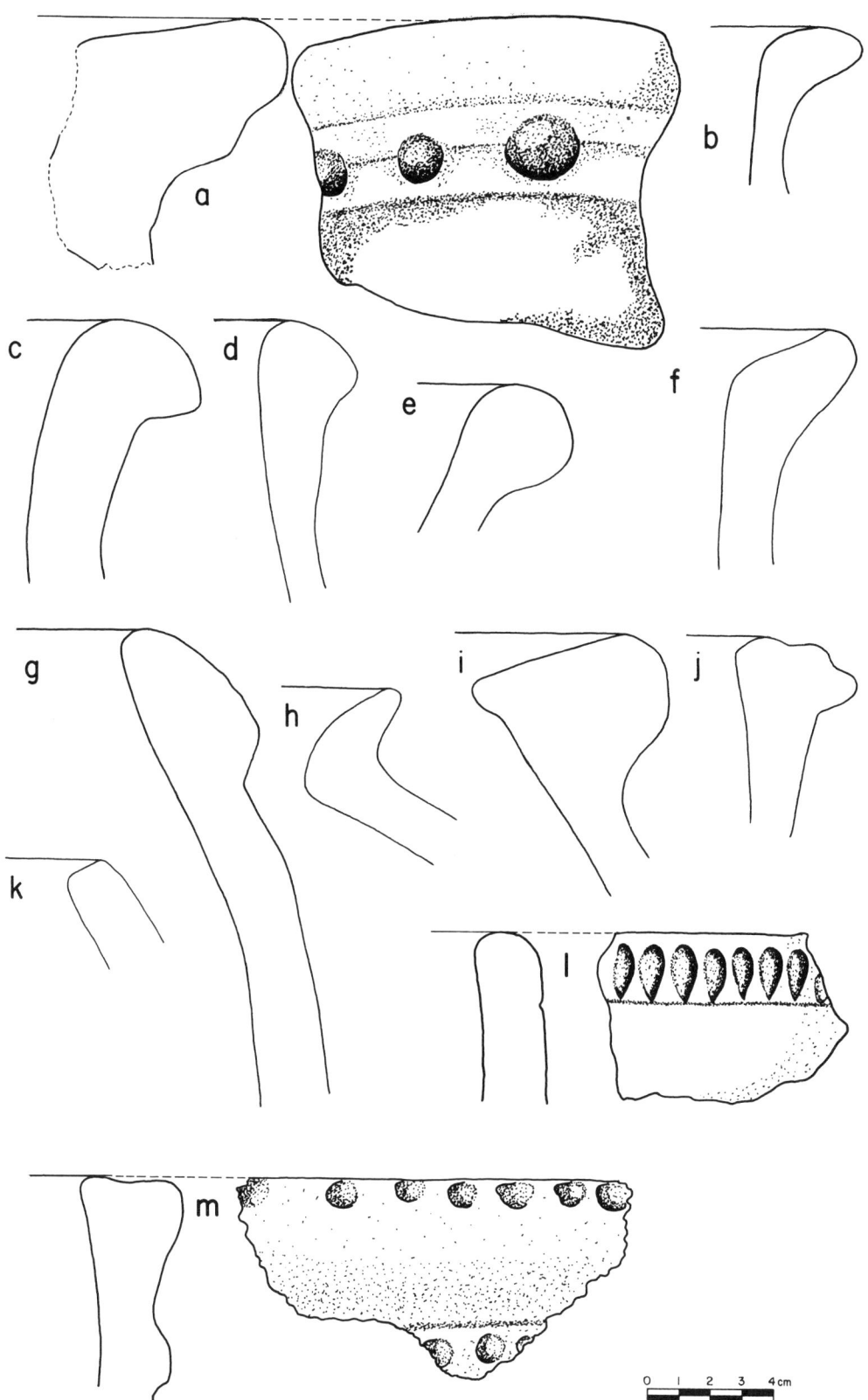

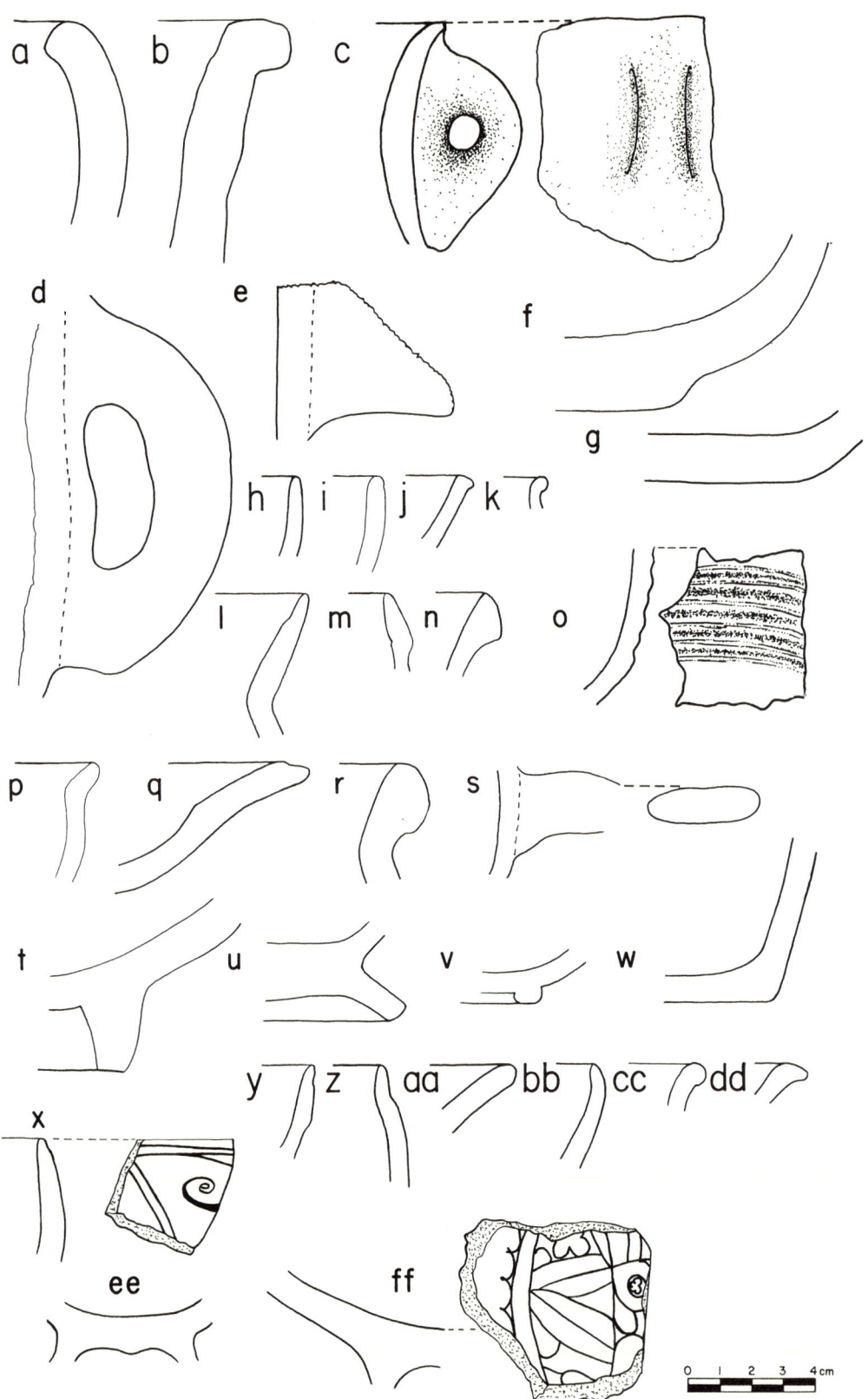

FIGURE 47

MEDIEVAL COARSE WARE

a. N52/2, Sq. A47. Exterior and interior: red-brown. Core: dark gray center to orange. Rim diameter: 30 cm.

b. 055/4, Sq. 14. Exterior: dark gray. Core: gray to orange. Interior: orange-gray. Rim diameter: ?

c. 055/8, Sq. 30. Exterior: light red-brown. Core: black. Interior: red-brown.

d. 055/1, Gen'l. Exterior: red-brown. Core: rust to gray. Interior: gray.

e. 054/8, Sq. D25. Exterior and interior: red-buff. Core: dark gray.

f. 054/8, Sq. D99. Exterior: brown. Core: dark gray center to orange-red. Interior: gray-brown.

g. 054/2, Sq. 158. Exterior: mottled gray and red-brown. Core: black. Interior: ?

MEDIEVAL GLAZED WARE

for h-v Exterior and interior: dark to light green glaze. Core: light buff to orange.

h. 054/25, Sq. A12. Rim diameter: 12–14 cm.
k. 054/2, Sq. 142. Rim diameter: ?
l. 054/2, Sq. 154. Diameter of neck constriction: 34 cm.
m. 055/1, Gen'l. Rim diameter: 16 cm?
n. 054/25, Sq. A28. Rim diameter: ?
o. 054/13, Gen'l.
p. 055/8, Sq. 18. Rim diameter: 10 cm.
q. 054/25, Sq. A26. Rim diameter: 24 cm.
r. 054/2, Sq. 6. Rim diameter: 22 cm.
s. 054/11, Sq. A5.
t. 054/12, Gen'l. Basal diameter: 8 cm.
u. 054/2, Sq. 90. Basal diameter: 10 cm.
v. 054/8, Sq. C28. Basal diameter: 9 cm.
w. 054/12, Sq. A34. Exterior: brown glaze. Core: buff. Interior: green glaze. Basal diameter: 12 cm.

MEDIEVAL SGRAFFIATO WARE

for x-ff Exterior and interior: dark to light green or gray-green glaze. Core: orange to buff.

x. N52/2, Sq. A24. Rim diameter: 25 cm?
y. N52/2, Sq. A3. Rim diameter: ?
z. 054/2, Sq. 172. Rim diameter: 16 cm.
aa. N52/2, Sq. A10. Rim diameter: 20 cm?
bb. 054/12, Sq. A85. Rim diameter: ?
cc. 054/2, Sq. 173. Rim diameter: 16 cm.
dd. 054/8, Sq. D63. Rim diameter: ?
ee. 054/12, Gen'l.
ff. 054/12, Gen'l.

FIGURE 48 MEDIEVAL RED SLIPPED WARE

a. N52/2, Sq. A82. Exterior: buff-gray. Core: black center to buff. Interior: red. Rim diameter: 12 cm.
b. 054/4, Gen'l. Exterior and interior: red-brown. Core: black. Rim diameter: 24 cm.
c. 054/16, Sq. B16. Exterior and interior: red. Core: gray center to orange. Rim diameter: ?
d. 054/6, Sq. A41. Exterior and interior: red. Core: orange. Rim diameter: 20 cm.
e. 054/17, Gen'l. Exterior and interior: red. Core: orange. Rim diameter: 24 cm.
f. 054/10, Sq. A15. Exterior and interior: red. Core: brown. Rim diameter: 22 cm.
g. 055/4, Sq. 49. Exterior and interior: red. Core: brown center to red. Rim diameter: 20 cm.
h. N52/2, Sq. A30. Exterior and interior: red. Core: cream-buff. Rim diameter: 28 cm.
i. 054/25, Sq. A6. Exterior and interior: red. Core: red-brown. Rim diameter: 24 cm.
j. 054/12, Sq. A2. Exterior: red. Core: black. Interior: brown. Rim diameter: 10 cm.
k. 054/8, Sq. A40. Exterior and interior: red-brown. Core: black. Rim diameter: 26 cm.
l. 054/8, Sq. A58. Exterior and interior: red. Core: red-orange. Rim diameter: 26 cm.
m. 054/7, Gen'l. Exterior and interior: red-brown. Core: black center to red-brown. Rim diameter: 26 cm.
n. 054/10, Sq. A5. Exterior: red. Core and interior: red-brown. Rim diameter: 28 cm.
o. 055/4, Sq. 31. Exterior and interior: red. Core: orange. Rim diameter: 14 cm.
p. 054/8, Sq. A40. Exterior and interior: red-brown. Core: brown. Rim diameter: 26 cm.
q. 054/2, Sq. 115. Exterior: red-brown. Core: brown. Interior: red-orange. Rim diameter: 24 cm.
r. 054/10, Sq. A15. Exterior and interior: red. Core: orange. Rim diameter: 28 cm.
s. 054/16, Sq. A7. Exterior and interior: red. Core: brown. Rim diameter: 18 cm.
t. 054/17, Gen'l. Exterior and interior: red. Core: gray center to orange. Rim diameter: 22 cm.
u. 054/17, Gen'l. Exterior and interior: red. Core: brown. Rim diameter: 20 cm.
v. 054/17, Gen'l. Exterior: black. Core: gray. Interior: red. Rim diameter: 22 cm.
w. 054/11, Sq. A4. Exterior: brown-red. Core: brown. Interior: red. Rim diameter: 20 cm.
x. 054/8, Sq. C38. Exterior: red-brown. Core: brown. Interior: red. Rim diameter: 28 cm.
y. 054/8, Sq. C30. Exterior: red-brown. Core: buff. Interior: red. Rim diameter: 10 cm.
z. 054/8, Sq. D63. Exterior and interior: red-brown. Core: brown. Rim diameter: 10 cm.
aa. 054/8, Sq. C36. Exterior: red-brown. Core and interior: buff-orange. Rim diameter: 28 cm.
bb. 054/8, Sq. D55. Exterior and interior: red. Core: orange. Rim diameter: 18 cm.
cc. 054/10, Sq. A18. Exterior and interior: red. Core: black. Rim diameter: 24 cm.
dd. 054/8, Sq. A27. Exterior and interior: red-brown. Core: black. Rim diameter: ?
ee. 054/8, Sq. C97. Exterior: red-buff. Core: gray center to buff. Interior: red-brown. Rim diameter: 32 cm.
ff. 054/12, Sq. C42. Exterior: red. Core: buff to orange. Interior: orange-cream. Rim diameter: 32 cm.
gg. 054/8, Sq. C41. Exterior and interior: red-brown. Core: brown. Rim diameter: 28 cm.
hh. 054/8, Sq. D16. Exterior and interior: red-brown. Core: buff-orange. Rim diameter: 24 cm.
ii. 054/12, Sq. B10. Exterior and interior: red. Core: orange. Rim diameter: 30 cm.
jj. 054/11, Sq. A6. Exterior, core, and interior: red-brown. Rim diameter: ?
kk. 054/8, Sq. C32. Exterior and interior: red. Core: red-brown. Rim diameter: 24 cm.
ll. 054/9, Sq. A30. Exterior, core, and interior: red-brown. Rim diameter: 28 cm.
mm. 054/2, Sq. 153. Exterior: red-brown. Core: brown to buff. Interior: buff. Rim diameter: 22 cm.
nn. N52/2, Sq. C7. Exterior and interior: red. Core: brown. Rim diameter: 24 cm.

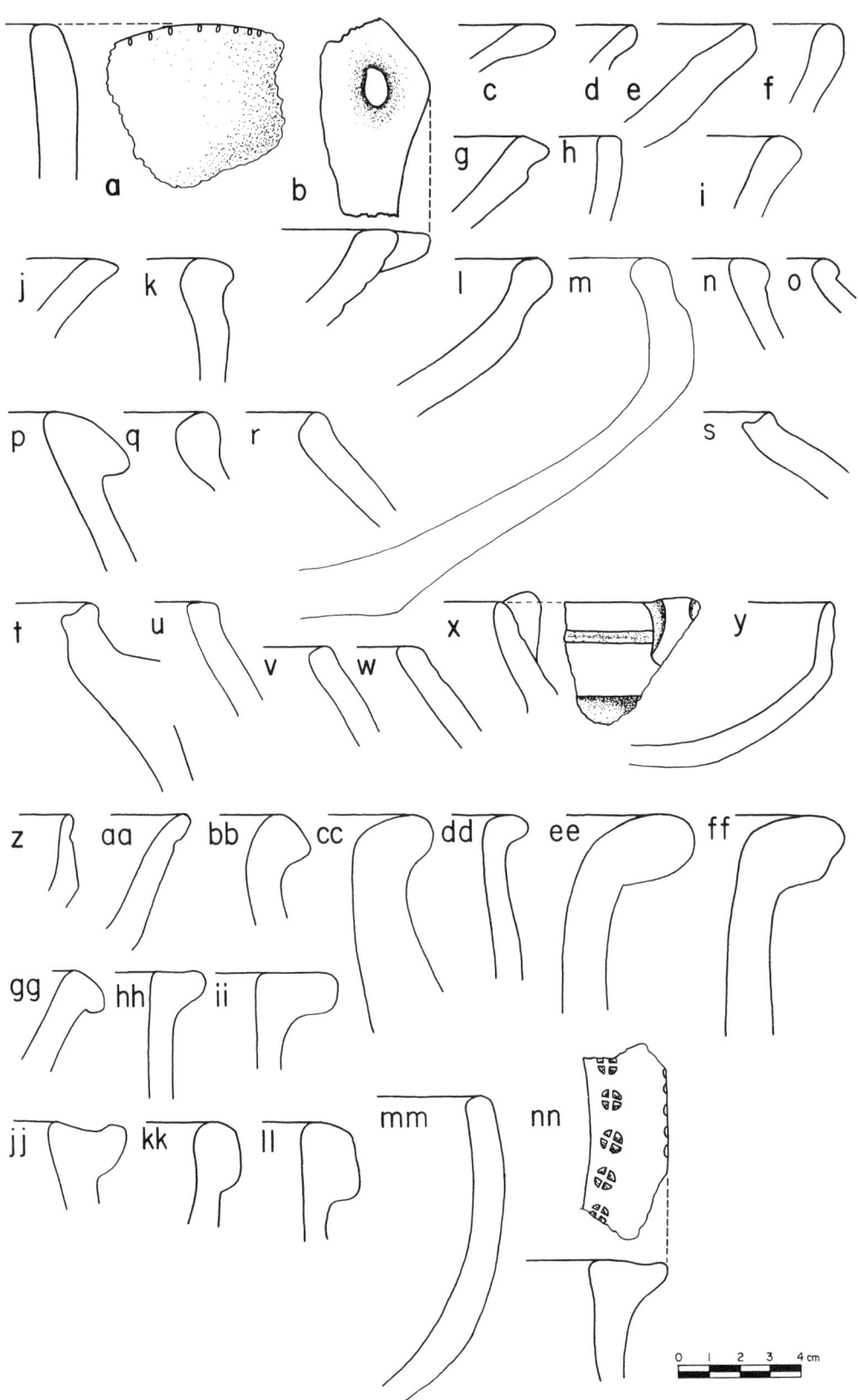

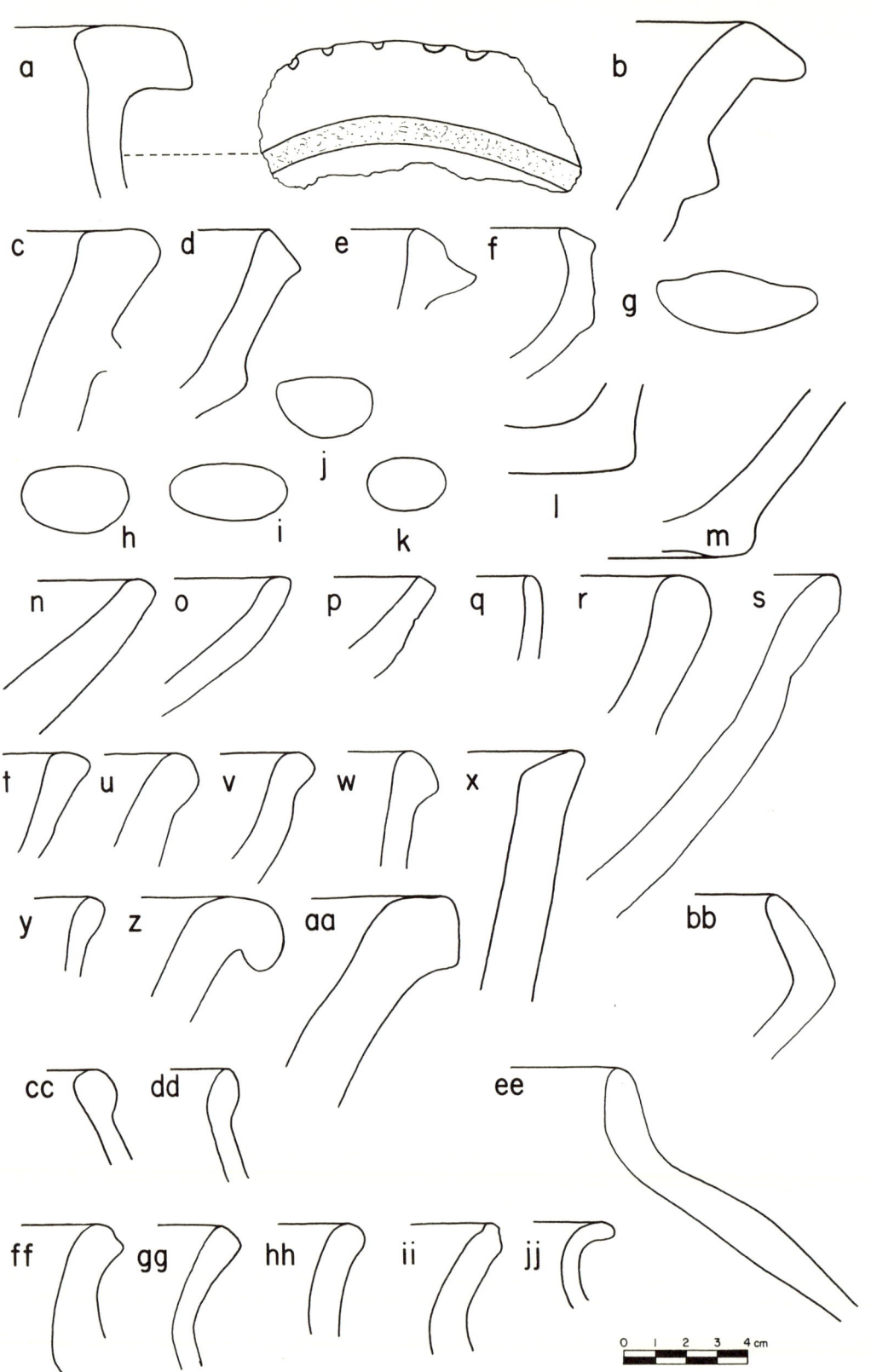

FIGURE 49

MEDIEVAL RED SLIPPED WARE

a. N52/2, Sq. A59. Exterior: red-brown. Core and interior: brown. Rim diameter: 26 cm.
b. 054/2, Sq. 170. Exterior: red. Core: black. Interior: red-brown. Rim diameter: 24 cm.
c. 054/11, Sq. A34. Exterior: red. Core: black. Interior: buff. Rim diameter: 20 cm.
d. 054/8, Sq. C46. Exterior: buff. Core: orange. Interior: red. Rim diameter: 32 cm.
e. 054/11, Sq. B15. Exterior and interior: red. Core: orange. Rim diameter: 30 cm.
f. 054/25, Sq. A27. Exterior: red. Core and interior: orange-brown. Rim diameter: 18 cm.
g. N52/2, Sq. A49. Exterior: red on buff. Core: buff. Interior: buff.
h. 054/2, Sq. 141. Exterior: red. Core: black center to buff.
i. N52/2, Sq. A54. Exterior: red. Core: brown.
j. 054/2, Sq. 118. Exterior: red-brown. Core: black.
k. N52/2, Sq. A61. Exterior: red-brown. Core: cream-buff. Interior: cream.
l. 054/10, Sq. A18. Exterior and interior: red. Core: black center to buff.
m. 054/2, Sq. 167. Exterior: red. Core: black center to brown. Interior: buff. Basal diameter: 16 cm.

MEDIEVAL WHITE SLIPPED WARE

n. N52/2, Sq. C7. Exterior: white slip over light orange. Core: gray center to orange. Interior: light orange. Rim diameter: 30 cm.
o. 054/6, Sq. B27. Exterior and interior: white slip on brick red. Core: gray. Rim diameter: 32 cm.
p. 054/8, Sq. D41. Exterior: white slip on orange-red. Core: gray center to orange. Interior: orange-red. Rim diameter: 30 cm?
q. 054/8, Sq. D52. Exterior: white slip on orange-red. Core: orange-red. Interior: ? Rim diameter: ?
r. 054/12, Sq. A19. Exterior and interior: white slip on orange. Core: gray center to orange. Rim diameter: ?
s. 054/8, Sq. A23. Exterior: white slip on orange. Core: orange. Interior: red-brown. Rim diameter: 40 cm.
t. 054/8, Sq. C31. Exterior: white slip on light gray. Core: light buff-orange. Rim diameter: 26 cm?
u. 054/6, Sq. A19. Exterior: white slip on brown. Core: black center to buff. Interior: brown-buff. Rim diameter: 40 cm.
v. 054/8, Sq. A46. Exterior: white slip on red-buff. Core: dark gray center to orange. Interior: white slip on brown-buff. Rim diameter: 28 cm.
w. 054/8, Sq. C27. Exterior: white slip on orange. Core: gray center to orange. Interior: cream. Rim diameter: 18 cm.
x. 054/25, Sq. A28. Exterior and interior: white slip on orange. Core: bright orange. Rim diameter: ?
y. 054/8, Sq. A49. Exterior and interior: white slip on buff. Core: buff. Rim diameter: 20 cm.
z. 054/8, Sq. A57. Exterior and interior: white slip on brown. Core: buff-brown. Rim diameter: ?
aa. 054/8, Sq. C55. Exterior and interior: white slip on orange. Core: gray center to orange. Rim diameter: ?
bb. 054/12, Sq. B10. Exterior: white slip on orange. Core: red-orange. Interior: orange. Rim diameter: 30 cm.
cc. 054/8, Sq. C17. Exterior: white slip on rust-brown. Core: black. Interior: rust-brown. Rim diameter: 22 cm.
dd. 054/12, Sq. B12. Exterior and interior: white slip on red-orange. Core: red-orange. Rim diameter: 14 cm.
ee. 055/1, Sq. 8. Exterior: white slip over brown. Core: orange-red. Interior: red-brown. Rim diameter: 40 cm.
ff. 054/6, Gen'l. Exterior and interior: buff slip on brick red. Core: black center to orange. Rim diameter: ?
gg. 054/8, Sq. D77. Exterior and interior: white slip on orange. Core: orange. Rim diameter: 18 cm.
hh. 054/8, Sq. A15. Exterior and interior: white slip on orange. Core: bright orange. Rim diameter: ?
ii. 055/4, Gen'l. Exterior and interior: white slip on orange. Core: gray center to orange. Rim diameter: 18 cm.
jj. 055/4, Sq. 16. Exterior and interior: white slip on orange. Core: bright orange. Rim diameter: 20 cm.

FIGURE 50

MEDIEVAL WHITE SLIPPED WARE

a. 054/27, Sq. A7. Exterior and interior: white slip on buff. Core: dark gray center to orange-buff. Rim diameter: 40+ cm?

b. 054/8, Sq. C47. Exterior and interior: white slip on buff. Core: buff. Rim diameter: 40+ cm.

c. 054/8, Sq. C28. Exterior: white slip on orange-brown. Core: gray center to orange. Interior: orange. Rim diameter: 38 cm.

d. 054/8, Sq. D74. Exterior and interior: white slip on red-brown. Core: gray center to red-orange. Rim diameter: 40+ cm.

e. 054/8, Sq. C16. Exterior: white slip on orange. Core: black center to orange. Interior: white slip on brown. Rim diameter: 34 cm?

f. 054/8, Gen'l. Exterior and interior: white slip on buff-orange. Core: orange. Rim diameter: 40+ cm.

g. 054/8, Sq. A29. Exterior and interior: white slip on orange. Core: black. Rim diameter: 40+ cm?

h. 054/8, Sq. C36. Exterior and interior: white slip on orange. Rim diameter: ?

i. 054/8, Sq. C36. Exterior and interior: white slip on orange. Core: bright red-orange. Rim diameter: 32 cm.

j. 055/8, Sq. 18. Exterior: red-brown. Core: gray center to orange. Interior: white slip on red. Rim diameter: ?

k. 054/8, Sq. C22. Exterior: white slip on orange. Core: gray center to orange. Interior: orange. Rim diameter: ?

l. 054/8, Sq. A9. Exterior: white slip on brown. Core: black center to orange.

m. N52/2, Sq. B36. Exterior: cream slip on cream-buff. Core: gray center to cream-buff.

n. 054/1, Gen'l. Exterior: white slip on orange. Core: dark gray center to orange. Interior: orange.

MEDIEVAL PAINTED WARE

for o-t Unless otherwise noted:
Exterior: red painted on cream-buff to gray. Core: cream-buff to gray. Interior: cream-buff to gray with red paint inside lip.

o. N52/2, Sq. A5. Rim diameter: 20 cm.
p. N52/2, Sq. B31. Rim diameter: 34 cm.
q. N52/2, Sq. A85. Exterior: spotty red painting. Rim diameter: ?
r. N52/2, Sq. A35. Red paint on flat top of lip. Rim diameter: ?
s. N52/2, Sq. B31. Rim diameter: 17 cm.
t. N52/2, Sq. A34. Rim diameter: ?

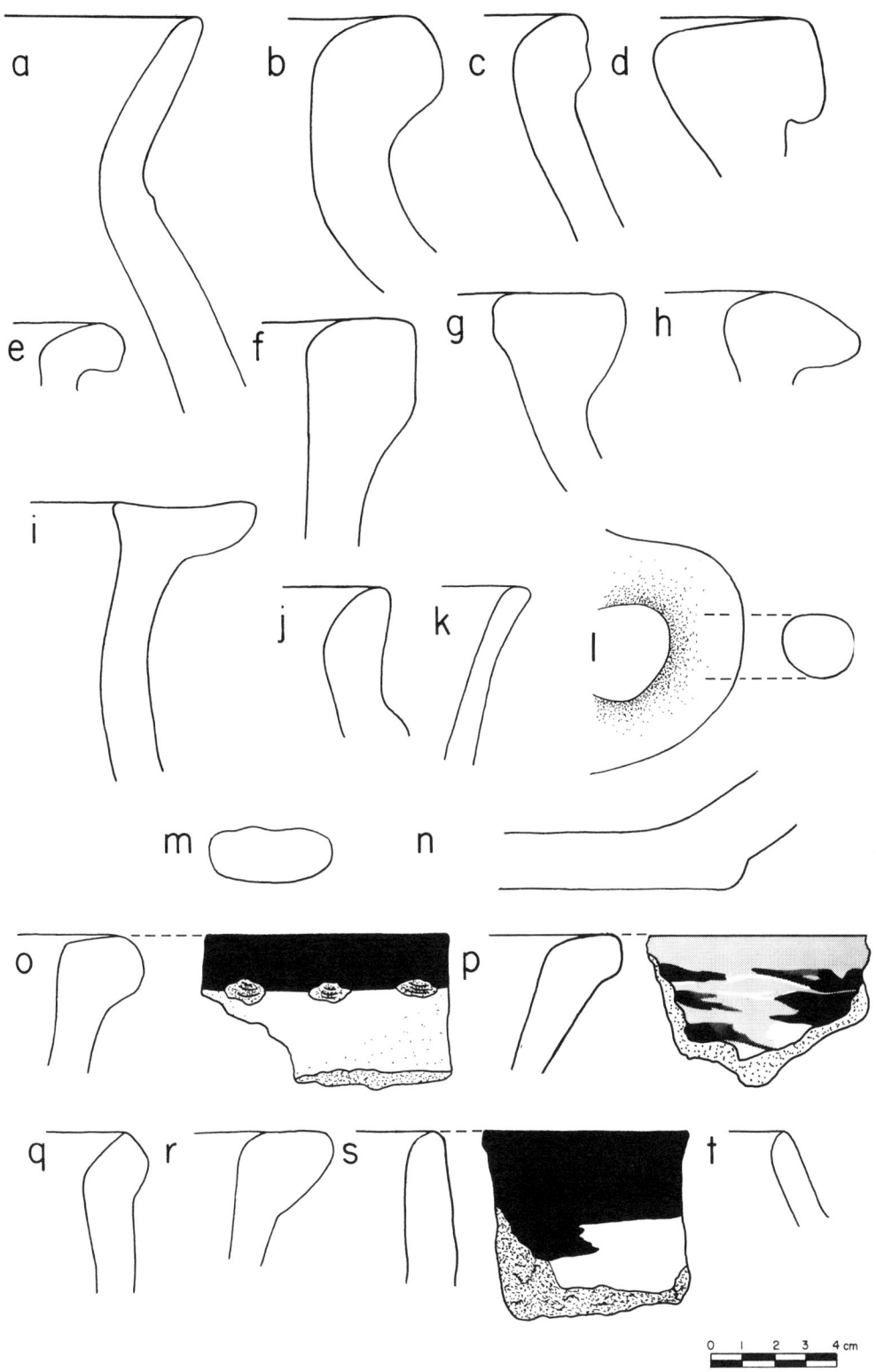

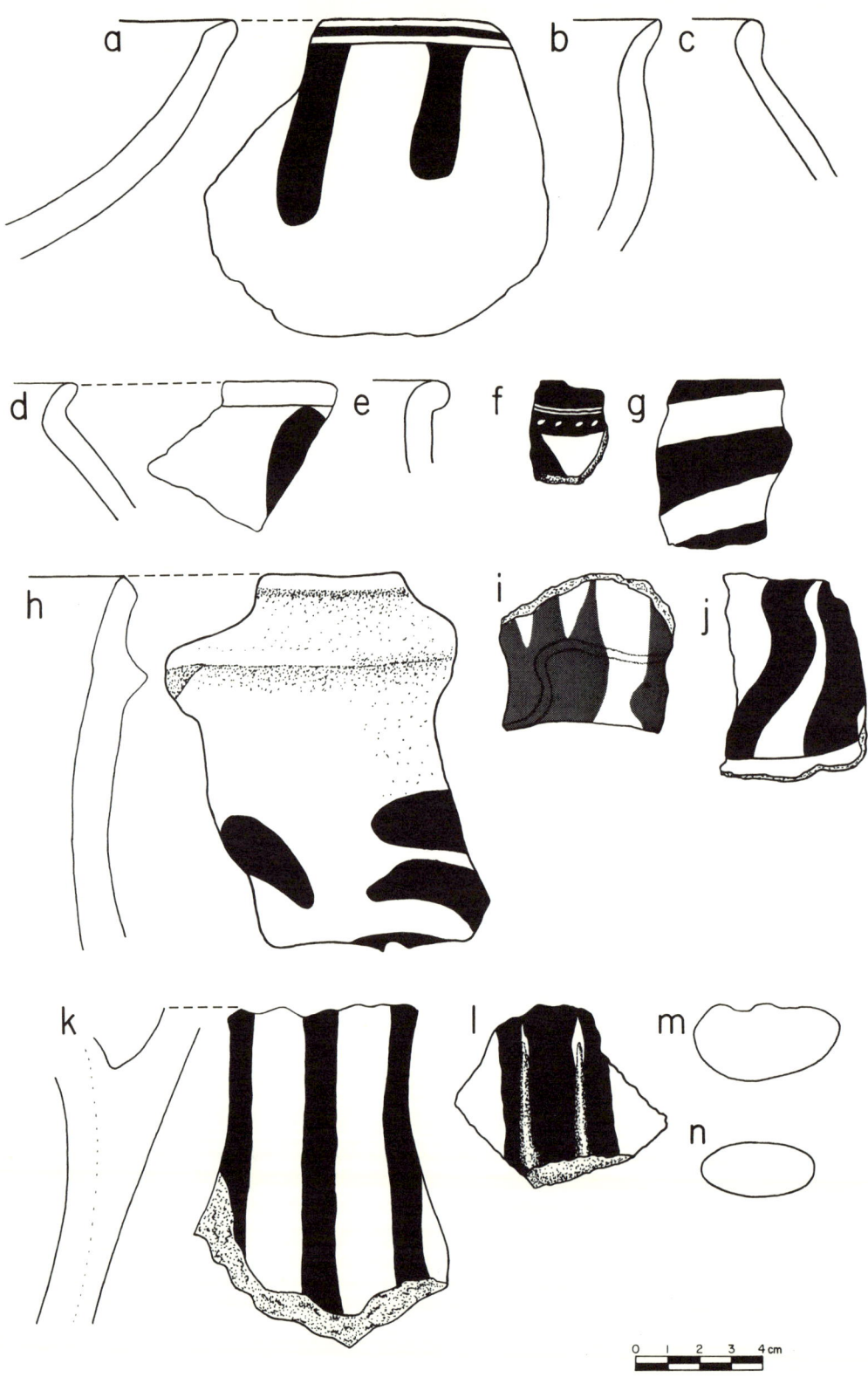

150

FIGURE 51 MEDIEVAL PAINTED WARE

All, unless otherwise noted: Exterior: red painted on cream–buff to gray. Core: cream–buff to gray. Interior: cream–buff to gray with red paint inside lip.

    a. O55/8, Sq. 21.   Rim diameter: 32 cm.
    b. O55/9, Sq. 5.   Rim diameter: 18 ? cm.
    c. N52/2, Sq. A40.   Rim diameter: 18 cm.
    d. O54/6, Sq. A12.   Rim diameter: 22 cm.
    e. O54/8, Sq. A41.   Core: dark orange. Rim diameter: ?
    f. N52/2, Sq. A36.
    g. N52/2, Sq. A5.
    h. O54/25, Sq. A26.   Rim diameter: 10 cm.
    i. O54/11, Sq. A32.
    j. N52/2, Sq. A4.
    k. O54/9, Sq. 31.   Exterior: red paint on cream slip. Core: orange. Interior: cream slip.
    l. O54/8, Sq. D68.
    m. N52/2, Sq. B27.
    n. N52/2, Sq. A57.

FIGURE 52 MEDIEVAL COOKING WARE

All, unless otherwise noted: Exterior, core, and interior: red-brown to black, varying on the same sherd.

a. N52/2, Sq. B9. Rim diameter: 8 cm.
b. 054/16, Sq. B9. Rim diameter: 20 cm.
c. N52/2, Sq. A41. Rim diameter: ?
d. 054/8, Sq. D34. Rim diameter: ?
e. 054/16, Sq. A12. Rim diameter: 15 cm.
f. 054/25, Sq. A25. Rim diameter: 11 cm.
g. 054/8, Gen'l. Exterior and interior: dark mottled brown-red burnished. Core: gray center to red-brown. Rim diameter: 17 cm.
h. 054/16, Sq. A17. Rim diameter. ?
i. 054/8, Sq. A53. Rim diameter: ?
j. 054/2, Gen'l. Rim diameter: ?
k. 054/8, Sq. C36. Rim diameter: 13 cm.
l. 054/13, Gen'l. Rim diameter: ?
m. 054/13, Gen'l. Rim diameter: 28 cm.
n. 054/25, Sq. A27. Rim diameter: 20 cm?
o. 054/13, Gen'l. Rim diameter: 18 cm.
p. 054/2, Sq. 160. Rim diameter: ?
q. 054/25, Sq. A30. Rim diameter: ?
r. 054/2, Sq. 170. Exterior and interior: red slip over dark buff orange. Rim diameter: 26 cm?
s. 054/11, Sq. A35. Rim diameter: ?
t. 055/4, Sq. 46. Exterior, core, and interior: gray-brown. Rim diameter: 22 cm.
u. 054/8, Sq. A76. Exterior: red-brown. Core: red-brown to black. Interior: black to gray. Rim diameter: ?
v. 054/8, Sq. A7. Exterior and interior: dark mottled red-brown burnished. Core: gray center to red-brown. Rim diameter: 31 cm.
w. 054/19, Gen'l. Exterior: red-orange smoothed, blackened. Core: red-orange. Interior: orange. Rim diameter: 15 cm.
x. 054/8, Sq. D56. Exterior and interior: dark mottled red-brown burnished. Core: gray center to red-brown. Rim diameter: 21 cm.
y. 054/8, Sq. D25. Exterior and interior: dark mottled red-brown burnished. Core: gray center to red-brown. Rim diameter: 24 cm.
z. 054/6, Sq. A40. Rim diameter: 18 cm.
aa. 054/8, Sq. C33. Rim diameter: 18 cm.
bb. 054/8, Sq. D72. Rim diameter: 14 cm?
cc. 054/8, Sq. A48. Rim diameter: 17 cm.
dd. 054/19, Gen'l. Exterior: buff slip, blackened. Core: dark gray center to buff-brown. Interior: gray. Rim diameter: 30 cm.
ee. 055/8, Sq. 19. Exterior, core, and interior: black. Rim diameter: 18 cm.
ff. 055/9, Sq. 7. Exterior, core, and interior: dark gray to black.
gg. 054/10, Sq. A10. Rim diameter: ?
hh. 055/9, Gen'l. Exterior: black. Core: black to brown. Interior: brown. Rim diameter: 18 cm.
ii. 055/9, Gen'l. Exterior: mottled light brown to black. Core: light gray. Interior: light brown. Rim diameter: 18 cm.
jj. 054/8, Sq. D68. Rim diameter: 30 cm.
kk. 054/6, Sq. B12. Rim diameter: 18 cm.
ll. 054/12, Sq. A28. Rim diameter: ?

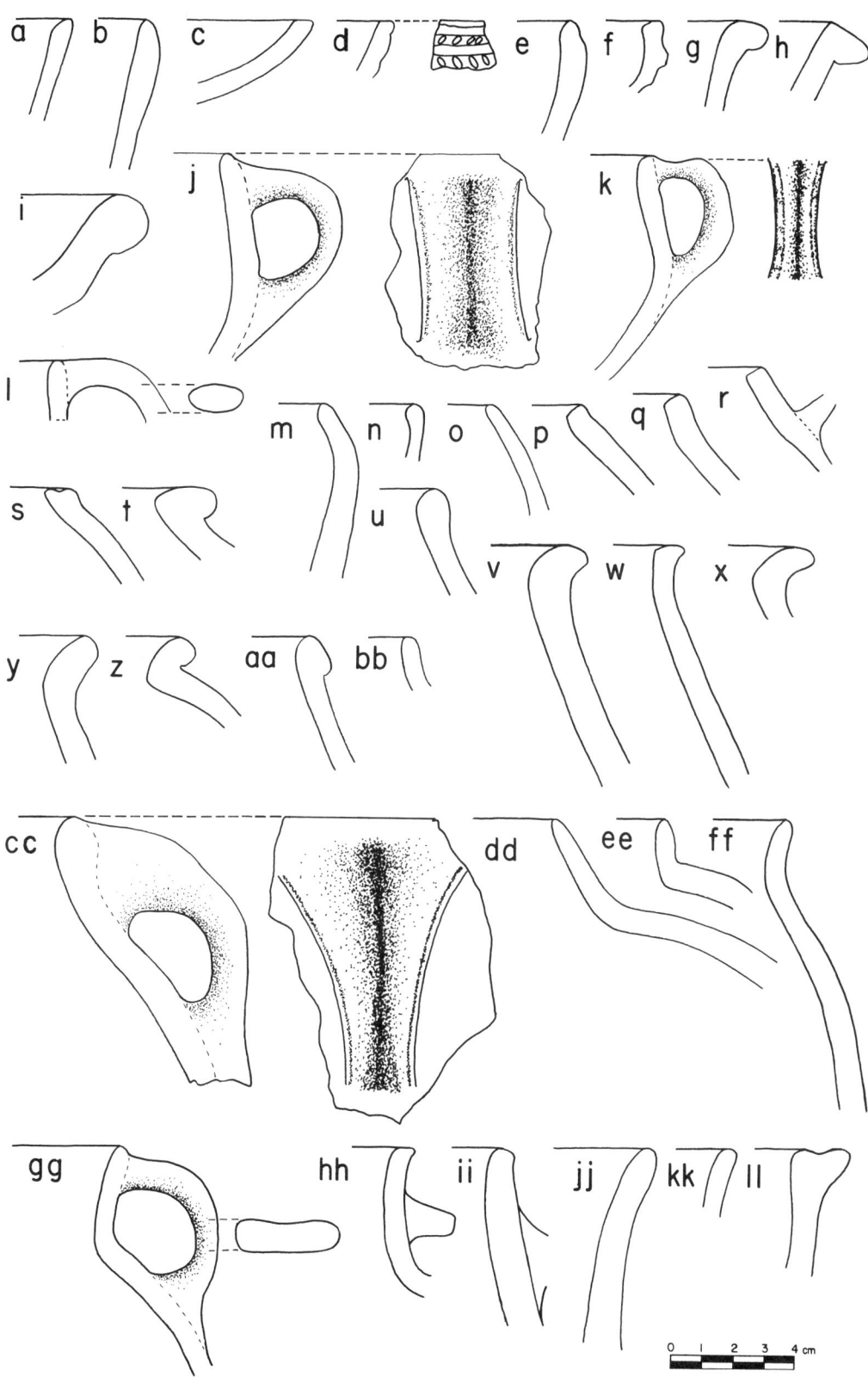

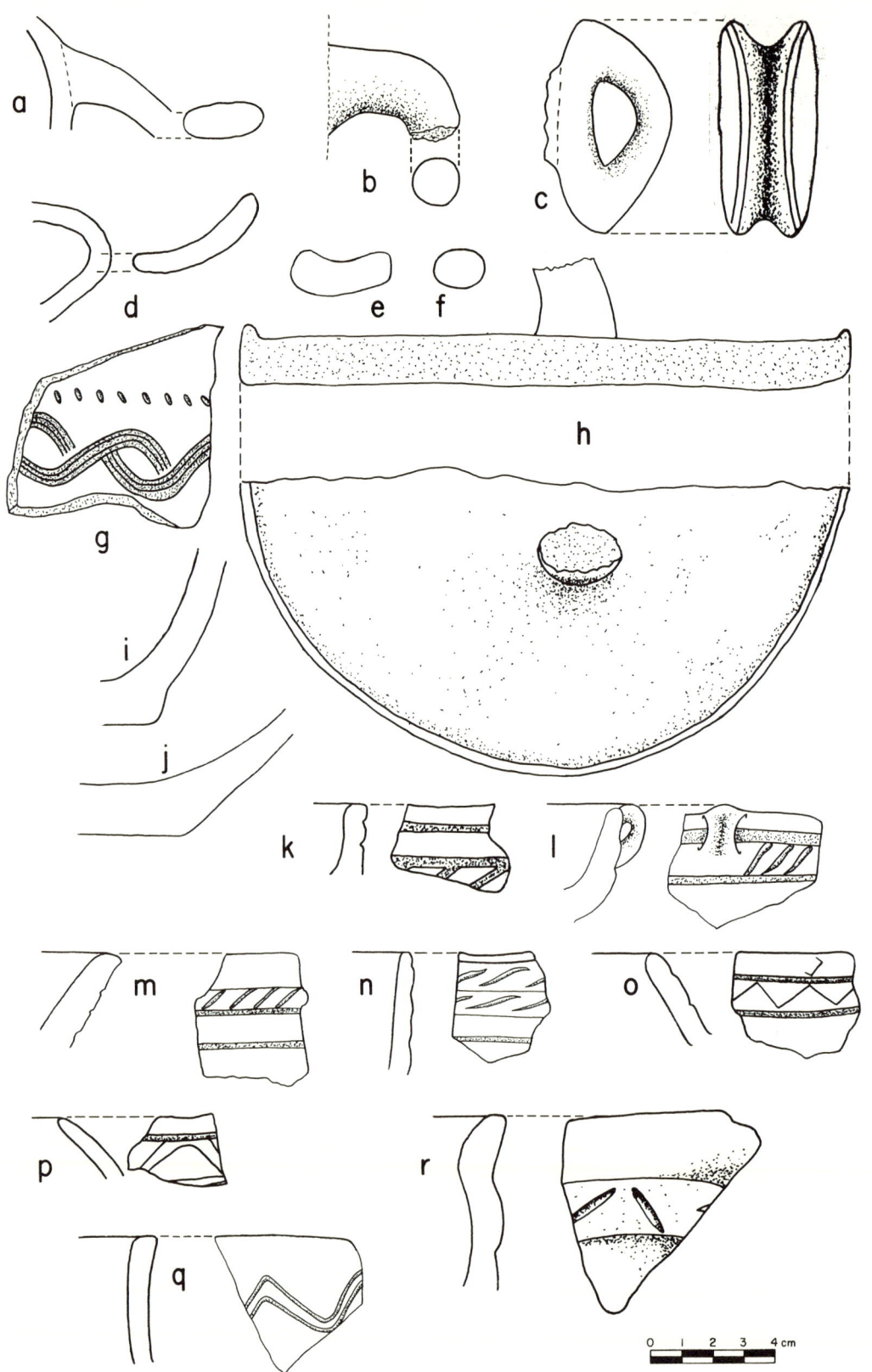

FIGURE 53

MEDIEVAL COOKING WARE

for a–j   Unless otherwise noted: Exterior, core, and interior: red–brown to black, varying on the same sherd.

    a. 054/2, Sq. 157.
    b. 054/8, Sq. C41.
    c. N53/3, Gen'l.
    d. 054/2, Sq. 126.
    e. N52/2, Sq. A33.
    f. 054/2, Sq. 141.
    g. 054/1, Gen'l.
    h. 054/2, Sq. 159.   Exterior: buff-orange. Core: buff to black. Interior: black.
    i. 054/2, Sq. 158.   Basal diameter: 11 cm.
    j. 054/2, Sq. 170.   Basal diameter: 10 cm.

MEDIEVAL MODELED WARE

    k. 054/8, Sq. D77.   Exterior and interior: red–brown. Core: orange. Rim diameter: 16 cm.
    l. 054/8, Gen'l.   Exterior and interior: orange burnished. Core: orange. Rim diameter: 16 cm.
    m. 054/8, Sq. D69.   Exterior and interior: red–brown. Core: black. Rim diameter: 18 cm.
    n. 054/8, Sq. A61.   Exterior and interior: brown burnished. Core: orange. Rim diameter: 14 cm.
    o. 054/8, Sq. B66.   Exterior: buff–brown burnished. Core: brown. Interior: red–brown burnished. Rim diameter: 26 cm.
    p. 054/8, Sq. C31.   Exterior and interior: red–brown. Core: orange. Rim diameter: 12 cm.
    q. 054/2, Sq. 162.   Exterior and interior: orange. Core: red–orange. Rim diameter: 16 cm.
    r. 054/8, Sq. C40.   Exterior and interior: red–brown burnished. Core: orange-brown. Rim diameter: 30 cm.

FIGURE 54 MEDIEVAL MODELED WARE

a. 054/8, Sq. C34. Exterior and interior: red–brown. Core: gray center to orange. Rim diameter: 32 cm.

b. 055/7, Gen'l. Exterior and interior: brown burnished. Core: orange-brown. Rim diameter: 8 cm.

c. 054/25, Sq. A30. Exterior and interior: brick red. Core: brown.

d. 054/2, Sq. 169. Exterior and interior: brown. Core: black.

e. N52/2, Sq. A44. Exterior: brown. Core: gray center to buff. Interior: gray–buff.

f. 054/2, Sq. 189. Exterior, core, and interior: buff.

g. 054/8, Sq. A51. Exterior and interior: brick red. Core: black center to brown.

h. 055/1, Gen'l. Exterior and interior: buff–orange. Core: orange.

i. 054/2, Sq. 171. Exterior, core, and interior: buff.

j. 054/28, Gen'l. Exterior: buff–orange. Core: gray center to orange. Interior: buff.

k. 055/7, Gen'l. Exterior: brick brown burnished. Core: orange to black. Interior: brown, blackened.

l. 054/25, Sq. A1. Exterior: brown. Core: dark gray. Interior: brown–black.

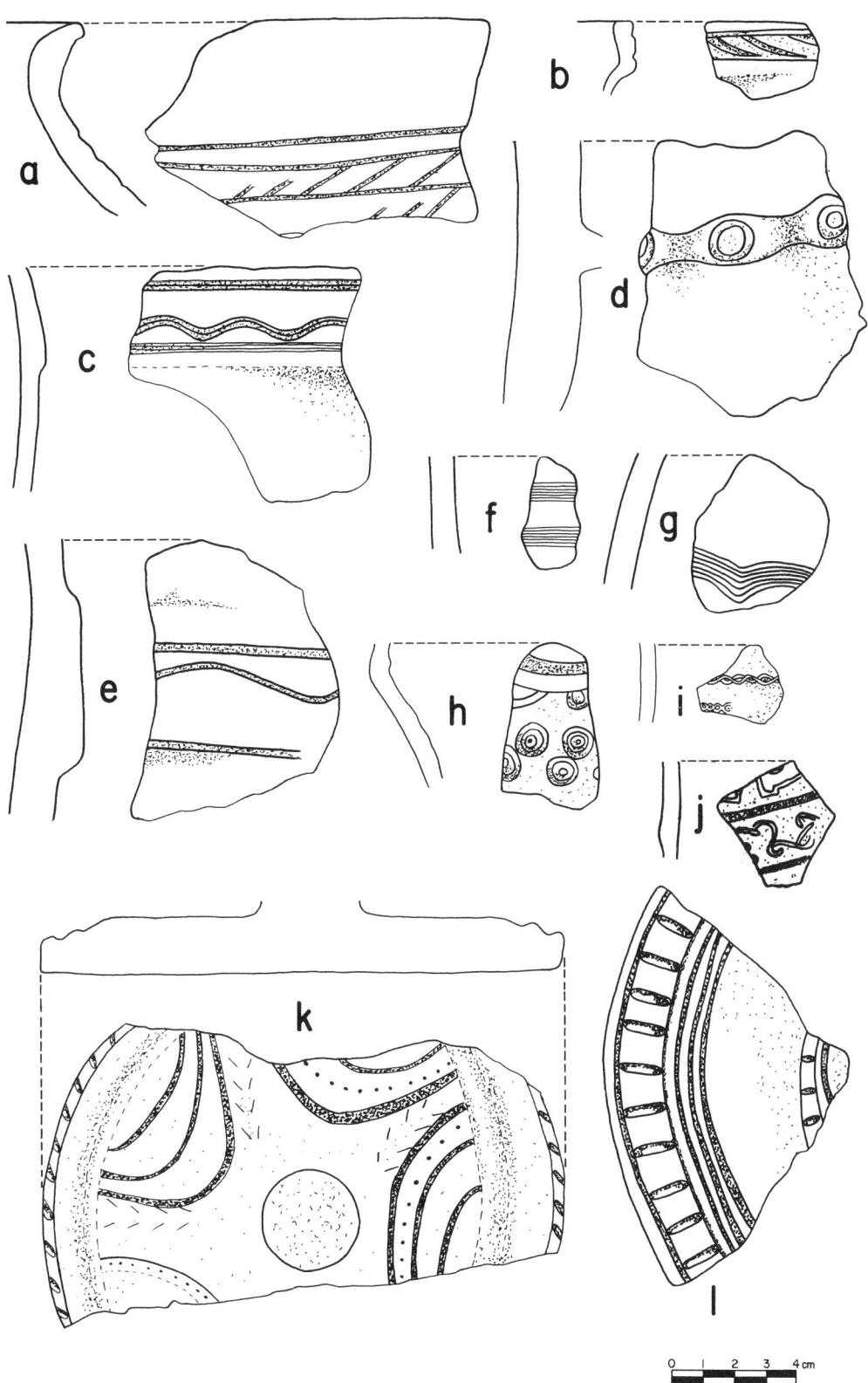

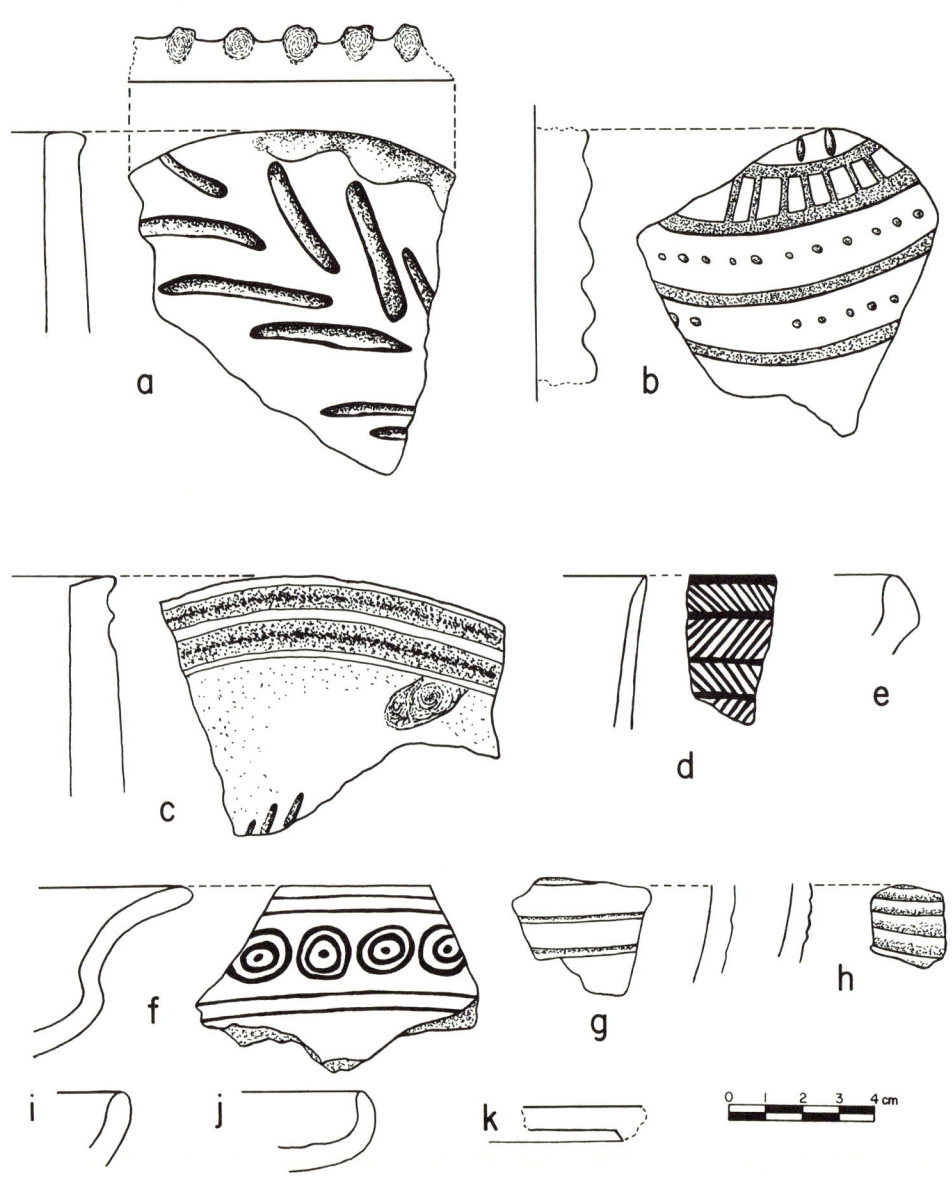

158

FIGURE 55

MEDIEVAL MODELED WARE
a. 054/1, Gen'l. Exterior, core, and interior: red–brown.
b. N52/2, Sq. B34. Exterior, core, and interior: brown.
c. N52/2, Sq. B39. Exterior: buff. Core: brown. Interior: red–brown.

HALAFIAN WARE
d. N55/1, Gen'l. Exterior: slightly glossy reddish brown paint on white slip. Core: buff. Interior: ? Rim diameter: 14 cm.

HITTITE RED WARE
e. 055/4, Gen'l. Exterior and interior: thick, dark red slip. Core: dark gray. Rim diameter: 22 cm.

PHRYGIAN (?) CERAMICS
f. 054/9, Gen'l. Exterior: white slip on buff–brown; black paint. Core: buff–brown. Interior: white slip on buff–brown. Rim diameter: 24–26 cm.
g. 054/8, Sq. B14. Exterior: black burnished. Core: black. Interior: gray–black.
h. 054/2, Sq. 177. Exterior: black burnished. Core and interior: black.

ROMAN RED WARE
i. 054/15, Gen'l. Exterior and interior: bright red slip, burnished.
j. N52/4, Gen'l. Exterior and interior: bright red slip, burnished.
k. 054/6, Sq. A52. Exterior and interior: bright red slip, burnished.

PLATE 2. Characteristic examples of Cream Chaff Ware.

3

The Sites

INTRODUCTION

The sites investigated by our survey are described in this chapter. We present first the general, descriptive information which was gathered uniformly for all sites (cf. Chapter 1). For those sites on which surface materials were collected in a controlled manner, this general information is followed by a detailed description of the collection procedures and the results of the more intensive surface survey. The data presented here are summarized in Chapter 4, which gives a synthesis of the survey results.

Excavations were made on a number of these sites after our survey. These are discussed, with reference to our survey results, in Chapter 5—Evaluation of Controlled Surface Collection.

N52/1

NAME: Taşkun Mevkii
    Vilayet: Elâzığ
    Kaza: Merkez kazası
    Nahiye: Balibey
    Village: —

NATURE: Mound

DESCRIPTION (Fig. 56): This is a low, broad, featureless mound, roughly oval in plan. It is cultivated, and there is no contemporary occupation. A small, dry channel runs along the eastern side of the site.

DIMENSIONS:
    Length: 190 m measured north-south
    Width: 120 m measured east-west
    Height: ca. 1.75 m on the south to ca. 2.5 m on the north

COLLECTIONS: Preliminary and gridded strip

OCCUPATIONS:
    Major—Early Chalcolithic
             Early Bronze Age I-II
             Hittite
    Minor—Chalcolithic–Early Bronze Age
             Transitional
             Medieval
    Trace— Middle Bronze Age
             Iron Age?

There is an abundance of Early Chalcolithic pottery on the surface here that is matched by only one or two other sites from the survey. In addition to hundreds of body sherds of Chalco-

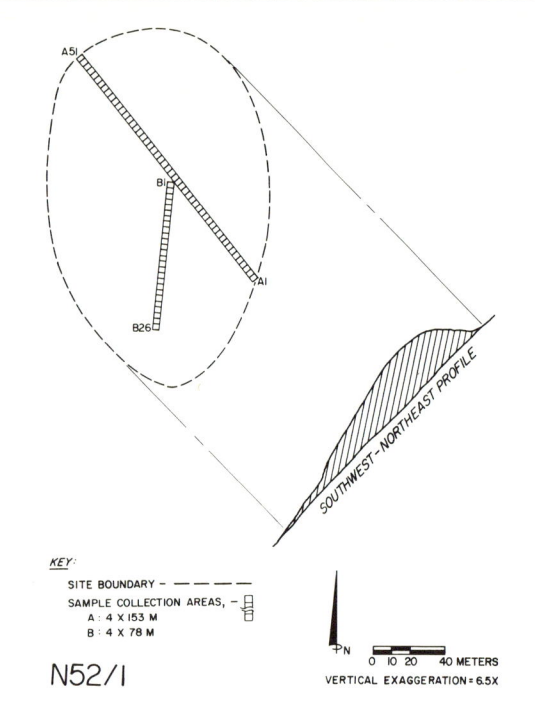

FIGURE 56. N52/1-Site plan and profile.

lithic Ware, a relatively large number of rimsherds were also recovered (e.g. Fig. 6:p-s,v,w; Fig. 7:k).

Next in quantity and also very numerous are sherds of Early Bronze Age pottery. This comprises primarily Early Bronze Age Burnished, including many rimsherds (e.g. Fig. 12:d,tt; Fig. 14:ll), a fair quantity of Early Bronze Age Plain (of which only one rim was found—Fig. 16:cc), and a few sherds each of Thick, Polished, Red Slipped, and Fine Grooved (Fig. 9:cc) wares.

Hittite body sherds were common and the variety of Hittite wares found on this site is great. They are noticeably less common than the earlier pottery, however. The most common wares are Hittite Plain (with rims such as Fig. 23:ss,tt; Fig. 25:s,v,kk; Fig. 26:d,e) and Hittite Buff-Orange Burnished (e.g. Fig. 28:kk), but there are a few sherds of Hittite Thick, Orange Smoothed, Red-Brown Burnished, Brown Burnished, White Slipped, Chaff Faced, Fine, and Brown Gritty Cooking wares also. One rim of both White Slipped (Fig. 33:e) and Brown Gritty Cooking Ware (Fig. 35:r) and three rim sherds of Hittite Fine pottery (e.g. Fig. 26:ff) were also recovered in the surface collection.

A few diagnostic sherds of the Chalcolithic-Early Bronze Age Transitional period were found, including rim sherds of Reserved Slip (Fig. 9:m) and Plain Simple wares (Fig. 9:z).

Medieval ceramics consist primarily of a few sherds of Medieval Brick Ware, plus three sherds of Red Slipped Ware, and one sherd of Medieval Cooking Ware.

The Middle Bronze Age is represented by a few sherds of Middle Bronze Age Gritty, Old Hittite Gray, and Old Hittite Light Faced Gray wares. No rimsherds of these wares were found.

A small quantity of body sherds were tabulated as Iron Age Ware. However, in view of their small number and the absence of any distinctive rims from this period, such identification must be uncertain.

CONTROLLED COLLECTION: A systematic surface collection of materials from this site was made with two gridded strips. One ran in a southeast to northwest direction, diagonally across the long axis of the mound. The other ran south from this strip. The grid units were 3 m long along the length of the strips by 4 m wide across the strips.

```
System:
    Strip A: Direction: 320°, length: 153 m (51
    squares)
        Squares A1–A18:    plowed field
                  A19:    plowed field and dry
                          grass
            A20–A36:      dry grass
            A37–A51:      plowed field
    Strip B: Direction: 185°, length: 78 m (26 squares),
    beginning at Square 27 of Strip A
        Squares B1–B18:    dry grass
                  B19:    dry grass and plowed
                          field
             B20–B26:     plowed field
```

Early Chalcolithic, Early Bronze Age I-II, and Hittite sherds occurred in sufficient quantity over the site to make a study of their patterns of distribution worthwhile.

The distribution of raw counts of Chalcolithic Ware along the two collection strips was smoothed by taking a moving average over six adjacent squares. Contour lines were then drawn on the site plan to enclose areas with greater than 3, 6, and 11 sherds respectively, in order to best represent the peaks and low spots of the smoothed frequency graphs (Fig. 57). The result is a clear picture of an Early Chalcolithic occupation that covers most of the site area, concentrated somewhat on the northern and eastern

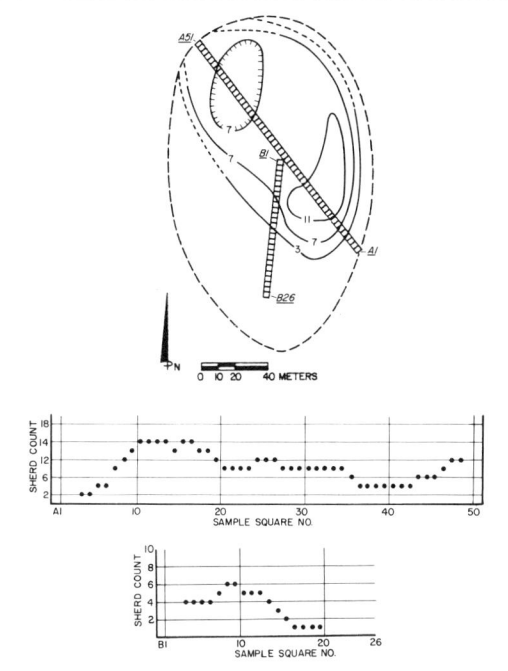

FIGURE 57. N52/1-Density contours of Early Chalcolithic ceramics.

portions of the mound. The area of occupation thus defined is approximately 140–150 m long by 80–90 m wide.

Early Bronze Age Polished, Red Slipped, Burnished, Plain, and Thick wares were grouped to form the Early Bronze Age I-II sample. The frequencies of occurrence of sherds of this group were smoothed along the collection strips by taking a moving average over five squares. Contoured over the site at intervals of 4, 6, and 8 sherds per square on the average, the distribution of Early Bronze Age pottery delineates a clear but relatively restricted area of occupation (Fig. 58). This Early Bronze Age occupation is located on the south to southeast portion of the site and is 70–80 m by 90–95 m in size.

All Hittite sherds were grouped together, and their frequencies along the collection strips were smoothed by using a moving average over five squares. Using contours of 3, 5, and 7 sherds per square, a localized occupation of this period becomes clear slightly south and west of the center of the mound (Fig. 59). The central area of this occupation measures roughly 80×40 m, while the maximum outline for the scatter of Hittite sherds covers an area roughly 130×60–70 m in size. The safest estimate of the size of the Hittite

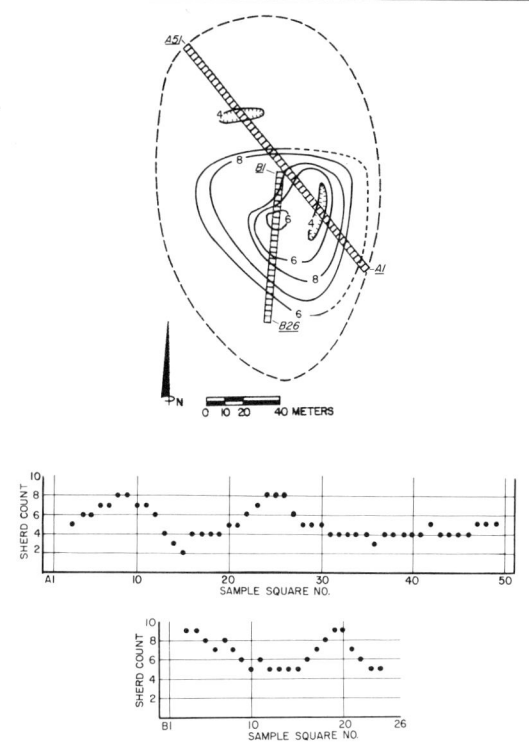

FIGURE 58. N52/1-Density contours of Early Bronze Age I-II ceramics.

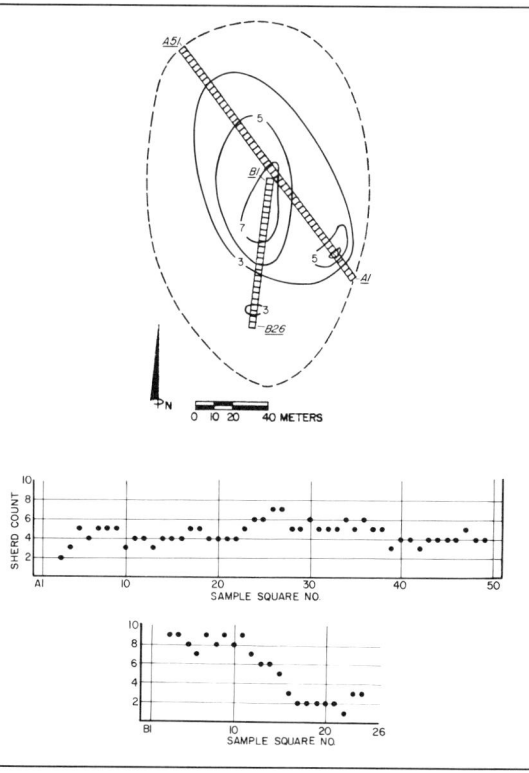

FIGURE 59. N52/1-Density contours of Hittite ceramics.

164 Archaeological Survey of the Keban Reservoir

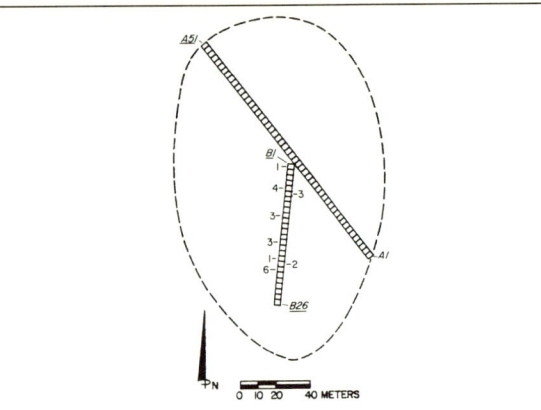

FIGURE 60. N52/1-Counts of Medieval sherds.

occupation might be an average of these two areas. This Hittite occupation is located in an area where both the Early Chalcolithic and the Early Bronze Age occupations tend to fade out. This effect may be due in part to the covering of these earlier occupations by the debris from the Hittite settlement.

Medieval sherds were too few to make detailed plotting meaningful. They were present exclusively on strip B, however, running down the southern half of the site, and were particularly concentrated near the south end of this strip (Fig. 60). If these sherds are identified correctly, they represent a miniscule occupation, or area of activity, only some 50 m in diameter.

N52/2

NAME: Taşkun Kalesi
    Vilayet: Elâzığ
    Kaza: Merkez Kazası
    Nahiye: Balibey
    Village: —

NATURE: Mound

DESCRIPTION (Fig. 61): Taşkun Kalesi is a moderately large, high mound. It consists of a high, flat-topped peak flanked by a broad sloping "apron" which spreads out on the western and southern sides of the peak. The north and east slopes of the peak are steep, and on the east they drop rather abruptly to the bed of a small stream flowing north to join the Murat River. There are low ruins of rough stone house foundations on the apron to the west and southwest of the central mound. There is no contemporary occupation, but the site is partially cultivated on the peak and on the southwest part of the apron.

DIMENSIONS:
    Length: ca. 150 m
    Width: ca. 150 m. The flat top of the high peak measures 30 m in diameter
    Height: ca. 18–20 m

COLLECTIONS: Preliminary and gridded strip

OCCUPATIONS:
    Major—Medieval
    Minor—Early Bronze Age I-II
            Early Bronze Age III
            Hittite

The surface material at this site is virtually all Medieval. It is abundant and comprises every Medieval ware recognized. Many rim sherds were

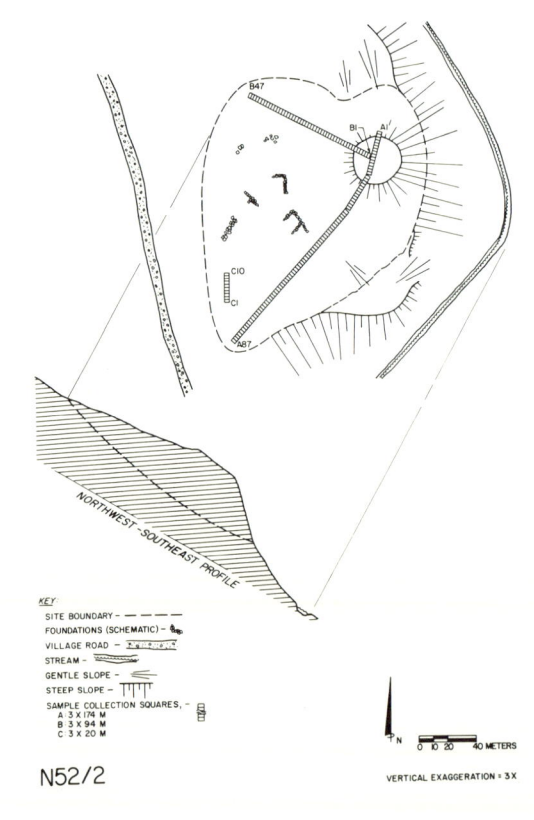

FIGURE 61. N52/2-Site plan and profile.

recovered. These pertain to Medieval Brick (e.g. Fig. 40:h; Fig. 41:g,t,dd,gg,ii,kk; Fig. 42:b,q; Fig. 43:g,w; Fig. 44:c,d,k), Thick (e.g. Fig. 45:d, f,g,i,j,m,n; Fig. 46:m), Coarse (e.g. Fig. 47:a), Red Slipped (e.g. Fig. 48:a,h,nn; Fig. 49:a,g,i,k), White Slipped (e.g. Fig. 49:n; Fig. 50:m), Cooking (e.g. Fig. 52:a,c; Fig. 53:e), Modeled (e.g. Fig. 54:e, Fig. 55:b,c), Painted (e.g. Fig. 50:o–t; Fig. 51:c,f,g,j,m,n), Sgraffiato (e.g. Fig. 47: x,y,aa), and Glazed wares.

A relatively modest amount of Early Bronze Age pottery was found on the mound. This consists primarily of Early Bronze Age Burnished sherds, including several rims (e.g. Fig. 14:m). A few sherds were also recovered of Early Bronze Age Plain, Red Slipped (e.g. Fig. 16:t), and Thick wares.

One sherd of Early Bronze Age III Red Painted and five sherds of Early Bronze III Black Painted ceramics (e.g. Fig. 19:n) show the existence of a small or brief occupation during this period.

A moderate amount of Hittite ceramics was also identified from the systematic collection. The most common wares were Hittite Plain, Thick, Buff-Orange Burnished, Brown Burnished, and Brown Gritty Cooking wares. Occasional sherds of Red–Brown Burnished, White Slipped, and Fine (e.g. Fig. 26:bb) wares also occurred.

CONTROLLED COLLECTION: Three gridded strips were collected at this site. Two strips were begun from the top of the mound. Strip A started running across the flat top of the high mound peak in a south-southwesterly direction. It then bent twice towards the west as it descended to eventually run southwest for two-thirds of its length out over the southwestern part of the lower apron flanking the mound peak. Strip B began part way along Strip A to run for a short distance across the flat top of the mound and then continue straight to the northwest down the mound slope and out onto the apron. Strip C was short and unconnected with the first two. It ran north-south on the southwestern part of the apron, one of the flatter areas of the lower mound.

The grid units of these strips were 3 m in width across the strips and 2 m in length along the strips.

System:
  Strip A: Segment 1: Direction 193°, length 30 m (15 squares)
  Segment 2: Direction 212°, length 26 m (13 squares)
  Segment 3: Direction 224°, length 118 m (59 squares)
  Squares A1–A15: plowed field
  A16–A30: dry grass
  A31: half plowed, half dry grass
  A32–A68: plowed field
  A69–A87: dry grass
Squares A69–A73 contained stone walls, ruins of house foundations, and it was impossible to collect surface materials in these squares. All together, then, 82 out of 87 squares contained material and were collected along this strip.
Strip B: Direction 296°, length 94 m (47 squares)
Begins at Square A10 of Strip A
  Squares B1–B10: plowed field
  B11–B13: dry grass
  B14–B28: plowed field
  B29–B30: rocky
  B31–B40: plowed field
  B41–B43: rocky
  B44: plowed field
  B45–B47: rocky
All squares contained material and were collected.
Strip C: Direction: 360°, length: 20 m (10 squares)
Squares C1–C10: rock foundations (ruins)

Only the Medieval ceramics occurred in enough quantity to make an analysis of surface distributional patterns meaningful. All Medieval types were grouped together, and the graphs of counts per grid unit were smoothed by taking a moving average over 6 squares. The resultant averages were contoured on the site at densities of 10, 14, and 18 sherds per square. The result (Fig. 62) shows a concentration of occupation around the high peak of the mound and a broad distribution of high sherd densities over the apron. The narrow band of very high counts (greater than 18 sherds per square), occurring roughly at the base of the high mound on Strip A, may very well be due to erosion from the peak and deposition at its foot. Medieval material then becomes abundant again on the apron. The distributional pattern indicates that this site is, in its present form, virtually entirely made up of debris from Medieval occupation.

N52/3

NAME: Kalecik (originally called Adsıztepe before this name was known)
  Vilayet: Elâzığ
  Kaza: Merkez kazası

166 *Archaeological Survey of the Keban Reservoir*

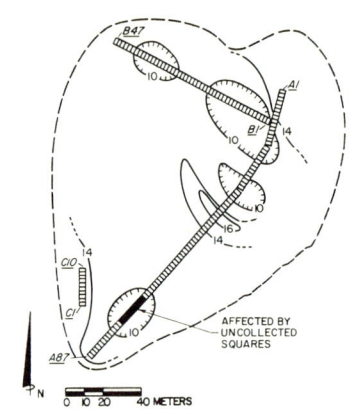

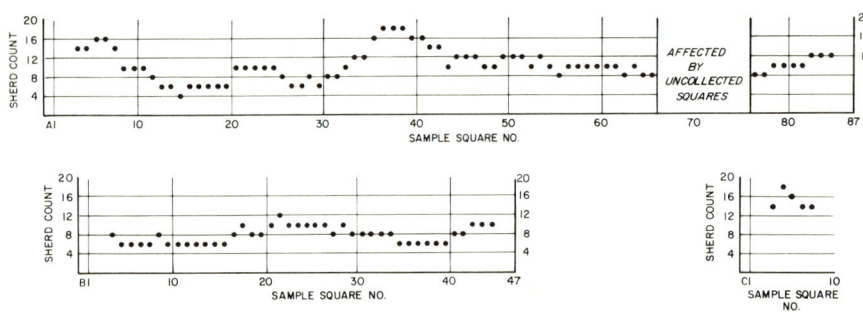

FIGURE 62. N52/2-Density contours of Medieval ceramics.

Nahiye: Balibey
Village: near Fatmalı

NATURE: Mound

DESCRIPTION (Fig. 63): This is a quite regular, round and rather low mound. There is no present day occupation. It is entirely cultivated, and a low and irregular stone wall which runs across most of the site separating two fields is the only surface feature. A spring is located just to the northwest.

DIMENSIONS:
  Length: 100 m measured east-west
  Width: 92 m measured north-south
  Height: ca. 3 m

COLLECTIONS: Preliminary and circular random gridded

OCCUPATIONS:
  Major—Early Chalcolithic
  Minor—Late Chacolithic

By far the most common pottery on this site is Chalcolithic Ware (e.g. Fig. 6:b–f,i,k–o,u,y–aa, cc,dd,ff,gg; Fig. 7:a,d,n–t; and Fig. 8:b,d,e,g,h). A much smaller but significant quantity of Late Chalcolithic Cream Chaff Ware was also found (e.g. Figs. 10:b,l,m,p,gg and 11:b,i,j,ee). Some sherds of Late Chalcolithic Grit Tempered Ware were among those found on the surface of this site (e.g. Fig. 17:g,h). No more than one or two odd sherds of other types were recovered.

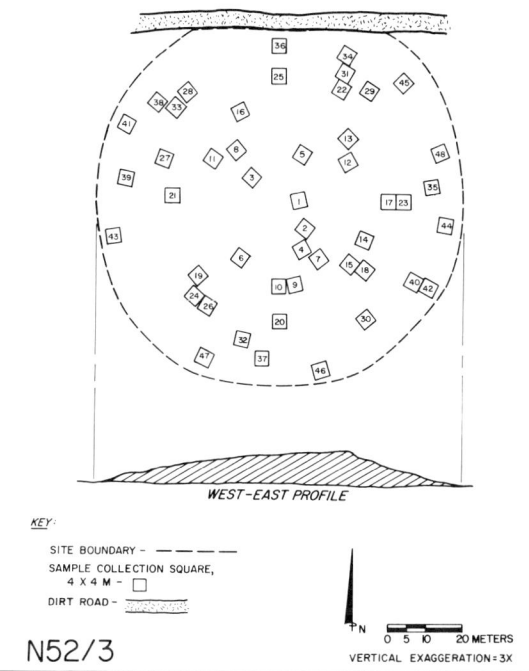

FIGURE 63. N52/3-Site plan and profile.

CONTROLLED COLLECTION: Systematic collection was carried out using a randomized circular grid. This is the only site at which this system was employed. It was particularly appropriate and successful here, but was possible primarily because the site was almost circular in outline and was a gently sloping, barren mound. The system was set up as follows:

A collection unit was established, in this case a square 4×4 m in size. On a plan of the site, then, concentric circles were drawn around the center of the mound, each circle having a radius 4 m greater than that of the preceding circle. A collection unit could thus fit exactly in the band between one circle and the next. The area of each band was then calculated and expressed as a fraction of the total site area. It was then arbitrarily decided to collect ten percent of this total area as a sample, and the 48 collection squares required to cover roughly ten percent of the site were divided among the concentric bands so that the number of squares assigned to each band was proportional to the relative area covered by the band. The exact location of each square within each band was determined by selecting a compass bearing at random. The square was then placed where the compass bearing crossed the band.

System:
> Mound radius = ca. 50 m. Collection squares = 4×4 m
> Mound area = ca. 7854 m², 48 squares = 768 m²
> = ±10 percent of the mound area

Establishment of 4 m concentric collection bands and the distribution of the 48 collection squares among them:

Circle	Outside radius (m)	Rel. Proportion of site area*	No. of sq.
1	4	.0069	.33 = 0
2	8	.0208	1.00 = 1
3	12	.0347	1.67 = 2
4	16	.0486	2.33 = 2
5	20	.0625	3.00 = 3
6	24	.0764	3.67 = 4
7	28	.0903	4.33 = 4
8	32	.1042	5.00 = 5
9	36	.1181	5.67 = 6
10	40	.1319	6.33 = 6
11	44	.1458	7.00 = 7
12	48	.1597	7.67 = 8
Totals			48

*$\left[\dfrac{\text{Area}/16\pi}{\text{Sum (Area}/16\pi)} \right]$

Establishment of the locations of the 48 collection squares:

Square no.	Inside radius of sq. (m)	Compass bearing (°)	Sq. no.	Inside radius of sq. (m)	Compass bearing (°)
1	4	83	25	32	360
2	8	131	26	32	215
3	8	313	27	32	290
4	12	154	28	36	319
5	12	25	29	36	39
6	16	216	30	36	140
7	16	144	31	36	27
8	16	321	32	36	194
9	20	170	33	36	311
10	20	180	34	40	24
11	20	304	35	40	83
12	20	61	36	40	360
13	24	47	37	40	184
14	24	115	38	40	308
15	24	131	39	40	278
16	24	335	40	40	120
17	28	88	41	44	296
18	28	127	42	44	119
19	28	230	43	44	258
20	28	180	44	44	98
21	28	274	45	44	46
22	32	29	46	44	165
23	32	89	47	44	206
24	32	222	48	44	75

168 *Archaeological Survey of the Keban Reservoir*

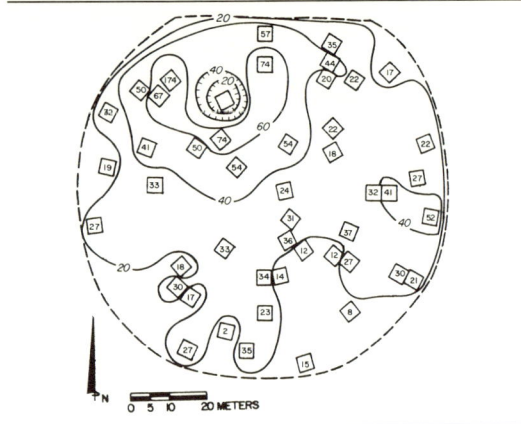

FIGURE 64. N52/3-Density contours of Early Chalcolithic ceramics.

The distribution of Early Chalcolithic sherds (Chalcolithic Ware) is shown (Fig. 64), with density contours drawn around squares containing more than 20, 40, and 60 sherds respectively. It is clear that sherds of this period are quite abundant over most of the site, with a concentration over the northern half of the site area. In contrast, the Late Chalcolithic sherds (Cream Chaff Ware), contoured at densities of five and ten sherds per square, show a distinct concentration on the southern portion of the site, with some extension to the eastern edge (Fig. 65). It is thus evident that a significant Early Chalcolithic occupation probably covers the majority of the area defined by the mound, and that a much smaller Late Chalcolithic occupation is superimposed upon it in the southern part of the site. That, of course, would explain the relative scarcity of

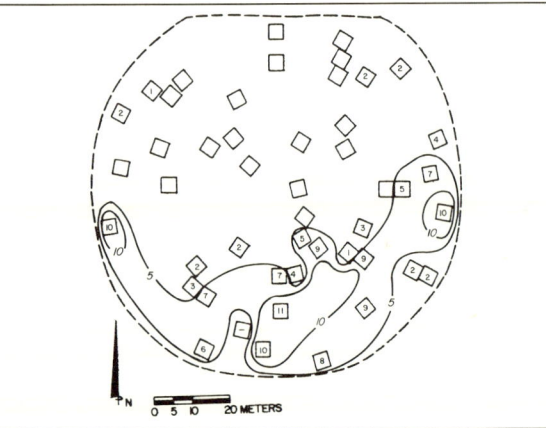

FIGURE 65. N52/3-Density contours of Late Chalcolithic ceramics.

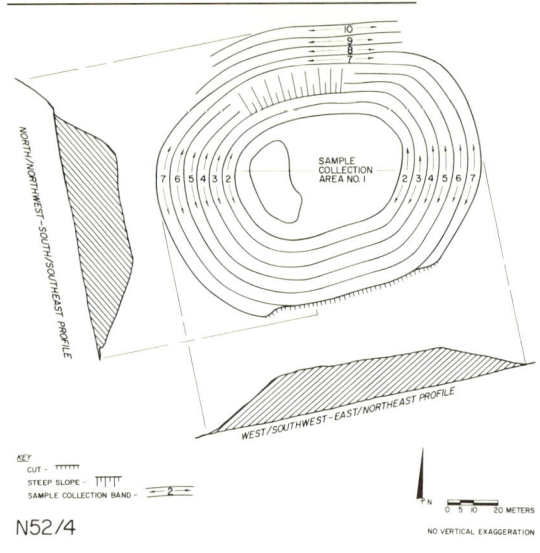

FIGURE 66. N52/4-Site plan and profiles.

Early Chalcolithic sherds in this part of the site. The Early Chalcolithic occupation area would therefore measure roughly 90–100 m in diameter. The Late Chalcolithic area is only 35–40 m by 75–80 m in size.

N52/4

NAME: Aşvan Kalesi
    Vilayet: Elâzığ
    Kaza: Merkez kazası
    Nahiye: Balibey
    Village: Aşvan

NATURE: Mound

DESCRIPTION (Fig. 66): The mound at Aşvan is large, high, and oval with steep sides and a broad, flat top. It is located directly on the edge of the terrace or bluff on the south side of the Murat River, high above the floodplain. The site is not presently occupied, but it is on the edge of the modern village of Aşvan, and on the south side of the mound earth has been removed over a length of about 30 m and to a height of about 5 m for house building, eating away an estimated 5 m or more of the extent of the mound at the base. In the resulting profile, stone walls of two types can be seen, one made of large boulders with intermediate fill of river pebbles and the other composed of rows of diagonally set, flat river cobbles. The mound is otherwise undisturbed and is not cultivated.

DIMENSIONS:
Length: Mound top = 65 m measured northeast-southwest. The mound as a whole is ca. 125 m long in the same direction
Width: Mound top = 45 m measured northwest-southeast. The whole mound is an estimated 95 m wide in this direction
Height: ca. 15 m

COLLECTIONS: Preliminary from the exposed profile, and complete, annular bands from the rest of the mound.

OCCUPATIONS:
Major—Early Bronze Age I-II
Medieval
Minor—Early Bronze Age III
Hellenistic-Roman
Trace— Middle Bronze Age (?)
Hittite (?)

The identification of periods of occupation is less certain for this mound than for most of the sites surveyed. The surface of the mound was covered with a tough, grassy vegetation, and relatively little archaeological material was to be found on the surface of the soil. The ceramics found tended to be small and highly fragmentary. Thus, almost no rim sherds, and even very few sherds large enough to be diagnostic of particular periods were recovered in the surface collection of this site (cf. Table 5).

It seems relatively certain, however, that there was a substantial Early Bronze Age occupation here. Sherds of this period are the most common of all those which definitely could be attributed to a period and include Early Bronze Age Burnished, Plain, Thick, Red Slipped, and Polished wares. Early Bronze Age III Red and Black Painted wares, however, were relatively infrequent.

The bulk of the tiny body sherds which were found appeared to be from Medieval Brick, White Slipped, and Medieval Cooking wares. There were, in addition, a number of certainly Medieval sherds, comprising Medieval Brick, Painted and Sgraffiato wares. All together this seems to indicate the presence of substantial Medieval occupation here.

A few characteristic Roman Red sherds were found (e.g. Fig. 55:j). This was considered adequate data on which to identify a Hellenistic-Roman occupation at this mound. Unfortunately, we were not able to identify the other, more common, wares of this period, and Hellenistic-Roman occupations were not consistently detected in our analysis of the survey materials (cf. Chapter 2).

The evidence for Middle Bronze Age and Hittite occupations comes from a large number of tiny body sherds of dubious identity. Among these sherds were many which we suspected were Middle Bronze Age Gray and Middle Bronze Age Gritty wares (including one possible rim—Fig. 20:d), as well as a substantial number which were thought perhaps to be Hittite Plain, Buff-Orange Burnished, and Fine Wares. This material was poor, and these identifications tenuous, however.

CONTROLLED COLLECTIONS: The broad, flat top and steep to extremely steep sides of the mound made designing a system of controlled surface collection difficult. It was decided that the collection of complete, concentric, annular bands would be the most expedient system. Such a collection would normally miss much of the distributional detail revealed by other methods, but it was felt that heavy erosion of the sides of the mound would have completely disturbed any such patterns of distribution and that the great scarcity of surface materials required collection units to be as large as possible. Concentric bands descending from the mound top would each encompass a large area, and the collection system would provide complete coverage of the mound except where slopes were too steep to stand on. Bands descending the sides of the mound would, in addition, allow at least some control over the vertical distribution of materials over the height of the mound.

The flat top of the mound was first collected as Band 1. Then a series of bands were collected, each 5 m in width, beginning at the clearly defined edge of the mound top. A number of these bands only could be collected over part of the circumference of the mound because of the steep slopes, the cut into the edge of the mound, or from having reached the base of the mound at some points. In all, six bands were almost completely collected around the circumference of the mound, and three others were collected over a portion of the north slopes of the mound, dropping down over the edge of the river terrace on which the mound is situated. This gave a total of ten collection units (Fig. 66).

System:

Collection Band Numbers:	Distance below Edge of Flat Mound Top
1	(Collection from the mound top itself)
2	0– 5m
3	5–10m
4	10–15m
5	15–20m
6	20–25m
7	25–30m
8	30–35m
9	35–40m
10	40–45m

The results of this collection procedure were disappointingly meager, considering the fact that virtually the entire surface of the mound was collected. The majority of the sherds recovered were tiny and, as mentioned, could usually not be identified with any confidence.

However, there are some general indications, even with this gross collection scheme and poor material, that there are distributional differences in surface materials which reflect the internal structure of the mound (Table 5). Early Bronze Age wares are definitely restricted to the lower portions of the mound slopes. They occur in significant quantities from Band 6 on down to Band 10. Early Bronze Age III painted wares are concentrated slightly higher on the slopes, particularly in the area of Bands 4 to 6. Definite Hittite sherds are too few to allow any statement. Roman Red pottery, however, is most highly concentrated on the flat top of the mound. Medieval wares occur over virtually the entire surface of the site.

These roughly observed patterns lead to some general conclusions concerning the occupation at this site. It appears that Early Bronze Age I-II occupation must make up a large part of the lower levels in the mound, perhaps as much as one-fourth or one-third of the bulk of the mound. Early Bronze Age III occupation must occur on top of these levels, but is probably relatively thin. Hittite occupation must be light. Hellenistic-Roman occupation was probably largely restricted to a small area such as the mound top. Medieval occupation was not long or intensive, judging from the relative quantity of material from this period, but it seems to have been extensive and to have lightly covered most of the mound.

From this, it is possible to guess at the relative sizes of occupations belonging to the various periods. This is obviously a rather risky procedure. Nonetheless, the Early Bronze Age I-II occupation will be considered to cover the entire basal area of the mound. The size of the mound at the base of Band 4 will be used for the size of the Early Bronze Age III occupation (assuming that most materials are eroding downward from their point of major exposure along the slopes of the mound). Hellenistic-Roman settlement will be counted as covering only the mound top. Medieval occupation, however, is thought of as extensive

TABLE 5 Identified ceramics* from the controlled surface collection of site N52/4 (Aşvan Kalesi).

	Collection Band Nos.									
	1	2	3	4	5	6	7	8	9	10
Early Bronze Age Burnished						23	35	21		15
Early Bronze Age Plain				3	1	4	35	3		18
Early Bronze Age Thick						10				
Early Bronze Age Red Slipped					1	2	2	1		3
Early Bronze Age Polished									3	
Early Bronze Age III Red Painted				1			1			
Early Bronze Age III Black Painted	1	1		3	2	1				
Hittite Plain										1
Hittite Chaff Faced				1						
Roman Red	5					2	1			
Medieval Brick	4	2				13	4			
Medieval Painted						3			2	
Sgraffiato	3	1			1					

*Note: There are also additional suspected but uncertainly identified sherds of the above wares, plus possibly Hittite Buff-Orange Burnished, Middle Bronze Age Gray, Middle Bronze Age Gritty, Medieval Cooking, and Medieval White Slipped wares.

and will be calculated as covering the entire site area. These estimates, just as the identifications of periods of occupation, are not particularly satisfactory, but they are the best possible with the survey data at hand.

N52/5

NAME: Pulur
    Vilayet: Tunceli
    Kaza: Vaskovan
    Nahiye: —
    Village: Pulur

NATURE: Mound

DESCRIPTION (Fig. 67): The most striking aspect of this mound is its high, steep-sided, flat-topped peak. This peak is relatively small and conical. The present day village of Pulur is clustered on the south side of the peak, and apparently a good deal of the lower portions of the mound lie under part of the village. The peak is cut into only slightly by borrow pits for village house construction and is otherwise unused today.

DIMENSIONS:
    Length: ca. 120 m east-west
    Width: ca. 80 m north-south (The high mound peak is approximately 75 m in diameter)
    Height: ca. 20 m

COLLECTIONS: Preliminary

OCCUPATIONS:
    Major—Early Bronze Age I-II
            Medieval
    Minor—Early Bronze Age III
    Trace— Early Chalcolithic (?)

The major period of occupation here appears to be the Early Bronze Age. The pottery is abundant, varied, and distinctive, comprising Early Bronze Age Burnished, Plain, Polished, and Relief Decorated wares. It seems that the bulk of the mound, and almost certainly all of the high peak of the mound, pertains to this period, perhaps running up to and including (on the basis of the finding of Early Bronze Age Red Painted Ware here) some occupation in Early Bronze III times, although distributional evidence to support this conclusion is lacking.

Medieval materials were also common, but perhaps pertain more to the lower slopes of the mound and to an occupation continuing into the present day than to former occupation of the high mound. The ceramics consist primarily of Brick Ware, although White Slipped Ware was also noted. Previous Armenian occupation seems likely from the original name of the contemporary village—Pulur—which means "mound" or "tell" in Armenian. Selcuk remains in the vicinity may also be indicative of historic Turkish occupation.

Early Chalcolithic occupation may occur at the base of the mound, but this is uncertain. Only a few sherds were identified as Chalcolithic Ware, and it is often easy to confuse a sherd or two of Early Bronze Age Burnished Ware with Early Chalcolithic ceramics.

N52/6

NAME: Kalecik (Kalaycık)
    Vilayet: Tunceli
    Kaza: Vaskovan
    Nahiye: —
    Village: —

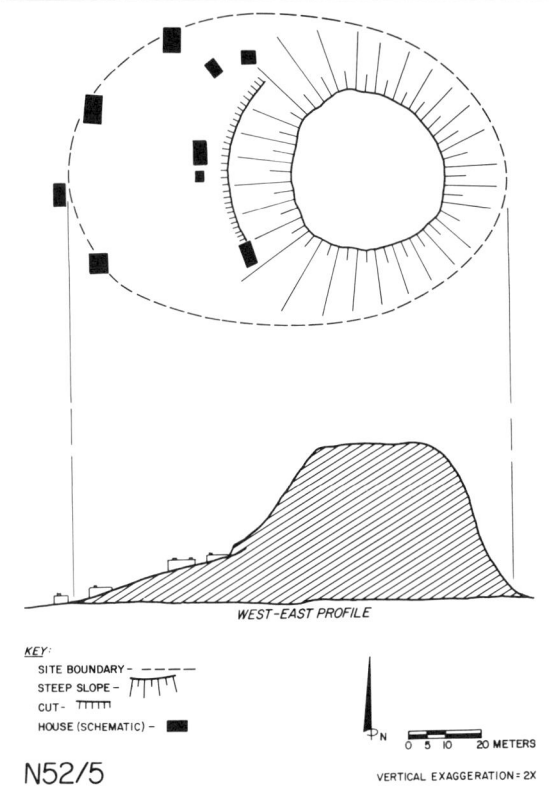

FIGURE 67. N52/5-Site plan and profile.

NATURE: Mound

DESCRIPTION (Fig. 68): This is a large, high mound with very steep sides. It is located on the tip of a promontory which overlooks the Euphrates far below on one side and which is bounded on two other sides by deep but dry valleys. The main mound rises to a relatively sharp peak, but to the southwest of the main peak there is a small, sloping terrace, running out to the tip of the promontory, on which ruined stone house foundations are visible. Rather high up the slopes of the main mound a large and heavy stone wall is partially exposed. There are also some small cuts, perhaps graves, dug into the high parts of the main mound on its east side. There is no modern occupation on or near the mound and it is not used agriculturally.

DIMENSIONS:
    Length: ca. 130 m northeast-southwest
    Width: ca. 70 m northwest-southeast
    Height: ca. 25–30 m

COLLECTIONS: Preliminary

OCCUPATIONS:
    Major—Early Bronze Age I-II
             Early Bronze Age III
             Medieval
    Trace— Middle Bronze Age
             Iron Age

The Early Bronze Age is well represented in the surface collection, both by Early Bronze Burnished Ware and the later Red and Black Painted wares of Early Bronze III times (e.g. Fig. 17:h). It seems clear that occupation during these periods was important. Medieval sherds are also common and represent a series of wares (Brick, Coarse, Cooking, Painted), although none of the most characteristic decorated wares (Glazed, Modeled, Sgraffiato) were recovered in the general collection.

The Middle Bronze Age is represented only by a single ceramic ware, Middle Bronze Age Gray, while Iron Age occupation is indicated by no more than a few sherds. Such occupations, if indeed present, should be considered only small or temporary settlements.

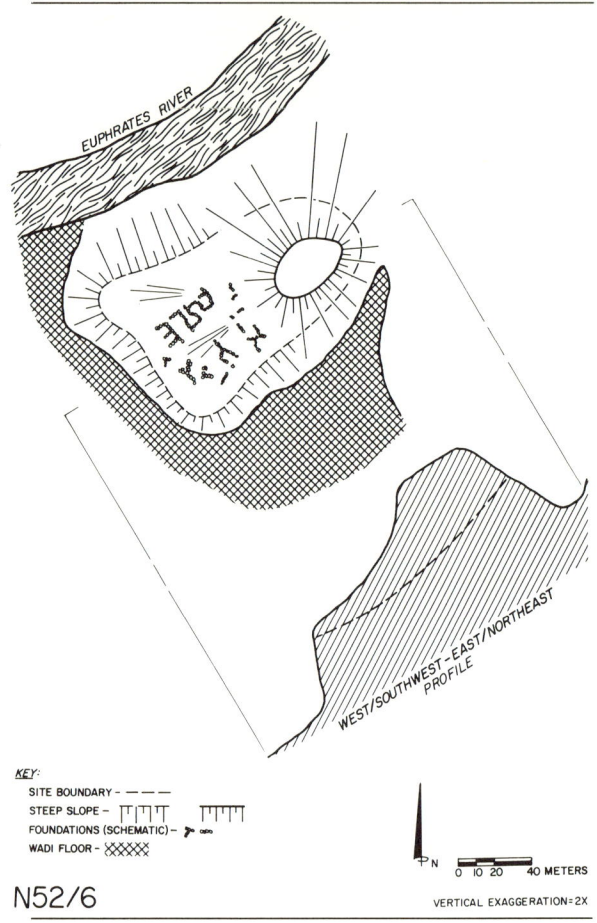

FIGURE 68. N52/6-Site plan and profile.

N52/7

NAME: —
    Vilayet: Elâzığ
    Kaza: Merkez kazası
    Nahiye: Balibey
    Village: —

NATURE: Surface scatter

DESCRIPTION: A scatter of material was found on a small, natural rise beside a small stream flowing north to the Murat River. The rise is bedrock with no soil cover.

DIMENSIONS:
    Length: ca. 40 m
    Width: ca. 40 m

COLLECTIONS: Preliminary

OCCUPATIONS: Major—Medieval

Virtually all the ceramic material from this site was Medieval Brick Ware. One rim was classified as possibly Middle Bronze Age Gritty Ware (Fig. 20:j) and one may be Hittite Plain (Fig. 25:e). It would seem, however, that this is a recent surface scatter. It does not represent a significant occupation in any case.

N52/8

NAME: —
    Vilâyet: Elâzığ
    Kaza: Merkez kazası
    Nahiye: Balibey
    Village: —

NATURE: Ruin (small mound?)

DESCRIPTION (Fig. 69): This site is a small rise on a hill slope, which is covered with the remains of stone house foundations. The rise is not clearly a mound, but the soil around and under the rubble looks like occupation debris. The foot of the slope is just beyond and to the east of the site. There, a small stream flows to the north. A spring lies on the other side of the stream. Today the site is not used in any way.

DIMENSIONS:
    Length: ca. 200 m north-south
    Width: ca. 100 m east-west
    Height: ca. 3 m on the east to ca. 1 m on the west

COLLECTIONS: Preliminary

OCCUPATIONS: Major—Medieval

All the ceramics from the surface of this site are Medieval, comprising Brick, Thick (e.g. Fig. 46:k) and Red Slipped wares. This, plus the fact that foundations still show on the surface, leads one to suspect that this is a relatively recently abandoned site.

N52/9

NAME: Çay Boyu or Köy Üstü
    Vilâyet: Elâzığ
    Kaza: Merkez kazası
    Nahiye: Balibey
    Village: near Aşvan

NATURE: Mound

DESCRIPTION (Fig. 70): This is a small, low, broad mound. Perhaps a little less than half of the original site has been eroded away by a stream flowing along its east side. The site is otherwise featureless and without contemporary occupation. It is cultivated.

DIMENSIONS:
    Length: 80 m measured north-south
    Width: There remain 60 m of mound measured east-west to the edge of the eroded area
    Height: ca. 1.5–2 m

COLLECTIONS: Preliminary and random gridded.

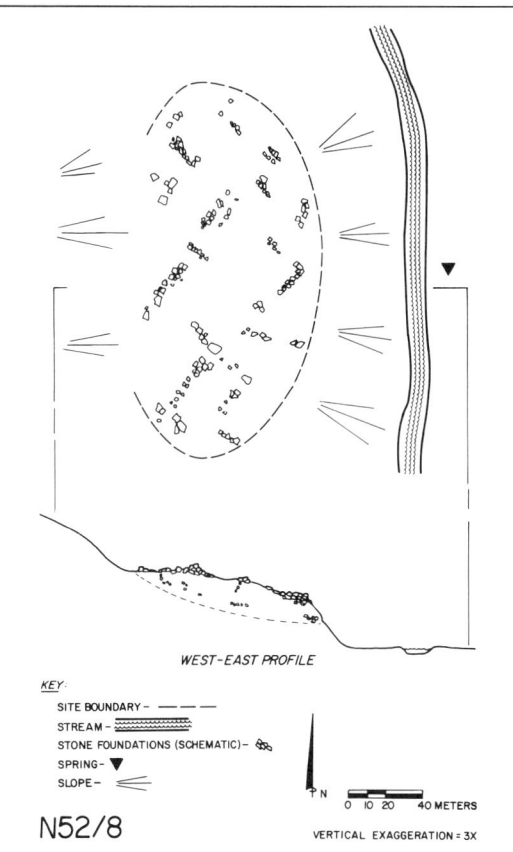

FIGURE 69. N52/8-Site plan and profile.

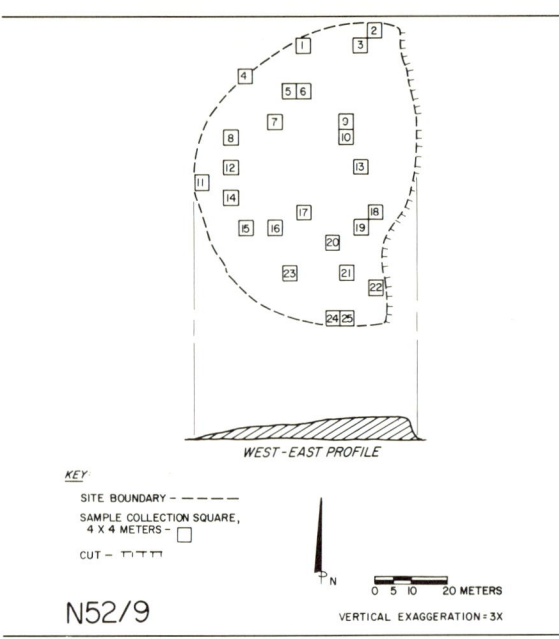

FIGURE 70. N52/9-Site plan and profile.

OCCUPATIONS:
    Major—Late Chalcolithic
               Early Bronze Age I-II
               Hittite
    Minor—Early Chalcolithic
               Medieval
    Trace— Early Bronze Age III (?)
               Middle Bronze Age

Late Chalcolithic occupation is abundantly represented by Cream Chaff Ware, both body and rim sherds (e.g. Fig. 10:a, mm; Fig. 11:ff).

The Early Bronze I–II period is also well represented by rim and body sherds, primarily of Early Bronze Age Burnished Ware (e.g. Fig. 14:o), but including also Early Bronze Age Polished (e.g. Fig. 16:k), Red Slipped, Thick, and Plain wares.

Hittite remains consist almost entirely of body sherds. However, a wide variety of wares is present here, including Hittite Plain, Thick, Buff–Orange Burnished, Red–Brown Burnished, Brown Burnished, Fine, and Brown Gritty Cooking wares. Only a single rim sherd of Buff–Orange Burnished ware was recovered from this site (Fig. 29:y). It might have been more appropriate to characterize the Hittite occupation here as minor, especially since its areal extent as defined from the controlled surface collection is limited (cf. below). It was called a major occupation largely because of the comparative abundance of body sherds, which are only slightly less in number than Late Chalcolithic sherds.

A number of Chalcolithic Ware sherds were found scattered randomly over the site. They were not sufficient to characterize a major occupation, but probably indicate the existence of an occupation layer of the Early Chalcolithic period underlying at least part of the remaining mound.

Medieval sherds also were not abundant, and they were concentrated on only part of the site. Medieval Brick Ware is the most common, but sherds were found of Medieval Thick, Coarse, White Slipped, Red Slipped, Cooking, and Sgraffiato wares also.

Two sherds identified as Early Bronze Age III Red Painted (e.g. Fig. 17:m) represent a "trace" of occupation from this period.

A handful of Middle Bronze Age Gritty, Old Hittite Gray, and Old Hittite Light Faced Gray wares suggest the possibility of a light occupation during the Middle Bronze Age as well.

CONTROLLED COLLECTION: A controlled surface collection was made from this mound using a random grid method for placing the collection squares. Twenty-five 4×4 m squares were scattered at random over the mound, covering slightly more than ten percent of the total site area.

Ceramics of the Late Chalcolithic, Early Bronze Age I-II, Hittite, and Medieval periods were present in great enough frequencies to allow density contours to be drawn to delineate their patterns of distribution over the site.

The Late Chalcolithic period was represented only by Cream Chaff Ware. Its distribution over the site can be represented by contours surrounding areas with densities of 5 and 10 sherds per grid square (Fig. 71). The area of occupation thus

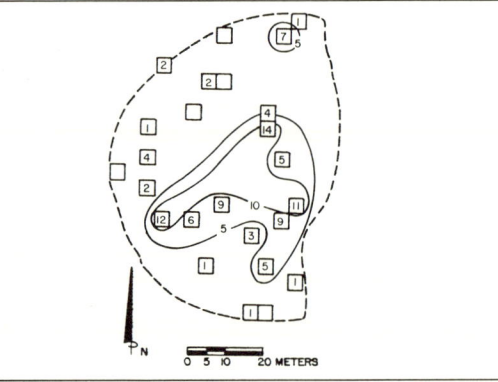

FIGURE 71. N52/9-Density contours of Late Chalcolithic ceramics.

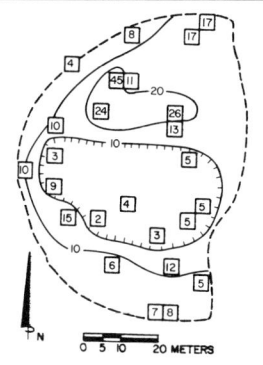

FIGURE 72. N52/9-Density contours of Early Bronze Age I-II ceramics.

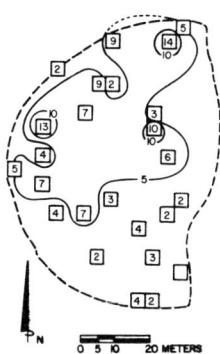

FIGURE 73. N52/9-Density contours of Hittite ceramics.

defined clearly seems restricted to the part of the site which has been preserved and does not seem to have extended over into the eroded area. It does cover most of the remaining area, however, with the 5-sherd contours enclosing an area roughly 40×45 m in size.

Early Bronze Age I-II occupation, on the other hand, definitely appears to have originally extended well into the now destroyed part of the site (Fig. 72). In fact, it appears to have been the major occupation of the site, and probably the bulk of the mound consists of debris from this period. Plotted and contoured as a group to define this pattern of occupation were Early Bronze Age Burnished, Plain, Thick, Polished, and Red Slipped wares. Contour lines were then drawn around areas of 10 and 20 sherds per collection square. The outline of Early Bronze Age I and II occupation is largely given by the 10-sherd contour line, which clearly extends out to the limits of the present mound on the north and east sides, allowing a projection on to the eroded eastern half of the site. The presently defined area is approximately 60×70 m, which can be projected into a reconstructed original size of roughly 70×100 m.

All Hittite wares were grouped together for plotting. Although the number of wares is considerably larger than for the Early Bronze Age, contours could still be drawn only for areas of 5 and 10 sherds per square. The area of occupation thus defined (Fig. 73) was also much smaller in size and definitely restricted to the northwest corner of the remaining mound. Hittite occupation was evidently small in area, measuring, from the indications of the surface survey, only ca. 45×65 m.

Medieval occupation was traced out from the distribution of all Medieval wares combined (Fig. 74). The occupation area is defined primarily by the distribution of squares with 5 or more sherds, with only one square having more than 10 Medieval sherds. This area is 30–45×70 m in size and appears fairly clearly restricted to the remaining mound area.

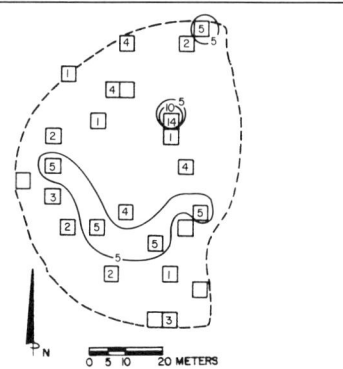

FIGURE 74. N52/9-Density contours of Medieval ceramics.

N52/10

NAME: —
    Vilayet: Elâzığ
    Kaza: Merkez kazası
    Nahiye: Balibey
    Village: Aslanbeyhan

NATURE: Mound

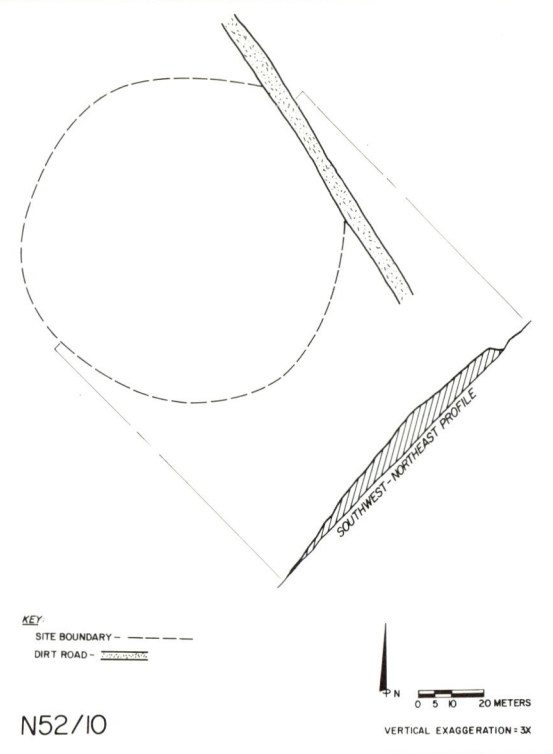

FIGURE 75. N52/10-Site plan and profile.

DESCRIPTION (Fig. 75): This is a very regular, round, low and broad mound. There is no contemporary occupation, but it is cultivated. Very close to the northwest is a spring around which one or two houses now stand. This mound lies outside of the reservoir area.

DIMENSIONS:
  Length: ca. 100 m
  Width: ca. 100 m
  Height: ca. 1.5–2 m

COLLECTIONS: Preliminary

OCCUPATIONS: Only a small amount of material was collected from this site outside the reservoir area. Identifications are generally not certain.
  Present—Late Chalcolithic (?)
    Early Bronze Age II (?)
    Middle Bronze Age
    Hittite (?)
    Medieval

The supposed Late Chalcolithic occupation is inferred from the presence of pottery initially classified as Hittite Chaff Faced, but now thought more probably to be Cream Chaff Ware. There were no diagnostic rim sherds in the collection, only body sherds, so attribution to any period is uncertain.

Early Bronze Age occupation is shown by the presence only of Early Bronze Age Plain Ware. Again, no rimsherds were collected, and these sherds might be related to a Late Chalcolithic component of the mound as easily as they might represent Early Bronze Age settlement. The lack of the typical and diagnostic burnished wares of the period either indicates that the identification of these ceramics as Early Bronze Age is incorrect or that the occupation is poor and late in the period. The former conclusion is probably correct.

Middle Bronze Age occupation seems relatively sure, although only one type of pottery was found—Old Hittite Gray. A rim sherd of this ware (Fig. 21:aa) was found here.

Hittite occupation is shown, with the exception of the doubtful Hittite Chaff Faced Ware, only by the presence of Hittite Plain Ware body sherds. Again, the possibility of misidentification is high.

Medieval settlement is represented by Medieval Brick Ware and Medieval Coarse Ware. A rim sherd of Brick ware (Fig. 42:o) was recovered.

N52/11

NAME: İviktepe
  Vilayet: Elâzığ
  Kaza: Merkez kazası
  Nahiye: Balibey
  Village: —

NATURE: Mound

DESCRIPTION (Fig. 76): This is a small but high mound with a small, flat top. It sits on the edge of a deep, steep-sided valley in the middle of an area which is now mostly wasteland. Cultivated fields are rare here. This site lies well outside the reservoir area and was found in passing through an area not otherwise surveyed.

DIMENSIONS:
  Length: ca. 120 m north-south
  Width: ca. 100 m east-west
  Height: ca. 7–8 m

COLLECTIONS: Preliminary

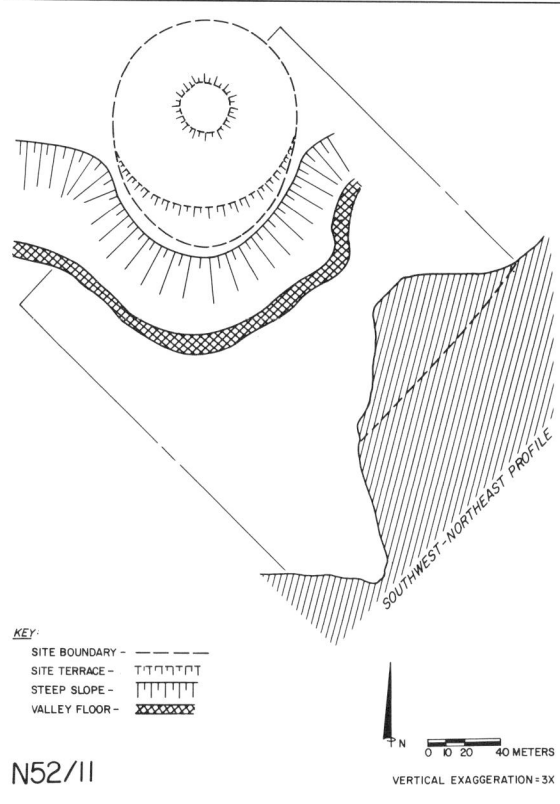

FIGURE 76. N52/11-Site plan and profile.

OCCUPATIONS:
- Major— Early Bronze Age I-II
- Present— Early Bronze Age III
  Hittite
  Medieval
- Trace— Late Chalcolithic (?)
  Iron Age

It is often difficult to estimate the relative importance of occupations of different periods from a preliminary surface collection. In this case it is sure that Early Bronze Age I-II occupation was substantial here, and that Late Chalcolithic and Iron Age occupations are not definitely demonstrated or are small, but for other periods it is only possible to state that they are represented at this mound. Although this was an interesting site, more intensive investigation was not undertaken because it lies well outside the Keban reservoir and was in no way threatened.

Early Bronze Age I-II materials were plentiful. Early Bronze Age Burnished, Polished and Plain wares were present, including a significant number of Early Bronze Age Burnished and Early Bronze Age Thick rims.

The Early Bronze Age III period was represented by characteristic Black Painted Ware, including one rimsherd.

No Hittite rimsherds were found. However, body sherds were recovered which were identified as Hittite Plain, Buff-Orange Burnished, Brown Burnished, and Fine wares. Hittite Chaff Faced Ware was also identified at first, but in the absence of any rims from this ware, it is quite possible that this is a misidentification and that there is some Cream Chaff pottery here, indicating a Late Chalcolithic occupation.

Medieval ceramics include Medieval Brick, Thick, and Cooking wares with some rims from the first two.

The Iron Age is only represented by body sherds. Identification is, of course, uncertain.

N53/1

NAME: —
    Vilayet: Elâzığ
    Kaza: Merkez kazası
    Nahiye: Harput
    Village: near Şıhıs

NATURE: Mound

DESCRIPTION (Fig. 77): This is a small, low, oval mound. It is located on the south bank of the Murat River, high above the river on the edge of

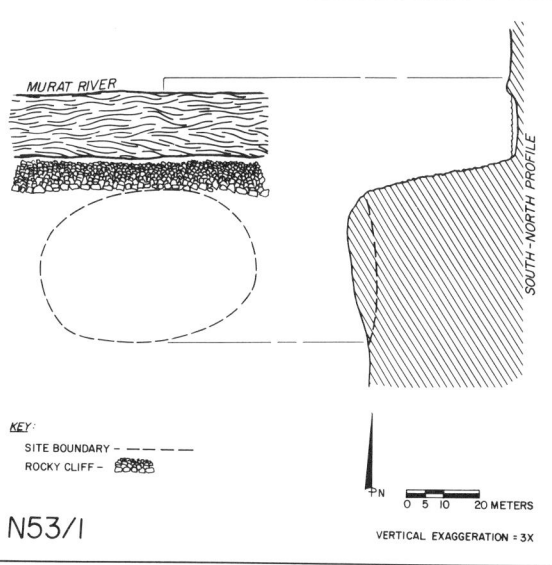

FIGURE 77. N53/1-Site plan and profile.

a steep, rocky cliff. The mound itself is wasteland, but it is surrounded by cultivated fields.

DIMENSIONS:
    Length: ca. 60 m east-west
    Width: ca 40 m north-south
    Height: ca 2 m

COLLECTIONS: Preliminary

OCCUPATIONS:
    Major—Early Bronze Age I-II
    Minor—Middle Bronze Age
            Medieval
    Trace— Hittite

Early Bronze Age Burnished and Thick wares are well represented in this preliminary collection, including a relatively large number of rims (e.g., Burnished—Fig. 13:m; Fig. 14:mm; Thick—Fig. 17:c-e).

The Middle Bronze Age is represented by Middle Bronze Age Gritty pottery, again with a few rims present in the collection (Fig. 20:q, r, z).

Occupation in the Medieval period is shown by body sherds of Medieval Brick, Thick, and Red Slipped wares.

A small Hittite occupation may be present, indicated by one rimsherd each of Hittite Plain (Fig. 25:u) and Fine wares.

N53/3

NAME: Hanibrahimşah (Esenkent)
    Vilayet: Elâzığ
    Kaza: Merkez kazası
    Nahiye: Balibey
    Village: Hanibrahimşah (Esenkent)

NATURE: Mound

DESCRIPTION (Fig. 78): The occupation mound sits on top of an isolated, natural peak with steep sides, the flat top of which is formed by a fossil reef. The area around this reef has been eroded, leaving this natural elevated platform. The occupation mound covers the whole top of the hill and rises with steep sides to a relatively small, flat top. An irrigation ditch passes by the west side of the hill and mound while a small stream flows by on the east. The slopes and mound top are currently unused and uninhabited. The site is just to the

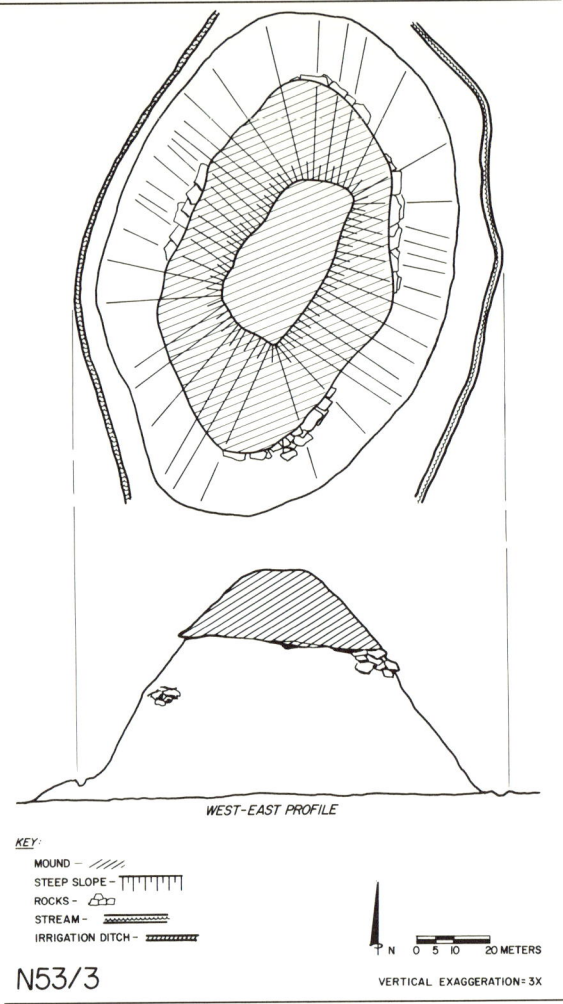

FIGURE 78. N53/3-Site plan and profile.

north of the contemporary village with its old caravansaray.

DIMENSIONS:
    Length: ca. 100 m north-south
    Width: ca. 60 m east-west
    Height: ca. 8 m

COLLECTIONS: Preliminary

OCCUPATIONS:
    Present—Early Bronze Age I-II
                Early Bronze Age IIIB
                Medieval
    Trace— Late Chalcolithic (?)
                Hittite (?)

No estimates of relative importance of the occupations of different periods are possible from the small preliminary collection from this large mound.

Occupation of the Early Bronze Age I-II period is shown by body sherds of Early Bronze Age Burnished and Plain wares, Fine Grooved Ware, and a fine rim from a small jar of Early Bronze Age Polished ware (Fig. 16:g).

Body sherds of Early Bronze Age III Black Painted pottery were also found.

The Medieval period is represented by Medieval Brick, Cooking (e.g. Fig. 53:m), Coarse, and Painted wares.

Late Chalcolithic and Hittite occupations are less clearly represented. Some body sherds initially identified as Hittite Chaff Faced Ware may well be Late Chalcolithic Cream Chaff Ware. Otherwise, Hittite ceramics are limited to rimsherds of Hittite Fine and Exterior Wheel–Marked wares, both relatively infrequent Hittite types. The absence of sherds of any of the several common Hittite wares is thus unusual and makes the identification of Hittite occupation here suspect.

N55/1

NAME: Göktepe
    Vilayet: Tunceli
    Kaza: Akpazar
    Nahiye: —
    Village: Göktepe

NATURE: Mound

DESCRIPTION (Fig. 79): This is a moderately large, high, rounded mound on the edge of a low terrace on the east side of the Munzur River. The modern village is clustered to the east and southeast of the mound, with a few of the village houses actually on the mound, and several borrow pits dug into the mound at various places. The damage to the mound is relatively slight, however, and the majority of the mound surface is wasteland.

DIMENSIONS:
    Length: ca. 300 m north-south
    Width: ca. 250 m east-west
    Height: ca. 10–15 m

COLLECTIONS: Preliminary

OCCUPATIONS: The preliminary surface collection was roughly divided over the mound so that the

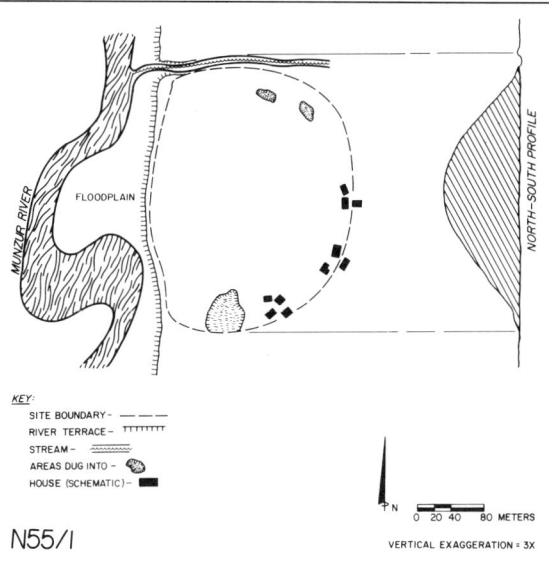

FIGURE 79. N55/1-Site plan and profile.

upper and lower parts of the mound were collected separately (dividing the mound at approximately half its height), and the lower half of the mound was collected separately on the east and on the west sides. The picture of occupation given by this rough areal breakdown of the mound was generally quite consistent, later materials dominating the collection from the upper part of the site, and the picture from the east and the west sides of the lower mound being for the most part identical.

Roughly estimating importance:
    Major—Early Bronze Age I-II
            Middle Bronze Age
            Hittite
            Medieval
    Minor—Middle Chalcolithic (Halaf)
            Chalcolithic–Early Bronze Age
              Transitional
    Trace— Early Chalcolithic
            Late Chalcolithic
            Early Bronze Age IIIA (?)
            Iron Age (?)

The Early Bronze Age is well represented on the mound. Relatively large quantities of Early Bronze Age Burnished and Polished (e.g. Fig. 16:i) pottery, including many rim sherds, were found, as well as lesser amounts of Red Slipped Ware (e.g. Fig. 16:q) and body sherds of Early Bronze Age Plain Ware. These materials were concentrated on the lower part of the mound, both east and west, but a few possible examples of Polished and Burnished ceramics were also found on the upper half of the site. It seems clear that Early Bronze Age I-II occupation is a major component of this mound.

The Middle Bronze Age is represented only in the collections from the lower half of the mound, but there it is found on both the east and west sides of the site. In both areas Middle Bronze Age Gray and Middle Bronze Age Gritty wares were found. Rims of both wares were also recovered.

Settlement in the Hittite period is clearly present, though not so abundantly demonstrated as the Early Bronze Age occupation. Again, evidence from the surface collection is largely limited to the lower slopes of the mound. A few sherds only, possibly representing Hittite Plain and Thick wares were recovered from the upper part of the site. Sherds of Hittite Plain, Brown Burnished, and Brown Gritty Cooking wares were found on both east and west sides of the mound. On the west Brown Gritty Cooking Ware was also present, while on the east Buff–Orange Burnished, Painted, Fine and perhaps Chaff Faced wares were collected. Almost all of these sherds were body sherds. Only a small handful of rims of Hittite Plain and one rim of Hittite Fine Ware were recovered. The significance of the Hittite period occupation here is attested, however, by the relative abundance, and particularly the variety, of Hittite ceramics found.

Medieval material is found over the whole surface of the mound. On the lower half of the mound Medieval Brick, Thick, Cooking, and Red Slipped wares are present. On the east was also found Medieval Painted Ware and on the west Coarse Ware. All of these wares also were present on the upper part of the site, where White Slipped and Green Glazed wares were also found. Rims of Medieval Brick, Thick, Cooking and Green Glazed wares were collected from the site. The occupation represented by these ceramics was undoubtedly extensive. Indeed, occupation may have been continuous to the present day. Modern sherds were noted over the mound surface, and on the lower east side of the mound, a fragment of an Ottoman pipe bowl was found.

A Halafian occupation may be indicated by one painted rimsherd originally thought to be of Early Bronze Age III Red Painted Ware. On closer inspection, however, this sherd appears clearly related to Halaf painted pottery (Fig. 55:d).

The Chalcolithic–Early Bronze Age Transitional period is surprisingly abundantly represented at this site by its characteristic Plain Simple and Reserved Slip wares, including a rim of Plain Simple Ware. All of this material was found on the east side of the lower half of the site, however, probably indicating that the area occupied in this period was rather small, perhaps only half or less of the total mound area.

One sherd (Fig. 7:f) appears to be of Chalcolithic Ware. The surface finish is not typical, however, and no other sherds of this ware were found. Although Early Chalcolithic occupation is possible, it cannot be considered demonstrated on the basis of this slim evidence.

The existence of Late Chalcolithic occupation at this site also is not at all sure. Some body sherds originally identified as Hittite Chaff Faced Ware may actually be Cream Chaff Ware, but this is highly uncertain, particularly with no rim sherds in the collection.

A few sherds identified as Early Bronze Age III Red Painted Ware were found on both sides of the lower part of the mound. They were not abundant, and Black Painted pottery was not found. At least one of these sherds was later re-identified as a Middle Chalcolithic painted ware (Halafian). There may have been an occupation here in the Early Bronze Age III period, but it was probably not extensive or long.

The Iron Age is represented by a single rim from the lower, eastern part of the mound. If this is indeed an Iron Age sherd, the occupation it indicates must have been small or temporary.

O54/1

NAME: Tülin Tepe
  Vilayet: Elâzığ
  Kaza: Merkez kazası
  Nahiye: Mollakendi
  Village: —

NATURE: Mound

DESCRIPTION (Fig. 80): This was apparently a relatively large, broad, and high mound. It was completely dug away prior to our survey (probably in 1966) to be used as fill for the new railroad embankment being constructed nearby to allow the railroad to bypass the future reservoir. A

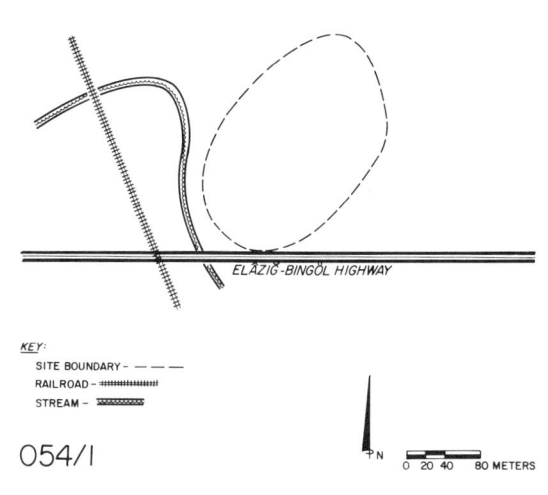

FIGURE 80. 054/1-Site plan.

photograph of this work in progress is published in *Doomed by the Dam* (1967:63) along with a few typical ceramics from the site. More material is preserved in the Elâzığ Museum but only a trifling proportion of what must have been contained in the mound. Collections were possible, however, both from the remaining basal area and from the railroad embankment itself.

A spring is located at the south edge of the mound from which a small stream flows to the northwest.

DIMENSIONS:
  Length: ca. 260 m measured across the remaining basal area
  Width: ca. 210 m similarly measured
  Height: (?)

COLLECTIONS: Preliminary

OCCUPATIONS: There were no striking differences between the collections from the basal area of the mound and the railroad embankment. Apparently the excavations for earth fill had so disturbed the strata that materials from all periods were strewn over the mound area and jumbled together in the earth carried to the embankment. The results of the collections in both places are therefore combined here to make a rough determination of the various periods of occupation formerly present in this mound.

Major— Early Bronze Age I-II
       Hittite
       Medieval
Present—Early Chalcolithic
        Middle Chalcolithic (Halaf)
        Late Chalcolithic
        Chalcolithic–Early Bronze Age Transitional
        Early Bronze Age IIIA
        Middle Bronze Age

Early Bronze Age Burnished (e.g. Fig. 14:h), Polished, Plain, and Red Slipped wares indicate an Early Bronze Age I-II occupation of some importance. A relatively large number of Early Bronze Age Burnished rimsherds was collected, and sherds of typical Early Bronze Age Relief Decorated Ware were recovered from the mound during its destruction in the year before our survey (*Doomed by the Dam*, 1967:63).

A substantial Hittite occupation is indicated by the wide variety of Hittite wares rather than the relative number of rimsherds, which was surprisingly small. Hittite Plain (Fig. 25:ff; Fig. 26:f), Buff–Orange Burnished, Orange Smoothed, Brown Burnished, White Slipped (Fig. 33:q), Exterior Wheel-Marked, Brown Gritty Cooking, Fine (Fig. 26:ii), and Chaff Faced wares were found.

The Medieval period is represented by Medieval Brick (e.g. Fig. 42:c), a Modeled lid (Fig. 55:a), Thick, Cooking (Fig. 53:g), Coarse, White Slipped (Fig. 50:n), and Sgraffiato wares. Again, rimsherds were not abundant but the variety of wares is relatively great.

Other periods of occupation are represented in the preliminary collections by only a few sherds from a limited range of wares. It is not possible, however, to conclude from their low representation in a preliminary collection that they were minor or insignificant occupations. They are therefore merely noted as being present.

The Early Chalcolithic is represented by the characteristic Graphite Slipped Ware. Painted pottery probably of Halaf type was found. A single rim of Cream Chaff Ware indicates a Late Chalcolithic presence at this mound. The Chalcolithic–Early Bronze Age Transitional period was evidently present as shown by the occurrence of Reserved Slip Ware. A small amount of Early Bronze Age III Red Painted pottery (e.g. Fig. 17:j) indicates some occupation during the Early

Bronze Age IIIA period. The Black Painted ware characteristic of the Early Bronze Age IIIB is absent. The Middle Bronze Age is represented by Old Hittite Gray and Middle Bronze Age Gritty wares.

O54/2

NAME: Makaraz Tepe (Tepecik)
    Vilayet: Elâzığ
    Kaza: Merkez kazası
    Nahiye: İçme
    Village: near Tepecik

NATURE: Mound

DESCRIPTION (Fig. 81): This is a fairly large, high mound. It consists of several topographic units. Near the center, and the highest, is a relatively narrow, round, steep sided peak with a flat top. From the base of this peak the mound slopes gently down to the surrounding land surface for slightly less than half its circumference, on the north. For the rest, a fairly clear, flat terrace surrounds the central peak, primarily on the south, but definitely curving around the east and west sides also. Then, fanning out from the foot of this terrace are relatively broad, gentle slopes which descend to natural ground level. These low slopes are broadest and extend the furthest from the center of the mound on its south side. They narrow around the east and west sides of the site merging with the top of the terrace where it disappears into the northern slopes of the mound.

Large portions of the mound are cultivated. The major exceptions are the central peak and most of the terrace. There is no contemporary settlement. The edges of the central peak have been dug into at several places, most to form small, rectangular niches, looking like small gun emplacements, but on the northeast side some extensive excavations have taken place. These excavations cut rather deeply into the peak and have left a high profile, up virtually the entire height of the peak. From this profile it can be seen that the central peak is composed primarily of collapsed mud brick or pisé buildings. No rubbish layers and consequently little artifactual material is apparent in most of this cut. Near the base of the profile, however, a number of levels, probably floors, and lenses are evident. It was from this area that the dated charcoal sample was obtained from the site (discussed under the dating of Early Bronze Age III Black Painted Ware in Chapter 2).

DIMENSIONS:
    Length: The central mound, including the north slopes and the terrace measures ca. 200 m long. The low slopes to the south of the terrace add an additional ca. 100 m
    Width: The central mound measures approximately 200 m wide. The southern slopes are slightly narrower, being 160–170 m in width
    Height: Total height is estimated at ca. 10 m

COLLECTIONS: Preliminary and stratified, gridded random.

OCCUPATIONS:
    Major—Early Bronze Age I-II
             Early Bronze Age III (A and B)
             Middle Bronze Age
             Hittite
             Iron Age (Early)
             Medieval
    Minor—Early Chalcolithic
             Late Chalcolithic
             Chalcolithic-Early Bronze Age Transitional.

This relatively large mound contains extensive and important occupations from a large number of periods. One of the more important of these occupations is that of the Early Bronze Age I-II. Sherds of every type of Early Bronze Age pottery recognized were recovered from the surface of this site (e.g. Early Bronze Age Burnished—Fig. 12:k,v,aa,mm,oo,rr; Fig. 13:d, f,h,u,bb,oo,rr,tt; Fig. 14:c,g,i,j,l,n,jj; Polished— Fig. 16:a,d,l; Thick—Fig. 16:ff; Fig. 17:a; Relief Decorated—Fig. 15:a; Plain—Fig. 16:z,aa; Red Slipped—Fig. 16:p,r,s,v). From the controlled surface collection alone no less than 96 rimsherds of Early Bronze Age Burnished Ware were recovered. This includes a number of "rail-rim" or "impressed neck" profiles typical of the early part of the Early Bronze Age (as in Fig. 12:a–g). A number of characteristic Relief Decorated sherds were also found (e.g. Fig. 15:a). These diagnostic sherds confirm what could probably have been concluded from the sheer bulk of

The Sites 183

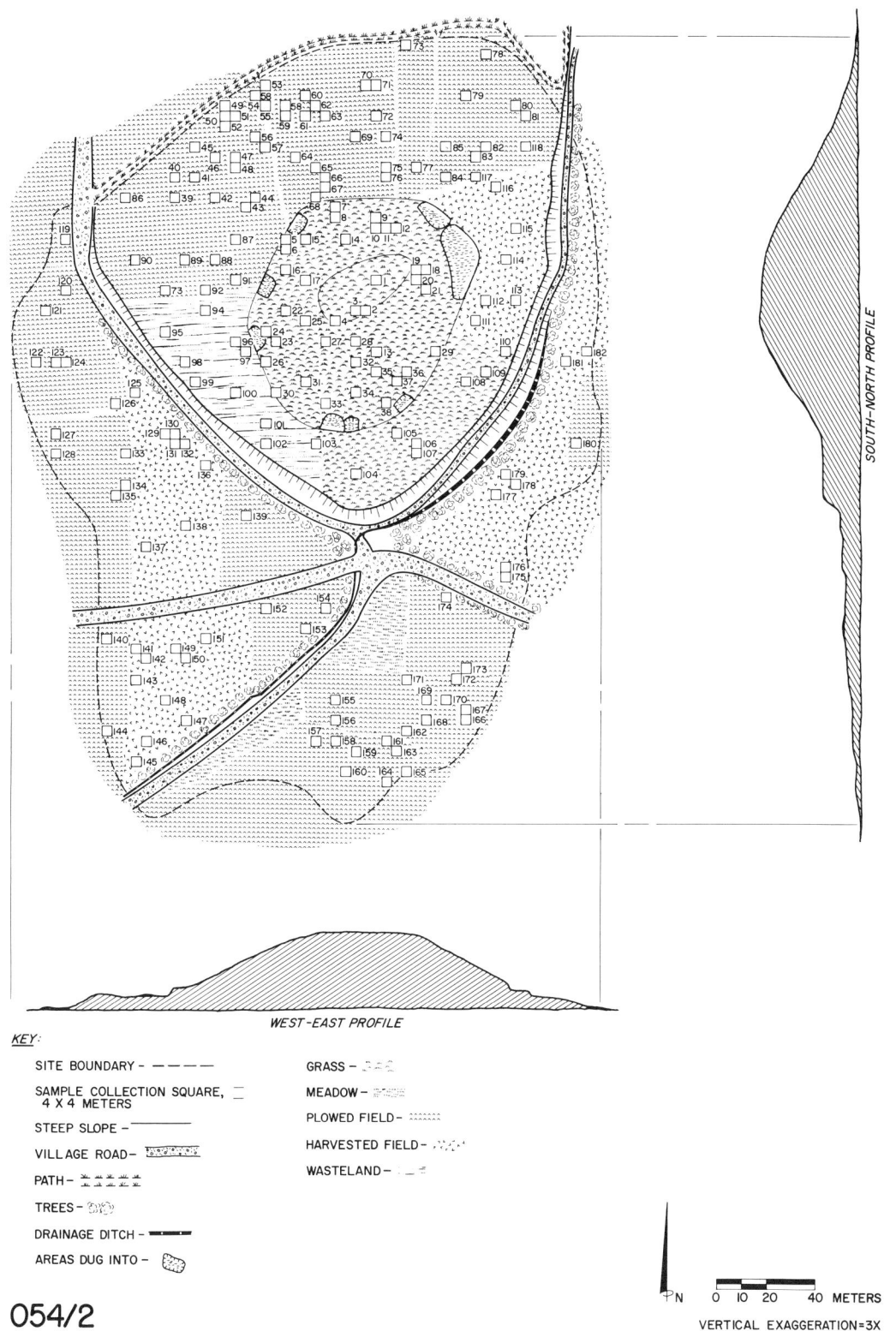

KEY:

SITE BOUNDARY – – – –
SAMPLE COLLECTION SQUARE, ☐
4 X 4 METERS
STEEP SLOPE –
VILLAGE ROAD –
PATH –
TREES –
DRAINAGE DITCH –
AREAS DUG INTO –

GRASS –
MEADOW –
PLOWED FIELD –
HARVESTED FIELD –
WASTELAND –

054/2

FIGURE 81. 054/2-Site plan and profiles.

Early Bronze Age Burnished Ware alone, that there is a substantial early settlement here and that the later Early Bronze Age III occupation is distinct and probably less important.

This is not to say that the Early Bronze Age III occupation was not a major or substantial one, however. Not only are there relatively numerous sherds of both Early Bronze Age Red Painted and Black Painted ceramics (e.g. Fig. 17:i, k,o,p,r; Fig. 19:e; Fig. 18:e,j,l–n,s,t), but the typically late grooved neck (as in Fig. 13:uu, vv) and hole-mouth jar profiles (as in Fig. 13:ff–ii) of Burnished ware are also present here in some numbers. Both the early and late phases of the Early Bronze Age III period are represented at this site, as is evident from the significant occurrence of both painted wares.

The Middle Bronze Age must also have seen a rather important settlement here. A relatively large quantity of Middle Bronze Age Gritty Ware was collected, including a large number of rims found in the controlled surface survey (e.g. Fig. 20:a,b,f–h,k,l,p.bb,dd,ee). Old Hittite Gray Ware was abundant, although primarily represented by body sherds. Still, a number of rims were gathered from the surface (Fig. 21:c,m,n,p,r,dd,ee). About the same number of Middle Bronze Age Gray Ware rims were found (e.g. Fig. 22:a,c–g,m,n,p,v–y), and there were occasional sherds of Old Hittite Light Faced Gray Ware (e.g. Fig. 22:bb–dd). This is one of the largest samples of Middle Bronze Age materials found in the survey.

Occupation during the Hittite period was also evidently extensive at this site. Every Hittite ware defined was found on the surface, with the single exception of Hittite Red, rare in the whole region. Rimsherds of almost all wares were common in the controlled collections, not so abundant as Early Bronze Age materials, but common enough to clearly demonstrate substantial Hittite occupation of the mound (e.g. Hittite Plain—Fig. 23:b,f,h,o,t,x,y,gg,ii,mm,nn,vv; Fig. 24:b,y,ii,oo; Fig. 25:z,hh,ll,nn,ss; Fig. 26:b,c,i, q,t,cc,mm; Thick—Fig. 27:a,b,r,s,x; Fig. 28: a,c,e; Buff–Orange Burnished—Fig. 28:m,s,w,y, ff,hh,mm,ww; Fig. 29:f,m–o,v,aa,hh,ii,oo,ww; Fig. 30:g,i,m; Orange Smoothed—Fig. 31:c,h; Red–Brown Burnished—Fig. 31:n,cc,ss; Brown Burnished—Fig. 32:g,i,k,v,w,dd,hh–jj,ll,oo,ss, aaa,bbb,eee; White Slipped—Fig. 33:a,c,f–h,m, r,v,x,aa,ff,kk,mm; Painted—Fig. 34:a,c,f–h, l,n,p,q; Fig. 35:a; Brown Gritty Cooking—Fig. 35:j). There is also a relative abundance of Hittite Fine Ware at this site, which may well indicate a relative importance of administrative or religious activities (i.e. activities not directly related to basic subsistence tasks).

Iron Age sherds are common, including many rimsherds from the controlled collection (e.g. Fig. 36:j,s,bb,tt; Fig. 37:a,r,ll,mm,oo,pp,vv,ww; Fig. 38:a,c,e,f; Fig. 39:a). In-turned bowls or hole-mouthed jars with multiple grooves running around the neck (as in Fig. 36:u–hh) were common; while open bowls with deeply grooved lips and necks (as in Fig. 36:a–f) were absent. It appears, therefore, that Iron Age occupation here is largely restricted to the Early Iron Age, but the settlement from this period must have been an important one. One sherd possibly of Phrygian type was found (Fig. 55:h).

Medieval materials are abundant. They include all ceramic wares identified for the period (e.g. Brick—Fig. 40:g,r,u; Fig. 41:n,w,cc,mm, Fig. 42:m,cc,tt; Fig. 43:n; Fig. 44:e,j,m; Thick—Fig. 46:c; Coarse—Fig. 47:g; Red Slipped—Fig. 47:z,cc; Fig. 48:q,mm; Fig. 49:b,h,j,m; White Slipped—Fig. 49:bb; Cooking—Fig. 52:j,p,r; Fig. 53:a,d,f,h–j; Modeled—Fig. 53:q; Fig. 54:d,f,i), including green Glazed (e.g. Fig. 47:k,l,r,u) and Sgraffiato pottery. The glazed ware is relatively common. Medieval occupation is extensive and important at this mound.

Early Chalcolithic occupation is not evidenced by any abundance of material. A few sherds of probable Chalcolithic Ware and especially of the distinctive Graphite Slipped Ware clearly define the presence of some occupation of this period. In all likelihood any Early Chalcolithic occupation level will be deeply covered by the overburden of debris from the many subsequent and important occupations of this site. The paucity of early materials on the mound surface is therefore not surprising.

Late Chalcolithic occupation at first was not thought to be present at this site. With the re-evaluation and reclassification of a number of rim profiles formerly thought to belong to Hittite Chaff Faced Ware, however, it became clear that there were at least some of sherds of Cream Chaff Ware in the collections (e.g. Fig. 10:r,ii; Fig. 11:bb,hh). Although the evidence is not abundant and the occupation is therefore probably relatively small (or deeply buried), it seems adequate to identify a Late Chalcolithic component at this site.

Several Reserved Slip Ware sherds (e.g. Fig. 9:l,n) and a few sherds of Plain Simple Ware (e.g. Fig. 9:y) may denote the presence of a Chalcolithic–Early Bronze Age Transitional settlement. They may, of course, be associated with the Early Bronze Age I-II Occupation, but they are not infrequent, and a separate occupation characterized by these ceramics may at least provisionally be suggested.

CONTROLLED COLLECTION: It was not possible to use a simple gridded strip or random grid system to make an adequate controlled surface collection from such a large and topographically complex mound as this. A system of "stratified" random grid sampling was therefore adopted. This is the only mound collected by this method during the survey. A "stratified" collection system has nothing to do with archaeological stratification of occupation layers in a site. In terms of sampling, it means simply that there are different areas to sample, which can be separately identified and defined before collecting. In this case the different topographic divisions of the mound are such areas. Within each area, then, a simple random grid system of collection squares is set up and collected. It was not possible, due to lack of time, to collect fully 10 percent of the total mound surface, as we attempted with most randomized grid samples. Over the three smaller topographic divisions, 10 percent of the surface area was collected. Approximately 5 percent of the surface area of the two larger divisions was collected. In all, almost 6 percent of the total site area was thus surveyed. Collection squares were all 4 m by 4 m in size. The final collection system is illustrated in Table 6 and Figure 81.

Density contours were drawn for the distribution of ceramic materials from the Early Bronze Age I-II, Early Bronze Age IIIA, Early Bronze Age IIIB, Middle Bronze Age, Hittite, Iron Age, and Medieval periods. Materials from other periods were too sparse to allow any meaningful analysis of their patterns of distribution over the mound.

Early Bronze Age Burnished, Plain, Thick, Polished, Relief Decorated, and Red Slipped wares were plotted together as a group, representative of Early Bronze Age I-II occupation debris. Density contour lines were then drawn around

TABLE 6 Stratified Random Grid Sampling Scheme For Site 054/2, Makaraz Tepe (Tepecik)

Topographic Division	No. grid squares in division	No. grid squares collected	Percent
Top of Mound Peak	38	4	10
Slopes of Mound Peak	343	34	10
Northern Lower Slopes	482	48	10
Terrace	607	32	5
Southern Lower Slopes	1620	64	4
(Collectable in this Division)	(1265)		(5)
Total	3090	182	6

areas of 10, 30, and 50 sherds per collection square (Fig. 82). These contours clearly show a large area of relatively continuous distribution of these Early Bronze Age materials over the center and western areas of the mound. All told, the area is roughly 230 m long in a northeast-southwest direction by roughly 150–160 m wide. The areas covered include the high mound or mound peak, the western half of the northern lower slopes, the terrace, and the northwestern quarter of the southern lower slopes. Interestingly and quite importantly, this relatively early material is abundantly represented over the central, high mound peak. None of the materials from other periods plotted, all later in time than this, were represented to any significant extent on the central mound peak, either on its top or its slopes. This strongly suggests that a great part of the mound, particularly of the high mound, is made up of Early Bronze Age occupation debris and that this was a major settlement of the period. The abundant occurrence of Early Bronze Age I-II materials over the terrace, out onto the northern lower slopes, and particularly over the southwestern lower slopes of the mound reinforces this picture of major occupation in this period and indicates that the areal extent of the occupation is considerably larger than the high mound alone. An estimate of 2.5–3.0 ha should adequately represent the size and importance of this Early Bronze Age settlement.

A crucible fragment was found in Square 88, well within the area of concentration of Early

Bronze Age I-II ceramics. The Hittite occupation area also covers this square, and it is impossible to tell exactly to what occupation a single find like this might belong. The presence of the crucible is important, however, in that it may indicate the presence of metal-working facilities at this site, probably in the Early Bronze Age, perhaps later in the Hittite period. There is other evidence for the importance of metallurgy in the Elâzığ region even before the Early Bronze Age, especially from the excavation at site N52/3 (Fatmalı-Kalecik—Whallon and Wright 1970).

Early Bronze Age IIIA and IIIB occupations were traced through the distributions of Early Bronze Age Red and Black Painted wares respectively. There was little difference between the patterns of distribution of these two wares (Figs. 83 and 84). They represent either a single occupation period or a continuity of occupation from the early to the late phases of the Early Bronze Age III at this site. These painted wares were sparsely scattered on the surface of the mound, but they occurred in numbers just adequate to allow a clear delineation of an area of occupation for the period. In these cases, with so little material on the mound surface, plotting individual sherd counts helps considerably to develop a picture of distributional patterns.

The most striking aspect of the distribution of Early Bronze Age III materials is their strong tendency to be concentrated on the terrace and northern lower slopes, peripheral to the central high mound. Sherd distributions outline two areas of major concentration, both on the terrace, one on the east and one on the west side of the central mound peak, with a more sparse scatter over the northern lower slope area. Of the areas bordering the mound peak, only the terrace area directly to its south failed to produce any sherds of this period. In addition, a few sherds were found directly on the lower slopes of the central mound peak, particularly on its western side, where materials from the Early Bronze Age I-II were relatively scarce. A few scattered and isolated sherds were also found over the southern lower mound slopes.

It seems fairly clear, then, that Early Bronze Age III occupation was located in a band which ran around the already existing central mound and which lapped up onto that mound to some degree. The two major concentrations of material indicated by the distributional contours measure approximately 15 × 100 m and 10 × 50 m, but this is probably an unrealistically low estimate for the area settled in this period. Taking into account the overall pattern of distribution of sherds, and counting both east and west terraces and the northern lower slopes as occupied, an estimate of 1.5–2.0 ha seems reasonable.

Middle Bronze Age Gritty, Middle Bronze Age Gray, Old Hittite Gray and Old Hittite Light Faced Gray wares were plotted together to represent the distribution of Middle Bronze Age materials over this site (Fig. 85). Density contours were then drawn around areas with five and ten sherds per grid unit. The distributional pattern was quite clear from these contours. All areas of high density of Middle Bronze Age ceramics were on the terrace and the northern lower slopes, with the exception of a single square on the lower slopes at the western periphery of the mound. The distribution does not extend up onto the slopes of the central high mound except in one, trivial instance. The conclusion is relatively clear, that settlement in the Middle Bronze Age was clustered around the foot of the mound peak, covering slightly more than .5 ha on the terrace and northern lower slopes, but not extending significantly beyond these areas.

Hittite sherds were abundant on the surface of the mound, and all wares except Hittite Red occurred. These were all grouped together in plotting the distribution of Hittite occupation debris on the site. Contour lines were drawn around squares with more than 10, 20, and 30 sherds. The resultant picture is one of a major occupation covering a large proportion of the total mound (Fig. 86). In fact, the only areas not covered with a significant number of Hittite sherds were the central high mound (the distribution of Hittite ceramics extends up onto the bottom slopes of this central mound peak only sporadically and not in significant density), the southeastern part of the terrace, and the central part of the southern lower slopes or apron. Judging from this distributional data, it would seem that the bulk of the occupation lies in the northern half of the site, surrounding the central mound peak on the west, north and east, with secondary but significant extensions onto the southern fringe of the mound. That the occupation should swing around the central high mound is understandable, but it is as yet unclear why the south–central area of the mound should be relatively barren of Hittite materials. The only period which is importantly represented in the surface collection data from this area of the mound is the Medieval period. Accepting the picture as it stands from the data of the stratified sampling scheme, one would have to estimate a central area of most intensive occupation roughly 150×230 m in size (less the central high mound area of ca. 80 m diameter) and add to that two secondary concentrations of occupation, 40×40 m in size on the southwest, and 40×100 m on the southeast corner of the mound. In all, this represents an estimated occupation area of approximately 3.4 ha.

Iron Age and Iron Age Thick pottery are distributed over the site in a manner much less clear than that of previous periods. Contoured at densities of four and eight sherds per square, a more or less discontinuous pattern of concentration appears on the northern lower slopes and on the terrace and lower slopes to the southwest of the central mound (Fig. 87). From this latter area, the distribution extends high up onto the central mound in one narrow area. It is a bit difficult to interpret this pattern of distribution, but it is possible to see it as a sparse scatter of material representing a short or light occupation over the northern and western areas of the site around the central mound peak. A short occupation would accord well with the presence of rim profiles characteristic only of the Early Iron Age. Such a liberal interpretation would give an estimate for total occupation area of 1 ha. Individually, the major areas outlined by the 4-sherd contour measure approximately 60×100 m, 20×100 m, and 20×90 m, or ca. .75 ha in total.

The grouped Medieval ceramics included Medieval Brick, Thick, Cooking, Coarse, White Slipped, Red Slipped, Painted, Modeled, Glazed, and Sgraffiato wares. These ceramics were quite abundant over the mound and, when contoured at 10, 20, and 30 sherds per collection square, show a distribution that virtually covers the entire mound with the exception of the central mound peak and minor sections of the terrace and the central and eastern parts of the northern lower slopes (Fig. 88). The bulk of the occupation seems to fall on the southern lower slopes, or the apron, stretching up around the central mound or terrace on the west and east sides. An independent plot of the diagnostic Glazed Ware sherds confirms this general impression that the area of major Medieval occupation was the southern apron of the mound (Fig. 89). As a whole, Medieval materials cover a large area, ca. 200×280 m (less the central high mound of ca. 80 m diameter). The major area of occupation covers a smaller, deeply V-shaped area of roughly 1.5 ha. A fragment of human skull found in Square 138 may very well relate to this late occupation on the mound. Medieval materials are the only ones to show a major concentration over the area around this square. Part of this large area of Medieval occupation may be devoted to cemetery use, therefore, thus effectively reducing the size of settlement which can be estimated for this site. The surface survey data as they stand are not capable of shedding further light on this problem, unless one relies on the independent pattern of distribution of the Glazed Ware to define an area roughly 80×160 m (ca. 1.25 ha) in size, restricted to the southern edge of the mound, as the most likely size for the true settlement area here in the Medieval period.

O54/3

NAME: Değirmen Tepe
   Vilayet: Elâzığ
   Kaza: Merkez kazası
   Nahiye: İçme
   Village: İlemil

NATURE: Mound

DESCRIPTION (Fig. 90): This appears to have been a moderately sized mound which has been eroded by two streams until at present only about a quarter of the mound remains. It seems to have been of simple form with little topographic variation. On the north flows a small stream, tributary to the Haringet Çayı, which runs along the east side of the remaining mound. What is left of the mound is currently under cultivation. It is not used as a borrow area for earth, so the two cut

188 *Archaeological Survey of the Keban Reservoir*

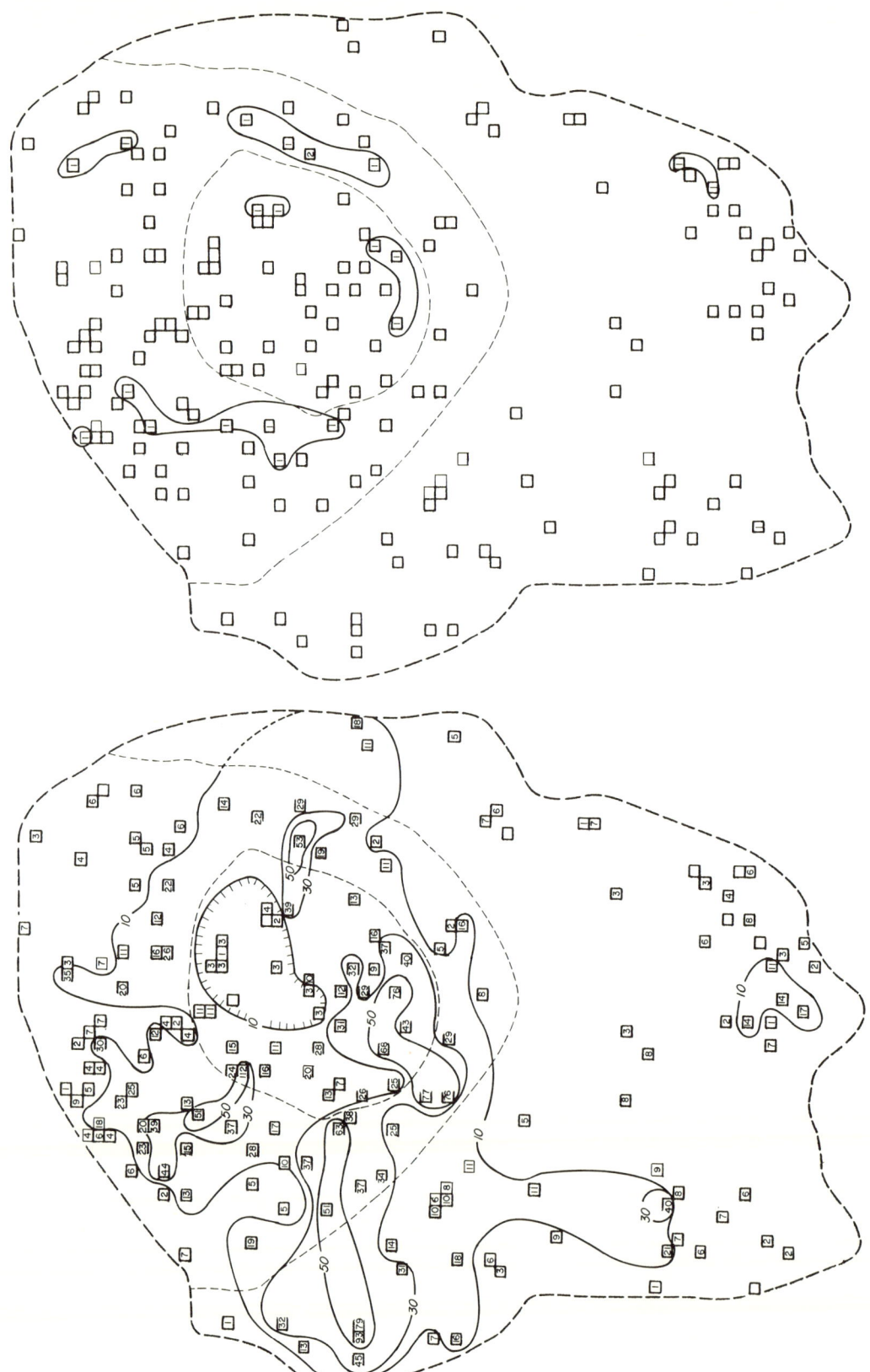

FIGURE 83. 054/2–Density contours of Early Bronze Age IIIA ceramics.

FIGURE 82. 054/2–Density contours of Early Bronze Age I-II ceramics.

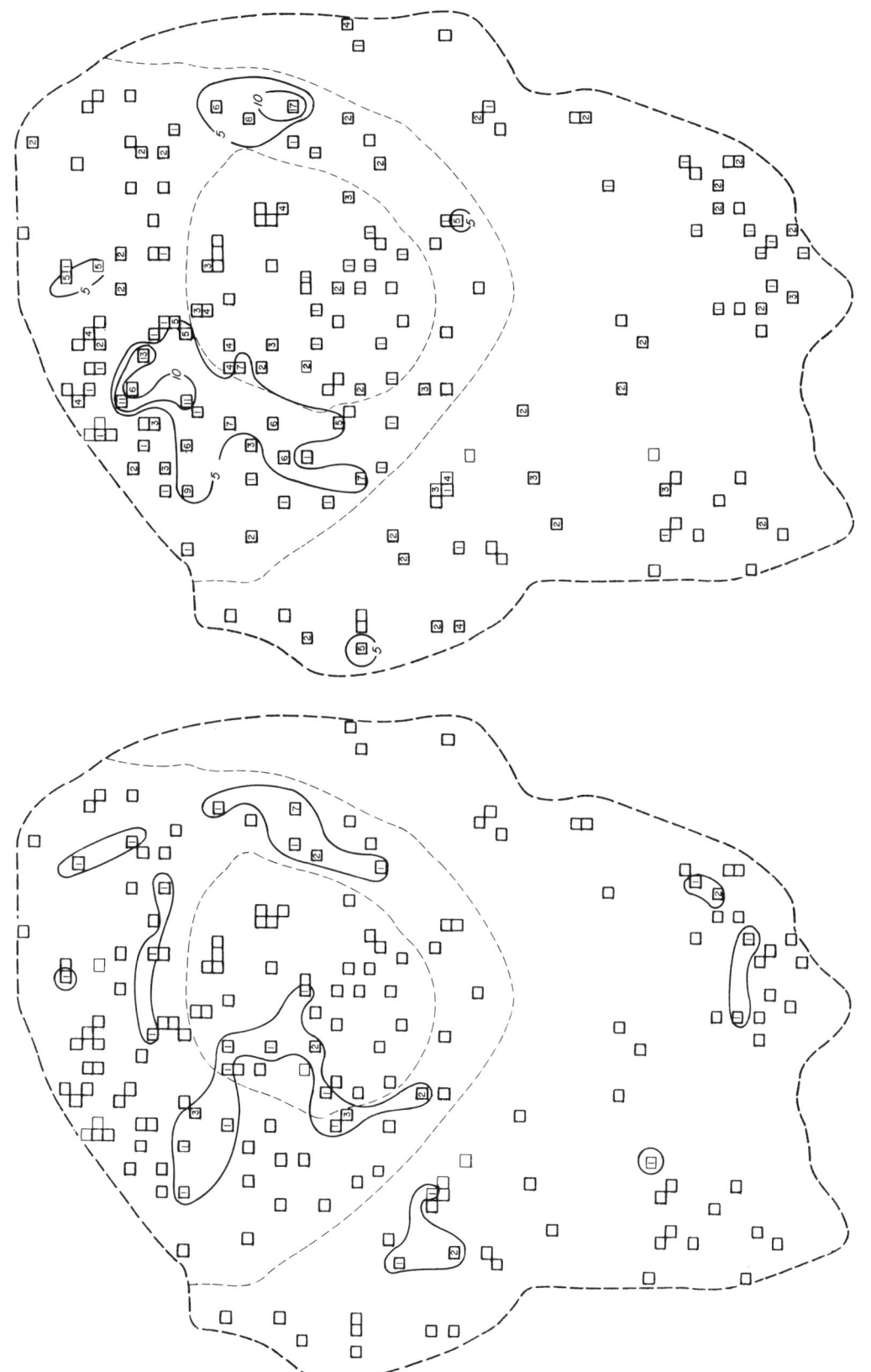

FIGURE 85. 054/2-Density contours of Middle Bronze Age ceramics.

FIGURE 84. 054/2-Density contours of Early Bronze Age IIIB ceramics.

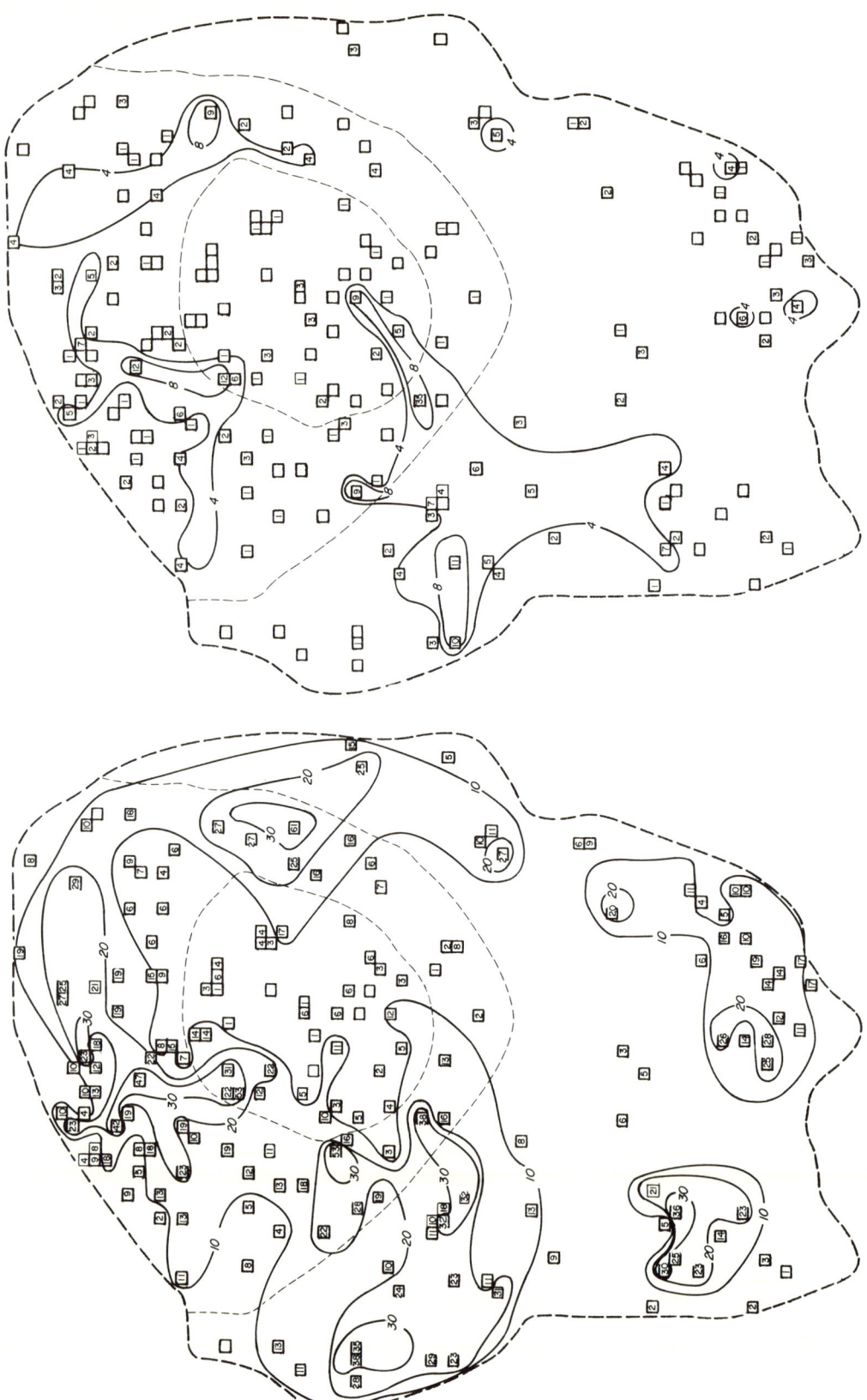

FIGURE 87. 054/2-Density contours of Iron Age ceramics.

FIGURE 86. 054/2-Density contours of Hittite ceramics.

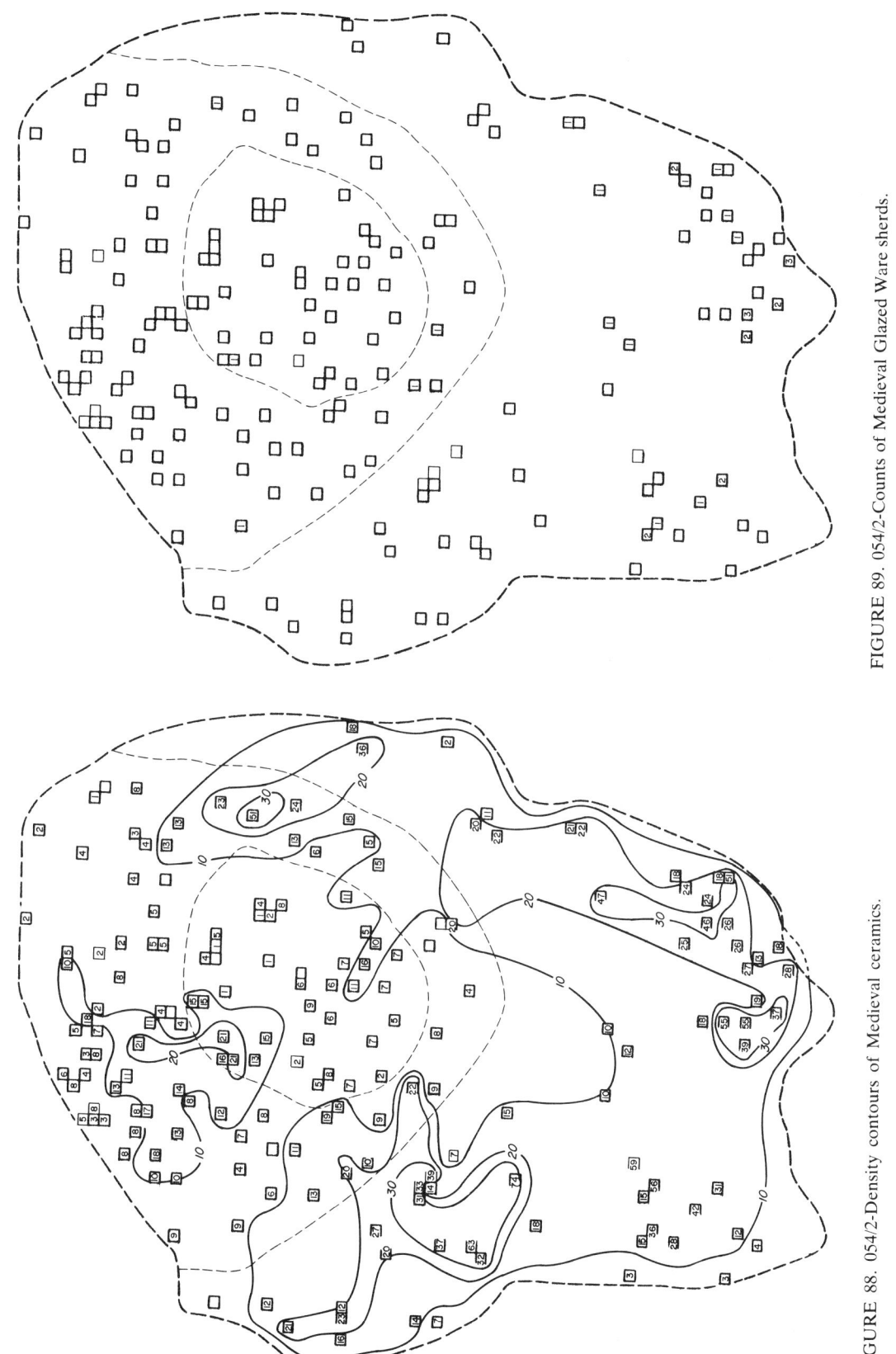

FIGURE 89. 054/2–Counts of Medieval Glazed Ware sherds.

FIGURE 88. 054/2–Density contours of Medieval ceramics.

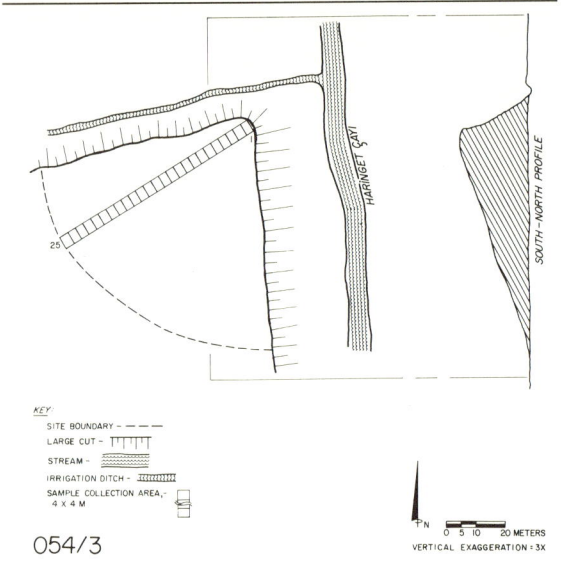

FIGURE 90. 054/3-Site plan and profile.

faces of the mound, having been naturally eroded, are covered by vegetation and nothing is visible in them, nor is much to be collected from them.

DIMENSIONS:
  Length: ca. 160 m originally, this is estimated from the measurements made of the remaining quarter of the mound, extrapolated by assuming an originally symmetrical, round form
  Width: An original ca. 150 m, similarly derived by extrapolation
  Height: ca. 7 m

COLLECTIONS: Preliminary and gridded strip

OCCUPATIONS:
  Major—Early Bronze Age I-II
    Hittite
    Medieval (Modern)
  Minor—Late Chalcolithic
    Iron Age (Early)
  Trace— Early Chalcolithic (?)
    Early Bronze Age IIIA (?)

The Early Bronze Age I-II is well represented here, particularly by an abundance of Early Bronze Age Burnished Ware. This includes a number of rims, the majority of which are of the characteristic "impressed neck" or "rail-rim" type. In addition, Early Bronze Age Polished, Red Slipped, Plain and Thick wares were found.

Hittite ceramics were also abundant here, comprising Hittite Plain (e.g. Fig. 25:w), Thick, Buff-Orange Burnished (e.g. Fig. 29:yy), Red-Brown Burnished, Brown Burnished (e.g. Fig. 32:a,l), White Slipped, Painted (e.g. Fig. 35:g), Fine, and Brown Gritty Cooking wares. Rimsherds were relatively scarce, however.

Occupation in the Medieval period was also evidenced by a relative abundance of sherds of Medieval Brick, Thick, Cooking, Coarse, White Slipped, Red Slipped, and Painted wares. None of the typical Modeled, Glazed, or Sgraffiato wares were present. This material may well represent a recent or "modern" occupation as suggested by a fragment of an Ottoman clay pipe.

The Late Chalcolithic period is represented by only a few sherds of Cream Chaff Ware, including two rims (e.g. Fig. 10:u).

Iron Age sherds (e.g. Fig. 37:dd) were considerably more abundant, but still relatively few compared to those from the major occupations. A moderate number of rims were recovered. Several of them were the typically Early Iron Age type with multiple, parallel, exterior grooves on the neck or rim.

Two sherds were identified as possibly Early Chalcolithic. Only one sherd was found which could be classified as perhaps Early Bronze Age Red Painted Ware.

CONTROLLED COLLECTION: Only an estimated quarter of the original site remained, consisting of a relatively high mound, roughly triangular in plan, with two steep faces and an apparently undisturbed mound surface sloping down from the mound top to the third side of the triangle. It was accordingly decided to run a gridded collection strip down this slope. This strip began at the top of the mound.

System:
  Strip A: Direction 240°, length 75 m (25 squares)
    Squares A1–A25:   cultivated field

Collection squares were 3×4 m in size, 3 m in length along the collection strip.

The frequencies of Early Bronze Age I-II, Hittite, Iron Age, and Medieval sherds along this strip were plotted.

The fluctuations in frequency of Early Bronze Age I-II sherds were smoothed by using a moving average calculated over groups of four collection squares. The resultant curve (Fig. 91) shows a clear and relatively high peak in frequency near the beginning of the strip. Mapped on the site plan and contoured at 4, 8, 12, and 16 sherds per square, one sees a strong tendency for materials of this period to be abundantly represented near the top of the present mound. They become progressively scarcer down the mound slope until there is a slight rise in frequency at the base of the mound. The depression in Early Bronze Age sherd frequencies along the lower slopes of the mound is quite likely the result of the accumulation of deposits from later periods on this area of the mound. The pattern of high concentration of materials from this early period near the top of the mound with later occupations more strongly or exclusively represented on the lower mound slopes is not unfamiliar in the area and strongly suggests that the bulk of the mound consists of occupation debris from the Early Bronze Age.

The materials of later periods are all concentrated further down the slope of the mound, perhaps indicating a tendency for later settlement to cluster around, rather than on, an original, high mound from the Early Bronze Age. A very similar situation has been demonstrated at site O54/2, Makaraz Tepe (Tepecik).

Hittite sherd frequencies, smoothed with a moving average across six squares, show a clear trend towards clustering well down the mound

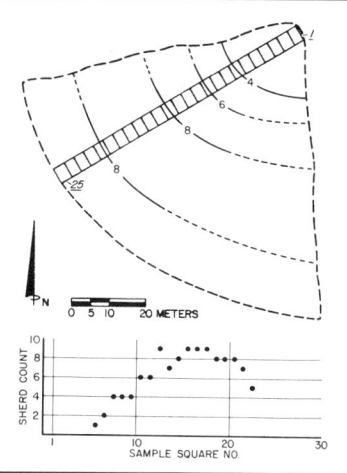

FIGURE 92. 054/3-Density contours of Hittite ceramics.

slopes (Fig. 92). The frequencies of Iron Age sherds are very low, but smoothed with a moving average over four squares, they appear clearly absent from the upper portion of the site and seem to peak in frequency in the middle of the slope (Fig. 93). Medieval materials are slightly more abundant, but the curve of their frequency in the collection squares, smoothed with a moving average over 4 squares, shows a broader representation over the middle of the mound slopes (Fig. 94).

None of these latter patterns is too revealing about the nature of distribution of occupation over the mound. Sherd counts are generally low, and a single collection strip running down a

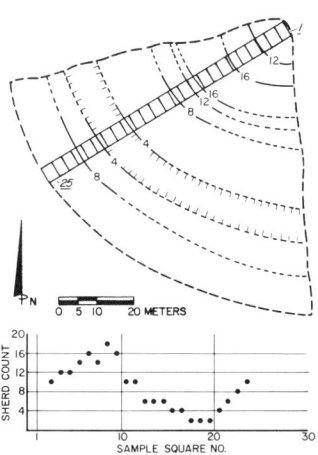

FIGURE 91. 054/3-Density contours of Early Bronze Age I-II ceramics.

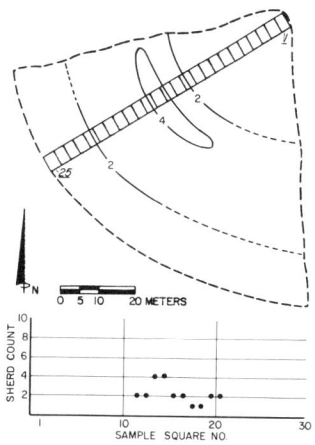

FIGURE 93. 054/3-Density contours of Iron Age ceramics.

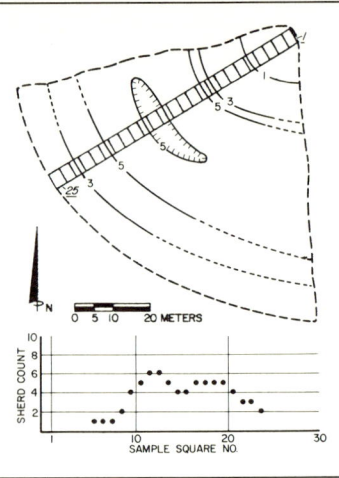

FIGURE 94. 054/3-Density contours of Medieval ceramics.

quarter of a mound seems inadequate to form any general picture or reconstruction of the site. The Early Bronze Age pattern appears definite, however, and the most reasonable interpretation seems still to be that given above of later occupations spreading over the lower slopes of the mound, around a central, high mound of earlier date.

If this interpretation is correct and the occupations later than the Early Bronze Age are distributed in bands encircling the central mound, as they are tentatively shown on the distributional maps, then approximate size estimates for them can be made. The Hittite occupation would lie in a band roughly 45 m in width, covering an area of some 1.75 ha. Iron Age occupation shows an unusually narrow width of 10–15 m, giving us an estimated area of .25 ha. Medieval occupation debris covers a band 35–40 wide, however, and allows us to estimate its size as about 1 ha.

All of the size estimates made for occupations at this site are based on the assumption that the diameters and widths indicated from the collection strip are continuous around the entire mound, forming complete circles about the present mound peak as the presumed original center. It is, of course unlikely that such was originally exactly the case, and so the estimates given here are likely to be somewhat inaccurate. (Note the asymmetrical growth of site O54/2, for example.) Judging impressionistically from the size of the mound both in drawings and in the field, however, they appear to be relatively reasonable approximations.

054/4

NAME: —
    Vilayet: Elâzığ
    Kaza: Merkez kazası
    Nahiye: İçme
    Village: near İlemil

NATURE: Surface scatter

DESCRIPTION: A small scatter of surface material was found in a dry gulch on the south side of a small, natural hill known as Garo Tepe.

DIMENSIONS:
    Length: Small and undefined
    Width: Small and undefined
    Height: None

COLLECTIONS: Preliminary

OCCUPATIONS:
    Present—Early Bronze Age I-II
              Hittite
              Medieval
    Trace— Middle Bronze Age
              Iron Age

The origin of this material is uncertain. It was not collected from the surface of an occupation deposit. It consists only of eroded and displaced surface material. There is therefore no reason to try to define relative importance of different periods of occupation and little sense in including this site on a map of settlements of any period.

Several characteristic rim sherds are illustrated from here, however: Hittite Exterior Wheel-Marked (Fig. 28:g), Buff-Orange Burnished (Fig. 28:vv), White Slipped (Fig. 33:hh), Painted (Fig. 34:o), Iron Age Decorated Fig. 38: i,l) and Medieval Red Slipped (Fig. 48:b).

054/5

NAME: Maşatlık (Sarpulu)
    Vilayet: Elâzığ
    Kaza: Merkez kazası
    Nahiye: Mollakendi
    Village: near Sarpulu

NATURE: Mound

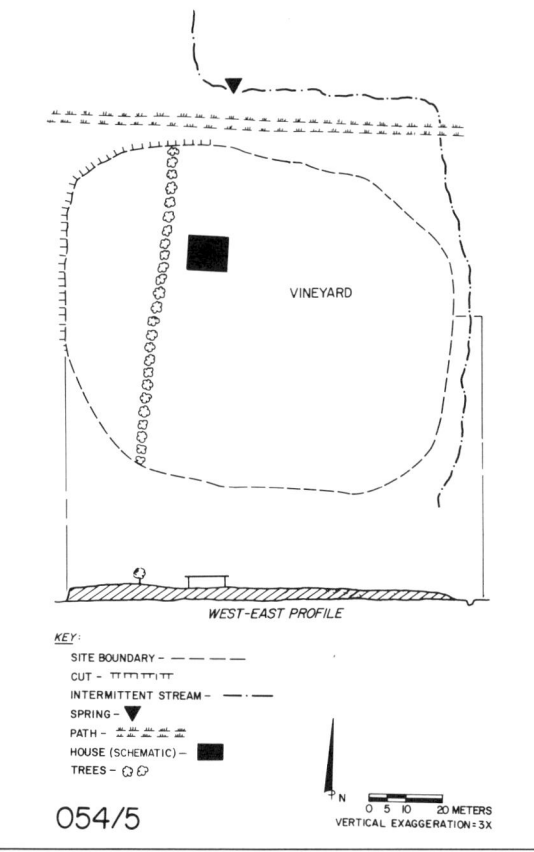

FIGURE 95. 054/5-Site plan and profile.

DESCRIPTION (Fig. 95): This is a small, low mound which is largely obscured by the fields, rows of trees, and vineyard on it. It is generally featureless except for modern disturbances, including a vineyard house built on the mound. On the west to northwestern edge, the mound has been cut into slightly to form a flat threshing area, leaving a low cut in which nothing is to be seen. A small stream runs along the east edge, curving around to the north side of the mound, where there is also a spring.

DIMENSIONS:
  Length: ca. 100–120 m east-west
  Width: ca. 80–100 m north-south
  Height: ca. 1.5 m

COLLECTIONS: Preliminary

OCCUPATIONS:
  Present—Hittite
      Medieval

The small preliminary collection from this site contained no rims and allows only the most general statement of periods present. The Hittite period is represented by Hittite Plain, Buff–Orange Burnished, Red–Brown Burnished, and Exterior Wheel–Marked wares. From the variety of wares it would appear that the Hittite occupation might comprise a substantial portion of this mound. Medieval occupation is indicated only by the presence of Medieval Brick and Coarse wares and may not be so important here.

054/6

NAME: Kazancı
  Vilayet: Elâzığ
  Kaza: Merkez kazası
  Nahiye: Mollakendi
  Village: near Sarpulu

NATURE: Mound

DESCRIPTION (Fig. 96): This is a broad, low mound with a featureless surface. It is presently entirely cultivated. It has a generally elongated, oval plan with the long axis running northwest-southeast. During collection it appeared that the nature of

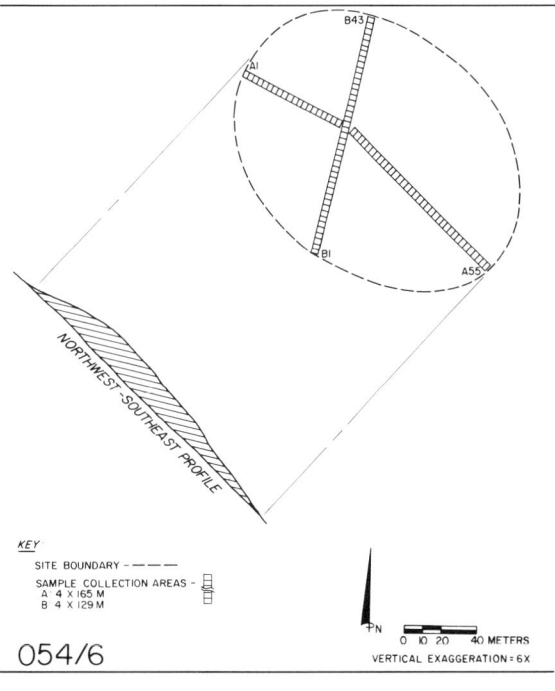

FIGURE 96. 054/6-Site plan and profile.

the surface material changed along this axis. This site is very close to 054/5.

DIMENSIONS:
    Length: 170 m measured in a northwest-southeast direction
    Width: 130 m measured northeast-southwest
    Height: ca. 2 m

COLLECTIONS: Preliminary and gridded strip

OCCUPATIONS:
    Major—Early Chalcolithic
             Late Chalcolithic
             Hittite
             Medieval
    Trace— Early Bronze Age I-II (?)
             Early Bronze Age III (?)
             Hellenistic-Roman

Early Chalcolithic occupation is evidenced by both Chalcolithic and Graphite Slipped wares. The former is more abundant, but Graphite Slipped pottery occurs in significant quantity. A number of rimsherds of both wares were recovered in the controlled collection (e.g. Chalcolithic—Fig. 7:c; Graphite Slipped—Fig. 9:e).

Late Chalcolithic ceramics were not at first recognized at this site. They were confused with Hittite White Slipped and Chaff Faced wares and with Iron Age pottery. Subsequent study of the rim profiles present at this site showed that virtually all the sherds originally classified in these three categories were in fact examples of Cream Chaff types (e.g. Fig. 10:e,q; Fig. 11:k). The existence of a substantial Late Chalcolithic occupation is thus clearly established.

Hittite occupation is represented by numerous sherds from a wide variety of wares. Leaving White Slipped and Chaff Faced wares aside as probably consisting of Cream Chaff ceramics for the most part, Hittite wares include both rim and body sherds of Hittite Plain (e.g. Fig. 23:u,cc; Fig. 26:r), Buff-Orange Burnished (e.g. Fig. 29:a), Red-Brown Burnished, Brown Burnished (e.g. Fig. 32:e,m,x,bb), and Thick (e.g. Fig. 27:f,m) wares and body sherds only of Orange Smoothed, Painted (e.g. Fig. 35:c), Fine, and Brown Gritty Cooking wares.

By far the most abundant pottery on the site was Medieval, however. This was primarily Brick (e.g. Fig. 40:o; Fig. 41:k,r,jj; Fig. 42:ll,vv,yy; Fig. 43:bb,cc), and Thick (e.g. Fig. 45:c; Fig. 46:g) wares, with a smattering of Cooking (e.g. Fig. 52:z,kk), Coarse, White Slipped (e.g. Fig. 49:o,u,ff), Red Slipped (e.g. Fig. 48:d), Painted (e.g. Fig. 50:d), and Glazed wares.

One or two sherds were identified as Early Bronze Age Burnished. They are so few that this identification is suspect. One sherd that could well be Early Bronze Age III Painted ware was recovered (Fig. 18:q). The paint was black, but the design, tapering triangles on the lip, more closely resembles typical red painted designs although it could be an earlier, perhaps Chalcolithic, motif.

One sherd of Roman Red pottery was found (Fig. 55:k). Its identification seems fairly sure, and some of the sherds identified as Medieval Brick ware may belong with it. It seems, however, highly unlikely that the picture of a substantial Medieval occupation should be changed by the discovery of this single sherd, particularly when there is also a sherd of Medieval Glazed pottery from this site.

CONTROLLED COLLECTION: Two gridded strips, crossing each other roughly in a T-shape pattern, were collected. The collection squares were 3 m long along the strips and 4 m wide across the strips.

    System:
        Strip A:
             First section - Direction: 118°, length: 60 m (20 squares)
             Second section - Direction: 134°, length: 105 m (35 squares)
             Squares A1-A35:   closely harvested field
        Strip B: Crosses Strip A at the junction between its first and second sections. Direction: 195°, length: 129 m (43 squares)
             Squares B1-B43:   closely harvested field

Materials of the Early Chalcolithic, Late Chalcolithic, Hittite, and Medieval periods were adequate to allow contouring of densities along the collection strips.

Chalcolithic and Graphite Slipped wares were plotted together as Early Chalcolithic occupation materials. The frequencies per grid square were smoothed by taking a moving average over six squares. The results, plotted at intervals of 1, 3, and 5 sherds, show a clear concentration of this material over the northwest portion of the mound

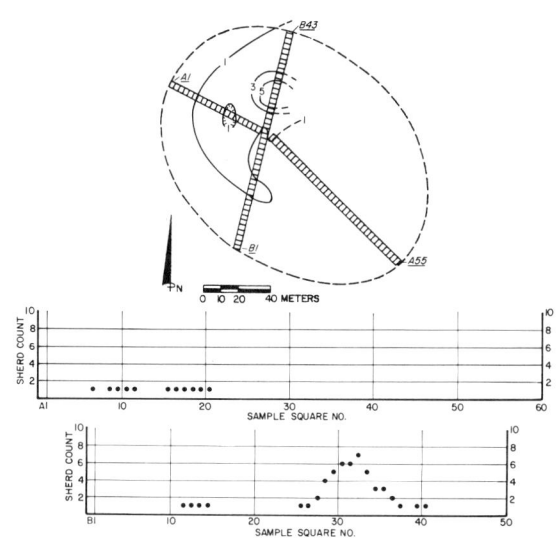

FIGURE 97. 054/6-Density contours of Early Chalcolithic ceramics.

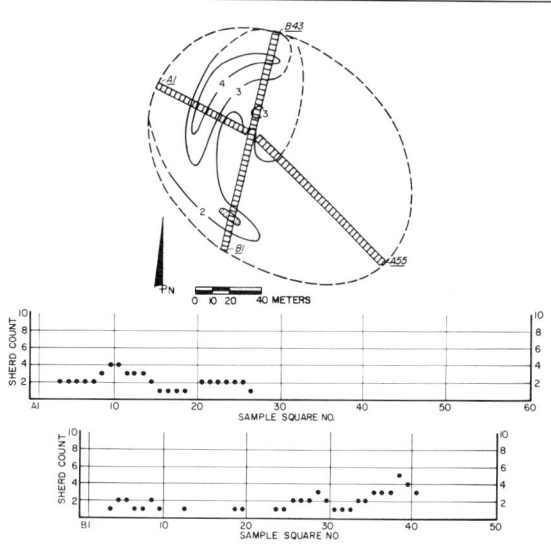

FIGURE 98. 054/6-Density contours of Late Chalcolithic ceramics.

(Fig. 97). A particularly dense concentration occurred in the middle of the northern half of Strip B. Estimating the total extent of the spread of this material from the one sherd contour line gives an area of approximately 80 × 100 m for the Early Chalcolithic occupation at this site.

Late Chalcolithic occupation is normally indicated by the presence and distribution of Cream Chaff Ware. Here, this ware was misclassified as Hittite Chaff Faced, Hittite White Slipped, and Iron Age wares, but this error was later evident with the discovery that all of the profiles of the rim sherds assigned to these three wares were definitely distinctive of Cream Chaff Ware. These three wares were accordingly combined and plotted as representative of Cream Chaff Ware and Late Chalcolithic occupation here. The picture they present is consistent and indicates a concentration of occupation over the west end of the site (Fig. 98). Counts per square were smoothed with a moving average taken over six squares, and contours of these average counts appear to represent the western end of an occupation area which can be estimated as 75 × 150 m in size.

Hittite occupation, on the other hand, seems clearly to be the most extensive on this mound and to cover the entire site (Fig. 99). Sherds of all Hittite wares present at the site, except White Slipped and Chaff Faced wares, were grouped together, and their counts smoothed with a moving average over four adjacent squares. Contours were drawn at 3, 6, and 9 sherds per square. The three sherd contour takes in virtually the entire mound, while the higher count contours on the Strip B appear to indicate the edges of an occupational level appearing at or close to the periphery of the visible mound. It seems safe to assume from this that Hittite occupation comprises the bulk of the site and is at least as extensive as the entire mound.

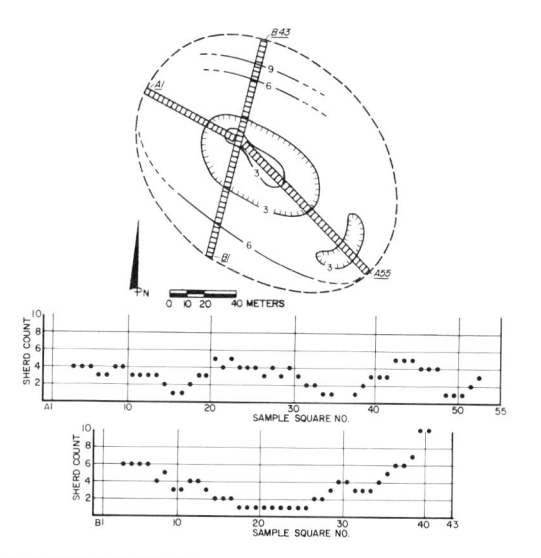

FIGURE 99. 054/6-Density contours of Hittite ceramics.

Medieval materials occur in much greater frequencies on the surface but are much more restricted in areal extent. All Medieval wares present were counted together, with a moving average taken over four collection squares being used to smooth the graphs of these counts. Contours made at the 24, 36, and 48 sherd levels of density show an occupation concentrated on the western half of the site (Fig. 100). The area of the concentration is approximately 100 × 120 m in size. Of course, the average density of Medieval materials is greater than 10 sherds per square over virtually the entire mound, and one could therefore assume that the entire site had been occupied in this period, but the density of materials clearly increases and is concentrated in the western half of the site. This is, thus, the area of primary or most intense occupation.

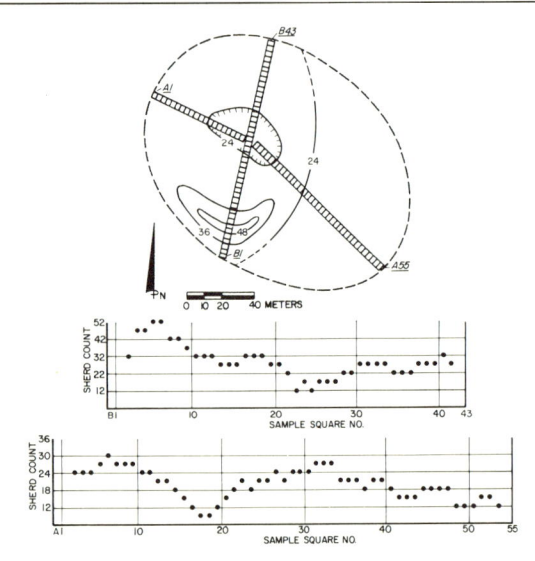

FIGURE 100. 054/6-Density contours of Medieval ceramics.

054/7

NAME: Könk
    Vilayet: Elâzığ
    Kaza: Merkez kazası
    Nahiye: Mollakendi
    Village: Könk

NATURE: Mound

DESCRIPTION (Fig. 101): This is a very large mound. It consists of a high peak at its north end

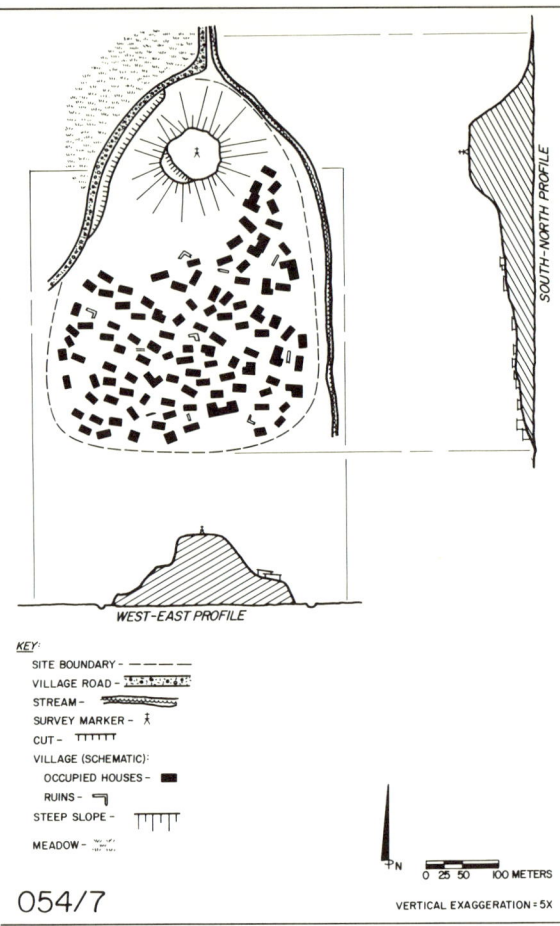

FIGURE 101. 054/7-Site plan and profiles.

and an apparently rather wide expanse of flat, broad, lower slopes fanning out to the south of the main mound peak. These lower slopes, forming the major area of the site, are covered by the contemporary village of Könk, with houses, gardens, small patches of mulberry trees, and other modern village and agricultural structures. The modern occupation and activities make it almost impossible to accurately observe the earlier mound and to make adequate collections from it. The high peak is essentially the only part of the mound which is currently free of occupation. It is relatively high and steep-sided and with a circular base and a flat, circular top. The western side of this peak has been deeply dug into, leaving a large cut. At several other places on the lower slopes long, low cuts are found. These are presumably all places from which earth was taken for the construction of modern village houses. Neither in the large cut, nor anywhere else on the peak or the rest of the mound, were any traces of construction or stratification noticed, however.

A contemporary triangulation point is located on the summit of the mound.

A spring on the south or southeast edge of the village feeds a small stream which flows around the east edge of the mound up to the northern peak, where it turns north and flows away.

DIMENSIONS:
- Length: 500 m very roughly estimated as the total length of the site, from the northern edge of the high mound peak to the southern fringe of the modern village. The mound proper may be only some 350 m in length, extending only partially under the village area. The diameter of the northern, flat-topped peak is estimated as ca. 100 m at the base and 10 m for the flat top
- Width: 250–350 m very roughly estimated. The lower figure is the maximum width of the mound around the high peak. The total width of the lower mound under the present-day village may be much broader, however
- Height: ca. 1–3 m for the lower slopes, ca. 16–18 m for the northern peak

COLLECTIONS: Preliminary

OCCUPATIONS:
Present—Early Chalcolithic
Early Bronze Age I-II
Early Bronze Age IIIB
Middle Bronze Age
Hittite
Iron Age
Medieval

The general surface collection was relatively small for such a large site. This was due largely to the extensive modern occupation covering most of the mound. There were few areas or exposures where earlier material was eroding out of the mound and was collectable from the surface. The range of periods represented by the ceramics collected is wide, but one may suspect that this is at best an imperfect and incomplete representation of the successive occupations at this site. In particular, no assessment of the relative importance or areal extent of the occupation of any period is possible.

The Early Chalcolithic period is represented by the distinctive Graphite Slipped pottery, including three typical rims (e.g. Fig. 9:a, f).

Early Bronze Age I-II occupation is indicated by the presence of Early Bronze Age Burnished, Polished, Plain, and Relief Decorated wares. One rim of typical Early Bronze Age Burnished Ware was found with the characteristic "impressed neck" or "rail-rim" profile. This and the Relief Decorated Ware indicate the definite existence of an occupation from the early phases of the Early Bronze Age.

Typical Early Bronze Age Black Painted pottery (e.g. Fig. 18:q) shows the existence also of an occupation from the Early Bronze Age IIIB period.

Old Hittite Gray Ware may relate to a Middle Bronze Age occupation of the mound.

Hittite occupation, however, is clear and attested by the presence of several diagnostic wares including Hittite Plain (e.g. Fig. 25:qq), Buff-Orange Burnished (e.g. Fig. 28:x), Orange Smoothed, Red-Brown Burnished, White Slipped, and Chaff Faced wares. (There are no rims from these latter two wares in the collection. It is therefore impossible to be sure that no sherds of Late Chalcolitic Cream Chaff Ware were misclassified as these Hittite wares as was frequently the case.)

There is a trace of Iron Age pottery in the collection. One rim was found which was of Early Iron Age type, with multiple, parallel horizontal grooves on the vessel neck.

Medieval ceramics included Brick, Red Slipped (e.g. Fig. 48m), Cooking, Coarse, and Glazed wares. Occupation presumably has been more or less continuous here from this period on up to the present day.

054/8

NAME: Norşun Tepe
  Vilayet: Elâzığ
  Kaza: Merkez kazası
  Nahiye: İçme
  Village: —

NATURE: Mound

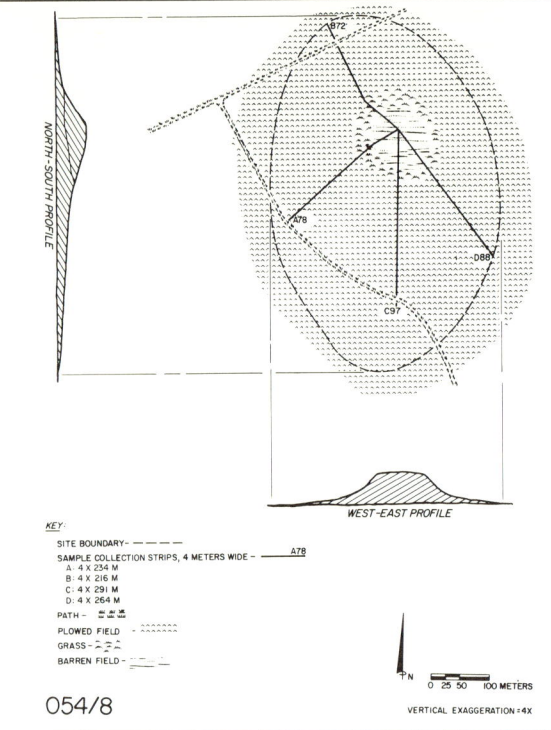

FIGURE 102. 054/8-Site plan and profiles.

DESCRIPTION (Fig. 102): Norşun Tepe is an extremely large mound, by far the largest in the survey area and very probably in the entire region around Elâzığ. It consists of a very high and steep-sided peak, surrounded on most sides by gentle lower slopes. The top of the high mound is moderately broad and more or less flat. From this top the sides of the mound descend steeply to the east, north, and west, less steeply to the south. On the east and northeast the steep slopes of the high mound descend directly from the top to the valley floor with no break to gentler lower slopes. The sides of the mound are too steep for standing or climbing here. On the north and southeast the sides of the high peak gradually become less steep and are climbable. This trend continues on the west side of the mound, but it is only on the south that the sides of the high peak become significantly gentler in slope. The mound therefore extends from the peak further to the south than in any other direction. Viewed from the east or west it is thus asymmetrically elongated to the south, while from the north or south it is approximately symmetrical in outline.

The steep slopes descending from the mound top run down to meet relatively gentle lower slopes on all sides except the east and northeast. This break in slope is quite marked and noticeable in most places. It is least striking on the south, where slopes are the gentlest, but even here the junction and topographic distinction of the two slopes is evident, especially when viewed from the side at some distance. The lower slopes descend most steeply on the north, somewhat less on the west and southeast, and most gently on the south, paralleling the differences in steepness of the upper mound slopes. The lower slopes thus extend furthest from the high mound peak on the south, here stretching away at an ever lessening angle to gradually merge with the valley floor. On the southeast, the outer edge of the lower slopes rapidly swings back in towards the high mound to join its slopes at the eastern base of the mound. On the west the lower slopes extend a considerable distance from the high mound, but still less than on the south, and they continue to draw rapidly back in, closer to the base of the high mound, as one rounds the north side of the site and finds the lower slopes vanishing against the steeply descending slopes of the high mound on its northeast side.

In general, then, Norşun Tepe appears as a massive, high mound, elongated towards the south, which is surrounded on most sides by an "apron" of lower slopes. These lower slopes extend the site most significantly to the south and to a lesser extent to the west. This large site dominates the central area of the Altınova.

The mound is uninhabited and undamaged by contemporary activities. The lower slopes are cultivated, but the steep upper slopes are left wild.

A small spring is located near the foot of the mound a short distance to the north.

DIMENSIONS:
   Length: ca. 500–600 m north-south
   Width: ca. 400 m east-west
   Height: ca. 25 m

COLLECTIONS: Preliminary and gridded strip.

OCCUPATIONS:
   Major—Early Bronze Age I-II
            Middle Bronze Age
            Hittite
            Iron Age (Early ?)
            Medieval

Minor—Early Chalcolithic
　　　Late Chalcolithic
　　　Early Bronze Age III
　　　Iron Age (Late ?)
Trace— Chalcolithic–Early Bronze Age
　　　　Transitional (?)
　　　Roman

Sherds of almost every ceramic ware recognized by us were found on this exceedingly large site. Its occupational history is obviously long and complex. Nevertheless, there are some clear differences in relative abundance of the wares of different periods.

One of the most abundant categories of material is that of the Early Bronze Age I-II ceramics. This includes Early Bronze Age Burnished, Plain, Thick, Polished, Red Slipped, Fine Grooved, and Relief Decorated wares (e.g. Early Bronze Age Burnished—Fig. 12:a–c,e–j,l–u,w–z,cc–ll, nn,pp,ss; Fig. 13:e,g,i–l,n–r,t,v–y,aa,cc–ee,gg–ii,kk,mm,nn,pp,qq,ss,uu,vv; Fig. 14:a,b,d,f,k,o–u,w,y–bb,dd,ee,gg,kk; Plain—Fig. 16:w–y,bb; Thick—Fig. 16:dd,ee; Fig. 17:b,f; Polished—Fig. 16:b,c,e,f,h,j; Red Slipped—Fig. 16:m; Fine Grooved—Fig. 9:aa). The Burnished and the Plain wares are the most common, numbering several thousand sherds from the controlled collection. Often there were several hundred Early Bronze Age Burnished and Plain sherds in a single collection square. Obviously this quantity of material argues for a substantial settlement of this period on the mound. The Plain Ware may well be associated with an Early Bronze Age III occupation, at least partially. Burnished pottery dominates, however, and among the distinctive rim profiles, those early forms with "impressed" necks or "rail-rims" (as on Fig. 12:a–g) outnumber later profiles by over four to one. In addition, a number of Relief Decorated sherds and decorated lids were found here (e.g. Fig. 15:b, c and Fig. 15:d–g, respectively), confirming the assessment of the other ceramics as indicative of an important Early Bronze Age I-II occupation at this site.

The Middle Bronze Age is amply represented by sherds of Middle Bronze Age Gritty (e.g. Fig. 20:e,i,m,o,t,w,aa), Middle Bronze Age Gray (e.g. Fig. 22:b,i,k,l,q–u), Old Hittite Gray (e.g. Fig. 21:a,b,d,f,g,i–l,o,p,s–v,x,ff–hh), Old Hittite Light Faced Gray (e.g. Fig. 22:z,aa), and Old Hittite Black Faced Gray wares. They are nowhere nearly as abundant as Early Bronze Age ceramics, but they number in the hundreds from the controlled surface collection and are diagnostic of a significant occupation from this period.

Hittite ceramics are plentiful. All wares except Hittite Red are found on the surface of the mound, and a series of rimsherds of Hittite Chaff Faced and White Slipped wares show that here they are for the most part indeed correctly identified as Hittite pottery. The number of typical Cream Chaff rim profiles found mixed in with these wares was relatively quite small at this site. The total number of Hittite sherds is in the low thousands, with the most common wares, Hittite Plain and Hittite Buff-Orange Burnished, numbering well over 1000 and close to 2000 sherds respectively (e.g.: Hittite Plain—Fig. 23:a, c–e,g,i,k–n,p–s,v,aa,bb,dd–ff,hh,jj–ll,oo–rr,uu, ww–eee; Fig. 24:a,c–f,h,j–n,p–t,w,x,aa,cc–ee, gg,hh,ll,nn,pp; Fig. 25:a,b,d,f,h,j–l,q,r,t,x,y,aa–ee,gg,jj,oo,pp,rr,uu; Fig. 26:g,j–n,p,s; Fine—Fig. 26:w,x,ee,gg,hh,kk,mm–oo; Thick—Fig. 27: d,e,k,n,p,q,w,y; Fig. 28:d; Exterior Wheel-Marked—Fig. 28:h; Buff-Orange Burnished—Fig. 28:i-k,n–r,t,bb,dd,gg,ii,ll,oo–qq,ss,tt; Fig. 29:c–e,g–j,l,p,q,u,w,x,bb–gg,jj,ll–nn,pp–vv,xx; Fig. 30:a–f,h,j,k,n,o; Chaff Faced—Fig. 30:r–t,v–y,bb,cc; Orange Smoothed—Fig. 31:d–f,k–m; Red-Brown Burnished—Fig. 31:o–q,s,u–w,y, z,bb,dd,ee,gg–qq; Brown Burnished—Fig. 32: b,c,f,h,j,o,q–s,aa,cc,ff,gg,kk,mm,nn,pp–rr,tt, vv–zz,ddd; White Slipped—Fig. 33:b,d, i,j,l,n–p,t,z,cc,dd,gg,ll,nn; Painted—Fig. 34:b,d,e,i,k; Fig. 35:d,e; Brown Gritty Cooking—Fig. 35:i,k–n). The large numbers and wide distribution of Hittite sherds on the site leave no doubt that an important component of this mound must date from Hittite times. Two hundred sherds of Hittite Fine wares may indicate functions at this site of more than simple farming and subsistence activities. Administrative and/or religious activities may well have been important here.

Several hundred Iron Age sherds were recovered in the controlled sample, including many characteristic rimsherds. The great majority of those rimsherds which could be identified as to sub-period were representative of the Early Iron Age. These were the typical rims with multiple exterior grooves (Fig. 36:u–aa,cc–hh). In contrast, only seven typically later (Fig. 36:a–f) rims were found. It seems therefore reasonable to postulate a relatively important occupation of the site in the Early Iron Age, to which the Iron Age

Painted sherds apparently also belong (cf. Fig. 38:o–q), dwindling in importance in the Middle Iron Age. Other rims were not immediately diagnostic of subdivisions of the Iron Age (cf. Fig. 36:g–i,k–m,o–r,t,ii–ll,nn–rr,uu; Fig. 37:c–e,g–q,s–x,z,bb,ee–kk,nn,qq–uu,xx,yy; Fig. 38:b,d,g,h,j,m,n). One sherd may be Phrygian or related to Phrygian ceramics (Fig. 55:g).

The greatest mass of material from the site was classified as Medieval. This amounts to almost 20,000 sherds, mostly of Medieval Brick, Thick, Cooking, White Slipped, and Red Slipped wares. Coarse ware was also present, but only insignificant quantities of Medieval Painted, Modeled, Glazed, and Sgraffiato wares were recovered. (Examples: Medieval Brick—Fig. 40:a,b,d–f,j,l–n,s,t,v–x; Fig. 41:b–e,h,i,l,n,s,x–aa,ff,hh,ll,nn–pp; Fig. 42:d–f,i–l,n,p,s,u–aa,dd–kk,mm,pp–rr,uu,ww–xx, Fig. 43:a,b,e,f,h–k,o,q–v,y,z; Fig. 44:a,b,f,h,l,n; Thick—Fig. 45:e,h,k,l; Fig. 46:b,e,f; Coarse—Fig. 47:e,f; Glazed—Fig. 47:v; Sgraffiato—Fig. 47:dd; Red Slipped—Fig. 48:k,l,p,x–bb,dd–hh,kk; Fig. 49:h; White Slipped—Fig. 49:p,q,s,t,v,w,y–aa,cc,gg,hh; Fig. 50:b–i,k,l; Painted—Fig. 51:e,l; Cooking—Fig. 52:d,g,i,k,u,v,x,y,aa–cc,jj; Fig. 53:b; Modeled—Fig. 53:k–p,r; Fig. 54:a,g.) Two interpretations come to mind. Either a vast amount of plain pottery (Brick, Thick, White and Red Slipped) has been misclassified, or the occupation is very late, mostly post-dating the periods of major occurrence of Modeled, Glazed, and Sgraffiato wares. For the moment the latter interpretation is preferred. The fact that the name of the mound is Armenian is suggestive of this interpretation. Abandoned and virtually obliterated Armenian sites dot the area, and the "Medieval" occupation here may date largely from this late period. Unfortunately, no pipe fragments or other items were found which would help to substantiate this interpretation. The small handful of Modeled, Glazed, and Sgraffiato sherds may hint at small, earlier Medieval occupation or may simply be random finds.

Early Chalcolithic occupation is definitely represented on the site, although the quantity of material is small. It is indicated by Chalcolithic Ware (e.g. Fig. 6:j,t), but especially also by the presence of Graphite Slipped Ware in equal or greater quantities (e.g. Fig. 9:b).

Late Chalcolithic occupation is represented by Cream Chaff Ware (e.g. Fig. 10:t; Fig. 11:s,x,cc,dd). Some sherds of this ware were found in the controlled surface collection. About half again as many were later identified from their rim profiles as having been incorrectly identified as Hittite Chaff Faced or White Slipped wares. This still totals only somewhat more than a dozen sherds, and it seems impossible to assume that most or all Hittite Chaff Faced and White Slipped body sherds are in fact misidentified Cream Chaff sherds. The number of Cream Chaff Ware rims found in the categories of Hittite Chaff Faced and White Slipped wares is very small compared to the profiles in these wares at this site which are characteristically Hittite. The evidence argues, therefore, for only a relatively minor Late Chalcolithic occupation here.

Early Bronze Age III ceramics are also definitely present. Early Bronze Age Black Painted sherds are moderately common. Over 150 were collected during the controlled surface sampling (e.g. Fig. 18:a–d,f–k,o,p,r; Fig. 19:f–i,k–m,o–r). These sherds outnumber Red Painted ceramics (e.g. Fig. 17:l,q,s; Fig. 19:a–d) by over five to one. It is tempting to say that the Early Bronze Age IIIB occupation is much more important here, but in actuality occupation is probably relatively continuous throughout the Early Bronze Age, and it is impossible to distinguish between a difference in importance of occupation from the early to the late part of the Early Bronze III period and simply a difference in the length of time each phase lasted. As mentioned above, Early Bronze Age Plain ware is quite abundant and may at least partially pertain to this period. Also, excurvate jar rims of Burnished Ware with multiple grooves on the neck (Fig. 13:uu, vv) are not uncommon, and some typical V-profiled hole-mouth jars (Fig. 13:gg–ii) have also been found. These are both late forms referable to the Early Bronze Age III, the former associated with the Red Painted ware and the latter with the Black Painted ware. Therefore, although the period cannot be considered as one of really major occupation of the mound, it is clearly present.

The indications for a minor occupation in the Middle Iron Age have been discussed above. The rim sherds are diagnostic but relatively scarce.

There are two Plain Simple Ware sherds (e.g. Fig. 9:s), and five Reserved Slip Ware sherds from the controlled collection. Comparatively, this is insignificant. One can therefore only speak of a trace of these wares and correspondingly of the possible transitional period occupation which they may represent. Their scarcity, however, may simply indicate that they pertain to the Early Bronze Age I-II occupation as minority wares and do not represent a separate occupation at all.

Five sherds of Roman Red pottery were also recovered (e.g. Fig. 55:1). They were widely scattered over the western, southern, and southeastern areas of the site, and hardly seem to represent a significant occupation of this period. They are perhaps more reflective simply of a Roman presence in the area than of any settlement on this mound.

CONTROLLED COLLECTION: The systematic collection of surface materials was carried out on this site with four gridded strips descending in different directions from the top of the mound. The slopes on the north, northeast and east sides of the mound were too steep to stand on and collect material. It was felt that these slopes would be severely eroded in any case. The four strips were thus run down the other sides of the mound, spaced so as to cover the collectable area as evenly as possible. The collection squares along these strips were the usual size for strip grids, 3 m along the length of the strip by 4 m wide across the strip.

System:
Strip A:
First section: Direction: 240°, length 24 m (8 squares)
Second section: Direction 230°, length 210 m (70 squares)

Squares	
A1-A8:	flat top of mound, sparse vegetation
A9-A11:	slope of high mound, sparse vegetation
A12-A15:	slope of high mound, barren ground
A16-A25:	slope of high mound, grass
A26-A78:	lower slopes, hard, barren surface

All squares contained material and were collected.

Strip B:
First section: Direction 300°, length 72 m (24 squares)
Second section: Direction 333°, length 144 m (48 squares)

Squares	
B1-B5:	flat top of mound, sparse vegetation
B6-B13:	slope of high mound, sparse vegetation
B14-B24:	slope of high mound, grass
B25-B59:	lower slopes, hard, barren surface
B60:	dirt road
B61-B72:	lower slopes, hard, barren surface

All squares contained material and were collected.

Strip C: Direction 181°, length 291 m (97 squares)

Squares	
C1-C8:	flat top of mound, sparse vegetation
C9-C23:	slope of high mound, sparse vegetation
C24-C26:	slope of high mound, grass
C27-C93:	lower slopes, hard, barren surface
C94-C95:	dirt road
C96-C97:	lower slopes, hard, barren surface

All squares contained material and were collected (C79 and C80 were collected together).

Strip D: Direction 143°, length 264 m (88 squares)

Squares	
D1-D8:	flat top of mound, sparse vegetation
D9-D25:	slope of high mound, sparse vegetation
D26-D31:	slope of high mound, grass
D32-D37:	lower slopes, sparse vegetation
D38-D41:	lower slopes, sparse vegetation, partially plowed
D42-D63:	lower slopes, plowed field
D64-D88:	lower slopes, hard, barren surface

Squares D31 and D46 contained no material. All other squares were collected.

Strip B ran down the steepest slope of the four strips, and it was apparent that greater erosion on this slope had exposed much more archaeological material than on the slopes down which the other three strips ran. This has to some extent biased the picture of distribution of materials and occupation of various periods, but it proves in practice not hard to compensate for this bias in looking at the density contour maps and to arrive at a fairly clear reconstruction of the occupational history of the mound.

The four collection strips do not, however, provide a detailed enough coverage of such a large and complex site to permit a meaningful study of the patterns of distribution of materials for every period represented. The periods of truly major occupation are represented by large vol-

204 *Archaeological Survey of the Keban Reservoir*

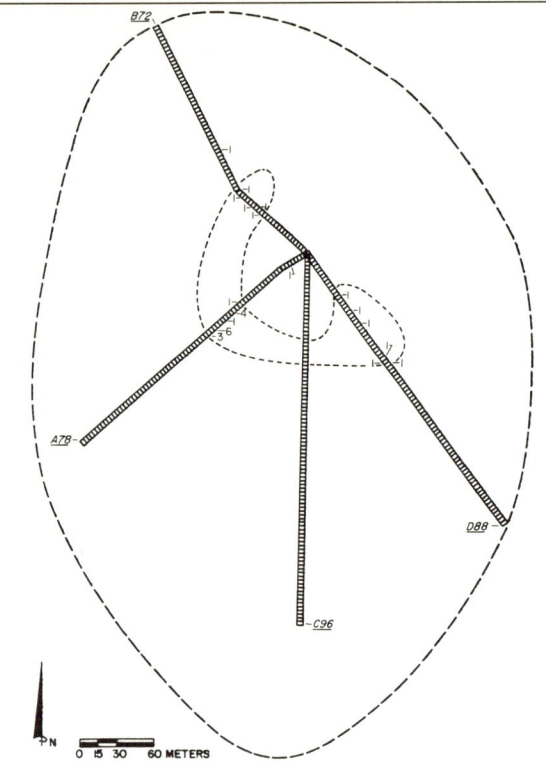

FIGURE 103. 054/8-Counts of Early Chalcolithic sherds.

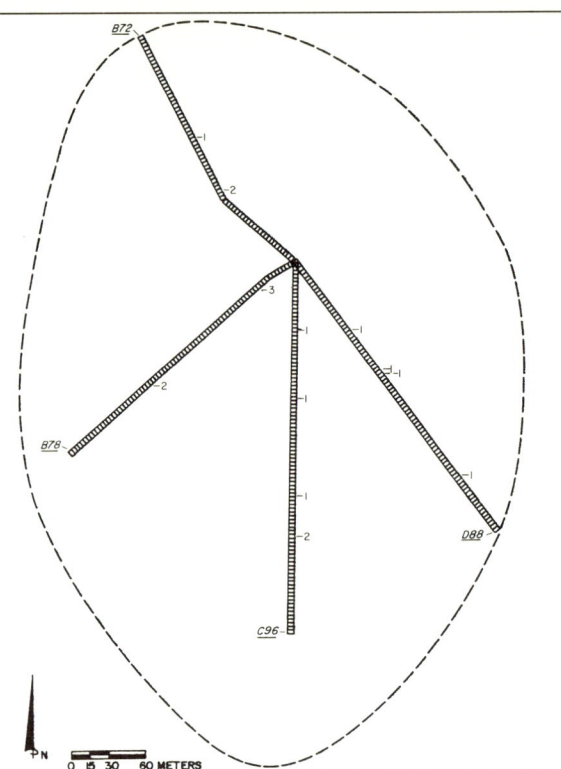

FIGURE 104. 054/8-Counts of Late Chalcolithic sherds.

umes of material on the mound surface which can easily be plotted and contoured from the data from the strip collections. These periods are the Early Bronze Age I-II, Hittite, Iron Age (as a whole, but predominantly early), and Medieval. To some extent the same can be done for the Early Bronze Age III and Middle Bronze Age materials, but here the materials are much less abundant and the results are not always as clear-cut. A few other materials can also be plotted and some conclusions drawn from their distributions even though it may not be possible to construct accurate density contours to represent their patterns of distribution.

A good example of this last type of material is the ceramics pertaining to the Early Chalcolithic period—Chalcolithic and Graphite Slipped wares. Sherds of these two wares are not abundant enough to form meaningful patterns when plotted as moving averages along the four strips. When the individual counts per grid square are plotted on a site map, however, it becomes quite evident that there is a strong tendency for these ceramics to be found within a restricted length along each of the strips (Fig. 103). If these relatively short lengths of the strips are roughly connected they define a band within which the great majority of Early Chalcolithic sherds are found. This band appears to run around the high part of the mound near the point where it meets the apron of lower slopes surrounding it. If such a distribution indicates the existence of an early Chalcolithic level in the high mound near its base, where it joins the lower slopes, it would give an area of occupation for this period roughly 165 × 195 m in size. Further, it would indicate that the high mound represents the focus of earlier occupations and that the lower slopes are the result of the accumulation of occupation debris of later periods.

Materials of the Early Bronze Age I-II were exceedingly abundant on the surface of the site. To represent their distribution, sherds of Early Bronze Age Polished, Relief Decorated, Red Slipped, Burnished, Plain, and Thick wares were combined and plotted as a group, using a moving average over three squares along the strips. The distributional picture which emerges (Fig. 105) shows a tremendous concentration of these wares on the north to northwest side of the high mound

(Strip B), spreading out onto the lower slopes in this area. A fair concentration occurs also on the west side of the high mound and out onto the adjacent lower slopes. A small area of concentration is also found on the southeast, but on the south slopes there is no appreciable quantity of material from this period. In the main areas of occurrence of Early Bronze Age I-II ceramics, that is on the north and west sides of the high mound, the concentrations ride well up onto the high mound, at least half-way and perhaps further up its steep slopes. Such a distribution would seem to argue strongly that the majority of the body of the high mound, as well as a significant part of the lower slopes at its base, is composed of occupation debris of this period. A certain amount of concentration of materials at the base of the high mound would be expected from erosion, and this is apparently what we see in the tremendous numbers of sherds concentrated on the north side of the mound. A relatively clear definition of a large area of probable Early Bronze Age I-II occupation, some 225 m long by an estimated 180 m wide, is possible from the distribution map, however. The great variety of ceramics from this period, their abundance, and the evidently great depth of Early Bronze Age I-II deposits in the high mound all indicate the substantial and important nature of this occupation.

If the Early Chalcolithic and Early Bronze Age I-II occupations are localized in the high mound, it would seem reasonable that the Late Chalcolithic occupation identified here would be stratigraphically between them. In this case, materials from this period should be found concentrated on the lower slopes of the high mound. Unfortunately, Late Chalcolithic occupation was identified from a small series of characteristic rim sherds. Body sherds were probably confused with the more numerous Hittite Chaff Faced sherds, but a large series of Hittite rim sherds shows clearly that this is not a consistent misidentification as it was occasionally at other sites. Hittite Chaff Faced pottery is indeed present and has obscured the Late Chalcolithic ceramics here. Of the six Cream Chaff rims from the controlled collection, three were found on the lower slopes of the high mound, lending some slight support to the idea that a relatively brief occupation characterized by this ware lies near the base of the high mound. Thus, it would measure approximately 150 m in diameter. The few identified Cream Chaff body sherds are widely scattered over the whole site, however (Fig. 104).

Early Bronze Age III ceramics are not abundant, but they are clearly localized on the site, well up on the slopes of the high mound, in this case consistently concentrating at half-way or more up the sides of this part of the site (Fig. 106). This consistent and clear distribution indicates a small occupation of only roughly 100 m diameter. It was probably also a short occupation, judging by the relative scarcity of materials from the period.

The distribution of Middle Bronze Age materials is more complicated. To represent this period, sherds of the Middle Bronze Age Gritty, Middle Bronze Age Gray, Old Hittite Gray, Light Faced Gray, and Black Faced Gray wares were combined. Plotted as a short moving average over three squares, counts for this group are low, but a moderately clear and convincing picture of occupation areas on both the high mound and the lower slopes appears (Fig. 107). The occupation area indicated on the high mound is, as might be expected, relatively high up on the slopes and seems to represent only a small area of ca. 90 m diameter. The major area of occupation lies on the lower mound slopes, principally on the north and west, extending slightly around to the south. The area covered is approximately 60 m by 360–400 m although this may represent only an exposed portion of an area originally somewhat larger, particularly on the south where late occupations tend to be located, perhaps on top of this one.

With Hittite ceramics there are adequate counts to allow a fairly clear and definite picture to be drawn of distribution over the mound (Fig. 108). All wares except Hittite Red were present on the site and were grouped together for the purpose of studying the distribution of the Hittite occupation. The counts were smoothed with a moving average taken over six squares. The materials are concentrated largely on the lower mound slopes, primarily on the northwest, but seeming to form a band which may run entirely around the high mound. As plotted from the ceramic distributions, this band varies from 60–100 m in width and has outside dimensions of roughly 300 × 400 m. The main focus of concentration of Hittite ceramics is a much smaller area of ca. 100 × 300 m on the northwest lower slopes. There is, in addition, some indication of a small amount of occupation near the top

206 *Archaeological Survey of the Keban Reservoir*

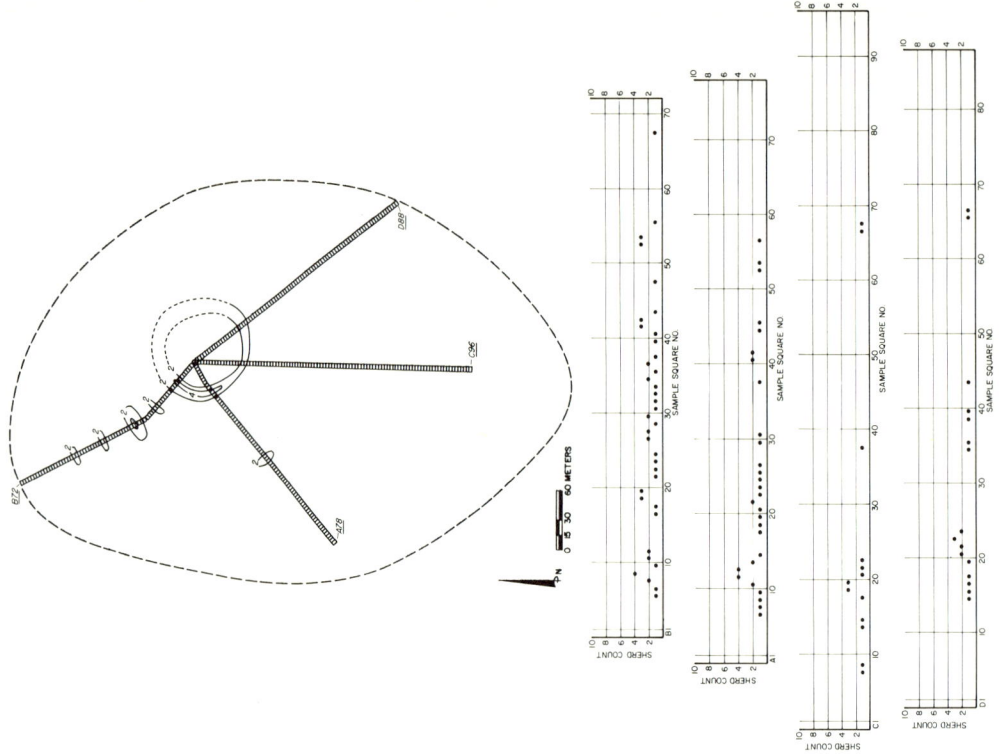

FIGURE 106. 054/8-Density contours of Early Bronze Age III ceramics.

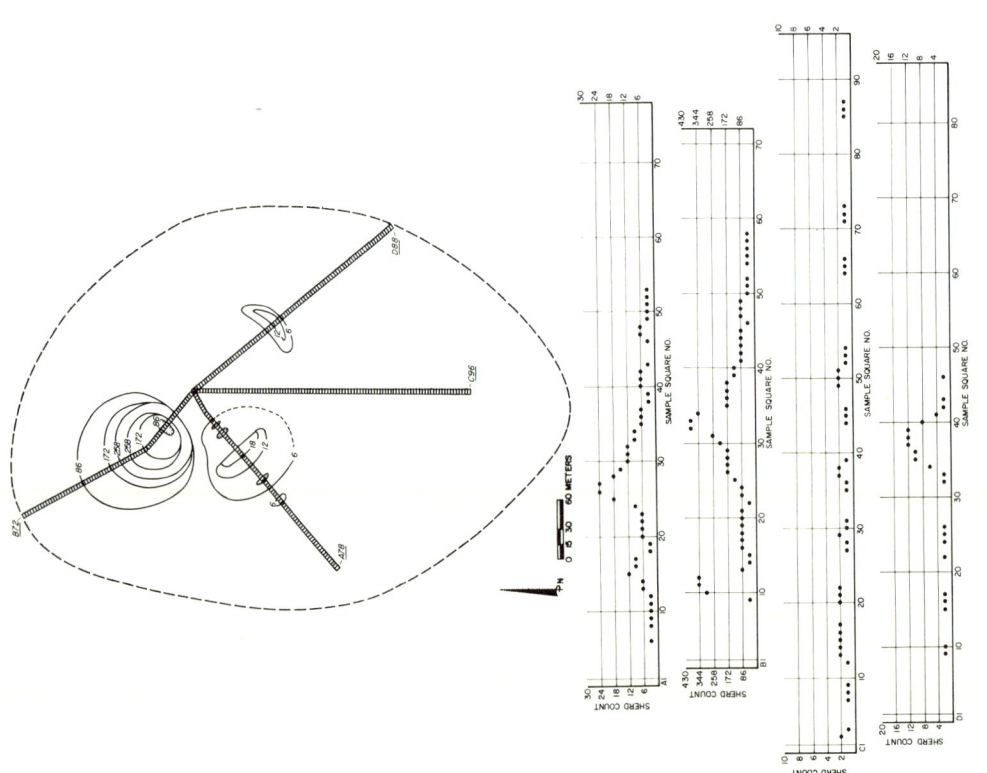

FIGURE 105. 054/8-Density contours of Early Bronze Age I-II ceramics.

The Sites 207

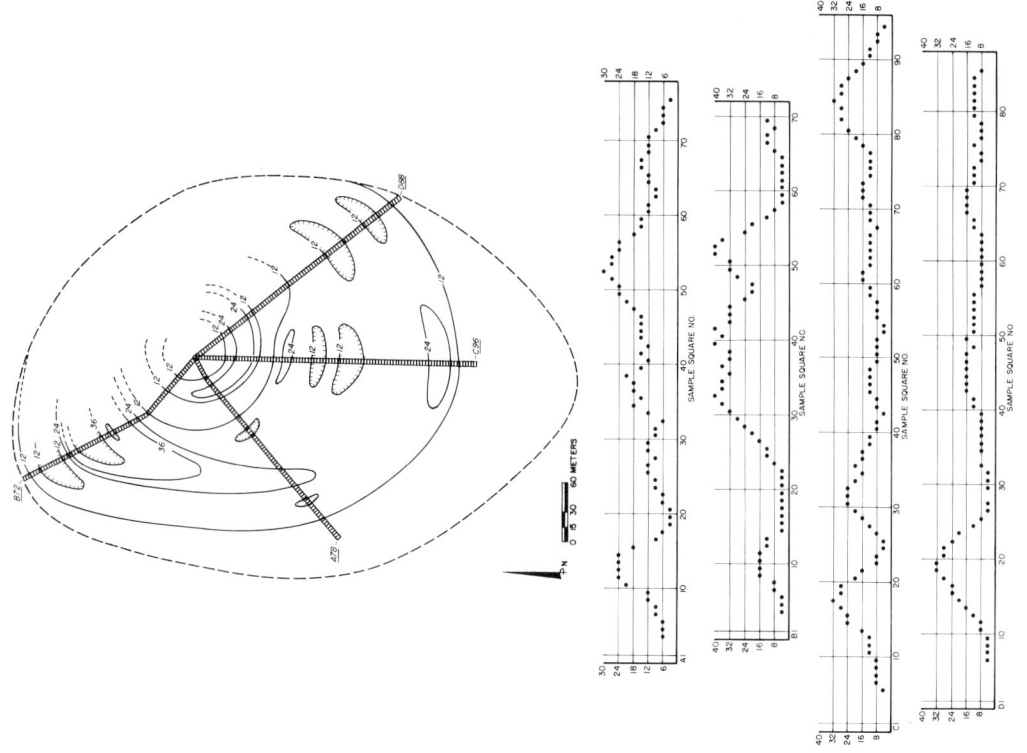

FIGURE 108. 054/8-Density contours of Hittite ceramics.

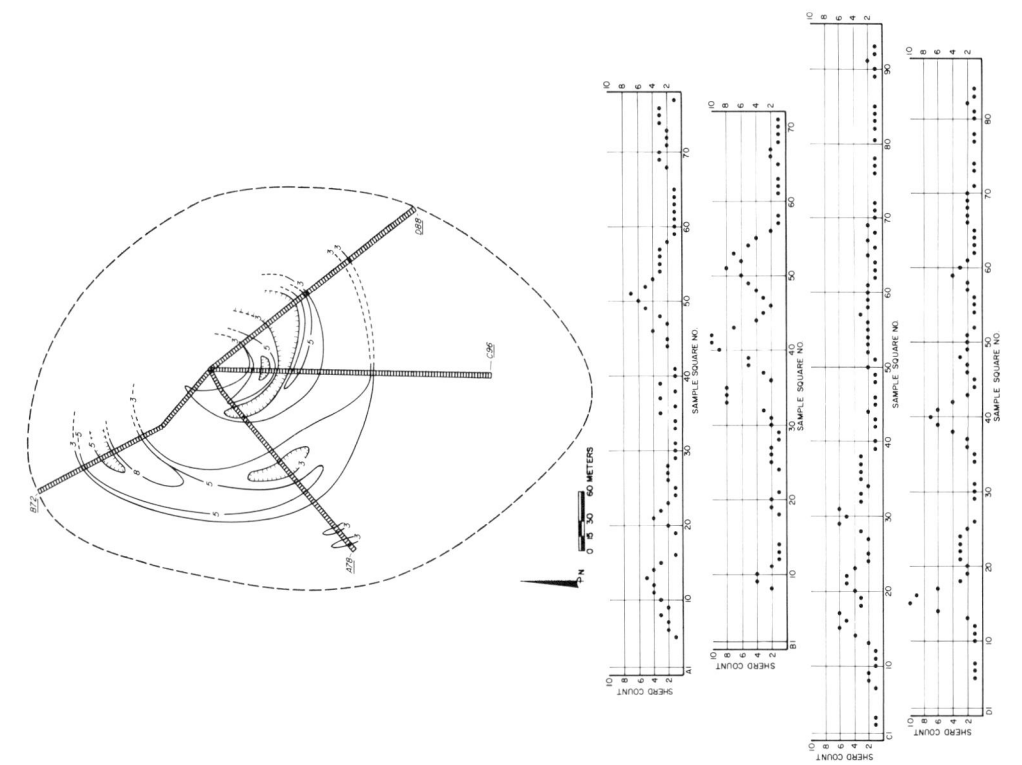

FIGURE 107. 054/8-Density contours of Middle Bronze Age ceramics.

208 *Archaeological Survey of the Keban Reservoir*

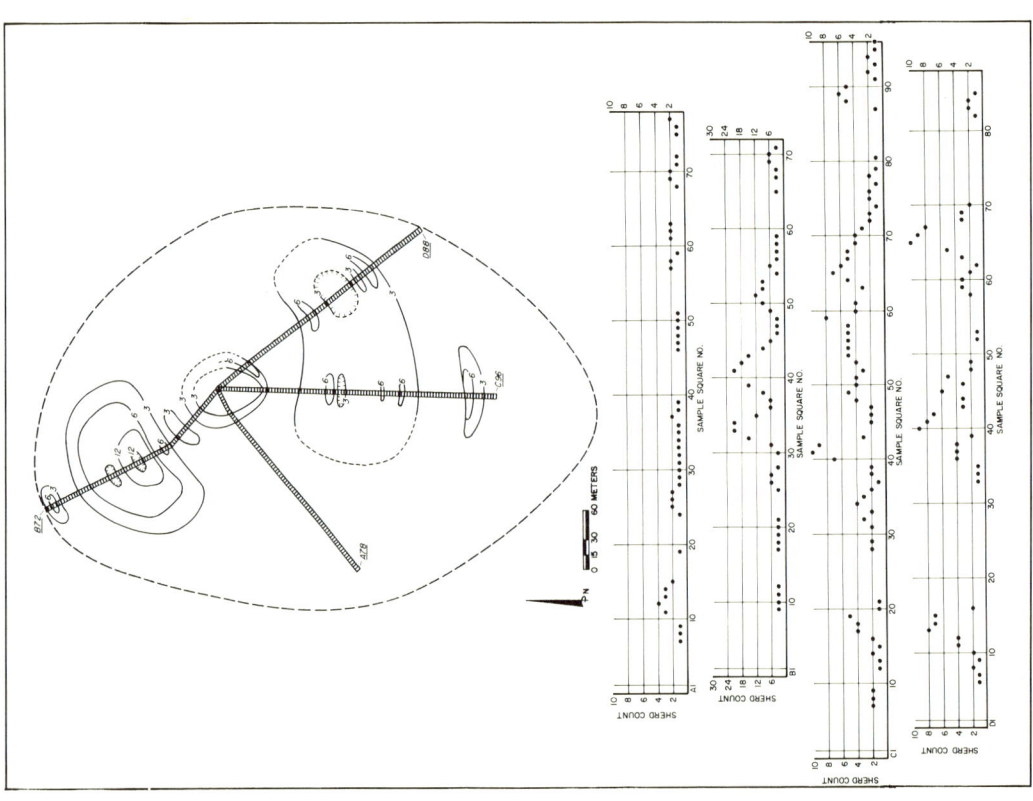

FIGURE 109. 054/8-Density contours of Iron Age ceramics.

of the high mound which would measure approximately 100 m in diameter. In all, the total area covered by Hittite occupation debris can be estimated as 8–8.5 ha.

Iron Age ceramics are not as abundant as Hittite, but they also are concentrated primarily on the lower mound slopes, with some indication of minor occupation near the top of the high mound (Fig. 109). Individual counts per square were smoothed with a moving average over three squares. There appear to be two major areas of concentration of Iron Age materials—on the northwest lower mound slopes and on the southern and southeastern lower mound slopes. Their sizes can only be measured approximately or estimated as 90 × 150+ m and 120 × 200+ m respectively. The area near the top of the high mound is tiny, measuring only about 75 m in diameter.

Certain of the Iron Age rims are assignable to either the Early Iron Age or the Middle Iron Age. A large number of such assignable rims belong to the Early Period. Only seven from the controlled collection are Middle Iron Age in date. The Early Iron Age rims (Fig. 110) are widely scattered over

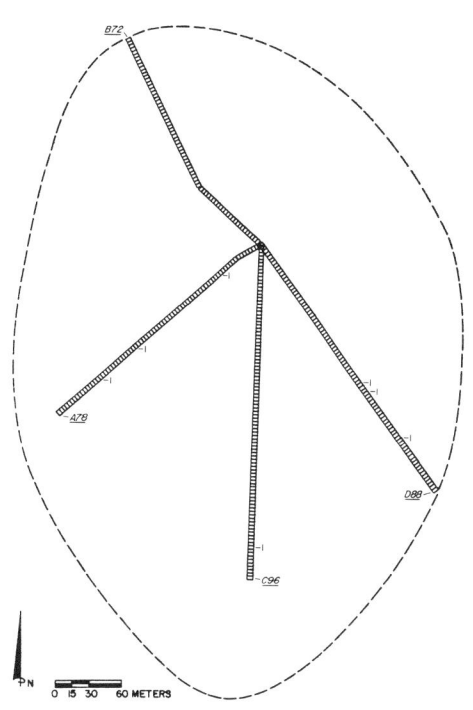

FIGURE 111. 054/8-Counts of Middle Iron Age rim sherds.

the mound, but do show some tendency to cluster, particularly along Strips B and C, less so along Strip A. The clusters along Strips B and C roughly parallel the distribution of Iron Age sherds in general, perhaps simply because most Iron Age material is from the Early period. A minor departure from this parallelism is the slight tendency for the rimsherds to concentrate more along Strip A than along Strip D. Unfortunately the seven Middle Iron Age rims are too few to demonstrate any clear tendencies or patterns of spatial distribution (Fig. 111). Of these seven, however, three lie on Strip D and three on Strip A. Weak as it is, this is perhaps a hint that within the area of Iron Age occupation as a whole, the weight of the Early occupation is on the south, west, and northwest portions of the lower slopes, while that of the later occupation lies more to the west, south, and southeast.

Medieval ceramics were the most abundant of any period on the site surface. All recognized wares were found and were grouped together to plot the distribution of occupation from this period. (Fig. 112) A moving average over four adjacent squares was used to smooth the individ-

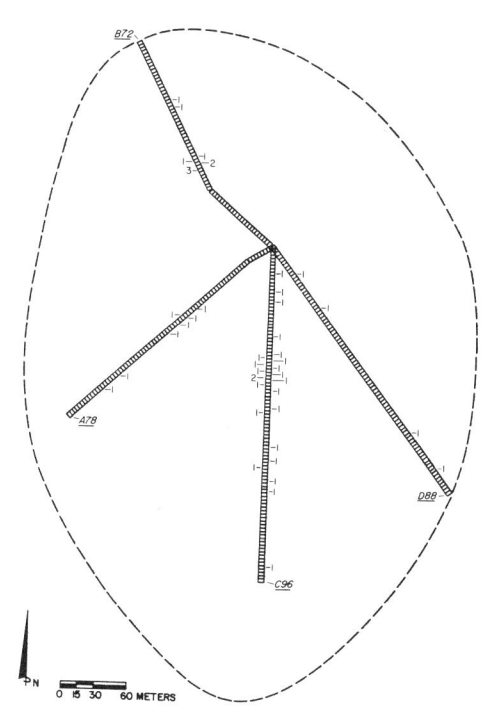

FIGURE 110. 054/8-Counts of Early Iron Age rim sherds.

210 *Archaeological Survey of the Keban Reservoir*

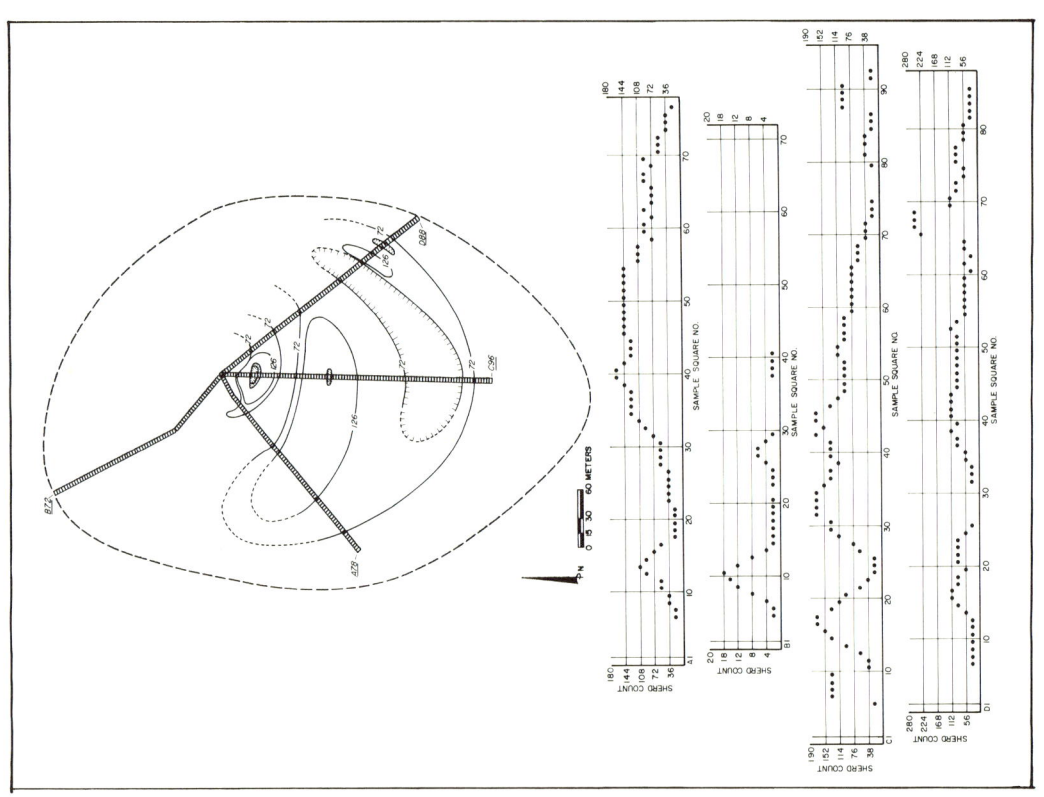

FIGURE 112. 054/8-Density contours of Medieval ceramics.

ual counts, and a quite clear picture of Medieval occupation area emerged from the plot. Medieval occupation is concentrated over the southern lower slopes of the mound, sweeping around to the western and southeastern lower slopes. This is a large area which may be estimated as being about 120–150 × 450 m in size. There is, in addition, a substantial area on the southern side of the high mound over which Medieval materials occur in substantial quantity. This area lies on the upper stretches of the sides of the high mound, which are here relatively gentle in slope. It appears as though this were an area of occupation covering the side of the high mound at this spot, rather than the ege of a more sizable occupation layer which is eroding. If so, this tiny supplementary area of Medieval occupation is only approximately 50 × 75 m in size. The major and important Medieval occupation area is spread out over the lower slopes below.

054/9

NAME: —
    Vilayet: Elâzığ
    Kaza: Merkez kazası
    Nahiye: İçme
    Village: —

NATURE: Mound

DESCRIPTION (Fig. 113): This is an extremely low, broad and flat mound of small size. It is barely visible as a mound but can be seen as a very gentle elevation which is somewhat egg-shaped in plan. It lies close to Norşun Tepe (054/8) on the field road leading to Norşun Tepe from the northwest. The site is under cultivation.

DIMENSIONS:
    Length: 100–110 m measured north-south
    Width: 70–75 m measured east-west at the broadest part of the visible mound
    Height: ca. .5 m

COLLECTIONS: Preliminary and gridded strip

OCCUPATIONS:
    Major—Hittite
              Medieval
    Minor—Middle Bronze Age
              Iron Age

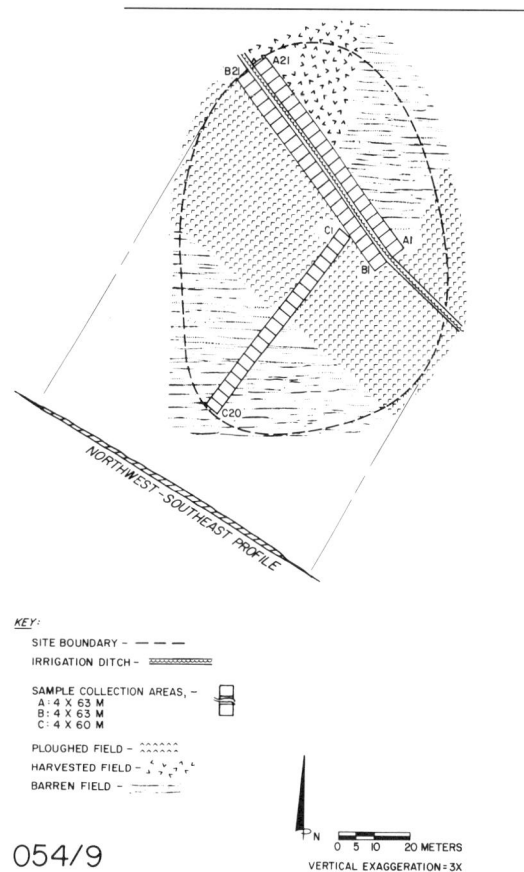

FIGURE 113. 054/9-Site plan and profile.

The most abundant pottery on this site is Hittite. All Hittite wares recognized by us were found on the surface except Hittite Exterior Wheel-Marked. Rim sherds of Hittite Plain (e.g. Fig. 23:j,w; Fig. 24:kk), Buff-Orange Burnished (e.g. Fig. 30:l,q), Red-Brown Burnished (e.g. Fig. 31:r,t,aa,ff,rr), Brown Burnished (e.g. Fig. 32:p,t,y,ss,ccc), White Slipped (e.g. Fig. 33:s, w,ee), Thick (e.g. Fig. 27:c; Fig. 28:b,aa, jj,rr), Fine, and Chaff Faced (e.g. Fig. 30:u,dd) wares were recovered.

Medieval pottery included all except Medieval Painted, Modeled, Glazed, and Sgraffiato. Rim sherds were rare, however, comprising only one of Medieval Brick (Fig. 41:ee), two of Thick (Fig. 45:o; Fig. 46:d), and one of Red Slipped ware (Fig. 48:ll). Medieval sherds were roughly half as common as Hittite sherds.

Only a small handful of sherds from this site were classified as Middle Bronze Age in date. These were for the most part Old Hittite Gray Ware sherds (e.g. Fig. 21:cc), with a few Old

Hittite Light Faced Gray fragments. All of the latter were body sherds. The Iron Age is represented by even fewer sherds, although in this case several rim sherds of both ordinary (e.g. Fig. 36:d,ss) and thick (e.g. Fig. 39:b,c,i) types were also present in the collection. One of these rims (Fig. 36:d) is a typical Middle Iron Age form. One sherd of possible Phrygian origin or related to Phrygian wares was also found (Fig. 55:f).

CONTROLLED COLLECTION: Three gridded strips were collected on this site. Two of the strips, A and B, were adjacent, running along either side of a shallow ditch separating several fields. Strip A, on the north side of this ditch, ran through barren or partially barren ("cut" or harvested) fields. Strip B, on the south of the ditch, ran through plowed fields. The distance between the two strips was only 2–3 m. These two parallel strips were collected in this way to allow a comparison and control of the results of surface collecting in essentially adjacent squares with totally different surface conditions. The difference between hard surfaced, barren fields and freshly plowed fields represented the two extremes of collecting conditions found in our survey. It was hoped that the collection of these two strips at this site might allow us to obtain an idea of the effect these differences might be having on the results of our collecting procedures.

The third strip, C, was laid out at roughly right angles to Strips A and B, forming a sort of L-shaped collection design. The squares collected along all three of these strips were 3 m in length along the strip and 4 m wide across the strip.

```
System:
    Strip A: Direction 320°, length 63 m (21 squares)
        Squares A1-A9:    barren field
                A10-A21:  harvested (cut) field
    Strip B: Direction 320°, length 63 m (21 squares)
        Square B1:        half harvested, half
                          plowed field
                B2-B21:   plowed field
    Strip C: Direction 220°, length 60 m (20 squares)
        Squares C1-C20:   plowed field
```

Only Hittite and Medieval sherds occurred in sufficient quantity to make a study of their distributional patterns possible. In neither case are these patterns very informative. Both show a tendency for counts to be low in the center of the site and to increase towards the site edges, particularly along Strip C. Most intriguing and disturbing is the total lack of any correspondence in the pattern of sherd counts between Strip A and Strip B. This lack of correspondence can clearly be seen in comparing the plots of the moving averages for Hittite and Medieval sherds along these strips (Figs. 114 and 115). In fact, in the case of Hittite ceramics Strips A and B seem to show exactly opposite trends, average count per square sharply decreasing to the northwest along Strip A and clearly increasing in the same direction along Strip B. Correlations of the counts and average counts per square along these strips illustrate this. Raw counts are correlated at $r = -.16$ for Hittite and $-.02$ for Medieval sherds while the moving averages show correlations of $-.70$ and $.07$ for Hittite and Medieval ceramics respectively.

However, contouring the average counts in the

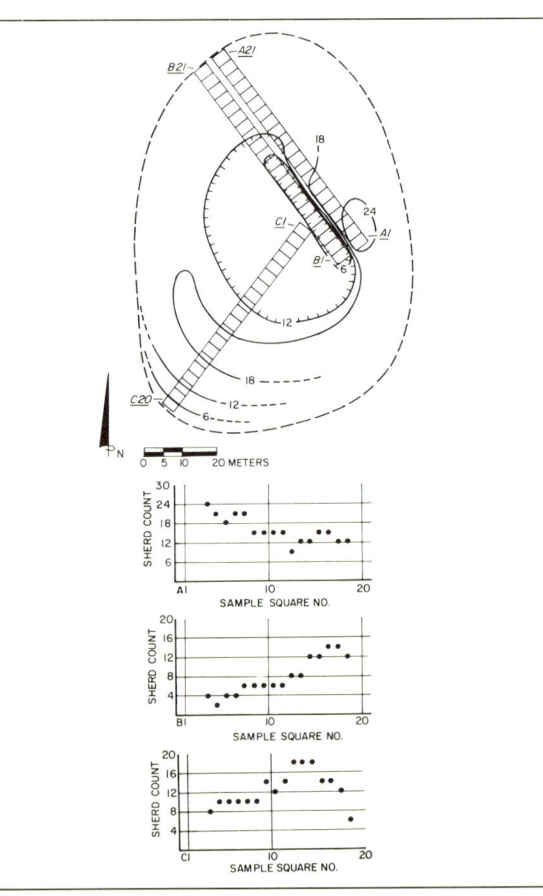

FIGURE 114. 054/9-Density contours of Hittite ceramics.

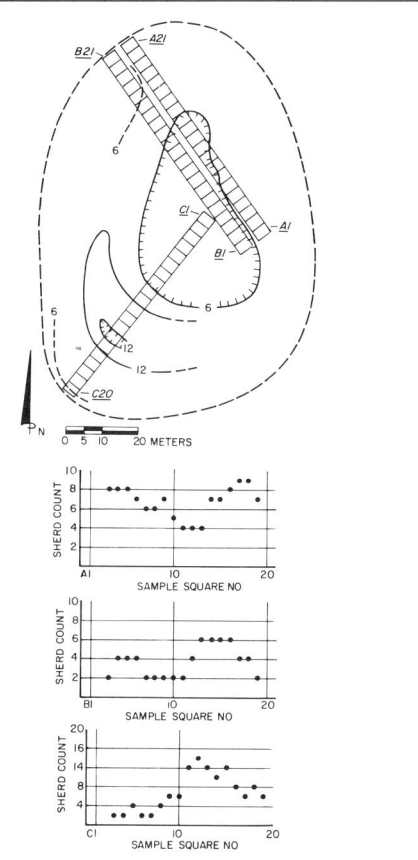

FIGURE 115. 054/9-Density contours of Medieval ceramics.

most reasonable and realistic way does give a rather clear picture of a scatter of Hittite materials (using a moving average over six squares) with the highest counts marking an area of roughly 50 × 75 m in size (Fig. 114). Inside and outside this area counts drop rapidly. Medieval sherds (with counts smoothed by using a moving average over five squares) exhibit a similar pattern, covering an area of approximately 50–60 × 60–70 m (Fig. 115). On most mounds such patterns might be interpreted as representing the edges of occupation levels eroding out of the sides of the mound. This site is so low and flat, however, that such an interpretation is impossible. It seems more likely that these patterns are formed in this case by the scattering of materials out from the center of the site through the action of plowing. In this case we should obviously take the lower of any size estimates as the best approximation of original site size.

054/10

NAME: Mezarlık Tepe
    Vilayet: Elâzığ
    Kaza: Merkez kazası
    Nahiye: Mollakendi
    Village: —

NATURE: Mound

DESCRIPTION (Fig. 116): This is a relatively small, moderately low mound, with a fairly regular circular plan. There are no distinct surface features related to early occupation, but there is a moderate amount of modern disturbance. The road from Yukarı Ağınsı to Alişam runs directly across the mound. Alongside the road runs a deep irrigation ditch. The southwest quarter of the mound has been extensively dug into, leaving a rather long cut in the body of the mound. A recent cemetery covers this area of the site. For the rest, the site is cultivated.

DIMENSIONS:
    Length: ca. 140 m measured in a northeast-southwest direction
    Width: ca. 140 m measured, northwest-southeast
    Height: ca. 2.5 m

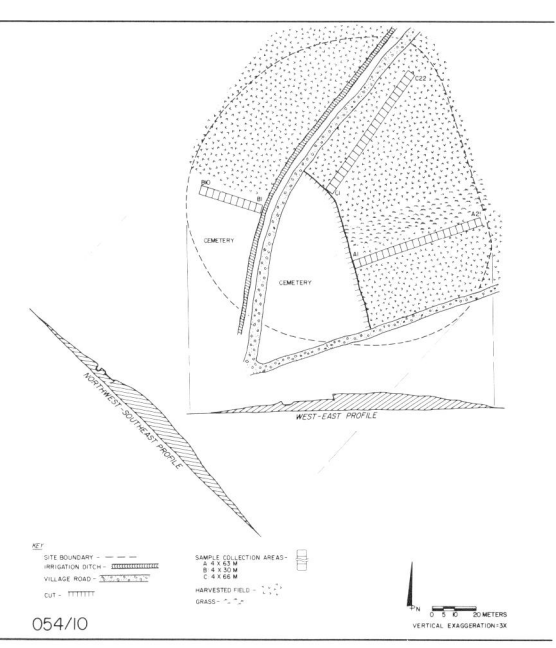

FIGURE 116. 054/10-Site plan and profiles.

COLLECTIONS: Preliminary and gridded strip

OCCUPATIONS:
    Major—Early Bronze Age I-II
            Medieval
    Minor—Middle Bronze Age
            Hittite
    Trace— Early Chalcolithic (?)
            Late Chalcolithic
            Early Bronze Age III (?)
            Iron Age (?)

The Early Bronze Age I-II is represented primarily by Early Bronze Age Burnished (e.g. Fig. 14:v) and Plain wares in more or less equal quantities. The relatively large proportion of Early Bronze Age Plain ceramics in this collection might argue for an occupation dating to the later part of the Early Bronze Age I-II period, or for a continuity of occupation throughout the whole of the Early Bronze Age. None of the distinctive Early Bronze Age Polished or Relief Decorated pottery was found, and Red Slipped and Thick sherds were relatively rare.

The proportion of Medieval material on this mound is enormous. Partially, this may relate to the presence of the rather large cemetery area on the site. It is obvious, nevertheless, that there was an extensive occupation here in Medieval times. Medieval Brick Ware is the most common ceramic on the site (e.g. Fig. 40:c,q; Fig. 42:oo; Fig. 43:ee). It occurs in almost overwhelming quantities relative to any other category of pottery. Medieval Thick, Coarse, Cooking (e.g. Fig. 52:gg), White Slipped, and Red Slipped (e.g. Fig. 48:f,n,r,cc; Fig. 49:l) pottery also occur in significant quantities. Modeled ware was not found, but a moderate number of Glazed and some Painted and Sgraffiato sherds were recovered.

The Middle Bronze Age is represented by Middle Bronze Age Gray (e.g. Fig. 22:j) and Old Hittite Gray wares (e.g. Fig. 21:e), with a few sherds of Middle Bronze Age Gritty (e.g. Fig. 20:n,v,cc) and Light Faced Gray wares.

Hittite occupation is indicated by the presence of a few sherds of every recognized Hittite ware except Hittite Red and Exterior Wheel-Marked.

Other periods of occupation are not so clearly attested. A few body sherds were classified as Chalcolithic Ware, but this could be a faulty identification given the quantity of Early Bronze Age Burnished pottery on the site. On the other hand, although no Cream Chaff body sherds were identified in the collection, three rims probably of this ware were found (e.g. Fig. 10:ee), and it is possible that a Late Chalcolithic level lies buried in this mound.

The Early Bronze Age III is indicated only by two sherds, one each of Red Painted and Black Painted ware. None of the rims of Early Bronze Age Burnished Ware characteristic of the Early Bronze Age III period were found. If, then, the two painted sherds are correctly identified, they must represent either accidental finds or indication of only a very small and/or very brief occupation.

A small handful of body sherds were classified as Iron Age in date. No rims were so identified. There may have been some small amount of Iron Age occupation of this site, but this is doubtful.

CONTROLLED COLLECTION: A systematic surface collection from this site was made in three gridded strips. These strips were placed so as to run out across the major surfaces of the mound undisturbed by roads, borrow pits, or the cemetery.

    System:
        Strip A: Direction 75°, length 63 m (21 squares)
            Squares A1-A21:   cut (harvested) field
        Strip B: Direction 300°, length 30 m (10 squares)
            Squares B1-B10:   cut field
        Strip C: Direction 35°, length 66 m (22 squares)
            Squares C1-C22:   cut field

The collection squares were 3 × 4 m in size, 3 m along the length of the strip, 4 m wide.

The Early Bronze Age I-II was represented by Early Bronze Age Burnished, Plain, Thick, and Red Slipped wares. Counts were smoothed along the strips by taking a moving average over five squares. The results of contouring these average counts (Fig. 117) reveal a broad, roughly circular area of Early Bronze Age I-II occupation, with a tendency toward lower counts in the center of the mound and over its southern quarter. This is the pattern one would expect from the exposure of the edge of an occupation level by erosion, with the center (and in this instance one other area) of the layer covered by deposits of later date. In this case, it can be seen clearly that it is the Medieval occupation debris which thickly covers both the center and the southern flank of the mound, obscuring materials from earlier occupations in these places (cf. Fig. 120). The size of the Early

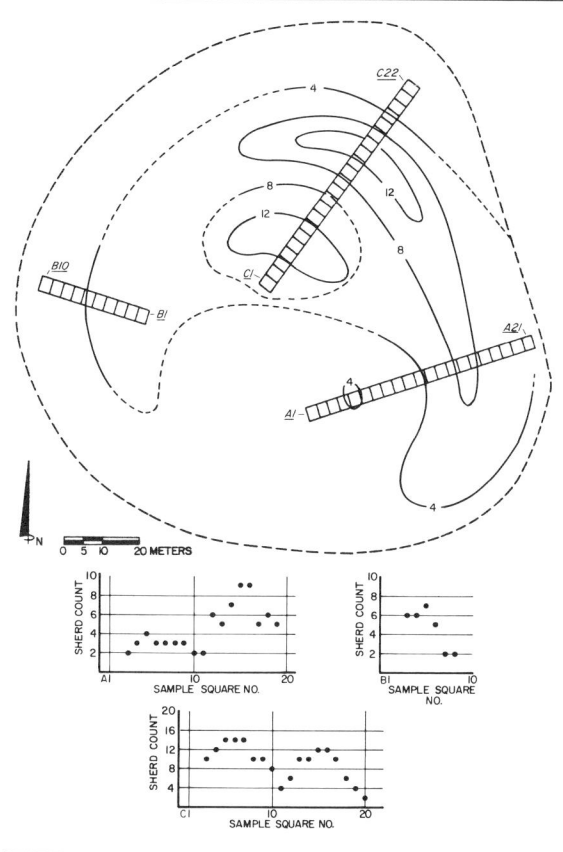

FIGURE 117. 054/10-Density contours of Early Bronze Age I-II ceramics.

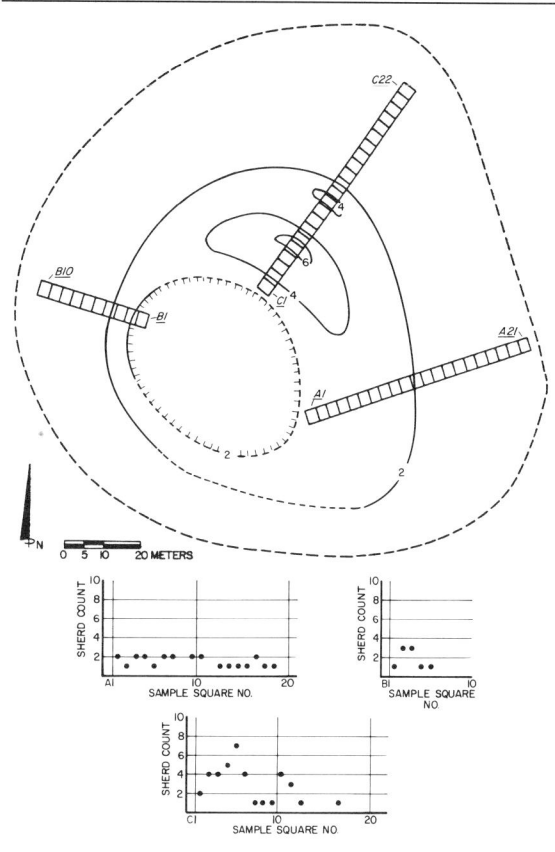

FIGURE 118. 054/10-Density contours of Middle Bronze Age ceramics.

Bronze Age I-II occupation as estimated from this contour plot would be roughly 120 m in diameter.

The Middle Bronze Age materials include here Middle Bronze Age Gritty, Middle Bronze Age Gray, Old Hittite Gray, and Old Hittite Light Faced Gray wares. Sherd counts of these wares were plotted as a moving average over two squares, and the results contoured. In spite of generally low counts over all, a fairly clear pattern of distribution was evident (Fig. 118). This shows an area of Middle Bronze Age occupation of approximately 80 × 90 m in size, with the same decline in average counts in the center and on the south side as found for the Early Bronze Age I-II materials.

Grouped together to represent Hittite occupation on this site were all the recognized Hittite ceramics present, which excluded only Hittite Red, and Exterior Wheel-Marked wares. Smoothing the generally low counts with a moving average over two squares, and contouring these counts, revealed a small, circular concentration of Hittite material only 85 m in approximate diameter, with the usual drop in counts in its center and on its southern side (Fig. 119).

Medieval materials include all Medieval wares except Medieval Modeled. Counts per square were high, much higher than for other periods, and they were smoothed by taking a moving average of counts over five squares. The contours of these averages clearly show a highly concentrated distribution of Medieval materials over the area where the three collection strips converge, the center of the areas of distribution of materials from other periods, and over the southern flank of the mound (Fig. 120). This concentration defines a relatively large occupation area approximately 100 × 150 m in size, and its location and density readily explain the low counts of materials from other periods over the same area.

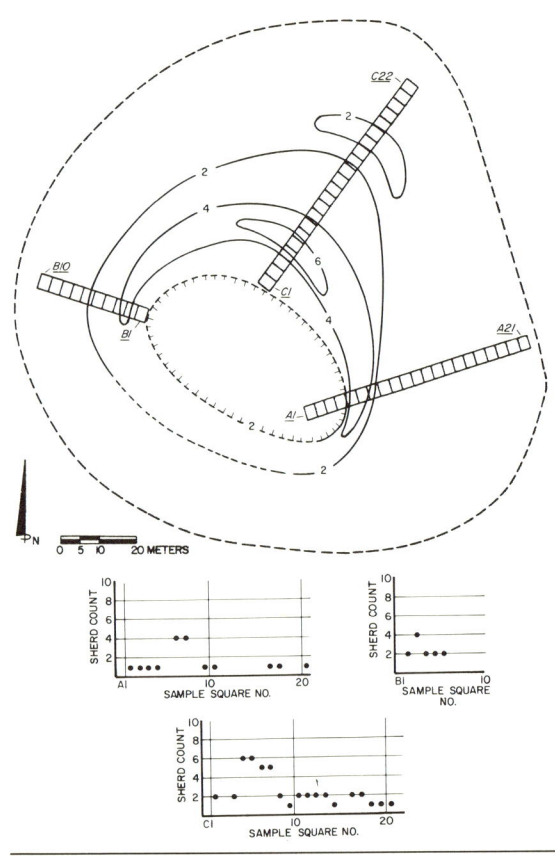

FIGURE 119. 054/10-Density contours of Hittite ceramics.

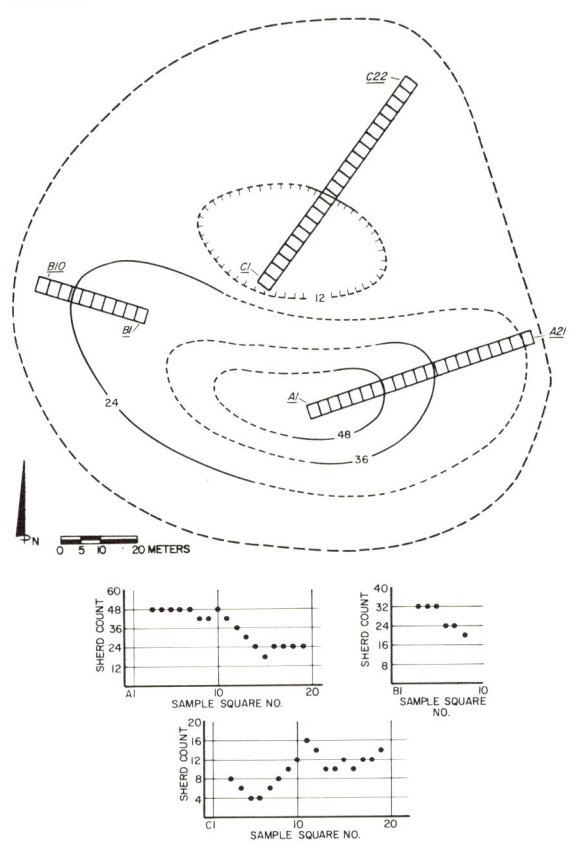

FIGURE 120. 054/10-Density contours of Medieval ceramics.

054/11

NAME: Yarık Tepe
  Vilayet: Elâzığ
  Kaza: Merkez kazası
  Nahiye: Mollakendi
  Village: —

NATURE: Mound

DESCRIPTION (Fig. 121): This is a relatively small, low mound with a roughly circular plan. The old main highway from Elâzığ to Bingöl cuts directly through the center of the mound. A slight distance from the road begin fields which cover the rest of the site. A small stream, the Karasu, is a short distance to the east of the mound.

DIMENSIONS:
  Length: 115 m measured north-south
  Width: 110 m measured east-west along the highway
  Height: ca. 1 m

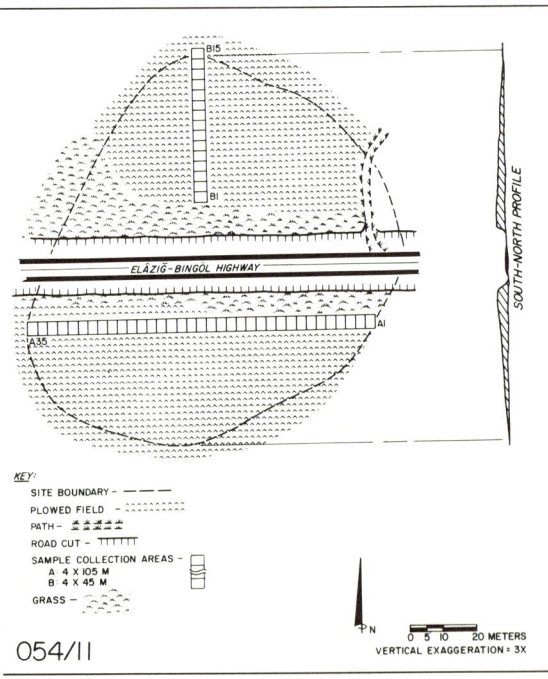

FIGURE 121. 054/11-Site plan and profile.

COLLECTIONS: Preliminary and gridded strip

OCCUPATIONS:
    Major—Hittite
              Medieval
    Minor—Early Chalcolithic
              Early Bronze Age I-II
              Middle Bronze Age
    Trace— Late Chalcolithic (?)
              Iron Age (?)

Not a particularly large amount of material was recovered from the surface of this mound. Of the periods of occupation listed above, only the Medieval occupation is represented by a really substantial quantity of ceramics.

The Hittite pottery comprises Hittite Plain, Thick, Buff-Orange Burnished, Red-Brown Burnished, Brown Burnished (e.g. Fig. 32:ee), Painted, Fine, and Brown Gritty Cooking wares. From among these, only three good rims were found, however.

Medieval ceramics include all our defined wares except Modeled, and at least ten rims from this period were found (e.g. Red Slipped—Fig. 48:w, jj; Fig. 49:c,e; Glazed—Fig. 47:s; Painted—Fig. 51:i; and Cooking Ware—Fig. 52:s). Included in this material were a significant number of sherds of Glazed and Sgraffiato wares, and at least one rim sherd of each.

Two characteristic Graphite Slipped sherds are probably adequate to show some degree of occupation of this site in the Early Chalcolithic period.

The Early Bronze Age I-II is marked only by body sherds. These include Early Bronze Age Burnished, Plain, Thick, and Red Slipped wares.

Middle Bronze Age occupation is evidenced primarily by sherds of Old Hittite Gray ware. A few Middle Bronze Age Gray and Light Faced Gray Ware sherds were also found, and several rim sherds of Old Hittite and Middle Bronze Age Gray wares were recovered.

A few body sherds identified as Cream Chaff and Iron Age wares allow one to suspect possible occupation here in the Late Chalcolithic and Iron Age, but are certainly far from conclusive.

CONTROLLED COLLECTION: Since the main highway cuts straight through the middle of this site, it was impossible to fully traverse the mound with collection strips. As close an approximation to this as possible was made, however, by running two gridded collection strips across the plowed portions of the site at right angles to each other. One strip paralleled the highway across the broadest remaining portion of the site, south of the road, while the second strip was run perpendicularly from the edge of the highway shoulder across the center of the remaining mound on the north side of the road.

System:
    Strip A: Direction 90°, length 105 m (35 squares)
        Squares A1-A35:   plowed field
    Strip B: Direction 0°, length 45 m (15 squares)
        Squares B1-B15:   plowed field

Collection squares were 3 × 4 m in size, running 3 m along the length of the collection strip.

Materials only of the Hittite and Medieval occupations were abundant enough to allow averaging, plotting, and contouring along the collection strips. Early Bronze Age materials were too sparse and too scattered.

With the ceramics of the Middle Bronze Age, however, a simple plot of sherd counts, without

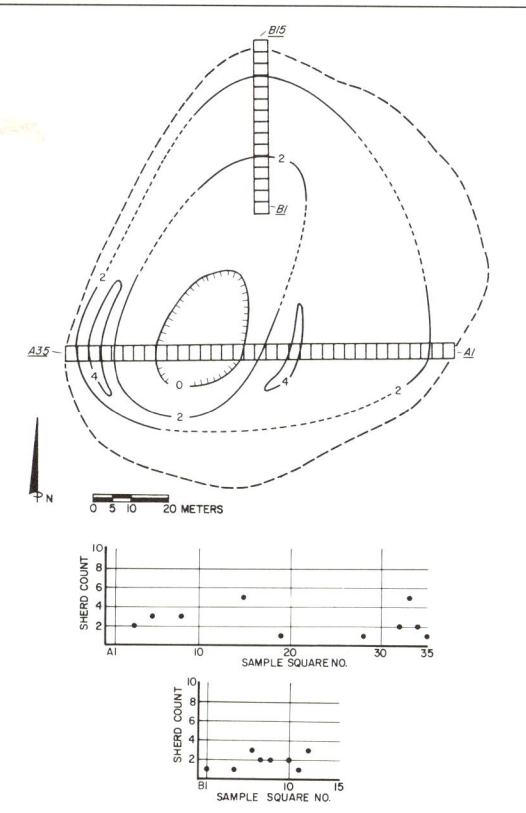

FIGURE 122. 054/11-Density contours of Middle Bronze Age ceramics.

averaging, did give some indication of the pattern of distribution of materials from this occupation period over the site. An approximate contouring of these counts provides a relatively plausible picture of an area of Middle Bronze Age occupation concentrated on the west and southwest parts of the mound (Fig. 122). This area is about 90 × 100 m in size.

All of the various Hittite wares found at this site were grouped together, and their counts per square were expressed as a moving average over four squares. The contours connecting these averages show a fairly clear area of approximately 90 × 100 m in size concentrated on the central and south-central areas of the site (Fig. 123), which we can take as a fair representation of the area of Hittite occupation here.

The Medieval ceramics, grouped together and expressed as a moving average over five squares, allow a contour map of densities per square to be constructed which gives a picture of an occupation area running northwest-southeast over the center of the mound in a long, oval form (Fig.

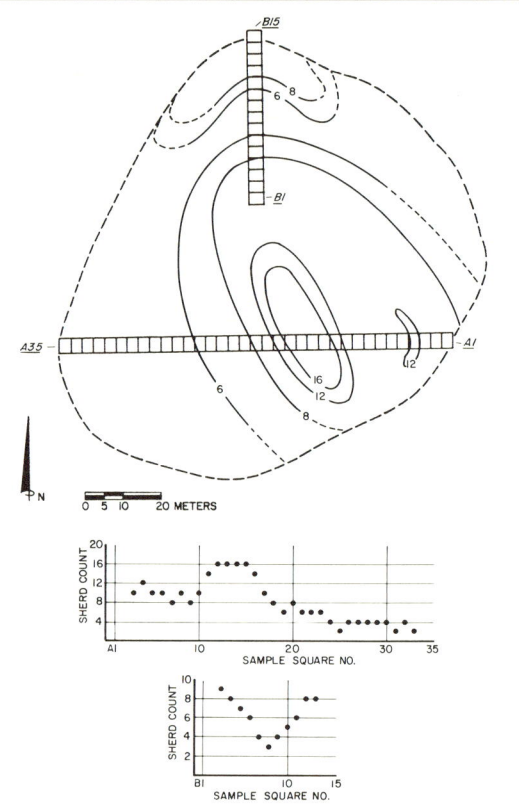

FIGURE 124. 054/11-Density contours of Medieval ceramics.

124). If one takes the clearest contour, that of eight sherds per square, an area of 50 × 100 m is defined. The visual impression is of a rather larger area, however, which must be estimated from the four sherd contour line and the general configuration of the contours as about 85 × 120 m in size.

From the three occupations just described, a fairly clear progression of settlement from west to east over the mound, with a constant tendency for concentration over the southern part of the site, can be seen. The sizes of these occupations are closely similar, however, in keeping with the small size of the mound as a whole.

054/12

NAME: Kuruçayır Tepesi
    Vilayet: Elâzığ
    Kaza: Merkez kazası
    Nahiye: Mollakendi
    Village: just east of Könk

NATURE: Mound

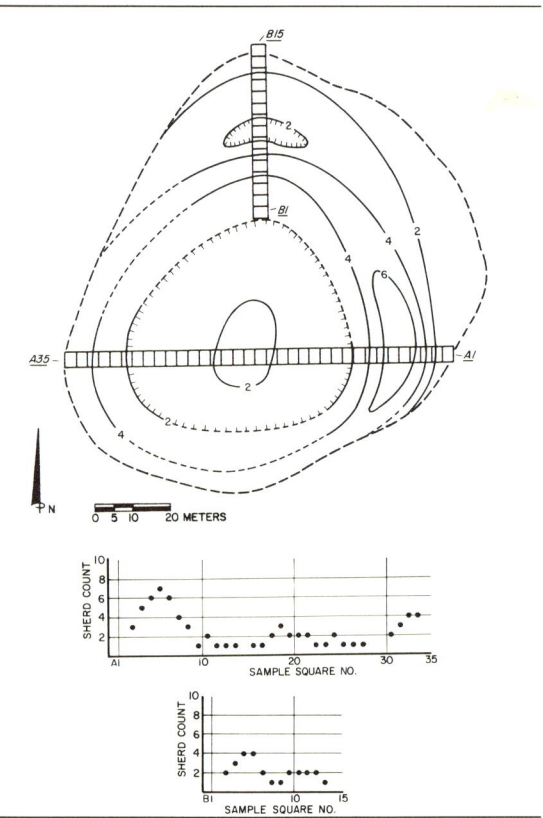

FIGURE 123. 054/11-Density contours of Hittite ceramics.

DESCRIPTION (Fig. 125): This is a moderately low, broad, relatively featureless mound. The surrounding land surface slopes to the north, and at the north end of the mound a small village road runs along the front of the site, making a low cut where, apparently, a fair portion of the mound has been removed, probably by erosion or by digging and agricultural activities. Perhaps a fourth or slightly more of the site is gone. Here also, at the northeast corner of the remaining mound is a spring which has cut itself a deep depression. The site is now under cultivation.

DIMENSIONS:

    Length: 85 m north-south, measured up to the village road where the present mound ends. The original length of the mound may have been some 120–130 m
    Width: 90 m measured east-west
    Height: ca. 2 m

COLLECTIONS: Preliminary and gridded strip

OCCUPATIONS:

    Major—Early Bronze Age I-II
           Medieval

    Minor—Late Chalcolithic
           Middle Bronze Age
           Hittite
    Trace— Iron Age

A significant number of body sherds of Early Bronze Age Burnished and Plain wares shows the presence of Early Bronze Age I-II occupation at this small site. A few rims were also recovered (e.g. Fig. 13:z), and several sherds of Early Bronze Age Thick and a single sherd both of Red Slipped and Polished wares complete the collection from this period.

In comparison, the Medieval materials from this site are overwhelmingly abundant. All the recognized Medieval wares except Medieval Modeled were found in large numbers. Rim sherds of most wares were also found (e.g. Medieval Brick—Fig. 40:i,k; Fig. 42:nn,aaa; Glazed—Fig. 47:t,gg; Sgraffiato—Fig. 47:bb, ee,ff; Red Slipped—Fig. 48:j,ii; White Slipped—Fig. 49:r,dd; Cooking ware—Fig. 52:ll).

Late Chalcolithic pottery is typically Cream Chaff Ware (e.g. Fig. 10:ll; Fig. 11:a). In classifying and tabulating the rimsherds from this site, two rims were identified as of Cream Chaff form. Later, a third rim, originally called Hittite Chaff Faced, was recognized as a Cream Chaff rim. There is thus some evidence for the presence of at least a small Late Chalcolithic occupation here, and there is a strong likelihood that many of those body sherds first called Hittite Chaff Faced are in fact Late Chalcolithic pottery.

The Middle Bronze Age is represented in the collection by ten body sherds of Old Hittite Gray Ware and one sherd of Old Hittite Light Faced Gray Ware. One rim of Middle Bronze Age Gritty Ware was found.

Hittite sherds were more common, comprising Hittite Plain (e.g. Fig. 25:n), Thick (e.g. Fig. 27:h), Buff-Orange Burnished, Red-Brown Burnished, Brown Burnished, White Slipped, Painted, Chaff Faced, Fine, and Brown Gritty Cooking wares (e.g. Fig. 35:q). The few Chaff Faced sherds may, in fact, be misidentified sherds of Cream Chaff Ware as mentioned above.

A small handful of body sherds were identified as possibly Iron Age in date. None were absolutely diagnostic, however.

CONTROLLED COLLECTION: The systematic surface collection was made here with two gridded strips

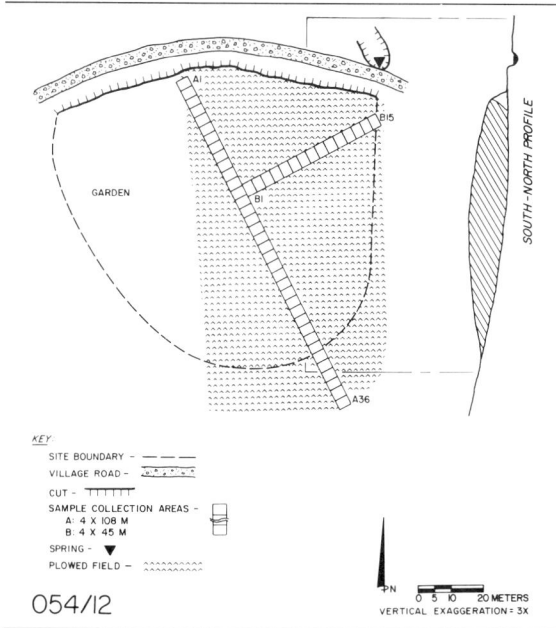

FIGURE 125. 054/12-Site plan and profile.

laid out in the form of a T. These strips were placed over the central and eastern part of the mound. The western one-third of the site was cultivated as a watermelon patch and was not collectable.

System:
    Strip A: Direction 153°, length 108 m (36 squares)
        Squares A1-A36:   barren field
    Strip B: Direction 63°, length 45 m (15 squares)
        Squares B1-B15:   barren field

Materials of the Early Bronze Age I-II, Hittite and Medieval periods were abundant enough to average and contour along the collection strips.

The various Early Bronze Age I-II wares, when added together and averaged over six squares, showed generally low densities everywhere. Their distribution was clearly concentrated towards the north-central side of the mound, however, in a pattern which strongly suggests that a major part of the occupation area of this period has been removed by the erosion of the northern portion of the mound (Fig. 126). As it stands, the area

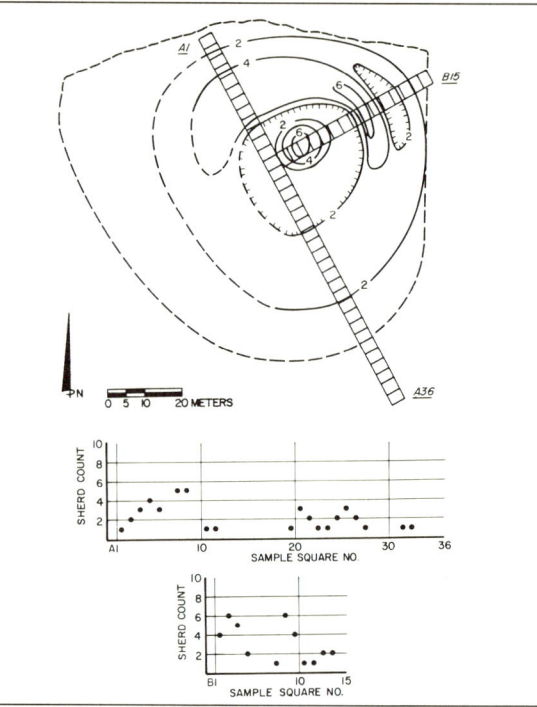

FIGURE 127. 054/12-Density contours of Hittite ceramics.

covered by Early Bronze Age I-II materials is ca. 50 × 65 m in size, but if we estimate from the form of the contour lines that about half the former occupation has been eroded we then arrive at a possible area of 65 × 100 m for Early Bronze Age I-II occupation here.

Hittite sherds, even when all Hittite wares are combined and plotted as a group, are relatively sparse. The counts of all Hittite ceramics were averaged over two squares and contoured (Fig. 127). The patterns of distribution along the two strips are rather clear and seem to allow a fairly clear contouring to be made. This shows an area of concentration squarely over the center and just east of center of the present-day mound. The form of the contours as given over the two strips collected is a rather regular semi-circle. Projecting this onto the uncollected western part of the mound would give a picture of a circular occupation roughly 70 m in diameter.

All Medieval wares were combined, and the graphs of their counts along the collection strips were smoothed with a moving average taken over six squares. Contouring these averages at 12, 24, 36, and 48 sherds per square shows an occupation

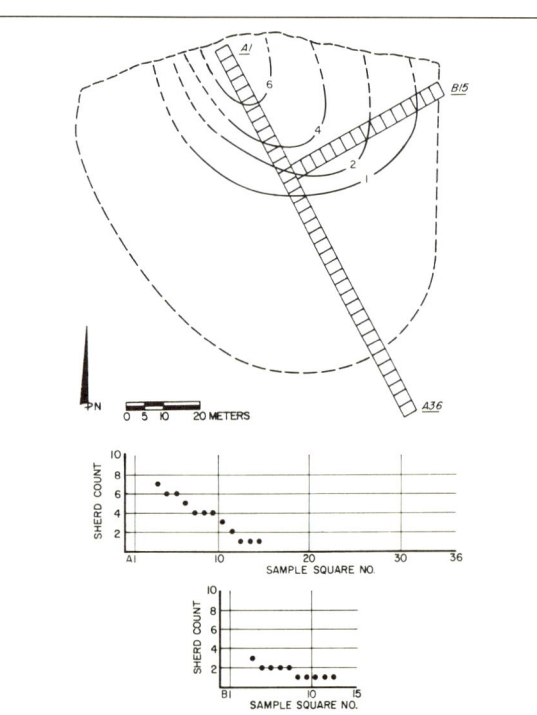

FIGURE 126. 054/12-Density contours of Early Bronze Age I-II ceramics.

NATURE: Surface scatter, perhaps an occupation site.

DESCRIPTION (Fig. 129): A scatter of sherds, and occasionally other kinds of occupation debris, defines this site. There may be a barely perceptible mound at this spot. The site gives an impression of an occupation which lasted an extremely short time. The site is now an open field.

DIMENSIONS:
  Length: 90 m east-west, as measured from the apparent edges of the scatter
  Width: 60 m north-south, similarly measured
  Height: 0 m to perhaps .25 m

COLLECTIONS: Preliminary

OCCUPATIONS: Major—Medieval

The only ceramics found on this site were Medieval. These include Medieval Brick, Thick (e.g. Fig. 45:b; Fig. 46:a) Cooking (e.g. Fig. 52:l, m,o), and Glazed (e.g. Fig. 47:o) wares. One rim sherd of Medieval Glazed pottery was found (Fig. 47:i).

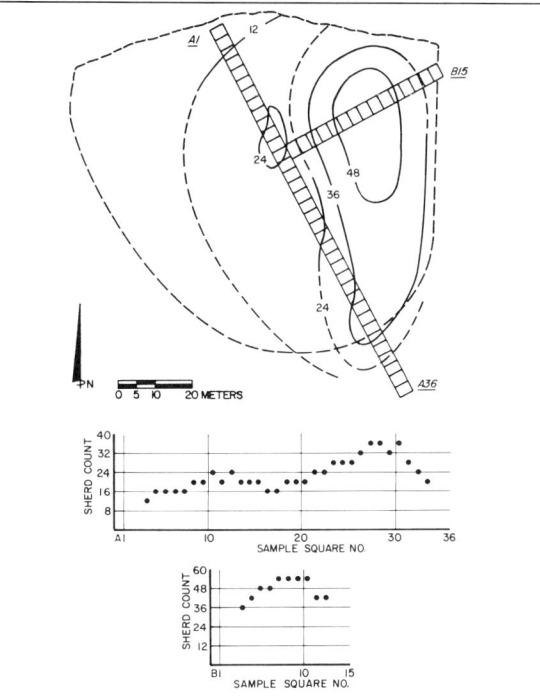

FIGURE 128. 054/12-Density contours of Medieval ceramics.

heavily concentrated on the east and southeast sides of the mound, running, according to the contours of sherd density, well beyond the borders of the recognizable mound (Fig. 128). On the mound proper, the area covered by the occupation is roughly 65 × 90 m in size, running from the 12 sherd contour to the recognized edge of the mound. The actual size of the occupation must be larger, however, and can be roughly estimated from the contours as at least 80 × 100 m.

From the Early Bronze Age I-II through the Hittite to the Medieval occupation of this site, then, we have a relatively clear progression of settlement from the northern side of the mound, over the center and slightly towards the east, to the far southeast and eastern edges of the site.

054/13

NAME: Peylik
  Vilayet: Elâzığ
  Kaza: Merkez kazası
  Nahiye: Mollakendi
  Village: just north of Könk

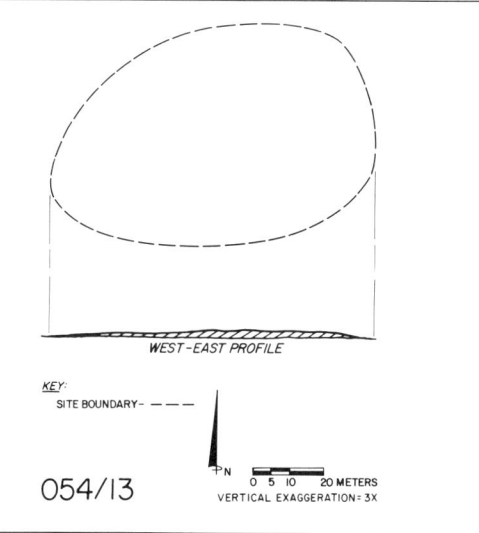

FIGURE 129. 054/13-Site plan and profile.

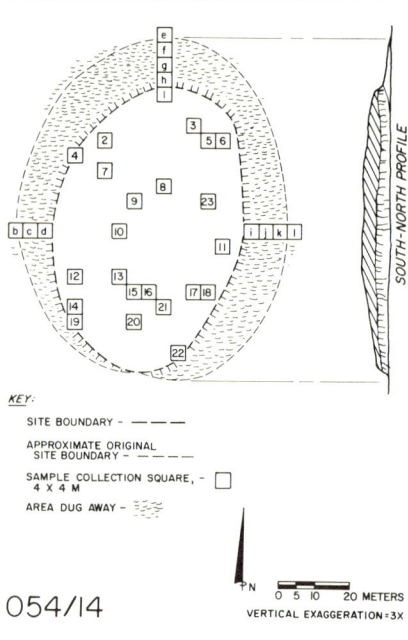

FIGURE 130. 054/14-Site plan and profile.

054/14

NAME: Körtepe (Cayırlar Tepesi, Boztepe, Tilkitepe)
    Vilayet: Elâzığ
    Kaza: Merkez kazası
    Nahiye: Mollakendi
    Village: near Sarpulu

NATURE: Mound

DESCRIPTION (Fig. 130): This is a small, low, broad mound. It has been quite extensively dug into around almost its entire periphery. Now, only an oval center section remains intact. The mound, and thus the profiles left from this digging, are low, and no features or structures are evident in them. The mound appears to have been more or less circular, or slightly elongated in a north-south direction. It is not cultivated. Just to the north of the site is a good spring, called Körpınar, on a tiny stream.

DIMENSIONS:
    Length: 85–90 m measured north-south over both the destroyed and remaining area
    Width: 50 m of remaining mound was measured east-west, the original width was probably approximately 75 m
    Height: ca. 2–2.5 m

COLLECTIONS: Preliminary and gridded random with short gridded strips over the cut-away areas

OCCUPATIONS:
    Major—Early Bronze Age I-II
              Middle Bronze Age
              Hittite
              Medieval
    Minor—Early Chalcolithic
              Early Bronze Age III
    Trace— Iron Age

Ceramics of the Early Bronze Age I-II period are overwhelmingly preponderant over other periods at this site. Mostly they consist of Early Bronze Age Burnished and Plain wares, with only occasional examples of Thick, Red Slipped and Polished wares. No Early Bronze Age Relief Decorated ware was found. The Burnished Ware is the most common and the frequency of it and Plain Ware together is such as to suggest that a large bulk of the mound must consist of debris from this period.

The Middle Bronze Age is represented by a relatively large number of Old Hittite Gray and Middle Bronze Age Gritty wares, supplemented by occasional sherds of Old Hittite Light Faced Gray Ware. Two rims of Old Hittite Gray Ware (e.g. Fig. 21:w) and 6 rims of Middle Bronze Age Gritty Ware (e.g. Fig. 20:c,s,u,y) were also recovered in the collection.

Hittite ceramics include small to moderate quantities of all Hittite wares defined (e.g. Buff-Orange Burnished—Fig. 29:z), with the exceptions of Hittite Orange Smoothed, and Exterior Wheel-Marked wares.

Similarly, the Medieval pottery includes single examples to moderate quantities of all plain Medieval wares, excluding Medieval Painted, Modeled, Glazed, and Sgraffiato wares.

Early Chalcolithic occupation is definitely present at this site, as evidenced by both Chalcolithic Ware and Graphite Slipped Ware. One rim of the former was found, but there was slightly more Graphite Slipped pottery in the collection. In total, however, only some 30 sherds of this period were found.

Only three sherds both of Early Bronze Age Red Painted and Black Painted wares were identified.

A few body sherds were tentatively identified as Iron Age pottery.

CONTROLLED COLLECTION: Intensive surface collection of this site consisted of a mixture of random grid square and gridded strip sampling. A grid of 4 × 4 m squares was drawn over the remaining area of intact mound, and 23 squares were chosen at random for collection. Then, three short strips of 4 × 4 m squares were run out across the flat areas obviously remaining from the borrow-pit digging which had destroyed a considerable portion of the peripheries of the mound. One strip of three such squares ran to the west, one of four squares to the north, and a strip of four to the east of the remaining mound. Thus, in total, 34 squares were collected, representing a combined surface area of somewhat more than 10 percent of the remaining mound surface.

System:
    Random squares - 23
    All squares: waste grassland
Strips:
    West: Squares B-D
    North: Squares E-H
    East: Squares I-L
    All squares: waste grassland

The counts per collection square were plotted on a site plan for the grouped ceramics of each period of major and minor occupation. In all cases at least some idea of the relative size and location of the occupation was gained. In every case the east to northeast sector of the remaining mound appeared as an area of very low counts or no material, however. It seems that local conditions here affect the surface densities of materials of all periods equally and that a paucity of sherds in this area should not necessarily be interpreted as a lack of occupation here. The form and trends of density contours over other parts of the site will be a more accurate guide to estimation of occupation area.

Early Chalcolithic sherds (Chalcolithic and Graphite Slipped wares) are few, but they are clearly localized on the south side of the remaining mound (Fig. 131). From this admittedly slight evidence, we might estimate a small occupation over this southern third of the site, an area of roughly 40 m diameter.

The various Early Bronze Age I-II wares, grouped together, show rather considerable densities over certain parts of this site (Fig. 132). The highest densities are on the western side of the remaining mound, but significant quantities of these ceramics are found over virtually the entire mound area. In contrast, densities are relatively low on the three strips running out over the dug-away areas of the mound. Only on the eastern strip is there a small area of low concentration of these sherds, on the very periphery of the site. It is as though the bulk of the Early Bronze Age I-II occupation were centered over the entire area of the remaining mound and had been slightly dug into on its eastern border. Such a reconstruction would give an approximate, estimated area of occupation 70 m in diameter for this period.

The Middle Bronze Age ceramics are very sparsely distributed over the site, even with sherds of all wares grouped together. Their pattern of distribution seems quite clear, however

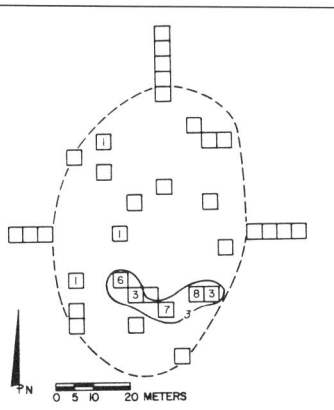

FIGURE 131. 054/14-Density contours of Early Chalcolithic ceramics.

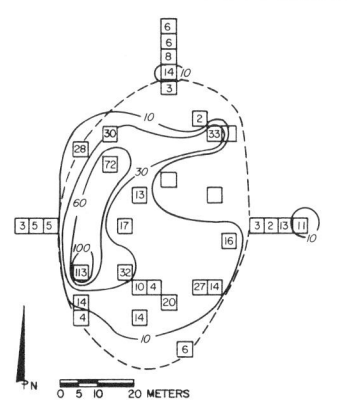

FIGURE 132. 054/14-Density contours of Early Bronze Age I-II ceramics.

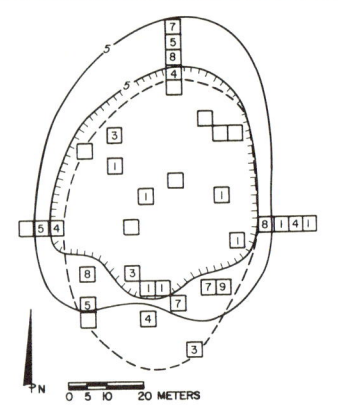

FIGURE 133. 054/14-Density contours of Middle Bronze Age ceramics.

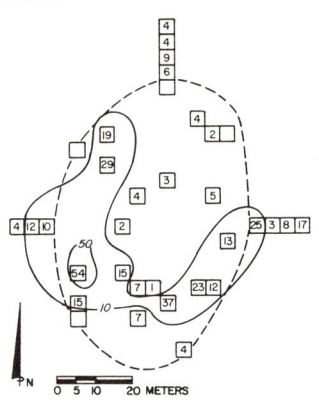

FIGURE 134. 054/14-Density contours of Hittite ceramics.

(Fig. 133). Over the center of the site, that is over most of the remaining mound, they are very rare or absent. Their areas of concentration lie in a band running over the southern portion of the mound and in the three strips collected across the dug-away parts of the mound. If these areas are joined, one sees a broad band roughly running around the periphery of the site, probably marking the edge of the occupation or where it has been dug into. If this band can be taken as the edge of the occupation layer, it represents an area of some 65 × 85 m in size. It seems contradictory then that sherds of an earlier period, the Early Bronze Age I-II, should occur in large quantities over the central area of the mound where materials of the Middle Bronze Age are scarce. A possible explanation may be that the occupation layer of Middle Bronze Age date is relatively thin, and easily destroyed or covered by later occupations, while a thicker Early Bronze Age layer still contributes much material to the surface scatter on the mound. A relatively thin Middle Bronze Age level would thus be visible on the surface of the mound only where it was either exposed or dug into as we have proposed above. Such an interpretation should, of course, be checked by excavation, but it must here serve the temporary purpose of allowing us to estimate the size of the Middle Bronze Age occupation at this site.

Hittite occupation is more clearly concentrated over the southwestern area of the site. Grouped counts of all Hittite wares show moderately high densities over this part of the site, running up the west side and over onto the southeast quarter of the site area (Fig. 134). The northeast quarter of the site is typically rather empty. It can be noted that significant densities of Hittite material occur on both the mound and the dug-away areas near the edge of the remaining mound. Perhaps this can be interpreted as an indication that Hittite occupation covered most of the remaining mound area and extended slightly into the area now dug away. If so, this gives us an estimated area for this occupation of roughly 55 × 65 m.

Medieval ceramics, in contrast, are very largely restricted to the surface of the remaining mound, and here they are concentrated over the center and northwestern portion of the mound. They are virtually absent from the southern part of the site and are few in number in the dug-away areas (Fig. 135). All Medieval wares were combined to

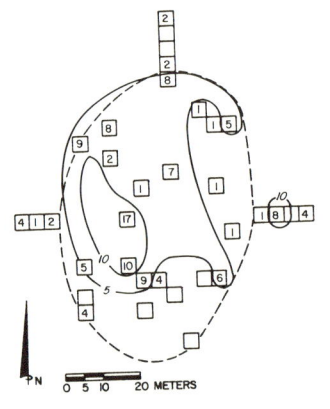

FIGURE 135. 054/14-Density contours of Medieval ceramics.

produce this picture of Medieval occupation area. It seems, though, that the occupation is relatively restricted to an area of only about 55 m in diameter.

054/15

NAME: Çakıltepe (Körtepe)
Vilayet: Elâzığ
Kaza: Merkez kazası
Nahiye: Mollakendi
Village: near Sarpulu

NATURE: Mound

DESCRIPTION (Fig. 136): This is a small, low, broad mound. It is somewhat irregular in plan, having a projection to the north. Around the south to the southeast edge it has been slightly bitten into by the construction of an irrigation ditch. The site is under cultivation for the most part, but there is unusually little material on the surface.

DIMENSIONS:
Length: 90 m measured in a northeast-southwest direction
Width: 70 m measured in a northwest-southeast direction
Height: ca. 2.5–3 m

COLLECTIONS: Preliminary and gridded strip

OCCUPATIONS: Materials of no period are abundant enough on this site to really allow the designation of periods of occupation as "major" or "minor" in the same sense as for other sites surveyed. We will therefore characterize the occupations evidenced here as either "present" or as "trace."
Present—Early Chalcolithic
Early Bronze Age I-II
Hittite
Medieval
Trace— Iron Age (?)
Hellenistic-Roman

Two sherds of Chalcolithic Ware and one distinctive Graphite Slipped sherd indicate the probable presence of a small Early Chalcolithic occupation here.

The Early Bronze Age is represented here by only Early Bronze Age Burnished and Plain

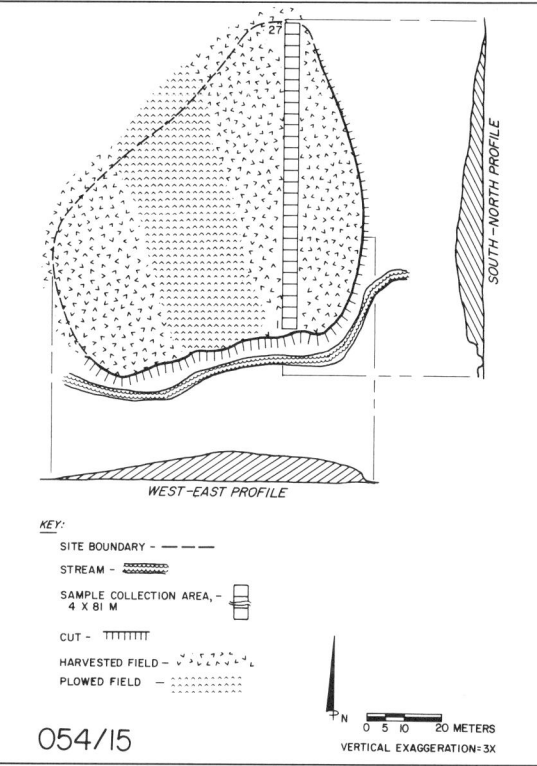

FIGURE 136. 054/15-Site plan and profiles.

wares, primarily the latter. The occupation indicated is therefore placed in the general period of the Early Bronze Age I-II, although it probably dates more toward the late end of this period than to its early part.

Hittite ceramics consist of body sherds of all Hittite wares except Hittite Orange Smoothed, White Slipped, Red, and Exterior Wheel-Marked. Of the wares present, though, only Hittite Plain and Brown Burnished occur in any abundance. The other wares occur as small handfuls of sherds or often as single examples.

Medieval pottery is certainly the most common on this site. The range of wares present is quite restricted, however, comprising only Medieval Brick (e.g. Fig. 43:d), Thick, Cooking, and Red Slipped wares.

Two body sherds were called Iron Age, but the certainty of this identification is questionable. One sherd probably of Roman Red Ware was also recovered (Fig. 55:i).

CONTROLLED COLLECTION: This being a tiny site with extremely little material on the surface, it was sampled with only a single gridded strip

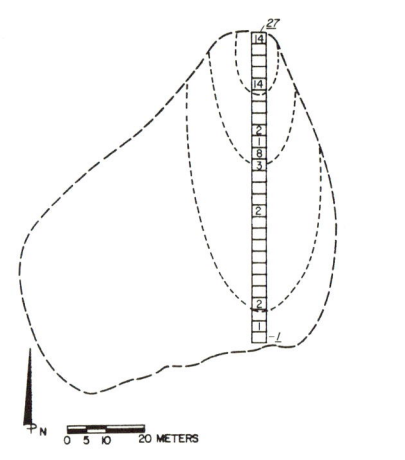

FIGURE 137. 054/15-Counts of Hittite sherds.

placed across the longest part of the site, where it appeared that the greatest amount of surface material was to be found.

System:
  Strip A: Direction 0°, length 81 m (27 squares)
  Squares A1-A27:   harvested (cut) field

The collection squares were 3 × 4 m, 3 m along the length of the strip.

Only the Hittite and Medieval ceramics showed high enough counts along this strip to give any kind of a picture of the distribution of occupation on the site.

Hittite sherds were not common enough to allow a meaningful averaging of counts along the strip, even though all Hittite wares were combined. A simple plot of the actual counts per square, however, shows a clear tendency toward concentration near the north end of the collection strip (Fig. 137). The bulk of the Hittite materials thus lie to the north of square A15. If this is in any way truly indicative of the location of the Hittite occupation of this site, it represents an extremely small area of only some 40 m diameter.

The counts of all Medieval sherds taken together show a greater density and, smoothed with a moving average over three squares, a clear pattern of concentration toward the southern end of the collection strip (Fig. 138). Average counts are still low and it is hard to generalize accurately from the pattern along this single strip, but the concentration is clear enough to allow at least a provisional estimate of the area of Medieval occupation as being ca. 50–60 m in diameter.

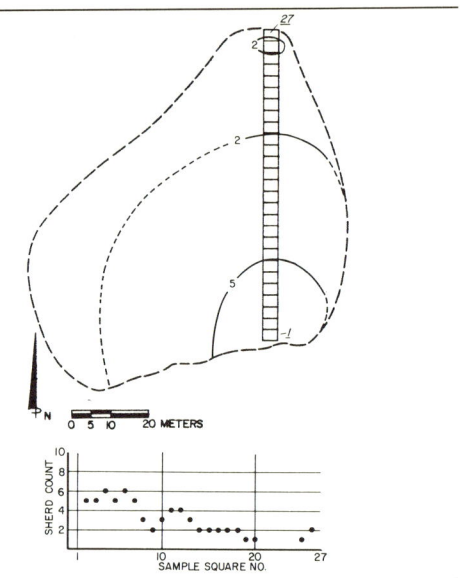

FIGURE 138. 054/15-Density contours of Medieval ceramics.

The differential distribution of Hittite and Medieval materials is rather striking. Early Bronze Age I-II sherds, insofar as they show any pattern, tend to follow the Hittite distribution, concentrating on the northern side of the site.

054/16

NAME: Çıplak Tepe
  Vilayet: Elâzığ
  Kaza: Merkez kazası
  Nahiye: Mollakendi
  Village: —

NATURE: Mound

DESCRIPTION (Fig. 139): The site is very small, low, almost flat. It is roughly oval in shape and located on the edge of the Haringet Çayı. It is partially under cultivation and without surface features or disturbances.

DIMENSIONS:
  Length: 90 m measured northwest-southeast
  Width: 65 m measured northeast-southwest
  Height: ca. 1 m

COLLECTIONS: Preliminary and gridded strip

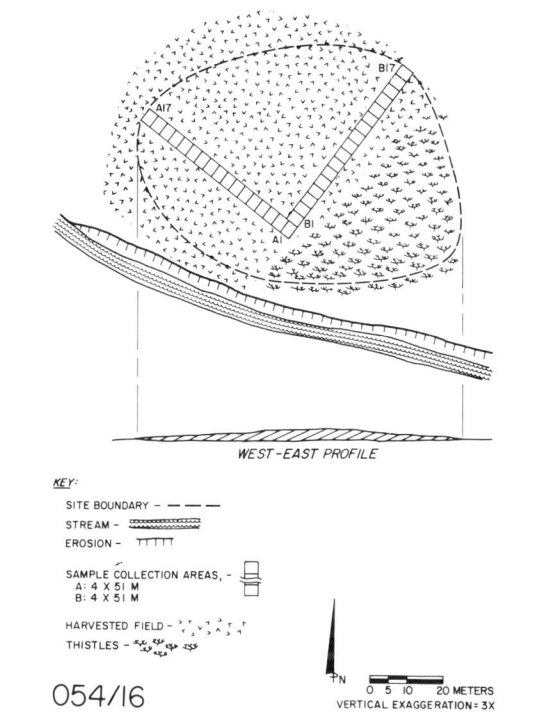

FIGURE 139. 054/16-Site plan and profile.

OCCUPATIONS: Major—Medieval

The only period significantly represented in the surface pottery from this site is Medieval. All Medieval wares except Painted and Modeled are represented in the collection, some with several rims (e.g. Red Slipped—Fig. 48:c,s; Cooking—Fig. 52:b,e,h) in addition to body sherds. Medieval Brick ware was the most common by far, but the majority of it was chaff-tempered here, which is not typical of this pottery at most sites.

One or two sherds were identified as other than Medieval. Two rims (similar to Fig. 16:x, y) were classed as Early Bronze Age Plain, and one lid was also called Early Bronze Age in date. The rim profiles and the plain pottery are not completely diagnostic. Quite similar lids also occur in the Medieval wares. One sherd was identified as Hittite Thick and one as Buff-Orange Burnished Ware. Within the context of the whole collection none of these few, trivial exceptions is totally convincing evidence for any occupation here earlier than the Medieval period.

CONTROLLED COLLECTION: A systematic surface collection was made from this site in two gridded strips joined together in an L shape and placed over the two fields covering the northwestern half of the site.

System:
    Strip A: Direction 307°, length 51 m (17 squares)
        Squares A1-A17:   cut (harvested) field
    Strip B: Direction 37°, length 51 m (17 squares)
        Squares B1-B17:   cut (harvested) field

The different Medieval wares were all grouped together and the graphs of their counts per square along each strip were smoothed by taking a moving average over five squares. These averages were then contoured over the two strips, and the results clearly showed the general distribution of the Medieval materials over the entire site (Fig. 140). The higher average counts are near the periphery of the mound as would be expected either from movement of materials off the top of the mound by plowing or erosion, or most likely from the exposure by erosion of the Medieval occupation layer(s) on the slopes at the edge of the mound. Taking the entire mound as Medieval, then, we arrive at an area of occupation some 65 × 90 m in size here.

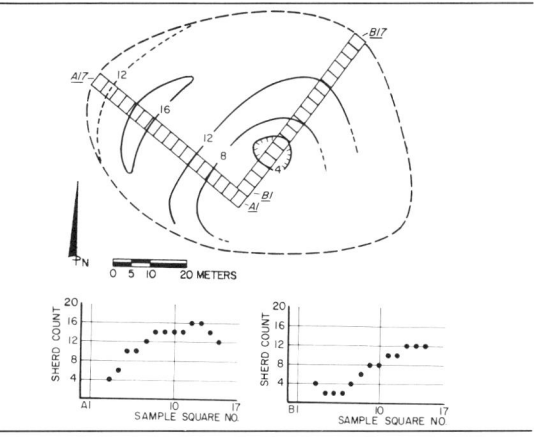

FIGURE 140. 054/16-Density contours of Medieval ceramics.

054/17

NAME: Eski Maşatlık
    Vilayet: Elâzığ
    Kaza: Merkez kazası
    Nahiye: İçme
    Village: —(between Munzuroğlu and Ahur)

NATURE: Surface scatter

DESCRIPTION: Evidences of an apparently brief occupation were found on the surface of a field which slopes gently down to the bank of the Haringet Çayı. There are no surface features, but villagers in the area say that stones and "foundations" are found when they plow the field. From the name of the site ("old cemetery") it is of course possible that these stones and "foundations" come from graves rather than from houses or other structures.

DIMENSIONS:
    Length: The area of main concentration is not more than 100 × 100 m in size
    Width: cf. above
    Height: 0 m

COLLECTIONS: Preliminary

OCCUPATIONS: Major—Medieval

Only Medieval sherds were recovered from the surface of this site. These included examples of Medieval Brick, Thick, Cooking, White Slipped, and Red Slipped (e.g. Fig. 48:e,t–v) wares. In addition to ceramics one fragment of a crucible was found, strongly suggesting, in spite of the local name for the site, that this was an occupation or, more likely, a special activity site rather than a cemetery.

054/18

NAME: Körpınar
    Vilayet: Elâzığ
    Kaza: Merkez kazası
    Nahiye: İçme
    Village: —(between Tepecik and Munzuroğlu)

NATURE: Surface scatter

DESCRIPTION: Here, some occupation material was collected from the surface of a slightly sloping field. No other surface indications of a site were present.

DIMENSIONS:
    Length: The area of the scatter was no larger than ca. 100 × 100 m
    Width: cf. above
    Height: 0 m

COLLECTIONS: Preliminary

OCCUPATIONS:
    Present—Medieval
    Possibly present—Early Bronze Age I-II (?)
        Hittite (?)

There is relatively little material to go on in assessing the periods of occupation of this site. Two rimsherds have been identified as Medieval Brick ware (Fig. 42:a, t), and some body sherds of the same ware and of Thick Ware were found.

Three body sherds were questionably classed as Early Bronze Age Burnished. One rather undiagnostic rim (like Fig. 17:f) was called Early Bronze Age Thick. One rim similar to Fig. 28:x was identified as Hittite Buff-Orange Burnished Ware.

In sum, this site might best be interpreted as a random scatter of late (Medieval) material, representing an area of activity in a field, rather than an occupation in the true sense.

054/19

NAME: —
    Vilayet: Elâzığ
    Kaza: Merkez kazası
    Nahiye: İçme
    Village: Kıraç

NATURE: Mound

DESCRIPTION (Fig. 141): This low mound of occupation debris is located relatively high up on the slopes on the north side of the Altınova, apparently on top of a small natural rise among quite heavily eroded gullies. It is extremely small and may represent a tiny occupation or may have been largely eroded. It is presently cultivated.

DIMENSIONS:
    Length: ca. 50 m north-south
    Width: ca. 30 m east-west
    Height: ca. .5-1 m (?)

COLLECTIONS: Preliminary

OCCUPATIONS:
    Present—Early Bronze Age I-II
        Middle Bronze Age
        Hittite
        Iron Age
        Medieval

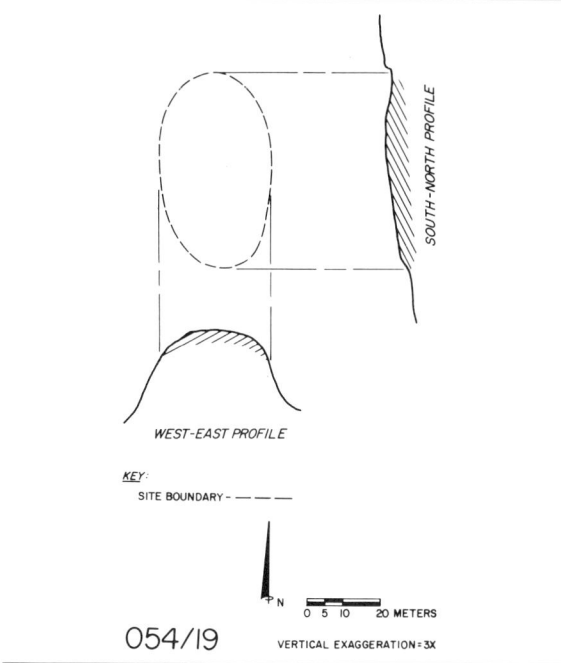

FIGURE 141. 054/19-Site plan and profiles.

All of the above periods are weakly represented. The Early Bronze Age I-II is shown only by body sherds of Early Bronze Age Burnished and Plain wares. The Middle Bronze Age is known from a rim sherd of Old Hittite Gray (Fig. 21:z). Hittite Plain and Buff-Orange Burnished sherds were found, including a rim of the latter ware (similar to Fig. 29:d). The Iron Age is present as a single rim sherd, but it is a typical, slightly grooved neck, jar form (Fig. 37:aa). And, finally, some sherds were classified as Medieval Brick (e.g. Fig. 40:p) and Cooking (e.g. Fig. 52:w,dd) wares. All in all, there is no clear picture of any dominant or even major occupation here, but only small quantities of material from several periods.

054/20

NAME: Kilise Tepe
    Vilayet: Elâzığ
    Kaza: Merkez kazası
    Nahiye: İçme
    Village: Habusu (İkizdemir)

NATURE: Mound and architectural remains

DESCRIPTION (Fig. 142) This mound appears to be moderately large, although it is virtually entirely covered by a modern village, so that it is difficult to define the limits of the site accurately. A relatively large amount of digging into the mound has occurred, undoubtedly for earth to make the walls of the present village houses. Small pits are found in a number of places. On the northeast and northwest sides of the mound it has been dug into leaving low profiles. A very large area, perhaps almost a fourth of the original mound, has been extensively dug into in the southwest quarter of the site, destroying the upper layers. An apparently fairly old, stone-paved road cuts across the northern edge of the mound, leading to a spring on the northwest. The rest of the site is capped by the contemporary village of Habusu. Habusu clearly was formerly an Armenian village. The partly standing ruins of a church are found at the center of the mound on its summit. A corner, four arches in the walls, and a large number of fallen stone columns remain.

DIMENSIONS:
    Length: ca. 250 m east-west
    Width: ca. 200 m north-south
    Height: ca. 7–8 m

COLLECTIONS: Preliminary

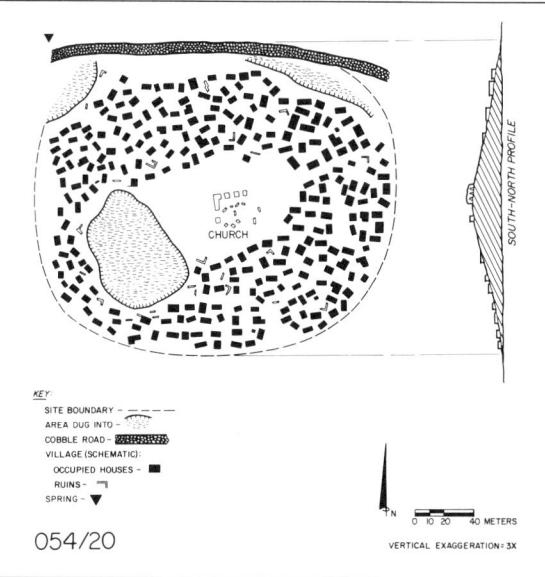

FIGURE 142. 054/20-Site plan and profile.

OCCUPATIONS:
>   Major—Medieval
>   Present—Early Bronze Age I-II
>   Possibly present—Early Chalcolithic
>   Hittite

The variety of Medieval wares in the general collection from this site is great. Sherds of Medieval Brick, Coarse, Cooking, White Slipped, Red Slipped, Painted, Glazed, and Sgraffiato wares are all present. From this diversity of ceramics, it seems fair to characterize the Medieval occupation of this site as "major."

The Early Bronze Age I-II is represented by body sherds of both Early Bronze Age Burnished and Plain wares. Hittite occupation is possibly shown by the occurrence of a rare type, Hittite Exterior Wheel-Marked, and a questionable example of Hittite Chaff Faced Ware. The former could well be a misidentification of a Medieval sherd while the questionable chaff tempered sherd could also be an Early Bronze Age piece. One sherd was thought perhaps to be of Early Chalcolithic date.

Earlier occupations may be effectively obscured by the extensive Medieval and Modern settlements here, but from the surface collection none of them can be securely identified as important at this site.

054/21

NAME: Kemaksı Mevkii Maşatlık
>   Vilayet: Elâzığ
>   Kaza: Merkez kazası
>   Nahiye: İçme
>   Village: —(near Alişam)

NATURE: Mound

DESCRIPTION (Fig. 143): This is a very small, low, almost flat mound. It is roughly circular in plan. There are no surface features, and the site appears to be simply left as a small piece of waste or grazing land today. It is located on the west bank of the Karasu, a small branch of the Harınget Çayı.

DIMENSIONS:
>   Length: The mound is almost circular with a
>   measured diameter of ca. 72 m
>   Width: cf. above
>   Height: ca. .75 m

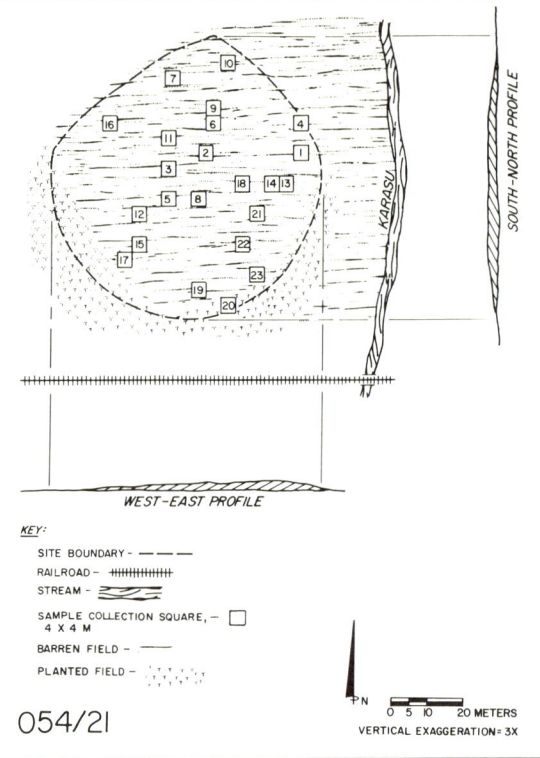

FIGURE 143. 054/21-Site plan and profiles.

COLLECTIONS: Preliminary and gridded random

OCCUPATIONS:
>   Major—Medieval
>   Minor—Hittite
>   Trace— Early Bronze Age I-II (?)
>   Middle Bronze Age (?)

The amount of Medieval pottery on this site far exceeds that of all other periods together. The bulk of this pottery was classified simply as Medieval Brick Ware (e.g. Fig. 41:m; Fig. 43:x; Fig. 44:g), but small to substantial quantities of all other wares except Painted and Modeled were also found (e.g. Glazed Ware—Fig. 47:j).

Enough Hittite pottery was found to clearly indicate occupation here in that period, but in contrast to the abundance of Medieval ceramics it assumes the aspect of a minor occupation. Hittite Plain and Buff-Orange Burnished were the only relatively common wares on this site, and together they numbered only 32 sherds (including one Buff-Orange Burnished rim) from the controlled sample collection. One to four sherds each were also found of Red-Brown Burnished, Brown

Burnished, White Slipped, Fine (e.g. Fig. 26:z), and Brown Gritty Cooking wares.

A handful of body sherds were classified as Early Bronze Age Plain, while about half that number were thought to be Early Bronze Age Burnished Ware. These identifications may not be accurate. Also, the identification of a half dozen body sherds as Middle Bronze Age Gritty and Old Hittite Light Faced Gray wares may well be in error.

CONTROLLED COLLECTION: The controlled surface collection was carried out here with a series of 23 squares, each 4 × 4 m in size, randomly selected from a grid covering the site. The area thus collected represents somewhat more than 10 percent of the site surface.

System:
23 randomly placed grid squares

Squares 1–23:   Smooth, barren (vegetationless) soil

Only the distribution of Medieval materials over the site could be meaningfully contoured. In addition, plotting the counts of all Hittite sherds made some sense in spite of their low density.

All Hittite sherds, counted and plotted over the site, show a general coverage of almost the whole mound (Fig. 144), letting us estimate a size for this occupation of some 60 × 70 m.

The Medieval ceramics, plotted and contoured together, show a relatively consistent pattern of increasing densities toward the center of the site,

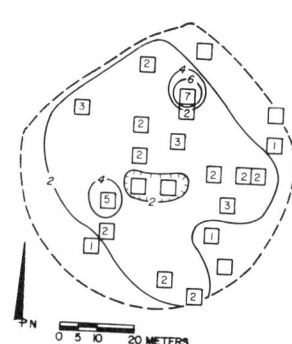

FIGURE 144. 054/21-Density contours of Hittite ceramics.

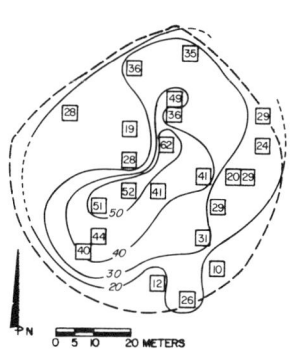

FIGURE 145. 054/21-Density contours of Medieval ceramics.

with a general distribution showing significant amounts of material over the entire area (Fig. 145). In short, it is clear that Medieval occupation covers the entire site, some 72 m in diameter. In contrast to some other small sites which are entirely covered by a late occupation (e.g. 054/16), the concentration of materials is here toward the center of the site and not around the site edges. Perhaps this shows the lack of plowing here, the fact that the site is largely treated as "wasteland."

054/22

NAME: Bahçeler Mevkii Körtepe
  Vilayet: Elâzığ
  Kaza: Merkez kazası
  Nahiye: İçme
  Village: —(near Alişam)

NATURE: Mound

DESCRIPTION (Fig. 146): This was a small, broad, and low mound which is now largely destroyed by borrow pit diggings. Some fields have also cut into and removed part of the mound. The relatively small remaining portion is grassland with no surface features. The site is located on the east edge of the small Karasu, a branch of the Haringet Çayı.

DIMENSIONS:
  Length: 80 m measured north-south to the apparent original edges of the mound

232 *Archaeological Survey of the Keban Reservoir*

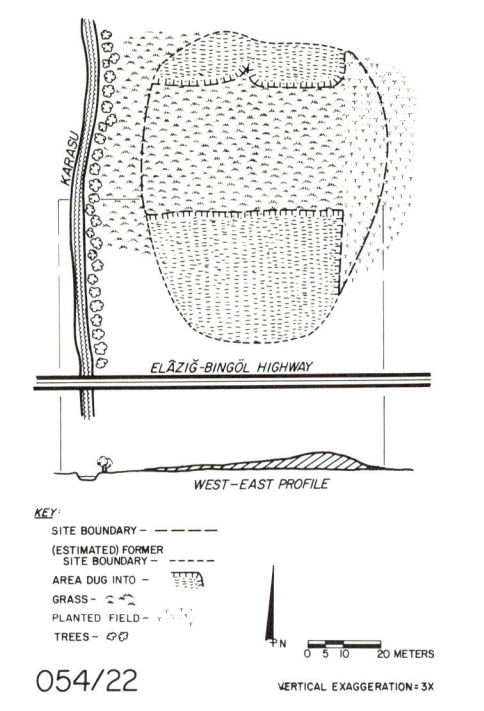

FIGURE 146. 054/22-Site plan and profile.

Width: 65 m measured east-west to the apparent edges of the original mound

Height: 1.2 m measured from the profile left by the modern diggings

COLLECTIONS: Preliminary

OCCUPATIONS:
Present—Early Chalcolithic
Hittite

It is impossible to make any kind of judgment about the relative importance of various occupations here from the small preliminary collection. Chalcolithic Ware (e.g. Fig. 6:ee; Fig. 7:l) is present, as are sherds of Hittite Plain (e.g. Fig. 24:v,bb), Fine (e.g. Fig. 26:pp), and Chaff Faced wares. Rims of Hittite Plain and Fine wares were found, but not of the Chaff Faced pottery. This is unfortunate because body sherds of this latter ware were often easily confused with the Late Chalcolithic Cream Chaff Ware. From the present data it appears that this mound was the location of small Early Chalcolithic and Hittite occupations.

054/23

NAME: Taşköprü
    Vilayet: Elâzığ
    Kaza: Merkez kazası
    Nahiye: İçme
    Village: —

NATURE: Mound

DESCRIPTION (Fig. 147): This site is relatively large in area but low. It is mostly meadow now. A small corner is cultivated. The surface of the mound is quite distinctive. It is extensively pitted by shallow depressions, like pockmarks. It gives the impression of a relatively recently abandoned settlement area where the foundations of the collapsed houses have rapidly been covered with a blanket of soil and grass. Vegetation is comparatively rich at this point, where a small stream running from a nearby spring joins the Haringet Çayı.

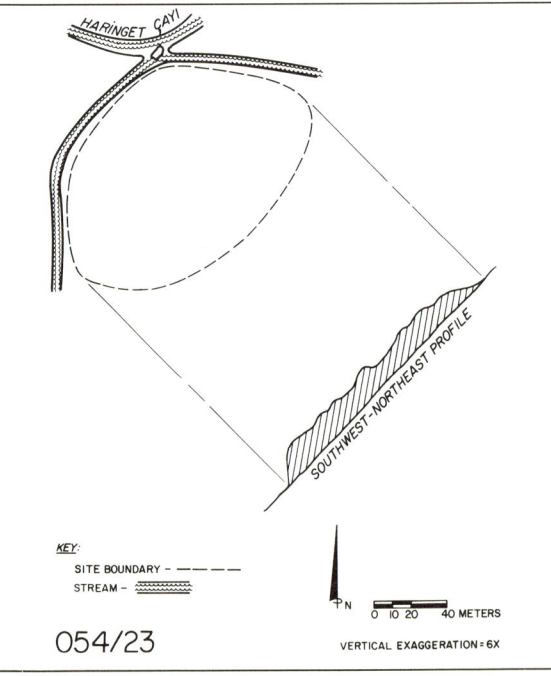

FIGURE 147. 054/23-Site plan and profile.

DIMENSIONS:
    Length: ca. 150 m northeast-southwest
    Width: ca. 100 m northwest-southeast
    Height: ca. 1.5–2 m

COLLECTIONS: Preliminary

OCCUPATION:
    Major—Medieval
    Present—Early Bronze Age I-II
              Hittite (?)

The relative importance of Medieval occupation here is shown clearly by the great variety of pottery of this period. Medieval Brick, Thick, Coarse, Red Slipped, Painted, Glazed, Sgraffiato, and even the rare Modeled ware were all recovered in the preliminary collection. The dominance of this late occupation accords well with the surface indications of relatively recent abandonment, with grass-covered irregularities resembling partially standing foundations still visible.

Some sherds were identified as Early Bronze Age Burnished, and there were also pieces classed as Hittite Plain, Exterior Wheel-Marked, and Painted. All of these were body sherds. In the case of the latter two Hittite wares particularly, confusion with later, Medieval materials is quite possible.

054/24

NAME: Şavka Tepe
    Vilayet: Elâzığ
    Kaza: Merkez kazası
    Nahiye: Mollakendi
    Village: near Haceri

NATURE: Mound

DESCRIPTION (Fig. 148): This is a very regular, round, low mound with no surface features. It is now under cultivation and lies on a small village road.

DIMENSIONS:
    Length: 110 m measured north-south
    Width: 100 m measured east-west
    Height: ca. 1.5 m

COLLECTIONS: Preliminary and gridded strip

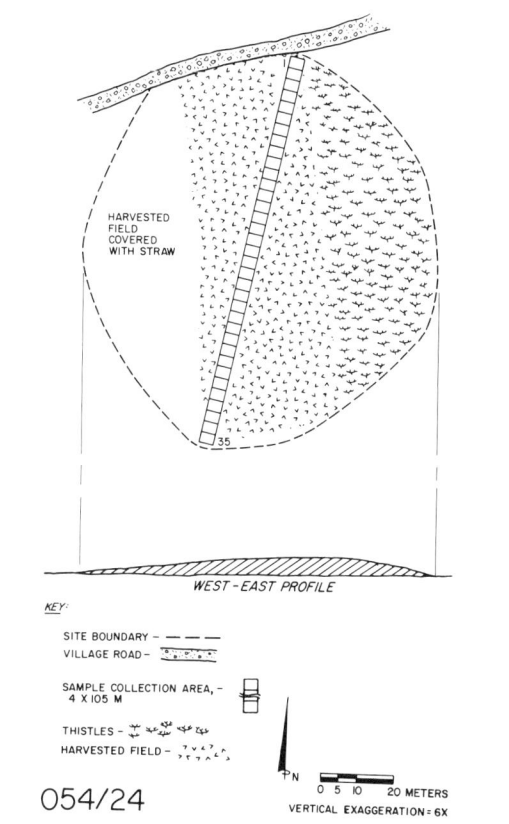

FIGURE 148. 054/24-Site plan and profile.

OCCUPATIONS:
    Major—Early Chalcolithic
              Late Chalcolithic
              Early Bronze Age I-II
              Hittite
              Medieval
    Minor—Early Bronze Age III
              Middle Bronze Age
    Trace— Iron Age

The variety of pottery of different wares and periods on this small site is amazing. One would be tempted to suspect a high degree of misidentification, but in most cases the evidence of the body sherds is supplemented and corroborated by the presence of more easily identifiable and diagostic rim sherds.

Only two body sherds were identified as Chalcolithic Ware in the first sorting and classification of the material from the systematic survey. Among the rim sherds were found ten of Chalcolithic Ware (e.g. Fig. 6:bb) and one of

Graphite Slipped Ware, however. This is a relatively large number of rims, and it seems rather probable that a number of body sherds identified as belonging to other wares, perhaps mostly to Early Bronze Age Burnished, are actually Chalcolithic. In any case, the evidence of the rims for a significant Early Chalcolithic occupation here is quite convincing.

Similarly, for the Late Chalcolithic occupation indicated by the presence of Cream Chaff Ware, 18 rims of this ware were identified (e.g. Fig. 10:g,kk; Fig. 11:d,e,k,jj), but the body sherds were initially classified as Hittite Chaff Faced Ware. This misidentification of the body sherds was evident from the exaggeratedly high count of the Hittite Chaff Faced Ware, higher even than Hittite Plain Ware here, whereas Hittite Chaff Faced pottery is relatively uncommon in all Hittite occupations.

The Early Bronze Age I-II is represented almost entirely by body sherds, only two rims of Early Bronze Age Burnished Ware (e.g. Fig. 16:ff) having been identified from the collection. Even if some of the pottery identified as Early Bronze Age is really Early Chalcolithic, there is still enough Early Bronze Age material here to indicate a significant occupation. Early Bronze Age Plain is even more common than Burnished ware, and the occupation may be relatively late in this period. Only three pieces of Early Bronze Age Thick ceramics were found.

Hittite occupation is weakly represented, at least in comparison with other small Hittite sites. Relatively modest quantities of Hittite Plain, Buff-Orange Burnished, Red-Brown Burnished, Brown Burnished, and White Slipped (e.g. Fig. 33:u) wares, and small amounts of Thick, Painted, Orange Smoothed, Fine, and Brown Gritty Cooking wares were present in the collection. There was also some Hittite Chaff Faced pottery, although it is hard to tell how much, since it was so clearly largely confused with Cream Chaff Ware here. Relatively few rimsherds were found. All together there were only five from three different wares.

The predominant period at this site in terms of the quantity of ceramics recovered was Medieval. In spite of relatively great quantity, the range of wares is limited and is restricted to the simpler, undecorated wares. Most of the Medieval pottery is Brick Ware, including 11 rim sherds (e.g. Fig. 41:j; Fig. 42:r). In addition, small quantities of Medieval Thick, Cooking, Coarse, White Slipped, and Red Slipped pottery were present in the collection.

A half-dozen sherds of Early Bronze Age III Red and Black Painted wares were also found. Perhaps these belong at least partly with the large quantity of Early Bronze Age Plain Ware mentioned above.

A relatively small amount of material was identified as Middle Bronze Age in date. This was for the most part Old Hittite Gray Ware (e.g. Fig. 21:h). There were also minor quantities of Middle Bronze Age Gritty, Old Hittite Light Faced Gray Ware, and Middle Bronze Age Gray Ware.

A moderate number of body sherds were called Iron Age, but only one rim of Iron Age Thick pottery was identified.

CONTROLLED COLLECTION: This being a small, almost circular, and low site, it was thought adequate to make a systematic surface collection from a single gridded strip run straight across the center of the mound. Squares measured 3 × 4 m, 4 m being the width across the strip.

System:
    Strip A: Direction 10°, length 105 m (35 squares)
    Squares A1-A35:   a cut (harvested) field

Early Bronze Age I-II, Hittite, and Medieval sherds were abundant enough to average, plot, and contour by average density along this strip. In addition, Late Chalcolithic Cream Chaff rims were plotted individually (Fig. 149), but this last

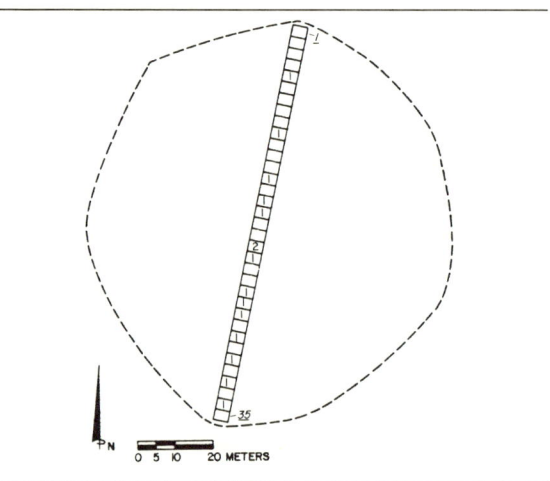

FIGURE 149. 054/24-Counts of Early Chalcolithic sherds.

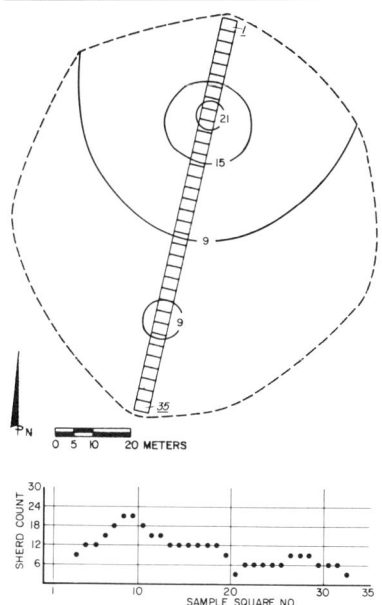

FIGURE 150. 054/24-Density contours of Early Bronze Age I-II ceramics.

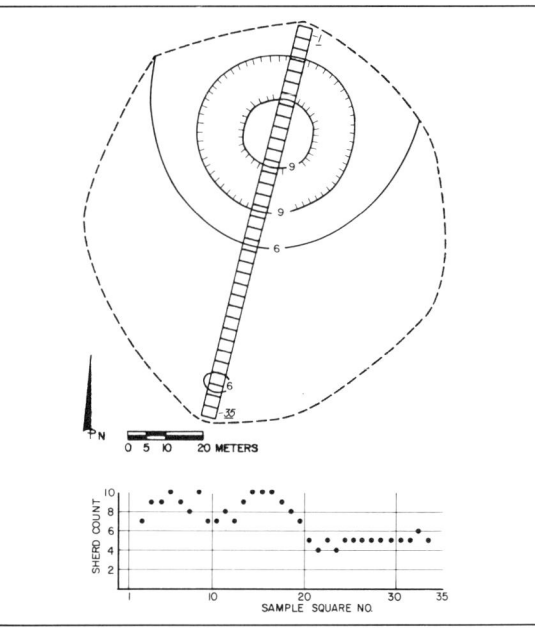

FIGURE 151. 054/24-Density contours of Hittite ceramics.

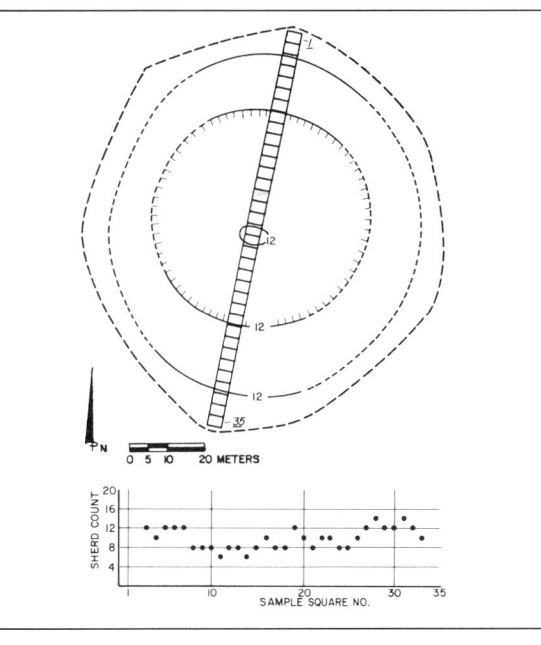

FIGURE 152. 054/24-Density contours of Medieval ceramics.

plot shows only the slightest tendency for these rims to be concentrated over the center of the southern half of the site. It is uncertain how much this tells us about the size and location of Late Chalcolithic occupation here. It seems in distribution and density to be relatively substantial, and a coverage of at least ca. three-quarters of the total site area seems a fairly reasonable estimate.

All Early Bronze Age I-II sherds taken together and averaged with a moving average over six squares show a clear localization over the northern half of the site (Fig. 150). This would give an estimated area of occupation some 70 m in diameter.

The sherds of all Hittite wares, expressed as a moving average over four squares, show an equal or stronger tendency to concentrate over the northern part of the site, in this case over an area estimated as some 60–65 m in diameter (Fig. 151).

Medieval materials on the other hand, averaged over five squares, show a pattern of distribution over the strip which suggests the existence of a band of high density running more or less around the periphery of the site (Fig. 152). Such a distribution is not surprising and strongly indicates that this late occupation covers the entire site area (ca. 100 × 110 m).

054/25

NAME: Körtepe
    Vilayet: Elâzığ
    Kaza: Merkez kazası
    Nahiye: Mollakendi
    Village: near Haceri

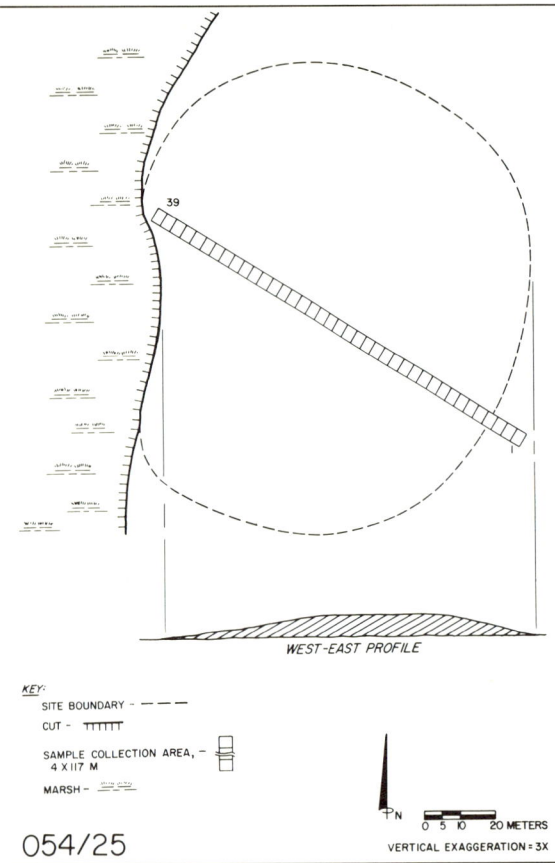

FIGURE 153. 054/25-Site plan and profile.

NATURE: Mound

DESCRIPTION (Fig.153): This is a small, regular, round mound of low height. There are no surface features, and it is presently cultivated. To the north and northwest there is a small drop, down into a wet, swampy area which appears to have encroached slightly on the west side of the mound.

DIMENSIONS:
  Length: 125 m measured north-south
  Width: 110 m measured east-west
  Height: ca. 2 m

COLLECTIONS: Preliminary and gridded strip

OCCUPATIONS:
  Major—Hittite
        Medieval
  Minor—Early Bronze Age I-II
        Middle Bronze Age

A substantial number of Hittite body sherds was collected from this site, including examples of Hittite Plain, Thick, Buff-Orange Burnished, Red-Brown Burnished, Brown Burnished, White Slipped, Painted, Fine, Brown Gritty Cooking, and perhaps Chaff Faced wares. Very surprisingly, only one rimsherd was identified as Hittite from this collection (Buff-Orange Burnished ware—Fig. 28:u).

The overwhelming majority of the ceramics on this mound were Medieval. Medieval ceramics included examples of all recognized wares, including the Modeled, Glazed, and Sgraffiato wares. Many rims were found, from a wide variety of Medieval wares. (For example: Brick—Fig. 41:u,v; Fig. 42:zz; Thick—Fig. 46:l; Glazed—Fig. 47:h,n,q; Red Slipped—Fig. 48:i; Fig. 49:f; White Slipped—Fig. 49:x; Fig. 51:h; Cooking—Fig. 52:f,n,q; Modeled—Fig. 54:c, l).

The Early Bronze Age I-II period is represented by a number of body sherds of Early Bronze Age Burnished, Plain, and Thick wares.

One sherd of Middle Bronze Age Gray and a handful of sherds of Old Hittite Gray and Old Hittite Light Faced Gray wares constitute the evidence for Middle Bronze Age occupation at this site.

CONTROLLED COLLECTION: A systematic surface collection was made from this small mound with a single gridded strip placed straight over the center of the site. Squares were 3 × 4 m in size, 3 m along the length of the collection strip.

System:
    Strip A: Direction 312°, length 117 m (39 squares)
    Squares A1-A39:   barren field

Analysis of the distributional patterns of both Hittite and Medieval material was possible.

All Hittite wares were grouped together, and the graph of their raw counts per square along the collection strip was smoothed by taking a moving average over six squares. These averages could be contoured easily. The results show a clear concentration of Hittite ceramics on the south-east side of the site, and it appears that this concentration represents an occupation area some 50–60 m in diameter (Fig. 154).

The counts of all Medieval wares, smoothed by taking a moving average over five squares, allowed a contouring of densities which indicates that essentially the entire site was covered by the Medieval occupation (Fig. 155). This gives an area of roughly 110 × 125 m for the occupation.

054/26

NAME: Maşatlık
    Vilayet: Elâzığ
    Kaza: Merkez kazası
    Nahiye: İçme
    Village: Habusu (İkizdemir)

NATURE: Mound or old cemetery.

DESCRIPTION (Fig. 156): Just to the north of the village of Habusu (also a mound—cf. 054/20, Kilise Tepe) is a small cemetery on an elevation, which may be a small mound. The cemetery is non-moslem (maşatlık as opposed to mezarlık) and is said by the villagers to be an old Armenian burial ground. This would, of course, accord well with the ruined church on the top of the mound on which Habusu is built, and neither church nor cemetery need be very old in archaeological terms. There were numerous sherds on the surface of this slight elevation, many of which were Medieval or later and could very well

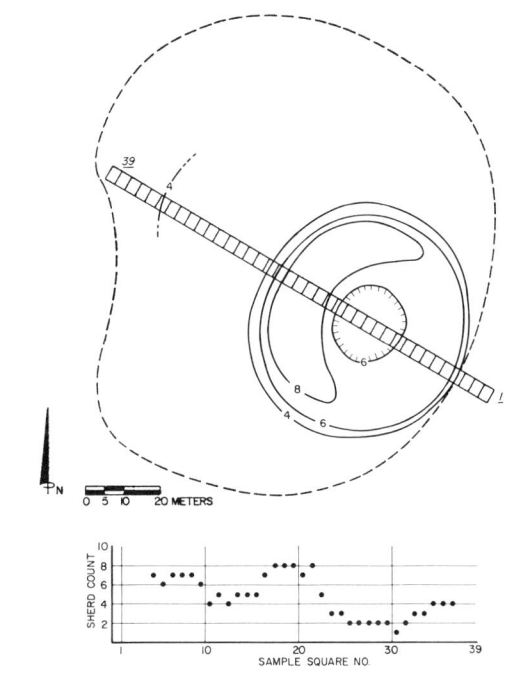

FIGURE 154. 054/25-Density contours of Hittite ceramics.

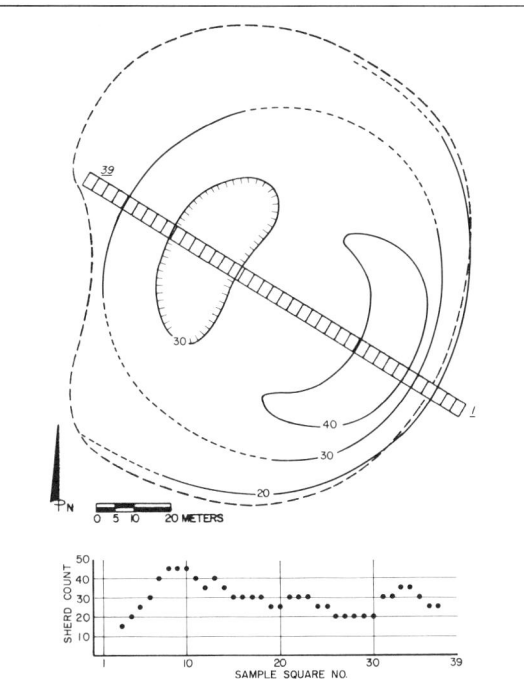

FIGURE 155. 054/25-Density contours of Medieval Ceramics.

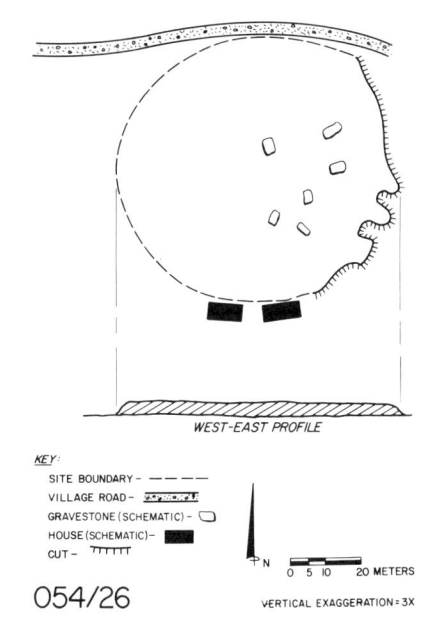

FIGURE 156. 054/26-Site plan and profile.

pertain to the Armenian occupation, but also others which were earlier. If these earlier sherds are not just materials from the main mound, 054/20 immediately to the south, which were dug up in the making of the cemetery, this could be a small, early mound. It is also possible that the elevation is simply due to grave digging. It seemed to us that some prehistoric occupation had occurred here but this is not absolutely certain.

The mound is presently left as grassland with some brush here and there. It seems to have been cut into irregularly on the east side, leaving a small profile. Village houses come right up to its edge on the south. On the surface, largely restricted to the eastern half of the mound, are several fallen gravestones. These stones are very eroded and mostly smooth and featureless, though on a few some sculpturing is still evident, seemingly mostly of human faces and figures.

DIMENSIONS:
    Length: 76 m measured east-west up to the cut where part of the mound has been dug away
    Width: 70 m measured north-south
    Height: ca. 1–1.25 m

COLLECTIONS: Preliminary

OCCUPATIONS:
    Present—Early Bronze Age I-II
    Middle Bronze Age (?)
    Hittite
    Medieval

No rim sherds were collected from this site. All wares were identified from body sherds.

The Early Bronze Age I-II is represented by Early Bronze Age Burnished and Plain wares. The Middle Bronze Age is represented only by Old Hittite Gray Ware and is therefore listed as questionably present. Hittite Plain, Buff-Orange Burnished, and Brown Burnished wares were identified in the collection. Medieval pottery included Medieval Brick, Cooking, Red Slipped, and Modeled Wares.

054/27

NAME: Gülüşanbaba Tepesi
Vilayet: Elâzığ

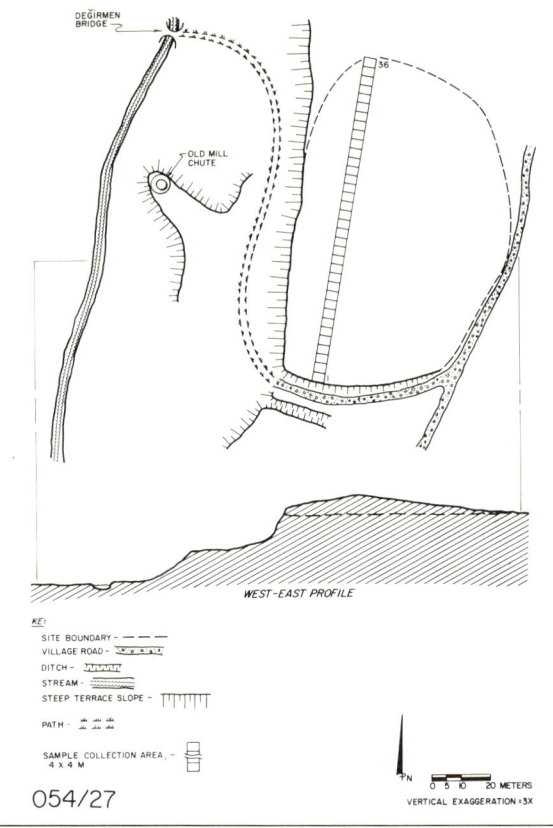

FIGURE 157. 054/27-Site plan and profile.

Kaza: Merkez kazası
Nahiye: İçme
Village: near Alişam (Harmanpınar)

NATURE: Mound

DESCRIPTION (Fig. 157): This is a very low, broad mound perched on the edge of the eastern terrace above the small stream the Karasu (tributary to the Haringet Çayı). Two village roads run alongside it, and it is situated just above an old mill, of which the stone foundations for the fall pipe are still standing. An early bridge crosses the Haringet Çayı at this point (*Doomed by the Dam* 1967:62). The mound has no surface features and is cultivated at present.

DIMENSIONS:
    Length: 110 m measured north-south
    Width: 75 m measured east-west
    Height: ca. 1.5–2 m

COLLECTIONS: Preliminary and gridded strip

OCCUPATIONS:
    Major—Hittite
            Medieval
    Minor—Late Chalcolithic
            Early Bronze Age I-II
            Middle Bronze Age
    Trace— Iron Age

The Hittite occupation here is manifested by a moderate quantity of sherds. These comprise primarily Hittite Plain, Buff-Orange Burnished (e.g. Fig. 29:k,r), and Brown Burnished wares. A relatively large number of Chaff Faced sherds was also counted, but there is some likelihood that most of these are actually misidentified Cream Chaff Ware. Small quantities of Hittite Thick, Red-Brown Burnished, White slipped (e.g. Fig. 33:k), and Fine wares were also found.

The overwhelming majority of the ceramics from this site were Medieval, however. Most of these were simply Medieval Brick Ware, (e.g. Fig. 43:c), but significant amounts of Medieval Thick, Cooking, and Red Slipped pottery, as well as a few sherds of Coarse, White Slipped (e.g. Fig. 50:a), and Painted wares, were recovered.

Late Chalcolithic occupation was first shown by the identification of one rim sherd as a Cream Chaff Ware type. (It had at first been classified as Middle Bronze Age Gray Ware.) It was then noted that the counts for Hittite Chaff Faced Ware were relatively high, and since the two wares were often confused in our first sorting and counting, it seems highly likely that many of these sherds are actually of Cream Chaff Ware. A small Late Chalcolithic occupation at this site is therefore very probable.

The Early Bronze Age I-II is evidenced only by some sherds of Early Bronze Age Burnished Ware and considerably fewer Early Bronze Age Plain sherds. A relatively large number of Burnished rims was found, however, and the presence of a small occupation here during this period seems probable.

The Middle Bronze Age is represented by some Old Hittite Gray Ware sherds, a few Old Hittite Light Faced Gray Ware sherds, and three Middle Bronze Age Gritty rims (e.g. Fig. 20:x).

Only a handful of sherds were identified as Iron Age.

CONTROLLED COLLECTION: This low, regular, and relatively small mound was collected in a systematic way with a single strip of grid squares run down its length over its highest part.

System:
    Strip A: Direction 10°, length 108 m (36 squares)
    Squares A1-A36:   harvested field

The collection squares were 3 × 4 m, 3 m along the length of the strip.

Hittite and Medieval ceramics were abundant enough to be averaged over several collection squares and plotted on the collection strip.

All Hittite wares were grouped including sherds designated as Chaff Faced Ware, although it may actually in large part be Cream Chaff Ware. It is only a small part of the total quantity of Hittite pottery, however, and even if it is partially misclassified, this should not effect the general results to a great degree. The counts of Hittite sherds were smoothed by taking a moving average over six squares. These averages were then contoured along the collection strip (Fig. 158). The results made it fairly clear that Hittite materials are generally distributed over the entire site area.

Medieval ceramics taken all together were treated in exactly the same way. The contour map

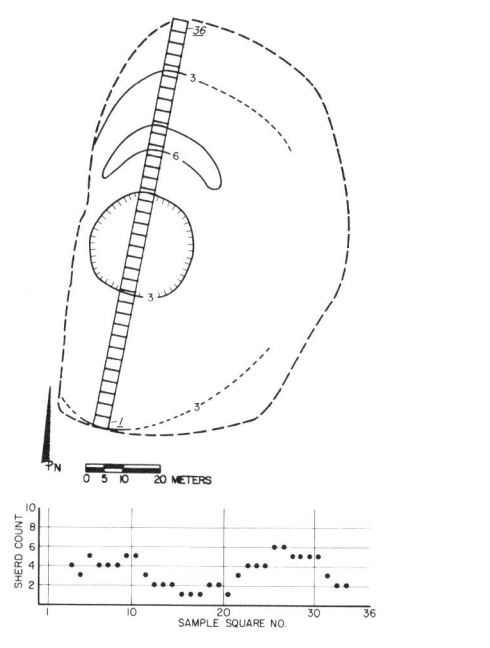

FIGURE 158. 054/27-Density contours of Hittite ceramics.

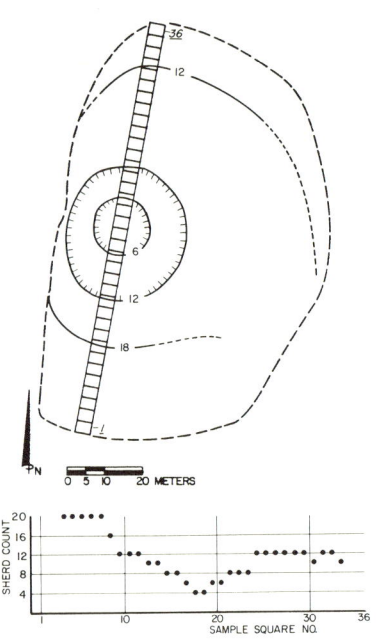

FIGURE 159. 054/27-Density contours of Medieval ceramics.

(Fig. 159) also indicates general distribution over the entire site. For both Hittite and Medieval occupations, then, we can simply use total site area as an estimate of occupation area.

054/28

NAME: Körtepe
    Vilayet: Elâzığ
    Kaza: Merkez kazası
    Nahiye: Mollakendi
    Village: near Şemsi

NATURE: Mound

DESCRIPTION (Fig. 160): This is a small, low and broad mound. It is located on the west bank of the Haringet Çayı. Irrigation ditches run from the Haringet Çayı here, one around the north edge of the mound cutting into it slightly, and another roughly east-west, straight through the center of the mound. The northern half of the mound is now used as a cemetery. The southern half is cultivated.

DIMENSIONS:
    Length: 120 m measured north-south
    Width: 100 m measured east-west
    Height: ca. 2 m

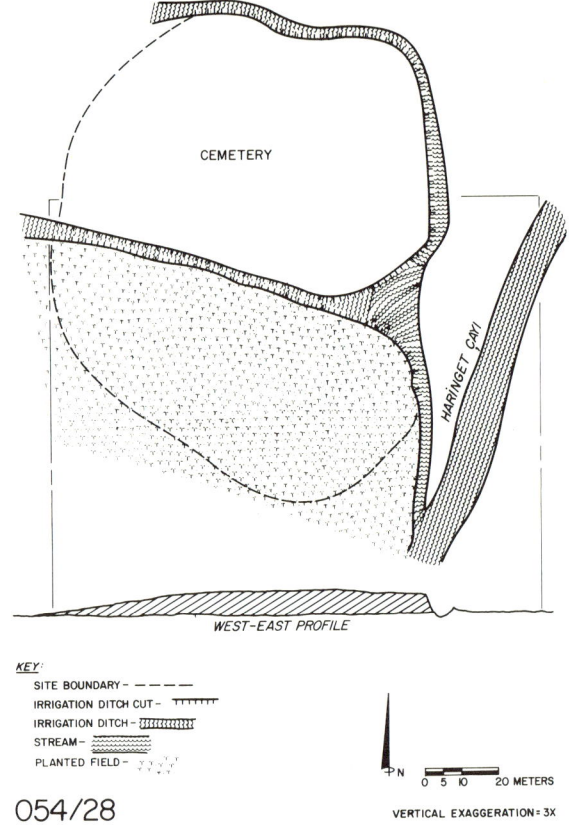

FIGURE 160. 054/28-Site plan and profile.

COLLECTIONS: Preliminary

OCCUPATIONS:
    Present—Early Bronze Age I-II
                Middle Bronze Age (?)
                Hittite
                Iron Age
                Medieval

The periods with the widest range of wares present on this site are the Hittite and Medieval periods. The Hittite ceramics include Hittite Plain, Buff-Orange Burnished, Red-Brown Burnished, Brown Burnished, and White Slipped wares. One rim sherd of Buff-Orange Burnished ware was found (Fig. 28:z). The Medieval pottery includes Medieval Brick, Modeled (e.g. Fig. 54:j), Thick, Coarse, and Cooking wares. Iron Age pottery is also relatively common, and the finds include one rim. For the rest, some Early Bronze Age Burnished and Plain ware body sherds and Old Hittite Gray Ware sherds were recovered in the preliminary collection.

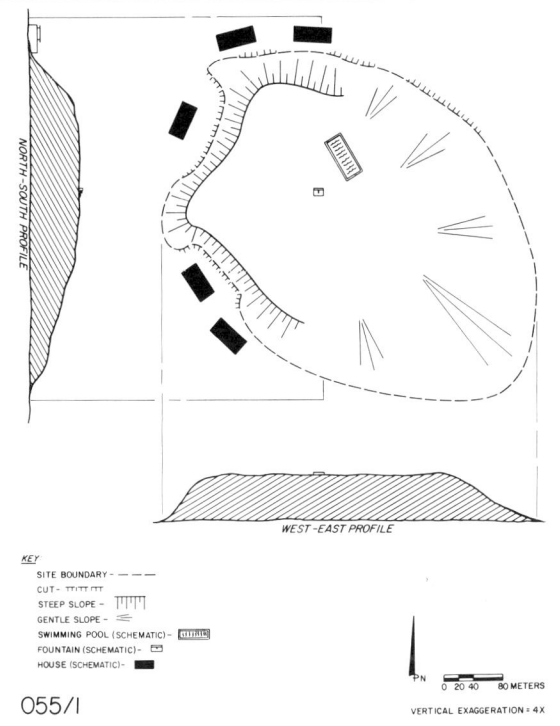

FIGURE 161. 055/1-Site plan and profiles.

055/1

NAME: Korucu Tepe
  Vilayet: Elâzığ
  Kaza: Merkez kazası
  Nahiye: İçme
  Village: —

NATURE: Mound

DESCRIPTION (Fig. 161): Korucu Tepe is a large, high mound. It lies in the old Elâzığ Sugar Factory farm (before relocation of the factory due to the Keban Dam project), and has been rather extensively damaged by the construction of buildings and other farm activities. On the western side of the mound a series of farm buildings have been built, and in back of some of them a very large and high cut has been dug back into the mound. At other areas around the edges of the mound smaller holes and cuts have been dug into it. The top of the original mound is relatively flat, with a slightly higher spot near the north end, again flat. On this latter area both a fountain and a large pool have been built.

In the large cut on the west side, mud brick walls can be seen, some burned, along with several burned floors. In at least two places houses cut through by the profile can be seen. Stone walls also show in the profile. At one point, a relatively heavy stone wall can be seen.

It is evident from its size and the evidence of construction visible in profile that this mound must have been the site of substantial and important occupation in several periods.

DIMENSIONS:
  Length: ca. 210–220 m northwest-southeast
  Width: ca. 150 m northeast-southwest
  Height: ca. 15–17 m

COLLECTIONS: Preliminary and from the large profile cut on the western side of the mound

OCCUPATIONS:
  Major—Early Chalcolithic
         Late Chalcolithic
         Early Bronze Age I-II
         Hittite
         Medieval
  Trace— Halaf
         Early Bronze Age III
         Middle Bronze Age
         Iron Age

The collection from this mound was not large. Consequently, the relative importance of various periods of occupation is not always as clear as at other sites and often has to be judged from the variety of ceramics present as well as from their quantity.

Chalcolithic Ware is relatively common, however, and several typical rimsherds were found (e.g. Fig. 6:g; Fig. 7:i).

Only one piece of Late Chalcolithic Grit Tempered Ware was recovered. The Late Chalcolithic period is otherwise well represented, however, by rimsherds (e.g. Fig. 10:d,f,j,z,aa) and a number of body sherds of Cream Chaff Ware.

The Early Bronze Age I-II ceramics are the most abundant from the site and include Early Bronze Age Burnished, Plain, Thick, and Red Slipped wares. Quantities are large, and rims are present from all wares except Early Bronze Age Plain (illustrated are one Thick rim on Fig. 16:i and one Red Slipped rim on Fig. 16:u). It is only surprising that, at such a large site with a major Early Bronze Age occupation, none of the typical Relief Decorated pottery of this period was recovered in the surface collection or from the deep cut.

With the Hittite period, we find evidence for a major occupation, not so much in the relative quantity of Hittite pottery as in the great variety of wares present. Only Hittite Red Ware was not found in the surface collections. Rim sherds were relatively common, especially of Hittite Plain (e.g. Fig. 24:g,i,mm; Fig. 25:g,i,p; Fig. 26:h,o,u), but also of Buff-Orange Burnished (e.g. Fig. 28:l), Brown Burnished (Fig. 32:d), Exterior Wheel-Marked (Fig. 28:f), Thick, Fine (e.g. Fig. 26:v,y,dd), Chaff Faced (Fig. 30:z), White Slipped (Fig. 31:a,b,g,i,j).

Similarly to the Hittite material, the Medieval ceramics are important at this site not for their relative quantity but for their variety. Medieval Brick, Thick, Coarse, White Slipped, Modeled, Painted, and Glazed wares were present in the surface collections. Rims were found for Brick Ware (Fig. 41:f,bb; Fig. 44:o), Thick Ware (Fig. 45:a), Coarse Ware (Fig. 47:d), White Slipped Ware (Fig. 49:ee), Modeled Ware (Fig. 54:h), and Glazed Ware (Fig. 47:m).

A single sherd was identified as "Halafian." A possible trace of Early Bronze Age III occupation was found in the form of one sherd of Red Painted Ware (Fig. 17:d). Middle Bronze Age ceramics from this mound comprise only a handful of Old Hittite Gray Ware sherds, including one or two rims (e.g. Fig. 21:y). The Iron Age is represented only by two rim sherds (Fig. 37:y; Fig. 38:k).

CONTROLLED COLLECTION: The majority of the surface of this mound was uncollectable due to recent construction, grassy surface, or thick growth of weeds and trees. On the western side of the mound, however, the large cut made recently for the construction of farm buildings offered the possibility of making at least an approximate stratigraphic collection of sherds. A number of general layers, delimited by color, texture, ash levels, burnt layers, etc., were visible in this cut as well as at least two cross-sections of houses and two or three house floors. Materials were therefore collected from this cut in 29 provenience units, of which one (No. 27) was reserved for material fallen to the floor of the cut and collected there (Fig. 162). To facilitate comparisons and interpretations, these individual provenience units were grouped into rough stratigraphic divisions (Table 7). Ceramics pertaining to the different periods of occupation were tabulated according to these divisions. The quantities of sherds from the Early Chalcolithic, Late Chalcolithic, Early Bronze Age I-II, Hittite, and Medieval periods were adequate for this purpose.

A rough stratigraphic sequence of these occupations can be seen from the sherd counts alone. This is made clearer by the addition of the percentage of the ceramics from each period which is found in each of the stratigraphic

TABLE 7   Sherd Counts from Stratigraphic Units in the Large Profile Collected at 055/1 (Korucu Tepe)

Stratigraphic Unit	Original Collection Units in Stratum	Early Chalcolithic		Late Chalcolithic		Early Bronze Age I–II		Hittite		Medieval	
		Counts	%	Counts	%	Counts	%	Counts	%	Counts	%
1	28	0	0	0	0	9	3.0	4	7.5	8	20.5
2	29	2	3.2	0	0	3	1.0	8	15.1	5	12.8
3	8, 21	2	3.2	1	9.1	20	6.6	13	24.5	7	17.9
4	7, 11, 16	3	4.8	3	27.3	25	8.3	1	1.9	1	2.6
5	5, 9, 17, 22	0	0	4	36.4	37	12.2	12	22.6	13	33.3
6	13, 14	3	4.8	1	9.1	20	6.6	0	0	0	0
7	4, 12, 18	13	20.6	2	18.2	64	21.1	2	3.8	3	7.7
8	3	2	3.2	0	0	3	1.0	0	0	0	0
9	23	1	1.6	0	0	1	.3	1	1.9	0	0
10	19, 24	14	22.2	0	0	35	11.6	3	5.7	1	2.6
11	25	12	19.0	0	0	24	7.9	0	0	0	0
12	20, 26	3	4.8	0	0	16	5.3	1	1.9	1	2.6
13	2, 6, 10, 15	6	9.5	0	0	44	14.5	8	15.1	0	0
14	1	2	3.2	0	0	2	.7	0	0	0	0

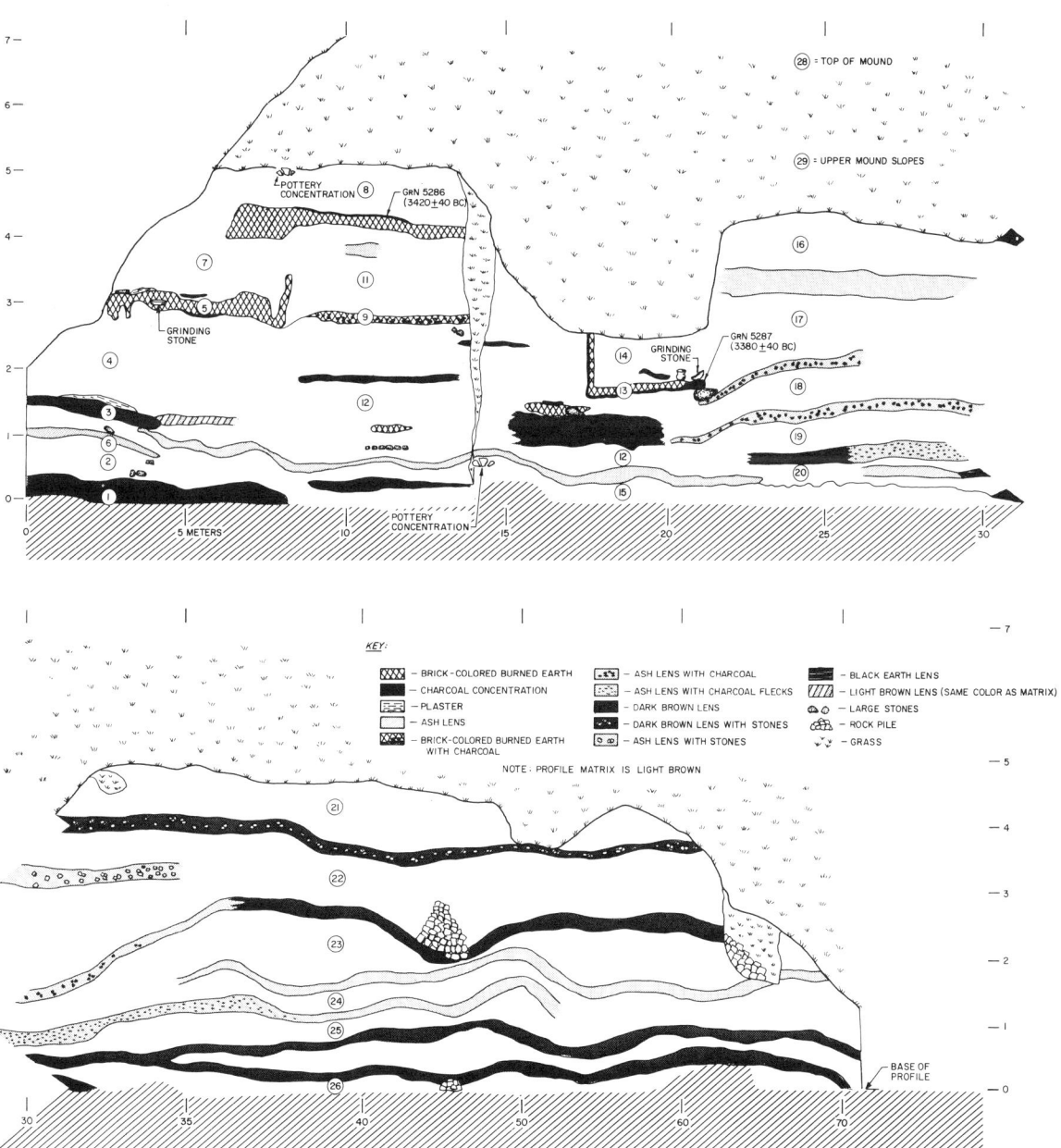

FIGURE 162. 055/1-Profile of large cut on northwest side of mound (split in half for purposes of presentation).

divisions (Table 7). It is also evident from this table that a good deal of detritus had accumulated over the face of this cut, in pockets and on ledges, bringing a considerable number of later ceramics down to lie on the exposed lower levels of the mound. This can be seen from the significant proportions of Early Bronze Age and Hittite ceramics, and even occasional Medieval sherds, that are found on the surface of the basal layers of the mound from our level 10 down to level 13. That these layers are Early Chalcolithic in date is clear from the relatively large numbers of Early Chalcolithic sherds found in higher levels, the significant quantities of these sherds in levels 10–13, and their continuous distribution on to level 14. With the degree of downward movement of materials evident from this tabulation, it was obvious that the major chronological divisions had to be defined from the tops of the distributions of each group of ceramics. In other words, the top of each occupation period had to be defined as the highest level in which a significant number or proportion of the ceramics of that period occurred.

Proceeding in this manner, the sequence is clear. Early Chalcolithic pottery covers a deep succession of layers extending from our level 7 down to the bottom of the cut at level 14. The Late Chalcolithic Cream Chaff Ware extends from level 4 down to level 7. Early Bronze Age I-II ceramics show a very long distribution, covering all or part of the distribution of practically all other periods. However, a high concentration of these materials begins above the Late Chalcolithic layers, in level 3. And significant quantities of Hittite pottery begin in level 2, although it, too, covers a long stratigraphic sequence. In the cases of both Early Bronze Age I-II and Hittite ceramics, a great deal of their occurrence over a broad stratigraphic range seems to be due to their downward movement as detritus over the face of this cut. Perhaps the higher levels were more dug into and disturbed than the lower levels of the mound so that relatively more material has eroded out and moved downward from them. Medieval ceramics are naturally most abundant at the top of the cut, coming from level 1, the upper mound surface, and extending a short way down the face of the cut.

From the results of this tabulation, we can generally say that the bottom levels, from level 7 on down, are Early Chalcolithic, levels 4–6 are Late Chalcolithic in date, level 3 belongs to the Early Bronze Age I-II, and level 2, above the main face of the cut, is Hittite, while Medieval material belongs to the top layers of the mound. Translating this picture into the original provenience units and plotting it out on the profile (Fig. 162) shows us a picture of a very substantial Early Chalcolithic deposit at the base of the mound, with much detritus on its lower levels. At least one, and possibly other house floors are visible in these layers. The profile recedes rapidly above this point, and Early Bronze Age I-II, Hittite and Medieval levels seem significant in terms of the quantity and variety of pottery recovered from them, but their real thickness cannot be seen in this cut.

An absolute character is given to this stratigraphic sequence by two radiocarbon dates, one of 3380 ±40 B.C.. (GrN-5287) from a house floor in the Late Chalcolithic levels and one of 3420 ±40 B.C. (GrN-5286) from a charcoal layer on a slightly higher floor (Fig. 162). These two dates agree nicely and place the Late Chalcolithic here at around 3400 B.C. in standard, uncorrected radiocarbon years.

Unfortunately little can be said directly about the absolute sizes of these occupations from the kind of collections and analysis made here. One would suspect, from the overall size of this mound and the relative importance of these four occupations in this cut, that they would all have been important in extent as well.

055/2

NAME: Altıntepe
    Vilayet   Elâzığ
    Kaza: Merkez kazası
    Nahiye: İçme
    Village: —

NATURE: Mound

DESCRIPTION (Fig. 163): This is a very small, low, round mound. There are no surface features, and it is not cultivated today.

DIMENSIONS:
    Length: 67 m measured north-south
    Width: 60 m measured east-west
    Height: ca. 2–2.5 m

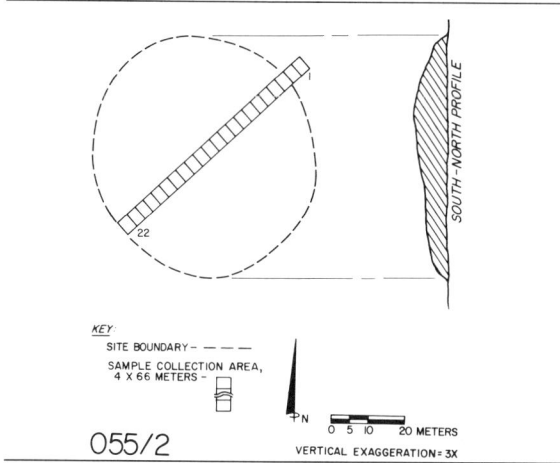

FIGURE 163. 055/2-Site plan and profile.

COLLECTIONS: Preliminary and gridded strip

OCCUPATIONS:
    Major—Early Chalcolithic
              Early Bronze Age I-II
    Minor—Late Chalcolithic
              Hittite
    Trace— Middle Bronze Age (?)
              Iron Age (?)
              Medieval (?)

The Early Chalcolithic pottery from this site comprises some Chalcolithic Ware and a relatively abundant quantity of Graphite Slipped Ware, including one rimsherd. The Early Bronze Age I-II period is, however by far the dominant period of occupation here. Early Bronze Age Burnished pottery is overwhelmingly abundant, while Early Bronze Age Plain Ware is quite common, Early Bronze Age Thick is well represented, and there are one or two sherds of Early Bronze Age Red Slipped Ware (e.g. Fig. 16:n).

The presence of Late Chalcolithic occupation at this site was largely noticed in the classification of the rimsherds. Several Cream Chaff rims were noted (e.g. Fig. 11:n), and it is likely that the relatively high count of Hittite Chaff Faced pottery here is indicative of some misidentification of Cream Chaff Ware as Hittite pottery.

A fairly wide variety of Hittite wares was found, although none of them in large quantity, and the total amount of Hittite ceramics from this site is not great. Hittite Plain, Thick, Buff-Orange Burnished, Red-Brown Burnished, Brown Burnished, White Slipped, Chaff Faced, Fine, and Brown Gritty Cooking wares were identified in quantities from one to 11 sherds. No Hittite rimsherds were identified. As mentioned above, some of the Chaff Faced sherds may actually be Cream Chaff Ware.

Only four sherds of Middle Bronze Age date, all Old Hittite Gray Ware were found. Five sherds of Iron Age pottery, including one rimsherd (Fig. 36:mm), were recovered. Medieval pottery consists of four sherds of Brick Ware and one sherd of Red Slipped Ware.

CONTROLLED COLLECTION: This being a simple, low, and regularly shaped mound, a systematic surface collection was made from a single gridded strip running over the center of the mound. Collection squares were 3 × 4 m in size, 3 m along the length of the strip.

    System:
        Strip A: Direction 228°, length 66 m (22 squares)
        Squares A1-A2:   a rocky field
               A3-A22:   a grassy wasteland

The Early Bronze Age I-II and the Hittite materials were abundant enough to average over several collection squares and plot over the site.

Counts of all Early Bronze Age wares were smoothed with a moving average over four squares. Contouring these average counts at six, ten, and 14 sherds per square shows rather clearly that occupation of this period covers the entire site area (Fig. 164).

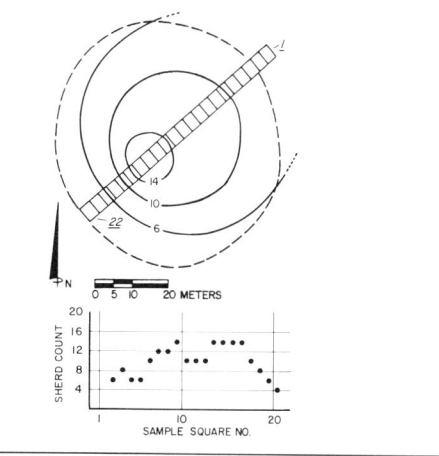

FIGURE 164. 055/2-Density contours of Early Bronze Age I-II ceramics.

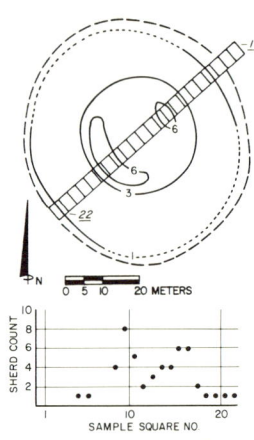

FIGURE 165. 055/2-Density contours of Hittite ceramics.

Similarly, grouping all Hittite ceramics and taking a moving average over two squares allows a reconstruction of the Hittite occupation area as also extending over the whole mound (Fig. 165). In neither case is this particularly surprising on such a small site.

055/3

NAME: Boy Tepe
    Vilayet: Elâzığ
    Kaza: Merkez kazası
    Nahiye: İçme
    Village: near Zertariç (Değirmenönü)

NATURE: Mound

DESCRIPTION (Fig. 166): There seem to be two distinct topographic parts to Boy Tepe. To the southeast there is a small but distinct mound with a flat top and abundant rubble from former stone construction. Southeast of this mound are some short, gentle mound slopes, but to the north and northwest the site extends a considerable distance as a series of sharply defined terraces. The terraces are undoubtedly of modern origin, with stone walls to keep the fields now cultivated on them from eroding, and perhaps to hold rainwater back for the crops. The distinctiveness of the two parts of the site (as well as the distinctively different materials that were found on each) seem to indicate that the mound to the southeast is a small, later occupation superimposed on a much broader area of earlier occupation.

The rocky, small mound is left wild. The site is otherwise largely under cultivation.

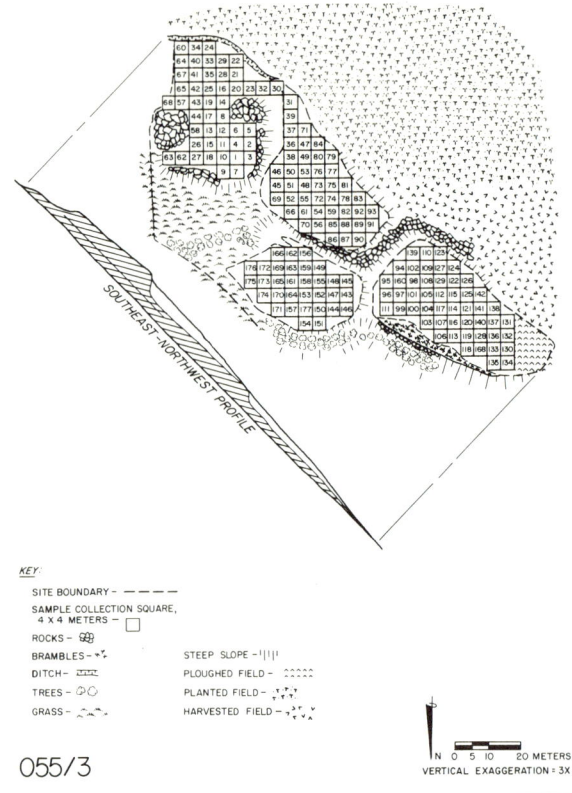

055/3

FIGURE 166. 055/3-Site plan and profile.

DIMENSIONS:
    Length: ca 150 m measured southeast-northwest
    Width: ca. 50 m measured southwest-northeast
    Height: ca. .75 m for the terraces, ca. 2 m more for the mound on the southeast

COLLECTIONS: Preliminary and complete gridded

OCCUPATIONS:
    Major—Preceramic
            Early Bronze Age I-II
            Hittite
            Medieval
    Minor—Late Chalcolithic
            Chalcolithic-Early Bronze Age Transitional
            Middle Bronze Age
            Iron Age
    Trace— Early Chalcolithic
            Early Bronze Age III

There appears to be a smattering of material from almost every period scattered over this site. A substantial quantity of material is found from only a few of these periods, however.

The Preceramic period has not been mentioned before, and it appears uniquely at this site in our survey. It is represented by a very distinctive chipped stone industry. The primary material is apparently obsidian, and the most distinctive tool types are made from this material. Flint appears to be closely associated with the obsidian, although the flint tools are not so immediately diagnostic for this industry. The preceramic chipped stone assemblage from this site will be described in detail elsewhere. It has, however, close affinities to the chipped stone industry from Çayönü Tepesi over the mountains to the south (Braidwood, Çambel and Watson 1969; Braidwood, Çambel, Redman and Watson 1971), suggesting a date perhaps as early as the seventh millenium B.C.

The Early Bronze Age is represented here by a large quantity of sherds. The majority of these are Early Bronze Age Plain Ware, which, along with the presence of sherds of Early Bronze Age Red and Black Painted wares, might suggest that the major occupation was late in this period, i.e. Early Bronze Age III. Only three sherds of painted pottery were found in a total surface collection of the site, however. The Early Bronze Age Burnished pottery was abundant, although less than Plain Ware, in addition, some 46 rimsherds of Burnished Ware were found as against none of Plain or Painted wares. From this, we have judged it reasonable to suggest that the major period of Early Bronze Age occupation is somewhat earlier than the Painted pottery, and that the few sherds of Painted ware indicate only a minor or insignificant occupation in Early Bronze Age III times. A handful of Early Bronze Age Polished, Red Slipped, and Fine Grooved Ware sherds completes the inventory of Early Bronze Age materials from the site.

Ceramic wares of the Hittite period are generally well represented at this site. All wares except Hittite Orange Smoothed, Painted, Red, and Exterior Wheel-Marked are present, in almost every case in significant quantities. Rim sherds of Hittite Plain (e.g. Fig. 23:z; Fig. 24:o), Buff-Orange Burnished, Thick (e.g. Fig. 27:t,u), and Fine (e.g. Fig. 26:aa) wares were also found.

There is no doubt of a relatively substantial Hittite occupation here.

There is equally surely a significant Medieval occupation of the site. Medieval Brick Ware is abundant, and Medieval Thick, Cooking, Coarse, White-Slipped, Red Slipped, and Glazed wares are also present. Unfortunately, very few rim sherds were found on the surface (one example is Medieval Brick—Fig. 43:l), but the existence and extent of the occupation are nonetheless evident from the large quantity of body sherds.

Of the less important or extensive occupations, the Late Chalcolithic was recognized largely from the reclassification of rim sherds. In this process a number of rims were seen to be of Cream Chaff Ware. These rims had for the most part been classified previously as Hittite Chaff Faced Ware, although one had been identified as Iron Age. These were not uncommon misidentifications of Cream Chaff Ware, and the somewhat higher than usual counts of Hittite Chaff Faced and of cream colored Iron Age body sherds undoubtedly reflect some confusion of Cream Chaff sherds with these other wares. The counts are not exceptionally high, however, and Late Chalcolithic occupation here can not be seen as extensive.

Several sherds of Reserved Slip Ware were found along with a number of pieces of Plain Simple Ware. The quantity is small but perhaps indicative of some presence at this site in the Chalcolithic-Early Bronze Age Transitional period.

The Middle Bronze Age may also have seen some light occupation of the mound, as evidenced by small quantities of Middle Bronze Age Gritty, Old Hittite Gray, Old Hittite Light Faced and Old Hittite Black Faced Gray wares.

A small amount of Iron Age pottery was also present in the surface collection. Although some cream colored sherds which were at first identified as Iron Age Ware were actually the much earlier Cream Chaff Ware, true Iron Age pottery did occur, including several rim sherds (e.g. Fig. 36:n; Fig. 37:f).

Finally, a small handful of sherds were identified as Early Chalcolithic. There are so few that we must think either of a very small occupation, one deeply buried, or the misidentification of a few sherds. Of these possibilities, the last is perhaps the most probable.

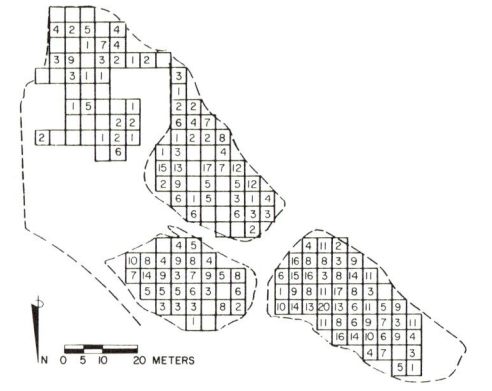

FIGURE 167. 055/3-Counts of all obsidian.

CONTROLLED COLLECTION: Because of our particular interest in the preceramic materials from this site it was collected as completely as possible. It was covered by a grid of 4 × 4 m squares, and all squares which were located on plowed field surfaces were totally collected. The plowed surfaces were the only areas where archaeological materials could be seen and collected in any significant quantity. The rocky and grassy surfaces were almost completely devoid of material. In this way a total of 177 squares were collected, of which 11 produced no remains.

There is a general separation of the early, preceramic occupation area from that of the later occupations in general. A plot of all obsidian from the site shows a clear and strong tendency for this material to be concentrated over the lower terraces (Fig. 167). In contrast, a plot of all ceramics shows them to be located primarily on the middle and upper terraces and on the small

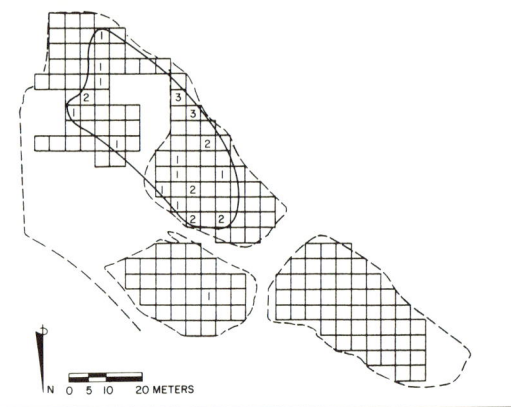

FIGURE 169. 055/3-Counts of Chalcolithic-Early Bronze Age Transitional sherds.

mound at the southeastern end of the site (Fig. 168). From among these ceramics, the specific distributions of materials from the Chalcolithic-Early Bronze Age Transitional, the Early Bronze Age I-II, the Middle Bronze Age, the Hittite, and the Medieval periods were abundant enough to show clear distributional patterns when plotted separately.

Ceramics of the Chalcolithic-Early Bronze Age Transitional period show a sparse, but relatively widespread distribution over the small mound and highest terrace, an area some 25 × 50 m in size (Fig. 169).

The Early Bronze Age materials are the most extensively distributed, yet they form a clear pattern of concentration over the entire area of the small mound and the highest terrace of the site in its present condition (Fig. 170). This

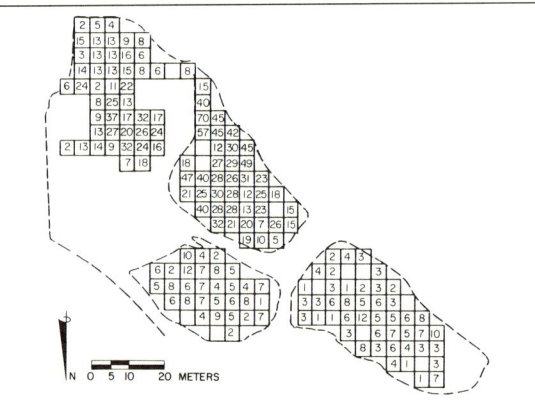

FIGURE 168. 055/3-Counts of all ceramics.

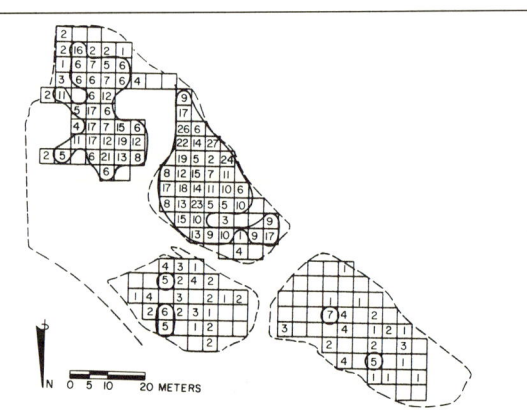

FIGURE 170. 055/3-Counts of Early Bronze Age I-II sherds.

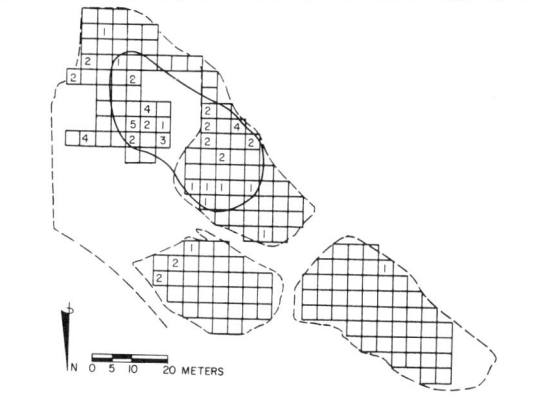

FIGURE 171. 055/3-Counts of Middle Bronze Age sherds.

distribution thus covers an area roughly 25 × 75 m in size.

Pottery of the Middle Bronze Age is not densely distributed over the site, but a plot of the counts per square nevertheless shows a relatively clear area of concentration over parts of the small mound and the highest terrace (Fig. 171), an area of approximately 20 × 40 m.

Hittite ceramics cover an area virtually identical to that of the Middle Bronze Age materials (Fig. 172).

Medieval wares, on the other hand, clearly are concentrated on the highest terrace only (Fig. 173). This is an area of some 20 × 30 m in extent. Medieval materials are generally absent from the other areas of the site. A small area at the southernmost tip of the site may show a slight, secondary concentration, but this is most likely nothing more than an insignificant, random scatter, such as is seen at a few spots elsewhere.

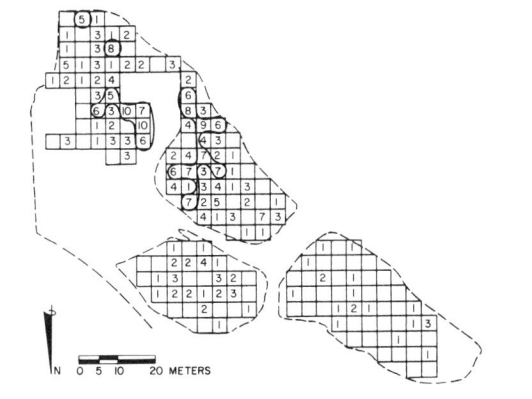

FIGURE 172. 055/3-Counts of Hittite sherds.

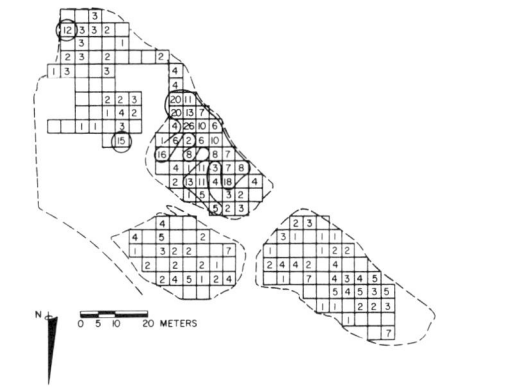

FIGURE 173. 055/3-Counts of Medieval sherds.

055/4

NAME: Körtepe
    Vilayet: Elâzığ
    Kaza: Merkez kazası
    Nahiye: İçme
    Village: —

NATURE: Mound

DESCRIPTION (Fig. 174): This is a very low, broad mound of small size. There are no surface features. It is now cultivated.

DIMENSIONS:
    Length: 145 m measured in a northwest-southeast direction
    Width: 110 m measured northeast-southwest
    Height: ca. 1.5 m

COLLECTIONS: Preliminary and gridded strip

OCCUPATIONS:
    Major—Hittite
        Iron Age
        Medieval
    Minor—Halaf
        Early Bronze Age I-II
        Middle Bronze Age

All recognized Hittite wares, with the exception of Hittite Painted Ware, were recovered from this site, most in moderate to abundant quantities. The most common wares were Hittite Plain and Buff-Orange Burnished, sherds of which occurred in

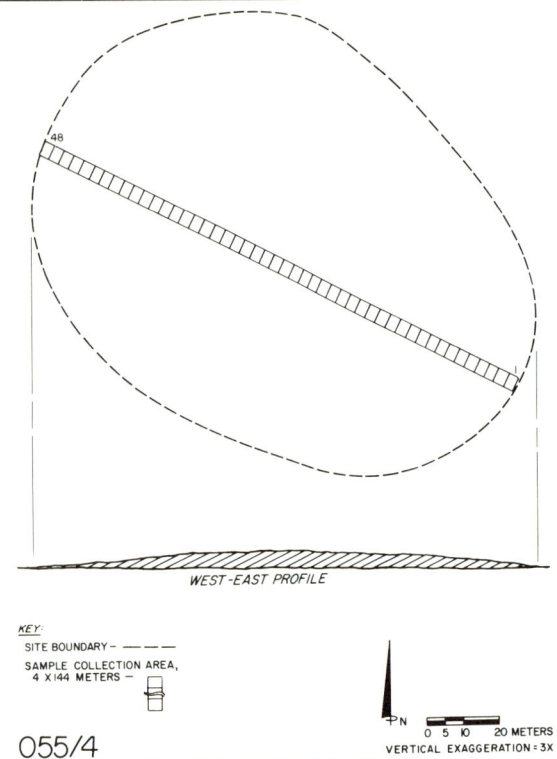

FIGURE 174. 055/4-Site plan and profile.

large numbers. Several rimsherds were also recovered (e.g. Hittite Plain—Fig. 24:ff; Fig. 25:c,m,ii; Thick—Fig. 27:g,i,j,l,o,v; Buff-Orange Burnished—Fig. 28:ee; Fig. 29:b,kk; Brown Burnished—Fig. 32:n,u; Red—Fig. 55:e).

Iron Age sherds were much less common than Hittite, but nonetheless, they were found in significant quantities. One rimsherd (Fig. 37:cc) was also found.

Medieval ceramics occurred in extraordinary abundance. All wares except Medieval Painted, Modeled, and Sgraffiato are represented in the collections. Medieval Brick, Red Slipped, and Cooking wares were by far the most common ceramics. A large number of rims of Brick (Fig. 41:p,q; Fig. 42:g,h,bb,ss; Fig. 43:p,aa), Thick (Fig. 45:p; Fig. 46:h,j), Coarse (Fig. 47:b), Red-Slipped (Fig. 48:g,o), White Slipped (Fig. 53:ii,jj), and Cooking (Fig. 45:t) wares were also found.

The Halaf period is represented here by a single sherd.

Occupation during the Early Bronze Age I-II is indicated by a tiny handful of Early Bronze Age Burnished and Thick ceramics, including several rims of the former (e.g. Fig. 12:qq; Fig. 13:c) and one of the latter (Fig. 17:g).

There are only a few more sherds of Middle Bronze Age pottery. These include one rim of Middle Bronze Age Gray Ware (Fig. 22:h), a rim (Fig. 21:h) and a few body sherds of Old Hittite Gray Ware, and a few sherds of Old Hittite Light Faced Gray Ware.

CONTROLLED COLLECTION: A single gridded strip laid down the center of the mound, over its longest dimension was collected in the systematic surface survey of this site. The squares were 3 × 4 m in size, being 4 m in width across the strip.

System:
 Strip A: Direction 295°, length 144 m (48 squares)
 Squares A1–A48: plowed field

Sherds of the three major occupations were common enough to allow averaging and plotting. The results were very similar for all three. All pottery wares of the Hittite, Iron Age, and Medieval periods respectively were grouped together and their counts per square smoothed by a moving average over six squares. Inspection of these graphs plus the contouring of these averages (Figs. 175, 176, 177) indicates for all three occupa-

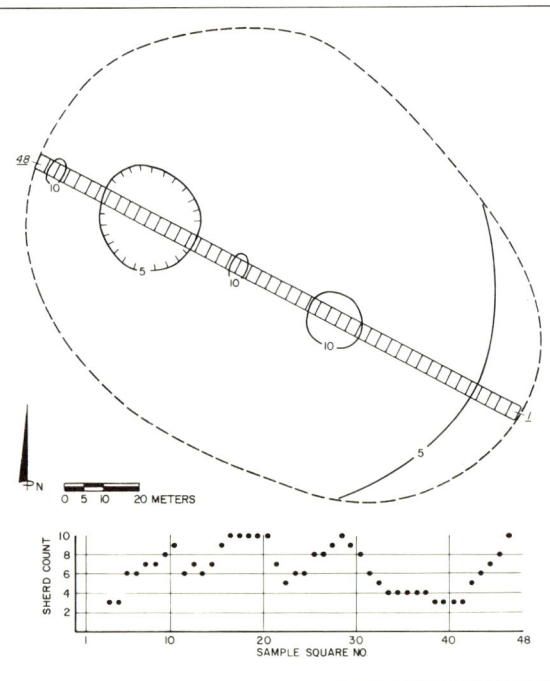

FIGURE 175. 055/4-Density contours of Hittite ceramics.

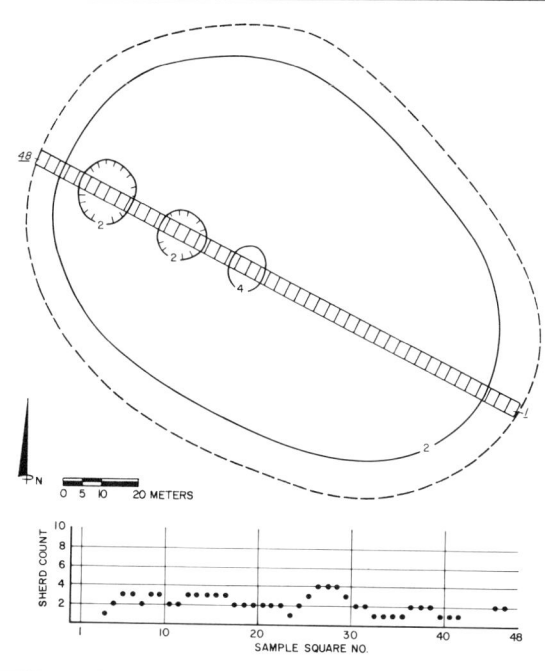

FIGURE 176. 055/4-Density contours of Iron Age ceramics.

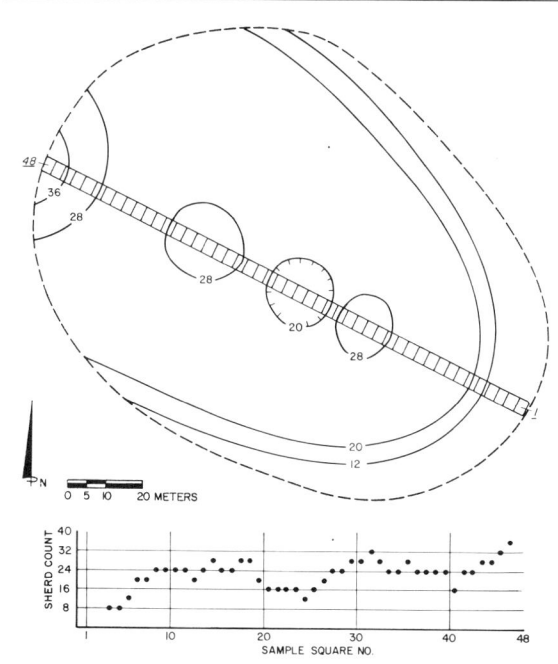

FIGURE 177. 055/4-Density contours of Medieval ceramics.

tions a general coverage of the entire site, with only local fluctuations in counts.

055/5

NAME: —
    Vilayet: Elâzığ
    Kaza: Merkez kazası
    Nahiye: İçme
    Village: Ahur (Saraybaşı)

NATURE: Surface scatter

DESCRIPTION (Fig. 178): A concentration of sherds was found here, in a field on a promontory high above the Murat River on its west side. The field is relatively flat and is just north of the village of Ahur. It sticks out on a point of land from which

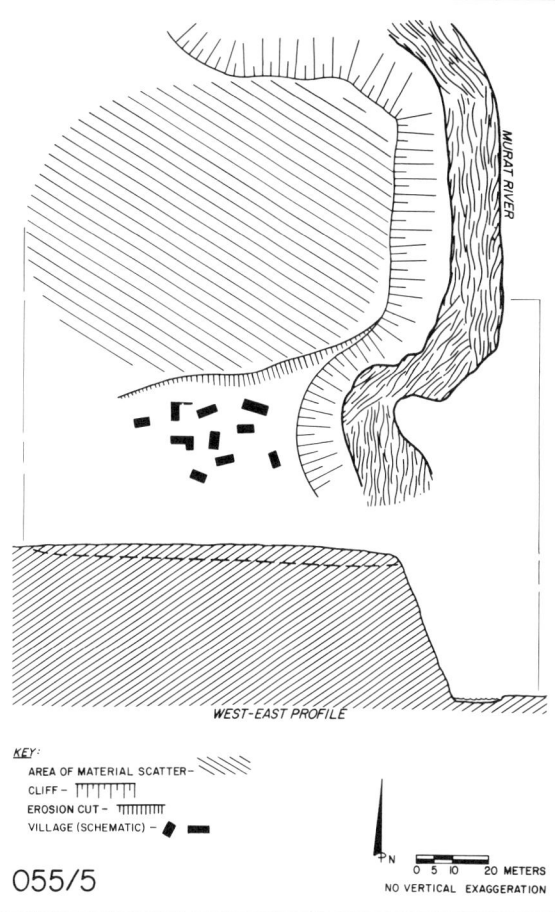

FIGURE 178. 055/5-Site plan and profile.

steep bluffs fall on three sides to the river far below.

DIMENSIONS:
  Length & Width: Materials were found in an area roughly 100 m east-west by 80 m north-south

COLLECTIONS: Preliminary

OCCUPATION: Present—Medieval

All of the sherds collected from this field appeared to be Medieval. Brick, Coarse, Cooking, Red Slipped, and Painted wares were identified in the collection. No rimsherds were found.

055/6

NAME: —
  Vilayet: Elâzığ
  Kaza: Merkez kazası
  Nahiye: İçme
  Village: —

NATURE: Surface scatter

DESCRIPTION (Fig. 179): This is a thin scatter of sherds in a field on a promontory high up on the western bluffs above the Murat River, north of the village of Ahur and of site 055/5. There was little archaeological material. According to the local villagers, however, stone foundations have been found while plowing.

DIMENSIONS:
  Length & Width: The materials are found over an area of roughly 50 m east-west by 30 m north-south

COLLECTIONS: Preliminary

OCCUPATIONS:
  Present—Early Bronze Age I-II
            Hittite
            Medieval

No rims were among the few sherds collected here. The ware identifications were made from body sherds. Early Bronze Age Burnished Ware was present. Hittite Plain and Brown Burnished wares were found. Medieval ceramics included Brick, Coarse, and White Slipped wares.

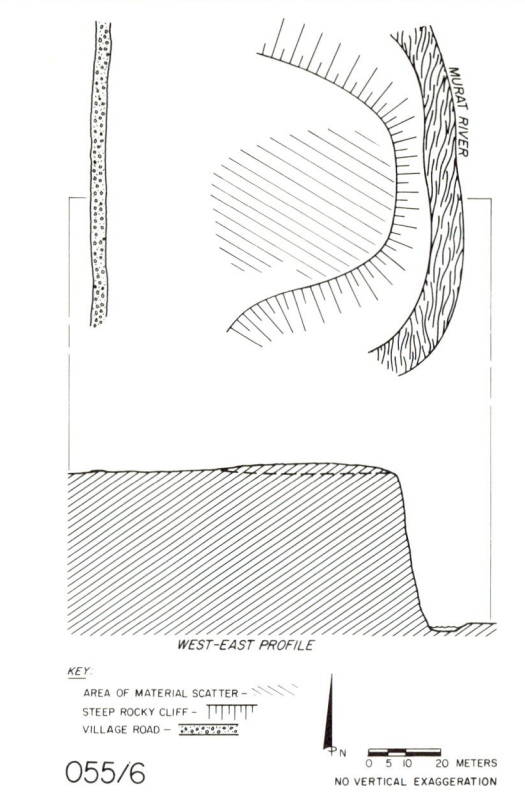

FIGURE 179. 055/6-Site plan and profile.

055/7

NAME: —
  Vilayet: Elâzığ
  Kaza: Merkez kazası
  Nahiye: İçme
  Village: —

NATURE: Ruin

DESCRIPTION (Fig. 180): A series of ruined, rough stone foundations were found here on a promontory projecting out over the Murat River, which is far below at the base of the bluff. Artifactual materials were scarce.

DIMENSIONS:
  Length: ca. 40 m east-west
  Width: ca. 15 m north-south
  Height: ca. .5 m

COLLECTIONS: Preliminary

OCCUPATIONS: Present—Medieval

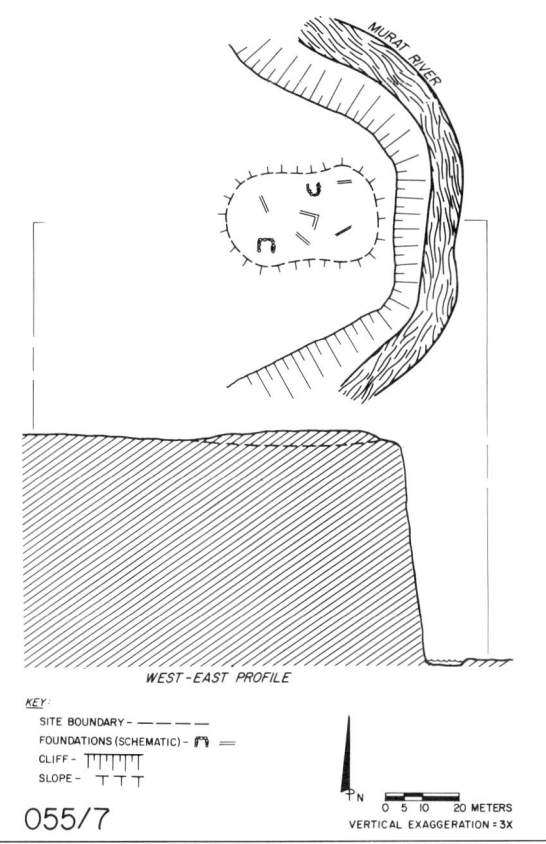

FIGURE 180. 055/7-Site plan and profile.

The only sherds found at this site were Medieval. Brick Ware naturally was found, but more distinctive wares, comprising Medieval Glazed, Modeled (Fig. 54:b,k), and Sgraffiato, were also collected here.

055/8-9

NAME: Körtepe
  Vilayet: Elâzığ
  Kaza: Merkez kazası
  Nahiye: İçme
  Village: near Habusu

NATURE: Mound

DESCRIPTION (Fig. 181): First recorded and collected as two separate, small mounds, 055/8 and 055/9 actually form a single, long, oval mound cut through by the old Elâzığ-Bingöl highway and the railway. As a whole, the site is relatively low and broad with no surface features. It is cultivated.

The Sites 253

North of the highway the mound has been rather extensively damaged. A village road and an irrigation channel cut into the base of the mound around the east and north sides, and the central area of the mound on the south edge has, in addition to the road cut, been extensively dug into and removed, perhaps as fill for the elevated roadbeds of the highway and railway. Archaeological material, particularly of the earlier periods of occupation, is exceedingly abundant in this disturbed area. South of the highway, the site has remained considerably more intact. The road and railway cut, and presumably borrowing activities, have cut a profile back into the mound that appears to be almost as deep as the occupation deposits. Beyond this cut, though, the mound appears undisturbed.

The overall shape of the mound is an elongated

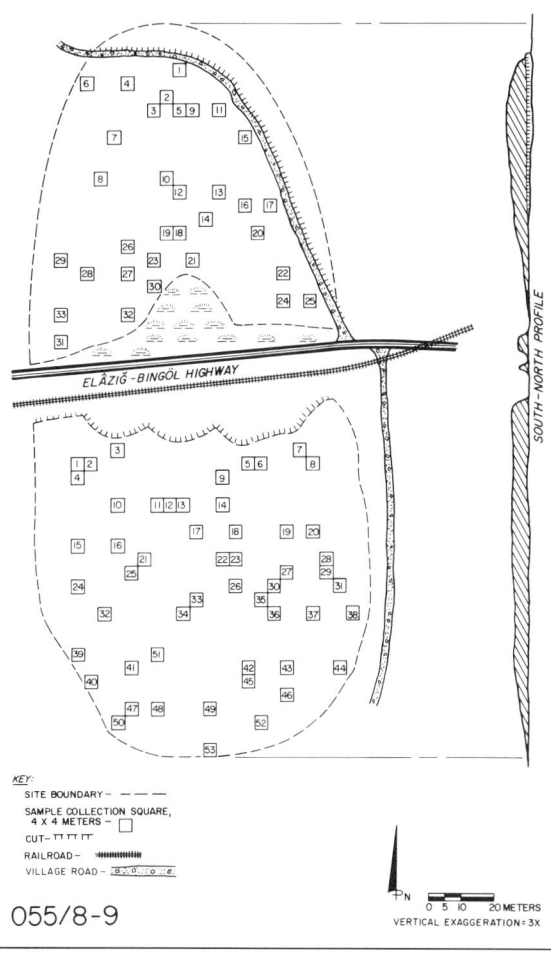

FIGURE 181. 055/8-9-Site plan and profile.

egg shape, with the narrow end to the north and the broader end to the south.

DIMENSIONS:
- Length: ca. 210–215 m measured north-south
- Width: ca. 100 m measured at the broadest point east-west
- Height: ca. 2 m

COLLECTIONS: Preliminary and gridded random

OCCUPATIONS:
- Major—Early Chalcolithic
  - Late Chalcolithic
  - Chalcolithic-Early Bronze Age Transitional
  - Early Bronze Age I-II
  - Hittite
  - Medieval
- Minor—Early Bronze Age III
  - Middle Bronze Age
  - Iron Age

The collection of pottery from this site is exceptionally rich, both in quantity and variety of material. This may in part be a result of the extensive disturbance of the site, but other sites at least equally dug into and disturbed do not show nearly this richness of surface materials. It appears that there has been almost continuous occupation of this relatively small mound from the Early Chalcolithic to the Medieval periods.

The Early Chalcolithic is well represented by both Chalcolithic and Graphite Slipped wares. Both occur in substantial quantities. Chalcolithic Ware is more common than Graphite Slipped Ware. Many characteristic Chalcolithic rims were recovered (e.g. Fig. 6:a,h,x; Fig. 7:b,e,h,j,m; Fig. 8:a,c,f), and a few of Graphite Slipped Ware were also found (e.g. Fig. 9:c,d).

Cream Chaff Ware is diagnostic of Late Chalcolithic occupation. Unfortunately, the collection from this site was classified and tabulated early in our laboratory work, and virtually all the sherds, especially body sherds, of this ware were confused with either Hittite Chaff Faced Ware or a cream colored variety of Iron Age Ware. This error can be largely corrected, however. Of the typical Cream Chaff Ware, 64 or 65 rims could be separated in the process of classifying the rimsherds (e.g. Fig. 10:c,h,i,k,n,o,s,v-y,bb-dd,ff,hh,jj; Fig. 11:c,f,g,l,m,o-r,t-w,y-aa,gg,ii). It is also obvious from the very unusual high counts of Hittite Chaff Faced and cream colored Iron Age wares that most, if not all, of the body sherds tabulated under these two wares are in fact Cream Chaff Ware. There is thus abundant and adequate evidence for a major Late Chalcolithic occupation at this site, and the distributional plotting of the identified Cream Chaff rims along with the almost entirely misclassified Hittite Chaff Faced and cream colored Iron Age wares allows a good picture to be drawn of the extent of this occupation.

The Transitional period between the Chalcolithic and the Early Bronze Age is indicated by two distinctive ceramic wares. Reserved Slip Ware and Plain Simple Ware are both new and clearly different from the usual Chalcolithic and Early Bronze Age pottery in this region. Both occur on this site, but the Plain Simple Ware is by far the most abundant, and several rimsherds were recovered (Fig. 9:p,r,u,w,x).

Ceramics of the Early Bronze Age I-II are extraordinarily abundant, by far the most abundant category of material on the site. The most common ware is, of course, Early Bronze Age Burnished. There are well over 1000 sherds of this ware, plus many typical rims (e.g. Fig. 13:a,i,jj,ll; Fig. 14:x,cc,ff,nn,ii). Next most common is Early Bronze Age Plain Ware, probably also at least partly related to the minor Early Bronze Age III occupation discussed below. In addition, Early Bronze Age Thick, Polished, and Red Slipped (including one rim—Fig. 16:o) wares and Fine Grooved Ware (also including one rim—Fig. 9:bb) are present.

Hittite sherds are also very abundant, and all wares except Hittite Red are present in the collection. A very few Orange Smoothed and Exterior Wheel-Marked sherds were found. All other wares occurred in moderate to relatively large quantities. Rimsherds of all these other wares, with the exception of Hittite Brown Burnished, were also recovered (e.g. Hittite Plain—Fig. 24:u,z,jj; Fig. 25:o,mm,tt; Hittite Buff-Orange Burnished—Fig. 28:v,nn,uu; Fig. 29:s,t; Hittite Fine—Fig. 26:x,jj; Hittite Chaff Faced—Fig. 30:aa; Hittite White Slipped—Fig. 33:y,jj; Hittite Painted—Fig. 34:j,m; Fig. 35:f). The count of Hittite Chaff Faced sherds is abnormally high, and as mentioned above, this is undoubtedly the result of misclassifying a large number of Cream Chaff sherds as Hittite Pottery. With only a little distortion, then, we can treat the category of Chaff Faced Ware as being in fact Cream Chaff Ware.

The Medieval period is also fairly well represented by sherds of all Medieval wares except Sgraffiato. Only Brick Ware is present in great abundance, however. Medieval Thick and Cooking wares are common, and the remaining Medieval wares are present in quantities ranging from a handful to single sherds. A number of rims of different wares are present in the material from this site, including Medieval Brick (Fig. 41:a; Fig. 43:m,dd; Fig. 44:i), Thick (Fig. 46:i), Coarse (Fig. 47:c), White Slipped (Fig. 50:j), Painted (Fig. 51:a,b,k), Cooking (Fig. 52:ee,ff,hh,ii), and Glazed (Fig. 47:p) rims.

Of the minor occupations, the Early Bronze Age III is represented by a handful both of Early Bronze Age Red and Black Painted pottery. Some of the common Early Bronze Age Plain Ware undoubtedly also belongs to this period, but none of the distinctive late forms of Early Bronze Age Burnished pottery were found here.

Pottery of the Middle Bronze Age Gritty, Old Hittite Gray, and Old Hittite Light Faced Gray wares was found, but only a few sherds of each, indicating only the possibility of some slight Middle Bronze Age occupation here.

The Iron Age is similarly slightly represented. At first, the counts of Iron Age Ware were high, but it was found that this was primarily due to large quantities of a cream colored variety. Later, this variety of pottery was recognized to be Cream Chaff Ware, from the Late Chalcolithic period. There is only a modest amount of true Iron Age pottery, including one or two rims (e.g. Fig. 37:b).

CONTROLLED COLLECTION: Both sections of this mound were gridded into 4x4 m squares, and a random sample of collection squares selected. Enough squares were chosen on each section of the site to cover at least ten percent of the remaining mound surface. This resulted in the collection of 33 squares on the northern part of the site (055/8) and 53 squares on the southern part (055/9). The sherds of all the wares pertaining to each period of occupation were grouped together and plotted over the site. Ceramics of the periods of major occupation were numerous enough to allow density contouring of these

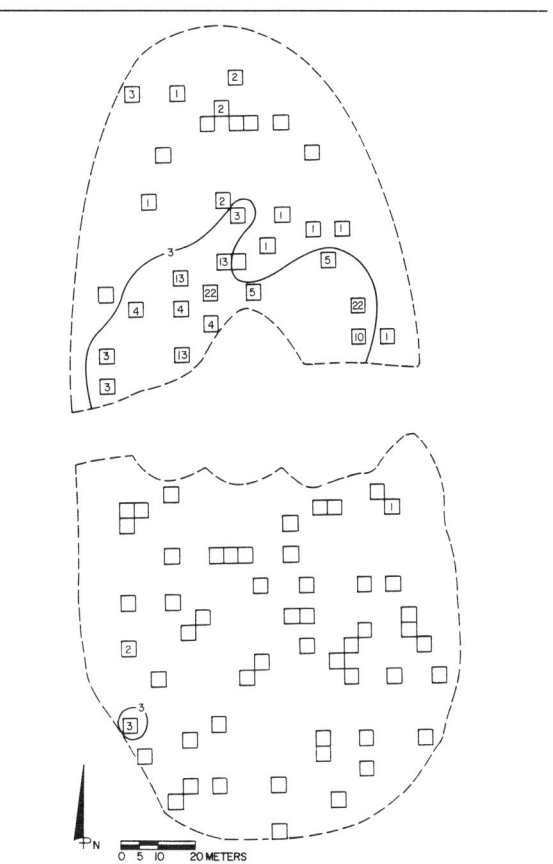

FIGURE 182. 055/8-9-Density contours of Early Chalcolithic ceramics.

grouped counts and an estimate of the extent of each occupation.

The counts of Early Chalcolithic materials are very variable from square to square (Fig. 182). It is difficult to contour them. Inspection of the raw counts indicates a clear concentration, however, and enclosing the area of concentration simply with a contour line representing a density of at least three sherds per square rather neatly defines an area approximately 60 x 80 m in size. This is probably a minimal area, since the concentration occurs in the area where the mound has been deeply dug into. Virtually no sherds of this period are found on the southern portion of the mound, however, and although it is perhaps minimal and influenced by disturbance, the area delimited by this contour line is probably not too far from a good representation of the extent of Early Chalcolithic occupation here.

The Late Chalcolithic occupation was plotted using the distribution of identified Cream Chaff rims, Hittite Chaff Faced Ware, and the cream

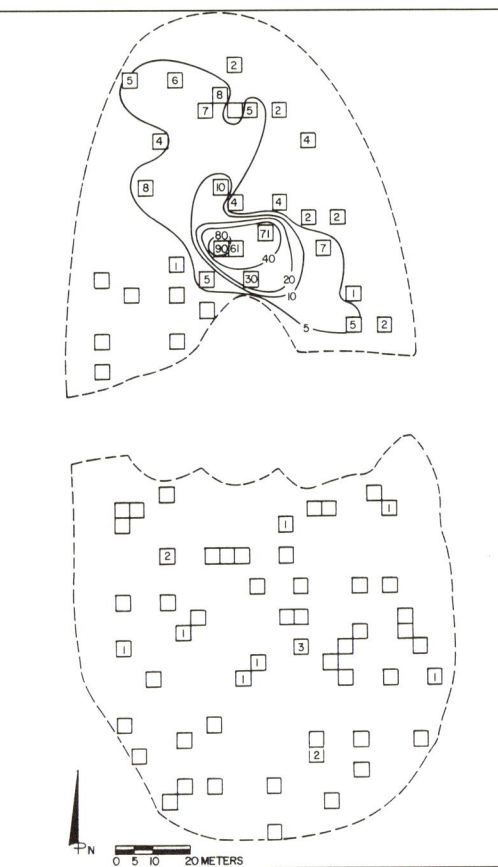

FIGURE 183. 055/8-9-Density contours of Late Chalcolithic ceramics.

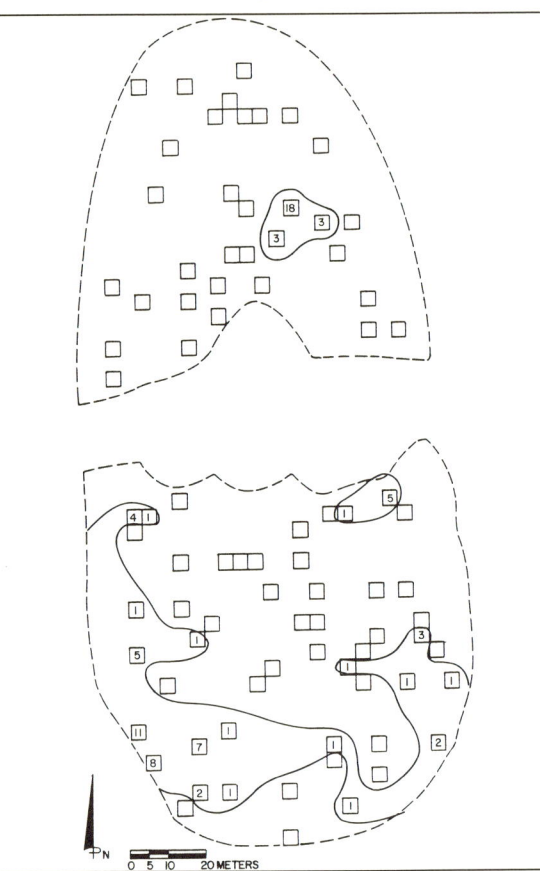

FIGURE 184. 055/8-9-Density contours of Chalcolithic-Early Bronze Age Transitional ceramics.

colored variety of Iron Age Ware. Although there is very likely some true Hittite and Iron Age material mixed in with this grouping, it is, as discussed above, likely to be only minor with respect to the Cream Chaff Ware which it represents. This can also be seen clearly from the fact that the distribution of body sherds of these two "Hittite" and "Iron Age" wares corresponds very closely to that of the identified Cream Chaff rims. Contours drawn around these counts show a clear and highly concentrated distribution of Late Chalcolithic materials over the northern portion of the mound (Fig. 183). Densities are unusually and exceedingly high in the area of mound disturbance here, and it seems clear that the Late Chalcolithic level has been directly dug into. The general distribution of this pottery, particularly of the rim sherds, is much more extensive, however, and the suggested total occupation area seems to be almost 200 x 80 m in size.

Sherds of the two wares from the Chalcolithic-Early Bronze Age Transitional period are rela-

tively rare. Plotting the counts of Reserved Slip and Plain Simple wares shows no clear way to contour them other than to simply enclose the entire area within which these wares are found by a single line (Fig. 184). This reveals a pattern of distribution largely restricted to the southern portion of the site, and a largely peripheral distribution there. Such a pattern could best be interpreted as reflecting the erosion of the edge of an underlying occupation layer covering this whole area of the mound, an area approximately 100 x 110 m in extent.

For the Early Bronze Age I-II, the situation is much more clear-cut. Plotting and contouring the counts of all Early Bronze Age I-II ceramics together (Fig. 185) makes it evident that materials of this period are distributed in significant numbers over the entire mound, an area roughly 100 x 210 m in size.

The same is true for the Hittite materials. Here all Hittite wares except Hittite Chaff Faced were grouped and plotted (Fig. 186). Again, it is

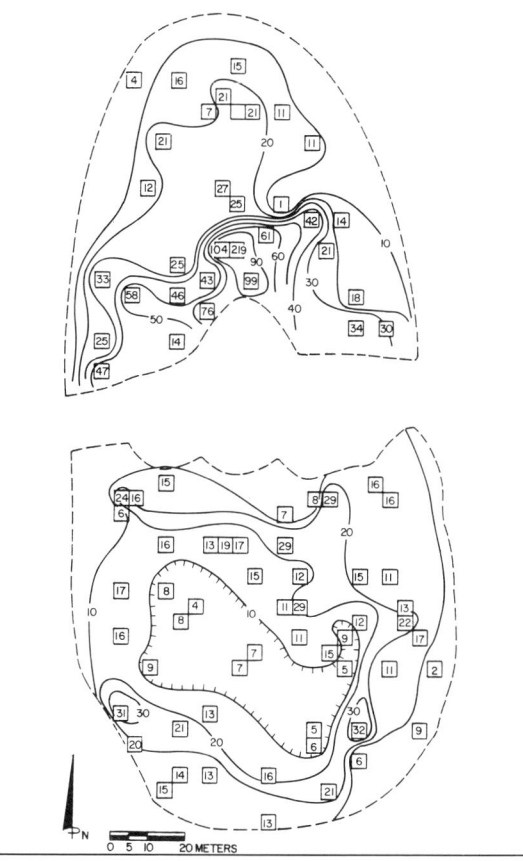

FIGURE 185. 055/8-9-Density contours of Early Bronze Age I-II ceramics.

evident that occupation of this period extended over the whole site.

When all Medieval ceramics are plotted together, there appears a light coverage of the whole site, but it is the central area, where contour lines representing densities of 6–12 sherds per square can be drawn, that seems to be the major location of this occupation (Fig. 187). Although it could be argued from this picture that a short occupation had covered the entire mound, we prefer to interpret this pattern as the result of a smaller occupation, perhaps some 60 x 180 m in size, as estimated from the area enclosed by the density contour lines, away from which a light, secondary scatter of sherds has been spread.

055/10

NAME: Aşağı Şeyhacı Tepesi
    Vilayet: Elâzığ
    Kaza: Merkez Kazası
    Nahiye: İçme
    Village: Aşağı Şeyhacı

NATURE: Mound

DESCRIPTION (Fig. 188): This appears to be a moderately large and high mound, but it is difficult to tell exactly, since it is completely covered by a modern village. In addition, the location is near the edge of the Altınova valley floor, where the terrain begins to be hilly, and the mound proper may be situated on a natural hill. It does appear, however, that at least a substantial proportion of the height consists of occupation deposits. In the village there are only one or two places where the mound has been dug into in a small way. All together it was not possible to make good observations on this mound, and little archaeological material could be collected.

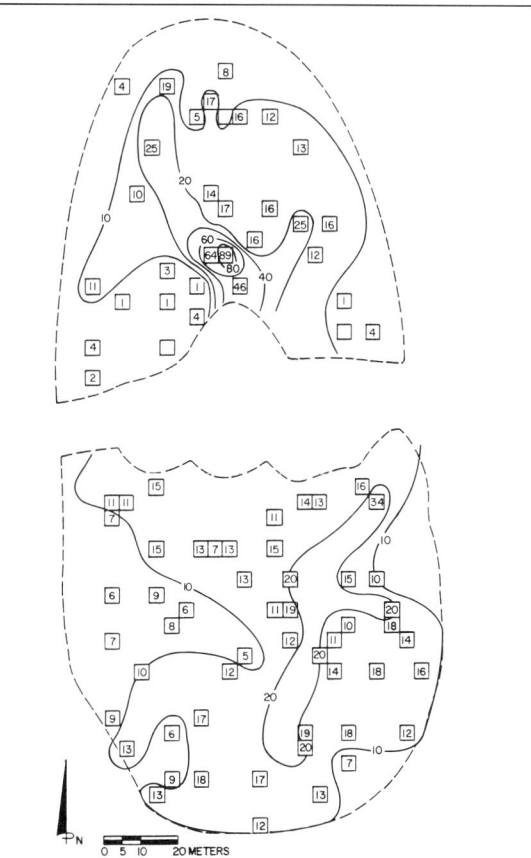

FIGURE 186. 055/8-9-Density contours of Hittite ceramics.

DIMENSIONS:
   Length: ca. 150 m north-south
   Width: ca. 100–125 m east-west
   Height: ca. 8–9 m

COLLECTIONS: Preliminary

OCCUPATIONS:
   Present—Early Bronze Age I-II
            Early Bronze Age IIIA
            Medieval
   Trace— Hittite

Unfortunately no rimsherds were recovered from this mound. Early Bronze Age ceramics were nevertheless easily identified. Early Bronze

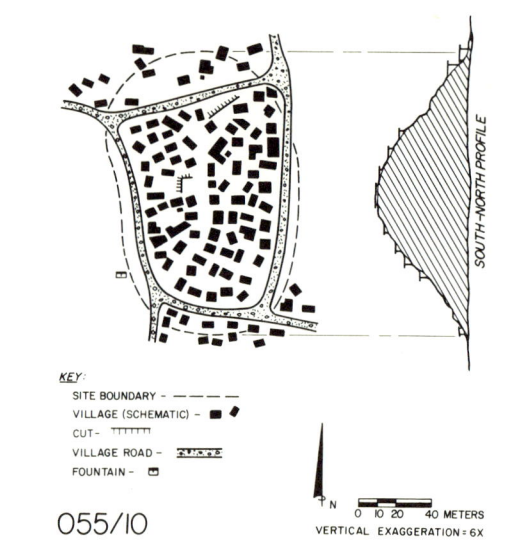

FIGURE 188. 055/10-Site plan and profile.

Age Burnished, Plain, and Polished wares were found in some numbers, and a sherd or two identified as Early Bronze Age Red Painted Ware were also present. There is nothing more available from the small preliminary collection to tell us whether these materials represent an occupation running from the Early Bronze Age I up into the early part of the Early Bronze Age III period or whether only the later period is present. None of the distinctively earlier Relief Decorated Ware was found, but it is generally rare, and aside from the occasional painted pieces no distinctive forms or decorative elements were noted from either early or late in the sequence. Impressionistically, judging by the preponderance of Burnished, Plain, and Polished wares, we would guess that at least the Early Bronze Age II-IIIA periods are present at this site.

Medieval ceramics include Brick Ware, Cooking Ware, White Slipped and Red Slipped wares, and Glazed pottery. Some of this pottery could be modern, and the mound has very likely been continuously occupied for some time.

The presence of Hittite occupation is uncertain and is based only on the identification of Hittite Plain Ware from the body sherds in the collection.

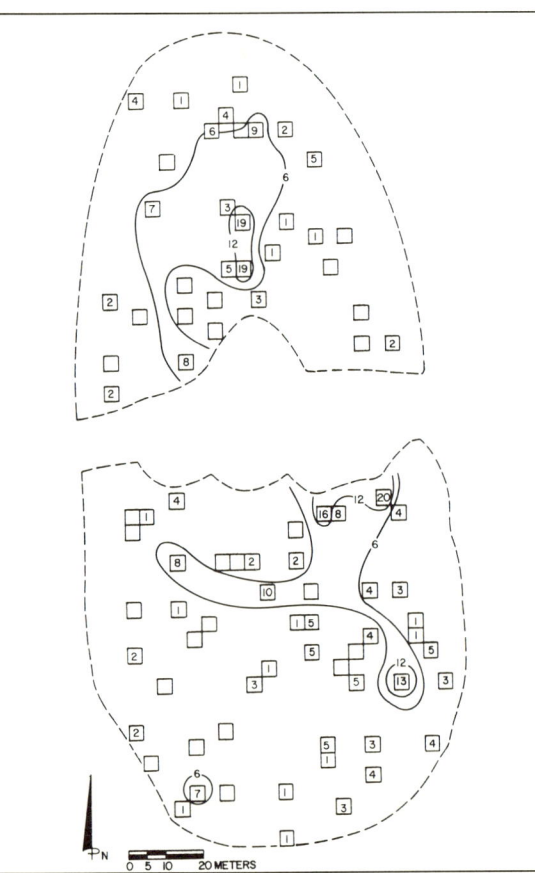

FIGURE 187. 055/8-9-Density contours of Medieval ceramics.

4

Settlement Patterns

We can now present a rough outline of the settlement pattern revealed by the survey for each of the major periods recognized. There are two major aspects of settlement pattern—site distribution and site size—which we can consider with the data at hand (Table 8). Together, they give us some idea of population distribution, aggregation, and density for each period. In addition, it is often possible to show that size is related to site position in a regional network of sites. This then allows some inference of centralized functions for larger sites, depending on the degree of size differentiation among the sites.

For each period, therefore, we begin with a tabulation of occupation size as determined from the results of controlled surface collections. To this is added a tabulation of estimated areas of occupation from those sites on which only general surface collections were made or for which the results of the controlled collections were not clear. Only occupations which were characterized as "major," "minor," and definitely "present" are included in this analysis. Questionable and "trace" occupations are not considered.

From frequency histograms of these occupation areas, several size classes are defined, and the distributions of occupations in these classes are plotted over selected portions of the survey area for each period. It is from these distribution maps that inferences about regional networks of sites and about central place locations and functions of various sites in these networks are made. Such inferences are generally only possible for the broad Altınova plain. To a much lesser extent they are sometimes possible in the Aşvan area.

Finally, from a chronological plot of the sum of all occupation areas (both measured and estimated) in each period, we can attempt to say something about trends and patterns in relative population density for the survey area.

ESTIMATION OF OCCUPATION AREA

In order to combine the data on size of occupation from sites on which this had been measured by controlled surface collections and sites from which only general surface collections were available, some method for estimating occupation sizes for these latter sites was necessary. Total site size was known for these sites. However, the size of individual occupations was very rarely equal to total site size on any of the sites at which occupation areas were measured, with the exception of extremely small sites and the few single-occupation sites. This can be seen clearly in Figs. 189 and 190, where occupation areas are plotted against total site size for all occupations on all sites at which more than one occupation was measured from the results of controlled surface collections.

These graphs were used to establish a procedure for estimating occupation size at other sites.

TABLE 8 Summary of site sizes and known and measured occupations on surveyed sites in the Keban Reservoir area*

Site	Total Site Size†	Preceramic	Early Chalcolithic	Middle Chalcolithic (Halaf)	Late Chalcolithic	Transitional
N52/1	1.8		1.0			+
N52/2	ca. 2.0					
N52/3	.7		.7		.2	
N52/4	.9					
N52/5	.8					
N52/6	.7					
N52/7	.1					
N52/8	1.6					
N52/9	ca. .5		+		.1	
N52/10	.8					
N52/11	.9					
N53/1	.2					
N53/3	.5					
N55/1	2–3 est.			+		+
O54/1	4 est.		+	+	+	+
O54/2	5.3		+		+	+
O54/3	ca. 2.0				+	
O54/4	Insignificant					
O54/5	.8					
O54/6	1.7		.6		.9	
O54/7	ca. 6.9		+			
O54/8	ca. 16.0		2.5		1.8	
O54/9	.6					
O54/10	1.5					
O54/11	1.0		+			
O54/12	ca. .8				+	
O54/13	.4					
O54/14	.5		.1			
O54/15	.5		+			
O54/16	.5					
O54/17	.8					
O54/18	.8					
O54/19	.1					
O54/20	ca. 4.0					
O54/21	.4					
O54/22	.4		+			
O54/23	1.2					
O54/24	.9		+		.7	
O54/25	1.1					
O54/26	.4					
O54/27	.7				+	
O54/28	.9					
O55/1	ca. 2.5		+		+	
O55/2	.3		.3		+	
O55/3	.6	.6			+	.1
O55/4	1.3			+		
O55/5	.6					
O55/6	.1					
O55/7	.1					
O55/8–9	1.7		.4		1.3	.9
O55/10	1.3					

Early Bronze Age I–II	Early Bronze Age III‡	Middle Bronze Age	Late Bronze Age (Hittite)	Iron Age‡	Hellenistic-Roman	Medieval-Modern§
.6			.5			.2
+	+ A&B		+			ca. 2.0 B-S
.9	.5 A&B				.2	.9 B-S
.4	+ A					.3 O-M
+	+ A&B					+
						+ O-M
						1.6 O-M
.5			.2			.2 B-S
		+				+
+	+ B		+			+
+		+				+
+	+ B					+
+			+	+		+ O-M
+	+ A		+			+ B-S
2.7	1.8 A&B	.6	3.4	.8–1.0 E		1–1.5 B-S
ca. 2.0			ca. 1.7	+ E		ca. 1.0 O-M
			+			+
			1.7			.9
+	+ B	+	+	+ E		+ O-M
3.2	.8 A&B	2.5	8.2	3.4 E&M		4.8 O-M
		+	.3	+		.3
1.1		.6	.6			1.2 B-S
+		.7	.7			.8 B-S
.5		+	.4			.6 B-S
						.4
.4	+ A&B	.4	.3			.2
+			.1			.2
						.5 B-S
						.8
						.8 O-M?
+		+	+	+		+
+						+ B-M
			.3			.4 B-S
			+			
						1.2 B-S
+	+ A&B	+	.3			.9
.4		+	.2			1.1 B-S
+			+			+ O-M
+		+	.7			.7
+			+	+		+ B-S
+			+			+ B-S
.3			.3			
.2		.1	.1	+		.1
+		+	1.3	1.3		1.3
						.6
.1			.1			.1
						.1 B-S
1.7	+ A&B	+	1.7	+		.8
+	+ A					+ O-M

*Sizes are given to the nearest .1 hectare. A + indicates the presence of an occupation whose extent could not be measured. The sizes of these occupations must be estimated from the total site size.

†ca. = roughly measured. est. = estimated by eye.

‡Underlining indicates occupation primarily of that sub-period. No notation indicates uncertainty about the specific sub-periods represented. E = early. M = middle.

§B-S = occupation of the Byzantine-Selcuk period. O-M = occupation in Ottoman to modern times. B-M = occupation from Byzantine to modern times. Lack of specific notation indicates uncertainty about the exact periods represented.

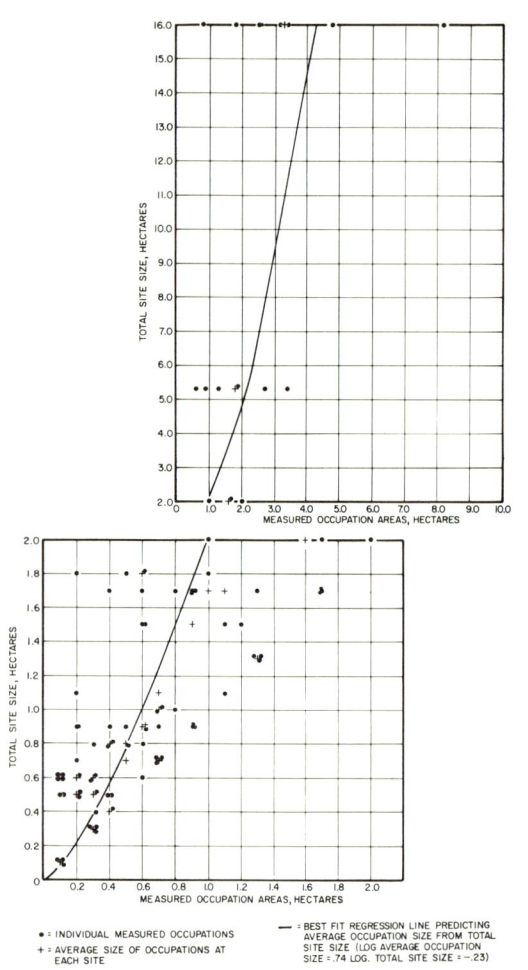

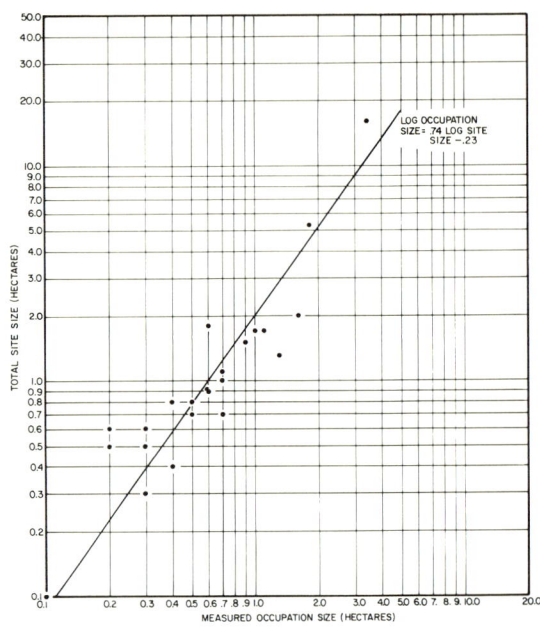

FIGURE 190. Log-log plot of total site size against average size of occupation at sites in the Keban Reservoir survey.

tion of total site size covered by an average occupation rapidly and continuously decreases for sites larger than 0.4 ha. This proportion is best given for these sites by a curvilinear relationship of the form:

$$\log y = .74 \log x - .23$$
where y = the area of an average occupation
x = total site size

We therefore come to the following solution (Table 9). For sites below 0.4 ha in size, occupations are considered to cover the entire site. Occupation areas on larger sites are estimated from the above formula by using a series of fractions representing the proportion of total site area we would expect to be covered by an average occupation on sites which were occupied more than once. Single occupations, of course, are most reasonably considered to have covered the entire site where they occur.

Using the above procedure for estimating the size of occupations on sites where we had not made a controlled surface collection, we were able to combine information on occupation from all sites in the survey area for the representation

FIGURE 189. Plot of total site size against measured and average sizes of occupation areas in the Keban survey data.

First, the average size of occupation at each site was indicated on the graphs. This immediately gave a clearer idea of the relationship between site size and the sizes of individual occupations, and it was obvious that on the average, and for the great majority of occupations, occupation size was regularly smaller than site size. It would have been easiest and most desirable to express this difference as a simple fraction of total site size.

This was tried in several ways, but it was quickly obvious that no simple rule gave a good fit to the data over its entire range. Below approximately 0.4 ha, occupations consistently seem to cover the entire site area. However, the propor-

TABLE 9 Fractional multipliers for estimating average occupation size from total site size*

Total Site Size (ha)	Multiplied By	Predicted Average Occupation Size (ha)
0– .3	1.00	0– .3
.4– .5	.8	.3– .4
.6– .9	.7	.4– .6
1.0– 1.4	.6	.6– .8
1.5– 3.0	.5	.8–1.5
4.0– 6.0	.4	1.6–2.4
7.0–16.0	.3	2.1–4.8

*Note: based on the regression: Log Average Occupation Size = .74 Log Total Size − .23.

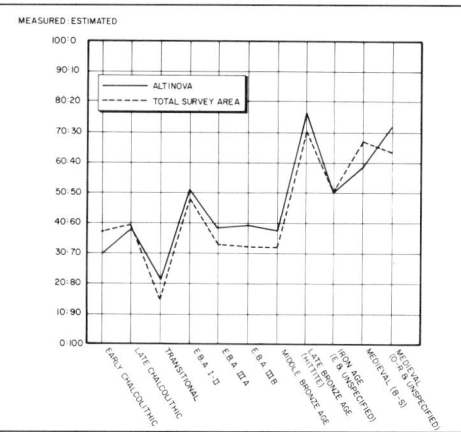

FIGURE 191. Relative proportions of total measured to total estimated occupation area by period within the Altınova and the survey area in general.

and analysis of settlement patterns. Generally, for those periods for which controlled collections had defined the sizes of enough occupations to provide a clear picture of the size classes present in this region, the estimated occupation sizes closely followed and strengthened the pattern already seen in the measured data (cf. especially the Early Bronze Age I–II and Hittite periods). We are thus encouraged to accept the above estimation procedure as relatively accurate.

An interesting pattern emerges when the total occupation area determined for each period is divided into the percentage actually measured from controlled collections versus the percentage estimated from site sizes (Fig. 191). There is a clear and strong trend from earlier to later periods toward a larger percentage of actually measured occupation area. We interpret this as a consequence of the superposition of later occupation layers over earlier occupations. Earlier materials are more deeply buried and therefore generally fewer on the surfaces of sites with multiple occupations. The degree to which controlled surface collection can provide a clear picture of the size and location of an occupation on a site is to a large extent a function of the quantity of materials eroding from exposures of the occupation layer at the surface of the site. Obviously then, the more deeply buried and less exposed a layer, the less likely it will be that there will be adequate material from this layer on the site surface to allow any collection procedure to define it clearly. Thus, many earlier occupations will be known only to be present at a site, and their sizes must be estimated.

Similarly, the more substantial an occupation level, the more likely it is that enough materials from it will be found on the surface of the site for a clear definition of its size and location by controlled collection. It is not surprising, therefore, to find that the sharp peaks in the graph of percentage of measured occupation area correspond exactly to the periods of peak population in this area as measured by total occupied area—Early Bronze Age I–II, Hittite, and Ottoman–Recent. The concentration of our attention on the plains of Altınova is shown by the fact that Altınova sites taken alone show a higher percentage of actually measured site area than the entire survey area in most periods.

Geographical Bases of Settlement Pattern

There are only two parts of the survey area which are large enough and have enough sites in them to make discussion of settlement patterns meaningful—the Aşvan area and the Altınova. In both areas geographical features play a significant role in determining settlement pattern.

At Aşvan, sites are concentrated in two small, steep-sided stream valleys leading, after a short distance, to the south side of the Murat River valley. The availability of water from these streams, from the Murat, and from the springs along the sides of these two small valleys seems to have been of great importance in influencing the location of sites of all periods here.

In the Altınova, the breadth of valley floor available for settlement is considerable. The north, south, and to some extent the east boundaries of this plain are sharply delimited by steep, rocky, mountain slopes, however. These are inhospitable slopes and quite clearly delimit habitable and cultivable valley land. The plain formed by this valley floor is well watered, but there is a strong patterning to the distribution of water sources. A stream, the Haringet Çayı, runs through the center of the plain. A number of small sites are located along this stream. In addition to the stream, there are numerous springs in the Altınova. These are very clearly distributed in lines which parallel the valley edges on both sides of the plain (Fig. 4). These appear to be strong and regular sources of water. Small streams flow away from several of them only to disappear through absorption into the alluvium of the valley floor, and several areas are made marshy from the strong flow of these springs. Most sites are located near one or more of these springs. Particularly, the large mounds in the Altınova are found at fairly regular intervals along the north and the south sides of the valley, always near or among one or more springs.

These natural influences on the distributions of sites of all periods must be borne in mind when considering the settlement patterns of the various individual periods of occupation. A great deal of resemblance exists among most of the settlement pattern maps. This is a consequence of the strength of these natural factors in determining the location of human occupations in the Aşvan and Altınova areas from the Early Chalcolithic period until the present day.

Defining Settlement Patterns

A simple method was used to define the settlement patterns presented here. For each period, the measured and the estimated occupation sizes were tabulated and compiled in a histogram. Rough divisions of the occupations into size categories—"small," "medium," "large," and "major"—were made from these histograms. Such modal categories seemed to be evident and definable in most histograms, although in several cases sample sizes were very small. After every period had been treated in this way, the ranges of the various size categories were compared among all periods. A striking uniformity in the boundaries of the "small" and "medium" size classes was found. "Small" occupations range up to approximately 1.25 ha in size. "Medium" occupations run from ca. 1.25 ha to about 2.15 ha in size. There is then, generally, a small gap between these occupations and the few "large" ones. There is some variability in the sizes of "large" occupations, but a range from 2.15–ca. 5 ha encompasses all of them. A single, very large occupation, measured from controlled surface collection as over 8 ha in area, was termed "major" for want of a better term. The overall impression of uniformity among the results of the various periods encourages our confidence in them. Estimated values closely followed the pattern of distribution of measured sizes in most cases, as mentioned above.

The distribution of occupations in these general size classes was then plotted on maps of the survey area for each period. These maps gave a good picture of the distribution, relative density, and the degree of concentration of human population in the various periods, particularly for the Altınova and to a lesser extent for the Aşvan area. A number of sites seem consistently to have been "large," sometimes "medium"-sized, centers of occupation. In the Altınova these sites are spaced at relatively regular intervals along the sides of the valley in two lines which correspond well to the lines of springs discussed above. These consistently larger occupations are found in sites 054/1, 054/2, and during many periods 054/3 along the north side of the Altınova and sites 054/7, 054/8, 055/1, and during some periods 055/10 along the south side of the Altınova. These lines of larger sites probably continue to the west at least as far as Hoğu on the north and Kövenk and Tilenzit on the south, all large mounds with known Early Bronze Age occupations recorded by Burney (1958—as sites 277, 273, and 274 respectively). In addition, site 054/20 seems to have had substantial occupation in certain periods.

In an effort to more clearly present and illustrate the settlement patterns of the various periods, polygonal (roughly hexagonal) "territories" were fitted around each of the above sites, including 054/20 for those periods in which it was extensively occupied. This manner of presenting the settlement pattern data is not intended to be a rigorous locational analysis. Nonetheless, we felt that it does provide a useful and informative frame of reference within which to view the spacing, density, and pattern of distribution of occupations in this area. For example, a partial conformity to this frame of reference may suggest that some occupations were missed or that the importance of certain occupations on some sites was misestimated.

These polygonal "territories" look convincing in another way, also. They were constructed without regard for the natural, geographical features of the Altınova plain, simply as polygons with sides equidistant between the sites being considered (Thiessen polygons) and outside edges drawn as hexagons commensurate in size with the distances to the sides between sites. Yet the outer boundaries of these "territories" run quite regularly along the sides of the valley floor, close to the break in slope between flatter, alluvial land and rocky talus from the mountains. And more interestingly, their inner borders, where the "territories" of the two lines of sites meet, run very neatly along the Haringet Çayı, the only natural barrier, boundary, or dividing line in the entire plain.

Finally, after the presentation of the individual settlement patterns, we tabulate total areas of occupation for each period in the Altınova and the entire survey area. This tabulation can be used as a rough indicator of relative levels of population here, and as such allows us to say something about the relative importance of the Altınova and of the region as a place of human habitation and activity through time.

EARLY CHALCOLITHIC (Table 10; Figs. 192 and 193)

The Early Chalcolithic is well represented, with 13 occupations in the Altınova and three near Aşvan. The three sites near Aşvan are small and widely separated, one near the head of each of the tributary valleys and one in the small plain near Aşvan itself. The occupations in the Altınova can be divided into small, medium, and large categories. The large and medium-sized occupations are found on most of the large mounds in the area. Small sites are virtually all located roughly equidistant between pairs of the larger sites, at the midpoints of the borders of the hexagonal "territories" defined for these larger sites. The pattern looks regular, and we suspect that it likely continues with important occupations at Hoğu, Kövenk etc. Such a spatial distribution would suggest a "transport" principle of organization of settlement location (Berry 1967:65). However, the ratios of large to medium

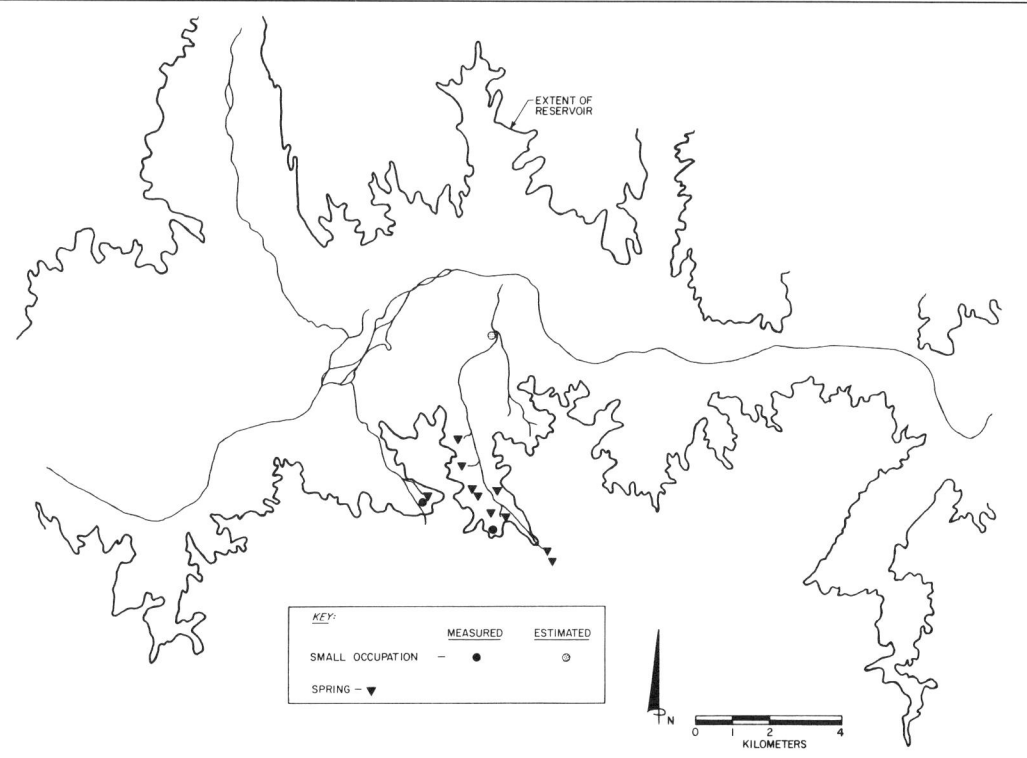

FIGURE 192. Distribution map of Early Chalcolithic occupations by size class in the Aşvan area.

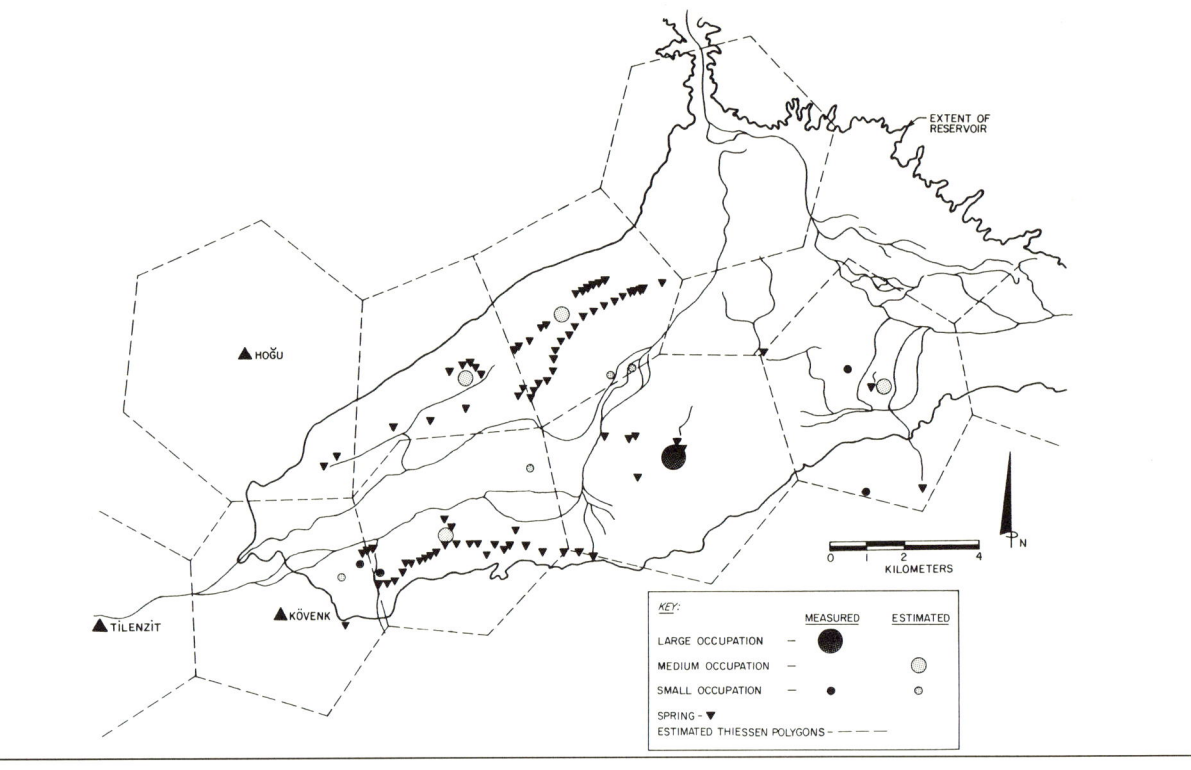

FIGURE 193. Distribution map of Early Chalcolithic occupations by size class in the Altınova.

to small occupations in the Altınova are 1:4:8, while the expected ratios among size classes in a "transport"–organized settlement pattern are 1:4:16. This discrepancy may simply be the result of our having missed a number of small occupations from this period in our survey. This is not unlikely, considering the early date of the period and the probability that such occupation levels are deeply buried under later overburden in many sites.

On the other hand, it must be remembered that the survey area is not a "natural" one. It is artificially defined by the height of the water in the Keban Reservoir, and we are restricted to considering that small part of the total, regional settlement pattern which happens to fall within this reservoir area. As will be seen below, the settlement patterns defined for the Altınova area of the reservoir clearly continue directly to the west onto the broad plains south of Elâzığ in many periods beside the Early Chalcolithic. In these circumstances, the picture of settlement patterns, and particularly such statistics as ratios among the numbers of occupations falling into different size classes, which are developed from the survey of the reservoir area alone may often be biased and not entirely accurate.

HALAF

Evidence for Halaf occupation was found at only three sites by our survey, two in the Altınova and one in the narrow valley of the Munzur River. Occupation was indicated by only one or two sherds in each case, and we have no confidence that our surface-collected materials give a representation or reliable picture of the occurrence of occupations of this period. Later excavations at Norşun Tepe (054/8), from which our controlled surface collection recovered several ten's of thousands of sherds, none of them Halafian, now reveal Halaf occupation there also (*Anatolian Studies* 1975:36), at 35 m below the top of the mound! Obviously, occupation levels of this date are deeply buried and material from them seldom reaches the surface of a site in any quantity.

LATE CHALCOLITHIC (Table 11; Figs. 194 and 195)

There are 14 Late Chalcolithic occupations found by our survey, 12 of them in the Altınova and two near Aşvan. Most of these appear to be small occupations. A few, on the larger mounds in the Altınova, seem to be of medium

Settlement Patterns 267

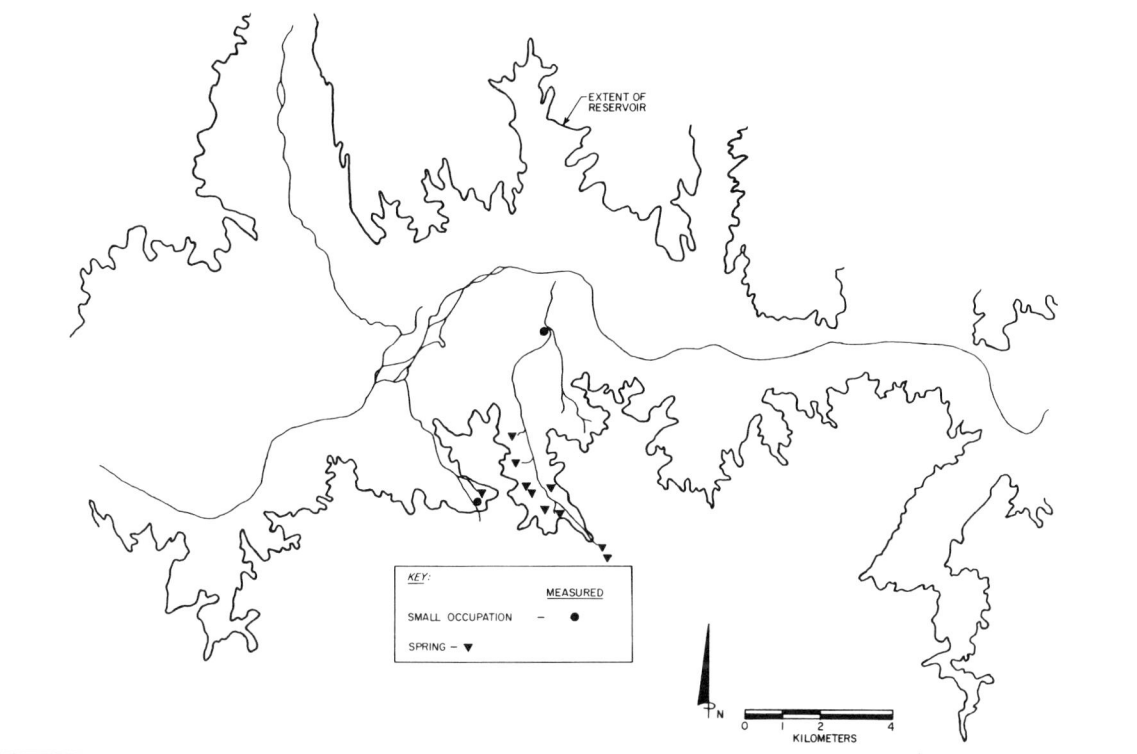

FIGURE 194. Distribution map of Late Chalcolithic occupations by size class in the Aşvan area.

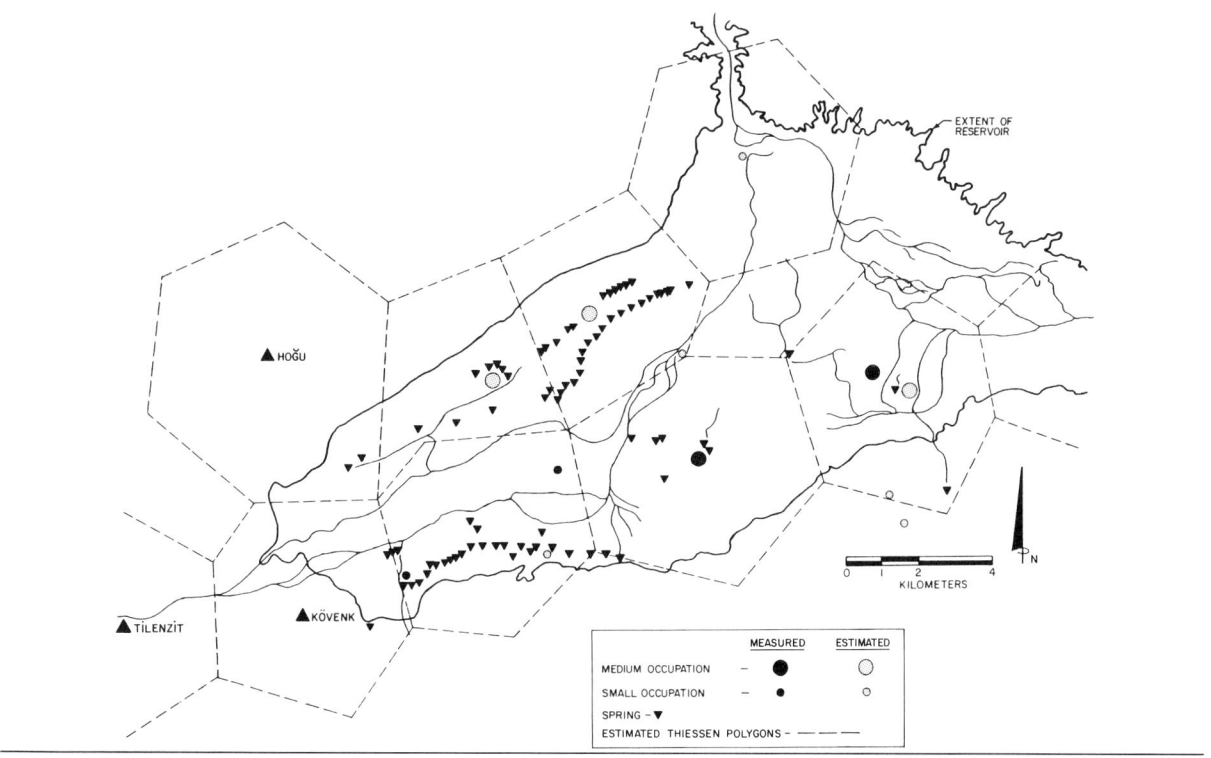

FIGURE 195. Distribution map of Late Chalcolithic occupations by size class in the Altınova.

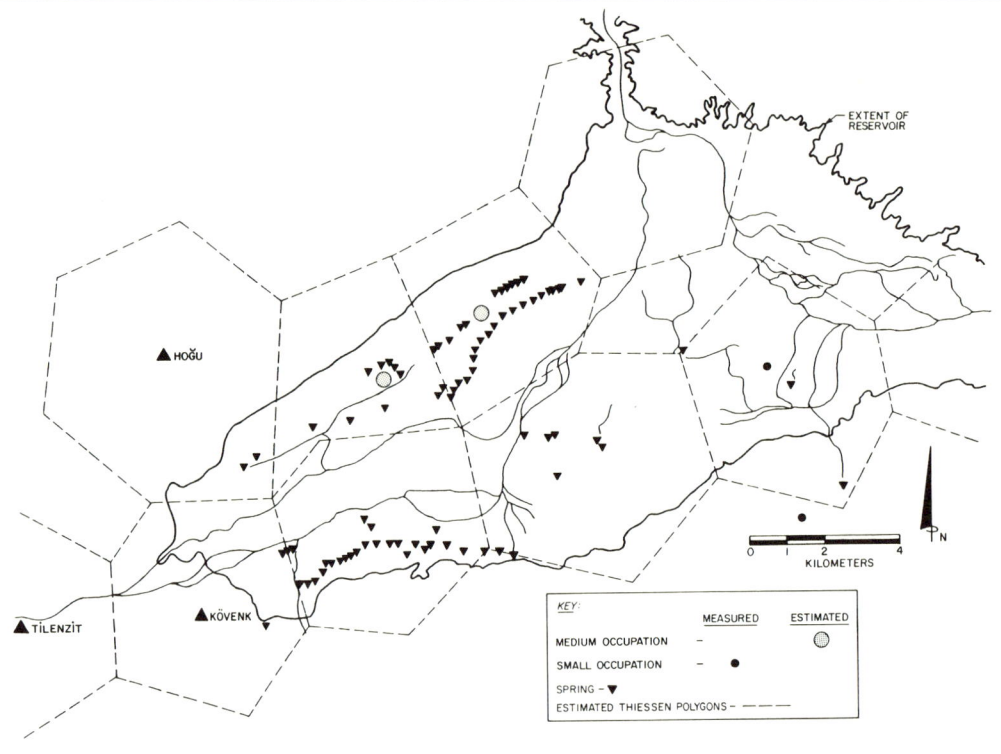

FIGURE 196. Distribution map of Chalcolithic-Early Bronze Age Transitional occupations by size class in the Altınova.

size. Smaller sites are widely dispersed around these slightly larger occupations rather than located at midpoints between them. The settlement pattern looks different from that of the Early Chalcolithic but it is difficult to characterize it specifically.

CHALCOLITHIC–EARLY BRONZE AGE TRANSITIONAL
(Table 12; Fig. 196)

Only seven occupations of this period were identified by us, of which only four are in the Altınova. Two medium–sized occupations are estimated for two of the large mounds here, but obviously little can be said about local settlement patterns from this small number of sites. In contrast to the preceeding periods, however, these occupations are more widely scattered throughout the survey area, occurring at sites N53/3 and N55/1 in addition to the Aşvan and Altınova areas.

EARLY BRONZE AGE I–II (Table 13; Figs. 197 and 198)

Many Early Bronze Age occupations were located in the Keban area. It had already been known from Burney's (1958) work in the area that the Early Bronze Age was extensively and plentifully represented here, and our survey amply confirmed this. A total of 35 occupations were recorded, 25 in the Altınova, four near Aşvan, and six scattered throughout the rest of the survey area. Occupations were divided into small, medium, and large categories.

The four occupations around Aşvan are all small. Two are in the tributary valley running down toward the small plain around Aşvan, and the other two occupations are located on the Aşvan plain itself.

In the Altınova, all the "large" and most of the "medium" occupations occur on the larger mounds strung along the north and south sides of the valley. This undoubtedly includes the mounds of Hoğu and Kövenk, recorded by Burney as having Early Bronze Age occupation, and from each of which he illustrates a typical Early Bronze Age "rail-rim" jar profile (Burney 1958:Figs. 174,176). It seems clear that a real hierarchy of sites existed in this period. Not only are there significant differences in size among the occupations, but the more elaborate decorated pottery of the period, the Relief Decorated Ware, is

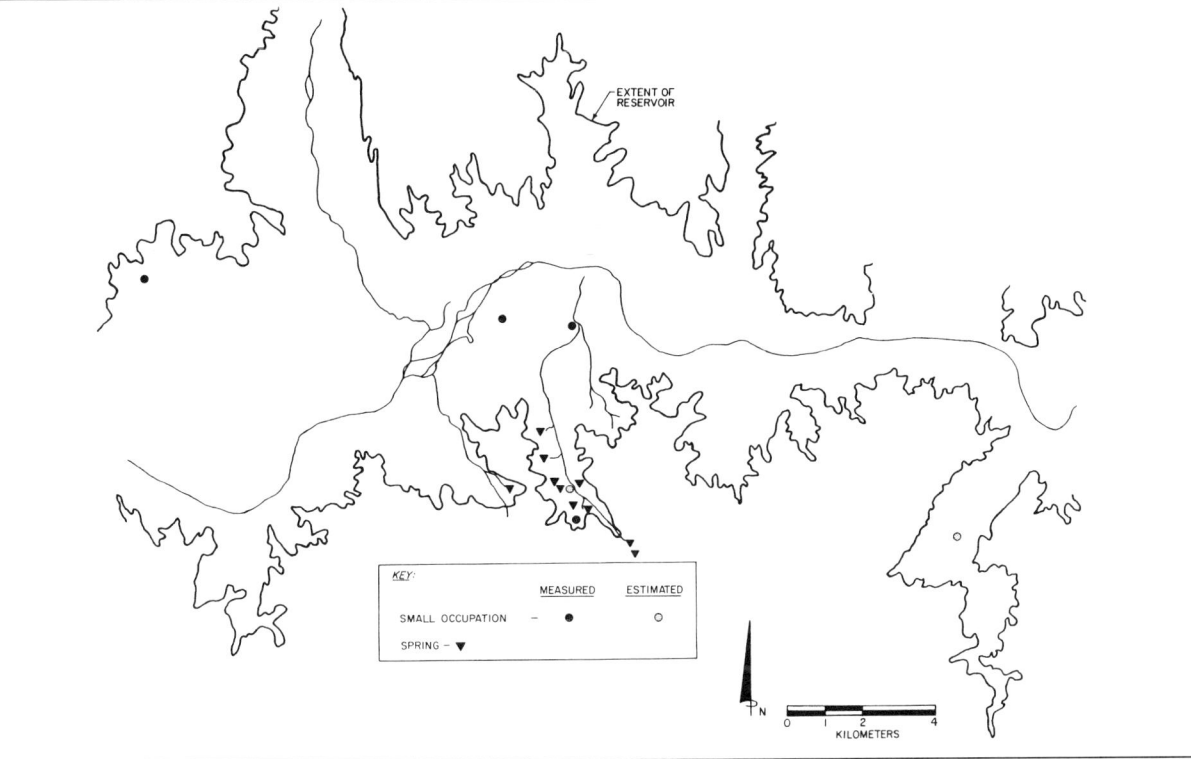

FIGURE 197. Distribution map of Early Bronze Age I-II occupations by size class in the Aşvan area.

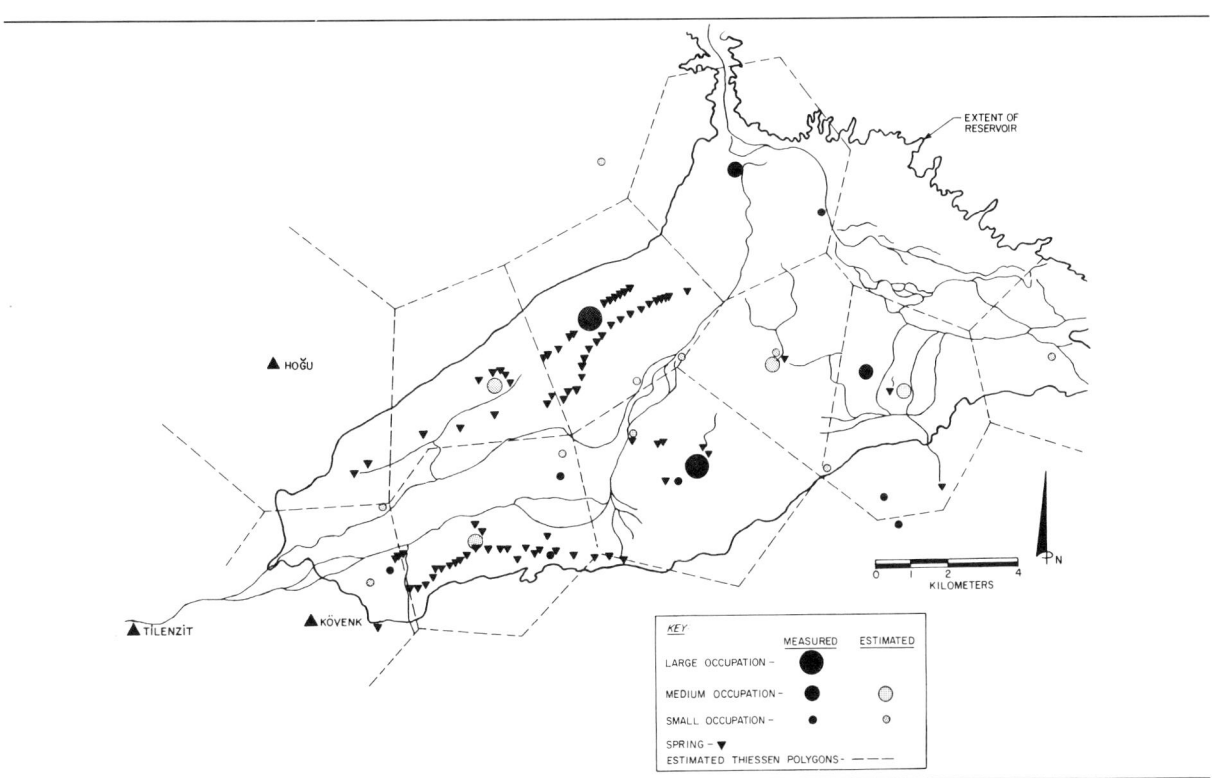

FIGURE 198. Distribution map of Early Bronze Age I-II occupations by size class in the Altınova.

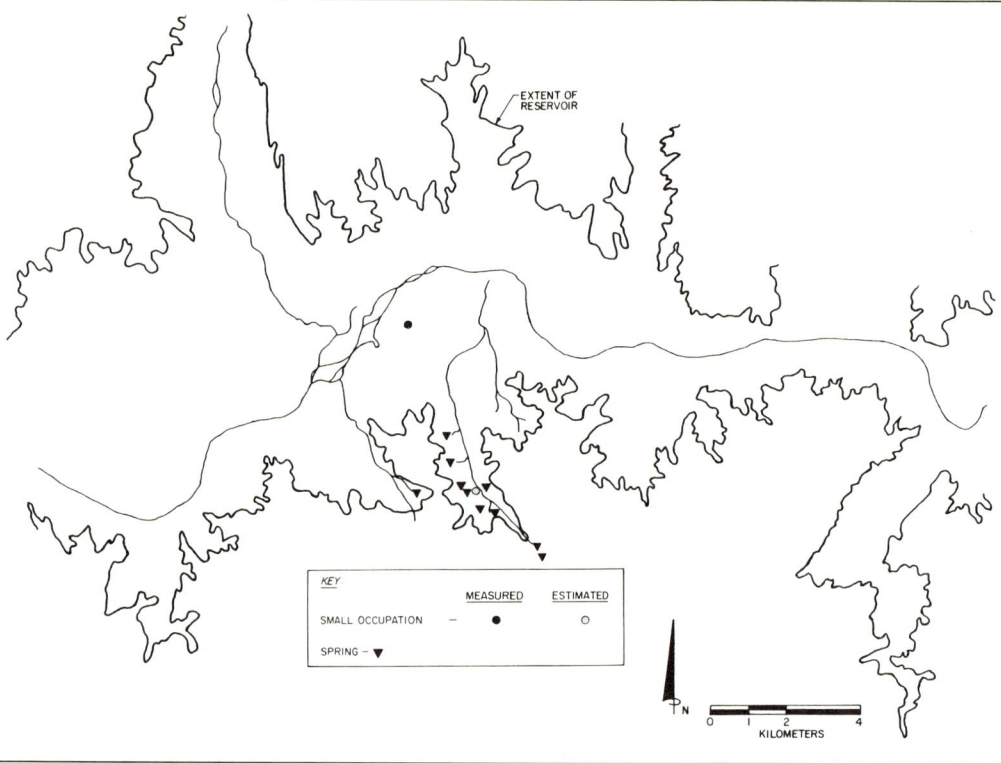

FIGURE 199. Distribution map of Early Bronze Age IIIA occupations by size class in the Aşvan area.

restricted to the larger sites in this hierarchy. In the Altınova it is found only on sites 054/1, 054/2, 054/7, and 054/8. Smaller sites are scattered around these larger centers, sometimes midway between them, but more often near the corners of the polygonal "territories" constructed around them. This pattern of site distribution would seem to indicate an organization based on a "marketing" principle (Berry 1967:65), and the ratios among large, medium, and small occupations (2:6:17) are very close to the theoretically expected ratios of 1:2:6 in this case, in which there are two sites in each class for every larger site.

EARLY BRONZE AGE IIIA (Table 14; Figs. 199 and 200)

Only seven occupations of this period were found in the Altınova, two in the Aşvan area, and two elsewhere in the survey area. Very little can be said about settlement patterns from such a sparse distribution of sites. In the Aşvan area one site is far up the tributary valley leading down to the small Aşvan plain, and one occupation is at Aşvan itself. In the Altınova, medium and small occupations seem to be regularly spaced along both the north and the south sides of the valley. The two medium occupations are found on the large mounds at the north edge of the valley. The five small sites run along the south valley edge.

EARLY BRONZE AGE IIIB (Table 15; Figs. 201 and 202)

Only six occupations of this period were identified in the Altınova, two in the Aşvan area, and three elsewhere in the survey area. Again, little can be said about settlement pattern from so few sites. The distribution of sites at Aşvan is identical to that of the Early Bronze Age IIIA. In the Altınova, occupations again appear to be regularly spaced. One medium occupation is found on a large mound at the north edge of the valley. The other medium occupation and all four small sites are spaced along the south side of the valley.

MIDDLE BRONZE AGE (Table 16; Fig. 203)

Middle Bronze Age occupations numbered 19 in our survey results. Of these, 16 were in the Altınova, and only three were scattered over

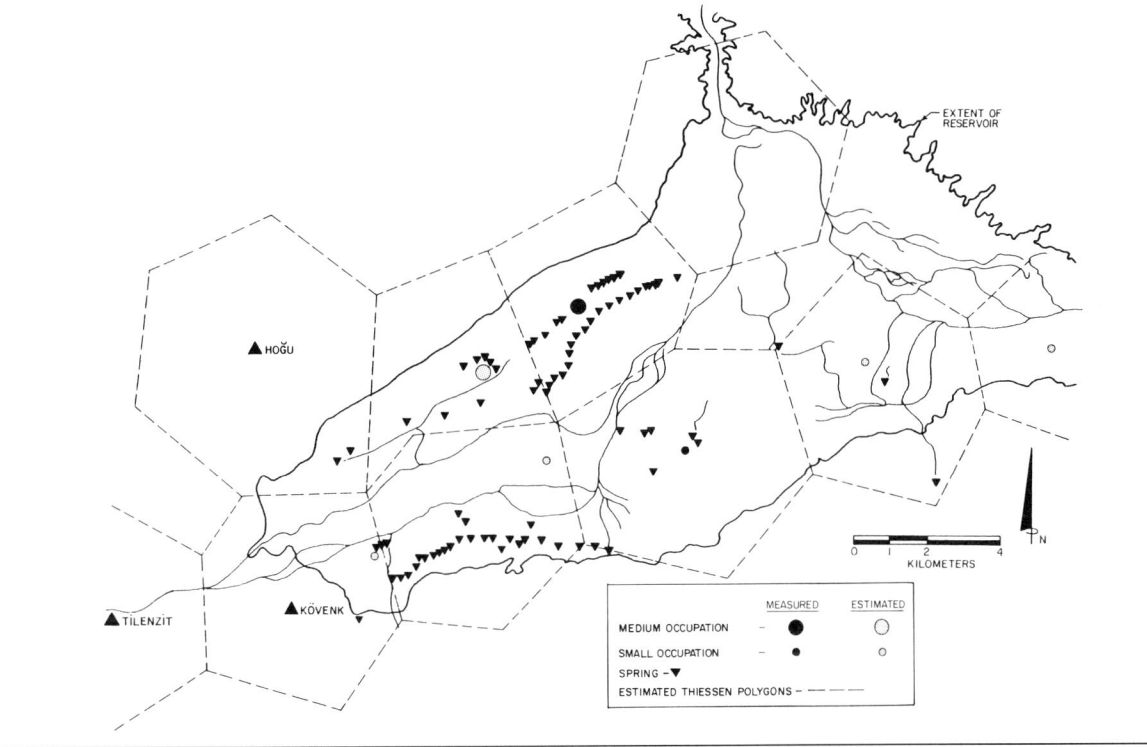

FIGURE 200. Distribution map of Early Bronze Age IIIA occupations by size class in the Altınova.

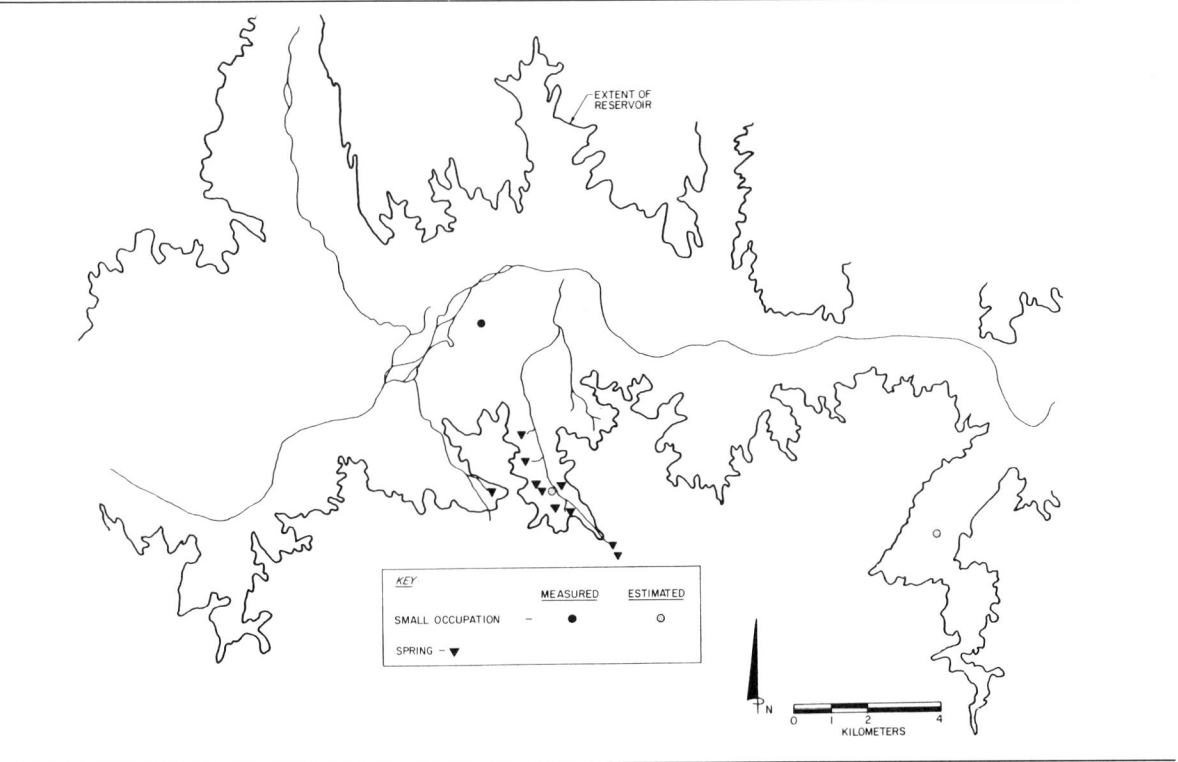

FIGURE 201. Distribution map of Early Bronze Age IIIB occupations by size class in the Aşvan area.

272 *Archaeological Survey of the Keban Reservoir*

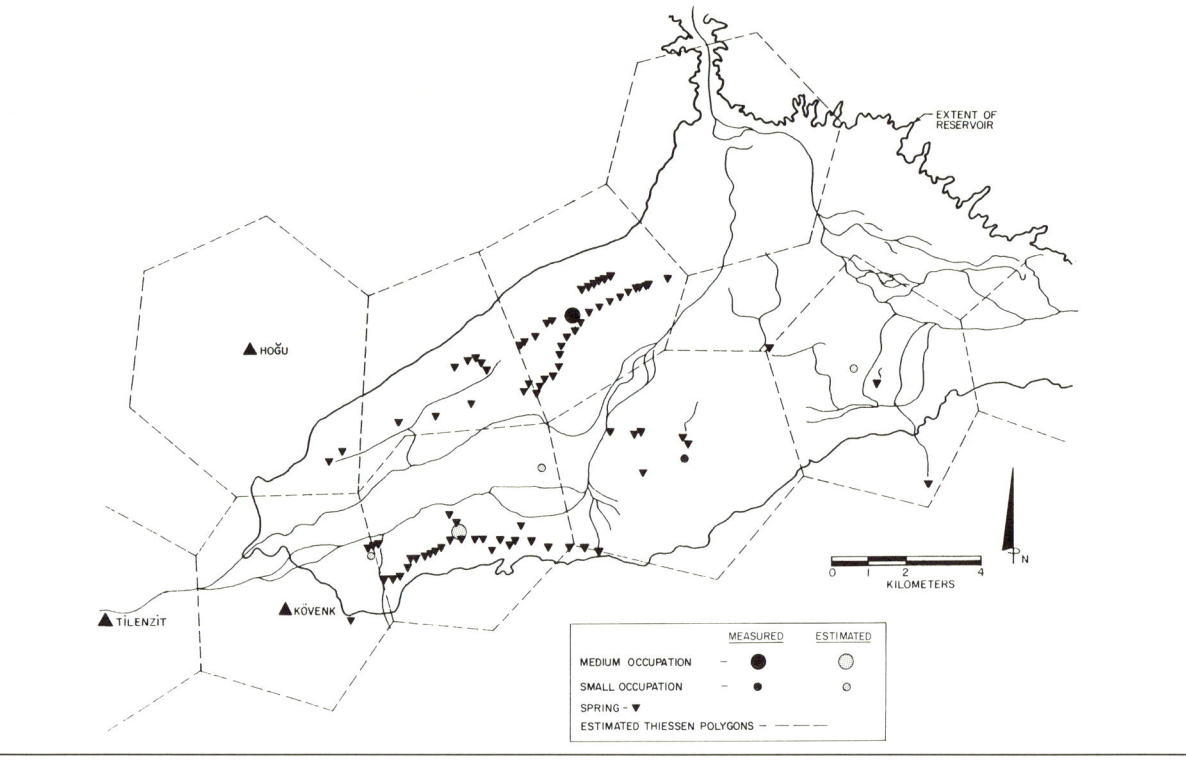

FIGURE 202. Distribution map of Early Bronze Age IIIB occupations by size class in the Altınova.

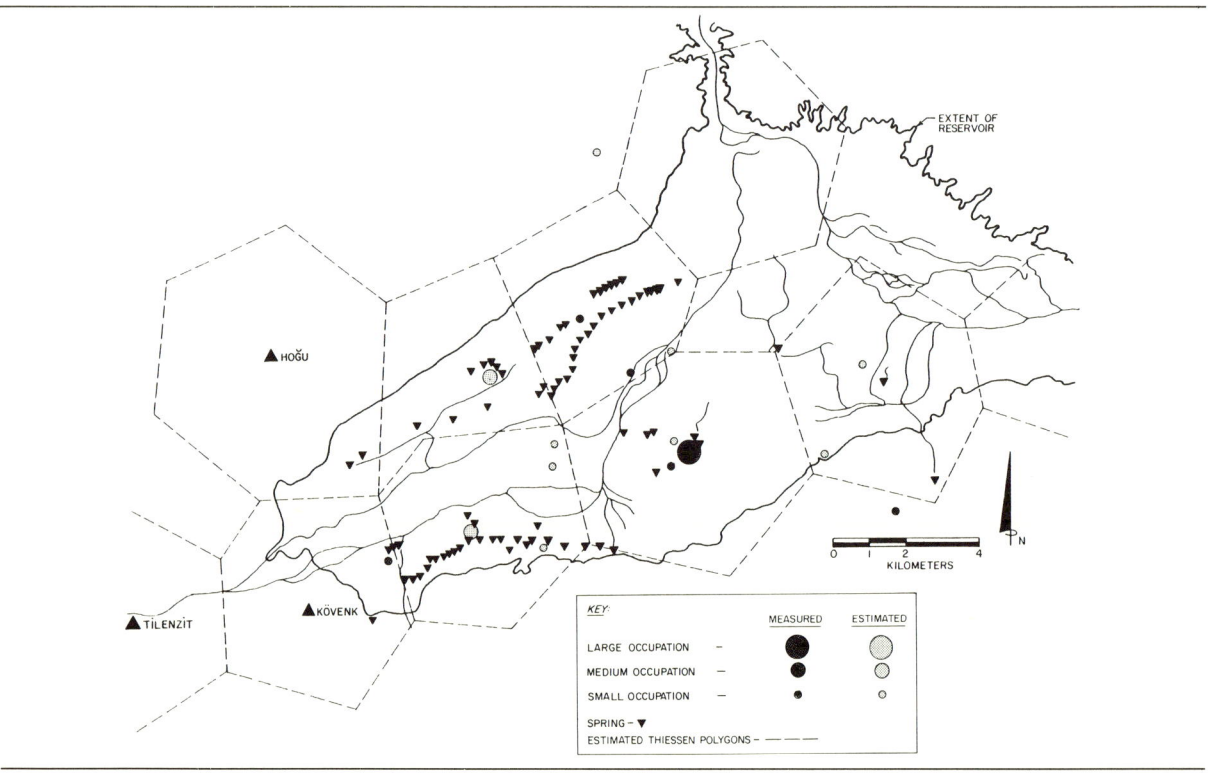

FIGURE 203. Distribution map of Middle Bronze Age occupations by size class in the Altınova.

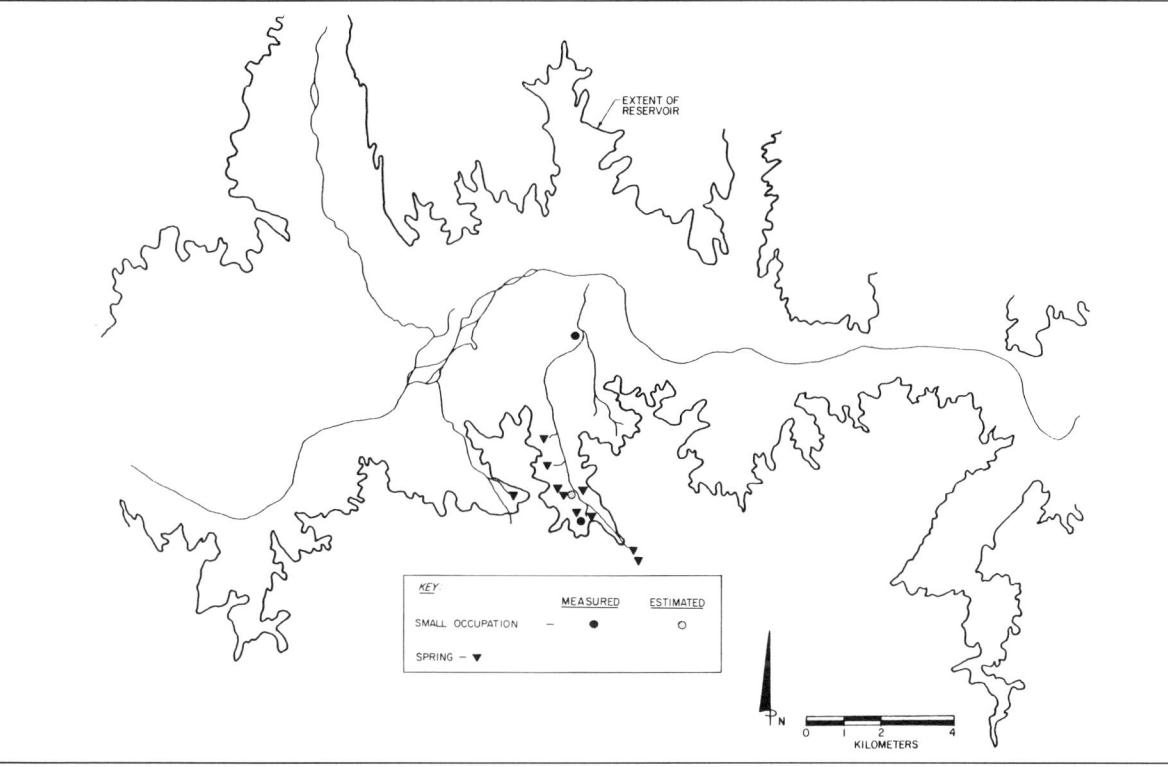

FIGURE 204. Distribution map of Late Bronze Age (Hittite) occupations by size class in the Aşvan area.

the rest of the survey area. One site could be called large. The others were of medium and small size. When plotted in the Altınova, the large and medium-sized occupations fell clearly on the lines of large mounds, particularly along the southern side of the plain. These occupations are surrounded by a scatter of small sites, which are generally dispersed toward the corners of the hexagonal "territories" around the larger sites.

LATE BRONZE AGE (HITTITE) (Table 17; Figs. 204 and 205)

Occupation of the Keban area in Hittite times was relatively important. A total of 27 occupations in the Altınova, three near Aşvan, and two elsewhere were found by our survey. The size distribution of these occupations forms two clearly defined classes—small and medium—with one large and one "major" occupation standing out from the rest.

The three sites near Aşvan are all small and are scattered over the Aşvan plain and its tributary valley.

In the Altınova, there are the "major" and the large sites, seven medium, and 18 small occupations, an almost perfect example of the 1:2:6:18 ratios representing the existence of two lower-level occupations for each occupation in a larger size class (Berry 1967:65). A slight error in our estimation of one site, calling it medium instead of large, would create the observed discrepancy.

The polygonal "territories" drawn around the large mounds in the Altınova provide a fair representation of the distribution of these occupations. Over half of the medium and all larger occupations are found on the large mounds at the centers of the "territories". The small sites are scattered among the larger ones, often being located at or near the peripheries of the "territories". Further, if sites are linked by a series of lines joining first the large sites and then extending from these sites to the smaller ones, a network appears which begins to approximate the hexagonal arrangement of a "market"-based settlement pattern (Berry 1967:65-66). This is congruent with the 1:2:6:18 ratios among sites of different size classes.

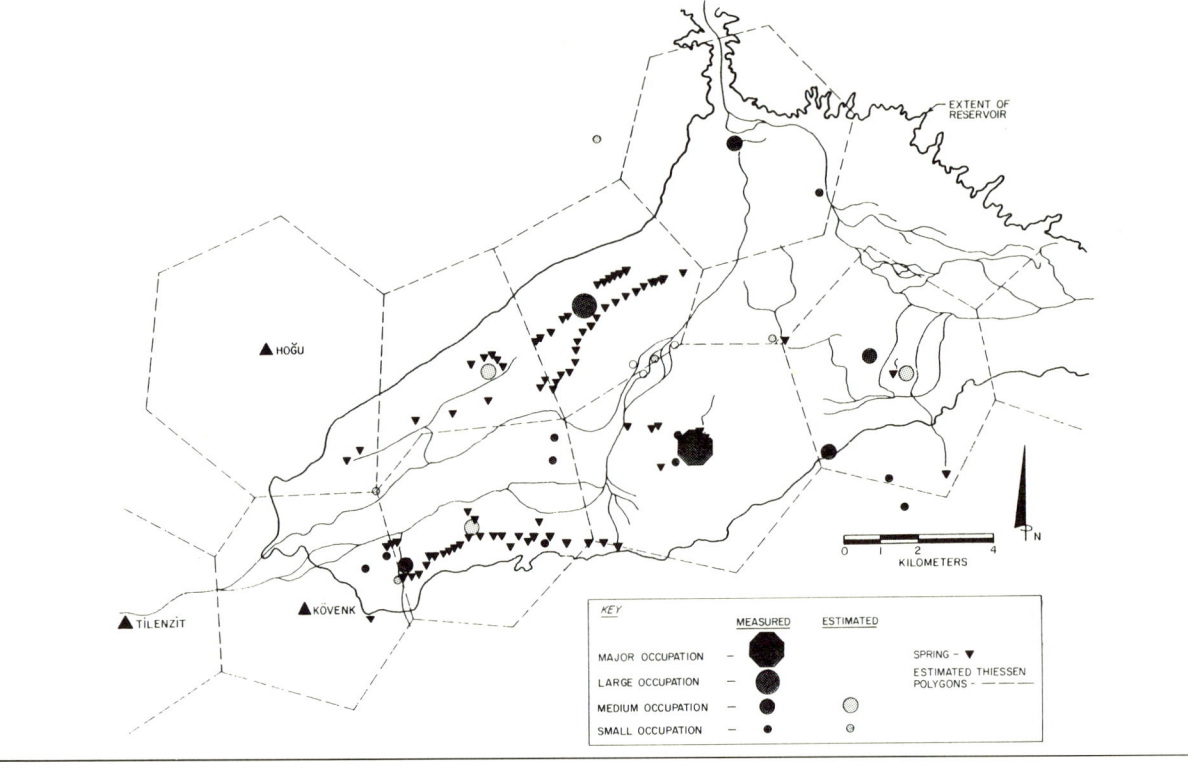

FIGURE 205. Distribution map of Late Bronze Age (Hittite) occupations by size class in the Altınova.

IRON AGE (Table 18; Fig. 206)

All the Iron Age occupations found by our survey were located in the Altınova. Four occupations were identifiable as Early Iron Age in date. Only one was identifiable as Middle Iron Age, and six were identifiable only as "Iron Age" without more specificity. Plotting the unspecified occupations together with those of the Early Iron Age, a sparse but fairly clear pattern of site distribution can be seen. For the most part, occupations are located at or near the centers of the hexagonal "territories" drawn around the large mounds on both sides of the valley. Two sites are at corners of these "territories," and two very small sites are located on the slopes above the valley floor.

HELLENISTIC–ROMAN

We were able to identify Hellenistic-Roman occupation on only one site in the survey area. Undoubtedly this is at least partly due to our unfamiliarity with pottery of these periods as well as to a conscious avoidance of the few already known Classical and historic sites outside our areas of most intense survey. Later excavations in the Keban Reservoir (Serdaroğlu 1970, 1971, 1972, 1974, 1976; Harper 1970, 1971, 1972; Öğün 1971, 1972) however, have uncovered substantial occupations from these periods, including Roman frontier fortifications.

MEDIEVAL (BYZANTINE-SELCUK) (Table 19; Figs. 207 and 208)

The "Medieval" period has been broken up very roughly into two divisions—the Byzantine–Selcuk and the Ottoman-Recent and Unspecified. The Byzantine–Selcuk occupations have been identified by the presence of Sgraffiato Ware and Islamic modeled pottery (e.g. Fig. 54:h–j). Sites with other Medieval wares, including Green Glazed Ware, were put into the Ottoman-Recent and Unspecified category. In some cases such sites had been occupied by Armenians (e.g. 054/2, Habusu—where the ruins of the Armenian church still stood). In others "Ottoman" pipe fragments were found. But on most sites only Brick Ware and other plain "Medieval" pottery was found. Such occupations were left "unspecified" in terms of more precise dating.

Identified Byzantine–Selcuk occupations num-

Settlement Patterns 275

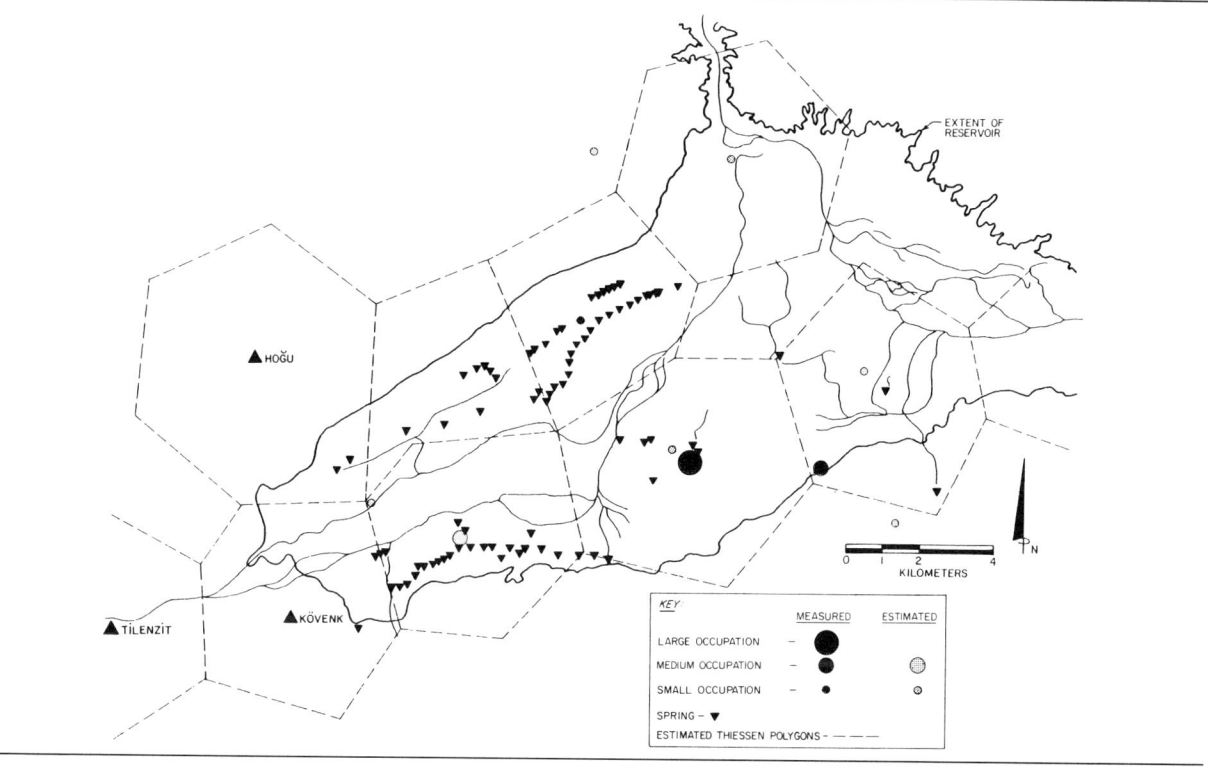

FIGURE 206. Distribution map of Iron Age (Early and Unspecified) occupations by size class in the Altınova.

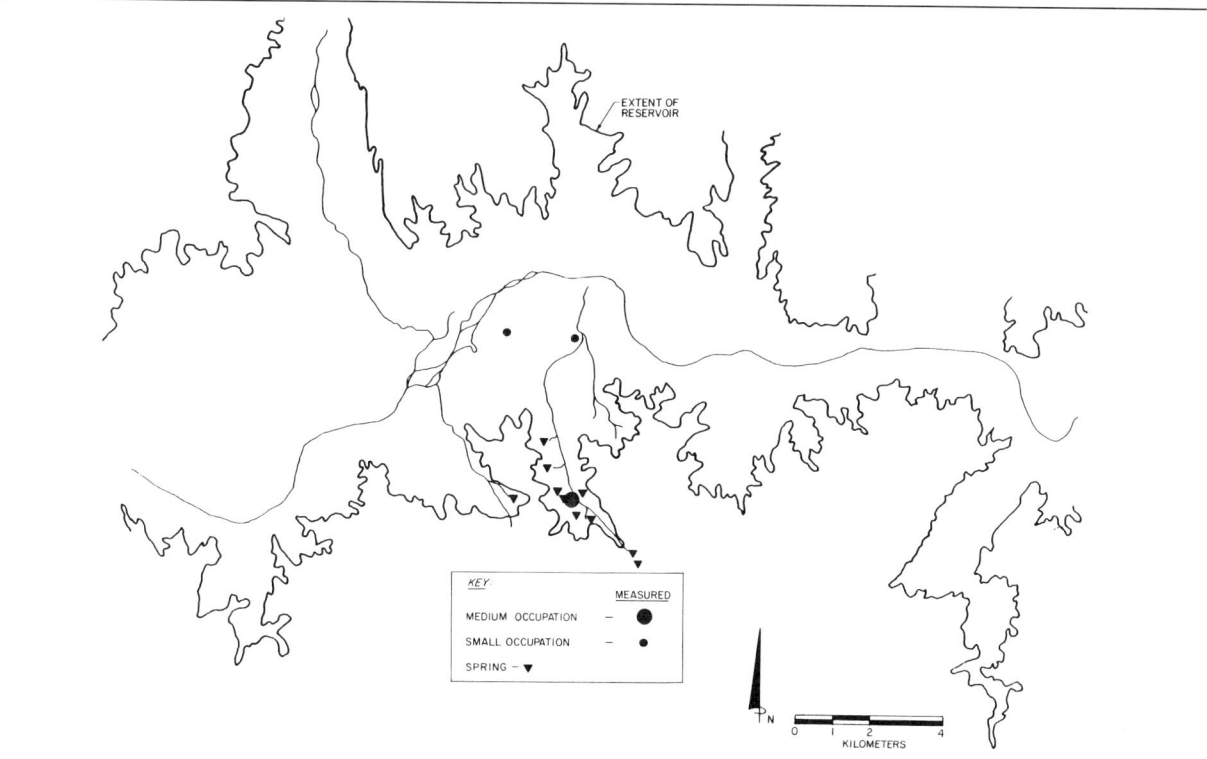

FIGURE 207. Distribution map of Medieval (Byzantine-Selcuk) occupations by size class in the Aşvan area.

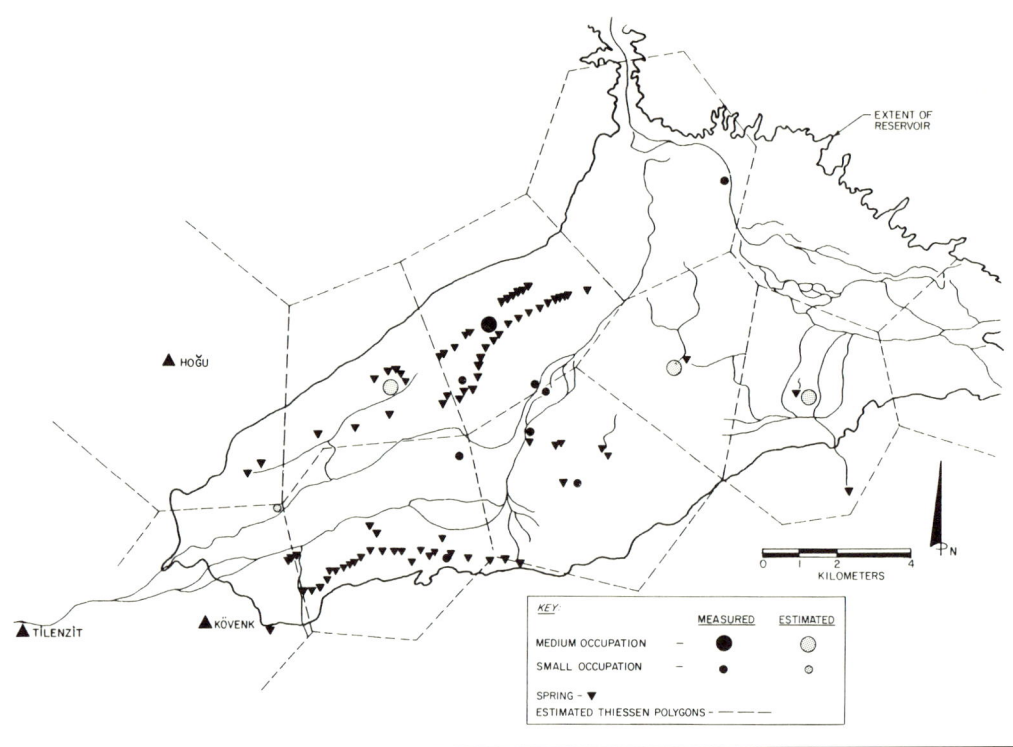

FIGURE 208. Distribution map of Medieval (Byzantine-Selcuk) occupations by size class in the Altınova.

ber three in the Aşvan area, 13 in the Altınova. The pattern around Aşvan is simple—a single medium-sized occupation far up the tributary valley with two small sites on the small Aşvan plain. In the Altınova, the ratio of medium to small sites is 4:9, close to the 1:2 ratio seen near Aşvan. However, the distribution of these sites shows no clear pattern. The larger sites no longer follow the lines of larger mounds along the north and south sides of the valley as obviously as in earlier periods, and the small sites seem to be randomly scattered with respect to the larger occupations. If any generalization can be made about the pattern of site distribution revealed for this period, it is that medium-sized occupations still may be located with respect to important springs in the valley, but that small occupations now tend to be located along streams and the river.

MEDIEVAL (OTTOMAN-RECENT AND UNSPECIFIED)
(Table 20; Figs. 209 and 210)

Of the 32 occupations placed in this period, three are in the area around Aşvan, 22 in the Altınova, and seven elsewhere in the survey area. Near Aşvan one medium occupation is located in the middle of a small tributary valley to the southwest of the main Aşvan plain, and single small sites are found far up both the two valleys in the area. In the Altınova, there are large, medium, and small occupations. Their ratios are 1:3:18, not far from the 1:4:16 ratios expected in a settlement pattern organized along a "transport" principle (Berry 1967:65) and quite different from the 1:2 ratio seen in the Aşvan area. However, the spatial pattern associated with such an organizing principle is not apparent from the distribution of these occupations. Neither the larger nor the small sites appear to follow any clear distributional pattern, and it is impossible to confirm the suggestion made above from the ratios among site classes.

In fact, for both this and the preceding period, it is probable that the data presented from our survey is only partially, and to some degree inaccurately, representative of the settlement patterns in this area because of our lack of expertise and precision in identifying and dating pottery from this range of time.

POPULATION TRENDS

Total area of occupation was calculated for each period by summing all of the areas measured

Settlement Patterns 277

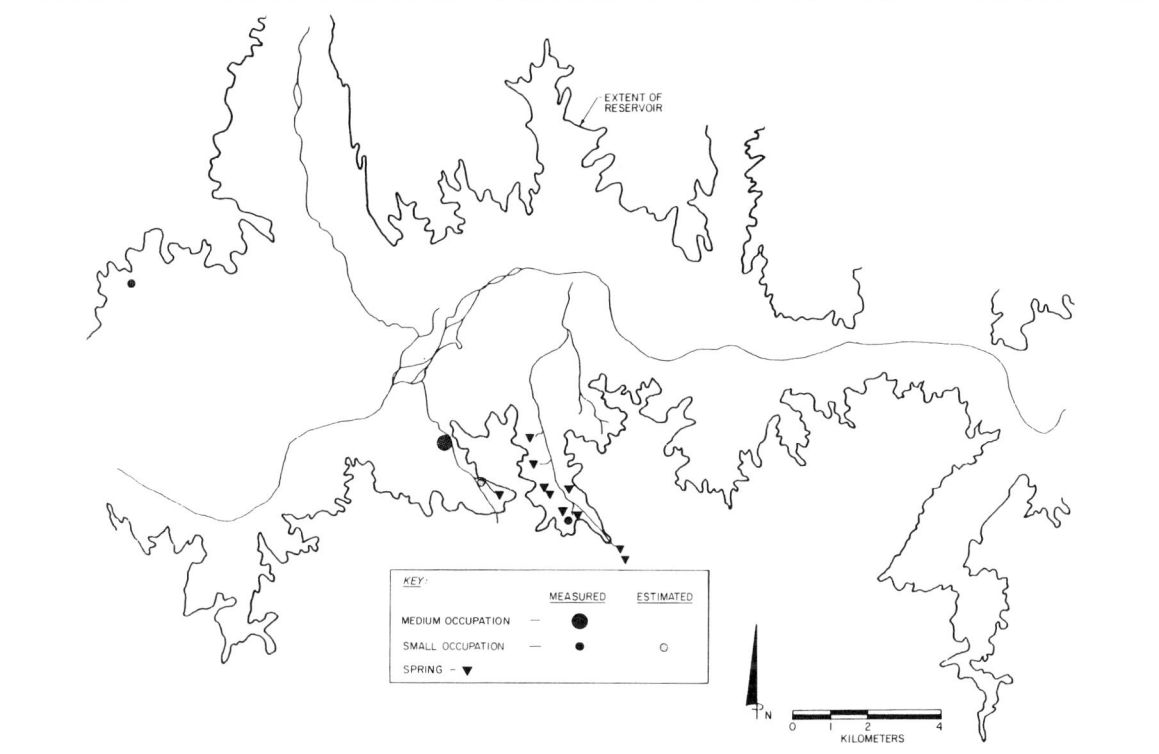

FIGURE 209. Distribution map of Medieval (Ottoman-Recent and Unspecified) occupations by size class in the Aşvan area.

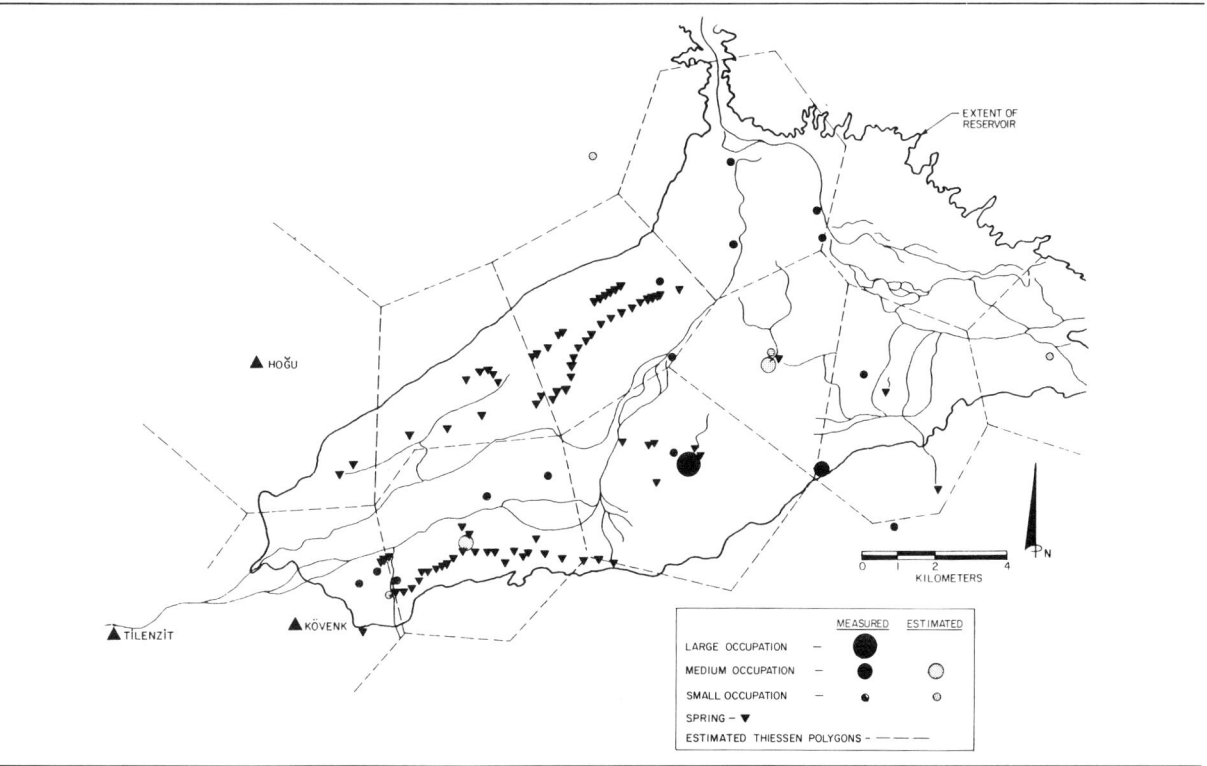

FIGURE 210. Distribution map of Medieval (Ottoman-Recent and Unspecified) occupations by size class in the Altınova.

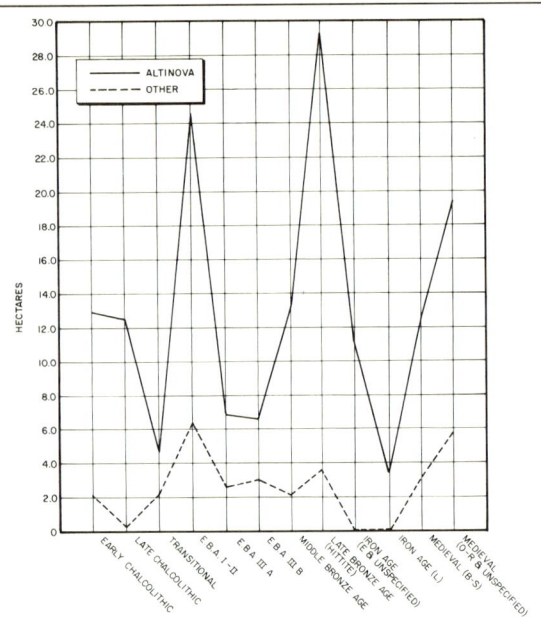

FIGURE 211. Total measured and estimated area of occupation by period within the Altınova and other parts of the survey area.

or estimated from all relevant sites (Fig. 211). This total area is assumed to be closely related to the population of the region in each period or at least to provide a comparative index of the importance or intensity of occupation in the various periods.

This index shows considerable variation from period to period. Fluctuating around an average total occupation area of almost 14 ha, noticeably low points occur in the Chalcolithic–Early Bronze Age Transitional period, the Early Bronze Age III (A and B), and the Late Iron Age. Striking high points are found in the Early Bronze Age I-II and the Hittite periods, with a smaller but probably significant peak in the Ottoman–Recent period. Whatever the exact levels of population to be attached to various totals of occupation area, the overall pattern of periods of relatively low and high population or relatively lesser and more important occupation of this region is very clear.

There are two interesting features of this picture of rise and fall in the importance of occupation of this region from the Chalcolithic to the Medieval period. First, periods of low population or less important occupation seem regularly to occur at transitions, as the directions or areas of major external contacts of this region change. Each successive period of high population or important occupation here shows a different orientation in terms of the region's contacts with the outside. Early, in the Chalcolithic periods, relationships are most obvious to the south, with northern Mesopotamia. The Early Bronze Age I-II is clearly related to the East Anatolian Early Bronze Age and ultimately to the Caucasus. This orientation begins to shift toward central Anatolia with the Early Bronze Age III, in which the painted wares show some resemblance to "Cappadocian" ceramics. The shift is completed by the Hittite period. Not only are the contacts with central Anatolia clear, but it is highly probable that the Altınova formed the center of the Hittite sub-kingdom of Išuwa (Güterbock 1973:140). The last time of extensive occupation identified by our survey is in the Medieval period, in which the region formed part of first the Byzantine, then the Ottoman, Empires.

The second interesting point about this picture of rise and fall in population or occupation is the apparent coincidence of high points in occupation with either extensive trade or with incorporation of this region in a much more extensive empire. Community specialization in copper smelting appears to begin here in the Late Chalcolithic (e.g. at N52/3, cf. Whallon and Wright 1970:70, and at O54/8, cf. *Anatolian Studies* 1975:38)—when the primary external relationships of this region seem to be with northern Mesopotamia. The case for the possible importance of Early Bronze Age trade in metals, wood, etc., with Mesopotamia has been made elsewhere (Whallon 1969). In both the Hittite and Medieval periods the survey area was clearly incorporated within extensive and powerful empires.

The above discussion of settlement patterns within the survey area is brief and often sketchy. It does, however, cover the essential outlines of what our survey revealed about human occupation in this region prior to the present. Naturally it is not a complete picture. The area inundated by the Keban Reservoir does not form a natural geographical unit. Many sites are located outside the borders of the reservoir, and in many cases the pattern of settlement distribution noted within the survey area easily can be seen to continue on beyond it. However, a preliminary picture can usefully be presented from our data.

TABLE 10 Early Chalcolithic Occupation Areas

	Site	Measured Occupation Area (ha)	Site	Total Site Size (ha)	Fraction	Estimated Occupation Area (ha)	Totals (ha)
Altınova	O54/6	.6	O54/1	4.0 est.	.4	1.6	
	O54/8	2.5	O54/2	5.3	.4	2.1	
	O54/14	.1	O54/7	ca. 6.9	.3	2.1	
	O55/2	.3	O54/11	1.0	.6	.6	
	O55/8–9	.4	O54/15	.5	.8	.4	
	Subtotal	3.9	O54/22	.4	.8	.3	
			O54/24	.9	.7	.6	
			O55/1	ca. 2.5	.5	1.3	
					Subtotal	9.0	12.9
Other Areas	N52/1	1.0	N52/9	ca. .5	.8	.4	
	N52/3	.7			Subtotal	.4	2.1
	Subtotal	1.7					
	Totals (ha)	5.6				9.4	15.0

```
              O
              O
              O
         O    O
         X    X              O
         X    X   X    X   O    O   O         X
    ────────────────────────────────────────────────
    0   .35  .65  .95  1.25  1.55  1.85  2.15  2.45  2.75  3.05  3.35
```

Histogram: X = Measured   0 = Estimated

280 Archaeological Survey of the Keban Reservoir

TABLE 11 Late Chalcolithic Occupation Areas

	Site	Measured Occupation Area (ha)	Site	Total Site Size (ha)	Fraction	Estimated Occupation Area (ha)	Totals (ha)
Altınova	O54/6 O54/8 O54/24 O55/8–9 Subtotal	.9 1.8 .7 1.3 4.7	O54/1 O54/2 O54/3 O54/12 O54/27 O55/1 O55/2 O55/3	4.0 est. 5.3 ca. 2.0 ca. .8 .7 ca. 2.5 .3 .6 Subtotal	.4 .4 .5 .7 .7 .5 1.0 .7	1.6 2.1 1.0 .6 .5 1.3 .3 .4 7.8	12.5
Other Areas	N52/3 N52/9 Subtotal	.2 .1 .3					.3
	Totals	5.0				7.8	12.8

```
              O    O
              X    O    X              O    O
              X    O    X    O    X    X    O
          0  .35  .65  .95 1.25 1.55 1.85 2.15 2.45 2.75 3.05 3.35
```

Histogram: X = Measured   O = Estimated

TABLE 12 Chalcolithic-Early Bronze Age Transitional Occupation Areas

	Site	Measured Occupation Area (ha)	Site	Total Site Size (ha)	Fraction	Estimated Occupation Area (ha)	Totals (ha)
Altınova	O55/3 O55/8–9 Subtotal	.1 .9 1.0	O54/1 O54/2	4.0 est. 5.3	.4 .4 Subtotal	1.6 2.1 3.7	4.7
Other Areas			N52/1 N55/1	1.8 2–3 est.	.5 .5 Subtotal	.9 1.3 2.2	2.2
	Totals	1.0				5.9	6.9

```
                   O
              X    X              O    O    O
          0  .35  .65  .95 1.25 1.55 1.85 2.15 2.45 2.75 3.05 3.35
```

Histogram: X = Measured   O = Estimated

TABLE 13 Early Bronze Age I–II Occupation Areas

	Site	Measured Occupation Area (ha)	Site	Total Site Size (ha)	Fraction	Estimated Occupation Area (ha)	Totals (ha)
Altınova	O54/2	2.7	O54/1	4.0 est.	.4	1.6	
	O54/3	ca. 2.0	O54/7	ca. 6.9	.3	2.1	
	O54/8	3.2	O54/11	1.0	.6	.6	
	O54/10	1.1	O54/15	.5	.8	.4	
	O54/12	.5	O54/19	.1	1.0	.1	
	O54/14	.4	O54/20	ca. 4.0	.4	1.6	
	O54/24	.4	O54/23	1.2	.6	.7	
	O55/2	.3	O54/25	1.1	.6	.7	
	O55/3	.2	O54/26	.4	.8	.3	
	O55/6	.1	O54/27	.7	.7	.5	
	O55/8–9	1.7	O54/28	.9	.7	.6	
			O55/1	ca. 2.5	.5	1.3	
	Subtotal	12.6	O55/4	1.3	.6	.8	
			O55/10	1.3	.6	.8	
					Subtotal	12.1	24.7
Other Areas	N52/1	.6	N52/2	ca. 2.0	.5	1.0	
	N52/4	.9	N52/6	.7	.7	.5	
	N52/5	.4	N52/11	.9	.7	.6	
	N52/9	.5	N53/1	.2	1.0	.2	
	Subtotal	2.4	N53/3	.5	.8	.4	
			N55/1	2–3 est.	.5	1.3	
					Subtotal	4.0	6.4
	Totals	15.0				16.1	31.1

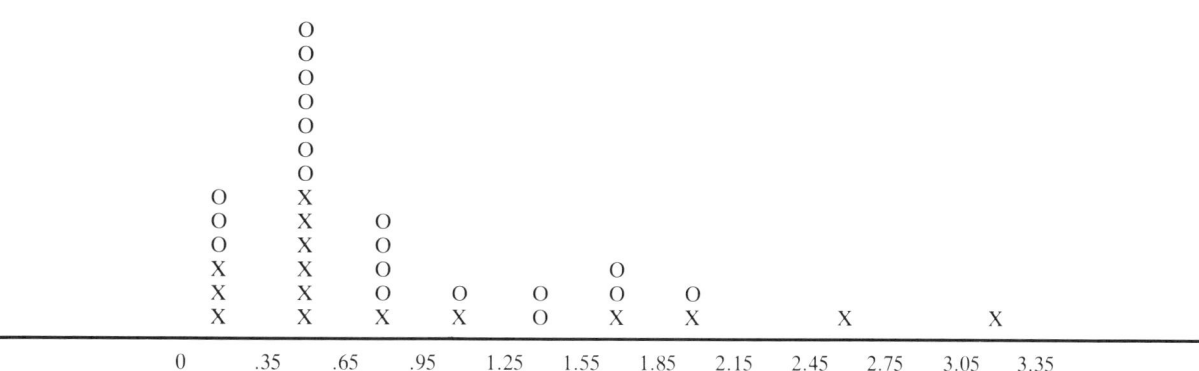

Histogram: X = Measured O = Estimated

TABLE 14 Early Bronze Age IIIA Occupation Areas

	Site	Measured Occupation Area (ha)	Site	Total Site Size (ha)	Fraction	Estimated Occupation Area (ha)	Totals (ha)
Altınova	O54/2 O54/8 Subtotal	1.8 .8 2.6	O54/1 O54/14 O54/24 O55/8–9 O55/10 Subtotal	4.0 est. .5 .9 1.7 1.3	.4 .8 .7 .5 .6	1.6 .4 .6 .9 .8 4.3	6.9
Other Areas	N52/4 Subtotal	.5 .5	N52/2 N52/5 N52/6 Subtotal	ca. 2.0 .8 .7	.5 .7 .7	1.0 .6 .5 2.1	2.6
	Totals	3.1				6.4	9.5

```
            O
            O
            O   O
            O   O                   O
            X   X    O              X
   0   .35 .65 .95 1.25 1.55 1.85 2.15 2.45 2.75 3.05 3.35
```

Histogram: X = Measured   O = Estimated

TABLE 15 Early Bronze Age IIIB Occupation Areas

	Site	Measured Occupation Area (ha)	Site	Total Site Size (ha)	Fraction	Estimated Occupation Area (ha)	Totals (ha)
Altınova	O54/2 O54/8 Subtotal	1.8 .8 2.6	O54/7 O54/14 O54/24 O55/8–9 Subtotal	ca. 6.9 .5 .9 1.7	.3 .8 .7 .5	2.1 .4 .6 .9 4.0	6.6
Other Areas	N52/4 Subtotal	.5 .5	N52/2 N52/6 N52/11 N53/3 Subtotal	ca. 2.0 .7 .9 .5	.5 .7 .7 .8	1.0 .5 .6 .4 2.5	3.0
	Totals	3.1				6.5	9.6

```
        O
        O
        O
        O
        O   O
        X   X    O         X    O
   0  .35 .65 .95 1.25 1.55 1.85 2.15 2.45 2.75 3.05 3.35
```

Histogram: X = Measured   O = Estimated

TABLE 16 Middle Bronze Age Occupation Areas

	Site	Measured Occupation Area (ha)	Site	Total Site Size (ha)	Fraction	Estimated Occupation Area (ha)	Totals (ha)
Altınova	O54/2	.6	O54/1	4.0 est.	.4	1.6	
	O54/8	2.5	O54/7	ca. 6.9	.3	2.1	
	O54/10	.6	O54/9	.6	.7	.4	
	O54/11	.7	O54/12	ca. .8	.7	.6	
	O54/14	.4	O54/19	.1	1.0	.1	
	O55/3	.1	O54/24	.9	.7	.6	
	Subtotal	4.9	O54/25	1.1	.6	.7	
			O54/27	.7	.7	.5	
			O55/4	1.3	.6	.8	
			O55/8–9	1.7	.5	.9	
						Subtotal 8.3	13.2
Other Areas			N52/10	.8	.7	.6	
			N53/1	.2	1.0	.2	
			N55/1	2–3 est.	.5	1.3	
						Subtotal 2.1	2.1
	Totals	4.9				10.4	15.3

```
            O
            O
            O
            O
            O     O
    O       X     O
    O       X     O
    X       X     X         O     O     O           X
  ─────────────────────────────────────────────────────────
    0   .35  .65  .95  1.25  1.55  1.85  2.15  2.45  2.75  3.05  3.35
```

Histogram: X = Measured   O = Estimated

TABLE 17 Late Bronze Age (Hittite) Occupation Areas

	Site	Measured Occupation Area (ha)	Site	Total Site Size (ha)	Fraction	Estimated Occupation Area (ha)	Totals (ha)
Altınova	O54/2	3.4	O54/1	4.0 est.	.4	1.6	
	O54/3	ca. 1.7	O54/5	.8	.7	.6	
	O54/6	1.7	O54/7	ca. 6.9	.3	2.1	
	O54/8	8.2	O54/19	.1	1.0	.1	
	O54/9	.3	O54/22	.4	.8	.3	
	O54/10	.6	O54/26	.4	.8	.3	
	O54/11	.7	O54/28	.9	.7	.6	
	O54/12	.4	O55/1	ca. 2.5	.5	1.3	
	O54/14	.3			Subtotal	6.9	
	O54/15	.1					
	O54/21	.3					
	O54/24	.3					
	O54/25	.2					
	O54/27	.7					
	O55/2	.3					
	O55/3	.1					
	O55/4	1.3					
	O55/6	.1					
	O55/8–9	1.7					
	Subtotal	22.4					29.3
Other Areas	N52/1	.5	N52/2	ca. 2.0	.5	1.0	
	N52/9	.2	N52/11	.9	.7	.6	
	Subtotal	.7	N55/1	2–3 est.	.5	1.3	
					Subtotal	2.9	3.6
	Totals	23.1				9.8	32.9

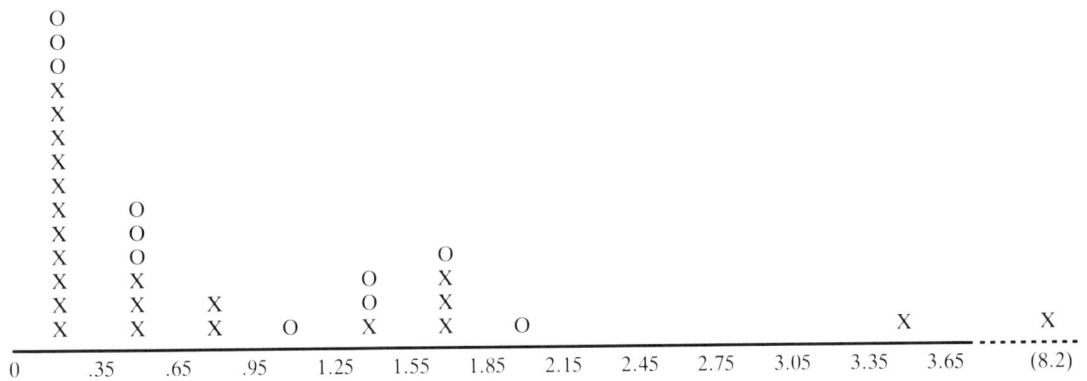

Histogram: X = Measured   O = Estimated

TABLE 18 Iron Age (Early and Unspecified) Occupation Areas

	Site	Measured Occupation Area (ha)	Site	Total Site Size (ha)	Fraction	Estimated Occupation Area (ha)	Totals (ha)
Altınova	O54/2	.8–1.0	O54/3	ca. 2.0	.5	1.0	
	O54/8	3.4	O54/7	ca. 6.9	.3	2.1	
	O55/4	1.3	O54/9	.6	.7	.4	
	Subtotal	5.6	O54/19	.1	1.0	.1	
			O54/28	.9	.7	.6	
			O55/3	.6	.7	.4	
			O55/8–9	1.7	.5	.9	
					Subtotal	5.5	11.1
	Totals	5.6				5.5	11.1

```
                    O
                    O    O
         O     O    X    O    X         O                              X
    ┼────┼────┼────┼────┼────┼────┼────┼────┼────┼────┼────┼────┼
    0   .35  .65  .95  1.25 1.55 1.85 2.15 2.45 2.75 3.05 3.35 3.65
```

Histogram: X = Measured   O = Estimated

TABLE 19 Medieval (Byzantine-Selcuk) Occupation Areas

	Site	Measured Occupation Area (ha)	Site	Total Site Size (ha)	Fraction	Estimated Occupation Area (ha)	Totals (ha)
Altınova	O54/2	1.0–1.5	O54/1	4.0 est.	.4	1.6	
	O54/10	1.2	O54/20	ca. 4.0	.4	1.6	
	O54/11	.8	O54/28	.9	.7	.6	
	O54/12	.6	O55/1	ca. 2.5	.5	1.3	
	O54/16	.5			Subtotal	5.1	
	O54/21	.4					
	O54/23	1.2					
	O54/25	1.1					
	O55/7	.1					
	Subtotal	7.2					12.3
Other Areas	N52/2	ca. 2.0					
	N52/4	.9					
	N52/9	.2					
	Subtotal	3.1					3.1
	Totals	10.3				5.1	15.4

```
                    O
                    X              X
        X    X      X    X    O    O
        X    X      X    X    X    O    X
      ┴────┴────┴────┴────┴────┴────┴────┴────┴────┴────┴────
      0   .35  .65  .95  1.25 1.55 1.85 2.15 2.45 2.75 3.05 3.35
```

Histogram: X = Measured   O = Estimated

Settlement Patterns 287

TABLE 20 Medieval (Ottoman-Recent and Unspecified) Occupation Areas

	Site	Measured Occupation Area (ha)	Site	Total Site Size (ha)	Fraction	Estimated Occupation Area (ha)	Totals (ha)
Altınova	O54/3	ca. 1.0	O54/5	.8	.7	.6	
	O54/6	.9	O54/7	ca. 6.9	.3	2.1	
	O54/8	4.8	O54/19	.1	1.0	.1	
	O54/9	.3	O54/20	ca. 4.0	.4	1.6	
	O54/13	.4	O54/26	.4	.8	.3	
	O54/14	.2	O55/10	1.3	.6	.8	
	O54/15	.2			Subtotal	5.5	
	O54/17	.8					
	O54/18	.8					
	O54/24	.9					
	O54/27	.7					
	O55/3	.1					
	O55/4	1.3					
	O55/5	.6					
	O55/6	.1					
	O55/8–9	.8					
	Subtotal	13.9					19.4
Other Areas	N52/1	.2	N52/6	.7	.7	.5	
	N52/5	.3	N52/7	.1	1.0	.1	
	N52/8	1.6	N52/10	.8	.7	.6	
	Subtotal	2.1	N52/11	.9	.7	.6	
			N53/1	.2	1.0	.2	
			N53/3	.5	.8	.4	
			N55/1	2–3 est.	.5	1.3	
					Subtotal	3.7	5.8
	Totals	16.0				9.2	25.2

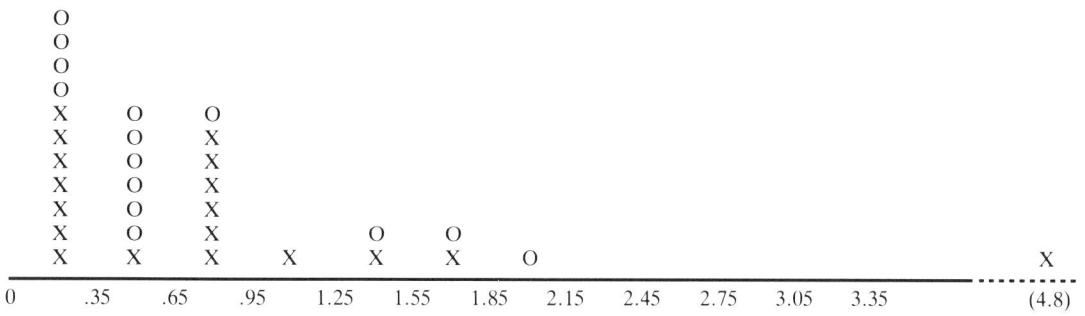

Histogram: X = Measured   O = Estimated

5

Evaluation of Controlled Surface Collection

This work has attempted to bring together and present the results of the 1967 archaeological survey of the Keban Reservoir area. These results have been summarized in the preceding chapters as a general contribution to our understanding of the history and patterns of human occupation of this area. The more detailed descriptions of each site surveyed have been presented as well. However, an important part of this survey was also the experimental application of a number of methods for the controlled collection of surface materials from both large and small mounds. The methods used and the history of their use in archaeological survey have been described and discussed in Chapter 1. A brief evaluation of these various methods and of controlled surface collections in general in the Keban survey may now be offered.

Comparison Among Methods

This evaluation concerns, first, the comparison of the different methods among themselves, primarily in terms of their effectiveness in providing a clear and complete picture of the patterns of distribution of different materials (different ceramic wares for the most part) over a mound. A second concern is the degree to which each method, and ultimately all methods of controlled surface collection together, accurately and adequately reveals the range of occupational periods present and the location and relative importance of each separate period within a mound.

First, we will consider the ease and effectiveness with which the different methods of controlled surface collection provide a picture of the distributional patterns of materials over a mound. Unfortunately, there is no objective standard against which to measure the degree of success of any particular collection system in this regard. Instead, we must resort to a more subjective evaluation, based largely on our experience in analyzing and interpreting the results of the numerous controlled collections made in this survey. We can also point to the results presented in Chapter 3 as evidence for this evaluation. What we are asking here is, how clearly and how thoroughly are patterns of distribution of surface materials revealed by the various controlled collections? A final consideration is, of course, how much effort and time does a given method require both in the field and in the laboratory?

These questions may be answered generally, in terms that apply to all collection methods used in this survey. All methods produced useful results on most sites, and none was clearly superior to all others in all aspects. Therefore, our general conclusions do not rank the various methods of controlled surface collection against each other.

Rather, they provide a series of guidelines in terms of which a particular method may be designed for the collection of any specific site, given the objectives of the collection and the time and means available for it.

In terms of time and effort, there is no difference among methods in the laboratory work required for processing and interpreting the collections. The amount of time and work required in the laboratory is simply a function of the size of the collection—the amount of material recovered. This, in turn, depends upon the size of the mound, the density of surface materials on the mound, and the proportion of the mound's surface which is covered by the collection units. No matter what survey or collection procedure is used, it will take more time and effort to survey a large mound than a small one.

The density of surface materials can be taken into account when using any of the controlled collection methods discussed below, and smaller or larger collection units can be used to obtain adequate quantities of material from sites with dense or sparse scatters of materials on the surface. The degree of coverage, the proportion of a mound's surface actually collected, can also be varied with any of the methods used and discussed here. To some extent this can even out the amount of time and work spent on mounds of different size. In the Keban survey, for example, the proportion of the mound covered by the collection of the largest mound, 054/8 (Norşun Tepe), is significantly less than that covered at the medium sized mound, 054/2 (Tepecik), which in turn is less than the proportion usually covered on smaller sites in the area. However, in practice, varying the intensity of collection is not so much a way of reducing the time and effort of surveying large mounds as it is a way of increasing the amount of information obtained on mounds which, for one or another reason, appear to be of particular interest to the archaeologist carrying out the survey, and of reducing effort while still obtaining the desired minimum of information from sites which seem of less interest or importance.

There are, however, fairly clear differences among collection methods in the ease, clarity and detail with which distributional patterns over a mound are revealed. A primary difference can be noted between the gridded strip collections and all collections made from a scatter of grid squares (random, circular random, stratified random), but within both of these groups, particularly among the various gridded strip collections, significant differences can also be seen. Considered together, these differences can, for the most part, be related to the degree of uniformity of coverage of the mound's surface given by each collection system.

For example, among the gridded strip collections, we can compare those collections made in a single strip across a mound with those made using two or more strips criss-crossing each other or radiating out from a central point. The results of the single-strip collections are generally more difficult to interpret, and the reconstructions of distributional patterns of materials over the whole mound are clearly more tenuous than are those made from multiple-strip collections.

Yet even among the single gridded strip collections there are noticeable differences. Compare the results of the collections from site 054/15, 054/24, 054/25, 054/27, and 054/4 with those from sites 054/3 and 055/2. The former are all moderately small mounds ranging from ca. 70×90 m to ca. 110×145 m in size, but the single strip of collection units across them generally shows only some variation in frequency of materials from the center of the mound towards the edges or from one side of the mound to the other. It requires a strong assumption that different occupation layers will be eroding and therefore most strongly contributing materials to the mound surface near the peripheries of the mound, and often some imagination in addition, to use such results to reconstruct a total picture of the various occupations, their sizes, and their locations on a mound. In contrast, 055/2 is a very small mound, only ca. 60×67 m in size, and only a small part of 054/3, a pie-shaped piece only ca. 75 m along a side, remained for investigation. In the case of 055/2 it was relatively easy to extend the variations in density of materials along the colletrion strip around the small circumference of this regular, circular mound, and it was similarly easy to extend the patterns from the collection strip running down the center of 054/3 to cover the small remaining portion of the mound.

A similar situation is found with the results of the collections made from multiple gridded strips. The majority of these results are reasonable to moderately good and are generally more satisfactory than the results obtained from most single-strip collections. Compare the analyses of the collections from sites N52/1, 054/6, 054/9, 054/10, and 054/11 with those from the sites discussed above. These sites are generally larger than those collected with a single gridded strip. Site 054/9 is relatively small, measuring only some 75×110 m, but the others range from 110×115 m to 120×190 m, 130×170 m, and 140×140 m in size. However, the multiple collection strips were run out over the mounds in several directions so that it is usually not too difficult to relate or connect the patterns of variation in the density of materials from one strip to another. The same assumption of maximum erosion of occupation layers around a mound's periphery is usually basic to this connection of patterns and the reconstruction of a total picture of distribution of various materials over these sites, but the assumption generally need not be so strong and is not quite so essential here. The situation is similar to that of the single-strip collections, however, in that the degree of coverage provided by the several collection strips, relative to the total area of these sites, can be seen to influence the adequacy of the results significantly.

On larger sites, the several gridded collection strips do not provide the degree of coverage of the mound's surface that they do on the sites mentioned above. For example, on 054/8 (Norşun Tepe), the largest mound in the survey area (400 × 500-600 m), four extremely long collection strips were run out from the top of the mound in such a manner as to provide as even a coverage of the collectable parts of the mound as possible, and an enormous quantity of material was collected from these strips. Nevertheless, it was quite difficult to connect the patterns of variation in density of the different materials from one strip to another. Such connections had to be made across wide areas of uninvestigated mound surface, and a very large amount of reliance had to be placed on the assumption that occupation layers would be regularly superimposed and eroding at the edges along the slopes of this mound. In short, both the survey coverage and the confidence felt in the final definition of surface distributional patterns over this mound leave something to be desired in comparison with results from other mounds in the area. Collection from even four extremely long and well spaced gridded strips did not easily provide a clear or very complete picture of surface distributions here because of this mound's exceptional size.

To a lesser extent the same problem is evident at N52/2, a site of some 150 × 150 m in size. Here, however, the problem is greatly mitigated because of the relatively simple picture of occupational history revealed by the surface materials. A few Early Bronze Age and Hittite sherds were found, but the overwhelming bulk of the surface material was Medieval. In this situation, the later occupation was so substantial and extensive, and earlier levels so deeply and thoroughly buried, that the rare pre-Medieval sherds found on the surface are only accidental finds which can do no more than hint at the presence of such earlier occupations. The only significant distribution of materials which can be observed on the surface of the mound is that of the Medieval ceramics, and they cover the entire site. The gridded strip collection is adequate to show this clearly, although large areas of the mound are not covered by the collection.

This introduces a second factor to consider in judging the adequacy of various methods of collection. Not only is the degree of uniformity of coverage of the mound surface important, but the degree of complexity of surface distributions also plays a large role in determining whether a given method or degree of survey coverage will provide a clear picture of the distribution of materials over a site. Other things being equal, less coverage will be necessary, and a simpler method of collection will be adequate, on a mound where only one or a limited number of occupations are represented by any quantity of materials on the surface.

Both of these factors play a role in conditioning the results from the remaining sites collected with multiple gridded strips. At 054/12, the collection strips effectively covered one side of this small (85x90 m) mound. Consequently, results are relatively clear and satisfactory for this half of the site and quite ambiguous for the other half. 054/16 is a very small site, only 65 × 90 m in size and was apparently occupied in only one period. Here, obviously, there was no difficulty in interpreting the results of the controlled surface collection in two gridded strips.

The collection of complete, concentric, annular bands is a rather unusual method, applied only at site N52/4 because of the particular condition of the surface of that mound. While it did provide some results in this rather difficult situation for surface collection, it really cannot be considered to be a method for defining patterns of distribution of surface materials on a site. It can only provide the general picture of the sequence and depth of the occupation levels in a mound, and it must rely completely upon the assumption of uniform superpositioning of levels and of their erosion along their edges on the mound slopes or at the mound's periphery. It is a method to be applied only in exceptional circumstances.

In considering methods of controlled surface collection which use a scatter of individual collection units over the site area, we can immediately note a generally striking improvement over gridded strip collection methods in the ease with which clear and relatively detailed patterns of distribution of materials can be defined.

Both the simple random scatters at N52/3, N52/9, 054/21, and 055/8-9 and the stratified random scatter of squares at 054/2 produced results noticeably better than those of the gridded strip collections. Primarily, this is due to a better overall coverage of the mound surface by the scattered collection squares, which greatly reduces the distances over which patterns and density contours must be extrapolated without confirming information from a collection unit.

We will make no distinction in this discussion between collection from a series of squares placed at random over a mound according to a rectangular grid system and collections from a similar series of squares located according to a circular grid system. In theory and results these two methods are identical. In practice it was convenient to use a circular system at the very regular, circular site N52/3.

The only difference in method among these particular collections lies in the contrast between the stratified random scattering of grid squares at 054/2 and the simple random placement of squares at all other sites. The simple random scatters of collection squares covered about 10 percent of the area of the mounds on which they were used. The density of coverage of 054/2 was not uniform and averaged a good deal less than 10 percent over the whole mound. Nevertheless, the controlled surface collection results were at least as good and generally even superior to the results of the simple random collection methods. Very likely, this is because stratification in sampling tends to produce a more even coverage of the entire survey area.

We can now summarize the above comparisons. They do not allow any clear–cut or fixed ranking of the various methods of controlled surface collection used in the Keban survey. Rather, they point to a series of factors which play a role in such collection, condition its results, and should be taken into account in the planning, carrying out, and interpretation of the results of a controlled collection on any specific site. These factors are:

1. The uniformity of coverage of the mound surface provided by each method

2. The degree of complexity of the occupational history or of the patterns of material distribution over the mound (or—the degree of detail desired in the picture of distributional patterns revealed by the collection)

3. The density of material on the mound surface

4. The relative efficiency or speed of application of each method in the field.

It is clear from the above discussions that the primary factor governing the success of any collection method is the degree to which it provides an adequate coverage of the mound's surface. There must be some approximation to a uniform coverage of all parts of the site. This determines the extent to which one must extrapolate observed patterning across uncollected areas of the site. The less one has to extrapolate in this manner, the more clear cut and obvious are the patterns of surface distribution over the site and the greater the reliance we may place on their accuracy. Thus, gridded strip collections are adequate and quite successful in those instances where the mound being surveyed is small and regular enough that a single strip covers a good portion of its surface and all of its topographic features (e.g. 055/2) or where enough strips are run over the mound to adequately cover it in this way (e.g. N52/1, 054/6, 054/9, 054/10, 054/11).

However, collections made from gridded strips are not efficient in one way, even when they are effective. The continuous pattern of variation in the frequency of occurrence of various materials along such a strip across the mound is not generally necessary for a good reconstruction of the overall picture of the distributions of these materials. It was initially thought that such continuous strips would be useful under the assumption of relatively uniform superpositioning of occupations and the erosion of their edges along the sides or peripheries of a mound. Clearly this is not a very accurate assumption in most cases, and furthermore, even where it is, it is more effective to have an accurate estimate of the density of material at a series of points or over a series of given areas scattered as evenly as possible over a mound.

From this, several things follow. First of all, it is important to adjust the size of the collection units to the density of materials on the site surface. The 3×4 m units that were generally standard in the gridded strip collections on the Keban area mounds seem, by and large, to have been somewhat too small. It was for this reason that, rather than raw counts per collection unit, moving averages over several units, commonly as many as six, were usually needed to define surface distributional patterns from these strip collections. The 4×4 m squares used in the various randomized grid collection systems were somewhat better in this respect, and even larger collection units might have been preferable, on at least some sites.

A second point which follows from the above considerations is that the more uniform the coverage of the entire mound, the more satisfactory the results of the surface collection in general. This is one explanation for the good results obtained with a stratified random scatter of collection squares over 054/2 in comparison to the results obtained at other sites using only a simple random scatter, even though the percentage of the surface area of 054/2 covered by the collection was significantly less than at these other sites. Gaps or open areas can be noted on all the sites over which a simple random scatter of squares was placed in the Keban survey. This is normal for a random scatter. To avoid this problem, a special method for areal sampling has been developed—systematic stratified unaligned distribution of sample units (Berry 1962; Haggett 1965:196–197). Some archaeologists have simply filled in the evident gaps or spaces in an otherwise random scatter of units (Redman and Watson 1970). These methods have been developed using randomization as an essential part of the placement of collection or survey units in order to avoid problems which might arise if uniformity or periodicity in the data being sampled happens to correspond to the uniformity or periodicity in the lay-out of sample units. In our earlier experiences with controlled surface collections in eastern Turkey (Whallon n.d.), we had no problems in using a uniform distribution of collection squares to obtain clear and useful results, however. The question remains open, but since no statistical inferences are generally drawn from the data of such surface collections, which would require careful random sampling, there seems little reason to slavishly adhere to strict random sampling procedures. Perhaps one should try to approach these, but the value of a uniform coverage of the entire site should also be kept in mind when planning a controlled surface collection.

Finally, to temper all the above considerations, the factor of efficiency and time spent in the field will always play an important role in planning any collection strategy. It must be remembered that the time and effort in the laboratory always remains long, and is directly related to the size of the site and the collection made from it, no matter what method is chosen for collection in the field. Nonetheless, there are differences among the methods which may influence one's choice in a given situation. Any gridded strip collection is, of course, somewhat faster and more efficient in the field than any randomized grid collection. A uniform grid of equally spaced collection squares would fall somewhere in between these two methods in speed and ease. In our experience, any finer distinction than these general differences is unimportant. Even these general differences are not great, and the other factors discussed above must all play a greater role in the planning of any collection procedures.

Of course, if time and effort are of no consequence, the ultimate solution is total collection within a grid covering the entire site. Such a collection was made in the course of the Keban survey at 055/3 because of our particular interest in the preceramic materials from this site. (These will be reported elsewhere). Unfortunately, this solution will be feasible for only a few sites and naturally will be restricted to sites of particular interest and importance. The controlled collection of samples of material from site surfaces will remain important, therefore. Hopefully our experiences in the Keban Reservoir survey and their discussion herein may prove useful in the planning and execution of similar ventures in the future.

COMPARISON OF SURVEY AND EXCAVATION RESULTS

A number of the mounds investigated by the Keban Reservoir survey were subsequently excavated. Some of these excavations were no more than small soundings, but others were extensive. A comparison of the results of these excavations, particularly of the extensive excavations, provides some measure of the accuracy and usefulness of the results of surface survey. The relevant sites for such comparison are:

1. Sites at which controlled surface collections were made and at which excavations were extensive enough or located in such a way as to provide a check on the distributional patterns revealed by the surface collections:

054/2 (Tepecik)
054/8 (Norşun Tepe).

2. Sites at which a similar check is possible to a lesser degree:

N52/2 (Taşkun Kalesi)
N52/3 (Fatmalı-Kalecik)
054/3 (Değirmen Tepe).

3. Sites at which controlled surface collections were made but at which excavations were too restricted to do more than indicate the presence of certain occupation layers in one part of the mound:

N52/1 (Taşkun Mevkii)
N52/4 (Aşvan Kalesi)
N52/9 (Çay Boyu)
055/8-9 (Habusu Körtepe).

4. Sites at which only preliminary surface survey and collections were made, for which it is possible to compare the survey and excavation results only in terms of occupations of various periods:

N52/5 (Pulur)
N52/6 (Kalaycık)
N53/3 (Hanibrahimşah)

054/2 TEPECİK

This moderately large mound in the Altınova was extensively and deeply excavated over several seasons (Esin 1970, 1971, 1972, 1974). Without going into the details of the abundant results of these excavations, a general picture of the occupational history and of the structure of this mound can be put together, with which the results of the controlled surface collections can be compared. Fortunately, these important excavations were well planned and clearly reported so that information is available not only on the occurrence and stratigraphic succession of occupations here but also to a large extent on the locations and sizes of these occupations.

In the first place, we can note that the list of occupations present in this mound, as defined from the results of our surface collections (Chapter 3), is identical to that revealed by the excavations. Even the assessment of relative importance of these occupations was quite accurate and understandable in terms or the stratigraphy of the mound. All of the periods for which major occupations were suggested by the surface survey are, in fact, represented on the mound by substantial building levels or extensive areas of activity. The Chalcolithic–Early Bronze Age Transitional period was ranked as a minor phase of occupation by the analysis of the surface survey materials. Excavation results seem to suggest that this evaluation may be generous and that only a slight trace of occupation in this period occurs on the mound (cf. Esin 1974:134–135). The Early Chalcolithic and Late Chalcolithic occupations said were to be minor from the survey results. In fact, they are probably more important than this. However, the Late Chalcolithic is quite deeply buried and, at least partially, seems to occur well off the mound proper. As was suggested in the discussion of the survey results, the Early Chalcolithic (called Neolithic by Esin) is even more deeply buried under the many succeeding occupation levels. Consequently, very little material from these occupations has a chance of being brought to the mound's surface by any minor erosion or other disturbance such as the digging of borrow pits, small irrigation channels, or village roads.

In reviewing the interpretation of the distributional patterns revealed by the controlled surface collection, a similarly good correspondence can be seen with the results of the excavations. The picture of Early Bronze Age I-II occupation comprising a large part of the high mound and extending widely out over the lower slopes, particularly to the southwest of the high mound, seems to be essentially confirmed by the excavations. The Early Bronze Age III occupation was portrayed as being concentrated around a pre-existing central mound largely made up of Early Bronze Age I-II debris, extending somewhat up onto that central mound, and except on the north, generally being absent from the wider area of the lower mound slopes. This seems also to be largely accurate, with the exception that it seriously underestimates the degree to which occupation in this period occurred over the central, high mound. In fact, substantial Early Bronze Age III layers appear to cover most or all of the high mound, occurring in some spots immediately under the present-day surface. Otherwise, the picture presented from the surface survey data of a significant occupation, yet one noticeably more restricted in extent than the Early Bronze Age I-II settlement is fairly close to the mark.

The distribution of Middle Bronze Age ceramics from the survey collection indicated an occupation clustered around the base of the high mound, extending also out over the northern slopes. This is exactly the picture of Middle Bronze Age settlement revealed by excavation. The buildings of this period were specifically noted by the excavator as having been placed up against the base of the old Early Bronze Age mound or on a terrace cut into the base of this mound (Esin 1972:152-153), and this occupation level was also traced out across the northern lower mound slopes.

Hittite occupation was described from the survey results as being concentrated on the northern half of the site, surrounding the central high mound on the west, north, and east, with significant extensions onto the southern fringe of the mound. The central mound, the southeastern portion of the terrace, and the central southern slopes of the mound were judged to be relatively free of Hittite materials. Insofar as it can be checked against excavation data, this description holds up remarkably well. Excavation revealed substantial Hittite building levels on the north slopes and around the northern base of the high mound, in effect forming a secondary part of the high mound in this area. Hittite levels were also found partly over the southwestern slopes of the high mound, on small portions of the eastern slopes and of the eastern lower slopes, and on the southwestern lower slopes. Hittite levels were not found on the south-central slopes of the high mound, nor on the south-central portions of the terrace and lower mound slopes. The interpretation of the survey results did not adequately stress the extension of occupation in this period over the northern half of the high mound, although, in restrospect, some indications of this can be seen in the density contours of surface finds over at least part of this area. Unfortunately much of the area over which surface survey indicated substantial occurrence of Hittite remains, particularly areas of the lower slopes at some distance from the central mound, was not explored by excavation so no test of the meaning of these distributions is possible.

This is even more true for the Iron Age. Most of the areas indicated by controlled surface collection as having concentrations of Iron Age materials were not tested by excavation. Iron Age occupation levels were found on the southwestern part of the central mound. Survey had shown a strong extension of surface materials over this area, but this was largely disregarded in interpreting the surface distributions because it appeared to be an exception to a more general pattern of concentration of Iron Age ceramics over the lower slopes at some distance from the central mound. The distribution of surface materials was more accurate in this case than we were ready to accept. An Iron Age house was found in a sounding on the east edge of the mound terrace. This structure was not far from a small concentration of Iron Age surface finds, but the wide scatter of collection squares and the isolation of this small sounding do not allow us to draw any general conclusions here.

In the case of Medieval materials, surface collection correctly pinpointed the major area of occupation as the far southern slopes or apron of the mound. At the time these plots were made, however, initial excavation had already revealed the existence of a large cemetery area of this period over most of the older mound. This knowledge was incorporated into the discussion of the results of the controlled collection, and it is likely that the inferred area of occupation would have been much larger had this fact not been known. This problem is briefly mentioned in Chapter 3.

In summary, the accuracy of the results of the controlled surface collections at this site was excellent when checked against the results of large-scale excavations.

054/8 (NORŞUN TEPE)

Very large and deep excavations were made on this mound over the course of a number of years (Hauptmann 1969/70, 1970, 1971, 1972, 1974, 1976a, 1976b; Anatolian Studies 1975). The mound is enormous, though, so that most of the mound area unfortunately remains unexcavated in spite of the very great amount of digging carried out here. In fact, the areas over which three of the four gridded strips of our controlled surface collection passed remain untouched by excavation with the exception of the top of the high peak of the mound. Only along the path of strip C, running straight across the southern slopes and apron of the mound, do we find an extensive series of shallow excavation areas. Nevertheless, enough was excavated to give a clear picture of the occupational history of this mound and to provide at least some idea of the extent and importance of many of the occupations.

Simply in terms of occupational periods represented on this mound and of their relative importance, the correspondence between the results derived from the controlled surface collection and the excavation results is rather good. The existence of major Early Bronze Age I-II, Hittite, and Early Iron Age occupations inferred from the survey collection is borne out by the results of the excavations. Middle Bronze Age levels also were certainly present but seem to be of somewhat lesser importance in the areas excavated, while Medieval occupation was revealed by excavation only as a cemetery on the top of the mound. However, if the situation here parallels that at 054/2 (Tepecik), Medieval settlement may well be on the lower mound slopes. Such a possibility is certainly suggested by the distributional pattern of the Medieval ceramics, as discussed below.

On the other hand, the four occupations suggested to be relatively minor on the basis of surface materials, the Early Chalcolithic, Late Chalcolithic, Early Bronze Age III, and Middle Iron Age, in fact show up as very substantial and important in the excavations. Both the Middle Iron Age and the Early Bronze Age III building levels were near or at the surface of the mound. However, the Early Chalcolithic and Late Chalcolithic occupation levels were deeply buried.

The Chacolithic-Early Bronze Age Transitional occupation layer was also quite deeply buried, and the results of the surface survey indicated only a trace of materials from this period. There is a trace of Roman occupation shown by the surface collection but this was not corroborated by excavation. However, only one occupation revealed by excavation (the deeply buried Halafian, cf. Chapter 3) was missed by the controlled surface collection.

The occupation levels of the Early and Late Chalcolithic, the Chalcolithic-Early Bronze Age Transitional, and, to a large extent, of the Early Bronze Age I-II were found by the excavators only in a relatively small, deep sounding on the west slopes, near the base of the high mound peak. No real test of the conclusions reached from the analysis of surface distributions concerning the extent of these occupations on the mound can be made from such a limited exposure by the excavations. However, the concentrations of Early Chalcolithic and Early Bronze Age I-II ceramics along the gridded strips were also in this same general zone, the slopes near the base of the high, central mound, and this fact suggests that the surface distributions of these materials may, indeed, have some validity. Apparently an Early Bronze Age I-II city wall runs along this zone in the sounding on the western slope.

The location and size of the Early Bronze Age III (A and B) occupation, as inferred from the results of controlled surface collection, was virtually identical to that revealed by excavation. This occupation was concentrated on the top of the central, high mound and was approximately 90 × 60 m in size. Also, the suggestion of a continuity of occupation of the mound throughout this period is well confirmed by the excavations.

A good comparison of survey and excavation results is impossible for the Middle Bronze Age and the Hittite periods. The small amount of occupation indicated for the high mound seems to be confirmed, but the areas of major surface concentration of the materials from both these periods are far from any excavation areas on the mound. No real tests or conclusions are possible here.

For the Early Iron Age, a small area on the mound top and two large areas, one on the northwest and one on the south and southeast lower slopes, with some hint of an area on the western lower slopes, were indicated as concentrations of occupation by the controlled collection. Excavation confirms the presence of Early Iron Age occupation levels on the mound top and on the western and southern slopes. The occupation of the top of the mound was more extensive and substantial than the surface collection had indicated. The picture of Early Iron Age occupation of the southern lower slopes corresponds very closely to that indicated by the surface materials, however. Unfortunately, the large concentrations on the north and the southeastern lower slopes are in unexcavated portions of the mound, and no further control on their accuracy as indicators of occupation areas can be made.

The location and extent of Middle Iron Age occupation were not well predicted by the results of the controlled surface collection. Partly, this was the result of distinguishing Early Iron Age and Middle Iron Age ceramics only on the basis of certain rim forms. A reanalysis of the surface collections from this mound might produce better results. It was suggested that the occupation of this period might be concentrated over the western, southern, and southeastern areas of the lower mound slopes. In fact, there is significant occupation on the top of the mound and also over the southern slopes, but it is concentrated here primarily at the southernmost end of the collection strip and beyond. None of this showed up in the results of the survey.

Medieval occupation was found in the excavations only as a cemetery over the top of the mound. This was seen in the results of the controlled surface collections as a small, secondary area of occupation. The suggested coverage of the southern mound slopes did not materialize in the excavations, which run well across this area, but the plot of the surface materials shows a particularly high concentration in the unexcavated southeastern portion of the lower slopes. A good deal of this occupation may be almost modern (perhaps Armenian, cf. Chapter 3) and it may be largely eroded and no longer recognizable as an occupation or building level. On the other hand, the situation is reminiscent of that at 054/2 (Tepecik), and a smaller residential area may exist on some part of the large unexcavated areas of the lower mound slopes (perhaps on the southeast), with the high mound top being used as a cemetery area.

At 054/8 the correspondence between the results of the controlled surface collection and the excavations is, by and large, quite good. A few discrepancies occur due to lack of expertise in the identification of certain ceramics or the deep burial of certain occupation levels in the mound. In several instances the coverage of the mound provided by the surface collection and by the excavations was rather different, and a cross–check between the results of the two kinds of investigation was not possible. All in all, largely because of the unusual and enormous size of this mound, neither the coverage by the surface collection procedure nor by excavation was proportionally as great as that at 054/2, and an overall knowledge of the whole site as an area of multiple occupations and activities, therefore, cannot be as complete as it would be with proportionally greater coverage. The positive comparisons between survey and excavation results here are encouraging, however.

N52/2 (TAŞKUN KALESİ)

The excavations at this site were very limited (McNicoll 1973). However, they suffice to confirm our conclusion, drawn from the results of the controlled surface collection, that in its present form this site is essentially a Medieval mound. A tiny sounding on the mound peak also revealed Early Bronze Age I-II levels with "rail-rim" pottery, an occupation which was recognized but labeled minor from the surface survey. Hittite and Early Bronze Age III occupations, identified from surface materials, were not found in the excavations, but this is not surprising, considering their very limited extent and depth.

N52/3 (FATMALI-KALECİK)

The excavation at this mound was no more than a single small trench, but this was placed so that the results of the controlled surface collection, which had indicated a boundary or overlap in this area between Early and Late Chalcolithic occupations on the mound could be tested (Whallon and Wright 1970). Confirmation of the surface survey results was clear and complete. A Late Chalcolithic level overlaps and tapers out on top of an Early Chalcolithic deposit in exactly the spot where the controlled surface collection had indicated this should occur. These two occupations make up the entire mound as indicated both by surface survey and excavation.

054/3 (DEĞİRMEN TEPE)

The apparently small excavations on this mound have only been reported in a preliminary notice (Anatolian Studies 1974). However, some picture of the findings is available from this source and may be compared to the results of the controlled surface collections.

These surface collections had indicated a major concentration of Early Bronze Age I-II ceramics on the high part of the mound, which suggested that the bulk of the mound was formed of occupation materials from this period. The situation was considered parallel to that at other sites in this area (e.g. 054/2, 054/8). In fact, the excavation results support this conclusion, with the exception that the uppermost levels on the top of the mound belong to the Early Bronze Age III period, including painted pottery, of which only a single sherd was recovered from the surface. This occupation was thus recorded only as a "trace" from the results of the surface survey. It is not clear how extensive or important the levels of this period were in the excavations. Underlying them, however, were the earlier Early Bronze Age layers, and the general conclusion that the central high part of this mound consists of Early Bronze Age materials is the same from both the surface collection and the excavations.

Also, the excavations revealed first millennium B.C. Iron Age wares from levels on the lower slopes of the mound. This corresponds well with the finding of the controlled surface collection that the Iron Age ceramics here were concentrated over what we called the middle slopes of the mound.

Other occupations identified from the surface collections either were not found in the excavations or not mentioned in the brief note summarizing the major results of the excavations. The only period for which this is somewhat unexpected is the "Medieval," from which material was shown by the controlled surface collection to be concentrated over the middle range of the slopes. This appears to have been virtually modern, with an Ottoman pipe fragment and no Medieval Islamic wares appearing in the collections, and it may be entirely eroded or only a surface scatter here. Hittite sherds showed a concentration further down the mound slopes than the Iron Age ceramics, and by inference beyond the range of the excavations as well. Chalcolithic levels, if indeed present at this mound, would lie deeper than the apparent limits of the soundings made.

Again, the situation at this site is not ideal for testing the adequacy or accuracy of controlled surface collections, but certain major conclusions agree and were independently reached, and the correspondence between results of controlled surface collection and excavation was good where it could be checked.

N52/1 (TAŞKUN MEVKİİ)

Only a very small area on the north–central part of this mound was excavated (Helms 1973). A single period, the Chalcolithic-Early Bronze Age Transitional, was represented by several building levels here. Some Early Bronze Age IIIA material was found in the surface layers and in pits extending down from the topsoil. The controlled surface collection had revealed the Chalcolithic-Early Bronze Age Transitional period as only a "trace" and had missed the Early Bronze Age III phase completely. On the other hand, the surface collection recovered materials of a number of other periods and showed significant concentrations of them on various parts of the mound. None of these occupations were represented in the excavations.

However, this is not a good test of the relationship between patterns of surface distribution revealed through controlled collection and the actual occupation layers in a mound as discovered by excavation. The very small excavation area was apparently located at the northern tip of the area covered by the controlled surface survey. Thus it lies essentially outside the areas of concentration of the different surface materials found by the controlled collection.

N52/4 (AŞVAN KALESİ)

A number of seasons of excavations were carried out at this site, concentrating on the large, flat top of the mound (French 1971; Mitchell 1973, 1974). Only a roughly controlled surface collection was made here, this being the one site at which concentric, annular rings were used as collection units. The agreement between the results of the surface collection and the excavations was expected to be very general and vague. Instead, with one or two gaps, it was surprisingly good.

Both the Early Bronze Age I-II and the Medieval occupations of the mound were considered to have been major on the basis of the surface survey results. The Early Bronze Age III and Hellenistic–Roman occupations were considered to have been minor. In terms of distribution, the Medieval materials seemed to cover the entire site. The Early Bronze Age I-II materials covered an area from collection Strip 6 down to the base of the mound at Strip 10, while those of the Early Bronze Age III period were concentrated from Strip 4 down to Strip 6. All of this accords rather well with the results indicated by the excavator. Although Medieval building levels are said to be confined to the north and west sides of the mound, the period is represented elsewhere by pits producing abundant materials, which are said to honeycomb the upper levels of the site. The exact area covered is not clear, but even if we assume reference is being made only to the flat mound top, this picture fits well with that of a major occupation here in the Medieval period, with a wide scatter of debris covering the mound.

Also, the distribution of all Early Bronze Age materials together corresponds remarkably well with the excavator's assessment that Early Bronze Age layers begin about two-thirds of the way up the mound and continue all the way to its base.

Hellenistic–Roman occupation was thought to be small and was counted as covering only the mound top. In fact it is small, and was not found in all excavated areas. However, since these areas were apparently restricted to the top of the mound, it is not sure that occupation of this period is, indeed, confined to this location.

The identifications of the Middle Bronze Age and Hittite materials from the controlled surface collection were considered tenuous and in fact, no occupation of either period was uncovered in the limited excavation of the mound.

Although the potential for correspondence between the inferences made from the results of the controlled surface survey and the situation revealed by excavation was considered to be slight, and although the restriction of excavation to the flat mound top made a strong test of such correspondence impossible, the degree of agreement between the results of the surface collection and of the excavations here is surprisingly good.

N52/9 (ÇAY BOYU)

The excavations at this mound were exceedingly small, consisting only of a 2×2 m sounding made in the cut which forms the present east edge of the mound (Diamant and Aksoy 1972, 1974; Aksoy and Diamant 1973). Only two phases were identified from the occupation levels in this sounding. They were clearly Early and Late Chalcolithic in date. Both periods had been definitely identified as present from the surface survey of the mound. The Late Chalcolithic was characterized as a "major" occupation, and the Early Chalcolithic was called a "minor" one. Of course, nothing can be said from a 2×2 m excavation concerning the relative extent and importance of these occupations. The Early Chalcolithic deposit seems substantial, however, and the characterization of this period as one of "minor" occupation here may simply be due to its being well covered by later overburden.

None of the several other occupations identified from the controlled surface collections were found in the excavations. Major occupation in the Early Bronze Age I-II and Hittite periods, minor occupation in Medieval times, and a trace of Middle Bronze Age occupation were suggested by the surface survey, in addition to the Chalcolithic occupations already mentioned. There was also a possible trace of Early Bronze Age III occupation. Of these other occupations, the surface distributional patterns could be plotted for the Early Bronze Age I-II, Hittite, and Medieval materials. The ceramics of the two latter periods showed distinct concentrations within the remaining area of the mound, with little indication of any spread or extension over the area of the cut onto the eroded portion of the site. It is, thus, not surprising that no indication of occupation in these periods was found in a sounding at the cut. The Early Bronze Age I-II materials, however, did seem originally to have extended well across the cut and onto the now eroded part of the mound. Some trace of this period might therefore have been expected in excavations along the face of this cut. On the other hand, an excavation of only 2×2 m cannot be expected to produce very reliable coverage of any site area, and no conclusive test of the results of the controlled surface collection can be made at this site.

O55/8-9 (HABUSU KÖRTEPE)

Here, also, only a small sounding was made. In this case the sounding was made on a spot already partially dug away for road fill, exposing the early, basal layers of the site (Hauptmann 1976c). The only occupation levels excavated in this sounding were Early Chalcolithic, a period for which controlled surface collection had indicated a major occupation at this site. Further surface collections by the excavators produced materials of all periods, from Early Chalcolithic to Early Iron Age, a picture identical to that revealed by controlled collection. However, lack of any further excavation precludes any determination of what these surface materials and their patterns of distribution mean in terms of actual occupation levels within the mound.

N52/5 (PULUR)

Only a preliminary surface collection was made from this extensively excavated site (Koşay 1976). The conclusions drawn from this general collection fit very well with the results of excavation, however. The Early Bronze Age I-II was considered a period of major occupation, thought perhaps to make up the bulk of the high mound. A minor occupation in Early Bronze Age IIIA times was suggested for the upper levels of the high mound. In fact, excavations show that levels I-VIII of the high mound were Early Bronze Age IIIA in date, with the bulk of the mound below level VIII consisting of Early Bronze Age I-II layers.

The major Medieval occupation suggested from the surface collections was considered to be late and possibly connected to the occupation of this spot up to the present day. No Medieval levels were found in the excavation of the high mound, and it must be concluded that these "Medieval" materials are virtually modern and relate to occupation around the foot of the high mound, where a contemporary village was located.

The Late Chalcolithic occupation uncovered by the excavations in levels XII-XIII at the base of the mound was entirely missed by the surface survey. However, a single illustrated sherd from the excavations (Koşay 1976: Colored Pl. IVb) looks very much like an Early Chalcolithic sherd and is the same sort of evidence from which a questionable "trace" of occupation in this period was postulated from the surface collections.

N52/6 (KALAYCIK)

A number of seasons of excavation were carried out at this site, from which only a preliminary surface collection was made (Serdaroğlu 1970, 1971, 1972, 1974). The occupations of various periods covered different areas and were found in different excavation units. The over-all sequence however, appears to be: Islamic, Byzantine, Roman, First Millennium (Iron Age), Late Bronze Age, Early Bronze Age IIIA, and Early Bronze Age I-II.

Of these, the Roman and Late Bronze Age occupations were not identified or detected by the preliminary surface collection. Grouping Byzantine and Islamic together, all the other occupations were identified at this site, although it was impossible to judge their relative importance accurately. On the other hand, a Middle Bronze Age occupation, although only a "trace," was thought from the results of the surface survey to occur here. No trace of such an occupation was mentioned in the excavation reports.

N53/3 (HANİBRAHİMŞAH)

Excavations at this mound revealed a succession of occupation layers running from Byzantine to Early Bronze Age IIIB to Early Bronze Age IIIA to Early Bronze Age I-II, terminating on solid bedrock (Ertem 1972, 1974). Preliminary surface collection had identified the presence of Medieval, Early Bronze Age IIIB and Early Bronze Age I-II periods here. The substantial occupation of Early Bronze Age IIIA date was missed. Traces of Late Chalcolithic and Hittite occupation were considered questionable from the surface collection results, and, in fact, no trace of these periods was noted in the excavations.

SUMMARY

There are, naturally, discrepancies between the conclusions reached from surface collection and the results of excavation. This is to be expected. However, we feel that the discrepancies revealed above are relatively minor when viewed in light of the really extensive and sometimes surprising correspondences and confirmations between surface survey and excavation results. This is extremely encouraging, and it gives us a great deal of confidence in the survey results even where they were not checked by later excavations.

The best correspondences come from mounds on which both extensive, controlled surface collections and extensive excavations, covering a large portion of the area of the mound, had been made. More discrepancies were noted when the degree of surface survey coverage was less extensive or when excavations were more limited in extent and coverage.

This is indicative of two things. First, surface survey, particularly well planned, controlled collection, can be a quite accurate method for revealing the occupational history of a mound as well as the sizes and locations of most of the occupation levels within the mound. Second, excavation, also, is not immune to the problems of failing to discover occupations or of giving an inaccurate or incomplete picture of the location and extent of an occupation. The same principles of good sampling and well planned coverage of a site are as necessary in excavation as they are in surface survey.

Bibliography

Aksoy, Behin and Steven Diamant
    1973 Çayboyu 1970–71. Anatolian Studies 23:97–108.
Altınlı, İ. Enver, Hamit N. Pamir and Cahit Erentöz
    1963 Erzurum. 1:500,000 Ölçekli Türkiye Jeoloji Haritası (Explanatory Text of the Geological Map of Turkey). Ankara: Maden Tetkik ve Arama Enstitüsü.
Amiran, Ruth B.K.
    1952 Connections between Anatolia and Palestine in the Early Bronze Age. Israel Exploration Journal 2:89–103.
Anatolian Studies
    1974 Recent Archaeological Research in Turkey, Norşuntepe, 1973. Anatolian Studies 24:43–44.
    1975 Recent Archaeological Research in Turkey, Norşuntepe. Anatolian Studies 25:35–38.
Bakırer, Ömür
    1974 The Excavations at Korucutepe, Turkey, 1968–70: Preliminary Report, Part VII: The Medieval Glazed Pottery. Journal of Near Eastern Studies 33:96–108.
Baykal, Fuat and Cahit Erentöz
    1966 Sivas. 1:500,000 Ölçekli Türkiye Jeoloji Haritası (Explanatory Text of the Geological Map of Turkey). Ankara: Maden Tetkik ve Arama Enstitüsü.
Berry, Brian J.L.
    1962 Sampling, Coding, and Storing Flood Plain Data. U.S. Dept. of Agriculture, Farm Economics Division. Agriculture Handbook 237.
    1967 Geography of Market Centers and Retail Distribution. Englewood Cliffs, New Jersey: Prentice Hall.
Bier, Carol Manson
    1973 The Excavations at Korucutepe, Turkey, 1968–70: Preliminary Report, Part II: The Fortification Wall. Journal of Near Eastern Studies 32: 424–434.
Binford, Lewis R., Sally R. Binford, Robert Whallon, and Margaret Ann Hardin
    1970 Archaeology at Hatchery West. Memoirs of the Society for American Archaeology No. 24.
Bittel, Kurt
    1970 Hattusha. New York: Oxford University Press.
Braidwood, Robert J.
    1972 Prehistoric Investigations in Southwestern Asia. Proceedings of the American Philosophical Society 116:310–320.
Braidwood, Robert J. and Linda Braidwood
    1960 Excavations in the Plain of Antioch. Oriental Institute Publications 61. Chicago: University of Chicago Press.
Braidwood, Robert J. and Bruce Howe
    1960 Prehistoric Investigations in Iraqi Kurdistan. The Oriental Institute, Studies in Ancient Oriental Civilization 31. Chicago: University of Chicago Press.
    1962 Southwestern Asia Beyond the Lands of the Mediterranean Littoral. In : Courses Toward Urban Life, ed. Robert J. Braidwood and Gordon R. Willey, pp. 132–146. Chicago: Aldine.
Braidwood, Robert J., Halet Çambel, Charles L. Redman and Patty Jo Watson
    1971 Beginnings of Village-Farming Communities in Southeastern Turkey. Proceedings of the National Academy of Sciences 68:1236–1240.
Braidwood, Robert J., Halet Çambel and Patty Jo Watson
    1969 Prehistoric Investigations in Southeastern Turkey. Science 164:1275–1276.
Brandt, Roelof W.
    1973 The Excavations at Korucutepe, Turkey, 1968–70: Preliminary Report, Part IV: The Chalcolithic Pottery. Journal of Near Eastern Studies 32:439–444.
Burney, Charles A.
    1958 East Anatolia in the Chalcolithic and Early Bronze Age. Anatolian Studies 8:157–209.

Burney, Charles and David Marshall Lang
 1972 The Peoples of the Hills. New York: Praeger.
Çambel, Halet and Robert J. Braidwood
 1970 An Early Farming Village in Turkey. Scientific American 222 (3): 50–56.
Diamant, Steven and Behin Aksoy
 1972 Çayboyu. Anatolian Studies 22:14.
 1974 Çayboyu. In: Keban Project 1971 Activities, pp. 48–49. Ankara: Middle East Technical University, Keban Project Publications, Series I., No. 4.
Doomed by the Dam: A Survey of the Monuments Threatened by the Creation of the Keban Dam Flood Area.
 1967 Ankara: Middle East Technical University, Faculty of Architecture, Publ. No. 9.
Ebasco Services Inc.
 1964 Keban Dam & H.E. Project General Reservoir Plan (Keban Barajı ve Hidroelektrik Tesisleri Genel Baraj Gölü Planı). Ankara: Elektrik İşleri Etüt İdaresi Genel Direktörlüğü. No. G-176933.
Emre, Kutlu
 1969 The Urartian Pottery from Altıntepe. Türk Tarih Kurumu, Belleten 33: 291–301.
Erinç, Sırrı
 1953 Doğu Anadolu Coğrafyası. İstanbul Üniversitesi Yayınları No. 572. İstanbul Üniversitesi Edebiyat Fakültesi Coğrafya Enstitüsü Yayınları No. 15.
Ertem, Hayri
 1972 Han İbrahim Şah Excavations, 1970. In: Keban Project 1970 Activities, pp. 69–74. Ankara: Middle East Technical University, Keban Project Publications, Series I, No. 3.
 1974 Han İbrahim Şah Excavations, 1971. In: Keban Project 1971 Activities, pp. 65–70. Ankara: Middle East Technical University, Keban Project Publications, Series I, No. 4.
Esin, Ufuk
 1970 Tepecik Excavation 1968 Campaign, Preliminary Report. In: 1968 Summer Work, pp. 159–172. Ankara: Middle East Technical University, Keban Project Publications, Series I, No. 1.
 1971 Tepecik Excavations, 1969. In: Keban Project 1969 Activities, pp. 119–128. Ankara: Middle East Technical University, Keban Project Publications, Series I, No. 2.
 1972 Tepecik Excavations, 1970. In: Keban Project 1970 Activities, pp. 149–158. Ankara: Middle East Technical University, Keban Project Publications, Series I, No. 3.
 1974 Tepecik Excavations, 1971. In: Keban Project 1971 Activities, pp. 123–136. Ankara: Middle East Technical University, Keban Project Publications, Series I, No. 4.
Fischer, Franz
 1963 Die Hethitische Keramik von Boğazköy, Boğazköy-Hattuša, Ergebnisse der Ausgrabungen des Deutschen Archäologischen Instituts und der Deutschen Orient Gesellschaft, Vol. IV. Wissenschaftliche Veröffentlichung der Deutsche Orient-Gesellschaft 75, Berlin: Verlag Gebr. Mann, Kurt Bittel.
Flannery, Kent V.
 1969 Origins and Ecological Effects of Early Domestication in Iran and the Near East. In: The Domestication and Exploitation of Plants and Animals, edited by Peter J. Ucko and G.W. Dimbleby, pp. 73–100. London: Gerald Duckworth & Co. Ltd.
French, David H.
 1970 1968 Aşvan Excavations Preliminary Report. In: 1968 Summer Work, pp. 57–60. Ankara: Middle East Technical University, Keban Project Publications, Series I, No. 1.
 1971 Aşvan Excavations, 1969. In: Keban Project 1969 Activities, pp. 35–37. Ankara: Middle East Technical University, Keban Project Publications, Series I, No. 2.
French, David and Stephen Mitchell
 1976 Aşvan Excavations, 1972. In: Keban Project 1972 Activities, pp. 19–24. Ankara: Middle East Technical University, Keban Project Publications, Series I, No. 5.
Gökmen, Halil
 1962 Türkiyede Orman Ağaç ve Ağaççıklarının Yayılışı (Distribution of the Forest Trees and Shrubs in Turkey). Map. Ankara: Harita Genel Müdürlüğü.
Great Britain, Admirality
 1942 Turkey, Vol. 1. Naval Intelligence Division, Geographical Handbook Series, B.R. 507.
Griffin, Elizabeth E.
 1974 The Excavations at Korucutepe, Turkey, 1968–70: Preliminary Report, Part VI: The Middle and Late Bronze Age Pottery. Journal of Near Eastern Studies 33:55–95.
Güterbock, Hans G.
 1973 Hittite Hieroglyphic Seal Impressions from Korucutepe. Journal of Near Eastern Studies 32:135–147.
Haggett, Peter
 1965 Locational Analysis in Human Geography. London: Edward Arnold.
Harper, Richard P.
 1970 1968 Pağnık Öreni, Kaşpınar Excavations Preliminary Report. In: 1968 Summer Work, pp. 135–138. Ankara: Middle East Technical University, Keban Project Publications, Series I, No. 1.
 1971 Pağnık Öreni Excavations, 1969. In: Keban Project 1969 Activities, pp. 95–101. Ankara: Middle East Technical University, Keban Project Publications, Series I, No. 2.
 1972 Pağnık Öreni Excavations, 1970. In: Keban Project 1970 Activities, pp. 123–125. Ankara: Middle East Technical University, Keban Project Publications, Series I, No. 3.
Hauptmann, Harald
 1969/1970 Norşun Tepe. Istanbuler Mitteilungen 19/20:21–78.

1970 Die Grabungen auf dem Norşun-Tepe 1968. In: 1968 Summer Work, pp. 115–130. Ankara: Middle East Technical University, Keban Project Publications, Series I, No. 1.
1971 Die Grabungen auf dem Norşun-Tepe, 1969. In: Keban Project 1969 Activities, pp. 81–90. Ankara: Middle East Technical University, Keban Project Publications, Series I, No. 2.
1972 Die Grabungen auf dem Norşun-Tepe, 1970. In: Keban Project 1970 Activities, pp. 103–117. Ankara: Middle East Technical University, Keban Project Publications, Series I, No. 3.
1974 Die Grabungen auf dem Norşun-Tepe, 1971. In: Keban Project 1971 Activities, pp. 87–99. Ankara: Middle East Technical University, Keban Project Publications, Series I, No. 4.
1976a Die Entwicklung der Frühbronzezeitlichen Siedlung auf dem Norşuntepe in Ostanatolien. Archäologisches Korrespondenzblatt 6:9–20.
1976b Die Ausgrabungen auf dem Norşun-Tepe, 1972. In: Keban Project 1972 Activities, pp. 71–90. Ankara: Middle East Technical University, Keban Project Publications, Series I, No. 5.
1976c Die Ausgrabungen auf dem Körtepe, 1972. In: Keban Project 1972 Activities, pp. 33–34. Ankara: Middle East Technical University, Keban Project Publications, Series I, No. 5.

Helms, Svend
1973 Taşkun Mevkii 1970–71. Anatolian Studies 23:109–120.

Huntington, Ellsworth
1902 The Valley of the Upper Euphrates River and Its People. Bulletin of the American Geographical Society of New York 34:301–393.

Kelly-Buccellati, Marilyn
1974 The Excavations at Korucutepe, Turkey, 1968–70: Preliminary Report, Part V: The Early Bronze Age Pottery and its Affinities. Journal of Near Eastern Studies 33:44–54.

Kökten, İ. Kılıç
1947 1945 Yılında Türk Tarih Kurumu Adına Yapılan Tarihöncesi Araştırmaları. Türk Tarih Kurumu, Belleten 11:431–472.

Koşay, Hamit Zübeyr
1976 Keban Projesi Pulur Kazısı 1968–1970. Keban Project Pulur Excavations 1968–1970. Ankara: Middle East Technical University, Keban Project Publications, Series III, No. 1.

McNicoll, Anthony
1973 Taşkun Kale. Anatolian Studies 23:159–180.
1974 Taşkun Kale. In: Keban Project 1971 Activities, pp. 50–51. Ankara: Middle East Technical University, Keban Project Publications, Series I, No. 4.

Mallowan, Max E.L.
1947 Excavations at Brak and Chagar Bazar. Iraq 9.

Mellink, Machteld J.
1965 Anatolian Chronology. In: Chronologies in Old World Archaeology, edited by Robert W. Ehrich, pp. 101–131. Chicago: University of Chicago Press.

Mitchell, Stephen
1973 Aşvan Kale. Anatolian Studies 23:121–151.
1974 Aşvan Kale. In: Keban Project 1971 Activities, pp. 44–48. Ankara: Middle East Technical University, Keban Project Publications, Series I, No. 4.

Öğün, Baki
1971 Haraba Excavations, 1969. In: Keban Project 1969 Activities, pp. 43–46. Ankara: Middle East Technical University, Keban Project Publications, Series I, No. 2.
1972 Haraba Excavations, 1970. In: Keban Project 1970 Activities, pp. 77–78. Ankara: Middle East Technical University, Keban Project Publications, Series I, No. 3.

Özgüç, Tahsin and Mahmut Akok
1958 Horoztepe. Ankara: Türk Tarih Kurumu Publications, Series 5, No. 18.

Redman, Charles L. and Patty Jo Watson
1970 Systematic, Intensive Surface Collection. American Antiquity 35:279–291.

Rowton, M.B.
1967 The Woodlands of Ancient Western Asia. Journal of Near Eastern Studies 26:261–277.

Ryan, Christopher W.
1957 A Guide to the Known Minerals of Turkey. Ankara: Mineral Research and Exploration Institute of Turkey and the Office of International Economic Cooperation, Ministry of Foreign Affairs, in cooperation with the U.S. Operations Mission to Turkey, International Cooperation Administration. Reprinted 1960.

Saraçoğlu, Hüseyin
1956 Doğu Anadolu, Cilt: I. (Türkiye Coğrafyası Üzerine Etüdler) Istanbul: Maarif Basımevi.

Sarıbeyoğlu, Mahmut
1951 Aşağı Murat Bölgesinin Beşeri Coğrafyası. Istanbul: Anıl Matbaası.

Serdaroğlu, Ümit
1970 Ağın and Kalaycık Excavations, 1968, Preliminary Report. In: 1968 Summer Work, pp. 41–51. Ankara: Middle East Technical University, Keban Project Publications, Series I, No. 1.
1971 Ağın and Kalaycık Excavations, 1969. In: Keban Project 1969 Activities, pp. 27–30. Ankara: Middle East Technical University, Keban Project Publications, Series I, No. 2.
1972 Ağın and Kalaycık Excavations, 1970. In: Keban Project 1970 Activities, pp. 25–43. Ankara: Middle East Technical University, Keban Project Publications, Series I, No. 3.
1974 Ağın and Kalaycık Excavations, 1971. In: Keban Project 1971 Activities, pp. 19–24. Ankara: Middle East Technical University, Keban Project Publications, Series I, No. 4.

  1976 Researches in Ağın and its Vicinity, 1972. In: Keban Project 1972 Activities, pp. 11–12. Ankara: Middle East Technical University, Keban Project Publications, Series I, No. 5.

Tanoğlu, Ali, Sırrı Erinç and Erol Tümertekin
  1961 Türkiye Atlası: Atlas of Turkey. Istanbul: Milli Eğitim Basımevi.

Tobler, Arthur J.
  1950 Excavations at Tepe Gawra, Vol. 2, Levels IX-XX. Philadelphia: University of Pennsylvania Press.

Türkiye Maden Zuhurları
  1960 (Distribution of Mineral Occurrences in Turkey). Ankara: Maden Tetkik ve Arama Enstitüsü.

van Loon, Maurits
  1973 The Excavations at Korucutepe, Turkey, 1968–70: Preliminary Report, Part I: Architecture and General Finds. Journal of Near Eastern Studies 32:357–423.

van Loon, Maurits and Giorgio Buccellati
  1970 The University of Chicago-University of California Excavations at Korucutepe—1968. In: 1968 Summer Work, pp. 89–102. Ankara: Middle East Technical University, Keban Project Publications, Series I, No. 1.

van Zeist, Willem
  1972 Palaeobotanical Results of the 1970 Season at Çayönü, Turkey. Helenium 12: 3–19.

Walter, H.
  1956 Vegetationsgliederung Anatoliens. Flora 143: 295–326.

Whallon, Robert Jr.
  n.d. The Systematic Collection and Analysis of Surface Materials from a Prehistoric Site in Southeastern Turkey. Unpublished ms.

Whallon, Robert Jr. and Sönmez Kantman
  1969 Early Bronze Age Development in the Keban Reservoir, East-Central Turkey. Current Anthropology 10:128–133.
  1970 The Survey of the Keban Dam Reservoir, 1967. In: 1968 Summer Work, pp. 7–12. Ankara: Middle East Technical University, Keban Project Publications, Series I, No. 1.

Whallon, Robert Jr. and Henry T. Wright
  1970 1968 Fatmalı-Kalecik Excavations Preliminary Report. In: 1968 Summer Work, pp. 67–71. Ankara: Middle East Technical University, Keban Project Publications, Series I, No. 1.

World Almanac
  1978 The World Almanac & Book of Facts, ed. George E. Delury. New York: Newspaper Enterprise Association, Inc.

Wright, Henry T., James A. Neely, Gregory A. Johnson, and John Speth
  1975 Early Fourth Millennium Developments in Southwestern Iran. Iran 13:129–147.

Appendix

APPENDIX: Sherd Counts of Wares Recovered by the Controlled Collections (Keban Reservoir Survey)

	N52/1	N52/2	N52/3	N52/9	O54/2	O54/3	O54/6	O54/8	O54/9	O54/10	O54/11
Chalcolithic	495	4	1644	26	3	2	46	14	0	16	0
Graphite Slipped	0	0	0	0	3	0	41	16	0	0	2
Cream Chaff	1	0	143	100	5	9	9*	17	0	3	1
Reserved Slip	4	0	0	0	13	0	0	5	0	0	0
Plain Simple	5	0	0	0	6	0	0	2	1	0	0
Fine Grooved	2	0	0	0	2	0	0	4	0	0	0
Early Bronze Age Burnished	294	125	0	175	2206	166	4	5008	1	178	32
Early Bronze Age Relief Decorated	0	0	0	0	5	0	0	15	0	0	0
Early Bronze Age Polished	5	0	1	4	24	3	0	90	0	0	0
Early Bronze Age Red Slipped	4	2	0	8	41	10	0	80	0	7	2
Early Bronze Age Plain	120	26	0	80	550	28	2	2393	1	160	26
Early Bronze Age Thick	2	4	0	7	101	26	0	409	0	6	6
Early Bronze Age Red Painted	0	1	0	2	24	1	0	30	0	1	0
Early Bronze Age Black Painted	0	6	0	0	51	0	0	159	0	1	0
Middle Bronze Age Gritty	12	0	0	9	126	0	0	268	0	7	0
Old Hittite Gray	6	0	1	2	144	1	6	312	15	64	32
Old Hittite Light Faced Gray	2	0	0	6	14	0	0	57	7	4	1
Old Hittite Black Faced Gray	0	0	0	0	0	0	0	1	0	0	0
Middle Bronze Age Gray	0	0	0	0	47	0	0	22	1	10	3
Hittite Red	0	0	0	0	0	7	0	0	1	0	0
Hittite Plain	126	44	0	52	417	26	85	1227	177	33	34

O54/12	O54/14	O54/15	O54/16	O54/21	O54/24	O54/25	O54/27	O55/1	O55/2	O55/3	O55/4	O55/8-9
0	13	2	0	0	2	0	0	63	5	4	0	99
0	17	1	0	0	0	0	0	0	20	0	0	52
3*	0	0	0	0	18*	0	1*	11	3*	6*	0	62*
0	0	0	0	0	0	0	0	0	0	5	0	7
0	0	0	0	0	0	0	0	0	0	20	0	74
0	0	0	0	0	0	0	0	0	0	3	0	6
82	334	9	0	6	173	11	19	125	119	389	3	1310
0	0	0	0	0	0	0	0	0	0	0	0	0
1	1	0	0	0	0	0	0	0	0	4	0	15
1	4	0	0	0	0	0	0	23	2	2	0	9
23	197	13	2	11	210	19	5	138	77	485	0	481
3	12	0	0	0	3	2	0	17	19	12	1	138
0	3	0	0	0	2	0	0	0	0	1	0	7
0	3	0	0	0	4	0	0	0	0	2	0	14
1	10	0	0	2	5	0	0	0	0	15	0	10
10	83	0	0	0	29	10	11	8	4	12	8	16
1	7	1	0	4	8	2	4	0	0	10	4	3
0	1	0	0	0	0	0	0	0	0	0	0	0
0	0	0	0	0	0	1	0	0	0	0	1	0
0	0	0	0	0	0	0	0	0	0	0	1	0
45	82	16	0	18	51	50	36	27	11	120	103	471

	N52/1	N52/2	N52/3	N52/9	O54/2	O54/3	O54/6	O54/8	O54/9	O54/10	O54/11
Hittite Fine	43	5	1	6	128	1	10	200	33	2	2
Hittite Thick	12	25	0	5	73	6	4	94	42	2	6
Hittite Exterior Wheel-Marked	0	0	0	0	12	0	0	10	0	0	0
Hittite Buff-Orange Burnished	106	51	1	30	992	23	134	1842	269	21	35
Hittite Chaff Faced	3	0	0	0	43	1	(97)‡	185	53	4	0
Hittite Orange Smoothed	4	0	0	0	12	0	1	18	8	1	0
Hittite Red-Brown Burnished	20	2	0	2	295	22	29	273	60	11	8
Hittite Brown Burnished	16	16	0	9	313	28	48	405	66	8	33
Hittite White Slipped	14	3	0	0	114	9	(62)‡	485	60	1	0
Hittite Painted	0	0	0	0	24	0	5	56	2	1	1
Hittite Brown Gritty Cooking Ware	20	19	0	24	87	9	1	283	13	2	6
Iron Age	15	0	0	2	369	28	(8)‡	978	15	10	6
Roman Red	0	0	0	0	0	0	1	5	0	0	0
Medieval Brick	21	734	2	53	1695	49	1952	16811	300	991	187
Medieval Thick	0	168	0	9	105	4	309	976	11	89	29
Medieval Coarse	0	5	0	2	19	2	22	91	3	24	63
Medieval Glazed	0	15	0	0	33	0	1	5	0	13	5
Medieval Sgraffiato	0	14	0	1	3	0	0	1	0	5	3
Medieval Red Slipped	3	259	0	3	390	11	41	1064	14	99	68
Medieval White Slipped	0	20	0	2	90	9	98	1233	42	27	16
Medieval Painted	0	51	0	0	4	4	3	7	0	2	5
Medieval Cooking	1	131	3	3	138	3	43	525	12	78	37
Medieval Modeled	0	1	0	0	3	0	0	7	0	0	0

*Cream Chaff Ware sherds were misidentified at this site, and a significant number of additional sherds of this ware will be found tabulated under Hittite Chaff Faced, Hittite White Slipped, or Iron Age wares.

‡Most of these sherds are, in fact, Cream Chaff Ware.

O54/12	O54/14	O54/15	O54/16	O54/21	O54/24	O54/25	O54/27	O55/1	O55/2	O55/3	O55/4	O55/8-9
4	5	1	0	4	6	5	1	2	1	49	10	155
0	11	2	1	0	2	1	8	1	6	3	10	59
0	0	0	0	0	0	0	0	0	0	0	0	4
12	37	5	2	14	25	60	29	19	10	47	132	242
(5)‡	4	1	0	0	(71)‡	1	(21)‡	4	(11)‡	(46)‡	2	(165)‡
0	0	0	0	0	0	0	0	3	0	0	1	1
4	30	6	0	1	20	21	7	3	2	24	20	71
3	90	10	0	3	50	35	23	0	3	22	49	80
5	7	0	0	3	21	1	2	0	4	23	4	40
3	2	1	0	0	1	1	0	1	0	0	0	20
2	79	3	0	1	8	5	7	0	5	19	7	30
9	28	2	0	2	73	5	13	0	3	(57)‡	118	(176)‡
0	0	0	0	0	0	0	0	0	0	0	0	0
1031	80	46	211	642	312	767	335	19	4	438	753	172
46	7	23	7	20	17	50	28	0	0	22	76	28
36	1	0	6	5	8	28	3	0	0	7	5	1
21	0	0	6	4	0	18	0	7	0	2	7	1
34	0	0	2	2	0	1	0	0	0	0	0	0
170	6	8	50	54	12	149	18	0	1	34	226	22
60	13	0	7	14	11	83	8	0	0	9	19	26
13	0	0	0	0	0	26	1	3	0	0	0	1
130	16	4	45	31	9	81	32	9	0	24	119	18
0	0	0	0	0	0	2	0	0	0	0	0	1